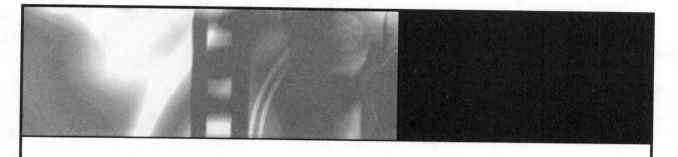

Movie Time

A Chronology of Hollywood and the Movie Industry from Its Beginnings to the Present

GENE BROWN

Mary Ann Lynch, Photo Editor

MACMILLAN • USA

To the Memory of

Bill Anderson, Pat Dagler, and Evelyn Rousso

MACMILLAN
A Simon & Schuster Macmillan Company
1633 Broadway
New York, NY 10019

Lists of the top stars at the box office and the stars of tomorrow were originally published in the *Motion Picture Herald* and the *Motion Picture Almanac* and are being used by permission of the Quigley Publishing Company.

MACMILLAN is a registered trademark of Macmillan, Inc.

Library of Congress Cataloging-in-Publication Data
Brown, Gene.
Movie time : a chronology of Hollywood and the movie industry from its beginnings to the present / Gene Brown.
p. cm.
Includes bibliographical references and index.
ISBN 0-02-860429-6 (pbk)
1. Motion pictures—United States—History—Chronology.
I. Title
PN1993.5.U6B687 1995
791.43'0973—dc20 95-9091
CIP

10 9 8 7 6 5 4 3 2 1

Printed in the United States of America

Design by Nick Anderson

Contents

Acknowledgments

For research material and other assistance, I would like to thank Brian Alweiss, Jennifer Alweiss, Linda Alweiss, Estelle Brown, Ed Chilcott, Paul Fargis, Sandy Izhakoff, Ken Keller, Harilyn Rousso, Dorothy Taylor, and Jerry Williams.

Invaluable assistance was provided by Marilyn Annan of the *New York Times* Reference Library, Nancy Dubin of the Central Branch of the Indianapolis Public Library, Ricardo Pla of the Queens College Law School Library of the City University of New York, and Margaret Rose of the Raymond Fogelman Library of the New School for Social Research. Also helpful were the staffs of the Grand Army Plaza branch of the Brooklyn Public Library, and of the Bobst Library of New York University.

Most of all, I would like to thank the librarians of the Billy Rose Theater Collection of the Lincoln Center Library for the Performing Arts. Their help, patience, and tolerance for the endless supply of call slips emanating from what must have seemed like the permanent occupant of seat number twenty-five were more valuable than they will ever know. I am also grateful to the pages, who without complaint delivered to me so many heavy bound volumes of *Daily Variety* and the *Hollywood Reporter*.

Natalie Chapman, my publisher at Macmillan Books, recognized what I hope will turn out to have been a diamond in the rough. I am grateful to her for her faith in this project and help in getting it going. My editor, Mary Ann Lynch, did me the favor of insisting on nothing but my best—and gave me her best, with careful editing and sage advice. Her knowledge and love of films and enthusiastic dedication to this book helped and energized me when I needed it most—and it's also fun to talk to her about the movies. I would also like to thank Michael J. Freeland for his marvelous, hot-buttered cover design.

Sheree Bykofsky, my agent, was always supportive. Without her tireless efforts, the cameras would never have rolled.

Harilyn Rousso, as always, with everything from love to a constructively critical perspective to chocolate brownies, was there when I needed her. Thanks to her, it's finally "a wrap."

Introduction

Describing declining business support for President Clinton in May 1993, advertising executive Jerry Della Femina said, "This was the fastest honeymoon since Ernest Borgnine married Ethel Merman."

In fact, the Borgnine-Merman state of bliss, which began June 27, 1964, was considerably shorter than Clinton's period of grace. It was all over between them after six loud weeks.

The movies and their personalities, when used to mark the times of our personal lives rather than the chronicle of politics, have an even richer and more resounding resonance. For example, many people can remember the movie they went to on their first date, what their lives were like when Elizabeth Taylor and Richard Burton were carrying on while filming *Cleopatra*, and what they were doing the day James Dean, Marilyn Monroe, Elvis Presley, John Belushi, or River Phoenix died.

The Way We Were, for example, which opened in 1973 with Barbra Streisand and Robert Redford, is a landmark film for me. It will always evoke strong feelings and significant events in my life. Nothing I've ever seen in a history book can bring back that year as vividly as that Sydney Pollack film.

There must be thousands of moments in movie history that have this effect on people. But although we have many chronologies of political and social events, there are no detailed ones of the incidents and people that often ring a clearer bell in our psyches. Hollywood creates more landmarks in our thoughts, feelings, and imagination than does Washington. Its milestones in our memories are worth marking.

The idea for *Movie Time*, which I hope will serve this purpose and more, came to me while I was reading Thomas Schatz's superb book, *The Genius of the System: Hollywood Filmmaking in the Studio Era*. I was a little confused about when certain events took place with respect to other events, and I checked for a chronology in the back of the book. There was none, nor could I find one anywhere else in my large library of movie books, or anything in the public library that approached what I thought was needed.

In trying to fill this gap, I kept two things in mind. First, I aimed to provide as accurate a chronological account of the movies in America as I could, and as complete as space would allow. In doing this, I have included only information that could be linked to a precise date or month. As a result, some time periods may appear less well covered than others. And second, and just as important, I worked to make it as comprehensive as I could. That meant covering every aspect of movie culture—the scandals, the romances, and the fascinating highlights about the stars as celebrities and about celebrityhood as a phenomenon; as well as aesthetic, business, and technological developments. In other words, I made sure to include all of what most people—including the film scholars I know—talk about when they discuss the movies.

The value of presenting this information in a chronological format is twofold. First, of course, it is the clearest way of organizing facts to answer the question "When did it happen?" So that the information is even easier and quicker to access, each year is organized into four categories: Personalities; Movies; Business and Society; and Births, Deaths, Marriages, and Divorces.

But this book is also for browsing. The advantage a chronology offers the casual reader is that one can pick a year or a topic and peruse as wide or narrow a stretch as one's mood or memories dictate. This is not only informative, it's also fun.

Wherever possible, information for *Movie Time* was taken from primary sources: the Hollywood trade press and contemporary newspaper and magazine articles. Some of what is in this book can be found in no other book; much comes from widely scattered sources and has never before been gathered in one place.

In choosing dates and types of information to include, I have tried to keep in mind what sorts of facts movie fans, movie buffs, students, and film scholars might want to know. I've also selected information with a desire to capture the spirit and flavor of the times. For example, specific films are listed in terms of premieres, not release dates, whenever a premiere date could be found.

Many people wrongly assume that the "release" date is synonymous with a film's premiere. In fact, throughout most of the history of the industry, the term has been used to designate the date of wide or general release, and is not necessarily the date of a film's premiere.

In *Movie Time*, films are introduced through release dates for the early years, when accurate information about premieres is not readily available; and for the period from 1980 to the present, since premieres are no longer so frequently held today. Premieres for the most part no longer serve as a platform to build interest in a picture before it moves into other houses and ultimately into neighborhood theaters. Now movies "open" in multiplexes, most of the time on Friday but sometimes on Wednesday, on as many as twenty-five hundred screens simultaneously, with breathless attention devoted to the first three days' gross.

In the 1930s and 1940s, the big downtown theaters often accompanied pictures with stage shows, which I have noted. I, for one, would love to have seen the opening of *Key Largo* at the Strand in New York on July 16, 1948. Included in the price of admission to the movie was the performance—live, onstage—of Count Basie and his Orchestra with Billie Holiday. Or imagine going to the Roxy on March 5, 1947 to see Elia Kazan's *Boomerang*. With it, newspaper columnist Ed Sullivan emceed a variety show onstage—no doubt a prototype of the TV program he was about to launch—featuring, "direct from the Copa," Sid Caesar.

HOW TO USE THIS BOOK

The following should be helpful as a guide to using this book.

YEARLY OVERVIEW The opening page of each year will usually contain some movie statistics. Occasionally, if you follow a particular series of figures over the years, such as the number of theaters, you may see an unusually big increase or decrease. Unfortunately, we do not have a consistent set of annual numbers for this and for many other important facets of the movies. Statistics were collected by different organizations in different eras, each using a different method of cumulating and tabulating the results—surveys, estimates, averages, and so forth. I've used what appeared to be the most reliable numbers available and indicated when the source for the figures changes. Top rental earnings, based on figures reported in *Variety*, have been rounded off to the nearest $50,000.

In compiling the numbers, lists, and highlights in these overviews, I used information appearing in the *Film Daily Almanac*; the Quigley Publication's *Motion Picture Herald and Fame* and their annual *Motion Picture Almanac*;

Variety; and the *New York Times*. The Motion Picture Association of America was especially helpful for statistics from recent years. I also drew from Joel W. Finler's *The Hollywood Story* and from *The Guinness Book of Movie Facts and Feats*.

PERSONALITIES Movie stars are, of course, public personalities. Everything in their lives is potential newspaper and magazine copy. Given their fame, wealth, and, often, power, much of the news they make tends to be sensational. It would be tempting, and a mistake, to assume that from their public behavior, and reports about it, we know the whole person. I can think of no better example than Frank Sinatra, whose occasionally outright antisocial behavior—chronicled here—is matched by frequent and substantial acts of private charity and compassionate assistance to colleagues in need in the industry.

MOVIES Space limitations required that coverage be limited to English-language films. For convenience and brevity, and because New York has been the media capital of the country during the rise of the movie industry, theaters not identified by location are New York houses. Two theaters in Los Angeles and two in New York figure frequently in major openings and premieres:

Grauman's Chinese Theater, now called the Chinese Theater, was built by showman Sid Grauman, and opened on Hollywood Boulevard in 1927. It is known for the handprints and footprints of the stars, preserved in cement in its forecourt.

The Carthay Circle, at Wilshire Boulevard, opened in 1926 and hosted many important premieres until it closed in 1969.

The Roxy Theater, once the world's largest movie house, was located in mid-Manhattan, at 50th Street and Seventh Avenue. From 1927 until its demolition in 1960, its stage shows and premieres of many 20th Century Fox pictures made it one of America's most notable movie palaces.

The Radio City Music Hall, "the Showplace of the Nation," and in its time probably the most famous movie theater in the world, opened in New York's Rockefeller Center in 1932. The Rockettes still delight audiences with their high-kick routine, but, except for special events, the theater stopped showing movies in the 1970s.

BUSINESS AND SOCIETY Organizations to which frequent reference is made include the following:

Academy of Motion Picture Arts and Sciences Begun in 1927 and intended to advance the industry in general and hold off efforts to organize film workers into unions in particular, it is primarily known to the public as the organization that annually awards the Oscars.

Famous Players–Lasky A 1916 amalgamation of two studios, which used a distributor called Paramount Pictures; audience familiarity with the name "Paramount" caused the Famous Players–Lasky studio to take the name "Paramount Pictures" as its own in the 1920s.

The Hays Office The part of the motion picture industry's governing body, headed by former Postmaster General Will Hays, that censored films by granting a seal of approval. Most theaters would not exhibit a film without this seal. The collection of rules about what could and couldn't be shown in a film was called the Hays Code, which the industry began to enforce in 1934. The censorship office was run for many years by Joseph Breen. The Hays Office was replaced by the rating system in the 1960s.

IATSE International Alliance of Theatrical Stage Employees, Hollywood's most important union, organized in 1893.

Loew's, Inc. The parent company of MGM, founded by Marcus Loew; he orchestrated the formation of Metro-Goldwyn-Mayer in 1924 by joining the Metro and Goldwyn studios with the operations of independent producer Louis B. Mayer.

MPAA Motion Picture Association of America, the industry's major organization through which the studios communicate with the public. It was formed in 1922 as the Motion Picture Producers and Distributors of America.

RKO Radio-Keith-Orpheum, a studio founded in 1928 by Joseph P. Kennedy, father of the President, and David Sarnoff, head of RCA. Ultimately acquired by Howard Hughes, it stopped making theatrical films in the late 1950s.

20th Century Fox The studio that resulted from the 1935 merger of the Fox Film Corporation, founded by William Fox, with Twentieth Century Pictures. Run by Darryl Zanuck, it was originally spelled with a hyphen: 20th Century-Fox. Throughout the book, however, we have chosen to delete the hyphen.

Universal Pictures Founded by Carl Laemmle in 1912, it merged with International Pictures in 1946 to create Universal-International, which was taken over by MCA (Music Corporation of America) in 1962.

United Artists Founded by Charlie Chaplin, Mary Pickford, Douglas Fairbanks, and D.W. Griffith in 1919 to release their own films, it eventually became the releasing organization for Hollywood's major independent producers, including Samuel Goldwyn and David O. Selznick. It is now part of MGM.

BIRTHS, DEATHS, MARRIAGES, AND DIVORCES I have used the following abbreviations: b. = "is born"; d. = "dies"; m.= "marries." Entries for births and deaths, and the first name in an entry for a marriage or divorce, are always an actor or actress unless otherwise identified. Names in parentheses are the real names of stars before they were given—or took—the names by which we know them. For this section I chose people who were important in their own era, so a few names, especially from the silent film period, may be unfamiliar. When I thought this might be the case, I identified them.

PHOTOGRAPHS AND ILLUSTRATIONS Sources for the photographs and illustrations are cited throughout. For reasons of space, the following abbreviations have been used: LC=the Lynch Collection; MSN=Movie Star News; MOMA=Museum of Modern Art.

Finally, anyone who seeks to peg Hollywood events to specific dates, for the most part cannot say, with Samuel Goldwyn, "I'll give you a definite maybe." One takes the risks entailed in being precise. This book has been carefully and exhaustively researched, but errors may have crept in. The author would appreciate hearing from readers about such mistakes—with documentation—in order to correct them in future editions. You can reach me by e-mail on the Internet: genebrown@delphi.com or you can write to me in care of Macmillan Books.

Photo opposite: D.W. Griffith and his cameraman Billy Bitzer (at the camera), courtesy the Lynch Collection

The Beginnings of the Film Industry

1830–1909

*T*he movies, like photography, have no single inventor. As the following chronology shows, the motion picture emerged by the 1890s as the product of several developments: the creation of the photographic process; the invention of celluloid roll film; and the realization that successive still pictures of anything in motion, when viewed consecutively, produced the illusion of motion—the phenomenon known as "persistence of vision."

Within a few years of Edison's 1889 development of the Kinetoscope—motion picture peep shows—the basic technology of making and showing films that would be used for the next forty years was in place. But movies as a technological achievement were one thing; the art of filmmaking—all the techniques that seamlessly result in the finished film—and the organization of film production, distribution, and exhibition, would take many more years to evolve.

Early movies were mostly slices of life. Nonfiction films constituted more than half of all titles produced until about 1908. The novelty of the new medium was itself enough to carry the day. When people could be amazed and thrilled by a shot of an approaching train or a passing parade, a story did not seem that necessary. At its most elaborate, this nonfiction filmmaking could record in motion a current event. In 1897, for instance, the Veriscope Company filmed the heavyweight fight between James Corbett and Bob Fitzsimmons.

Inevitably, creative individuals began to see how movies could offer unique ways to tell a story, using methods that could be employed on the stage only with great difficulty or not at all. As early as 1895, for example, the Edison Studio, in *The Execution of Mary, Queen of Scots*, was already using trick photography. The camera was stopped during the beheading scene so that the actress playing Mary could be replaced by a dummy. Films made in these early years ran between fifteen and ninety seconds. This one lasted less than thirty.

Then in 1902, George Méliés, a French filmmaker, made a narrative movie, *A Trip to the Moon*, that pioneered surreal special effects, including a rocket plunging into the face of the "man in the moon." Here was an early example of cinema art depicting something that "happened" only in the imagination.

A Trip to the Moon, 1902   LC

As early as 1904, real and imaginary events were depicted in a way that is perhaps even more cinematic than the photographing of people or things in motion. This same year, J. Stuart Blackton, a founder of the Vitagraph Company, produced *Humorous Phases of Funny Faces*, generally recognized as the forerunner of the animated cartoon. Vitagraph, Biograph, and the Edison Company were the major movie production companies of this period.

3

Technological advances gradually increased the tools available to the early filmmakers. By 1905, Cooper Hewitt mercury lamps made indoor shooting without sunlight practical. It was becoming easier to put together interior and exterior scenes to tell a whole tale. Gradually, the dramatic conventions that were to lend familiarity and excitement to early fiction films were also coming into use. The 1904 Biograph film, *Personal*, for instance, features the first comic chase scene—around Grant's Tomb in New York City. Biograph's production was beginning to shift toward the fiction, or "story," film. In a few years it would give director D.W. Griffith and actresses Mary Pickford and Lillian Gish the opportunity to create some of the first popular fiction films in America.

In these early years, even more so than today, the movies were first of all a business—one in which the most effective business methods had yet to be invented. It began with companies called "factories"—not, yet, "studios"—turning out films on rooftops and empty lots in New York and New Jersey. These film factories issued mail-order catalogs through which owners of amusement parlors and managers of vaudeville houses—the separate movie theater was yet to come—could buy films. Films were sold by their length, and they *were* sold, not rented. Soon, however, in 1902, in San Francisco, Henry Miles set up the first film exchange. Exhibitors could now rent films from a distributor instead of buying them directly from the company that made them, making it affordable for exhibitors to change shows more often.

By the middle of the first decade of the twentieth century, the elements of a major industry were in place: the producers, the distributors, and the theaters. A large urban audience, much of it foreign-born, provided a market for cheap, easily assimilated entertainment. A product was available that was beginning to tell short, simple stories, ideally suited to this audience. Still needed were the entrepreneurs to more widely exploit this opportunity and create the means by which the movies could be brought to the millions.

The nickelodeon—a small, storefront theater where films were shown with piano accompaniment—fit the bill. A nickelodeon required a small investment and the skills of business people willing to take a chance on something new. Such businessmen included Adolph Zukor, a furrier; Marcus Loew, the owner of urban amusement arcades; Jesse Lasky, whose résumé listed gold prospector and vaudeville performer; Sam Goldwyn, a glove salesman; the Warner brothers, who operated a bicycle repair business; Carl Laemmle, haberdasher; William Fox, garment manufacturer; and Louis B. Mayer, who literally sold junk—an occupation he would one day live down by running the movie studio known for quality, MGM.

These men, immigrants themselves, could identify with their audience. They were not afraid to be associated with an industry still just outside the realm of respectability. Perhaps as outsiders—Jews in a society predominantly gentile—

they were best prepared to showcase entertainment that was not yet considered genteel.

By 1907, the *Saturday Evening Post* was reporting that daily attendance at nickelodeons had broken the two-million mark, barely a decade after the first customers had paid to see images projected on the screen. The 35mm film format in a ratio of 1.33 x 1 (a screen image slightly wider than high) had been adopted as an international standard. Companies in the U.S. and Europe were turning out thousands of films a year. An important industry and a new, major art form seemed to be in the making. Yet, the most basic kinds of questions remained to be answered.

How would this industry be organized? Film production by scores of small, independent firms seemed to go against the trend of American business. Companies of all kinds were being grouped together in huge corporations—"trusts"—in an attempt to monopolize everything from railroads and steel to food packaging. In fact, in 1908, the Motion Picture Patents Company was set up to do the same for moving pictures. Would it work?

Where would films be shown? Could the nickelodeon suffice once the middle class began to go to the movies in large numbers, or would theaters like the ones that presented stage plays be needed? And what was to be the nature of this new art? The model for the early narrative films was still the stage. Many pictures were no more than abbreviated, filmed plays. In fact, in France, a company called Société du Film d'Art was formed to produce "art" films, linked to classical theater. Casts were assembled from the Comédie Française and from individual performers such as Sarah Bernhardt. One of these films, *The Assassination of the Duc de Guise*, even had a score written for its accompaniment by Camille Saint-Saens.

Could film become a distinct art with its own "grammar" and conventions? Would audiences accept the ideas of a "close-up" and complicated editing that bent time and space to the needs of the screen? Would the movies get away from the printed page and the pictorial limits of the theater's proscenium arch?

How long should a movie be? The ten- to twelve-minute, one-reel film was still standard in 1909. Would the movies finally emulate the theater, unreeling a plot at a leisurely pace over as much as several hours?

It was also not clear what role the performers on the screen would play in the new industry. In film, as late as 1909, they were anonymous. Stage actors called the movies "the flickers." They did not take them seriously, working in them in the summer to make ends meet when Broadway's boards got a rest. Would the moving pictures develop their own matinée idols to compete with those on Broadway?

The movies in their first decade in America were far from achieving acceptance and respectability. In 1909, Boston's Twentieth Century Club expressed concern with the "growing tendency toward a lower and less desirable form of recreative amusement." They meant the movies. The New

York Society for the Prevention of Cruelty to Children attacked "the pernicious moving picture" for showing children how to commit crimes.

If anything, demands for censorship, which had started with Edison's *The Kiss* in 1896, with its closeup shot of lips meeting, were growing. There was also concern over fires in nickelodeons, caused by the highly inflammable nitrate film, the standard stock.

It was by no means clear that America would lead the way in moviemaking. The biggest film company in the world in the first decade of the new century was the French Pathé, which opened a New York office in 1904. The only thing certain was that by 1910, this new industry, where the rules of art and commerce had yet to be set, was offering a product already immensely popular, and opportunities to create from the ground up a new art and entertainment medium.

1830s

• W.H. Fox Talbot in Britain and Louis Daguerre in France discover and begin to perfect the technology that will lead to modern photography.

1832

• Joseph Plateau, a Belgian, builds what he calls the Phenakistoscope. Using rotating disks, a mirror, and drawings, he produces images that seem to move. The phenomenon of persistence of vision that produces this illusion, in which the eye supplies the missing motion between the successive still pictures, will be crucial for the development of movies.

1834

• William G. Horner perfects a device similar to the Phenakistoscope. It depicts movement through images attached to a revolving drum. Sold as a toy, it is called the Zoetrope (the name that director Francis Ford Coppola will later choose for his studio).

1847

FEBRUARY 11 Inventor Thomas A. Edison b.

1867

JANUARY 17 Carl Laemmle, founder of Universal, b.

1870

MAY 7 Marcus Loew, founder of MGM, b.

1873

JANUARY 7 Adolph Zukor, founder of Famous Players, forerunner of Paramount Pictures, b.

1875

JANUARY 22 Director D.W. Griffith (David Wark Griffith) b.

1878

APRIL 28 Lionel Barrymore b.

JULY 8 Photographer Eadweard Muybridge, who has devised a method of taking successive photographs of animals and people to show how they move, projects these images for the San Francisco Art Association.

1879

JANUARY 1 William Fox (Wilhelm Fried), founder of the Fox Film Corporation, b.

FEBRUARY 10 W.C. Fields (William Claude Dukenfield) b.

JULY • Independent producer Samuel Goldwyn (Schmuel Gelbfisz, later Samuel Goldfish) b.

NOVEMBER 4 Will Rogers b. **5** Will Hays, who will become "czar" of the movie industry, b.

1880

JANUARY 6 Tom Mix b. **17** Mack Sennett (Michael Sinnott) b.

SEPTEMBER 13 Jesse L. Lasky, founder of the Jesse Lasky Feature Play Company, forerunner of Paramount Pictures, b.

1881

AUGUST 6 Columnist Louella Parsons (Louella Rose Oettinger) b. **12** Director Cecil B. DeMille b.

1882

• Etienne Marey in France develops a camera in the form of a photographic revolver that can take twelve pictures per second (he will later raise it to 100). This may be the source for the term "shooting," when making movies.

FEBRUARY 15 John Barrymore b.

OCTOBER 20 Bela Lugosi (Béla Blaskó) b.

NOVEMBER 6 Silent-screen producer Thomas Ince b.

1883

JANUARY 10 Silent-screen star Francis X. Bushman b.

MAY 23 Douglas Fairbanks (Douglas Ulman) b.

APRIL 1 Lon Chaney (Alonso Chaney) b.

1885

• George Eastman produces paper roll film. • Louis B. Mayer (Lazar Meir) b. (The date often given, July 4, appears to have been chosen by Mayer in hindsight to express his feelings for America.)

APRIL 1 Wallace Beery b.

MAY 2 Columnist Hedda Hopper b. (She will later lie about both the day and year, switching to 1890 for youth and June 2 for what she thought was a better astrological sign.)

1886

MAY 26 Al Jolson (Asa Yoelson) b.

1887

FEBRUARY 1 Real-estate developer Harvey Wilcox files a subdivision map for a tract in the Cahuenga Valley, near Los Angeles, that he bought last year for $150 an acre. Marked "Hollywood," the origin of the name is not certain, but is usually attributed to his wife, Deida, who, it has been said, liked the way the word sounds.

1889

• George Eastman introduces commercial celluloid roll film, refining an invention of Hannibal W. Goodwin. • Thomas Edison and W.K. Dickson develop the Kinetoscope, a box in which rolled film is moved past a light. Viewers look into the box to see moving images, peep-show style.

FEBRUARY 18 Director and actor Erich von Stroheim b. (Sometimes his birthdate is given as September 22, 1885.)

APRIL 16 Charlie Chaplin b.

1890

JUNE 16   Stan Laurel b.

OCTOBER 2   Groucho Marx (Julius Marx) b.

1891

JULY 23   Harry Cohn, founder of Columbia Pictures, b.

1892

JANUARY 18   Oliver Hardy b.   **31**   Eddie Cantor (Edward Israel Iskowitz) b.

APRIL 8   Mary Pickford (Gladys Smith) b.

JULY 29   William Powell b.

AUGUST 2   Jack Warner, a founder of Warner Bros., b.   **17**   Mae West b.

NOVEMBER 9   Mabel Normand b.

1893

• Edison is granted a patent for his movie camera, the Kinetograph, and for the Kinetoscope.

FEBRUARY   Edison builds the first movie studio to produce films for his Kinetoscope. This $635 semi-enclosed stage with a camera mounted inside rotates to catch sunlight through its open roof, illuminating the scene being filmed. Workers call the tar paper–covered structure the "Black Maria," slang for a police wagon, which it resembles.

Thomas Edison   LC

APRIL 20   Harold Lloyd b.

MAY 9   In what is probably the first picture show, Edison demonstrates his Kinetoscope in Brooklyn. The film shows three of his workers pretending to be blacksmiths.

JULY 17   The International Alliance of Theatrical Stage Employees, better known as IATSE, is founded. This stage union will become the primary labor organization in the movie industry.

OCTOBER 14   Lillian Gish b.

DECEMBER 12   Edward G. Robinson (Emmanuel Goldenberg) b.

1894

JANUARY 7   The Library of Congress issues the first copyright for a film—deposited in the form of successive paper print photographs—to Thomas Edison for a movie of a man named Fred Ott sneezing. Edison shot the film in 1891.

APRIL 14   Edison's coin-operated Kinetoscope makes its commercial debut in a New York City amusement arcade, which has installed ten of his machines. The short films consist mostly of unedited slices of life, vaudeville acts, odd sights—almost anything that moves. Soon there are complaints that some of the films, such as *How Bridget Served the Salad Undressed*, are too suggestive.

1895

FEBRUARY 1   Director John Ford (Sean O'Feeney) b.   **13**   In France, Louis and August Lumière, inspired by Edison's Kinetoscope, patent a combination movie camera-projector, the Cinématographe. Unlike the bulky Kinetoscope that allows only viewing, the Cinématographe is portable, capable of projecting a movie that many people can watch at the same time, and can be used to shoot films as well.

MARCH 22   The Lumière brothers give the first public demonstration of the Cinématographe.

APRIL 21   In New York City, brothers Otway and Gray Latham, and their father, Woodville, demonstrate the Eidoloscope, a movie projector they built with the help of W.K. Dickson, who has worked with Edison. In probably the first projected movie show in America, they show scenes of boys playing in a park and a man smoking a pipe.

MAY 6   Rudolph Valentino (Rudolfo Guglielmi) b.

JULY 10   Silent-screen star John Gilbert b.

SEPTEMBER 22   Paul Muni b.

OCTOBER   The Phantascope, a movie projector invented by C. Francis Jenkins and Thomas Armat, notable for its intermittent motion mechanism, is shown at Atlanta's Cotton States Exposition.   **2**   Bud Abbott (William Abbott) b.   **4**   Buster Keaton (Joseph Francis Keaton) b.

DECEMBER 28   The Lumières, in Paris, give the first commercial exhibition of projected motion pictures in the first movie theater—at the Grand Café. Their show includes the first comedy: a prank played on a gardener, who is squirted with his own hose. In the next five years photographers employed by the Lumières will shoot scenes from life all over the globe, as well as a number of short fiction films. They will have produced about two thousand films by 1900. The word "cinema" will be derived from their Cinématographe. They also establish the standard film width at 35mm, used virtually everywhere, and a speed of sixteen frames per second.

1896

APRIL 20   Projected motion pictures have their commercial theatrical debut in America. The Edison Company, using the projector built by Thomas Armat and C. Francis Jenkins, now called the Vitascope, shows a variety of hand-tinted moving images, including dancers, at Koster & Bial's Music Hall in New York City. The show, presented as one of the vaudeville acts, is well received. (In 1902, Koster & Bial's will be demolished to make way for Macy's department store.)

Early movies are sometimes used as "chasers" in vaudeville houses to clear the audience after the last live act. Gradually, areas in amusement arcades will also be set aside for projected films.

MAY 30   Director Howard Hawks b.

OCTOBER 12   The American Mutoscope and Biograph Company demonstrates its Biograph projector at Hammerstein's Olympia Theater in New York.

DECEMBER   Showman Lyman Howe puts together the first traveling film exhibition, bringing movies to the hinterlands.

1897

• American Mutoscope and Biograph begins to make movies on a New York City rooftop.

MARCH   • J. Stuart Blackton and Albert E.

Program from Koster & Bial's Music Hall, including Edison's Vitascope selections
LC

Smith form the Edison Vitagraph film company, known later as American Vitagraph, and then just Vitagraph. **27** Gloria Swanson (Gloria Swenson) b.

MAY 16 Vitagraph shoots its first picture, *The Burglar on the Roof*. **18** Director Frank Capra b. **26** Silent-screen star Norma Talmadge b.

AUGUST 31 Thomas Edison is granted a patent for his movie camera, the Kinetograph.

1898

MAY 13 Edison files the first of many patent-infringement suits, claiming that others in the business are using equipment based on his Kinetograph camera. Biograph is his major target. Patent suits will color the history of the business for the next decade.

1899

JANUARY 23 Humphrey Bogart b.

MAY 10 Fred Astaire (Frederick Austerlitz) b. **30** Producer Irving Thalberg b.

JULY 17 James Cagney (Jr.) b.

AUGUST 13 Director Alfred Hitchcock b.

1900

APRIL 5 Spencer Tracy b.

1901

FEBRUARY 1 Clark Gable (William Clark Gable) b. **21** A vaudeville performers' strike allows movie exhibitors to make inroads at theaters where films are needed to fill out the bill.

MAY 7 Gary Cooper (Frank Cooper) b.

JUNE 18 Jeanette MacDonald b. **29** Nelson Eddy b.

DECEMBER 5 Walt Disney b. **27** Marlene Dietrich (Maria Magdalena Dietrich) b.

1902

MARCH 10 In *Edison v. American Mutoscope Company*, the U.S. Court of Appeals rules that Edison did not invent the movie camera, as he claimed, but does credit him with developing the mechanism of sprockets on the edge of the film to move it along.

APRIL 16 Thomas L. Talley's Electric Theater in a storefront in Los Angeles becomes the first theater showing movies exclusively.

MAY 10 Producer David O. Selznick, son of producer Lewis J. and brother of agent Myron Selznick, b.

JULY 1 Director William Wyler b.

AUGUST 11 Norma Shearer b.

SEPTEMBER 5 Producer Darryl F. Zanuck b.

1903

JANUARY • Edwin S. Porter, chief of production at the Edison studio, in his *Life of an American Fireman*, uses the technique of editing creatively and cuts from place to place rather than scene to scene, even from the inside to the outside of a house on fire. The film also includes a chase sequence. The extent to which Porter originated these techniques is in dispute.

FEBRUARY • The forty-room Hollywood Hotel is completed.

MARCH 10 Biograph patents a three-blade shutter, lessening the annoying flicker effect of early films. They also switch from

70mm to 35mm film.

APRIL 20 In *Edison v. Lubin*, a federal court rules that a film may be copyrighted in its entirety, not just each frame separately

MAY • Biograph opens the first indoor studio, on 14th Street in New York City. **29** Bob Hope (Leslie Hope) b.

NOVEMBER 14 The citizens of Hollywood vote to incorporate as a village.

DECEMBER • Edwin S. Porter uses editing techniques to build a narrative in *The Great Train Robbery*, made in New Jersey. This one-reel, approximately twelve-minute movie is probably the first film shot out of chronological sequence. It is also the first western—and the movies' first smash hit. "Broncho Billy" Anderson, the movies' first cowboy, falls off his horse during the film's production.

1904

JANUARY 18 Cary Grant (Archibald Leach) b.

MARCH 23 Joan Crawford (Lucille LeSeur) b.

MAY 2 Bing Crosby (Harry Lillis Crosby) b.

NOVEMBER 14 Dick Powell b.

1905

MAY 16 Henry Fonda b.

JUNE 19 Harry Davis, a local showman and real-estate speculator in Pittsburgh, opens the first nickelodeon. These small, storefront theaters show films with piano accompaniment and generally charge $.05 (sometimes $.10). This first one is on Smithfield St. and has ninety-six seats. The opening attraction is *The Great Train Robbery*. One block away is the jewelry store of Lewis J. Selznick, future movie pioneer, and father of agent Myron and producer David O. Selznick.

The name "nickelodeon" catches on and within months similar establishments are springing up all over. Some feature continuous showings of their typically fifteen-minute film programs, running as late as midnight. A few vaudeville acts, a lecture, or a slide show often accompany the movies. Nickelodeons are popular with immigrants, as well as with working-class audiences in general. These storefront theaters will dominate the exhibition business for the next five years, after which the modern movie theater will begin to replace them.

JULY 29 Clara Bow b.

AUGUST 2 Myrna Loy (Myrna Williams) b.

SEPTEMBER 13 Claudette Colbert (Claudette Lily Chauchoin) b. **18** Greta Garbo (Greta Gustafsson) b.

DECEMBER 16 *Variety*, "The Bible of Show Business," begins publication. **24** Producer Howard Hughes b.

1906

MARCH 6 Lou Costello b.

APRIL 26 *Views and Film Index*, the first trade paper devoted solely to movies, begins publication.

JUNE 22 Director Billy Wilder (Samuel Wilder) b.

AUGUST 5 Director John Huston, son of actor Walter Huston, b.

OCTOBER 6 Janet Gaynor (Laura Gainer) b.

NOVEMBER • Vitagraph opens America's most modern film studio in Brooklyn.

DECEMBER 5 Director Otto Preminger b.

1907

• The first film companies arrive in Los Angeles. The Selig Company's *The Count of Monte Cristo* is the first production filmed there—on the beach at Santa Monica.

JANUARY 19 *Variety*, begun two years ago, publishes its first film reviews, grouped with its coverage of new vaudeville acts. The review praises the seven-minute comedy *An Exciting Honeymoon*, and describes the thirteen-minute *The Life of a Cowboy* as "so melodramatic in treatment that it acted on the audience like a vivid play."

MAY 22 Laurence Olivier b. **26** John Wayne (Marion Morrison) b.

JULY 11 Douglas Fairbanks m. Anna Beth Sully. **16** Barbara Stanwyck (Ruby Stevens) b.

SEPTEMBER 29 Gene Autry b.

NOVEMBER 4 Chicago is the first city to censor movies, granting police the power to ban a movie prior to its first showing. Newspaper editorials and judges, who see film as inciting juvenile crime, have been calling for such a measure. Across the country, the nickelodeons, a cheap entertainment that attracts the working class and draws money and attention away from vaudeville and the churches, are beginning to be blamed for all kinds of social unrest, real and potential. **8** Katharine

Hepburn b. **28** Louis B. Mayer enters the movie business, opening a theater, the Orpheum, "home of refined amusement," in Haverhill, Massachusetts.

DECEMBER 3 Mary Pickford, making $25 a week, opens in the Broadway play *The Warrens of Virginia*, also starring Cecil B. DeMille

1908

• The International Alliance of Theatrical Stage Employees charters the first movie craft union, The Motion Picture Machine Operators.

APRIL 5 Bette Davis (Ruth Elizabeth Davis) b.

MAY 20 James Stewart b.

JULY 14 Biograph releases the first film directed by D.W. Griffith, *The Adventures of Dollie*. It concerns a gypsy thief and child kidnapper. In a month he will finish *The Fatal Hour*, a story about a Chinese man—a "saffron-skinned varlet," according to the Biograph press release—who forces pretty, young white girls into prostitution. In it, Griffith will use cross-cutting, a cinematic adaptation of a stage technique showing two simultaneous actions, to build toward a suspenseful climax. Over the next five years at Biograph, in more than four hundred pictures, Griffith will blend cross-cutting, close-ups, and other techniques into a new, cinematic style of narrative that will bring the one-reel film to its peak.

AUGUST 17 Biograph signs D.W. Griffith to a contract at $50 per week plus a small royalty on each film he directs. **30** Fred MacMurray b.

SEPTEMBER 9 The Motion Picture Patents Company—also known as the Patents Trust—is formed by the nine leading film companies in order to monopolize film production. It includes Biograph, Vitagraph, the Edison Studio, Essanay, Kalem, Selig, Lubin, Pathé, Méliés, and George Kleine, an importer. They agree to share rights to the various machine patents and not to sell or lease to any distributor buying from any other production company. Kodak agrees to sell raw film stock only to member companies. The Patents Company hopes to stop all others from breaking into the quickly growing industry. They distribute only to exhibitors who agree to their terms, charging each exhibitor $2 per week for the right to use the equipment covered by their patents. When any of the scores of lawsuits they file don't work, the Patents Company will use violence against defiant filmmakers, sending goons to break up their filming.

One goal of the Company is to upgrade the audience for movies. Toward this end, they give preferential treatment to exhibitors who open in middle-class areas, away from downtown sections populated by immigrants and working-class families.

The Patents Company, by ending the struggle over patents, brings stability and predictability to the business, enabling the studios to expand production and dominate their market, which had been under pressure from foreign competitors. **29** Greer Garson b.

OCTOBER 6 Carole Lombard (Jane Alice Peters) b.

DECEMBER 24 In a controversy over bribery for licensing movie houses and immorality in films, New York City temporarily shuts down all of its 600-plus nickelodeons. They will reopen under police supervision.

1909

• There are about nine-thousand movie theaters in the U.S. Newspapers are beginning to print stories about the movies, but not yet regular reviews.

FEBRUARY 11 Screenwriter-director Joseph L. Mankiewicz b. **13** D.W. Griffith has begun to make an impression on the critics, although, due to the lack of screen credit for his work, it is at first anonymous. The *New York Dramatic Mirror* says of his *A Fool's Revenge*: "This is the first American film that we have felt justified in pronouncing the equal in smoothness of construction and power of dramatic action of any of the Pathé 'film d'art'." **25** Members of The Motion Picture Patents Company submit the first films for review to the newly organized Board of Censorship in New York State. Made up of private citizens, the Board achieves the voluntary cooperation of the companies, which are afraid that the government will step in if the movie makers don't censor themselves. The Board soon becomes a national organization. By 1916 it will be known as The National Board of Review.

MARCH 16 In *Harper and Bros. v. Kalem Co.*, a federal court rules that Kalem's 1907 *Ben-Hur*, filmed without the author's permission, infringed on his copyright. The purchase of rights to a literary or stage property will become an important part of the movie business

APRIL 3 Screen comedian Ben Turpin is the first movie actor to be mentioned by name when written about in a publication—in the *Moving Picture World*, a trade journal. **12** Film distributor Carl Laemmle defies the Patents Company by setting up his own Independent Motion Picture Company,

known as IMP, using raw film stock obtained from abroad. Over the next three years Laemmle will have to fight 289 lawsuits, some of which involve the Edison equipment he begins to use surreptitiously. **20** Stage actress Mary Pickford begins her film career, working at Biograph on *Her First Biscuits*.

MAY 15 James Mason b.

JUNE 20 Errol Flynn b.

JULY • Tom Mix, who has already served with the Texas Rangers and won a national rodeo championship, comes upon a crew from the Selig Company filming *Ranch Life in the Great Southwest* in Oklahoma. Already on horseback, Mix joins up on the spot and ropes a steer on camera. He is also roped

into a career that will make him America's greatest silent-film cowboy star. From the late teens through the early twenties, he and his horse, Tony, will be two of the most familiar figures on the screen, especially to young moviegoers.

DECEMBER 18 Carl Laemmle institutionalizes the star system. Until now, studios generally avoided publicizing players by name. Their faces appeared in ads and on posters, and fans recognized them from film to film but could identify them by nothing more specific than descriptive nicknames such as "the Biograph girl." Laemmle hires the Biograph girl, Florence Lawrence, and in an ad in today's *Moving Picture World*, he publishes her photograph, proclaiming: "She's an Imp!"

Tom Mix, America's greatest silent-film cowboy star

LC

Photo opposite: Rudolph Valentino, courtesy the Lynch Collection

The Silent Film Era

1910–1926

*C*arl Laemmle creates the first movie personality to be known by name—Florence Lawrence, formerly the "Biograph Girl." Theaters begin to display still photos of the players in what are now called "photoplays," and Mary Pickford's curls are responsible for the first movie-inspired "look." Studios begin to pay for the rights to film literary properties. Films of the "Great White Hope" fight cause racial tension, the Patents Company tries to control film distribution, and Los Angeles annexes the incorporated village of Hollywood. Stage actor John Bunny joins Vitagraph, becoming the movies' first prominent comedian, and Norma Talmadge becomes the first of the three Talmadge sisters to appear in films, beginning her career with the same studio. Mack Sennett begins his directing career at Biograph, while D.W. Griffith is filming in California for the first time.

- Number of theaters: about 13,000
- Average length of a show: 3 reels—about 30 minutes
- Frequency shows are changed: daily
- Average cost of a ticket: $.07
- Population of Hollywood: 5,000
- Mary Pickford's salary: $175 per week
- First movie fashion fad: Mary Pickford's curls
- First sale of movie rights: $100 paid by Biograph for novel *Ramona*

Florence Lawrence, the Biograph Girl   LC

January	February	March	April	May	June	
• Exhibitors want promotional photos of players	**28** Vincente Minnelli b.	**1** David Niven b.	• Patents Trust organizes the General Film Company	**23** *Ramona*	• Phrase "Motion Picture Star" used in article	

July	August	September	October	November	December	
2 Fire destroys negatives of early Vitagraph films	**8** Sylvia Sidney b.	**1** John Barrymore m. Katherine Harris	**3** Charlie Chaplin and Stan Laurel tour U.S.	**10** Clune's Theater opens	• Mary Pickford leaves Biograph	

Personalities

• Pathé films imported into the United States introduce comedian Max Linder, a Charlie Chaplin prototype.

JANUARY 15 *Moving Picture World* notes that exhibitors are beginning to ask film companies for promotional photos of their players. **20** D.W. Griffith and his stock company arrive in Los Angeles for the first time to film.

FEBRUARY 4 *The Moving Picture World* reports that "Little Bebe Daniels, the well-known professional child actress . . . has given up picture work for the present . . ."

APRIL 16 A writer in the *New York Dramatic Mirror* states that Mary Pickford "has

a future if she doesn't permit her head to get swelled." Her golden curls are setting off the first movie-driven fashion fad.

MAY • The name of "the Vitagraph Girl," Florence Turner, appears on a studio advertising poster, and she begins to make personal appearances.

JUNE • Florence Turner is the subject of an article, "A Motion Picture Star," in the *New York Dramatic Mirror*, probably the first use of that expression to describe a player.

OCTOBER 3 Charlie Chaplin and Stan Laurel, members of Fred Karno's British vaudeville company, arrive to tour in the U.S. Later, in 1926, Laurel will find a partner and the famous team of Laurel and Hardy will be born.

DECEMBER • Mary Pickford leaves Biograph to work for Carl Laemmle at the Independent Moving Picture Company for $175 a week. Laemmle crows that "Little Mary is an Imp now."

Movies

• A contest conducted by the Essanay Company comes up with the word "photoplay" as a synonym for "pictures."

MARCH 7 D.W. Griffith features Mary Pickford in *The Thread of Destiny*. This film is notable for his use of multiple "shots" to build scenes, jumping from image to image to construct a narrative in a way that is unrelated to viewing a play on the stage.

MAY 23 Released today and starring Mary Pickford, *Ramona*, a D.W. Griffith picture

about the injustices done to the American Indian, is notable for the $100 Biograph pays for the right to film the Helen Jackson novel. It may be the first sale of movie rights.

NOVEMBER 23 Kalem releases *The Lad from Old Ireland*, the first U.S. film shot on location abroad.

DECEMBER 2 Vitagraph's *Jack Fat and Jim Slim at Coney Island*, probably the first of the 150 pictures rotund comedian John Bunny will make for the studio, is released.

Business and Society

FEBRUARY • Loew's Consolidated Enterprises—Adolph Zukor treasurer, Nicholas Schenck, secretary—combines Marcus Loew's theaters, amusement arcades, and other entertainment interests.

APRIL • The Patents Company, which has been trying to monopolize the production of films, now attempts the same thing with

film distribution by organizing the distributors they lease their films to into the General Film Company. Previously, independent "exchanges," operating as middle-men, handled distribution. General Film, by buying them out, will put the movie distribution and production business under one roof, a model for the coming Hollywood studio system. However, theater chain and exchange owner William Fox will not give up his independent distribution business. In fact, he now begins to make pictures to

compete with those produced by the members of the Patents Company.

JULY 2 A fire in New York destroys the only existing negatives of early Vitagraph films. **4** The Motion Picture Patents Company has purchased exclusive rights to film tonight's fight, in which black boxer Jack Johnson defeats James Jeffries (the "Great White Hope"). **23** Georgia, in response to the "Great White Hope" fight film, prohibits the showing of interracial

Births, Deaths, Marriages, and Divorces

FEBRUARY 27 Joan Bennett, sister of Constance Bennett, b. **28** Director Vincente Minnelli b.

MARCH 1 David Niven (James David Niven) b.

MAY 8 Samuel Goldfish (later Goldwyn) m. Blanche Lasky, sister of Jesse Lasky.

AUGUST 8 Sylvia Sidney b.

SEPTEMBER 1 John Barrymore m. Katherine Harris.

OCTOBER 27 Jack Carson b.

DECEMBER 13 Van Heflin (Emmett Evan Heflin, Jr.) b.

Laurel and Hardy in *Leave 'Em Laughin'*, 1928

LC

boxing films, fearing that they will provoke violence. Several cities throughout the country follow suit.

AUGUST • Edison reintroduces his Kineto-phone, which combines the phonograph with movies to produce talking pictures and which was developed in his laboratory in 1889. It was a commercial failure in Kineto-scope parlors in the 1890s, and it will fail again in movie theaters.

OCTOBER 8 The founding of the American Film Manufacturing Company, an inde-pendent distribution operation set up by members of several film exchanges, is announced. Its aim is to thwart the Patent Company's attempt to monopolize film distribution.

NOVEMBER 10 Clune's Theater in Los Angeles, a nine-hundred-seat auditorium for movies, opens.

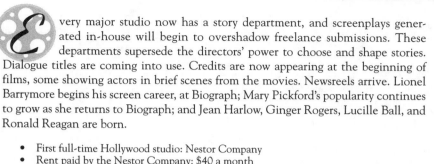

*E*very major studio now has a story department, and screenplays generated in-house will begin to overshadow freelance submissions. These departments supersede the directors' power to choose and shape stories. Dialogue titles are coming into use. Credits are now appearing at the beginning of films, some showing actors in brief scenes from the movies. Newsreels arrive. Lionel Barrymore begins his screen career, at Biograph; Mary Pickford's popularity continues to grow as she returns to Biograph; and Jean Harlow, Ginger Rogers, Lucille Ball, and Ronald Reagan are born.

- First full-time Hollywood studio: Nestor Company
- Rent paid by the Nestor Company: $40 a month
- Movies' first bankable name: Mary Pickford
- Mary Pickford's salary: $275 per week
- First state to pass a film censorship law: Pennsylvania
- D.W. Griffith's first two-reeler: *Enoch Arden*

Mary Pickford   *LC*

January	February	March	April	May	June	
• *His Trust and His Trust Fulfilled*	• *Motion Picture Story Magazine* begins publication	**25** The *Moving Picture World* criticizes close-ups	**11** Mae West m. Frank Wallace	**27** Vincent Price b.	**12–15** *Enoch Arden*	

July	August	September	October	November	December	
16 Ginger Rogers b.	**8** First U.S. newsreel		**27** First Hollywood studio opens	**18** *The Courting of Mary*	• Mary Pickford returns to Biograph	

Personalities

FEBRUARY • Vitagraph begins publication of *Motion Picture Story Magazine*, a forerunner of the movie fan magazine. It relates the plots of the studio's films, and features pictures and information about the stars.

OCTOBER 14 A court voids Mary Pickford's contract with the Independent Moving Picture Company because she was a minor when she signed it. She will leave IMP to work for the Majestic company at $275 a week. Her presence at that studio is the key to its viability—the beginning of the "bankable" name in movie making.

DECEMBER • *Motion Picture Story* magazine publishes what may be the first interview with a star, Florence Lawrence. She says she doesn't miss the theater, likes opera, and is a Suffragette. • Mary Pickford returns to Biograph.

Movies

JANUARY • With two- and three-reel films running thirty minutes and more becoming common in Europe, D.W. Griffith finally gets Biograph to permit him to make a two-reeler. But it releases the film in two parts, to be shown a week apart: *His Trust* and *His Trust Fulfilled*. **9** Mary Pickford's first IMP film, *Their First Misunderstanding*, is released.

MARCH 25 The *Moving Picture World* comments on close-ups: "There are very many moving pictures made nowadays, even by reputable makers, in which the figures are too near the camera . . . . Filmmakers have the idea that the public wants to see the faces of the figures large . . . ."

JUNE 12–15 Biograph releases D.W. Griffith's *Enoch Arden*, a two-reeler, in two parts. But the week-long wait between sections disappoints audiences, who let it be known that they want to see them closer together. Theater managers begin to show the sections on consecutive days, and finally Biograph relents and releases them as a whole. It is a harbinger of the American "feature-length" film.

AUGUST 8 *Pathé's Weekly* is the first newsreel to be regularly released in the U.S.

NOVEMBER 18 Majestic releases *The Courting of Mary*, its first film starring Mary Pickford.

Business and Society

JANUARY 7 *Moving Picture World* introduces its first California correspondent.

FEBRUARY 14 Kodak breaks with the Patents Company and resumes selling its film stock to all who wish to buy it.

APRIL 8 An article in the *Moving Picture World* states that "Los Angeles within the short period of two years has reached a position in the moving picture manufacturing field where it is second only to New York." The major studios are still headquartered in the East. Edison, Biograph, and Vitagraph are in the New York area. Kalem is in Stamford, Connecticut. Essanay and Selig, in Chicago, are the western outposts.

JULY 19 Pennsylvania is the first state to pass a law censoring movies.

AUGUST • The Motion Picture Exhibitors' League, the first national theater owner's group, is established. **27** Twenty-five people are trampled to death in a panic caused by a small fire in a Canonsburg, Pennsylvania, movie theater.

OCTOBER • Director Thomas Ince leases thousands of acres of California land for what will become known as "Inceville," a fully equipped outdoor movie facility. **27** The Nestor Company is the first to

Births, Deaths, Marriages, and Divorces

JANUARY 7 Mary Pickford m. Owen Moore.

FEBRUARY 6 Ronald Reagan b. **19** Merle Oberon (Estelle Merle O'Brien Thompson) b.

MARCH 3 Jean Harlow (Harlean Carpenter) b.

APRIL 11 Mae West m. Frank Wallace.

MAY 16 Margaret Sullavan (Margaret Brooke) b. **17** Maureen O'Sullivan b. **27** Vincent Price b.

JUNE 3 Paulette Goddard (Marion Levy) b. (When she dies, in Switzerland, in 1990, the authorities will list her year of birth as 1905.) **29** Composer Bernard Herrmann b.

Jean Harlow (left) and Lucille Ball (right) are both born this year. While the glamorous Harlow will die an early death in 1937, Ball will begin her career as a film actress and then become one of television's all-time greats before her death in 1989.   *LC*

open a full-time studio in Hollywood—at Sunset and Gower.

JULY 16   Ginger Rogers (Virginia McMath) b.

AUGUST 5   Robert Taylor (Spangler Arlington Brugh) b.   **6**   Lucille Ball b.

OCTOBER 5   Larry Fine (Louis Fineburg) of the Three Stooges b.

DECEMBER 8   Lee J. Cobb b.   **9**   Broderick Crawford (William Broderick Crawford), son of actress Helen Broderick, b.

he Patents Company begins to lose in the courts. Carl Laemmle forms what will become Universal Pictures, and Adolph Zukor starts Famous Players. The Copyright Act of 1912 is the first to specifically protect films. Neighborhood theaters charging $.10 to $.15 are replacing the smaller, store-front nickelodeons, as the middle class begins to go to the movies. Thomas Ince creates the role of film producer, and the four-reel, feature-length *Queen Elizabeth* foreshadows the demise of the one-reel film. The Keystone Kops and Dorothy and Lillian Gish debut. Carbon arc lamps, which give off dirty carbon particles and irritate the eyes, come into regular use in filming. And Hollywood has its first nightclub.

- Number of theaters: 13,000
- Number of feature-length films released: 2
- First Keystone comedies: *Cohen Collects a Debt* and *The Water Nymph*
- First Keystone Kop film: *Hoffmeyer's Legacy*
- First gangster film: Griffith's *The Musketeers of Pig Alley*
- Number of film companies in Hollywood: 15
- First Hollywood nightclub: the Vernon Country Club
- Number of Chicago theaters declared unsafe by that city's Buildings Commissioner: 50

Mack Sennett, genius of the Keystone Company   *LC*

January	February	March	April	May	June	
• *War on the Plains*	**24** Variety reviews The Marx Bros. & Co. vaudeville act		**8** Sonja Henie b. • Francis X. Bushman: America's favorite movie actor	**2** First Hollywood nightclub opens	**2** Universal Film Manufacturing Company (Universal) formed	

July	August	September	October	November	December	
12 *Queen Elizabeth*	**23** Gene Kelly b.	**23** First Keystone comedies	• Mary Pickford leaves Biograph again	• Roy Rogers b.	**23** Keystone's first "Kop" film	

Personalities

• Probably the first player to do so, actress Helen Gardner forms her own production company, the Helen Gardner Picture Corporation.

FEBRUARY 24 *Variety* reviews a vaudeville act called The Marx Bros. & Co., "A lively set of youngsters, with four comedians." One of them "is a harpist, and a good one."

MARCH • *Motion Picture Story* magazine declares Francis X. Bushman to be America's favorite photoplay actor.

APRIL • Francis X. Bushman, America's favorite movie actor, is wounded in the arm when hit by the wadding from a blank shot while filming a detective story for Essanay.

Francis X. Bushman, America's favorite actor, in *Ben-Hur*   MSN

Movies

JANUARY • With the release of *War on the Plains*, director Thomas Ince brings a new realism to westerns by hiring an entire Wild West show to fill the screen with authentic detail. He is the first supervisor-producer, introducing the detailed shooting script to movie production.

JULY 11 Mae Marsh's career gets started with the release of Griffith's *Man's Genesis*. Mary Pickford and Blanche Sweet have passed on it because it required them to show their bare legs. **12** *Queen*

Elizabeth, a four-reel French film running close to forty-five minutes, imported by Adolph Zukor, opens in New York, marking the beginning of the end of the one-reel feature. The members of the Pat-

ents Company will stick doggedly to the shorter-length pictures. The film's American premiere also is a landmark on the path to middle class respectability for the movies. The audience, once mostly

Business and Society

• In Britain, a Board of Film Censors, a non-governmental organization, sets up a letter-based rating system. "U" designates Universal Exhibition; "A" requires children fifteen and under to be accompanied by an adult.

MARCH • The Mutual Film Corporation, an independent distributing and releasing

company, is formed. The power of the Patents Company to stymie such organizations is all but gone.

APRIL 27 The *Motion Picture World*, writing about *The Cry of the Children*, a film about child labor, states: "The value of a moving picture as a means of agitating for the betterment of social conditions is self-evident. Nothing affects us more powerfully than the truth when it is preached in pictures."

JUNE 1 Adolph Zukor incorporates the Famous Players Film Company, which initially features stars of the Broadway stage. It is a future building block of Paramount Pictures. **2** Carl Laemmle merges IMP with several other independent studios to form the Universal Film Manufacturing Company, known as Universal. It will become the first major Hollywood studio.

AUGUST 4 A *New York Times* article complains that movies have brought "a new

Births, Deaths, Marriages, and Divorces

NOVEMBER Roy Rogers (Leonard Slye) b.

JANUARY 8 Jose Ferrer b.

APRIL 8 Sonja Henie b.

MAY 5 Alice Faye (Alice Lippert) b. **23** John Payne b.

AUGUST 23 Gene Kelly b.

MAY 2 Hollywood's first nightclub, the Vernon Country Club, opens.

JULY • Dorothy Gish, fourteen, and Lillian Gish, sixteen, are taken by their mother to call on Mary Pickford, with whom they used to board, at the Biograph studios in the Bronx. Mrs. Gish hopes to get her daughters into the pictures. D.W. Griffith hires them, and the next day they make their first film, *The Unseen Enemy*.

AUGUST 28 Mack Sennett and Mabel Normand arrive in Los Angeles to begin work at Keystone.

OCTOBER • Mary Pickford leaves Biograph again.

working class, is beginning to change, as the movies become more respectable and the middle class gets the movie-going habit. **26** The release of *What Happened to Mary*, a series of twelve films and a precursor of the serial, begins. They are filmed by the Edison Company and appear simultaneously in *McClure's Ladies World* as short stories. Each movie, though, is complete, and is not "to be continued."

SEPTEMBER 23 The first Keystone comedies, *Cohen Collects a Debt* and *The Water Nymph*, featuring Mabel Normand, are released. The *New York Dramatic Mirror* calls *Cohen* "idiotic horseplay."

OCTOBER 31 Biograph releases D.W. Griffith's *The Musketeers of Pig Alley*. Filmed in the slums of New York City, it is sometimes cited as the first gangster movie. Lillian Gish stars, and scholar Kevin Brownlow has pointed out that Elmer Booth, playing a gangster called the Snapper Kid, has the look and air of the early James Cagney movie hoods. Biograph is promoting the picture with claims that real gangsters are playing in it. Future real-life mobster Lucky Luciano is now a fifteen-year-old, living two streets away from where this movie was made.

NOVEMBER • Essanay's release, *The House*

of Pride, features the first teaming of Francis X. Bushman and Beverly Bayne, the screen's first great love duo.

DECEMBER 5 D.W. Griffith's *The New York Hat*, starring Mary Pickford and based on the first screenplay by teenager Anita Loos, is released. Loos mailed the manuscript to the Biograph studio from her home in San Diego and was paid $25. **23** Keystone releases its first "Kop" film: *Hoffmeyer's Legacy*. These films will be made through 1920. Mack Sennett will make a brief appearance in *Abbott and Costello Meet the Keystone Kops* in 1955.

capriciousness to the public mind, a feverish desire for change which is new even to the amusement world." Trends and fashion in work and play had been lasting two or three years, but with the advent of movies, they last only two or three months. **12** The formation of the Keystone Film Company is announced. Mack Sennett, actor, director, and screenwriter, who has worked with D.W. Griffith at Biograph, starts the company with the backing of the New York Motion Picture Company's

Charles O. Bauman and Adam Kessel. **16** The U.S. government sues the Motion Picture Patents Company and its distributing arm, the General Film Company, charging that it is a trust in restraint of trade. It is the beginning of the end for the Patents Company. **24** The U.S. Circuit Court rules against the Motion Picture Patents Company on their claim to exclusive rights to the mechanism used in movie cameras.

*V*ariety begins to devote several pages in the back of the paper to the movies. Theaters start to use lobby cards to promote their shows. The first American serial appears, Fatty Arbuckle and Mabel Normand are paired for the first time, Lon Chaney has his initial makeup-dependent role, and Mary Pickford joins Famous Players. D.W. Griffith leaves Biograph. Players are demanding screen credits; *Photoplay*, the first real fan magazine, debuts; and Cecil B. DeMille, with the newly formed Jesse Lasky Company, films *The Squaw Man*, the first feature-length picture made in Hollywood. British vaudevillian Charlie Chaplin makes his first picture. And Loretta Young, Burt Lancaster, Alan Ladd, and Vivien Leigh are born.

- Number of theaters in New York City: 1,000
- Theaters in U.S. catering to black audiences: 214
- Number of feature-length films released: 12
- Average feature film budget: $13,000
- First serial: *The Adventures of Kathlyn*
- First major exploitation film: *Traffic in Souls*
- First film pie-in-the-face: Mabel Normand to Fatty Arbuckle
- Mary Pickford's salary: $500 per week
- Charlie Chaplin's salary at Keystone: $150 a week
- Fatty Arbuckle's pay as a Keystone Kop: $3 per day
- Ticket price for first-run of *Quo Vadis*: $1.50

Fighting Blood, with Blanche Sweet, 1911, one of the hundreds of films D.W. Griffith directed for Biograph.   *LC*

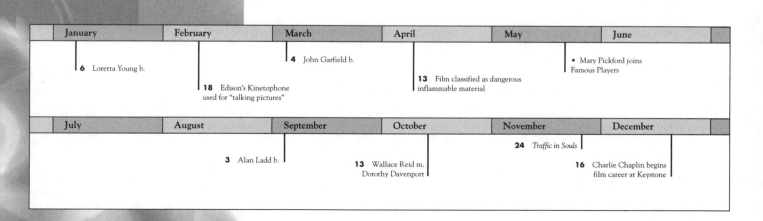

January	February	March	April	May	June	
6 Loretta Young b.	**18** Edison's Kinetophone used for "talking pictures"	**4** John Garfield b.	**13** Film classified as dangerous inflammable material		• Mary Pickford joins Famous Players	

July	August	September	October	November	December	
	3 Alan Ladd b.	**13** Wallace Reid m. Dorothy Davenport		**24** *Traffic in Souls*	**16** Charlie Chaplin begins film career at Keystone	

Personalities

MAY • Mary Pickford joins Adolph Zukor's Famous Players Company at $500 a week, where producer B.P. Schulberg will dub her "America's Sweetheart."

SEPTEMBER 25 Charlie Chaplin signs with Keystone to appear in the movies. **29** Unhappy with his treatment at Biograph and about to leave for greener pastures, D.W. Griffith takes out an ad in the *New York Dramatic Mirror*, listing his accomplishments and declaring himself "Producer of all great Biograph successes, revolutionizing Motion Picture drama and founding the modern technique of the art."

NOVEMBER 21 "Picture Actors Are Asking for Names on the Screen," according

Movies

APRIL 21 *Quo Vadis*, an epic, eight-reel Italian film, opens at the Astor Theater, where it will play for twenty-two weeks. It is the first film to play its initial engagement in a respectable Broadway theater. Its $1.50 admission price is also a first. **29** Roscoe "Fatty" Arbuckle's first Keystone film, *The Gangsters*, is released.

JUNE 13 Fatty Arbuckle and Mabel Normand make their first joint screen appearance in *The Waiter's Picnic*, released today.

Mabel Normand, the gifted Mack Sennett comedienne, delivers the first recorded pie-in-the-face on film.   *LC*

Business and Society

JANUARY 13 The Thanhouser Company's studios in New Rochelle, New York, burn down. On February 4 it will release *When the Studio Burned Down*, about the fire.

FEBRUARY 18 The headline on a *New York Times* article reports: "New York Applauds The Talking Picture." The show, from the Edison Company, consists of several shorts in the inventor's Kinetophone process, which synchronizes a phonograph record with a film. One of the films, shown at four theatres, features a minstrel show. The process is technologically rough, and doesn't always work right. In fact, on March 21, *Variety* will report that sound films were booed at a New York theater.

APRIL • Biograph, its days as a major studio numbered, finally begins to identify its players by name. **13** The Interstate Commerce Commission classifies film as dangerous and inflammable material for the purpose of regulating its shipment.

OCTOBER 3 Marcus Loew secures rights to film the World Series.

NOVEMBER 26 The Jesse Lasky Feature Play Company is formed. Playwright Cecil B. DeMille is the company's first director and Lasky's brother-in-law, Samuel Goldfish (later Goldwyn), manages sales.

Births, Deaths, Marriages, and Divorces

JANUARY 6 Loretta Young (Gretchen Young) b. **18** Danny Kaye (David Daniel Kominski) b.

MARCH 4 John Garfield (Julius Garfinkle) b.

MAY 5 Tyrone Power (Jr.) is born, son of actor Tyrone Power. **6** Stewart Granger (James Stewart) b. **8** Hedda Hopper m. actor De Wolf Hopper. **26** Peter Cushing b.

SEPTEMBER 3 Alan Ladd b. **23** Producer/director Stanley Kramer b.

OCTOBER 13 Wallace Reid m. actress Dorothy Davenport, daughter of character actor Harry Davenport.

to a *Variety* headline.

DECEMBER • Cecil B. DeMille wants a more realistic place to film *The Squaw Man* than New Jersey, which Jesse Lasky prefers, so DeMille takes the train to Flagstaff, Arizona. When the director doesn't like what he sees there, he keeps going. Reaching the coast, he sends one of the most famous telegrams in Hollywood history to Lasky: HAVE PROCEEDED TO CALIFORNIA. WANT AUTHORITY TO RENT BARN IN A PLACE CALLED HOLLYWOOD FOR SEVENTY-FIVE DOLLARS A MONTH. REGARDS TO SAM. Samuel Goldfish and Lasky approve, but caution that DeMille should rent by the month, without "any long commitment." That barn will become the legendary birthplace of Paramount's Hollywood studio. • *Photoplay*, the first true movie fan magazine, debuts. The cover story is "Children of the Photoplays," about child actors. **16** Charlie Chaplin begins his film career at Keystone at $150 per week. **29** Filming begins on the first feature-length movie made in Hollywood: Cecil B. DeMille's *The Squaw Man*, starring Dustin Farnum. Farnum and leading lady Winifred Kingston are soon carrying on the first on-the-set romance. **31** W. Somerset Maugham escorts Billie Burke to a New Year's Eve party at the Hotel Astor in New York, where she meets Flo Ziegfeld, her future husband. **31** D.W. Griffith, after directing close to five hundred films for Biograph, leaves to direct for the independent company, Mutual, which will allow him to make one picture of his own, annually. He takes with him his cameraman "Billy" Bitzer and the Griffith company of actors. Biograph was shocked at Griffith's extravagance in letting his latest film, *Judith* *of Bethulia*, starring Blanche Sweet, run to four reels and double its original budget, and had relieved him of his directing duties. None of the Patent Trust firms want the multi-reel, expensive film to become the norm. (The company, however, will release the film in March 1914.)

JULY 17 In Keystone's *A Noise from the Deep*, released today, Mabel Normand delivers the first recorded pie-in-the-face to Roscoe "Fatty" Arbuckle. Mack Sennett will later say that Ben Turpin was the recipient, but the comedian will not join Keystone until 1917.

AUGUST 22 *The Sea Urchin*, in which Lon Chaney plays a hunchback—his first makeup-dependent role—is released.

NOVEMBER 24 Universal's *Traffic in Souls*, about "white slavery" (prostitution), the first major exploitation feature, is released. Although costing $25,000 to make, it's billed as "a $200,000 spectacle... showing the traps cunningly laid for young girls by vice agents." The ads imply a link to the recent Rockefeller White Slavery Report, but John D. Rockefeller, Jr. disavows any such connection. The movie, directed by George Loane Tucker, will gross about $450,000. One thousand moviegoers are turned away from Joe Weber's Theatre on Broadway on opening night — helping to pay for much of the building of Universal City in Hollywood.

DECEMBER 29 The Selig Company releases the first of thirteen chapters of the first American serial, *The Adventures of Kathlyn*, starring Kathlyn Williams. The *Chicago Tribune*, which runs the story serially in its pages, coproduces it.

NOVEMBER 2 Burt Lancaster b. **4** Gig Young b. **5** Vivien Leigh b. **9** Heddy Lamarr (Hedwig Kiesler) b.

Also this year: • Pola Negri m. Count Eugene Dambski. • Claude Rains m. actress Isabel Jeans.

A typical four-reel program sent out by Universal consists of a two-reel drama, one-reel comedy, and a one-reel travelogue or documentary. Max Factor introduces the first special screen makeup: Supreme Greasepaint—required for indoor shooting with artificial light. Chicago sets up America's first rating system, restricting certain types of films to people over the age of twenty-one. These films are issued "pink permits." Charlie Chaplin introduces the "tramp." Pearl White is a star in *The Perils of Pauline*, and the first movie "palace" opens. Beverly Hills incorporates.

- Number of one-reel films released in December: 306
- Five-reel films released in December: 52
- Number of episodes in the serial *Hazards of Helen*, begun this year and running through 1917: 119
- Charlie Chaplin's debut as the "tramp" in *Kid Auto Races at Venice*
- Value of U.S. film exports (1913–14): $6,500,000
- Mary Pickford's salary: $2,000 a week
- Charlie Chaplin's salary: $1,250 a week
- First screen makeup: Max Factor's Supreme Greasepaint
- First prominent cartoon character: "Gertie the Dinosaur"
- First city to set up a rating system: Chicago

"Gertie the Dinosaur," one of the first animated characters, drawn by Winsor McKay   *LC*

January	February	March	April	May	June	
28 Beverly Hills incorporated			**25** *Neptune's Daughter*		**9** Eddie Cantor m. Ida Tobias	
	15 *The Squaw Man*	• "Gertie the Dinosaur," first prominent cartoon character		**8** Paramount Pictures, a distributor, formed		

July	August	September	October	November	December	
			26 Jackie Coogan b.		**10** Dorothy Lamour b.	
4 Griffith begins filming *The Birth of a Nation*				**14** *Tillie's Punctured Romance*		

Personalities

• Louella Parson's first movie column appears in the *Chicago Record-Herald*.

JANUARY • Mexican rebel Pancho Villa agrees to accommodate American moviemakers by scheduling his fighting, whenever possible, for their filming convenience. It will result in *The Life of General Villa*, Raoul Walsh and Christy Cabanne, directors. **28** Beverly Hills, future home of the stars, is incorporated.

MARCH 20 *Variety* praises the vaudeville dance act of Mae Murray and Clifton Webb.

JULY • The readers of the *Ladies World* vote Francis X. Bushman "the typical American hero." **4** D.W. Griffith begins four

months of filming on *The Clansman* (later retitled *The Birth of a Nation*). Battle scenes are shot on land now partly occupied by Forest Lawn Cemetery.

OCTOBER • Sessue Hayakawa becomes one of the first foreign actors to establish a career in American films. His third picture, *Typhoon*, is a big hit. In it, a woman says to him: "You yellow whining rat—and your Japan, a yellow blot on the ocean."

NOVEMBER • Adolph Zukor raises Mary Pickford to $2,000 a week. **14** Charlie Chaplin leaves Keystone to sign with the Essanay company at $1,250 per week. He will make fourteen films for them in 1915.

DECEMBER 13 Mack Sennett says that Mabel Normand will henceforth direct all films in which she appears.

Movies

FEBRUARY • Mary Pickford is a hit in *Tess of the Storm Country*, the credits of which bill her as "America's Foremost Film Actress." **2** *Making a Living*, featuring Charlie Chaplin's first appearance in a Mack Sennett comedy, of which he will make thirty-five this year, is released. Chaplin, who will direct twenty-three of these films himself, is an immediate hit. **7** Charlie Chaplin debuts as "The Tramp," with mustache, derby, baggy trousers, and cane, in *Kid Auto Races at Venice*, released today. **15** The Lasky Company releases *The Squaw Man*.

MARCH • "Gertie the Dinosaur," a character created by newspaper illustrator Winsor McKay in 1909, debuts in a cartoon at the Palace Theater in Chicago. McKay drew each frame by hand. Gertie becomes the movies' first prominent cartoon character. • Biograph releases D.W. Griffith's four-reel *Judith of Bethulia*. **3** Pathé releases *The Perils of Pauline*, a serial starring Pearl White. In one episode she saves the life of a child, played by six-year-old Milton Berle. White, a former circus trapeze artist, does her own stunts. *The Moving Picture World* declares: "The motion picture serial has come to stay."

APRIL 12 The Strand, in Times Square, the first movie "palace," built specifically to exhibit films, opens. It has a two-story lobby, seats about three thousand, and is managed by Samuel "Roxy" Rothapfel. The opening attraction is *The Spoilers*, starring William Farnum. **25** Swimming star Annette Kellerman makes her film debut in *Neptune's Daughter*, released today.

JUNE 1 *Cabiria*, an Italian spectacle about ancient Rome's defeat of Carthage, opens in New York and becomes a big hit despite its three-hour running time. The screenplay for *Cabiria* is attributed to poet Gabriele d'Annunzio, the first prominent

Business and Society

FEBRUARY 19 The mayor of Pittsburgh orders movie theaters to set aside a section for unaccompanied women, who have been harassed by men when the lights go out.

MARCH 18 Georgia Senator Hoke Smith introduces a bill to set up a federal motion picture censorship commission. **27** Fire damages Edison's Bronx film studio.

MAY 8 Paramount Pictures is formed by W.W. Hodkinson to finance and distribute nationally the feature films of several independent producers. On May 15 Adolph Zukor and Jesse Lasky will agree to distribute through Paramount. **26** A *New York Times* editorial acknowledges the legitimacy of the verb, "to film." It also gives its nod to the new word "movie."

JUNE • Fire destroys the prints and negatives of the Lubin Company's early films.

6 Carl Laemmle declares in the *Universal Weekly* that feature-length films are a fad, two-reelers, the future.

JULY • Lewis J. Selznick, father of Myron and David O. Selznick, becomes vice president and general manager of the World Film Company.

OCTOBER 29 Moviemakers can now purchase Kodak film in Los Angeles instead of sending to Rochester, New York, for it.

Births, Deaths, Marriages, and Divorces

JANUARY 4 Jane Wyman (Sarah Jane Mayfield, later Sarah Jane Fulks) b. **30** John Ireland b.

FEBRUARY 15 Kevin McCarthy, brother of author Mary McCarthy, b. **17** Arthur Kennedy (John Arthur Kennedy) b.

MARCH 22 Karl Malden (Malden Sekulovich) b. **24** Richard Conte (Nicolas Conte) b.

APRIL 2 Alec Guinness b. **12** Billie Burke m. Flo Ziegfeld.

Charlie Chaplin makes his first appearance as "the Tramp" this year. This scene is from *Sunnyside*, 1919.   *LC*

literary figure to be so credited in a film. This film introduces the tracking shot to America. It will be screened at the White House for President Wilson, the first movie shown there.

NOVEMBER 14 *Tillie's Punctured Romance* is released. Charlie Chaplin and Mabel Normand co-star with stage actress Marie Dressler in this six-reel film, Mack Sennett's first feature-length picture. The film, based on Dressler's 1910 Broadway hit, *Tillie's Nightmare*, is Chaplin's last appearance in a film that he does not direct himself.

MAY 11 Alice Joyce m. Tom Moore.

JUNE 9 Eddie Cantor m. Ida Tobias.

OCTOBER 26 Jackie Coogan b.

NOVEMBER 24 Geraldine Fitzgerald b.

DECEMBER 10 Dorothy Lamour b. **14** Dan Dailey b. **26** Richard Widmark b.

Also this year: • Barbara LaMarr m. twice: cowboy Jack Lytell, who dies, and, in June, Lawrence Converse, arrested for bigamy the day after their wedding. He will die in jail. • Lon Chaney divorces Cleva Creighton and m. Hazel Bennett.

1915

𝒯he feature film of five or more reels is slowly gaining dominance. D.W. Griffith transforms American filmmaking with *The Birth of a Nation*, which engenders protest over its overt racism. The Fox film corporation is formed and turns Theodosia Goodman into Theda Bara, "the vamp." Douglas Fairbanks, W.C. Fields, and Harold Lloyd begin their picture careers. The Bell & Howell 2709 camera begins to replace the Pathé model used since the early days of the movies. The new camera has a turret lens that acts like a zoom, facilitating special effects shots and closeups without camera movement. It will become the standard until replaced in the 1920s by a model made by the Mitchell Company. Meanwhile, film is beginning to receive serious consideration as an art form.

- Number of theaters: about 17,000
- Number of feature-length films released: 419
- Value of U.S. film exports (1914–15): $5,100,000
- Douglas Fairbanks's salary: $2,000 per week
- Mary Pickford's salary: $4,000 a week
- Ethel Barrymore's fee for making movies: $40,000 per picture
- First movie sex symbol: Theda Bara

Top male and female box office stars, based on a Quigley publications poll of exhibitors:
male: William S. Hart
female: Mary Pickford

William S. Hart (center, facing camera) moved from stage productions to movie westerns. He is shown here in a scene from *The Gun Fighter*, 1916.   *LC*

January	February	March	April	May	June
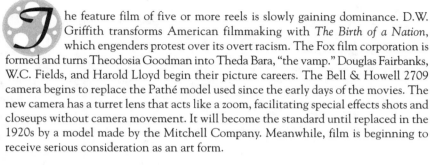 **12** *A Fool There Was*, with "vamp" Theda Bara	**8** *The Birth of a Nation*	• Mary Pickford making $4,000 a week	**27** Opera singer Geraldine Farrar signs movie contract	**1** Francis X. Bushman leaves Essanay for Metro	**3** "Dead End Kid" Leo Gorcey b.

July	August	September	October	November	December
20 The Triangle Film Corporation formed	**29** Ingrid Bergman b.	**10** Edmond O'Brien b.	**13** Cornel Wilde b.	**19** Technicolor is in business	**14** Ethel Barrymore signs with Metro

Personalities

- Although Hollywood has taken over from New York City and Ft. Lee, New Jersey, as the world's film capital, many of Hollywood's residents continue to look down their noses at the people they refer to as "the movies." Ads for rooms to rent still carry the line: "no movies."

JANUARY • James Quirk becomes editor of *Photoplay*, and turns it into the fan magazine that will dominate its field for the next two decades, chronicling and helping to create the careers of innumerable stars and playing a large role in the growth of the celebrityhood phenomenon.

FEBRUARY • Charlie Chaplin is becoming so popular that theaters are holding con-

tests in which people imitate him. **27** In an article on Francis X. Bushman, the movies' first matinee idol, the *Moving Picture World* observes: "Only yesterday a gentleman of the stage could 'get away with anything,' first because he was an actor, and second because the public didn't care so long as he pleased them. Today we know what our favorite star eats for breakfast, whether he prefers lavender or red hosiery, and innumerable other things associated with private life. He must conduct himself true to the ethics of propriety lest he be ostracized by the very fans whose favor he would curry."

MARCH • Mary Pickford's salary at Famous Players has reached $4,000 a week.

APRIL 27 Jesse Lasky announces that opera singer Geraldine Farrar has signed a movie

contract. She will get $20,000 for three films and a private railroad car from New York to Los Angeles.

MAY 1 Francis X. Bushman leaves Essanay for Metro.

SEPTEMBER • With the opening of *The Lamb*, his first film and first big splash at the box office, stage actor Douglas Fairbanks suddenly finds himself a movie star. But on the set the crew dislike his constant athletic workouts—D.W. Griffith calls him "The Jumping Jack"—and find his condescending airs obnoxious, and they respond by sabotaging his makeup. Triangle has put Fairbanks under the general supervision of D.W. Griffith, who is oblivious to Valentino's screen charm. Griffith appears to have a much better sense of female movie talent than of male.

Movies

JANUARY 1 D.W. Griffith shows *The Clansman* (*The Birth of a Nation*) at a sneak preview—a practice he has been credited for starting—in Riverside, California. **12** *A Fool There Was* premieres in New York. Fox makes its star, Theda Bara, Hollywood's first sex symbol and temptress—the "vamp"—and the first Hollywood-fabricated celebrity persona, complete with pre-release publicity tour. It was cheaper to create a Theda Bara than to pay a big salary from the beginning to a prominent Broadway actress with an

Theda Bara, the "vamp"   *MSN*

Business and Society

FEBRUARY 1 William Fox combines his motion picture production, distribution, and theater chain into the Fox Film Corporation, which will feature Theda Bara and Tom Mix. **18** President Woodrow Wilson, a Virginian and college friend of Thomas Dixon, sees *The Clansman* at the White House. Wilson is supposed to have said: "It is like writing history with Light-

ning. And my only regret is that it is all terribly true." He will also write (March 15) that it is "a splendid production." **23** The U.S. Supreme Court, in *Mutual Film Corp v. Industrial Commission of Ohio*, rules that

government may censor movies, upholding state laws enacted in the last two years.

MARCH 5 Metro pictures is incorporated. **6** The NAACP denounces the portrayal

Births, Deaths, Marriages, and Divorces

JANUARY 29 Victor Mature b.

FEBRUARY 21 Ann Sheridan (Clara Lou Sheridan) b.

APRIL • William Powell m. Eileen Wilson. **21** Anthony Quinn b. **26** Silent screen comedian John Bunny d.

MAY 6 Orson Welles (George Orson Welles) b.

JUNE 3 "Dead End Kid" Leo Gorcey b.

JULY 12 Yul Brynner is born (various sources also cite 1917, 1920, and 1922 as the year).

AUGUST 29 Ingrid Bergman b.

SEPTEMBER 10 Edmond O'Brien b.

D.W. Griffith's *The Birth of a Nation*

Walter Long, a white actor in blackface, is surrounded by the film's "heroes," the Ku Klux Klan.   *LC*

panying score, becomes a hit, the first generated by a movie. It will also become the theme music of radio and TV's *Amos 'n Andy* show.

MARCH 3   *The Clansman*, retitled *The Birth of a Nation*, opens at New York City's Liberty Theater. A 40-piece orchestra with chorus accompanies the film. Tickets cost up to $2.00 for the two-a-day showings, an unheard of price for a movie. Ads for the film boast that it used 18,000 people, 3,000 horses, took eight months to film, cost $500,000, and expresses "genius in a new realm of art."

Mae Marsh, the "little sister" in *The Birth of a Nation*   *LC*

FEBRUARY 8   D.W. Griffith's $100,000, two-hour, forty-minute *The Clansman* premieres at Clune's Auditorium in Los Angeles (owned by an investor in the film). It features Lillian Gish, Mae Marsh, and a cast of thousands, including Erich von Stroheim, Elmo Lincoln (the movies' first Tarzan), John Ford (under a Ku Klux Klan hood), Raoul Walsh, Donald Crisp, and Eugene Pallette. Featured black roles are played by whites. The picture presents the Ku Klux Klan as heroes and Southern blacks as villains. Aesthetically, with its advancement of the craft of editing, multiple camera angles, and close-ups to tell a story on an epic scale, it is a stunning, landmark American film. "The Perfect Song," part of the accom-

of blacks in *The Birth of a Nation* as "the meanest vilification of the Negro race." The film has caused disturbances in several cities.   **12**   Responding to attacks on racism in *The Birth of a Nation*, D.W. Griffith submits a slightly toned-down version to the National Board of Censorship, which will approve it on November 15.   **15**   The opening of the 250-acre Universal City in Los Angeles is attended by Henry Ford, Thomas Edison, and Buffalo Bill.

APRIL •   In reaction to the uproar over *The Birth of a Nation*, Woodrow Wilson's secretary states that "the President was entirely unaware of the character of the play before it was presented and has at no time expressed his approbation of it. Its exhibition at the White House was a courtesy extended to an old acquaintance."   **5**   V-L-S-E, the Vitagraph-Lubin-Selig-Essanay Motion Picture Company, is set up to release the feature films of the member companies. Vitagraph will later control it.

JULY 12   Vaudeville's United Booking Office, run by the powerful Keith-Albee circuit, says it will reduce the salary of any vaudeville performer who appears in a movie.   **20**   The Triangle Film Corporation is formed, with directors D.W. Griffith, Thomas Ince, and Mack Sennett representing the core of its creative talent.

SEPTEMBER 9   The Motion Picture Board of Trade, the industry's first major trade group, is formed.   **11**   Fire destroys Famous

OCTOBER 13   Cornel Wilde (Cornelius Wilde) b.

DECEMBER 7   Eli Wallach b.   **12**   Frank Sinatra b.

Also this year: •   Florence Arto m. director King Vidor, becoming Florence Vidor, the name under which she will achieve fame as a silent film star.

Personalities

OCTOBER 16 Stage matinee idol Tyrone Power Sr., acknowledging the importance of the movies in a *Picture Play Weekly* interview, says: "Mrs. Power and I have a son . . . when he grows in years, the art of the motion picture will do much for his education."

NOVEMBER 16 "W.C. Fields Speaks," headlines the *Detroit News*. The normally pantomime juggler, appearing with Bert Williams and Ed Wynn, has "a lovely voice which reminds you of stripping gears on a flivver," says the paper.

DECEMBER 14 Ethel Barrymore signs with Metro for $40,000 per picture.

Movies

already established public personality. The money saved is spent on the massive publicity campaign.

MARCH 3 New York opening of *The Birth of a Nation*.

APRIL 11 *The Tramp*, the first film in which Charlie Chaplin uses his signature waddle, is released. **19** The release of the "Lonesome Luke" series short *Just Nuts* marks the first billed role for Harold Lloyd.

SEPTEMBER 9 Vitagraph's *The Battle Cry of Peace* opens in New York to excellent reviews and ticket sales. The studio hires Charles Emerson Cook, David Belasco's publicity man, to run an intensive press campaign for this film, which advocates preparedness for war. **19** W.C. Fields makes his first screen appearance in *Pool Sharks*, released today. **23** Among the Triangle Company's first releases is Douglas Fairbanks's first feature film, *The Lamb*, the story of an eastern tenderfoot who has to find his manhood in the Old West. It opens today at the Knickerbocker Theater.

DECEMBER 13 *The Cheat*, starring Sessue Hayakawa, in which a Japanese man brands a white woman, is released. *Variety* describes Hayakawa as "one of the best yellow heavies that the screen has ever had . . ."

Business and Society

Players's New York offices and studios.

OCTOBER • *Wid's Films and Film Folks*, the trade paper that will become *Film Daily*, begins publication. **1** A federal court rules the Motion Picture Patents Corporation an illegal restraint of trade. The Patents Trust appeal won't be dismissed until 1918, but its power is already gone.

NOVEMBER–DECEMBER • *Photoplay*'s inauguration of Julian Johnson's "Department of Comment and Criticism on Current Photoplays" (November), and the publication of poet Vachel Lindsay's *The Art of the Moving Picture* (December), represent the beginning of the recognition of cinema as an art.

NOVEMBER 19 Herbert T. Kalmus sets up the Technicolor Motion Picture Corporation.

Births, Deaths, Marriages, and Divorces

At Triangle, Thomas Ince has mostly given up directing in favor of producing. He is developing the management technique of using producers to supervise groups of pictures. It enables the head of production to run a studio like a factory, with several films in production simultaneously. The pivotal role of the producer will become the mainstay of the studio system in the coming decades. Famous Players–Lasky and the Goldwyn Company are formed this year. D.W. Griffith's answer to criticism of *The Birth of a Nation* is *Intolerance*. The Lincoln Motion Picture Company, the first black-owned and -run movie company, is started. Its first film is *The Realization of a Negro's Ambition*.

- Number of feature-length films released: 677
- Average weekly movie theater attendance: 10,000,000
- Value of U.S. film exports: (1915–16): $9,000,000
- Douglas Fairbanks's salary: $10,000 a week
- Mary Pickford's salary: $10,000 a week minimum against 50% of the profits
- First star autobiography: Pearl White's *Just Me*
- First college film course: photoplay writing, at Columbia University

Major industries in America (according to the *New York Times*):
1. agriculture
2. transportation
3. oil
4. steel
5. motion pictures

Top male and female box office stars, based on a Quigley Publications poll of exhibitors:
male: William S. Hart
female: Mary Pickford

Intolerance   LC

January	February	March	April	May	June	
27 Woodrow Wilson addresses the Motion Picture Board of Trade	**26** Charlie Chaplin signs with Mutual	**14** Samuel Goldwyn and Blanche Lasky divorce	**17** *Civilization*	**1** Mabel Normand controls her own production company	**28** Famous Players–Lasky Corp. formed	

July	August	September	October	November	December	
1 Olivia de Havilland b.	**25** Van Johnson b.	**5** *Intolerance*	**14** Louis B. Mayer becomes a movie producer	**19** Goldwyn Company formed	**9** Kirk Douglas b.	

Personalities

FEBRUARY • Producer David Horsely announces that he will seek the Republican nomination for Congress in his California district, becoming the first Hollywood personage to try (unsuccessfully) for national office. **19** The first annual Movie Costume and Civic Ball draws sixteen thousand to New York's Madison Square Garden to see the likes of Fatty Arbuckle, Mabel Normand, Mary Miles Minter, Anita Stewart, Clara Kimball Young, Lionel Barrymore, and Pearl White. **26** Charlie Chaplin signs with Mutual.

MAY 1 Mabel Normand takes control of her own production company, the price Mack Sennett pays to keep her from jumping to Thomas Ince. The company produces only

OH, THOSE MARY PICKFORD CURLS

Mary Pickford   LC

JUNE 24 Mary Pickford signs with Adolph Zukor what the trade papers are calling the first "Million Dollar Contract." She receives a guaranteed minimum of $10,000 per week against fifty percent of the profits on a two-year contract that includes bonuses. She also has approval of all creative aspects of her films. The famous curls on America's Sweetheart are now being augmented by makeup man George Westmore, who gets the hair from Los Angeles prostitutes, employees of Big Suzy's French Whorehouse.

Movies

FEBRUARY • Japanese-Americans in Los Angeles protest the showing of *The Cheat*, which features villain Sessue Hayakawa. **13** *His Picture in the Papers*, starring Douglas Fairbanks, which D.W. Griffith at Triangle had wished to hold back for recutting, is released by mistake. It is shown at the Strand because the scheduled film has not arrived. The *New York Times* favorably reviews it and the movie makes a profit.

MARCH 26 *Hoodoo Ann*, starring Mae Marsh, is released.

APRIL 17 Thomas Ince's *Civilization*, which decries the horrors of war, billed as a "million dollar" picture, premieres in Los Angeles. An advertising poster declares that *Civilization* is "Dedicated to that vast army whose tears have girdled the Universe —The Mothers of the Dead." Woodrow Wilson's presidential campaign will make use of the film and its popularity to emphasize their candidate's theme: "He kept us out of war."

MAY • *Where Are My Children*, directed by Lois Weber and starring Tyrone Power Sr.,

is released. Dealing with birth control (which it supports) and abortion, it is banned in Pennsylvania.

SEPTEMBER 5 D.W. Griffith's *Intolerance*, starring Lillian Gish, Mae Marsh, Robert Harron, Bessie Love, and Constance Talmadge, premieres at the Liberty Theater in New York. Assistant directors on the film included Erich von Stroheim, Tod Browning, Allan Dwan, Christy Cabanne, and Victor Fleming. Ruth St. Dennis provided choreography. *Intolerance* cuts back and forth between four stories and four histori-

Business and Society

• Columbia University offers a course in photoplay writing, the first film course given at an American school.

JANUARY 27 President Woodrow Wilson addresses the first annual meeting of the Motion Picture Board of Trade, another sign that the movies have arrived.

APRIL • The National Board of Censorship changes its name to the National Board of Review. **1** Lewis J. Selznick Productions is created.

MAY 21 Adolph Zukor and Jesse Lasky acquire half the stock of Paramount Pictures and, on June 13, make Hiram Abrams Paramount's president. He replaces W.W. Hodkinson.

JUNE 28 The Famous Players Film Company and the Jesse L. Lasky Feature Play Company announce their merger to form Famous Players–Lasky Corporation, Adolph Zukor, president. It is the core of what will become Paramount Pictures. *Film Daily* describes it as the U.S. Steel of the movies.

JULY 5 New York City bans all children under age sixteen from theaters because of a polio epidemic. The ban, extending

Births, Deaths, Marriages, and Divorces

FEBRUARY • Director Raoul Walsh m. actress Miriam Cooper. **8** Geraldine Farrar, opera singer and movie star, m. actor Lou Tellegen. **26** Jackie Gleason (Herbert John Gleason) b.

MARCH 14 Samuel Goldwyn and Blanche Lasky divorce. **26** Sterling Hayden (John Hamilton) b. **27** Gloria Swanson, seventeen today, m. Wallace Beery.

APRIL 5 Gregory Peck (Eldred Gregory Peck) b.

MAY 1 Glenn Ford (Gwyllyn Ford), nephew of John MacDonald, first Prime Minister of Canada, b.

one film: *Mickey*. **6** The *New York Dramatic Mirror* reports that Francis X. Bushman has had to hire security guards to keep fans away from the house he bought in Baltimore three weeks ago. **6** "Mrs. De Wolf Hopper is in pictures for the first time," notes *Exhibitors Herald*. The "Mrs.," married to a prominent stage personality, is actress Hedda Hopper, the future gossip columnist.

NOVEMBER 12 While filming *Pride of the Clan* off the New England coast, director Maurice Tourneur saves Mary Pickford's life when their boat takes on water and she is knocked down by a wave.

cal eras, from ancient Babylon to the present, with Gish, a mother rocking a cradle, serving as a unifying image. The reviews are mixed and the film is not a commercial success. Griffith will refilm the crucifixion scene when the B'nai Brith protests the portrayal of Jews as Christ killers. **10** Douglas Fairbanks stars in *Manhattan Madness*, premiering at the Rialto.

OCTOBER 17 Premiering at the Lyric Theater is *A Daughter of the Gods*, starring swimmer and actress Annette Kellerman, playing the first nude scene in a major feature film.

NOVEMBER 13 Released today is *The Cossack Whip*, starring Viola Dana.

DECEMBER 25 Cecil B. DeMille's *Joan the Woman*, in which the flames that consume Joan of Arc are in color, is released. It stars Geraldine Farrar, Raymond Hatton, and Hobart Bosworth.

through the summer, causes the closing of two hundred theaters. **25** The National Association of the Motion Picture Industry, which will absorb the Motion Picture Board of Trade, holds its first meeting.

SEPTEMBER 14 Samuel Goldfish, unable to get along with Adolph Zukor, leaves Famous Players–Lasky.

OCTOBER 14 Louis B. Mayer becomes a movie producer with the beginning of film-

ing on the serial *The Great Secret*, starring Francis X. Bushman and Beverly Bayne.

NOVEMBER 19 Samuel Goldfish, with producer Edgar Selwyn, forms the Goldwyn Company. Goldfish finds the amalgamation of the two names so appealing that he adopts it as his own last name, becoming Samuel Goldwyn. **21** Fire destroys the Fox studio in Hollywood.

DECEMBER 4 Famous Players–Lasky ac-

quires the remaining fifty percent of Paramount.

JULY 1 Olivia de Havilland b. **27** Keenan Wynn (Francis Wynn), son of vaudville star Ed Wynn, b.

AUGUST 25 Van Johnson (Charles Van Johnson) b.

SEPTEMBER 28 Peter Finch (William Mitchell) b. **29** Trevor Howard b.

DECEMBER 9 Kirk Douglas (Issur Danielovitch) b. **18** Betty Grable (Elizabeth Ruth Grable) b. • Mae Murray m. Jay O'Brien.

Also this year: • The original Rin Tin Tin b. • Barbara LaMarr m. Phil Ainsworth. It lasts seven weeks, until he is imprisoned for forgery.

he war is allowing American films to dominate the European market and is also infusing Hollywood's pictures with patriotism and war themes. The government uses films for propaganda, and Hollywood cooperates with the war effort. Mack Sennett's bathing beauties become soldiers' pinups. Vaudeville performer Buster Keaton makes his film debut, and Harold Lloyd starts to wear glasses. Independent theaters form First National, and George Westmore establishes the first studio makeup department, at the Selig studio. In Germany, the government combines small film companies into one huge studio, the Universum Film A.G., later known as U.F.A.

- Number of feature-length films released: 687
- Value of U.S. film exports: $7,800,000
- Number of "first class" theaters, according to *Wid's Yearbook*: 6,000
- Buster Keaton's first film: *The Butcher Boy*

Top Male and female box office stars, based on a Quigley Publications poll of exhibitors:

male: Douglas Fairbanks
female: Anita Stewart

Fred Astaire debuts on Broadway this year.   *LC*

January	February	March	April	May	June	
• War making U.S. films dominant in Europe	**16** *Variety* reports popularity of war films	**5** *Poor Little Rich Girl*	**23** Buster Keaton film debut	• Jack Pickford m. Olive Thomas	**12** W.C. Fields, Eddie Cantor, and Will Rogers open in Ziegfeld's *Follies*	

July	August	September	October	November	December	
23 Mabel Normand leaves Mack Sennett	**27** *Straight Shooting*	**15** Louis B. Mayer announces signing of Anita Stewart	**20** Norma Talmadge m. producer Joseph Schenck	**28** Fred Astaire debuts on Broadway	• John Barrymore and Katherine Harris divorce	

Personalities

• Mary Pickford and Douglas Fairbanks have become lovers. When needed on the set at Famous Players, Pickford is often summoned from her meetings in her bungalow with Fairbanks by property man Howard Hawks.

JANUARY 1 Fatty Arbuckle, who has left Keystone, begins to make films for independent producer Joseph Schenck. **1** Mack Sennett, disaffected with Triangle, announces that his films may be shown anywhere, even in theaters unconnected to the company. Sennett had wanted Triangle to merge with Paramount. **2** Douglas Fairbanks says he will no longer distribute through Triangle. **30** Wallace Beery signs with Mack Sennett for $50 per week.

Movies

JANUARY 8 Mary Pickford stars in *Pride of the Clan*, released today. Director Maurice Tourneur complains that New York's Strand Theater has cut the film to reduce the length of the show. The Strand's manager says he "improved" the picture—a practice not uncommon at this time.

MARCH 5 *Poor Little Rich Girl*, starring Mary Pickford, is released. Director Maurice Tourneur had struggled unsuccessfully with Pickford to tone down a bit of her exuberance. She felt that he didn't understand

Harold Lloyd, one of the movies' greatest comedians, in *The Freshman*   LC

Business and Society

JANUARY 21 The National Board of Review, representing the movie studios, bows to public pressure and announces that its members will not permit nudity in its pictures.

MARCH • Secretary of the Navy Josephus Daniels informs all newsreel producers that their films will be censored.

APRIL 25 Independent theater owners form the First National Exhibitors Circuit to bypass major studios and obtain films directly from independent producers.

MAY 7 Chicago bans *The Spirit of '76*, about the American Revolution, because it disparages Britain, now an ally.

JULY 28 D.W. Griffith chairs a new group to coordinate the movie industry's war ef-

forts with those of the Committee for Public Information.

AUGUST • Adolph Zukor buys fifty percent of Lewis J. Selznick Productions, changing its name to Select Pictures.

SEPTEMBER 25 The U.S. government sets up a Division of Films under The Committee on Public Information, to promote the American cause in World War I.

Births, Deaths, Marriages, and Divorces

APRIL 13 Howard Keel (Harry Leek) b.

MAY • Jack Pickford m. Olive Thomas.

JUNE 7 Dean Martin (Dino Crocetti) b. **30** Lena Horne b.

AUGUST 6 Robert Mitchum b. **25** Mel Ferrer b.

OCTOBER 7 June Allyson (Ella Geisman) b. **20** Norma Talmadge m. producer Joseph Schenck. **22** Joan Fontaine (Joan de Beauvoir de Havilland), sister of Olivia de Havilland, b.

DECEMBER • John Barrymore and Katherine Harris divorce.

April 17 "Harold Lloyd, the star of Pathé's 'Lonesome Luke' Comedies has, in less than a year and a half, become one of the few great comedians in the country," says *Moving Picture World*. This is the year that he begins to wear his signature glasses.

JUNE • Thomas Ince leaves Triangle. **12** Future film stars W.C. Fields, Eddie Cantor, and Will Rogers open in Ziegfeld's *Follies*. **25** Triangle buys out Mack Sennett, retaining rights to the name "Keystone."

JULY 23 Mabel Normand leaves Mack Sennett to sign with Goldwyn.

SEPTEMBER 9 Jack Pickford, film star and Mary's brother, driving home from a Los Angeles party at four A.M. with Olive Thomas, hits a truck, seriously injuring the

driver. **15** Independent producer Louis B. Mayer announces that he's signed Anita Stewart, but her Vitagraph contract runs through January 31, 1918. Mayer has to make a financial settlement with Vitagraph, and she will not begin to film *Virtuous Wives*, her first film for Mayer, until August, 1918. **30** Mack Sennett joins Paramount.

NOVEMBER • Eighteen-year-old Irving Thalberg places this ad in the *New York Journal of Commerce*: SITUATION WANTED: Secretary-stenographer. Spanish. English. High School education. Inexperienced. $15. **28** Fred and Adele Astaire debut on Broadway in *Over the Top*.

her American spiritedness. **12** Fox's *A Tale of Two Cities*, released today, is notable for its use of double exposure.

APRIL • Margaret Sanger appears in a new film called *Birth Control*. Distributors receive an alternate set of publicity materials with the title *The New World*, for those who fear negative reaction or censor-ship. **23** Buster Keaton's film debut comes with the release of *The Butcher Boy*, a Fatty Arbuckle picture.

JUNE 24 Douglas Fairbanks stars in *Wild and Woolly*, released today, in which Victor Fleming directed the photography and

Erich von Stroheim worked as a technical director.

AUGUST 27 *Straight Shooting*, the first feature-length film directed by John Ford, is released. It stars Harry Carey as "Cheyenne Harry." Hoot Gibson also appears.

SEPTEMBER 9 Goldwyn Pictures releases its first film, *Polly of the Circus*, starring Mae Marsh. In its first ad in *Variety*, on January 19, Goldwyn Pictures promised "stars of tremendous personality and fame who have made their reputation because of their work—not stars created by dubious publicity and silly advertising." **21** *The Gulf*

Between, the first film in Technicolor, premieres before an invited audience at New York's Aeolian Hall, but technical difficulties keep it from going into general release.

OCTOBER 4 The new war commodities tax includes a footage tax on films. **9** Max Fleischer patents his "rotoscope," a method of photographing drawings to create animation. **27** The Secretary of War assigns the Signal Corps the task of recording the war on film.

Also this year: • Tom Mix and Olive Stokes divorce. • Mae Murray and Jay O'Brien divorce.

he word "cinema" comes into general use in the U.S., and "Hollywood" is now a generic word that describes the American film industry. Tarzan swings across the screen for the first time, Will Rogers makes his first movie, and Sid Grauman opens his first Los Angeles theater. In Hollywood's first major scandal, Francis X. Bushman, in a divorce case, turns out to be other than what people thought he was; Mary Pickford begins to be depicted as "the other woman" in another brewing divorce; and Charlie Chaplin marries sixteen-year-old Mildred Harris. Pickford, in the meanwhile, is now getting $250,000 per picture, and Gloria Swanson signs with Paramount for $150 a week. Oscar Micheaux, who will become the major figure in the independent black film industry, starts the Micheaux Film and Book Corporation.

- Number of feature-length films released: 841
- First Tarzan film: *Tarzan of the Apes*
- Number of flu deaths in large cities, September–November, causing theaters to close: about 82,000
- Mary Pickford's compensation: $250,000 per film
- Gloria Swanson's salary: $150 a week

Top male and female box office stars, based on a Quigley Publications poll of exhibitors:
male: Douglas Fairbanks
female: Mary Pickford

Charlie Chaplin in *Shoulder Arms*, 1918   LC

January	February	March	April	May	June	
27 *Tarzan of the Apes,* first Tarzan film	**5** Francis X. Bushman divorce case	**12** D.W. Griffith's *Hearts of the World*	**8** Fairbanks and Chaplin draw thousands to Wall St. war bonds rally		**30** Susan Hayward b.	

July	August	September	October	November	December	
29 Francis X. Bushman m. Beverly Bayne	**11** *Mickey*	• Stars making war propaganda films	**23** Charlie Chaplin m. 16-year-old Mildred Harris	**9** Mary Pickford signs with First National	**30** Wallace Beery divorces Gloria Swanson	

Personalities

JANUARY 15 Stan Laurel begins work at the Hal Roach studio.

FEBRUARY 5 Francis X. Bushman's wife sues for divorce, claiming that he is having an affair with an actress she will not name (but who, most people can guess, is his frequent co-star, Beverly Bayne). Fans are startled to find out that he is married and has five children, because his contracts had specified that he not publicize that fact (to preserve his romantic allure). Some theaters will now refuse to play Bushman-Bayne films.

APRIL • Newspapers publicize Douglas Fairbanks's wife's complaints about "another woman," who is clearly Mary Pickford.

JUNE 9 Louella Parsons is named movie columnist of the New York *Morning Telegraph.*

JULY 3 Five-year-old Alan Ladd, playing with matches with a friend, accidentally burns down the Hot Springs, Arkansas, building in which his family lives. No one is hurt. **26** *Variety* reports that producer William N. Selig, who has placed seventeen-year-old Colleen Moore under contract, "is convinced the young woman has starring qualities and is proceeding to 'make' her a stellar attraction." She will become the screen's first "flapper."

AUGUST • The managers of the Alhambra and Mall theaters in Cleveland announce that they will no longer play films with Francis X. Bushman and Beverly Bayne because of their scandalous romance. **9** Elias Leach signs a contract allowing his fourteen-year-old son, Archie (Cary Grant), to appear with the Bob Pender vaudeville troupe.

NOVEMBER • "Mrs. Charlie Chaplin" is how actress Mildred Harris, the comedian's recent bride, is now billed. **9** Mary Pickford, who has left Famous Players, signs with First National to produce her own films at $250,000 each. **11** John Gilbert is inducted into the army the day World War I ends. He will be sent home tomorrow with an honorable discharge.

DECEMBER 17 William S. Hart, accused by Elizabeth MacCauley of fathering her child, denies it, but agrees to pay her $30 a month to avoid even the hint of scandal. **30** Gloria Swanson, who on November 5 left Triangle to make *Don't Change Your Husband* with Cecil B. DeMille at Famous

Movies

JANUARY 21 *Stella Maris,* directed by Marshall Neilan and starring Mary Pickford, is released. **27** *Tarzan of the Apes,* the first Tarzan film, starring Elmo Lincoln, premieres at the Broadway Theater. *Variety* calls it "a freak picture that will cause talk."

FEBRUARY 1 Sid Grauman's Million Dollar Theater, his first in Los Angeles, opens with William S. Hart in *The Silent Man.*

MARCH 10 The New York premiere of *My Four Years in Germany* is also the debut of the Warner brothers' first feature film. **12** D.W. Griffith's war film, *Hearts of the World,* premieres at Clune's Auditorium in Los Angeles. Present at the gala opening—probably the first major West Coast premiere—are Blanche Sweet, the Gish sisters, Charlie Chaplin, Douglas Fairbanks, Mae Murray, Mary Miles Minter, Mack Sennett, Fatty Arbuckle, and Dustin Farnum. On April 30 it will be screened for free in Philadelphia when censors demand cuts in scenes of violence and seminudity before allowing any commercial showing. But it will reopen a few days later on a commercial basis with the cuts. **31** *The Bluebird,* notable for its use of color tinting and stylized backdrops, is released.

APRIL 15 *Black Sherlock Holmes* is the initial release of films with all-black casts by the Ebony Film Corporation.

AUGUST 11 *Mickey,* Mabel Normand's first feature-length comedy, is released. It is the first time prerelease publicity is tied to a song—"Mickey."

SEPTEMBER 30 *Laughing Bill Hyde,* Will Rogers's first film, opens at the Rivoli.

Business and Society

FEBRUARY • *Variety* opens a branch office in Los Angeles.

APRIL 8 Douglas Fairbanks and Charlie Chaplin draw a crowd of thousands in the financial district in New York City when they appear to sell war bonds.

JULY 6 The movies are classified an essential industry for purposes of the military draft, and employment in it may be considered a basis for exemption.

SEPTEMBER • Players making war propaganda films include William S. Hart (*A Bullet for Berlin*) and Mae Murray (*The Taming of Kaiser Bull*).

OCTOBER 7 A spokesperson for the War Department claims that propaganda films helped convince fifteen conscientious objectors at one base to take up arms. **15** The major film companies announce that they will release no new features for a month, beginning today, because the flu epidemic has closed many theaters. **18** *Variety* reports a "gentle-men's agreement" among studio heads to restrain their bidding war for top film stars. **25** In a *Variety* bylined article, Adolph Zukor, head of a studio that is about to go on a theater-buying splurge, writes: "The evil of producing and exhibiting coalitions is one of the

Births, Deaths, Marriages, and Divorces

FEBRUARY 4 Ida Lupino b.

APRIL 17 William Holden (William Beedle Jr.) b.

JUNE • Mae Murray m. director Robert Leonard. **8** Robert Preston (Robert Preston Meservey) b. **14** Dorothy McGuire b. **30** Susan Hayward (Edythe Marrener) b.

JULY 26 Francis X. Bushman and Josephine Flaudume divorce. **29** Francis X. Bushman m. Beverly Bayne.

AUGUST • Alma Rubens m. Franklyn Farnum. It lasts less than a month. **26** John Gilbert m. Olivia Burwell.

STORMY WEATHER

December hits the Hollywood community. William S. Hart (left) is accused of fathering Elizabeth MacCauley's child and agrees to pay her $30 a month to avoid a scandal. On the marriage front, Wallace Beery divorces Gloria Swanson (right), though in a little over a year she will marry again. *MSN*

Players–Lasky, agrees to a contract with the studio at $150 per week, rising to $350 after two years.

gravest perils that has ever confronted the motion picture industry."

NOVEMBER • Film ads are revised to play down references to the war, ended this month, as public taste shifts once more toward light entertainment. **1** Samuel Goldwyn takes over the former Triangle studios in Culver City. Triangle has been fatally hurt by the loss of D.W. Griffith, Thomas Ince, Mack Sennett, and Douglas Fairbanks.

OCTOBER 13 Robert Walker b. **17** Rita Hayworth (Margarita Cansino) b. **23** Charlie Chaplin m. sixteen-year-old Mildred Harris. **27** Teresa Wright (Muriel Teresa Wright) b.

DECEMBER 13 Wallace Beery divorces Gloria Swanson. **15** Jeff Chandler (Ira Grossel) b.

Also this year: • Barbara LaMarr m. her dance partner, Ben Deely. • Tom Mix m. Victoria Forde. • Director William Wellman m. actress Helene Chadwick.

The major studios begin to assemble the chains of first-run theaters that will eventually make them targets of antitrust action. United Artists is formed, and Loew's, Inc., is set up. Gloria Swanson is a new star, Erich von Stroheim is a newly prominent director, and the new Capitol Theater in New York is the world's largest. The Douglas Fairbanks divorce case names "unknown woman" as a co-respondent, and Harold Lloyd is injured in a bomb blast. Cameraman Billy Bitzer puts a silk net in front of his lens to photograph Lillian Gish, making her look younger. This is a precursor of the diffusion lens. And automatic change machines help speed up lines at the box office.

- Number of feature-length films released: 646
- Average feature film budget: $60,000
- Working title of D.W. Griffith's *Broken Blossoms*: "The Chink and the Child"
- Budget for Erich von Stroheim's *Blind Husbands*: $10,000
- Actual cost of von Stroheim's *Blind Husbands*: almost $200,000
- Rudolph Valentino's salary: $100 per week
- First movie star to live in Beverly Hills: Douglas Fairbanks
- Population of Hollywood: 35,000

Top male and female box office stars, based on a Quigley Publications poll of exhibitors:
male: Wallace Reid
female: Mary Pickford

Lillian Gish in *Broken Blossoms*   MSN

January	February	March	April	May	June	
26 *Don't Change Your Husband*		**2** Jennifer Jones b.		**13** *Broken Blossoms*		
	5 United Artists formed		**10** Lewis J. Selznick regains control of Select Pictures		• Famous Players signs Mary Miles Minter	

July	August	September	October	November	December	
• Expansion capital flows into Goldwyn Pictures		• Catholic Photoplay Pre-Review Service started		**30** Douglas Fairbanks and Beth Sully divorce	**7** *Blind Husbands*	
	27 Harold Lloyd is injured in bomb accident		**18** Loew's, Inc., set up			

Personalities

• Musso & Frank's restaurant is founded in Hollywood. • Wallace Reid, injured in a train crash while traveling to film *Valley of the Giants*, is given morphine, starting an addiction that will lead to an early death in 1923 and will add to the popular conception of Hollywood as a kind of Babylon where anything goes. • Eleven-year-old Bette Davis, playing Santa Claus at a school Christmas celebration, gets too near a candle, igniting her costume. Bystanders roll her in a rug to put out the fire, which leaves her face blistered.

MAY 4 In her movie column in the *Morning Telegraph*, Louella Parsons describes actress (and future rival columnist) Hedda Hopper as having "youth and good looks" and says that she likes Hopper's screen work. **11** Norma Talmadge's *The New Moon* is doing so well at New York's Rivoli Theater that the police have to order the box office to stop selling tickets to prevent overcrowding. When the star and her sisters try to get in, they are turned away.

JUNE • Famous Players signs Mary Miles Minter to a three-year contract, with the idea of making her the new Mary Pickford. She promises not to marry and to avoid any public scandal. They advertise her as the "Dainty Monarch of the Kingdom of Sweet Sixteen."

AUGUST 27 Harold Lloyd loses a finger and thumb when a trick bomb detonates while he's posing for publicity stills.

NOVEMBER 11 Charlie Chaplin denies that he is financing *The Liberator*, a left-wing magazine published by his friend, Max Eastman. **19** Director Marshall Neilen complains of supervising producers, such as Louis B. Mayer, who put their names in ads, taking undue credit for films.

Movies

JANUARY 26 Gloria Swanson achieves stardom with the release of Cecil B. DeMille's *Don't Change Your Husband*. The film is one of the first to deal in a sophisticated way with the sexuality and allure of a married woman, her temptations and compromises. Capitalizing on the success of this film, DeMille will also make *Why Change Your Wife?*

FEBRUARY • "Old" Charlie Chaplin films, re-released, do very well at the box office.

MAY 13 D.W. Griffith's *Broken Blossoms*, starring Lillian Gish, Donald Crisp, and Richard Barthelmess, opens at the George M. Cohan Theater. *Photoplay* calls this film, which had been known by the working title, "The Chink and the Child," "the first genuine tragedy of the movies." The theme is miscegenation. Griffith made *Broken Blossoms* for Adolph Zukor, who found it too arty and sold the film, which cost $88,000 to make, to United Artists, for $250,000. It will return a $700,000 profit.

AUGUST 26 *The Miracle Man*, starring Thomas Meighan, Betty Compson, and Lon Chaney, premieres in New York at the George M. Cohan Theater in Times Square. Several blocks uptown, Houdini is appearing in person, accompanying his film, *The Grim Game*.

OCTOBER 11 The Fox News newsreel makes its debut. **24** The Capitol Theater, the world's largest movie house, opens in New York with Douglas Fairbanks in *His Majesty, The American*, the first film made for United Artists to be released.

NOVEMBER 23 Cecil B. DeMille's *Male and Female*, starring Gloria Swanson and Thomas Meighan, with costumes by Mitchell Leisen, photography by James Wong Howe,

Business and Society

FEBRUARY 5 Charlie Chaplin, Mary Pickford, Douglas Fairbanks Sr., and D.W. Griffith form United Artists to distribute their films and those of other independent producers.

APRIL 10 Lewis J. Selznick buys back full control of Select Pictures from Adolph Zukor for $1 million. **18** Famous Players buys an interest in Sid Grauman's movie theaters in Los Angeles. The studio has $10 million for theater purchases from a stock issue underwritten by Kuhn, Loeb. **27** The National Association of the Motion Picture Industry announces that members have agreed to submit films to the trade group for approval to avoid government censorship.

JULY • Capital for expansion flows into Goldwyn Pictures as Dupont invests and Broadway producers J.J. and Lee Shubert, Al Woods, and Sam H. Harris buy in, helping Goldwyn also to corner the film rights to plays. **6** Carl Leammle promotes his secretary, Irving Thalberg, to an executive position, at a salary of $60 a week.

AUGUST 1 Famous Players gains control of the Stanley theater chain.

SEPTEMBER • A Catholic Photoplay Pre-Review Service is started to provide re-

Births, Deaths, Marriages, and Divorces

JANUARY 1 Carole Landis (Frances Ridste) b.

FEBRUARY 18 Jack Palance (Walter Jack Palahnuik) b.

MARCH 2 Jennifer Jones (Phyllis Isely) b.

APRIL 29 Celeste Holm b.

NOVEMBER • Rudolph Valentino m. Jean Acker. **19** Veronica Lake (Constance Ockelman) b. **30** Douglas Fairbanks and Beth Sully divorce, with "unknown woman" named as co-respondent.

Charlie Chaplin, Mary Pickford, D.W. Griffith, and Douglas Fairbanks Sr. form United Artists.　　　　　*LC*

and promotional ads sketched by eighteen-year-old Walt Disney, premieres at the Rivoli.

DECEMBER 7 Erich von Stroheim's *Blind Husbands*, which he directs and stars in, premieres at the Capitol. Despite his assurances to Universal's Carl Laemmle that he would keep within a $10,000 budget, the film cost almost $200,000. The original title, *The Pinnacle*, was changed when exhibitors didn't like it. Von Stroheim took out an ad in *Motion Picture News* on September 27, protesting the change. *Blind Husbands*, which succeeds with the critics and with movie audiences, is von Stroheim's directing debut, and is based on his own short story. He also designed the sets.

views of films to Catholic publications. **5** "Japs Buying Picture Houses Startle Whole West Coast," reads a headline in today's *Variety*. **15** The International Alliance of Theatrical Stage Employees (IATSE) strikes Los Angeles film studios. The strike lasts through November 6.

OCTOBER 18 Loew's, Inc., is set up to consolidate Marcus Loew's holdings. Gambler Arnold Rothstein is an investor.

NOVEMBER 8 Directors Thomas Ince, Allan Dwan, Marshall Neilan, Mack Sennett, Maurice Tourneur, and George Loane Tucker form Associated Producers to distribute their own films.

DECEMBER 17 A joint committee of the House and Senate asks the movie industry to make films that will "upbuild and strengthen the spirit of Americanism."

DECEMBER 20 Gloria Swanson m. Herbert K. Somborn.

arcus Loew takes over Metro. Douglas Fairbanks begins a series of popular swashbucklers with *The Mark of Zorro*. Fairbanks's marriage to Mary Pickford is a major cultural event. Automatic film developing begins to replace processing by hand in the lab. The first commercial radio station goes on the air. In Germany, the release of *The Cabinet of Doctor Caligari* marks the rise of the expressionist movement in film, characterized by the use of the camera and set design—often with distorted perspective—to express subjective feelings. The Mitchell camera, just coming into use, permits cinematographers to compose through the lens. It will eventually supplant the Bell and Howell as the camera of choice.

- Number of releases: 797
- Theater attendance: about 35 million a week
- Number of studios in the Los Angeles area: 49
- Number of studio employees: 20,000
- Number of unsolicited screenplays received by Hollywood studios each week: 8,000
- Value of life insurance on Lillian Gish for *Way Down East:* $1,000,000
- Number of cuts made in *Way Down East* by the Pennsylvania Board of Censorship: 60
- Number of cars owned by Douglas Fairbanks: 7
- Number of rooms in Pickfair: 22, situated on 18 acres with Beverly Hills's first swimming pool
- Settlement obtained by Mildred Harris in her divorce from Charles Chaplin: $200,000

Top male and female box office stars, based on a Quigley Publications poll of exhibitors:
male: Wallace Reid
female: Marguerite Clark

Top billing in Hollywood by gender, according to *The Guinness Book of Movie Facts and Feats*:
men: 43%
women: 57%

Archie Leach, 16, later to become Cary Grant, arrives in America in July. He will find a role model for elegance in Douglas Fairbanks. Here Grant is shown in mid-career.   *LC*

January	February	March	April	May	June	
	8 Lana Turner b.	**28** Douglas Fairbanks m. Mary Pickford	**7** Charlie Chaplin and Louis B. Mayer have a fistfight	**29** Goldwyn buys the Capitol Theater in New York	• First fan magazine article on Rudolph Valentino	
• Marcus Loew takes over Metro Pictures						

July	August	September	October	November	December
• 16-year-old Archie Leach (Cary Grant) sails to America	**17** Maureen O'Hara b.	**3** *Way Down East*	**17** Montgomery Clift b.	**28** *The Mark of Zorro*	

Personalities

JANUARY • Za Su Pitts, who has played supporting roles in several Mary Pickford films, signs a three-year contract with Lewis Selznick.

MARCH 28 Douglas Fairbanks and Mary Pickford are married. Her wedding present is the twenty-two-room "Pickfair," between Benedict and Coldwater Canyons in Beverly Hills. The couple is in the vanguard of the movement to the west of Hollywood, and they have the first swimming pool in the area.

APRIL 7 Charlie Chaplin and Louis B. Mayer have a fistfight in the dining room of Hollywood's Alexandria Hotel. Chaplin, reacting to remarks Mayer had made about

the comedian's divorce proceedings with Mayer's contract player Mildred Harris Chaplin, throws the first punch and is knocked down. **30** According to *Variety*, after Erich von Stroheim's *Blind Husbands*, "the trade is anxiously waiting to see if this director is a flash in the pan or the real thing." (On August 13, the paper will find his second film, *The Devil's Pass Key*, "wearisome.")

JUNE • *Motion Picture Classics* publishes the first movie magazine article on Rudolph Valentino, who is now filming *The Four Horsemen of the Apocalypse*. The article claims that Nijinsky had asked Valentino to teach him the tango. **10** *The Houston Post* carries a story about a fourteen-year-old boy who has built a "Light and Cheaper Motorcycle": Howard Hughes.

Lana Turner, born this year   LC

Movies

JANUARY 10 *Pollyanna*, released today, is Mary Pickford's first film for United Artists.

FEBRUARY 10 Rioters sack the Sun Theater in San Francisco at the opening of *Kathleen Mavourneen*, starring Theda Bara, because they claim the film misrepresents the Irish poor. **15** The Pathé serial released today, *Daredevil Jack*, directed by W.S. Van Dyke, stars boxer Jack Dempsey and features Lon Chaney. (In 1926, Gene Tunney will appear in the serial *The Fight-*

ing Marine, just before his fight with Dempsey.)

MARCH 28 John Barrymore stars in *Dr. Jekyll and Mr. Hyde*, premiering at the Rivoli.

AUGUST 8 Erich von Stroheim's *The Devil's Pass Key*, "A picture of wicked Paris—of an American playwright and the butterfly wife who was caught in the net of scandal," premieres at the Capitol.

SEPTEMBER 3 D.W. Griffith's *Way Down East* opens as a road show (noncontinuous showings with seats reserved) engagement

at the 44th St. Theater in New York City, with an unprecedented top price of $10 a ticket. It stars Lillian Gish and Richard Barthelmess. Gish gave her all for Griffith in this film, acting outdoors in a blizzard, protected only by a shawl. Many of her takes filmed on ice floes were not trick photography — she was where she seemed to be. The success of this picture is marred by the death, last night, of Robert Harron, once a Griffith leading man. The police theorize that he accidentally shot himself, but his recent displacement in the forefront of Griffith's players by Richard Barthelmess suggests the possibility of suicide. **25** Cecil B. DeMille's *The Affairs of*

Business and Society

JANUARY • Adolph Zukor holds a press conference to deny that the studios' increased dependence on Wall Street for financing means that the financiers will control the movies. • Marcus Loew takes over Metro Pictures. **24** The Americanization Committee, a group of movie executives and politicians intending to promote patriotism through the movies, announces

production of *The Land of Opportunity*, starring Ralph Ince as Abraham Lincoln. Committee members include Secretary of the Interior Franklin K. Lane, Lewis Selznick, and Adolph Zukor.

MAY 29 The Goldwyn Company buys New York's Capitol Theater.

JUNE 9 Hiram Abrams becomes president of United Artists. **30** Film industry representatives complain to the Los Angeles

Chamber of Commerce about continued discrimination against movie people who seek to rent apartments, gouging by merchants, stereotyping by newspapers, and general condescension by the local population.

JULY 19 Twenty-one hundred members of the Motion Picture Craftsmen strike thirty-eight film labs. The strike ends August 1.

AUGUST • Famous Players–Lasky tries to cor-

Births, Deaths, Marriages, and Divorces

FEBRUARY 8 Lana Turner (Julia Turner) b. **26** Tony Randall (Leonard Rosenberg) b.

MARCH 2 Mary Pickford divorces Owen Moore. **28** Douglas Fairbanks m. Mary Pickford.

AUGUST 5 John Barrymore m. Blanche Thomas (poet "Michael Strange"). **17** Maureen O'Hara (Maureen Fitzsimmons) b.

SEPTEMBER 10 Olive Thomas, actress and wife of actor Jack Pickford (Mary's brother),

21 Arriving in London on their honeymoon, Mary Pickford and Douglas Fairbanks experience the first of three days of wild public adulation, ushering in the age of the "celebrity."

JULY • Sixteen-year-old Archie Leach (Cary Grant) sails to America from England on the SS Olympic in second class with the Bob Pender vaudeville troupe. Archie catches sight of Mary Pickford and Douglas Fairbanks in first class, returning from their honeymoon. The boy never forgets Fairbanks's elegance. **28** Lawyer Jesse James, son of the outlaw, signs with Mecca Pictures to play his father in *Jesse James Under the Black Flag* and other films.

SEPTEMBER 10 Metro's ad in *Variety* for its new film, *One Week*, reads: "Here is the comedy sensation of the year, introducing

a new stellar comedian . . . Buster Keaton has graduated from vaudeville, where for years he was a member of the famous Three Keatons." **28** Sixteen-year-old chorus boy James Cagney makes his Broadway debut in *Pitter Patter* at the Longacre Theater. In his only previous stage experience, he was a female impersonator in an uptown revue.

NOVEMBER • According to California State Motor Vehicle Department records, Roscoe Fatty Arbuckle is first among film colony automobile owners, with four cars worth a total of $42,000. Douglas Fairbanks's seven cars are valued at only $37,000. • Mabel Normand has a nervous breakdown. **17** First National announces the signing of Constance and Norma Talmadge for a series of pictures to be produced by their independent production company.

Anatole, starring Wallace Beery, Gloria Swanson, and Bebe Daniels, is released.

OCTOBER 10 Fatty Arbuckle's first feature film, *The Round Up*, is released.

NOVEMBER 21 *The Last of the Mohicans*, starring Wallace Beery, with Boris Karloff in a bit part as an Indian, is released. **28** Douglas Fairbanks stars in *The Mark of Zorro*, opening at the Capitol.

DECEMBER 12 *Passion* (the American title for *Madame Dubarry*) has its U. S. premiere at the Capitol. It introduces to Americans director Ernst Lubitsch and Polish actress

Pola Negri. With memories of the European war still fresh, its German origins are played down, as is Negri's co-star, German actor Emil Jannings. More than 100,000 people see it in the first week and soon Lubitsch is being called "the Griffith of Europe."

---

ner the film rights to German drama by optioning the output of most of the major German dramatists.

SEPTEMBER 20 Famous Players–Lasky, supplementing its Los Angeles facilities, opens its Astoria studios in New York City.

OCTOBER • The Association of Motion Picture Advertisers, taking advantage of baseball's "Black Sox Scandal," in which several players took money from gamblers

to throw the World Series, presses newspapers to devote less space to sports and more to movies. The *New York World*, which recently put in a movie page, is held up as an example of what other publications might do.

NOVEMBER • Screenwriters organize their own branch of the Author's League of America. **2** KDKA in Pittsburgh, the first commercial radio station, goes on the air.

---

with whom she shares an addiction to heroin, dies in Paris, apparently a suicide. **18** Ronald Colman m. Thelma Raye. **23** Mickey Rooney (Joe Yule Jr.) b. **26** In a double ceremony, Constance Talmadge m. John Pialoglou and Dorothy Gish m. James Rennie.

OCTOBER 1 Walter Matthau (Walter Matuschanskavasky) b. **17** Montgomery Clift (Edward Montgomery Clift) b.

NOVEMBER 19 Charlie Chaplin and Mildred Harris divorce. **20** Gene Tierney b.

Also this year: • 15-year-old Lolita Dolores Negrette m. Jaime Del Rio, becoming Dolores Del Rio. • Alice Joyce and Tom Moore, often screen partners, divorce. • Claude Rains m. and divorces Marie Hemingway.

1921

*F*atty Arbuckle is arrested for the murder of Virginia Rappe, and the movie colony is coming under increasing scrutiny for its morals. Rudolph Valentino achieves stardom (and sheikhood), six-year-old Jackie Coogan becomes immensely popular, and Harold Lloyd begins to make feature-length films. The Cocoanut Grove opens in Hollywood. The recession hits the movie industry, decreasing the number of jobs for noncontract players. The studios cut wages, the government charges Famous Players–Lasky with violation of the antitrust laws, and film censorship becomes a hot issue in many state legislatures. And Greta Garbo appears in an advertising film, *How Not to Dress*, for Bergstrom's, a Stockholm department store.

- Number of releases: 854
- Number of theaters: 20,000
- Gloria Swanson's salary: $2,500 a week
- Fatty Arbuckle's annual earnings: about $1,000,000

Movie theater operation, based on a poll of exhibitors published in the Film Daily Yearbook:
Theaters open one day a week: 7%
Theaters open six days a week: 30%
Theaters open seven days a week: 32%
Theaters having only one show a day: 25%
Theaters showing serials: 35%
Theaters with live musical accompaniment: 85% (organ, 46%; orchestra—two or more musicians—30%; piano, 24%)
Theaters with stage shows: 6%

Top male and female box office stars, based on a Quigley Publications poll of exhibitors:
male: Douglas Fairbanks
female: Mary Pickford

Gloria Swanson   MSN

January	February	March	April	May	June
1 Gloria Swanson now making $2,500 per week	**6** *The Kid* **6** *The Four Horsemen of the Apocalypse*		**21** Cocoanut Grove nightclub opens in Hollywood	**31** Buster Keaton m. Natalie Talmadge	**21** Jane Russell b.

July	August	September	October	November	December
6 Nancy Davis (Reagan) b.	**31** FCC charges Famous Players–Lasky with antitrust violations	**11** Fatty Arbuckle arrested for murder	**16** Linda Darnell b.	**6** *The Sheik*	**28** *Orphans of the Storm*

Personalities

JANUARY 1 Gloria Swanson's new contract with Famous Players–Lasky calls for five pictures a year at $2,500 per week, eventually rising to $7,000 if the studio exercises an option clause.

MARCH 25 *Variety* reports that Clarence Brown, assistant to director Maurice Tourneur, "is to be given an opportunity to direct a picture on his own." He will eventually become a prominent director at MGM, working on several of Greta Garbo's films.

APRIL • A speeding conviction lands Bebe Daniels in a Santa Ana jail for ten days. Her next film, *The Speed Girl*, will be about an actress who is jailed for speeding.

21 The Cocoanut Grove nightclub, decorated with palm trees used in *The Sheik*, opens in Hollywood's Ambassador Hotel on Wilshire Boulevard.

JUNE 22 Spencer Tracy makes his stage debut in *College Days* at Ripon College, receiving a good review in the campus paper.

SEPTEMBER 11 Roscoe "Fatty" Arbuckle, screen comic star, is arrested in San Francisco for the murder of actress Virginia Rappe. In Hollywood's worst scandal to date, the 320-pound Arbuckle is accused of killing her at a party in his hotel suite, apparently during a sexual assault. The San Francisco detective in charge of the case says: "This woman, without a doubt, died as a result of an attack by Arbuckle. That makes it first degree murder without a doubt. We don't feel that a man like Fatty

Arbuckle can pull stuff like this in San Francisco and get away with it." (The charges will be rape and manslaughter.) The police have recovered Rappe's torn clothing. By tomorrow, theaters around the country will be withdrawing the comedian's films from exhibition. The 1974 film, *The Wild Party*, will be loosely based on this incident. **28** Fatty Arbuckle is released from jail on $5,000 bail.

DECEMBER 4 The first Fatty Arbuckle trial ends in a hung jury.

Movies

FEBRUARY 5 Loew's State Theater in Cleveland, seating four thousand, opens. **6** *The Kid*, released today, stars Charlie Chaplin and six-year-old Jackie Coogan.

MARCH 6 *The Four Horsemen of the Apocalypse*, Metro's greatest hit, starring Rudolph Valentino, Alice Terry, and Wallace Beery, premieres at the Lyric Theater. *Variety*'s review accords director Rex Ingram "a place alongside Griffith," but mentions Valentino only in passing. When Metro won't meet Valentino's demand for an increase from

$350 to $450 a week, based on the success of the film, he will jump to Famous Players–Lasky, where he will make *The Sheik*.

APRIL 3 *The Cabinet of Dr. Caligari* opens in New York at the Capitol. *Variety* praises it, but notes, "It is morbid. Continental creations usually are." On May 7, American Legionnaires, consisting mostly of men employed in the film industry, parade to a Hollywood theater showing *The Cabinet of Dr. Caligari*, to protest the importing of German films. Several thousand people, including U.S. sailors, join them, causing a riot that forces the withdrawal of the movie.

AUGUST 28 Douglas Fairbanks, Mary Pickford, Charlie Chaplin, and Jack Dempsey attend the premier at the Lyric of Fairbanks's *The Three Musketeers*, co-starring Barbara LaMarr. **29** Loew's State theater in Times Square, seating thirty-five hundred, opens. Celebrities on hand include Gloria Swanson, Theda Bara, Constance and Norma Talmadge, and Jack Dempsey.

NOVEMBER 13 Mary Pickford stars in *Little Lord Fauntleroy*, released today. **17** San Francisco's Granada Theater, seating thirty-two hundred, opens with Marion Davies in *Enchantment*. **21** Henry King's *Tol'able*

Business and Society

JANUARY • Famous Players–Lasky reaches agreement with Ufa, the German state film studio, to import its films into the U.S.

FEBRUARY • Walter Wanger, Famous Players–Lasky Production Manager, reports that the studio's experiment with having an accountant carefully supervise the budget of each film is working well. • Famous Play-

ers–Lasky issues a house production code, advising supervisors not to exploit sex, religion, or violence.

APRIL • Douglas Fairbanks appears in *The Non-Sense of Censorship*, a short subject made by the movie industry to ridicule censorship.

JUNE 24 Famous Players–Lasky announces a twenty-five-percent pay cut, which Metro and Goldwyn will adopt.

JULY 1 Hollywood craft workers respond to studio wage cuts with a strike that lasts well into August, when they drift back to work.

AUGUST 31 The Federal Trade Commission charges Famous Players–Lasky and theater groups and individuals associated with it with violating the antitrust laws through control of theaters and preventing the films of independent producers from being shown in them. The ensuing inquiry and court proceedings will drag on until 1932.

Births, Deaths, Marriages, and Divorces

JANUARY 27 Donna Reed (Donna Belle Mullenger) b. **31** Mario Lanza (Alfred Coccozza) b.

FEBRUARY 12 Renée Adorée m. Tom Moore, ex-husband of Alice Joyce. **26** Betty Hutton (Betty Thornburg) b.

APRIL 16 Peter Ustinov b.

MAY 31 Buster Keaton m. Natalie Talmadge, making him Constance and Norma Talmadge's and producer Joseph Schenck's brother-in-law.

JUNE 6 Constance Bennett m. Chester Moorehead. **21** Jane Russell (Ernestine Jane Russell) b.

RUDOLPH VALENTINO STARS AS THE SHEIK

Rudolph Valentino, *The Sheik*

NOVEMBER 6 *The Sheik*, starring Rudolph Valentino, Agnes Ayers, and Adolphe Menjou, opens at the Rivoli and Rialto theaters, the ads for which urge moviegoers to "SEE the auction of beautiful girls to the lords of Algerian harems." According to *Variety*, "Mr. Valentino is revealed as a player without resources. He depicts the fundamental emotions of the Arabian sheik chiefly by showing his teeth and rolling his eyes."

LC

David, starring Richard Barthelmess, is released.

DECEMBER 25 Harold Lloyd's *A Sailor-Made Man*, his first feature-length film, is released. **28** D. W. Griffith's *Orphans of the Storm*, starring Dorothy and Lillian Gish, and Joseph Schildkraut, premieres in Boston.

SEPTEMBER 21 Universal, responding to the Fatty Arbuckle scandal, announces that it will add a morality clause to all its actor contracts.

JULY 6 Nancy Davis (Anne Frances Robbins), the future Nancy Reagan, b.

SEPTEMBER 15 Jackie Cooper b. **30** Deborah Kerr (Deborah Kerr-Trimmer) b.

OCTOBER 16 Linda Darnell (Monetta Eloyse Darnell) b.

NOVEMBER • Alice Terry m. director Rex Ingram. **3** Charles Bronson (Charles Buchinsky) b.

DECEMBER 4 Deanna Durbin (Edna Mae Durbin) b. **7** William S. Hart m.

Winifred Westover. **29** Richard Barthelmess and Mary Hay divorce.

Also this year: • John Gilbert and Olivia Burwell divorce.

irector William Desmond Taylor is murdered, Fatty Arbuckle is acquitted, and Will Hays becomes the movies' "czar." Valentino is arrested (briefly) for bigamy and walks out of his Paramount contract. *Nanook of the North* is the first major nonfiction feature, *Our Gang* comedies debut, and costume dramas are popular. *Toll of the Sea* is the first feature-length film in (two-color) Technicolor, and the German *Nosferatu*, based on the novel *Dracula* and directed by F.W. Murnau, is the screen's first vampire movie.

- Number of releases: 748
- Number of states and municipalities with film censorship boards: 8 states and 90 municipalities
- First *Our Gang* comedy release: *One Terrible Day*
- Dimensions of the castle in Douglas Fairbanks's *Robin Hood*: 450 feet long, 90 feet high
- Ramon Novarro's salary: $125 per week
- Number of trials required to acquit Fatty Arbuckle of a charge of manslaughter: 3

Top male and female box office stars, based on a Quigley Publications poll of exhibitors:
male: Douglas Fairbanks
female: Mary Pickford

Our Gang

MSN

January	February	March	April	May	June
				20 Valentino arrested for bigamy	
		6 Will Hays starts work as movies' new "czar"			
11 *Foolish Wives*	**2** William Taylor, Paramount's leading director, found murdered		**12** Fatty Arbuckle found not guilty in third trial		**6** Studios post Hays warning to players to lead more moral lives

July	August	September	October	November	December
	5 *Blood and Sand*				• Famous Players drops Mary Miles Minter over Taylor scandal
23 Twenty-one-year-old Clark Gable plays a woman in play, *When Women Rule*		**1** Rudolph Valentino walks out of Paramount	**18** *Robin Hood*		
			26 *Toll of the Sea*, first feature in Technicolor		

Personalities

JANUARY • *Motion Picture Classic* runs a photo of sixteen-year-old Clara Bow of Brooklyn, winner of a movie magazine "Fame and Fortune Contest." Her prize includes a brief role in *Beyond the Rainbow* (released February 19, 1922), initially left on the cutting room floor but restored to the film in its re-release after Bow becomes famous.

FEBRUARY • Lowell Sherman files for bankruptcy. **2** William Taylor, Paramount's leading director, is found shot to death in his home. The police question Mabel Normand, who had seen him the night before his death. Actress Mary Miles Minter is also linked to him. The public perceives it as yet another Hollywood scandal.

3 The second Fatty Arbuckle trial results in a hung jury.

APRIL 12 In his third trial, Fatty Arbuckle is found not guilty of causing the death of Virginia Rappe. **18** Will Hays temporarily bans Fatty Arbuckle from the movie industry.

MARCH 2 Joseph Schenck changes the name of the Comique Film Corporation, which has been making Fatty Arbuckle's movies, to Buster Keaton Productions, to accommodate his new star. Arbuckle will still draw thirty-five percent of the profits.

MAY 20 Rudolph Valentino is arrested for bigamy in Los Angeles because of his May 13 marriage to Natacha Rambova. A judge declares that the January 10 interlocutory decree granting the star's divorce from Jean Acker required him to wait a year before

remarrying. Valentino spends several hours in jail, but the charge will be dropped on June 5.

JULY 23 Twenty-one-year-old Clark Gable appears in blackface as a female cook in the play *When Women Rule* in Astoria, Oregon.

SEPTEMBER 1 Rudolph Valentino says he will make no more pictures for Paramount, although his contract runs through February 7, 1924. He tells reporters of his experiences there: "I have been dissatisfied with the photography, management and direction—the handling of all my films. They do not live up to my artistic ambitions." Of *The Sheik*, he says: "I hate it." He also attacks the practice of block booking, in which theaters are forced to rent all or most of a studio's film output in order to exhibit the ones they really want, but

Movies

JANUARY 11 Erich von Stroheim's *Foolish Wives*, in which he plays a seducer and child molester, premieres at the Criterion. "Salacious junk," says *Variety*. Universal brags on a Broadway sign that this is the first $1 million picture, and in newspaper ads says of von Stroheim: "You will revel in your hatred for him." The studio cuts the film after the opening (von Stroheim's six-hour director's cut had already been reduced to two), insisting it's for length, not from pressure to censor it. Ohio will ban the picture.

MARCH 6 Boston's Loew's State, seating four thousand, opens, with fifteen thousand trying to get in to see *The Champion* and *The Cradle* and celebrities Theda Bara and Mae Murray, appearing in person.

JUNE 11 Robert Flaherty's *Nanook of the North*, a nonfiction film about Eskimos, opens at the Capitol. Frances Patterson, in the *New Republic*, calls it "the first photoplay of the natural school of cinematography … there are no fictionalized situations, yet the picture is dramatic in the highest sense of the word."

JULY 31 Rex Ingram's *The Prisoner of Zenda*,

starring Lewis Stone and Alice Terry, premieres at the Astor Theater. It will be remade in 1937 and 1952.

AUGUST 5 Rudolph Valentino stars in *Blood and Sand*, with Lila Lee and Nita Naldi, premiering in Los Angeles.

SEPTEMBER 10 Hal Roach releases his first *Our Gang* comedy, *One Terrible Day*. **14** Marion Davies stars in *When Knighthood Was in Flower*, premiering at the Criterion. Its success will set off a search for costume drama scripts and cause United Artists to step up the release of Douglas Fairbanks's *Robin Hood*. **27** *The Power*

Business and Society

JANUARY 28 Snow collapses the roof of the Knickerbocker Theater in Washington, D.C., killing ninety-seven.

MARCH 6 Former Postmaster General Will Hays starts work as the movies' new "czar." He will head the newly formed Motion Picture Producers and Distributors of America. His appointment is an attempt

by studio heads to use self-censorship to cut off demands for state or federal control of picture content in the wake of recent Hollywood scandals. **10** Samuel Goldwyn loses control of the Goldwyn Company he co-founded in 1916 and resigns. **10** "Radio Sweeping Country" is *Variety's* front-page headline.

MAY 17 The Motion Picture Producers and Distributors of America approves Will Hays's warning to the studios that players

must lead more moral lives (posted at the studios on June 6). They also establish a censorship office under the control of Hays, which comes to be known as the Hays Office. **31** Fire at Universal City causes $500,000 in damage and destroys the only negatives of footage for Tod Browning's *Under Two Flags*, which will have to be reshot.

JUNE • Famous Players–Lasky establishes a Paramount Stock Company school to in-

Births, Deaths, Marriages, and Divorces

JANUARY 10 Rudolph Valentino and Jean Acker divorce. **21** Paul Scofield b.

MARCH 3 John Gilbert m. actress Leatrice Joy a second time after questions about his

divorce from Olivia Burwell cast doubt on the legality of their first ceremony.

APRIL 4 Composer Elmer Bernstein b.

MAY 13 Rudolph Valentino m. Natacha Rambova (Winifred Hudnut, a millionaire's stepdaughter) in Mexico. **27** Christopher Lee b.

JUNE 1 Constance Talmadge divorces John Pialoglou. **8** Blanche Sweet m. director Marshall "Mickey" Neilan. **10** Judy

the newspapers do not report this. **17** Harold Lloyd begins to film the scene from *Safety Last* in which he climbs up the side of a building and hangs from a clock. Long thought to have been filmed without doubles, a stand-in is, in fact, used in the long shots, and Lloyd films the close-ups on sets constructed on top of several tall buildings so that camera angles can give the impression that he is defying death. **25** Polish actress Pola Negri arrives in Los Angeles to make films at Famous Players. **30** Famous Players–Lasky gets an injunction preventing Rudolph Valentino from making movies for any other company.

OCTOBER 3 Douglas Fairbanks, publicizing the October 30th New York opening of *Robin Hood*, poses for photographers atop the Ritz-Carlton Hotel with a bow and arrow. Fairbanks and a few other people "fool

Douglas Fairbanks as Robin Hood *MSN*

around" with the weapon, shooting it. A man in a nearby window is hit and slightly wounded, and only a visit from Fairbanks convinces him not to press charges.

NOVEMBER 19 Movie theater impresario Samuel "Roxy" Rothapfel begins to broadcast the Capitol Theater's stage show over WEAF in New York. It soon develops into radio's first variety show, *Roxy and His Gang*.

DECEMBER • Famous Players–Lasky drops Mary Miles Minter, who was involved in the William Desmond Taylor scandal. **20** Will Hays lets Fatty Arbuckle return to the movie industry. Arbuckle will leave acting to direct films. **21** The *New York Times* review of yesterday's opening of the play, *The Red Poppy*, notes: "Bela Lugosi is a newcomer of quite splendid mien, romantically handsome and young."

of Love opens in Los Angeles. Filmed in the Fairall stereoscopic process, it is probably the first 3-D feature film.

OCTOBER 8 *Fire Fighters*, released today, is the first *Our Gang* film for Allen "Farina" Hoskins. He will appear in more of the comedy shorts than anyone else. **18** The premiere in Hollywood of Douglas Fairbanks's *Robin Hood* is also the opening of Sid Grauman's Egyptian Theater and the first time searchlights have been used at a premiere. **29** Jackie Coogan and Lon Chaney star in *Oliver Twist*, premiering at the Strand. The accompanying stage show features the Russian Fokine Ballet.

NOVEMBER 12 Mary Pickford stars in *Tess of the Storm Country*, released today. She starred in a 1914 filming of the same story. **26** *Toll of the Sea*, premiering at the Rialto, is the first feature film in Technicolor: "Human beings made to live and breathe before your eyes!" The process, two-color Technicolor (compared with three-color, which will become familiar from the mid-1930s on), blends two negatives, one emphasizing red, the other, green.

struct its players in good behavior as well as to teach "the fundamentals of screen art."

AUGUST • The Federal Trade Commission issues a complaint against William Fox for rereleasing old films under new titles without identifying them as such. Other studios have done this in recent years. **16** Lee De Forest, in Berlin, demonstrates his photophone method of adding sound to pictures by recording it electronically on the edge of the film strip.

DECEMBER 8 New York State Supreme Court Justice Robert F. Wagner rules that a movie star can't prevent the re-editing and re-releasing of an earlier film in which he or she starred, as an author could prevent such a re-doing of a book. Douglas Fairbanks maintained that his earlier films, made under the supervision of D. W. Griffith at Triangle, could not be treated in this way.

Garland (Frances Gumm) b. **21** Judy Holliday b.

JULY 22 Jason Robards Jr., son of stage and screen actor Jason Robards, b. **30** Jack Pickford m. Ziegfeld Follies star Marilyn Miller (former mistress of Flo Ziegfeld).

AUGUST 18 Shelley Winters (Shirley Schrift) b.

DECEMBER • Lionel Barrymore and Doris Rankin divorce. **24** Ava Gardner b.

Also this year: • George Brent m. Helen Campbell. • James Cagney m. Frances

Vernon. • Walter Pidgeon m. Edna Pickles.

The Covered Wagon begins a cycle of 1920s Westerns, Hollywood starts to make films about itself, Lon Chaney proves that a leading man doesn't have to be handsome, Cecil B. DeMille brings his first version of *The Ten Commandments* to the screen, and director Ernst Lubitsch begins his American career. Scandal temporarily forces William S. Hart off the screen. Warner Bros. incorporates, and Irving Thalberg goes to work for independent producer Louis B. Mayer. Young women are flocking to Hollywood to try to get into pictures, and Mack Sennett, Harry Chandler, and the *Los Angeles Times* put up the HOLLYWOODLAND (later shortened to HOLLYWOOD) sign to publicize a real estate development.

- Number of releases: 576
- Number of theaters: 15,000
- Total film industry employment: 130,000
- Number of wagons in *The Covered Wagon*: 500
- Cost of the HOLLYWOODLAND sign: $21,000
- Amount of time needed to apply Lon Chaney's makeup for *The Hunchback of Notre Dame*: 4$\frac{1}{2}$ hours
- Annual compensation for 3$\frac{1}{2}$-year-old film star Baby Peggy (Peggy Montgomery): about $1,500,000 per year

Weekly star salaries, according to the Motion Picture Theater Owners of America:

1.	Norma Talmadge	$10,000	6.	Pauline Frederick	5,000
2.	Dorothy Dalton	7,500	7.	Lillian Gish	5,000
3.	Gloria Swanson	6,500	8.	Tom Mix	4,000
4.	Larry Semon	5,000	9.	Betty Compson	3,500
5.	Constance Talmadge	5,000	10.	Barbara LaMarr	3,500
			44.	Mary Astor	750

Top male and female box office stars, based on a Quigley Publications poll of exhibitors:
male: Thomas Meighan
female: Norma Talmadge

Norma Talmadge, #1 female star   *MSN*

January	February	March	April	May	June
		16 *The Covered Wagon*		• William S. Hart cleared in paternity case	
18 Wallace Reid d. from drug addiction and drinking			**4** Warner Bros. Pictures incorporates		• Tyrone Power Sr. arrested for non-support of Tyrone Jr. and his sister

July	August	September	October	November	December
	• Baby Peggy, age 3$\frac{1}{2}$, under contract for more than $1 million per year		**4** Charlton Heston b.	**12** *Flaming Youth*	**4** Cecil B. DeMille's *The Ten Commandments*
18 Rudolph Valentino and Famous Players settle feud		**2** *The Hunchback of Notre Dame*			

Personalities

JANUARY 11   Jackie Coogan signs with Metro. **18** Wallace Reed dies at age thirty-two in a sanitorium. The drug addiction and drinking of this actor, known for playing wholesome college men, fuels the demands for Hollywood to clean up its image. **22** Cecil B. DeMille, competing in a motorboat race in Los Angeles, is blown into the water when his gas tank ignites. **25** The *Los Angeles Times* reports Mary Miles Minter's decision to end her film career.

FEBRUARY 22   *Variety* reports that Hal Roach has signed Norma Shearer. "Miss Shearer, of Montreal, recently won a beauty contest."

MARCH • Cecil B. DeMille pays hush money to lawyers who threaten to reveal his star Gloria Swanson's alleged affair with director Mickey Neilan. Will Hays informed DeMille on February 18 that if news of the affair gets out, "she will be banned from pictures." Swanson's husband, Herbert K. Somborn, is suing her for divorce, claiming she has committed adultery with fourteen men. **2** The *Los Angeles Examiner* headlines: "Negri Jilts Chaplin." Actually, it's the other way around. Charlie Chaplin has given them the story to make it sound as if Pola Negri and not he broke off their engagement. **10** Will Rogers signs with the Hal Roach studio, where he will remain for two years. **27** Winifred Westover, suing William S. Hart for divorce, reveals that her husband was charged with fathering another woman's child in 1917. His career damaged, Hart retires. **29** Vaudeville star Harry Langdon signs to make pictures for Sol Lesser's Principal Pictures. But Lesser will sell the contract to Mack Sennett, where Langdon begins his movie career.

APRIL 15   The *New York Times* reviews favorably a collection of stories, *Habit*, by screenwriter Darryl F. Zanuck. **24** Former Assistant Secretary of the Navy Franklin D. Roosevelt, through an agent, submits to Adolph Zukor a treatment for a screenplay about John Paul Jones. Nothing comes of it.

MAY 23   Elizabeth MacCauley, to whom William S. Hart has been making payments for six years because she said he fathered her child, confesses that she lied about his paternity. **31** Jesse Lasky announces that William S. Hart, his name cleared, will return to the screen.

Movies

MARCH 16   *The Covered Wagon*, directed by James Cruze, the first of a cycle of 1920s westerns, opens at the Criterion. It was shot on location, and five hundred wagons lend authenticity. Many of the cast are unknowns, and few of the actors wear makeup.

APRIL 1   Harold Lloyd's *Safety Last* is released. **8** Samuel Goldwyn's *Souls for Sale*, "the Sensational Story of Hollywood which tears aside the veil of secrecy surrounding the lives of our screen celebrities," is one of the movie colony's first films about itself, with thirty-five stars making "cameo" appearances—a new concept. It opens today at the Capitol. On August 19, Paramount will release *Hollywood*, a similar film. **15** A program of shorts featuring vaudeville stars, produced using the De Forest Phonofilm sound process, opens at the Rivoli. The unclear sound diminishes its impact. Even so, it is thought that this "canned vaudeville" will substitute for live performers in rural areas and small cities where stage shows don't play. Little or nothing is heard about sound film replacing silent movies.

JULY 1   *Merry-Go-Round*, from which Irving Thalberg removed Erich von Stroheim as director, replacing him with Rupert Julian, premieres at the Rivoli. And the first Rin Tin Tin movie, *Where the North Begins*, is released.

SEPTEMBER 2   *The Hunchback of Notre Dame* premieres at the Astor. The *New York Times* describes Lon Chaney's Quasimodo as "a fearsome, frightful, crooked creature, one eye bulging but blind, knees that interfere, sharp, saw-edged protruding teeth, high, swollen cheek bones and a dented and twisted nose...."

Business and Society

• The movie industry, which employed thirty-five thousand people four years ago, now provides jobs for 130,000, one of whom is film cutter Gladys Baker, who in 1926 will give birth to Marilyn Monroe.

FEBRUARY • Lewis Selznick's Select Pictures is forced into bankruptcy, something his two sons—agent, Myron, and producer, David—will blame on the Hollywood establishment. **•** William Randolph Hearst's Cosmopolitan Pictures switches distribution from Paramount to Goldwyn. **15** Irving Thalberg at age twenty-four leaves Universal to become independent producer Louis B. Mayer's production assistant.

APRIL 4   Warner Bros. Pictures incorporates. **22** The FTC issues an ammended anti-trust complaint against Famous-Players Lasky. The studio denies all charges. **29** The Federal Trade Commission files a complaint against Eastman Kodak for trying to monopolize the sale of movie film.

MAY •   The Federal Trade Commission rules that ads for films reissued under new titles must display the old one in type of equal size.

JULY 27   Loew's announces that it has purchased a New York radio station, WHN, for use in broadcasting from the stage of Loew's State and publicizing its movies.

Births, Deaths, Marriages, and Divorces

JANUARY 17   Constance Bennett's 1921 marriage to Chester Moorehead is annulled on the grounds that they were underage. **18** Wallace Reid d.

FEBRUARY 10   Harold Lloyd m. Mildred Davis.

23   Geraldine Farrar and Lou Tellegen divorce.

MARCH 15   Rudolph Valentino remarries Natacha Rambova.

APRIL 21   Marjorie Daw m. director Edward Sutherland at Pickfair, with Mary Pickford and Charlie Chaplin matron-of-honor and best man, respectively.

JUNE 22 Al Jolson views the rushes for *Black and White*, the film he's just started to make with D.W. Griffith, and walks out, never to return, insecure about how he is coming across in his first film. Griffith will sue him, but win a settlement of just a few thousand dollars.

JULY 18 Rudolph Valentino and Famous Players–Lasky settle their differences. He will make two more films for them, over which he will exercise considerable control. Anticipating his departure from the studio, Famous Players–Lasky begins to groom Ricardo Cortez as its new Latin lover.

AUGUST 27 Baby Peggy, three-and-a-half years old, a Shirley Temple prototype who will star in such films as *Captain January* (remade by Temple in 1936), will be making more than $1 million per year under her new contract, it is announced today. **30** "David Selznick, youngest son of Lewis J., has entered the producing field for himself," reports *Variety*.

NOVEMBER 7 While filming, Harold Lloyd is knocked off a moving truck by a fire hose nozzle that swings into his face, cutting him. He will be out for two weeks. **19** Louella Parsons joins Hearst's New York *American* as motion picture editor and columnist.

DECEMBER 3 The Hollywood Chamber of commerce launches a campaign to dissuade young women from going West to try to get into the movies. At a rally addressing

Lon Chaney as Quasimodo, *The Hunchback of Notre Dame*   MSN

3 Ernst Lubitsch's first American film, *Rosita*, starring Mary Pickford, premieres at the Lyric Theater. Critics acclaim it for its beauty, but she hates its artiness. **26** Charlie Chaplin's *A Woman of Paris* premieres at the opening of the opulent Criterion Theater in Hollywood. Chaplin is not there, but present are Mabel Normand, Mack Sennett, Mary Pickford and Douglas Fairbanks, Will Rogers, and Irving Thalberg.

NOVEMBER 4 *Little Old New York*, starring Marion Davies, is released. **12** *Flaming Youth*, with Colleen Moore as a flapper, a

NOVEMBER • Ohio censors, who last year banned Erich von Stroheim's *Foolish Wives*, approve *The Toll of Justice*, the Ku Klux Klan's first film. It portrays the Klan's fight against vice and corruption. **19** The Supreme Court, in *Binderup v. Pathé Exchange*, holds that the shipment of films within a state is an extension of interstate commerce and may be regulated by the federal government.

MAY 5 Her marriage to Ben Deely annulled, Barbara LaMarr m. Jack Dougherty. **7** Anne Baxter, granddaughter of Frank Lloyd Wright, b. **17** Marlene Dietrich m. film production assistant Rudolf Sieber.

JUNE • Theda Bara m. director Charles Brabin.

JULY 14 Lionel Barrymore m. Irene Fenwick.

AUGUST 8 Esther Williams b. **10** Rhonda Fleming (Marilyn Louis) b. **18** Colleen Moore m. John McCormick, production chief at First National.

SEPTEMBER 7 Peter Lawford b. **12** Spencer Tracy m. Louise Treadwell. **19** Gloria Swanson is divorced by Herbert Somborn.

OCTOBER 4 Charlton Heston (Charles Carter) b.

Personalities

thousands, Mary Pickford warns that it takes a long time to make it in this industry. "Take mother along: you'll need her," she advises aspiring actresses.

Movies

type she will play in several films, is released.

DECEMBER 4   Cecil B. DeMille's epic, *The Ten Commandments* (remade in 1956), with Richard Dix, Rod La Rocque, Leatrice Joy, and Nita Naldi, premieres at Grauman's Egyptian Theater in Hollywood. It includes scenes in Technicolor.

Business and Society

Births, Deaths, Marriages, and Divorces

NOVEMBER 9   Dorothy Dandridge b. **31** Minta Durfee divorces Fatty Arbuckle.

Also this year: • Renée Adorée divorces Tom Moore. • Pola Negri divorces Count Eugene Dambski.

MGM, Columbia Pictures, and MCA are created. The Douglas Fairbanks Studio (the independent production company he started in 1916) is the first to buy a Moviola editing machine. Erich von Stroheim's *Greed*, diminished in length by the Goldwyn Studio, and in stature by the critics, premieres. Joan Crawford is discovered, and commercial artist Gary Cooper arrives in Los Angeles looking for work. Max and Dave Fleischer introduce "the bouncing ball" animations to audience sing-alongs. As the pianist or organist plays, the ball bounces onto each word of the lyrics on the screen as it comes up in the song.

- Number of releases: 579
- Number of theaters: 15,000
- Average ticket price: $.25
- U.S. films as a percentage of those shown in British theaters: 80%
- Price range of tickets at major downtown theaters:
  Stanley Theater (Philadelphia): $.50–.75
  Capitol (New York): $.35–1.65
  Roosevelt (Chicago): $.55

Top box office stars, according to a *Film Daily* poll of exhibitors:

1. Harold Lloyd
2. Gloria Swanson
3. Tom Mix
4. Thomas Meighan
5. Norma Talmadge
6. Corinne Griffith and Rudolph Valentino (tied)
7. Douglas Fairbanks
8. Colleen Moore, Mary Pickford, and Reginald Denny (tied)

The *New York Times* Ten Best Films

1. *The Dramatic Life of Abraham Lincoln*
2. *The Thief of Bagdad*
3. *Beau Brummel*
4. *Merton of the Movies*
5. *The Sea Hawk*
6. *He Who Gets Slapped*
7. *The Marriage Circle*
8. *In Hollywood with Potash and Perlmutter*
9. *Peter Pan*
10. *Isn't Life Wonderful?*

Gary Cooper arrives in L.A. seeking work this year. MSN

January	February	March	April	May	June	
10 Columbia Pictures comes into being	**20** Sidney Poitier b.	**18** *The Thief of Bagdad*	**17** Metro-Goldwyn (later Metro-Goldwyn-Mayer) formed	**20** *Innocent Eyes* opens on Broadway with chorus girl Lucille LeSeur (Joan Crawford)	**25** Director Sidney Lumet b.	

July	August	September	October	November	December	
4 Eva Marie Saint b.	**28** *The Iron Horse* / **16** Lauren Bacall b.	• 16 year-old Carole Lombard signs with Fox		**27** Gary Cooper arrives in L.A., seeking work as commercial artist	**4** *Greed*	

Personalities

JANUARY 1 Mabel Normand's chauffeur shoots millionaire Courtland Dines at Dines's home while Mabel and actress Edna Purviance are in the next room. This latest brush with scandal gets Normand's films banned in Ohio and Michigan.

MARCH • Tom Mix reports that he has accidentally wounded himself with his gun. (Ten years later, testifying in a lawsuit, he will acknowledge that his wife shot him—because he beat her, she will contend.) **2** Charlie Chaplin signs Lillita McMurray, not quite sixteen years old, to appear in *The Gold Rush* for $75 per week, changing her name to Lita Grey. Journalist Jim Tully is given the job of building her up in the press. An example, from an article syndicated in

June: "No love affairs have ever brought a quick beating to her heart, a flush to her cheeks. She idolizes Chaplin, but much as a child feels for some much older man who has shown her a great kindness." By November she and Chaplin will be married.

APRIL • The Secretary of War ends the granting of the honorary rank of "Colonel" when a newspaper complains about the newly appointed Col. Marion Davies. Mary Pickford is also a colonel.

MAY 20 An otherwise undistinguished revue, *Innocent Eyes*, opening at the Winter Garden in New York, has one chorus girl who will catch the eye of an MGM scout: Lucille LeSeur (Joan Crawford).

JUNE 10 D.W. Griffith signs with Paramount.

JULY 18 Johnny Weissmuller wins the Olympic four-hundred-meter free-style event.

AUGUST 3 Mabel Normand leaves Hollywood to try a New York stage career, in which she will flop. **12** The *Boston Advertiser* heralds the stage debut in that city of "Miriam Hopkins, chic, blondy and apparently sweet seventeen" in *Little Jessy James*.

OCTOBER • Sixteen-year-old Carole Lombard signs with Fox.

NOVEMBER 11 The opening of the Eugene O'Neill play *Desire under the Elms* on Broadway makes Walter Huston a major star in the American theater and draws his son John to the theater as a profession. **19** Producer/director Thomas Ince dies under mysterious circumstances on Will-

Movies

JANUARY 12 Erich von Stroheim screens his nine-hour, forty-two-reel rough cut of *Greed* for the Goldwyn studio executives. He will reduce it to twenty-two reels, and then the company will cut it to ten. *Motion Picture Magazine*, in April, will print a brief account by someone present at the screening. Harry Carr writes: "I can't imagine what they are going to do with it. It's like *Les Misérables*. Episodes come along that you think have no bearing on the story, then twelve or fourteen reels later, it hits you with a crash. For stark, terrible realism

and marvelous artistry, it is the greatest picture I have ever seen." By the time *Greed* is reduced to its final running time, the Goldwyn studio will have become part of the new MGM, and Louis B. Mayer will be responsible for the film's length. Von Stroheim will later recall: "Mayer thereupon gave it to a cutter, a man earning thirty dollars a week, a man who had never read the book nor the script, and on whose mind was nothing but a hat. He ruined the whole of my two year's work."

FEBRUARY 3 *The Marriage Circle*, the first of director Ernst Lubitsch's social satires, premieres at the Strand. Florence Vidor,

Monte Blue, Marie Prevost, and Adolphe Menjou star in "a *Sensational Story* of married lovers whose love is not always confined to their own mates." **21** D.W. Griffith's *America*, starring Lionel Barrymore, premieres at the 42nd St. Theater.

MARCH 18 *The Thief of Bagdad* premieres at the Liberty Theater, where ushers dressed as Arabs serve Turkish coffee to female patrons only. Police have to form a wedge to get star Douglas Fairbanks and Mary Pickford through the crowd outside. Fairbanks had originally entrusted the production design of this film to Maxwell

Business and Society

JANUARY • Paramount, the distribution company controlled by Famous Players–Lasky, has become more famous than its parent, causing a corporate identification problem. The solution is a new line in ads: "Production of Famous Players–Lasky, a Paramount Picture." **10** CBC Film Sales, founded in 1922 and known in the business as "Corned Beef and Cabbage," is

a cheap production studio—"Poverty Row"—led by Harry and Jack Cohn and Joseph Brandt, which now changes its name to Columbia Pictures Corporation, headed by Brandt.

APRIL 17 Metro Pictures, Goldwyn Pictures (with which Samuel Goldwyn is no longer connected), and the Louis B. Mayer Company announce their merger to form Metro–Goldwyn Pictures. Marcus Loew, whose large chain of theaters will showcase

their films, heads the new company, with Louis B. Mayer in charge of production. Mayer's production supervisor, Irving Thalberg, will hold the same post at the new company. The studio will use the Goldwyn Company's forty-acre Culver City lot (dedicated April 26 by Mayer). For the first few months, its films will be presented as "A Metro Goldwyn picture, produced by Louis B. Mayer," until at Mayer's insistence, the company becomes Metro–Goldwyn Mayer (MGM).

Births, Deaths, Marriages, and Divorces

JANUARY 24 Screenwriter Darryl F. Zanuck m. Virginia Fox.

FEBRUARY 19 Lee Marvin b. **20** Sidney Poitier b.

MARCH 15 Sabu (Sabu Dastagir) b. **24** Freddie Bartholomew b.

APRIL 3 Marlon Brando and Doris Day (Doris Von Kappelhoff) are born.

JUNE 20 Audie Murphy b. **25** Director Sidney Lumet b.

JULY 4 Eva Marie Saint b.

AUGUST 11 Arlene Dahl b.

SEPTEMBER 16 Lauren Bacall (Betty Joan Perske) b.

iam Randolph Hearst's yacht. Ince is rumored to have been shot by Hearst, who mistook him for Charlie Chaplin, who is having an affair with Hearst mistress Marion Davies. **27** Gary Cooper arrives in Los Angeles from Montana, seeking work as a commercial artist.

Gary Cooper   *MSN*

Parrish, but dissatisfied with the illustrator's work, he uses only the striking advertising poster Parrish created. It is William Cameron Menzies, early in his career, who is finally responsible for the look of the picture. **24** Norma Talmadge stars in *Secrets*, premiering at the Astor Theater. **30** *Beau Brummel*, starring Mary Astor and John Barrymore, premieres at the Astor.

APRIL 20 Harold Lloyd stars in *Girl Shy*, released today. **21** Buster Keaton's *Sherlock Jr.* is released.

AUGUST 18 Released today is *Monsieur Beaucaire*, starring Rudolph Valentino and

Bebe Daniels. **21** Loew's State in St. Louis, seating thirty-six hundred, opens with *Revelation*. **28** John Ford's *The Iron Horse*, starring George O'Brien and Madge Bellamy,

premieres at the Lyric Theater. Ford's first major film borrows from *The Covered Wagon* in its attention to realistic detail.

MAY 27 Jules Stein, to pay for medical school, starts a dance band booking agency called The Music Corporation of America (MCA).

JUNE • Actors' Equity, the stage actor's association founded in 1912, attempts to make inroads among movie players.

JULY 7 Fire at the Hal Roach studios causes $175,000 in damage.

SEPTEMBER 24 *Variety* begins a "Radio" page.

NOVEMBER • Theaters in some outlying areas and small cities—Providence, Rhode Island, for example—begin to show double features. **22** Independent producer Joseph M. Schenck becomes a partner in, and chairman of the board of, United Artists, bringing with him contract players Norma and Constance Talmadge and Buster Keaton. The company will now

finance and produce as well as distribute films. Among the creative producers they will eventually attract are David O. Selznick, Walt Disney, Howard Hughes, Alexander Korda, and Samuel Goldwyn.

DECEMBER 31 The Motion Picture Relief Fund is incorporated to provide medical and financial help to professionals in need.

OCTOBER 14 Director James Cruze m. film star Betty Compson.

NOVEMBER 24 Geraldine Page b. **26** Charlie Chaplin m. 16-year-old Lita Grey.

DECEMBER 13 Clark Gable m. his drama teacher, Josephine Dillon. **20** Ruth Chatterton m. Ralph Forbes.

Also this year: • Claude Rains m. Beatrix Thomas.

Personalities

Erich von Stroheim   *MSN*

Movies

NOVEMBER 9 *He Who Gets Slapped*, premiering at the Capitol, is MGM's first release. Starring Lon Chaney, John Gilbert, and Norma Shearer, it's directed by Victor Seastrom. Chaney plays a scientist who has become a circus clown. According to the *New York Times*, "Seastrom has directed this dramatic story with all the genius of a Chaplin or a Lubitsch, and he has accomplished more than they have in their respective works.. . . For dramatic value and a faultless adaptation of the play [by Leonid Andreyev], this is the finest produc-

tion we have yet seen."

DECEMBER 4 Erich von Stroheim's *Greed* premieres at William Randolph Hearst's Cosmopolitan Theater in New York. The *New York Times* calls it the "sour creme de

la sour creme de la bourgoisie [sic]," and *Variety* says it's "morbid and senseless from a commercial viewpoint.…"

Business and Society

Births, Deaths, Marriages, and Divorces

Paramount and Balaban & Katz theaters merge, Warner Bros. agrees to work with Western Electric on a sound system, and film executives are worried about competing with radio. John Gilbert achieves stardom in *The Big Parade*, and *Ben-Hur* opens. Tom Mix is making $20,000 a week, MGM signs Greta Garbo, Vilma Banky becomes an American movie star, Louise Brooks makes her film debut, and top stars are beginning to expect a dressing room–bungalow on the lot. In the Soviet Union, Sergei Eisenstein's *Potemkin*, in which meaning and emotion are conveyed through the editing of shots—a technique known as *montage*—is released.

- Number of releases: 578
- Population of Hollywood: 130,000
- Tom Mix's salary: $20,000 a week
- Ramon Novarro's salary: $10,000 a week
- Value of San Simeon, William Randolph Hearst estate: $50,000,000
- Number of theaters with fewer than 100 seats: 11, 5 of which are in Montana
- Material used to make the boots eaten by Charlie Chaplin in *The Gold Rush*: chocolate
- Number of cameras used to film the chariot race in *Ben-Hur*: 42, which record 200,000 feet of film, 750 of which make it into the release print

Top male and female box office stars, based on a Quigley Publications poll of exhibitors:
    male: Rudolph Valentino
    female: Norma Talmadge

The New York Times Ten Best Films

1. *The Big Parade*
2. *The Last Laugh*
3. *The Unholy Three*
4. *The Gold Rush*
5. *The Merry Widow*
6. *The Dark Angel*
7. *Don Q, Son of Zorro*
8. *Ben-Hur*
9. *Stella Dallas*
10. *A Kiss for Cinderella*

Louise Brooks makes her film debut this year.   MSN

January	February	March	April	May	June	
• Tom Mix signs Fox contract for $20,000 per week		**9** Valentino signs with United Artists	**20** Warner Bros. buys Vitagraph		**26** *The Gold Rush*	
	8 Jack Lemmon b.			• Louise Brooks becomes a movie actress		

July	August	September	October	November	December	
		18 MGM renames Lucille LeSeur "Joan Crawford"	• Carole Lombard cut on face in auto accident		**30** *Ben-Hur*	
	7 Greta Garbo arrives in U.S.	**17** Merger of Paramount and Balaban & Katz theaters		**5** *The Big Parade*		

Personalities

JANUARY • Tom Mix signs a new contract with Fox for $20,000 a week, the highest salary ever paid a movie star. **3** Lucille LeSeur, not yet "Joan Crawford," steps off the Sunset Limited in Los Angeles to begin work at MGM. **24** FREUD REBUFFS GOLDWYN—VIENNESE PSYCHOANALYST IS NOT INTERESTED IN MOTION PICTURE OFFER, headlines the *New York Times*. **29** Erich von Stroheim and MGM have made peace. After Mae Murray, female lead in *The Merry Widow*, called him a "dirty Hun," von Stroheim was temporarily removed from the film. When Irving Thalberg complains of too much attention devoted to the shoes in the baron's wardrobe, von Stroheim replies that the baron had a foot fetish. Thalberg's reposte is said to be: "And you

Greta Garbo   MSN

are a footage fetishist." **30** Greta Garbo signs her first MGM contract.

MARCH 2 Cecil B. DeMille, who left Famous Players–Lasky on January 10, sets up his own studio in Culver City. **8** Director Mickey Neilan and his wife, Blanche Sweet, exchange punches in the MGM commissary. (By the end of the month, Neilan, as well as Erich von Stroheim, will be gone from the studio.) **9** Valentino signs with United Artists. His contract stipulates that his wife, Natacha Rambova, who exercises great sway over him, will stay away while he works.

MAY • Louise Brooks makes her movie debut as she films *Street of Forgotten Men* at Famous Players–Lasky's Astoria Studio. **12** One of the first all-star broadcast ap-

Movies

JANUARY 25 A version of the 1924 German film *The Last Laugh* opens, shortened for American audiences. Its success opens the way for its director, F. W. Murnau, and its star, Emil Jannings, to work in the U. S.

FEBRUARY 8 *The Lost World* opens at the Astor. Starring Bessie Love, Wallace Beery, and Lewis Stone, it is the prototype for science fiction films about dinosaurs.

JUNE 26 At the premiere of Charlie Chaplin's *The Gold Rush*, fifteen thousand fans throng Grauman's Egyptian Theater in Hollywood to see the arrival of Chaplin, Cecil B. DeMille, Marion Davies and William Randolph Hearst, Harold Lloyd, Norma Talmadge, a caped-and-gowned Gloria Swanson, Douglas Fairbanks and Mary Pickford, John Barrymore, Mabel Normand, Fatty Arbuckle, Tom Mix in a white tuxedo, and Rudolph Valentino.

JULY 4 Noble Sissle and Eubie Blake become the first black performers to headline a major movie theater stage show, in St. Louis, at the Missouri Theater. **12** As

The Gold Rush   LC

Business and Society

JANUARY • Germany requires that at least fifty percent of all films shown there be made there as well. • MGM pulls its *Ben-Hur* production company out of Italy, bringing it home to Hollywood, where costs and quality can be better controlled.

MARCH • *Photoplay* editor James R. Quirk writes: "The motion picture theater own-

ers are lying awake nights worrying about the effect of radio on box office receipts." • Warner Bros. begins a theater building and buying program. Jack Warner takes charge of production. **3** Warners' Los Angeles radio station KFWB goes on the air.

APRIL 20 Warner Bros. buys the Vitagraph Company.

JUNE • According to Jack Warner, when Sam told Harry that dialogue might come to

films, brother Harry replied: "Who the hell wants to hear actors talk?" In fact, for the struggling studio, sound will boost its ability to compete with MGM, Paramount, and

Births, Deaths, Marriages, and Divorces

JANUARY 26 Paul Newman b. **28** Gloria Swanson m. the Marquis de la Falaise de la Coudraye.

FEBRUARY 8 Jack Lemmon (John Lemmon III) b.

APRIL 14 Rod Steiger b.

MAY 25 Jeanne Crain b. **26** Mae Murray divorces Robert Leonard. **29** John Gilbert and Leatrice Joy divorce.

JUNE 2 Francis X. Bushman and Beverly Bayne divorce. **3** Tony Curtis (Bernard Schwartz) b. **21** Maureen Stapleton, sister of Jean Stapleton, b.

JULY • Marjorie Daw divorces Edward Sutherland. **1** Farley Granger b.

pearances of movie personalities is made by Lillian Gish, Marion Davies, Barbara LaMarr, and Jackie Coogan on Philadelphia's WIP. On May 10 the Hearst papers gushed: "The movie fans who have seen their favorite screen star…will now have the opportunity to hear their voices [something new in the era of silent films]—and the next time you see them, you'll feel as if you really know the star!"

JULY 17 Hollywood's the *Film Mercury* asks: "Why are so many ladies of the screen having their hair cut like a man?" **26** "No one can convince me that the modern girl cares for nothing but cocktails, cigarettes and jazz," says Mary Pickford, according to today's Louella Parsons column.

AUGUST 12 *Variety* reports that "Samuel Goldwyn seems to have found one of the best leading women bets of the year in Vilma Banky, a blond Hungarian screen actress . . ." **18** *Movie Weekly* magazine ran a contest to pick a new name for MGM's Lucille LeSeur, which reminds producer Harry Rapf of "sewer." The studio has discarded the judges' choice, "Joan Arden," because several people sent it in and each would receive the $500 prize. Today, MGM selects "Joan Crawford," submitted by only one person.

OCTOBER • Fox starlet Carole Lombard sustains bad facial cuts from flying glass in an auto accident and has plastic surgery. **1** MGM's Fred Niblo directs the filming of the *Ben-Hur* chariot race on the studio's Culver City lot. The enormity of the spectacle draws an audience of Hollywood's elite, including Mary Pickford and Douglas Fairbanks Sr. They see 10,000 extras, 198 horses, 62 assistant directors (one of whom is William Wyler), and members of the U.S. Army serving as the Roman Imperial Guard. Director Niblo marshals his forces and 42 cameras from a tower 100 feet above it all.

NOVEMBER • William Randolph Hearst sends his movie editor, Louella Parsons, to Hollywood to report from the "front."

DECEMBER • William Powell signs a long-term contract with Famous Players–Lasky. He will become one of the silent screen's foremost villains. **25** William Randolph Hearst moves into San Simeon, his $50 million estate near the Pacific—the model for "Xanadu" in *Citizen Kane*. Movie stars will be his frequent weekend guests.

an experiment, New York's Rivoli Theater replaces its symphony orchestra—typical in big city, first run theaters—with Ben Bernie and his "jazz" band. Bernie also emcees the stage show.

AUGUST 2 *Sally of the Sawdust*, starring W.C. Fields and Carol Dempster, is released. **16** *The Unholy Three*, starring Lon Chaney and Mae Busch, is released. **26** Erich von Stroheim's *The Merry Widow*, starring John Gilbert and Mae Murray, premieres as the first attraction at the intimate, four-hundred-seat Embassy Theater, the latest in the Loew's chain. The *New York Times* review notes the "close-ups of ankles, of booted feet" from the director who is said to have a foot fetish.

SEPTEMBER 6 Lon Chaney, borrowed from Universal by MGM, stars in *The Phantom of the Opera*, which premieres at the Astor. **6** *Pretty Ladies*, released today by MGM, stars ZaSu Pitts, but three bit players foreshadow another generation of stars: Norma Shearer, Joan Crawford, and, in her film debut, Myrna Loy. **20** Harold Lloyd's most popular film, *The Freshman*, premieres at the Colony. *Don Q, Son of Zorro*, starring Douglas Fairbanks and Mary Astor, is released.

NOVEMBER 5 *The Big Parade*, King Vidor's World War I film that stars, and makes a star of, John Gilbert, premieres at Grauman's Egyptian Theater in Hollywood, with Gilbert, Darryl Zanuck, and Buster Keaton attending. Also starring in the film are Renée Adorée and Hobart Bosworth. **8** *The Eagle*, starring Rudolph Valentino and Vilma Banky, premieres at the Strand, with Valentino attending.

DECEMBER 30 MGM's *Ben-Hur*, inherited from the Goldwyn Company, premieres at the George M. Cohan Theater. It stars Ramon Novarro, Francis X. Bushman, and May McAvoy. The otherwise black-and-white film includes a few Technicolor sequences.

Universal. Pioneering sound films will increase its assets from a current $5 million to $230 million by 1930. **25** Warner Bros. agrees to work with Western Electric to develop an effective movie sound system.

SEPTEMBER 17 Paramount announces the merger of its theaters with those owned by Balaban & Katz. By November, Sam Katz will be managing the chain—soon to encompass over one thousand houses—that becomes the Publix Theaters Corporation.

Many local movie theaters will be christened "the Paramount."

NOVEMBER • B.P. Schulberg joins Famous Players–Lasky as an associate producer, bringing along the cream of his Preferred Pictures personnel: Clara Bow and director William Wellman. **21** In return for an infusion of cash for production, UFA, Germany's huge film company, grants Universal sole exhibition rights in its theaters. (On December 30, Famous Players–Lasky and MGM are cut in on the deal.) **27** Universal announces a plan to control one thousand theaters. William Fox is also acquiring theaters.

5 Silent screen actress Lina Basquette m. Sam Warner, one of the Warner brothers.

AUGUST 30 Donald O'Connor b.

SEPTEMBER 8 Peter Sellers b. **9** Cliff Robertson b.

OCTOBER 16 Angela Lansbury, granddaughter of future British Labor Party head George Lansbury, b.

NOVEMBER 10 Richard Burton (Richard Jenkins Jr.) b. **17** Rock Hudson (Roy Scherer Jr., later Roy Fitzgerald) b. **23** Constance Bennett m. Philip Plant, son of a millionaire. **28** Gloria Grahame (Gloria Grahame Hallward) b.

DECEMBER 8 Sammy Davis Jr. b.

Also this year: • Florence and King Vidor divorce.

arners's *Don Juan*, in the Vitaphone process, has sound but no dialogue. Greta Garbo debuts in *The Torrent* and becomes a romantic star in *The Flesh and the Devil*, the Paramount Theater opens in New York, Hollywood dabbles with a crude wide-screen process, and the word "documentary" is coined. There is almost mass hysteria at Valentino's funeral, and Louella Parsons becomes Hollywood's first major gossip columnist. Congress begins to promote the rental of American films and the purchase of American moviemaking equipment abroad. In Germany, Fritz Lang's futuristic fantasy, *Metropolis*, is released. And Abel Gance's *Napoleon* opens at the Paris Opéra. It was filmed in a wide-screen (three screens across) process.

- Number of releases: 740
- Number of theaters: 19,500
- Average weekly attendance: 50,000,000
- Number of trade and fan magazines: 60
- Total industry employment: 300,000
- First feature film with sound: *Don Juan*
- Greta Garbo's salary: $350 per week
- Number of film people owning homes in Beverly Hills: 109
- Number of times John Barrymore kisses Mary Astor and Estelle Taylor in *Don Juan* (according to Warners's publicity department): 127
- Lead character in *Gone With the Wind*, a novel begun by Margaret Mitchell: "Pansy" O'Hara

Top male and female box office stars, according to a Quigley Publications poll of exhibitors:
male: Tom Mix
female: Colleen Moore

The *New York Times* Ten Best Films

1. *Variety*
2. *Beau Geste*
3. *What Price Glory*
4. *Potemkin*
5. *The Grand Duchess and the Waiter*
6. *The Black Pirate*
7. *Old Ironsides*
8. *Moana*
9. *La Bohème*
10. *So This Is Paris*

Metropolis   LC

January	February	March	April	May	June	
16 Valentino in *Collier's* article: "Heaven knows, I'm no sheik"	• Gloria Swanson buys into United Artists	**16** Jerry Lewis b.	**5** Director/producer Roger Corman b.	**10** Pickford and Fairbanks meet Mussolini	**13** Norma Jean Mortenson (Marilyn Monroe) placed in foster home	

July	August	September	October	November	December	
6 *Don Juan*, in Vitaphone process	**29** Norma Shearer m. Irving Thalberg		**20** Ruby Stevens opens on Broadway with new name: Barbara Stanwyck	• Louella Parsons is Hollywood's first major gossip columnist **25** *The Flesh and the Devil*		

Personalities

JANUARY • Herman J. Mankiewicz leaves the drama staff of the *New York Times* to write screenplays in Hollywood. • *Photoplay*, in its review of *Old Clothes*, says that "Joan Crawford, a newcomer, is interesting." **14** Douglas Fairbanks tells reporters that Mary Pickford now has an armed guard protecting her because "We are the targets of all the 'nuts' who come to Los Angeles." **16** In an article in *Collier's*, Rudolph Valentino says: "Heaven knows, I'm no sheik." **27** *Variety* reports that Irving Thalberg intends to raise to stardom "Greta Garbo and Sally O'Neil."

FEBRUARY • Erich von Stroheim becomes an American citizen. • Gloria Swanson, who has left Paramount, buys into United Artists. She and Mary Pickford are now the only women producing major films independently. **4** The Western Association of Motion Picture Advertisers (WAMPAS) introduces its most promising group of forecasted future stars. Its "Baby Stars" include Dolores Costello, Joan Crawford, Dolores Del Rio, Mary Astor, Janet Gaynor, and Fay Wray. **6** Oliver Hardy signs a long-term contract with Hal Roach.

MARCH • In a review of *The American Venus*, *Photoplay* notes: "Watch Louise Brooks, a new face." **6** In what may be one of the first evocations of the joy of screen camp, Iris Barry writes in London's *The Spectator*: "There is a sort of perverse pleasure to be got out of a really unspeakable film." She offers as an example Norma Talmadge in *Graustark*. Barry will become the Museum of Modern Art's first film curator.

APRIL • Frank Capra, Harry Langdon's gag man, is promoted to director of the comedian's films.

MAY 10 Mary Pickford and Douglas Fairbanks, on a six-month tour of Europe, meet Benito Mussolini. "I have seen you often in the movies, but I like you better in real life," Fairbanks tells the Italian leader. When Doug and Mary arrive in the Soviet Union, 300,000 fans will greet them, and the Russians film a comedy, *A Kiss from Mary Pickford*, with roles for their guests, in honor of the occasion.

JUNE 13 The mother of twelve-day-old Norma Jean Mortenson (Marilyn Monroe), not up to the burdens of parenthood, gives her up to foster parents.

JULY 20 Rudolph Valentino says he wants

Movies

JANUARY 15 John Barrymore and Dolores Costello star in *The Sea Beast*, released today and based on *Moby Dick*.

FEBRUARY 8 John Grierson, filmmaker and writer, reviewing Robert Flaherty's *Moana* in the *New York Sun*, coins a new term to describe such nonfiction films. From the French *documentaire*, he creates "documentary." **15** Rex Ingram's *Mare Nostrum*, based on the story of Mata Hari, starring Antonio Moreno, a Latin-lover type, and Alice Terry, opens at the Criterion.

21 *The Torrent*, Greta Garbo's MGM debut, opens at the Capitol.

MARCH 8 *The Black Pirate*, in two-color Technicolor, starring Douglas Fairbanks, opens at the Selwyn. Fairbanks and Mary Pickford attend. On May 14 the movie will open at Grauman's Egyptian Theater on a double feature with *The Sparrows*, starring Mary Pickford, in the first dual Hollywood premiere.

MAY 18 The Carthay Circle Theater in Los Angeles opens with Cecil B. DeMille's *The Volga Boatman*, starring William Boyd.

JUNE 27 The movie *Variety*, starring Emil Jannings and Lya de Putti, opens at the Rialto. The *New Republic* says of de Putti: "She plays with a tempered abandon that none but a European actress ever has, an emotional intensity, that seems always destined to be lost with importation to our shores."

JULY 9 *The Son of the Sheik*, starring Rudolph Valentino and Vilma Banky, premieres at Grauman's Million Dollar Theater in Los Angeles.

AUGUST 6 Warners's *Don Juan*, starring John Barrymore, the first feature film with

Business and Society

JANUARY 6 *Variety*'s review of *Ben-Hur* notes that the sensitive portrayal of Jesus is the movies' "answer to the so-called reformer who cries that the industry is in the hands of the Jews." **25** Hollywood's Central Casting Bureau, a hiring pool for extras, is formally opened. By 1929, more than seventeen thousand extras will be registered.

FEBRUARY • Financier Joseph P. Kennedy buys the Film Booking Office of America.

APRIL 20 Warner Bros. and Western Electric announce the perfection of the synchronized sound process, in which sound is recorded on a record linked electronically to a film projector. Warners calls the system, and its new company, formed with Western Electric, "Vitaphone," after the old Vitagraph Company. They will license it to other producers. **28** *Variety* moves its "Pictures" section to the front of the newspaper, ahead of the legitimate theater and vaudeville.

MAY 23 Joseph Schenck announces the formation of the United Artists Theater Circuit. **26** *Variety* reveals that movie magazine publisher Eugene V. Brewster ordered his staff on April 15 to give favorable coverage to MGM. This appears to have been *quid pro quo* for the Metro contract secured by Corliss Palmer, Brewster's mistress.

Births, Deaths, Marriages, and Divorces

JANUARY 7 Gracie Allen m. her stage partner, George Burns. **19** Rudolph Valentino and Natacha Rambova divorce. **20** Patricia Neal b. **30** Barbara LaMarr dies at age 29, of crash dieting, drugs, alcohol, and tuberculosis. • Ricardo Cortez m. Alma Rubens.

FEBRUARY • Constance Talmadge m. Alistair MacIntosh.

MARCH 16 Jerry Lewis (Joseph Levitch) b.

APRIL 5 Director/producer Roger Corman b.

MAY 11 Miriam Hopkins m. Brandon Peters. **20** Humphrey Bogart m. Helen Menken.

to fight the author of the *Chicago Tribune* article blaming the actor for effeminate American men. The inflammatory writer, commenting on the powder puff vending machine installed in the men's room of a Chicago ballroom, referred to the star as a "painted pansy" and complained: "Homo Americanus! Why didn't someone quietly drown Rudolph Guglielmo, alias Valentino, years ago!"

AUGUST • Clara Bow signs with Famous Players for five years at a salary that will ascend from $1,750 to $4,000 per week. **25** Douglas Fairbanks, back from Russia, tells the *New York Times*: "The Russians are the finest picture makers in the world. Americans and Germans are not in it with them. I saw the film 'Potempkin,' called after the battleship and made by a Russian, Izenstein [*sic*]. It was simply wonderful in

HOLLYWOOD MOURNS SCREEN IDOL VALENTINO

Rudolph Valentino, *Blood and Sand*   LC

AUGUST 25 Public viewing of the body of Rudolph Valentino, who died two days ago, is cut short due to unruly behavior, at times verging on mass hysteria, among the tens of thousands who have come to see their idol at the Campbell Funeral Home in New York. **27** A *New York Times* editorial on the public's reaction to Rudolph Valentino's death sees it as "a reminder of what the moving pictures have done to standardize and make identical the sentiments of millions of people."

SEPTEMBER 7 Movie studios shut down, for the first time, during the Hollywood funeral of Rudolph Valentino. The legendary leading man and screen idol died August 23 at age thirty-one, of a perforated ulcer.

sound (but no speaking), premieres at the Warner Theater. The New York Philharmonic provides the film's music via the Vitaphone process. Introducing *Don Juan* is a short in which Will H. Hays, industry spokesperson, does speak. He begins: "No story written for the screen is dramatic as the screen itself." Several Vitaphone musical shorts, mostly opera arias, accompany the feature. Celebrities attending the premiere include Rudolph Valentino and Jack Dempsey. **9** Lillian Gish stars in *The Scarlet Letter*, directed by Victor Seastrom, premiering at the Central Theater. **9** All major first-run movie theaters on Broadway are now air-cooled. **25** Ronald

Colman, Victor McLaglen and William Powell star in *Beau Geste*, premiering at the Criterion. It will be remade three times.

OCTOBER 3 *The Temptress*, starring Greta Garbo, is released. **8** Warner Bros.' second Vitaphone program, released today, includes a short, *Al Jolson in Plantation Act*. **14** *The Winning of Barbara Worth*, the second of five films Ronald Colman and Vilma Banky will make together, premieres in Los Angeles.

NOVEMBER 19 The $3 million New York Paramount Theater opens with *God Gave*

Me Twenty Cents. Thomas Edison, Gloria Swanson, Flo Ziegfeld, and D.W. Griffith attend. **21** The release of the first episode of the serial *House without a Key* marks the first screen appearance of Charlie Chan. **23** Fox's *What Price Glory*, directed by Raoul Walsh and starring Victor McLaglen, Dolores Del Rio, and Edmund Lowe, premieres at the Harris Theater.

DECEMBER 5 *Battleship Potemkin*, Sergei Eisenstein's film about a mutiny on a Russian ship in 1905, opens in New York (the Moscow premiere was at the Bolshoi Theater on December 21, 1925). Its depiction

---

JULY • B.P. Schulberg becomes Hollywood production head at Famous Players–Lasky. **23** William Fox pays $60,000 for the patents to the Case-Sponable system of recording sound directly on film. He renames it "Movietone."

AUGUST 25 United Artists announces that it will distribute the films of independent producer Samuel Goldwyn.

SEPTEMBER • RCA incorporates NBC and

the more popular vaudeville entertainers begin to appear on radio.

NOVEMBER 29 The Studio Basic Agreement, which will govern labor-management relations in Hollywood, is signed by producers and the International Alliance of Theatrical Stage Employees (IATSE), Carpenters, Electricians, Painters and Musicians.

DECEMBER 8 *Variety* notes a "A new development in radio, Television . . . ."

JUNE • Louis Calhern m. Ilka Chase. **1** Marilyn Monroe (Norma Jean Mortenson) b. **27** Mae Murray m. Prince David Mdivani.

JULY 26 Louise Brooks m. director Edward Sutherland, ex-husband of Marjorie Daw.

AUGUST 23 Rudolph Valentino, 31, is dead following surgery for a perforated ulcer.

SEPTEMBER 15 Joan Bennett m. theatrical producer John M. Fox. **17** Mabel Normand m. actor Lew Cody on the spur of the moment after they have been drinking. **29** MGM star Norma Shearer

m. MGM production supervisor Irving Thalberg.

OCTOBER 12 Silent screen stars Doris Kenyon and Milton Sills marry. **15** Jean Peters (Elizabeth Peters) b.

Personalities

acting, photography, mounting and every other way." Fairbanks also praises Mussolini for making Italian trains run on time.

SEPTEMBER 8 John Gilbert and Greta Garbo are supposed to marry today in a double ceremony with King Vidor and Eleanor Boardman, but Garbo does not show up. Louis B. Mayer says to Gilbert about Garbo: "Why do you have to marry her for? Why don't you just fuck her and forget about it?" When Gilbert knocks him down, Mayer warns Gilbert he's "finished," and threatens to "destroy" him.

OCTOBER 20 Ruby Stevens opens tonight in the Broadway play *The Noose*. But she is billed by the name that producer David Belasco has just picked for her: Barbara Stanwyck.

NOVEMBER • Louella Parsons becomes motion picture editor of the Hearst United Press Service and Hollywood's first major gossip columnist. • Clara Bow, having been recently engaged to Gilbert Roland and Victor Fleming, takes up with Gary Cooper.

DECEMBER 4 Ginger Rogers wins a dance contest, is named "Charleston Champion of Texas," and receives a vaudeville booking.

Movies

of the Czar's troops marching on and firing at the people as they flee down the steps of Odessa is possibly the most famous scene in movie history. Brian de Palma's *The Untouchables* (1987) will quote it. **6** *Old Ironsides*, starring Charles Farrell, Esther Ralston, and Wallace Beery, premieres at the Rivoli. A few scenes are in a widescreen process called Magnascope, in which a special lens placed on the projector produces a longer—but grainy and fuzzy—image. **25** MGM's *The Flesh and the Devil*, starring John Gilbert "with" Greta Garbo,

Greta Garbo and John Gilbert in *Flesh and the Devil*   MSN

is released. Their torrid, prone love scenes, which *Photoplay* finds "smoulder-ingly fervent," reflect their off-screen passion for one another. Says *Variety* (January 12): "Miss Garbo, properly handled and given the right material, will be as great a money asset as Theda Bara was to Fox in years past. This girl has everything."

Business and Society

Births, Deaths, Marriages, and Divorces

NOVEMBER 14 Silent screen star Laura La Plante m. director William Seiter.

DECEMBER 2 Alfred Hitchcock m. Alma Reville.

Also this year: • Director Raoul Walsh and Miriam Cooper divorce.

EISENSTEIN'S *POTEMKIN*: A RUSSIAN CLASSIC

Photo courtesy the Lynch Collection and Janus Films.

Sergei Eisenstein's *Potemkin*, from which this still is taken, a Russian film released in the U.S. in 1926, was one of the classics of the silent era. During this period, reviewers, with varying degrees of sophistication, sometimes commented on the difference between the U.S. and European film cultures. *Variety*, for example, said of the German *The Cabinet of Dr. Caligari* that it was "morbid. Continental creations usually are." *The New Republic* noticed in Lya de Putti, star of the German film, *Variety*, "an emotional intensity, that seems always destined to be lost with importation to our shores."

But European and American films clearly had something important in common before the coming of sound: they were equally accessible to the audience in terms of the mechanics of viewing them. Only the relatively few title cards needed translating. Once the movies spoke, however, foreign language films, now requiring hundreds of subtitles and greater concentration on the part of viewers, would become a specialty market. They would foster the opening of big city and collegetown art theaters, making the likes of Renoir, Kurosawa, and Bergman available mostly to an elite instead of a mass audience.

Photo opposite: *The Wizard of Oz*, with Ray Bolger (The Scarecrow), Jack Haley (The Tin Man), Judy Garland (Dorothy), and Bert Lahr (The Cowardly Lion). Photo courtesy Movie Star News.

The Studio System—
Hollywood at Its Height

1927–1947

With box office receipts down as the year begins, a reflection of the growth of radio as an alternative source of entertainment, the industry needs a boost. *The Jazz Singer* provides it, bringing spoken dialogue to the screen through the Vitaphone disk process, which revolutionizes the movies. Fox presents its Movietone system, which adds a soundtrack directly on the film. The Motion Picture Academy is founded, and the Justice Department moves to investigate antitrust violations in the movie industry. The use of panchromatic film spurs a demand for incandescent tungsten lamps, which work well with it. This kind of lighting is also preferable for sound film because it doesn't sizzle like the carbon arc lamps.

- Number of releases: 743
- Number of theaters: 21,660
- Number of theaters showing newsreels: 802
- Average weekly attendance: 57,000,000
- Total industry employment: 350,000
- Ratio of box-office receipts, movies to legitimate theater: 60:1
- Number of seats at the Roxy: 6,214
- Marie Dressler's salary: $1,500 per week
- Back taxes owed by Charlie Chaplin: $1,000,000
- First feature-length talkie: *The Jazz Singer*
- Number of words in *The Jazz Singer*: fewer than 350
- Al Jolson's fee for *The Jazz Singer*: $75,000

Top male and female box office stars, according to a Quigley Publications poll of exhibitors:
male: Tom Mix
female: Colleen Moore

The first Academy Awards (covering films opening in Los Angeles between August 1, 1927 and July 31, 1928; the awards are not announced until February 18, 1929 and are given out on May 16 of that year)
Best Picture: *Wings*
Actor: Emil Jannings (*The Way of All Flesh* and *The Last Command*)
Actress: Janet Gaynor (*Seventh Heaven*, *Street Angel*, and *Sunrise*)
Director: Frank Borzage (*Seventh Heaven*)

Al Jolson, *The Jazz Singer*—"... you ain't heard nothin' yet!" LC

January	February	March	April	May	June	
11 Movie notables plan Academy of Motion Picture Arts and Sciences		• Laurel and Hardy become a comedy team	**15** First star prints in front of Grauman's Chinese Theater		**26** Vilma Banky m. Rod La Rocque	
	24 Fox demonstrates Movietone sound process		**18** Grauman's Chinese Theater opens			

July	August	September	October	November	December	
6 Janet Leigh b.	**12** *Wings*		**6** *The Jazz Singer* begins the sound era		• Cecil B. DeMille agrees to delete anti-Semitic material from *The King of Kings*	
		21 MGM's Leo the Lion in plane crash		**24** Gloria Swanson meets Joseph P. Kennedy		

Personalities

JANUARY • Dorothy Arzner, the second prominent woman director after Lois Weber, starts work at Paramount on her first film, *Fashions for Women*. **9** The former Laurel Canyon home of actress Alla Nazimova is opened as The Garden of Allah Hotel. **11** Court receivers freeze most of Charlie Chaplin's $16-million-dollar estate as his wife, Lita Grey Chaplin, sues for divorce.

FEBRUARY • Louise Brooks is on the cover of *Photoplay*. The article, which describes her rise to "the top" in a year's time, states: "It is hard to write about Louise Brooks. You have to see her." **23** Harry Langdon fires Frank Capra.

Laurel and Hardy   *MSN*

MARCH • "Laurel and Hardy Team Up in Film," reads a press release from the Hal Roach Studio. Although they had appeared separately in the same movie before, Stan Laurel and Oliver Hardy are working together for the first time in *Duck Soup* (no relationship to the later Marx Brothers film of the same title). Lost for years and barely known, a print will turn up in Europe in 1974. In the film, Laurel and Hardy play tramps who think they have found a plush spot to bed down in a vacant house. But when a couple seeks to rent it, the boys have to pretend they own the place.

APRIL 15 Norma and Constance Talmadge, Douglas Fairbanks, and Mary Pickford become the first stars to leave their footprints in cement in front of Sid Grauman's soon-to-be-completed Chinese Theater in Hollywood. The theater was built on the site

Movies

JANUARY 21 The first Movietone musical shorts open in New York, accompanying *What Price Glory*. **24** *The Pleasure Garden* is the first of Alfred Hitchcock's films to be released (in Britain).

FEBRUARY • With the opening of *It*, Clara Bow becomes the "It" girl. Paramount has paid novelist Elinor Glyn, from whose fiction the film is adapted, $50,000 to certify that Clara Bow has "It." Privately, Bow refers to Glyn as "that shithead." Asked by a reporter to explain exactly what "It" is, Bow

replies in her authentic Brooklyn accent: "I ain't real sure." One of the title cards in *It* reads: "So you're one of those Minute Men—the minute you know a girl you think you can kiss her." **5** Buster Keaton's *The General* is released. It does poorly at the box office and with the reviewers. The *New York Times*, which pans this picture on the same page that it pronounces Clara Bow's *It* worthless (February 13), complains of this future classic that "the fun is not exactly plentiful," and *Variety* calls it "far from funny." **14** Alfred Hitchcock's first suspense film, *The Lodger*, opens in London.

MARCH 6 Fritz Lang's *Metropolis* opens at

the Rialto. A product of UFA, Germany's dominant studio, *Metropolis* is a vision of revolt in a mechanized and dehumanized city of the future. The film is visually striking and its special effects and photography prove influential. Ads for the picture refer to the presence in it of television, "the newest miracle of science." In 1984 *Metropolis* will be reissued tinted, with a new musical soundtrack. **11** The Roxy Theater in New York, "The Cathedral of the Motion Picture," the world's largest movie theater, seating 6,214, opens with Gloria Swanson in *The Love of Sunja*. Swanson, Charlie Chaplin, Irving Berlin, and Norma Talmadge attend.

Business and Society

• William Fox's Movietone and Vitaphone sign a cross-licensing agreement.

FEBRUARY 2 RCA demonstrates its Photophone movie sound system in Schenectady, New York. Like Movietone, it records sound directly on the film in a "soundtrack," a term that will not come into use until 1929. **17** MGM, Para-

mount, Universal, First National, and the Producers Distributing Corporation agree that they will wait for a year before deciding whether to make talkies. If they adopt sound production, they will all use the same technology. **24** Fox demonstrates its new Movietone sound process for the press by filming the reporters this morning and showing the film to them tonight, allowing them to hear as well as see themselves.

MARCH • The Keith-Albee vaudeville cir-

cuit inserts a clause in performer contracts forbidding appearances in movies produced with the new Vitaphone sound process. **29** Famous Players–Lasky changes its name to Paramount, the more well-known name of the studio's distribution company.

MAY 11 In the planning stages since January 11, The Academy of Motion Picture Arts and Sciences—Douglas Fairbanks, president—comes into being at a banquet at the Biltmore Hotel in Hollywood. The

Births, Deaths, Marriages, and Divorces

JANUARY 21 Edward G. Robinson m. Gladys Lord. **28** Richard Arlen m. Jobyna Ralston.

FEBRUARY • Ilka Chase divorces Louis Calhern. **11** William S. Hart and

Winifred Westover divorce.

MARCH 1 Harry Belafonte (Harold Belafonte) b.

MAY 14 Pola Negri m. Prince Sergei Mdivani, making her Mae Murray's sister-in-law. **30** Fredric March m. Florence Eldridge.

JULY 6 Janet Leigh (Jeanette Morrison) b.

AUGUST 8 Carl "Alfalfa" Switzer b. (The year is sometimes given as 1926.) **9** Rob-

THE FIRST FEATURE-LENGTH TALKIE: THE JAZZ SINGER

Warners' Theatre premieres *The Jazz Singer*   LC

OCTOBER 6   Warner Bros.'s *The Jazz Singer*, featuring the Vitaphone sound process, premieres at Warners' Theatre— one day after the death of Sam Warner, who supervised Vitaphone sound pictures at Warners. This first feature-length talkie is mostly silent. Al Jolson speaks fewer than 350 ad-libbed words, beginning with "Wait a minute, wait a minute, you ain't heard nothin' yet!"

The Jazz Singer contains the first use of dubbing (or "doubling," as it is called). Swedish actor Warner Oland, soon to play Charlie Chan, plays Jolson's father, the cantor. Cantor Joseph Rosenblatt does the actual singing as Oland lip-synchs.

Variety (October 12) has a mixed review but no news story about the film, and it will be weeks before the meaning of its enormous popularity sinks in. Distribution is initially limited to the two hundred or so theaters in the country equipped for Vitaphone. A silent version will also be released to play in theaters that have not yet spent the approximately $20,000 it costs to wire a movie house for talkies.

A soundproof booth silenced the noise of the Vitaphone camera used to film *The Jazz Singer*. Conditions inside the booth were so stifling that takes had to be short so the cameraman could come out for air.   LC

ert Shaw b. **22** Lita Grey divorces Charlie Chaplin.

SEPTEMBER 5   Marcus Loew, head of the Loew's Theater chain, which controls MGM, d. **16** Peter Falk b. **21** 16-year-old Jean Harlow m. Charles McGrew II.

OCTOBER 15   Constance Talmadge divorces Alistair MacIntosh. **18** George C. Scott b.

NOVEMBER • Paulette Goddard m. Edgar James. • Louise Fazenda m. producer Hal Wallis. **2** Jack Pickford and Marilyn Miller divorce. **18** Humphrey Bogart and Helen Menken divorce.

Also this year: • Silent screen star Leila Hyams m. agent Phil Berg. • Miriam Hopkins and Brandon Peters divorce.

Personalities

of the former home of Francis X. Bushman. **19** Stage star Ray Raymond dies from injuries suffered in a fistfight yesterday with screen actor Paul Kelly. They were arguing over Raymond's wife, actress Dorothy MacKaye, with whom Kelly is in love. **19** Mae West is sentenced to ten days in jail for the indecent content of her Broadway play, *Sex*, about a gigolo and seduction. **19** John Gilbert is released from a Beverly Hills jail after a day of incarceration for disturbing the peace. **20** Charlie Chaplin agrees to pay the government $1 million in back taxes.

MAY • Production of Warners' *The Jazz Singer* is temporarily held up because star George Jessel wants extra pay for the sound part of the film. When Warners' and Jessel cannot reach an agreement, he leaves the production. Eddie Cantor will turn down the picture and finally Al Jolson will be hired. **25** Paul Kelly is convicted of manslaughter for the death of Ray Raymond and will serve time in San Quentin Prison, as will Raymond's wife, Dorothy MacKaye, for trying to cover up the crime. In 1931, Kelly and Raymond, having served their time, will marry.

JUNE 9 Roscoe "Fatty" Arbuckle returns to Broadway in *Baby Mine*, also starring Humphrey Bogart. **26** The wedding of stars Vilma Banky and Rod La Rocque becomes the six-hundred-guest spectacle that Samuel Goldwyn, Banky's employer, wants, not the elopement the couple intended. Bebe Daniels and Constance Talmadge are in the bridal party, Harold Lloyd and Ronald Colman are ushers, Cecil B. DeMille is best man, and Tom Mix arrives in a horse-drawn carriage. **27** Louis B. Mayer is indicted for involvement in the shady stock dealings of the Julian Petroleum Company. He and Cecil B. DeMille, indicted July 7 for a similar offense, will eventually be cleared.

JULY • *Motion Picture Magazine* interviews F. Scott Fitzgerald on his impression of movie flappers. The man who first described this social type calls Clara Bow: "Pretty, impudent, superbly assured, as worldly wise, briefly clad and 'hard-berled' as possible." He sees Colleen Moore as "the young collegiate—the carefree, lovable child who rules bewildered but adoring parents with an iron hand." "Sophisticated" Constance Talmadge is "the deft princess of lingerie—and love—plus humor." And Joan Crawford

Movies

APRIL 29 *Chang*, a docudrama about the Siamese jungle, premieres at the Rivoli. It was produced and directed by Merian Cooper and Ernest B. Schoedsack, who in a few years will make *King Kong*. **30** Fox Movietone News, "the first talking newsreel," debuts at the Roxy Theater, with a four-minute feature on West Point.

MAY 6 *Seventh Heaven* premieres in Los Angeles. In it, Janet Gaynor and Charles Farrell star in the first of the twelve romantic films they will make together. They will be known as "America's lovebirds," the screen's most popular couple. **18** The Hollywood premiere tonight of Cecil B. DeMille's *The King of Kings* (it opened in New York a month ago) inaugurates the twenty-two-hundred-seat Grauman's Chinese Theater on Hollywood Boulevard. As many as 100,000 crowd the streets for blocks around, held in check by five hundred policemen. Inside, D.W. Griffith is master of ceremonies, and speakers include DeMille and Mary Pickford. **20** In its first coverage of a major story, Fox Movietone News films Charles Lindbergh's takeoff for Paris this morning and has the newsreel on the screen at the Roxy tonight.

AUGUST • Irish-American protests against the derogatory stereotypes in *The Callahans and the Murphys*, with Marie Dressler and Polly Moran, force MGM to withdraw the film. **8** The revival last year of *The Cabinet of Dr. Caligari* and the just-released *Metropolis* have paved the way for the belated New York opening of the 1922 German expressionist film, *Doctor Mabuse, the Gambler*, directed by Fritz Lang. It is the story of a maniacal criminal who uses hypnotism to try to conquer the world. **12** *Wings*, a movie about air combat in World War I, opens at the Criterion. The only silent film to win the Academy Award for Best Picture, it stars Clara Bow, Charles

Business and Society

industry hopes that it will halt the unionization of the studios' workers. The Academy is divided into crafts: writers, actors, directors, producers, and technicians.

JUNE 22 Paramount announces pay cuts to keep the lid on costs. Tomorrow other studios will follow suit.

JULY • Movie contracts begin to stipulate forty rather than fifty-two weeks of work per year. **1** Responding to strong opposition, the studios call off their salary cuts. **7** Actors Equity steps up its drive to organize movie players, calling for an eight-hour day. **9** The Federal Trade Commission finds Paramount guilty of restraining trade, most notably through the process of block booking. The studio is told to stop this practice. **12** Paramount President Adolph Zukor says that his studio will ignore the FTC order, putting the matter into the courts. **23** The Justice Department announces that it will investigate the movie industry's violation of the antitrust laws.

SEPTEMBER • The Motion Picture Producers and Distributors of America issues to studios a "Don'ts and Be Carefuls" memo, specifying what to avoid, including nudity, illegal use of drugs, cursing, white slavery, and miscegenation. **19** Nicholas

Births, Deaths, Marriages, and Divorces

is "the dramatic flapper. The girl you see at the smart night clubs—gowned to the apex of sophistication...." • David O. Selznick is promoted to associate producer at MGM.

AUGUST 23 Critic Richard Watts, reviewing last night's screen debut of stage actress Claudette Colbert in *For Love of Mike*, writes in the *New York Herald Tribune*: "She looks lovely, of course; she seems at ease before the camera, and she does everything expected of her well enough, but the part itself is too characterless for one to judge her screen potentialities."

SEPTEMBER 21 A plane carrying MGM's Leo the Lion on a publicity flight from Los Angeles to New York crashes in Arizona. Leo survives.

OCTOBER • Frank Capra begins work at Co-

lumbia Pictures. • *Photoplay*'s picture of stage actress Claudette Colbert, who has begun a movie career, is captioned, "You are going to see a lot of this girl." **5** *Dracula*, the Broadway play, starring Bela Lugosi, opens.

NOVEMBER 24 Joseph P. Kennedy meets Gloria Swanson at the Savoy Plaza Hotel in New York. She is seeking financing for her films, which he will provide. They will

also become lovers.

DECEMBER • Paramount hires producer David O. Selznick to head its writing and story departments. He left MGM last month after quarreling with producers Hunt Stromberg and Irving Thalberg. **23** Louis B. Mayer calls on Secretary of Commerce Herbert Hoover and tells him that Hollywood backs him for president.

Buddy Rogers and Clara Bow, *Wings*

MSN

"Buddy" Rogers, and Richard Arlen, and is directed by William Wellman, who flew with the Lafayette Escadrille. *Wings* will be rereleased on January 5, 1929, with sound effects and music. *Wings* provides a few minutes of screen time to young Gary Cooper, who carried on an off-screen romance with Bow. The realistic combat sequences were filmed in Texas over a tract that the U.S. Army accommodatingly bombed and dug out to give it the cratered look of a war-torn land. **20** Josef von Sternberg's *Underworld*, the first filming of a Ben Hecht screenplay, opens at the Paramount. Starring George Bancroft, it is the beginning of the modern gangster film genre. It will

Schenck succeeds Marcus Loew as the head of Loew's, Inc., MGM's parent company. **22** The radio broadcast of the boxing match between Jack Dempsey and Gene Tunney cuts U.S. theater receipts by half.

OCTOBER • RCA agrees to buy into Joseph Kennedy's Film Booking Office, giving them an interest in a movie studio, and Kennedy access to the Phonofilm sound system. The combination of RCA and FBO forms the cornerstone of what will

become RKO (Radio-Keith-Orpheum). **11** Samuel Goldwyn becomes a partner in United Artists.

DECEMBER • Hollywood imports have overwhelmed the British film industry. Parliament responds with a film quota bill requiring that exhibitors devote a set percentage of their shows to British-made movies—the so-called "quota quickies." • After Jewish groups object to some scenes in *The King of Kings*, Cecil B. DeMille agrees

to delete the offending material, and Will Hayes says that in the future he will consult the B'nai Brith on films with subjects of Jewish interest. **19** Movie actors and their employers reach agreement on a labor pact under the auspices of the Academy of Motion Picture Arts and Sciences.

Personalities

Movies

win the first Oscar for best original story.

SEPTEMBER 9   *The Cat and the Canary*, the prototype for haunted house movies and the first American film for German director Paul Leni, is released.   **23**   Director F. W. Murnau's *Sunrise*, starring Janet Gaynor, premieres at the Times Square Theater. It is acclaimed for its beautiful photography—particularly its use of light to express emotion—and the acting of Janet Gaynor. Gaynor and the cinematography by Karl Struss and Charles Rosher will earn Acad-

emy Awards. It also contains a musical soundtrack recorded in the Movietone process. Murnau specifies that music by Gounod accompany it. Alfred Hitchcock will hear it and later use it as the theme for his TV show, "Alfred Hitchcock Presents." In the accompanying Movietone Newsreel, Italian Premier Benito Mussolini "speaks to you and lives before your eyes."

NOVEMBER 29   *Love* again couples John Gilbert and Greta Garbo, this time in a version of *Anna Karenina*. The film is released with two endings. In the happy one, Anna does not kill herself and instead reunites with Vronsky, played by Gilbert.

Theaters can show either one. Garbo will appear in a sound version, with Fredric March, in 1935.

Business and Society

Births, Deaths, Marriages, and Divorces

The industry begins to confront new issues raised by sound. Some film production shifts temporarily back East, where the studios can be closer to the reservoir of Broadway stage talent. Elocution lessons are becoming a necessity—"mike fright" is a new expression—and actors with good voices and stage experience, such as Conrad Nagel and Walter Pidgeon, are in demand. Noiseless movie cameras, with fiber gears and sound-insulated camera boxes, are coming on the market. RKO is formed. In France, Luis Buñuel and Salvador Dali collaborate on the surrealist *Un Chien Andalou*, which opens with a shot of an eyeball being slit.

- Number of releases: 820
- Number of all-talking pictures released: 10 (all by Warners)
- Number of theaters: 22,300 (wired for sound: 100–200)
- Average weekly attendance: 65,000,000
- Total industry employment: 235,000
- First all-talking film: *Lights of New York*
- Plane/train traveling time between Los Angeles and New York: 2 days
- Proportion of fan mail at Paramount coming from women: 75%
- First hit record from a movie: Al Jolson's "Sonny Boy," from *The Singing Fool*, which sells two million copies in less than a year

Top male and female box office stars, based on a Quigley Publications poll of exhibitors:
male: Lon Chaney
female: Clara Bow

The Academy Awards (covering mid-1928 to mid-1929 and presented April 30, 1930)
Best Picture: *Broadway Melody*
Actor: Warner Baxter (*In Old Arizona*)
Actress: Mary Pickford (*Coquette*)
Director: Frank Lloyd (*Divine Lady*, *Drag*, and *Weary River*)

Clara Bow, #1 female box office star   *LC*

January	February	March	April	May	June	
26 Buster Keaton signs with MGM	**14** *Tenderloin*, first sound film to have dialogue censored, opens			**23** Shirley Temple b.		
	• Darryl Zanuck heads production at Warner Bros.				**21** Mary Pickford bobs her hair	

July	August	September	October	November	December	
6 *Lights of New York*, first all-talking picture		**21** Al Jolson m. Ruby Keeler			**12** Katharine Hepburn m. Ludlow Ogden Smith	
	26 Barbara Stanwyck m. Frank Fay			**1** Von Stroheim and Swanson begin work on *Queen Kelly*		
			23 RKO Radio Pictures in business			

Personalities

• Clara Bow is receiving thirty-five thousand fan letters a month, more than any other star.

JANUARY 25 *Variety* runs an open letter from Francis X. Bushman, headlined "Jews Are My Friends." In it he repudiates a release issued by his press agent, which said that the actor was retiring because of his dislike for the "pants pressers and buttonhole makers" who run the film industry. **26** Buster Keaton signs with MGM.

FEBRUARY 25 Myron Selznick gives John Barrymore a black eye in a fight on the lawn of Hollywood's Ambassador Hotel. **29** According to *Variety*, Beth Brown, hired by William De Mille to write gags for

Buster Keaton   LC

the film *Tenth Avenue*, is the first woman to work in that capacity.

JUNE 12 Delegate Louis B. Mayer is present at the opening of the Republican presidential nominating convention. Mayer is the first Hollywood personage to play such a role. **21** Mary Pickford bobs her hair, cutting off the world's most famous blond curls.

JULY 25 *Variety* headlines: "Novelty of Talkies Smothering and Outdrawing Silent Film Names." The phenomenon is beginning to make many actors in Hollywood apprehensive about their marketability in the sound era.

AUGUST 8 Cecil B. DeMille signs a three-film contract with MGM. **15** *Variety* headlines: "1st Sound Film Bust, Negri's 'Loves.'" The problem is Pola Negri's Pol-

Movies

JANUARY 1 Douglas Fairbanks and Lupe Velez star in *The Gaucho*, released today. **7** *Sadie Thompson*, starring Gloria Swanson, Lionel Barrymore, and Raoul Walsh (who also directed) is released, as is Charlie Chaplin's *The Circus*. **21** *The Last Command*, directed by Josef von Sternberg and starring Emil Jannings, Evelyn Brent, and William Powell, is released.

FEBRUARY 18 King Vidor's *The Crowd*, starring Eleanor Boardman and James Murray, premieres at the Capitol. *Variety*'s verdict:

"A drab actionless story of ungodly length and apparently telling nothing." It will become a classic.

MARCH 14 *Tenderloin* opens at the Warner Theater. It is the first film promoted by a sound "trailer" (this word for "coming attractions" is now entering general use) and the first sound film to have its dialogue censored.

APRIL 26 The Warner Theater in Hollywood opens with *Glorious Betsy*.

MAY 12 Buster Keaton's *Steamboat Bill, Jr.* is released.

Business and Society

JANUARY 1 The first industry-drafted standard movie player contract comes into use.

FEBRUARY • Darryl Zanuck is made head of production at Warner Bros.

MAY 4 France alleviates the severity of its film import restrictions after U.S. studios threaten to abandon all production in that

country. **11** Loew's, United Artists, and Paramount contract to use the Movietone sound system. **15** Joseph P. Kennedy secures control of the Keith-Albee-Orpheum theater circuit, the exhibition base of the soon-to-be launched RKO. **16** *Variety* headlines: "Film Trade Goes Talker." **17** A *New York Times* editorial, "When the Movies Talk," declares: "With transatlantic broadcasting already a probability and with American films speaking to the world, he who does not understand English

will cut off his ears."

JUNE • MGM begins to build sound stages.

JULY • Paramount is the first studio to announce that it will go all-talkie, as of January.

AUGUST • *Photoplay*, the leading movie fan magazine, first mentions "talking" pictures.

OCTOBER 9 Warner Bros. announces its merger with First National Pictures and the

Births, Deaths, Marriages, and Divorces

FEBRUARY 24 Mary Astor m. director Kenneth Hawks, brother of Howard Hawks.

APRIL 3 Humphrey Bogart m. Mary Phillips. **7** James Garner b. **14** Rob-

ert Montgomery m. Elizabeth Allen. **20** Richard Barthelmess m. Jessica Sargeant. **23** Shirley Temple b.

JUNE 2 Miriam Hopkins m. screenwriter

Austin Parker. **7** Director James Ivory b. **15** Fay Wray m. screenwriter John Monk Saunders. **20** Louise Brooks divorces Edward Sutherland.

JULY • Joan Bennett divorces John M. Fox. **16** Irene Dunne m. Dr. Francis Griffen. **26** Director Stanley Kubrick b.

ish accent. **26** Barbara Stanwyck marries vaudevillian Frank Fay. The twenty-year-old bride says she will retire from the stage.

SEPTEMBER • *Photoplay*, on this month's article on Joan Crawford: "Every ambitious girl who is struggling for success against odds should read this story of Joan Crawford's brave fight."

OCTOBER • Raoul Walsh loses an eye in an auto accident while directing *In Old Arizona*. Irving Cummings finishes directing the film.

NOVEMBER 1 Erich von Stroheim and Gloria Swanson begin work on the never-to-be-completed *Queen Kelly*, the story of a convent-raised girl in Europe who inherits an East African whorehouse.

DECEMBER • Leo McCarey, who has supervised Hal Roach's Charlie Chase and Laurel and Hardy comedies, leaves the Roach studio. For a while Stan Laurel will direct his films with Oliver Hardy. **2** In *Caught in the Fog*, opening at the Strand, Conrad Nagel turns to the camera at the end and says: "Well, folks, that's all there is," predating Bugs Bunny's "That's all, folks" by several years.

JULY 6 Warner Bros.'s *Lights of New York*, the first all-talking picture (although it has twenty-four titles to explain transitions), has a midnight premiere at the Strand. This poorly made gangster film gives Americans a new catch-phrase: "Take him for a ride." **25** Fox releases the short, *The Sex Life of a Polyp*, featuring Robert Benchley's "lecture" on this beguiling subject. **31** *White Shadows of the South Seas*, MGM's first sound film release, has one word of dialogue: "Hello."

SEPTEMBER 19 *The Singing Fool*, Al Jolson's second talkie, is released.

OCTOBER 6 *Our Dancing Daughters*, Joan Crawford's breakthrough film—with music and sound effects but no dialogue—opens at the Capitol. **14** Erich von Stroheim's *The Wedding March* opens at the Rivoli. It stars ZaSu Pitts, Fay Wray, and "the man you love to hate, von Stroheim . . . Ruthless . . . Savage . . . Suave."

NOVEMBER 3 Victor Seastrom's *The Wind*—"It's in Sound!"—starring Lillian Gish, opens at the Capitol. **18** Mickey Mouse debuts in Walt Disney's *Steamboat Willie*, the first cartoon with synchronized sound, premiering at the Colony Theater.

DECEMBER 14 MGM's partial talkie, *Alias Jimmy Valentine*, is released.

Stanley Theater Company. **23** RKO Radio Pictures, a subsidiary of RKO (Radio-Keith-Orpheum) is in business. William Le Baron and Joseph Schnitzer head production. Nineteen bankers sit on its board of directors. Bankers are also becoming prominent at other studios, the result of the need for large sums of money to convert to sound.

AUGUST 16 Ann Blyth b. **17** Helen Hayes m. writer Charles MacArthur. **31** James Coburn b.

SEPTEMBER 17 Roddy McDowall b. **21** Al Jolson m. Ruby Keeler.

OCTOBER 1 Laurence Harvey (Lauruska Skikne) b. **1** George Peppard b. **2** George "Spanky" McFarland b. **14** Roger Moore b. **28** Anthony Franciosa (Anthony Papaleo) b.

NOVEMBER 12 Grace Kelly b. **19** John Barrymore and Blanche Thomas divorce. **24** John Barrymore m. Dolores Costello.

DECEMBER 12 Katharine Hepburn m. stockbroker Ludlow Ogden Smith. **26** Florence Vidor m. violinist Jascha Heifetz.

Also this year: • Claudette Colbert m. Norman Foster. • Ginger Rogers m. Edward Culpepper.

*T*he microphone boom comes into general use, and the use of process shots and two-color Technicolor is becoming widespread. *Variety*'s reviews of talkies include the percentage of dialogue actually spoken. Howard Hughes discovers Jean Harlow, and Walt Disney begins his "Silly Symphony" cartoon series with "The Skeleton Dance." Fox Grandeur, a wide-screen process, will have a brief vogue, and William Fox manages to (briefly) gain control of Loew's, Inc. The first lap dissolve in a sound film—the volume of one character's speech fades as another's rises to override it— is used in the filming of *Divorce Made Easy*. Also this year, the first Academy Awards—for films produced between August 1, 1927 and July 21, 1928—are awarded at last.

- Number of releases: 707
- Number of feature films using color: 60
- Number of theaters: 23,344
- Box office receipts: $720,000,000
- Theaters showing films aimed at black audiences: 400
- Average weekly attendance: 95,000,000
- Average ticket price: $.35
- Average typical programming required annually by a U. S. theater: 175 features and 350 shorts
- Amount that Groucho Marx loses in the stock market: $240,000
- Material used for the telephone eaten by Harpo Marx in *Cocoanuts*: chocolate
- Number of "Broadway Melody" films made by MGM, beginning with this year's *Broadway Melody* of 1929: 4, including the *Broadway Melody* of 1936, 1938, and 1940.

Top male and female box office stars, based on a Quigley Publications poll of exhibitors:
male: Lon Chaney
female: Clara Bow

The Academy Awards (covering mid-1929 to mid-1930 and presented November 5, 1930)
Best Picture: *All Quiet on the Western Front*
Actor: George Arliss (*Disraeli*)
Actress: Norma Shearer (*The Divorcée*)
Director: Lewis Milestone (*All Quiet on the Western Front*)

The Marx Brothers   LC

January	February	March	April	May	June
• Work stops on *Queen Kelly*, never to be completed		**3** William Fox announces that he controls Loew's		**24** *The Cocoanuts*, first Marx Brothers film	
	18 First Academy Awards announced (given out on May 16)		**28** 21-year-old Carl Laemmle Jr. heads Universal		**3** Joan Crawford m. Douglas Fairbanks Jr.

July	August	September	October	November	December
17 William Fox in auto accident		**11** Janet Gaynor m. Lydell Peck			**10** Fire at Pathé studio in New York kills ten
	17 Actor's Equity withdraws demand for closed shop in Hollywood		• Howard Hughes redoing *Hell's Angels* with sound	**27** Justice Department sues Fox for antitrust violation	

Personalities

JANUARY 20 Gloria Swanson is unhappy with a rough cut of footage of *Queen Kelly*. She will stop work and have financial backer Joseph Kennedy fire director Erich von Stroheim. The film will never be completed.

FEBRUARY • Paramount orders Maurice Chevalier not to take English lessons or do anything else to diminish his accent. **13** The *Los Angeles Times* reports that "Still another Broadway stage director has come to Hollywood to conquer new worlds in the realm of talking pictures. He is George Cukor. . . ." **16** Alma Rubens, movie star wife of Ricardo Cortez, is revealed to be a drug addict, getting her supply from a Beverly Hills doctor. She will spend six months in the State Insane Asylum, kicking the habit.

MARCH • Louis B. Mayer is President Hoover's first dinner guest at the White House. • The *American Mercury* carries John Huston's short story, "Fool," based on the author's experience as a boxer. • Ramon Novarro signs with RCA to record "The Pagan Love Song," from *The Pagan*, in which he stars. It will become one of the first hit records engendered by a sound film. **6** A *Variety* headline declares: "Film People Seeking Radio Dates as Mike Training for Voices." **22** Will Rogers signs with Fox to act in and write four films, for a total of $600,000. **24** Buster Keaton's *Spite Marriage* is pulled from the Capitol in New York after only five shows, so bad is the box office. **26** A *New York Times* review of the play *The Earth*

Ramon Navarro in a scene from *Ben-Hur*, 1925   *LC*

Movies

JANUARY 19 *In Old Arizona*—"Every Word, Every Sound Is Audible!"—opens at the Roxy. Warner Baxter stars as the Cisco Kid.

FEBRUARY 1 *The Broadway Melody*, starring Anita Page and Bessie Love, premieres at Grauman's Chinese Theater. It is the first original film musical and will be the first sound film to win an Academy Award for Best Picture. **18** The Academy of Motion Picture Arts and Sciences announces the names of the winners of its first Academy Awards on the back page of its *Bulletin*. On February 20, *Variety* will report the news—on page seven. The paper doesn't mention the Best Production award to *Wings* until almost the end of the article. The Awards will be given out at a banquet on May 16.

APRIL 18 *Small Talk* is released, the first "Our Gang" talkie. **26** *Innocents of Paris*, premiering at the Paramount, marks Maurice Chevalier's American debut. He makes a personal appearance at the theater today.

MAY 2 *Bulldog Drummond* premiering at the Apollo, makes Ronald Colman one of the early major stars of the sound film. Colman, in the audience, is besieged by excited fans. **10** Walt Disney releases *The Skeleton Dance*, the first "Silly Symphony" cartoon, in which mood rather than a featured character holds sway. **16** The first Academy Awards are given out, at the Roosevelt Hotel in Hollywood, covering films opening in Los Angeles between August 1, 1927 and July 31, 1928. **24** The Marx Brothers' first film, *The Cocoanuts*, opens at the Rialto. **27** Warner Bros.' *Broadway*, "The World's First Talking, Singing, Dancing, Dramatic Picture," with scenes in Technicolor, premieres at the Globe. **28** *On With The Show*, the first all-color,

Business and Society

JANUARY • Spyros Skouras becomes managing director of Warners' theater holdings. • Warners buys M. Witmark and Sons, music publishers. After purchasing several more music houses it consolidates them under Music Publishers Holding Corporation. The move is emblematic of the studios' new concern, with the coming of sound, to tie up the rights to musical compositions.

MARCH • The studios' belief that Broadway stage actors are what they need for the talkies has faded, and hastily added production facilities in the East are being closed. **3** William Fox announces that he has purchased controlling interest in Loew's by buying shares assembled by Loew's president Nicholas Schenck.

APRIL 3 RKO's first *Variety* ad proclaims: "Stalwart offspring of mighty industries, of science and of art, Radio Pictures assumes overnight a commanding position in the Amusement World . . ." **28** Carl Laemmle Jr. is made head of Universal as a twenty-first birthday present from his father. **30** Joseph Kennedy becomes chairman of Pathé.

JUNE 4 Actor's Equity tells its members not to work in Hollywood until producers agree to hire only members of their union (a closed shop). It also calls for rehearsal and overtime pay. **14** Adolph Zukor

Births, Deaths, Marriages, and Divorces

JANUARY 23 Marjorie Daw m. agent Myron Selznick. **31** Jean Simmons b.

FEBRUARY 10 Charles Laughton m. Elsa Lanchester.

APRIL 1 Jane Powell (Suzanne Burce) b. **28** Carolyn Jones b.

MAY 4 Audrey Hepburn (Edda Kathleen Hepburn van Heemstra) b. **8** Constance Talmadge m. Townsend Netcher. **9** John Gilbert m. Ina Claire, whom he met three weeks ago.

JUNE 3 Joan Crawford m. Douglas Fairbanks Jr., making her Douglas Fairbanks's daughter-in-law.

Between, at the Provincetown Playhouse, finds it "turgid," but also notes that one of the cast, "who is now making her first professional appearance, is an entrancing creature who plays in a soft, unassertive style." Her name is Bette Davis.

APRIL • Paramount and German actor Emil Jannings terminate their contract when Jannings opposes the studio's dubbing his voice in a film.

MAY • Charlie Chaplin, asked in *Motion Picture* how he feels about the talkies, says, "I loathe them." • Gary Cooper is denying persistent rumors that he will marry Lupe Velez.

SEPTEMBER • Marlene Dietrich takes a screen test in Berlin for *The Blue Angel*. She sings "You're the Cream in My Coffee," and

all-talking musical, opens at the Winter Garden. **29** Fox releases *Fox Movietone Follies*, in a 70mm wide-screen process with a 2.13 x 1 ratio it calls Fox Grandeur (the normal ratio is 1.37 x 1). Theaters need special equipment to show it.

JUNE • *Bosko the Talk-Ink Kid*, the first sound cartoon with dialogue, is created by Hugh Harmon and Rudolf Ising. It ends with "That's all, folks." In 1930, Warners will hire Ising and Harmon to create "Looney Tunes." **20** MGM's *Hollywood Revue of 1929* premieres at Grauman's Chinese Theater. It has most of MGM's stars talking and singing and includes color sequences and a

Joan Crawford marries Douglas Fairbanks Jr. in June 1929. *LC*

disastrous scene from Romeo and Juliet with Norma Shearer and John Gilbert. Gilbert's voice is mocked by audiences at previews. It also has a new song, "Singin'

in the Rain." Rival studio knockoffs include *Movietone Follies* (Fox), *Show of Shows* (Warners), and *Paramount on Parade*. **28** The opening of San Francisco's 4,650-

and William Paley announce that Paramount has bought fifty percent of CBS.

JULY • Warners announces that it is opening a voice culture school for its players. **3** Critic Gilbert Seldes, in *The New Republic*, writes of recent Russian film imports, all of which "are possessed of moral fervor far more intense than we are accustomed to, not only in our films (which almost entirely lack any element of morality), but in all our arts." **6** The U.S. Commerce

Department announces formation of a Motion Picture Division to promote film exports. **8** Two-day combined air/rail service between Los Angeles and New York is begun. Mary Pickford officiates at the first flight. The pilot is Charles Lindbergh. **17** Studio head William Fox is seriously injured in an auto accident.

AUGUST • RCA, in an early example of media corporate synergy, has the NBC radio network plugging songs from RKO's *Street*

Girl. **17** Actor's Equity withdraws its insistence on a closed shop in Hollywood, having failed to gain enough support for the move.

OCTOBER 8 A newsreel and two shorts are screened on an Air Transport transcontinental flight, the first in-flight movies in America. **23** Albert Warner announces that the merger of Warner Bros. and Paramount, rumored for several months, is "definitely off."

JULY 3 Dustin Farnum d.

SEPTEMBER 11 Janet Gaynor m. Lydell Peck.

DECEMBER • Constance Bennett and Philip Plant divorce. **9** John Cassavetes b. **27** Bessie Love m. producer William

Hawks, brother of directors Howard and Kenneth Hawks, making her Mary Astor's sister-in-law.

Also this year: • John Houseman m. Zita Johann. • George Brent and Helen Campbell divorce. • Paulette Goddard divorces Edgar James.

Personalities

shouts at the not-too-talented studio pianist. **9** The *New York Times* review of *Three Loves*, the German film that opened yesterday, sees "a rare Garboesque beauty in Marlene Dietrich." She "lacks a depth of temperament but is nevertheless a credible performer." **14** Joan Crawford leaves her prints outside Grauman's Chinese Theater.

OCTOBER 5 The *New York Times* reports that women at the Capitol for yesterday's opening of *His Glorious Night*, starring John Gilbert—"In His First Talking Picture," brag the ads—"giggle and laugh" at Gilbert's repeated line, "I love you." **24** Jean Harlow signs a three-year contract with Howard Hughes. **30** *Variety*

notes that Howard Hughes is redoing much of *Hell's Angels* with sound, and has replaced the original female lead, Norwegian actress Greta Nissen, with Jean Harlow, "understood to be a nineteen-year-old Chicago society girl...." Previously she made $5 a day shooting comedies for Poverty Row studios.

NOVEMBER 4 Dick Powell becomes the singing emcee of stage shows at the Stanley Theater in Pittsburgh.

DECEMBER 9 With a new director, Richard Boleslawsky, a new script, and plans to add sound, shooting resumes on *Queen Kelly*. **12** Joseph Kennedy stops filming of *Queen Kelly*, unhappy with the new scenes. **25** Ginger Rogers makes her Broadway debut in *Top Speed*.

> **The Virginian, "All-Talking! All-Outdoors!," opens at the Rialto. It builds the Gary Cooper strong-and-silent image and immortalizes his response to an insult from Walter Huston: "If you want to call me that, smile" (later corrupted to "Smile when you say that.").**
>
> December 22, 1929

Movies

seat Fox Theater draws tens of thousands to Market Street to see Norma Shearer, Will Rogers, and Bessie Love arrive to dedicate the largest movie palace west of the Mississippi. The opening attraction is *Behind That Curtain*, starring Warner Baxter.

AUGUST 14 At the opening of *The Hollywood Revue of 1929* at New York's Astor Theater, live chorus girls form a "human billboard" on the theater's facade. They are strapped to bars over each of the giant letters spelling out the film's title. A crowd of

15,000 gathers and the police put an end to the stunt, which is stopping traffic. **20** King Vidor's *Hallelujah* opens simultaneously at the midtown Embassy and the Lafayette in Harlem. It's the first Hollywood film with a black cast. Vidor was quoted in the *New York Times* (June 2): "A negro is a natural actor, singer and a born mimic. Any group of them can sing and dance in harmony. They are born that way."

OCTOBER 2 George Arliss and Joan Bennett star in *Disraeli*, premiering at the Warner Bros. Theater. **6** The musical *Rio Rita*, starring Bebe Daniels, RKO's first major film, opens at the Earl Carroll Theater.

7 Rouben Mamoulian's *Applause*, starring Helen Morgan, opens at the Criterion. **11** *They Had to See Paris*, Will Rogers's first sound film, opens at the Roxy. **26** *The Taming of the Shrew*, released today, is the only film co-starring Douglas Fairbanks and Mary Pickford. Richard Burton and Elizabeth Taylor will redo it in 1967.

NOVEMBER 19 Ernst Lubitsch's *The Love Parade*, starring Maurice Chevalier and Jeanette MacDonald, premieres at the Criterion.

Business and Society

NOVEMBER • Theaters do not seem immediately affected by the stock market crash, although business does decline around Thanksgiving. **3** Fox sells its shares of First National to Warner Bros. **27** The Justice Department sues both Fox for violation of the antitrust laws in its control of Loew's, and Warners for its control of First National.

DECEMBER 10 A fire at the Pathé Studio in New York kills ten people.

Births, Deaths, Marriages, and Divorces

1930

In a year of many firsts, John Wayne has his first starring role, Universal films the first modern horror movie, MGM beats Warner Bros. to the punch with the first prison movie, and Garbo talks. The *Hollywood Reporter* begins publication, but the brief vogue of wide-screen films peters out. At the Bijou they're beginning to give out dishes and a double feature for the price of a ticket. And Hollywood now has a not-yet-enforced Production Code. In France, René Clair begins to explore the use of sound to express emotion in *Under the Roofs of Paris*. In Germany, Josef von Sternberg's *The Blue Angel* makes a star of Marlene Dietrich.

- Number of releases: 595
- Number of theaters: 23,000 (wired for sound: 8,860)
- Average weekly attendance: 90,000,000
- Box office receipts: $732,000,000
- Total footage shot for *Hell's Angels*: 2,254,750 feet (560 hours)
- Fatalities in plane crash in filming of *Such Men Are Dangerous*: 10
- First film in which John Wayne stars: *The Big Trail*
- First modern horror film: *Dracula*
- Bela Lugosi's pay for *Dracula*: $3,500
- Marie Dressler's salary: $500 per week

Top male and female box office stars, based on a Quigley Publications poll of exhibitors:
male: William Haines
female: Joan Crawford

The Academy Awards (covering films opening mid-1930 to mid-1931 and presented November 10, 1931)
Best Picture: *Cimarron*
Actor: Lionel Barrymore (*A Free Soul*)
Actress: Marie Dressler (*Min and Bill*)
Director: Norman Taurog (*Skippy*)

Dracula   *MSN*

January	February	March	April	May	June	
2 Ten killed in plane crash filming *Such Men Are Dangerous*	**13** Spencer Tracy opens on Broadway	**31** Production Code adopted	• Double features revived	**27** *Hell's Angels*	**27** Hoot Gibson m. Sally Eilers	

July	August	September	October	November	December	
25 Laurence Olivier m. Jill Esmond	**26** Lon Chaney d.	**3** The *Hollywood Reporter* debuts, FDR subscribes **24** *The Big Trail*, with John Wayne in first starring role		• *Modern Screen* begins publication	**13** Bette Davis arrives in Hollywood	

Personalities

JANUARY • Marlene Dietrich records "Falling in Love Again," in English, which will be released in the U.S. before the *The Blue Angel* opens here. **2** Ten men are killed when planes collide during the filming of Fox's *Such Men Are Dangerous*, including director Kenneth Hawks, brother of Howard Hawks and husband of Mary Astor. **14** Filming begins on *Ladies of Leisure*, which leads to an affair between director Frank Capra and the film's star, Barbara Stanwyck.

FEBRUARY • Producer Merian C. Cooper, beginning to put together the scenario for a film about a giant ape, has an idea for the picture's climax when he sees a plane fly close to the New York Life Insurance

Building. • At a Hollywood night spot, John Gilbert challenges journalist Jim Tully over his critical articles about the actor. Tully knocks down Gilbert with one punch. **13** Spencer Tracy opens on Broadway in the play *The Last Mile*, which will bring him a film contract.

MARCH 5 Tom Mix pays $175,000 in back taxes. **12** *Variety* reports that Paramount has given Josef von Sternberg's "German find," Marlene Dietrich, a six-month contract. The director "found her a very original type, full of European sex appeal." She sails for New York on April 2.

APRIL • Fox begins to build up George O'Brien as Tom Mix's replacement. Mix left the studio over a year ago and the studio needs a new cowboy star. **1** Samuel Goldwyn drops Vilma Banky, whose Hun-

garian accent limits her roles in talkies. **2** Bert Lahr, in a letter published in *Variety*, accuses Joe E. Brown of stealing his mannerisms and material and using it in the movie *Hold Everything*. **11** James Cagney arrives in Los Angeles with a three-week contract to film the play *Penny Arcade* (retitled *Sinner's Holiday*), co-starring another newcomer: Joan Blondell. Al Jolson saw them in the play and alerted Warner Bros. **30** The Academy Awards ceremony for films opening 1928–1929 is at the Cocoanut Grove. Mary Pickford's Best Actress award for *Coquette*, many people will say, has more to do with her status as a charter member of the Academy than with the quality of her performance.

MAY • An article in *Photoplay* mourning the recent death of one of the silent screen's greatest stars begins: "Battered and beaten

Movies

MARCH 14 *Anna Christie*—"Greta Garbo Talks!" ("Gimme a visky, ginger ale on the side and don' be stingy, baby," she says.)—opens at the Capitol. **20** *Dance, Fools, Dance*, the first of eight films pairing Joan Crawford and Clark Gable, opens at the Capitol.

APRIL 29 *All Quiet on the Western Front*, directed by Lewis Milestone and starring Lew Ayres, opens at the Central Theater.

MAY 27 Howard Hughes's World War I

aviation epic, *Hell's Angels*, starring Ben Lyon, James Hall, and Jean Harlow (nicknamed the "platinum blonde" by Hughes's publicity department), premieres in Hollywood at Grauman's Chinese Theater. Fifty planes fly over Hollywood Boulevard to herald the opening, attended by Hughes, Harlow, Douglas Fairbanks, Mary Pickford, and Charlie Chaplin. This is the film in which Harlow says, "Would you be shocked if I put on something more comfortable?"

JUNE 24 MGM's *The Big House*, prototype of the prison drama that later becomes a Warner Bros. staple, opens at the Astor. Wallace Beery stars.

JULY 4 *The Unholy Three*, Lon Chaney's only sound film, opens at the Capitol, where Fred Waring and his Pennsylvanians are onstage.

AUGUST 22 "The Divine Garbo" (the ads now call her) stars in *Romance*, opening at the Capitol. She wears a Gilbert Adrian hat tilted down over one eye, helping to set a fashion trend for the rest of the 1930s. **28** The Marx Brothers' *Animal Crackers* opens at the Rialto. Groucho sings "Hooray for Captain Spaulding," years later the theme song for his "You Bet Your Life" TV show.

SEPTEMBER 18 *Outward Bound*, starring Leslie Howard and Douglas Fairbanks Jr.,

Business and Society

• Fox now controls more than five hundred theaters in the U.S. and 450 abroad, placing it second only to Paramount. Warner Bros. is buying theaters at the rate of 1.5 a day. • Theater owners report that cartoons are their most popular shorts and ask the studios for more. A market starts to develop in the U.S. for foreign-language films for ethnic audiences.

FEBRUARY • Theaters not wired for sound begin to struggle to find enough silent films as production dwindles. **17** In a new labor agreement, the studios guarantee actors a twelve-hour rest period between work days.

MARCH 31 The movie industry adopts the Production Code, a formal set of guidelines of what is not acceptable in matters of sex, religion, crime, violence, etc. The advent of sound has motivated the codifying of new standards.

APRIL • Double features are revived, with silent or independently made sound films paired with a major studio talkie. **7** William Fox loses his battle with financiers for control of Fox Film and Fox Theaters, and is forced to resign as president. Harley L. Clarke, a utilities executive, replaces him.

MAY • The film industry pulls back from the production of wide-screen movies. Theaters that have just converted to sound can't afford it. *Variety* reports (May 7): "Only

Births, Deaths, Marriages, and Divorces

JANUARY 26 Loretta Young m. actor Grant Withers.

FEBRUARY 10 Robert Wagner b. **23** Mabel Normand d. **27** Joanne Woodward b.

MARCH 19 Edith Mayer, daughter of Louis B. Mayer, m. producer William Goetz. **24** Steve McQueen (Terence Steven McQueen) b.

APRIL 1 Clark Gable and Josephine Dillon divorce. **14** Bradford Dillman b. **29** Producer David O. Selznick m. Irene Mayer, daughter of MGM head Louis B. Mayer.

MAY 13 Colleen Moore divorces John McCormick. **20** Betty Compson

by life, little Mabel Normand has gone home to the Great Heart who understands all."

JUNE 4 Columbia's full-page *Variety* ad heralds: "A New Star By Popular Acclaim": Barbara Stanwyck. **7** Clark Gable's flagging film career is boosted when he opens in Los Angeles in the play, *The Last Mile*. Spencer Tracy's success in the New York production has already marked him as movie material. **30** James Cagney signs a five-year contract with Warner Bros., starting at $400 a week.

AUGUST 29 A Beverly Hills miniature golf course in which Mary Pickford has a sizeable stake opens. The studios pressure her not to lend her name to publicity because the enterprise competes with theaters.

SEPTEMBER • Louis B. Mayer becomes vice chairman of the California Republican State Central Committee. **18** Erich von Stroheim has a private audience with the Pope. **29** The filming of *Dracula* begins. Bela Lugosi, who played the role on the stage, will make a mere $3,500 for his work on this landmark picture. Beginning October 10, a Spanish-language version of the movie will be filmed nightly on the same sets.

OCTOBER 15 Saxophonist Fred MacMurray makes his Broadway debut, playing—and doing a little acting—in the revue, *Three's a Crowd*, which stars song-and-dance man Clifton Webb.

NOVEMBER • According to *Variety*, the gossip around MGM is that Greta Garbo has been listening to Marlene Dietrich's records

John Wayne   *MSN*

---

opening at the Hollywood Theater in New York, in which characters move between life and death, is the prototype for *Death Takes a Holiday* (1934), *On Borrowed Time* (1939), *Here Comes Mr. Jordan* (1941), *Heaven Can Wait* (1943), and *Ghost* (1990). **30** *Whoopie!* premieres at the Rivoli, where star Eddie Cantor sings live for the opening night audience. Also in the film is chorus girl Betty Grable. Busby Berkeley is choreographing his first film.

OCTOBER 17 MGM's first major sound western, *Billy the Kid*, starring Johnny Mack Brown and Wallace Beery, opens at the Capitol in "Realife," a 70mm wide-screen

format, part of a cycle of wide-screen films begun with *Fox Movietone Follies 1929*. **24** Fox's *The Big Trail*, John Wayne's first starring role, opens at the Roxy. It was filmed in "Fox Grandeur," that studio's name for the 70mm wide-screen format, but shown in this version only at the Roxy and at Grauman's Chinese Theater in Hollywood. *Variety* says: "Young Wayne, wholly inexperienced, shows it, but also suggests he can be built up." The *New York Times* review refers to him as "a studio property man," picked for the part by director Raoul Walsh. The film will not do well, condemning Wayne to B roles for almost a decade.

---

should the public show marked signs of wearying of picture entertainment as they did before talk manifested itself will wide width be trotted out."

MAY • Paramount sets a minimum length for talkies of sixty-five minutes. The average length of features had been shrinking. **28** *Variety* quotes the composer, "Strawinsky," who says "The sound screen is the future medium of music art."

JUNE • West Coast theater owners complain that miniature golf is stealing away their younger patrons. **22** The movie industry adopts a code of advertising ethics, paralleling the production code announced in March.

JULY • RCA Photophone can now convert small theaters—the last holdouts—to sound, for as little as $2,500.

AUGUST • Hollywood studios begin to re-

spond to the Depression, cutting overhead and some employees.

SEPTEMBER • A trend begins to develop toward "dubbing" films for export. The new word usually appears in quotation marks. **3** The *Hollywood Reporter*, the first daily trade newspaper published in Hollywood, debuts, with news that newspapers plan to decrease the amount of free publicity they have been giving the movies. President Roosevelt will subscribe.

---

divorces director James Cruze. **31** Clint Eastwood b.

JUNE 14 Bebe Daniels m. actor Ben Lyon, with Louella Parsons as matron-of-honor. **27** Hoot Gibson m. Sally Eilers.

JULY 25 Laurence Olivier m. Jill Esmond.

AUGUST 6 Dolores Del Rio m. art director Cedric Gibbons. **25** Sean Connery (Thomas Connery) b. **26** Lon Chaney d. **28** Ben Gazzara b **29** Bing Crosby m. Dixie Lee.

NOVEMBER 6 Gloria Swanson and the Marquis de la Falaise de la Coudraye divorce.

DECEMBER 4 Tom Mix and Victoria Forde divorce. **8** Maximillian Schell, brother of Maria Schell, b.

Also this year: • Wallace Beery m. Rita Gilman. • Walter Pidgeon m. Ruth Walker.

Personalities

to see how close the German actress's accent comes to her own. • The *Modern Screen Magazine* (later *Modern Screen*), priced at $.10, begins publication. Kay Francis is on the first cover. **5** The Academy Awards, for films opening 1929–30, chosen for the first time by vote of all Academy members, are given out at the Ambassador Hotel. Norma Shearer's Best Actress award, some will later say, was the product of MGM pressure on its employees to vote for her.

DECEMBER • Director Josef von Sternberg orders off the set New York *Daily News* correspondent Florabelle Muir, who has been contemptuously referring to him in print as "Joe Stern." (His real name is Josef Sternberg—

the "von" is strictly Hollywood.) • In his first interview, John Wayne tells *Photoplay* that there is no danger that he will "go Hollywood." **4** Clark Gable signs his first long-term MGM contract and will appear in nine of their films in 1931. **8** The Bank of Hollywood, at Hollywood and Vine, fails. Depositors include Wallace Beery and Douglas Fairbanks Jr. **11** The Bank of Hollywood's failure has caused a run on the Guarantee Building and Loan Association, which goes under today. It, too, holds the money of many movie people. **13** Stage actress Bette Davis, traveling with her mother, finds no one from Universal at the train station to welcome their new contract player. The person sent by the studio did not spot anyone who looked like a movie star and left. **17** *Variety* reports that Paramount won't lend Sylvia Sidney for the female lead in *The Front Page* be-

cause the studio fears that the tough-girl role would conflict "with the sweet ingenue innocence they're planning for her cinematic career." **31** Erich von Stroheim and agent Myron Selznick exchange punches at a Hollywood New Year's eve party.

Movies

NOVEMBER 2 *Du Barry, Woman of Passion* opens at the Rivoli and ends Norma Talmadge's career. She is one of the few major silent movie stars whose voice actually forces her retirement. **14** Josef von Sternberg's *Morocco*, starring Marlene Dietrich, in her first American feature film, and Gary Cooper, premieres at the Rivoli. *Variety*'s review sees "nothing but Gary Cooper to be depended upon as a draw." Marlene Dietrich will matter only in the big cities, where they wonder "whether she's another Garbo." **21** *Min and Bill*, star-

ring Wallace Beery and Marie Dressler, opens at the Capitol. In 1933 they will be reteamed in *Tugboat Annie*.

DECEMBER 5 *The Blue Angel*, which premiered in Berlin on April 1, making Marlene Dietrich a star, opens at the Rialto in English (filmed simultaneously with the German version). Josef von Sternberg directs the first of his six films with Dietrich, and Emil Jannings co-stars. Dietrich, as Lola Lola, sings "Falling in Love Again."

Business and Society

NOVEMBER 12 In the first *Variety* ad boasting of an academy award, MGM shows Norma Shearer holding up her statuette for her performance in *The Divorcée*.

DECEMBER 11 Germany bans showing of the antiwar American film *All Quiet on the Western Front* after Nazis riot to protest it.

Births, Deaths, Marriages, and Divorces

On the "silver screen" (a new phrase) *Little Caesar* and *Public Enemy*, and *Dracula* and *Frankenstein* establish the gangster and horror genre pictures in the sound era. Clara Bow is brought down by scandal; Norma Talmadge, by sound. But Betty Grable and Cary Grant are just getting started in movies. John Wayne seems not destined for stardom after all, and producer Merian C. Cooper proposes a film about a giant gorilla. The soundtrack has triumphed over the Vitaphone disk, RCA's Noiseless Recording system, which takes the hiss out of sound movies, comes into use, and you can fly from New York to Los Angeles in thirty-four hours.

- Number of releases: 622
- Average shooting time for a feature film: 22 days
- Number of theaters: 21,993 (wired for sound: 13,128)
- Average weekly attendance: 75,000,000
- Box office receipts: $719,000,000
- Clark Gable's salary: $350 per week
- Joan Crawford's salary: $3,000 per week
- Greta Garbo's compensation: $250,000 per picture
- Number of takes in Chaplin's *City Lights* required for the scene in which Charlie buys a flower from a blind girl: more than 300
- Number of takes required for the scene in *Public Enemy* in which James Cagney shoves a grapefruit into the face of Mae Clark: just one

Top male and female box office stars, based on a Quigley Publications poll of exhibitors:
male: Charles Farrell
female: Janet Gaynor

The Academy Awards (covering films opening mid-1931 to mid-1932 and presented November 18, 1932)
Best Picture: *Grand Hotel*
Actor (a tie): Wallace Beery (*The Champ*) and Fredric March (*Dr. Jekyll and Mr. Hyde*)
Actress: Helen Hayes (*The Sin of Madelon Claudet*)
Director: Frank Borzage (*Bad Girl*)

Miriam Hopkins and Fredric March in *Dr. Jekyll and Mr. Hyde*   *LC*

January	February	March	April	May	June	
• Clara Bow's career damaged by testimony in Daisy Devoe trial	**12** *Dracula*	• Monogram begins to make B movies	• Paramount discards Jean Arthur, and Fox drops John Wayne	**8** Archie Leach (Cary Grant) signs with Paramount	• Greta Garbo stages walkouts at MGM	

July	August	September	October	November	December	
1 Leslie Caron and Tab Hunter b.	**23** The "Lady in Black" makes first appearance at Valentino tomb	**17** Anne Bancroft b.	• David O. Selznick joins RKO	• John Hertz heads committee to cut Paramount's financial losses	**4** *Frankenstein*	

Personalities

JANUARY 17   Duncan Renaldo, featured in the about-to-be-released *Trader Horn* (and the future "Cisco Kid" on TV) is arrested for making false statements on his passport. His ex-wife, with whom he is locked in a child custody battle, has turned him in. **23**   Clara Bow's assistant, Daisy Devoe, is found guilty of stealing from her employer. Trial testimony has characterized Bow as totally promiscuous, hurting her and her career. **30**   David O. Selznick and writer Herman J. Mankiewicz have a fistfight at a Hollywood Biltmore dance.

FEBRUARY 5   The *Hollywood Reporter* notes: "Young Joe Mankiewicz (he is still a boy) is clicking like an old-timer with his dialog and adaptations, and is pointed to the ace spot

Edward G. Robinson in *Little Caesar*   MSN

Movies

JANUARY 9   The three thousand people trying to get into the Strand to see the premiere of *Little Caesar* smash several of the theater's glass doors. Edward. G. Robinson and Douglas Fairbanks Jr. star. The *New York Times* says that Robinson, who will become identified with the role, makes the gangster Rico "a figure out of Greek epic tragedy. . . ." His character dies with the words, "Mother of mercy, is this the end of Rico?" **26**   *Cimarron*, premiering at the Globe, where star Richard Dix makes a personal appearance, will gain for RKO the

only Oscar for best picture the studio ever receives. **30**   John Barrymore, Gloria Swanson, Cecil B. DeMille, Marion Davies, and Albert Einstein attend the premiere of Charlie Chaplin's *City Lights* at the just opened Los Angeles Theater. A crowd of thousands smashes several department store windows attempting to get close to the arriving celebrities.

FEBRUARY 3   MGM's *Trader Horn*, starring Harry Carey, Edwina Booth, and Duncan Renaldo, filmed on location in Africa, opens at the Astor. *Trader Horn*'s ads hype the picture with: "Beautiful white goddess . . . she ruled a nation of blacks in savage Africa." Animal footage left over from the film will be used in next year's *Tarzan the Ape Man*. **12**   Bela Lugosi is *Dracula*, premiering at the Roxy. Universal claims

Business and Society

• The total amount paid to actors in salaries is down because many of the new talking picture stars, such as James Cagney, have risen quickly and are not yet getting top dollar.

JANUARY •   Warners is the last of the major studios to adopt the sound-on-film method of making talkies, abandoning the

Vitaphone disc recordings. **6**   RKO buys Pathé. **16**   Warners denies charges that it is raiding stars from other studios. Among players Warner Bros. has enticed are Ruth Chatterton and William Powell from Paramount, Constance Bennett from Pathé, and Bebe Daniels from RKO. **19**   Samuel Goldwyn announces that Coco Chanel will serve as fashion consultant to United Artists, helping to keep the company's costumes *au courant*.

MARCH •   Monogram Pictures begins to produce B movies that will play as the second half of double features. • The Hays Office warns Warner Bros. to keep horizontal lovemaking off its advertising posters.

APRIL •   Technicolor cuts the cost of prints by thirty percent to stimulate its flagging business. **29**   *Variety* reports that "Adolf Hitler, leader of the Nationalistic Party, may go into film production in Munich."

Births, Deaths, Marriages, and Divorces

JANUARY •   Jean Harlow divorces Charles McGrew II. **5**   Robert Duvall b. **17**   Loretta Young and Grant Withers divorce. • James Earl Jones b. **30**   Gene Hackman b.

FEBRUARY 8   James Dean b. **10**   Actor Paul Kelly m. actress Dorothy MacKaye. **28**   Johnny Weissmuller m. Bobbe Arnst.

MARCH 11   Director F.W. Murnau is killed

in a California auto accident. **22**   William Shatner b. **26**   Leonard Nimoy b.

APRIL 2   Pola Negri divorces Prince Sergei Mdivani. **5**   Melvyn Douglas m. actress Helen Gahagan, who as Helen Gahagan Douglas will run for the U.S. Senate against Richard Nixon in 1950.

for writers over at Paramount." **28** William [Stage] Boyd is arrested in Hollywood for possession of gambling equipment, liquor and obscene films. Arrested with him, for drunkenness, is Pat O'Brien. Boyd, who moved from the legitimate theater to films only two years ago, will cause problems for William [Bill] Boyd, the future Hopalong Cassidy, with whom he will be confused.

APRIL • Fox decides to change contract player Nancy Gordon back to her original name, Minna Gombell, when fans who followed her stage career object to her renaming. • Robert Young, spotted by Louis B. Mayer at the Pasadena Playhouse, signs with MGM. Young's low self-esteem and the pressure of working at Metro will aggravate his drinking problem. **5** Fox drops John Wayne. **18** Erich von Stroheim walks out of Universal when the studio will not let him re-

make his silent film, *Blind Husbands.*

MAY • According to *Variety*, executives at United Artists, which releases Samuel Goldwyn's films, are thinking of changing Betty Grable's name to "Frances Dean." **8** Archie Leach (Cary Grant) signs with Paramount for six days of work on the short, *Singapore Sue.* He's paid $150 for his first screen appearance. **13** Norma Talmadge and Samuel Goldwyn announce that she is being released from her contract with United Artists with two pictures remaining. They give as the reason her desire to pick her own stories for filming, but Talmadge's poor screen voice is a bigger factor. **23** "Metro working Clark Gable hard to build him to star ranking," reports *Variety*.

JUNE • Greta Garbo, caught up in an affair with Mercedes de Acosta and disappointed

with Clark Gable as a costar—the feeling is mutual—on the film they are making, *Susan Lenox, Her Fall and Rise*, stages several walkouts at MGM. **8** Paramount announces that Clara Bow has accepted the termination of her contract so that she might regain her health. Production boss B.P. Schulberg has already assigned her old dressing room to his new protégée (and lover) Sylvia Sydney, who describes Bow as "just a pathetic little girl." **11** The *Hollywood Reporter* notes: "Ginger Rogers' contract option was not renewed by Paramount last week. RKO-Pathé stepped in to sign her . . . ." **16–17** Bela Lugosi takes a screen test for the monster in *Frankenstein*. The lack of speaking lines and heavy makeup put him off.

JULY 17 About to begin filming *Forbidden*, Barbara Stanwyck tells Columbia's Harry Cohn she wants out because she needs to

---

to have moved the opening up a day to avoid a premiere on Friday the 13th. Lugosi will later say of the response to his vampire role: "Women wrote me letters. Ah, what letters women wrote me!"

MARCH 19 *The Front Page*, starring Adolphe Menjou, Pat O'Brien, Mary Brian, and Mae Clark, premieres at the Rivoli. It will be remade as *His Girl Friday* (1940) and under the original title in 1974. **20** Warner Oland plays Charlie Chan for the first time in *Charlie Chan Carries On*, opening at the Roxy.

APRIL 3 Jackie Cooper stars in *Skippy*, open-

ing at the Paramount. **5** *Rough House Rhythm*, released today, is the first of the ninety-eight shorts Edgar Kennedy will make for RKO through 1948. **23** James Cagney blasts his way to stardom in William Wellman's *Public Enemy*, opening at the Strand. Co-starring are Jean Harlow, Joan Blondell, and Mae Clark, who gets a grapefruit in her face from Cagney. Wellman switched Cagney from the second lead to the lead after a few days of filming.

MAY 1 *Svengali*, starring John Barrymore and Marian Marsh, opens at New York's Hollywood Theater.

JUNE 2 *A Free Soul*, premiering at the Astor, stars John Barrymore, Norma Shearer, and Clark Gable in a film that helps make Gable a star. Fans will write to MGM asking to see more of "the guy who slapped Norma Shearer." **18** "Together!" say the ads. *Smart Money*, the only film to pair Edward G. Robinson and James Cagney, premieres at the Winter Garden, and at Warners Hollywood and Downtown Theaters in Los Angeles.

OCTOBER 30 Helen Hayes, in her movie debut, stars in *The Sin of Madelon Claudet*, opening at the Capitol.

MAY • Warners cuts salaries of all non-contract personnel.

JUNE 6 France ends its restrictive quota on American movies. **28** The Federal Council of Churches charges that the movie industry has been making payments to clergymen to obtain from them favorable opinions about the film business.

AUGUST 11 Reporting on the movie Production Code, *Variety* says that the word

"pansy" has been removed from six films. It is the direct reference to homosexuality, not the derogatory term, that is found objectionable. *Variety* freely uses the word, even in headlines. It also uses the word "Chink."

OCTOBER • David O. Selznick becomes Vice President in Charge of Production at RKO.

NOVEMBER • Kuhn, Loeb & Co. gets John Hertz, rent-a-car pioneer, to head a com-

mittee to manage a failing Paramount's financial affairs. He slashes the production budget by a third, cuts salaries, releases featured players, and sells the company's shares of CBS. **3** Suspecting that the *Hollywood Reporter* is stealing its material, *Variety* plants a phony story about a management change at a studio. **4** The *Hollywood Reporter* repeats *Variety*'s planted story. *Variety* will sue in January, later dropping the matter. **7** Fox cuts salaries by as much as twenty-five percent. **26** Pro-

---

MAY 28 Carroll Baker b.

JUNE 19 Clark Gable m. Rhea Langham. **26** Carole Lombard m. William Powell. **29** Mary Astor m. Dr. Franklin Thorpe.

JULY 1 Leslie Caron and Tab Hunter (Arthur Gelien) are born. **21** Stu Erwin m. June Collyer.

AUGUST 4 John Gilbert and Ina Claire divorce. **16** Gloria Swanson m. Michael Farmer. She will remarry him on November 9 to clear up questions about the effective date of her divorce from her previous husband, the Marquis de la Falaise de la Coudraye.

SEPTEMBER 17 Anne Bancroft (Anna Maria Italiano) b. **30** Angie Dickinson (Angeline Brown) b.

OCTOBER 15 Arline Judge m. the first of her seven husbands, director Wesley Ruggles. **18** Thomas Edison d.

Personalities

be with her husband, Frank Fay, (a vaude-villian and alcoholic whose career is fading as her star is being born). But, she says, upping her fee from $30,000 to $50,000 could change her mind.

AUGUST 23 On the anniversary of Rudolph Valentino's death, the mysterious "Lady in Black" makes the first of her annual appearances at the cemetery where he is buried. **24** Universal's *Frankenstein* goes into production on a cemetery set. Tomorrow, *Variety* will report that Universal is negotiating a contract with Boris Karloff, the "English character actor who has been kicking around Hollywood for several years."

SEPTEMBER 7 Five-year-old Jerry Lewis,

Movies

NOVEMBER 9 *The Champ*, the first of four films with Wallace Beery and Jackie Cooper, "the Boy Star with Heaven in his face," premieres at the Astor. It will be remade in 1979. **27** *Possessed*, starring Clark Gable and Joan Crawford, playing the quintessential working girl with higher aspirations, opens at the Capitol.

DECEMBER 4 *Variety* reported on April 8: "Producers are *not* certain whether nightmare pictures have a box office pull, or whether 'Dracula' is just a freak." Today

Business and Society

ducer Merian C. Cooper begins work at RKO.

DECEMBER • The studios agree to limit raiding of each other's stars and to submit disputes on the matter to arbitration.

singing "Brother, Can You Spare a Dime," makes his stage debut at a Borscht-belt hotel where his father is the emcee. **15** Harry Cohn, having secured an injunction preventing Barbara Stanwyck from working for any studio other than Columbia, compels her to film *Forbidden*. But he also gives her the $50,000 she demanded in July.

OCTOBER 12 MGM picks Johnny Weissmuller to play Tarzan.

Clark Gable and Joan Crawford in *Possessed*
LC

NOVEMBER 10 The Academy Awards ceremony is held at Hollywood's Biltmore Hotel. Marie Dressler hears herself declared winner of the Best Actress award while holding Jackie Cooper on her lap.

DECEMBER • "The Comeback Champ" is what *Photoplay* calls Ricardo Cortez, who failed as Valentino's replacement after the Sheik's death but has now been revived in "bad guy" roles. **18** Producer Merian C. Cooper writes to RKO production head David O. Selznick concerning a film about a "Giant Gorilla, fifty times as strong as a man—a creature of nightmare horror and drama." Animator Willis O'Brien sketches the ape atop a skyscraper, attacked by airplanes as he clutches the human heroine. **24** Bette Davis signs her first Warner Bros. contract.

Frankenstein opens at the Mayfair, and its box office success ends the uncertainty. Only at the end is Boris Karloff identified—with fourth billing. Universal paid $20,000 for the rights to film *Frankenstein: An Adventure in the Macabre*, a London play that ran in 1930. The movie is based on the play, an updating of the novel. **31** Rouben Mamoulian's *Dr. Jekyll and Mr. Hyde*, starring Fredric March and Miriam Hopkins, opens at the Rivoli. It will be remade in 1941 with Spencer Tracy and Ingrid Bergman.

Births, Deaths, Marriages, and Divorces

NOVEMBER 4 Darla Hood of "Our Gang" comedies b. **6** Director Mike Nichols (Michael Peschkowsky) b. **22** Constance Bennett m. the Marquis de la Falaise de la Coudraye, ex-husband of Gloria Swanson.

DECEMBER 3 Clara Bow m. Westerns star (later lieutenant governor of Nevada) Rex Bell. **25** Henry Fonda m. Margaret Sullavan. It will last four months.

Also this year: • Miriam Hopkins and Austin Parker, William Powell and Eileen Wilson, and Ginger Rogers and Edward Culpepper divorce.

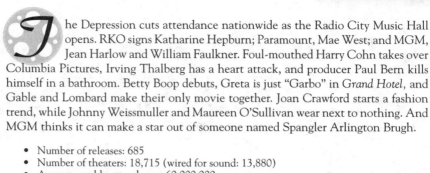

*T*he Depression cuts attendance nationwide as the Radio City Music Hall opens. RKO signs Katharine Hepburn; Paramount, Mae West; and MGM, Jean Harlow and William Faulkner. Foul-mouthed Harry Cohn takes over Columbia Pictures, Irving Thalberg has a heart attack, and producer Paul Bern kills himself in a bathroom. Betty Boop debuts, Greta is just "Garbo" in *Grand Hotel,* and Gable and Lombard make their only movie together. Joan Crawford starts a fashion trend, while Johnny Weissmuller and Maureen O'Sullivan wear next to nothing. And MGM thinks it can make a star out of someone named Spangler Arlington Brugh.

- Number of releases: 685
- Number of theaters: 18,715 (wired for sound: 13,880)
- Average weekly attendance: 60,000,000
- Box office receipts: $527,000,000
- First annual film festival: Venice (August 6–21)
- Seating capacity of the new Radio City Music Hall: 5,945
- Cary Grant's salary: $450 per week
- Number of gold medals won by Johnny Weissmuller in the 1924 and 1928 Olympics: 5
- Components of Tarzan's jungle call: reportedly, a hyena's yell played in reverse, a camel bleat, a soprano belting out a high C—and Johnny Weissmuller yelling
- Weissmuller's most vivid memory of filming *Tarzan the Ape Man:* "Once I was following my elephant by vine when he stopped. I ran into his ass and broke my nose."

Top male and female box office stars, based on a Quigley Publications poll of exhibitors:
male: Charles Farrell
female: Marie Dressler

The Academy Awards (covering films opening mid-1932 through 1933 and presented March 16, 1934)
Best Picture: *Cavalcade*
Actor: Charles Laughton (*The Private Life of Henry VIII*)
Actress: Katharine Hepburn (*Morning Glory*)
Director: Frank Lloyd (*Cavalcade*)

Johnny Weismuller as Tarzan   *LC*

January	February	March	April	May	June	
29 Harry Cohn becomes president of Columbia Pictures	**27** Elizabeth Taylor b.	**19** Jean Harlow begins work at MGM	**12** *Grand Hotel*	**19** Roxy Theater in receivership	**3** First National Bank of Beverly Hills fails	

July	August	September	October	November	December	
3 Katharine Hepburn boards train for Hollywood and her movie debut	**8** Buster Keaton and Natalie Talmadge divorce, and Rin Tin Tin d.	**5** Suicide of MGM producer Paul Bern, Jean Harlow's husband	• Bela Lugosi declares bankruptcy	**26** Don Ameche m. Honore Prendergast	**27** Radio City Music Hall opens	

Personalities

JANUARY 23　Shirley Temple's parents agree to a contract for their child's services with Educational Films, a Poverty Row studio that will put her in their "Baby Burlesks" short subjects.

FEBRUARY　• RKO signs Lon Chaney's son Creighton to a contract. • Claire Boothe Brokaw (later, Claire Booth Luce) writes in *Vanity Fair* of Greta Garbo that "as an actress, her memory will be dead when Helen Hayes's, Lynn Fontanne's, and Katherine Cornell's are beginning to grow greenest."

MARCH 19　Jean Harlow begins work at MGM.

APRIL　• Chico Marx is injured in an automobile accident on Wilshire Boulevard, holding up the filming of *Horse Feathers* for ten weeks. • MGM puts a stop to Clark Gable's Hollywood polo career playing, fearing he will be injured. **6** Darryl Zanuck is advised by a Warners' story editor that Robert E. Burns, author of *I Am a Fugitive from a Georgia Chain Gang*, will be arriving in Hollywood under the alias "Richard M. Crane." Burns, the subject of the studio's *I Am a Fugitive from a Chain Gang*, is still wanted by the state of Georgia for stealing $5.29 in 1920. The film, starring Paul Muni, will go into production in July. **18** "William Faulkner, a writer from the South, has been signed by MGM to a short-term contract and will leave for Hollywood in two weeks," according to the *Hollywood Reporter*. **26** James Cagney, demanding more money from Warners, walks out and is suspended.

MAY　• While filming *Blonde Venus*, Marlene Dietrich receives threats that her daughter Maria will be kidnapped. The culprit, who is arrested, turns out to be a disgruntled former Paramount employee.

JUNE　• Filming *Son of Oklahoma* for Monogram, western star Bob Steele is thrown from his horse, breaking an arm, his horse smashes the camera, and director Robert Bradbury, Steele's father, has a heart attack. **3** The First National Bank of Beverly Hills fails. Depositors include Greta Garbo, John Gilbert, Jack Warner, and Constance Bennett. **16** With a Paramount contract worth $5,000 a week for two months of work, New York stage sensation Mae West leaves for California.

JULY　• After years of being passed off as a "Spaniard" in romantic roles, Ricardo

Movies

FEBRUARY 13　The release of *Free Eats* introduces George "Spanky" McFarland to Hal Roach's *Our Gang* series. **17** "Many men loved 'Shanghai Lily,'" who is played by Marlene Dietrich in Josef von Sternberg's *Shanghai Express*, premiering at the Rialto.

MARCH 23　Maurice Chevalier and Jeanette MacDonald star in *One Hour with You*, premiering at the Rialto and Rivoli theaters. This remake of the 1924 *The Marriage Circle* was begun by director George Cukor and completed by Ernst Lubitsch. **25** *Tarzan the Ape Man*, opening at the Capitol, is the first of twelve films in which Johnny Weissmuller plays the Lord of the Jungle. (He does not say: "Me Tarzan, you Jane.") Co-starring is Maureen O'Sullivan.

APRIL 12　MGM's all-star *Grand Hotel* premieres at the Astor. The cast of this film, based on the Vicki Baum play and directed by Edmund Goulding, includes "Garbo" — that's how Metro is billing her—John Barrymore, Joan Crawford, Wallace Beery, Lionel Barrymore, and Jean Hersholt. Attending the premiere are Noel Coward and

Poster for *Tarzan the Ape Man*　　　　　　　　　　*LC*

Business and Society

• The University of Southern California sets up a Department of Cinematography, in which it grants a B.A. • Kodak brings out an 8-millimeter film for amateur photographers.

JANUARY　• Sidney Kent leaves Paramount to head the Fox Film Company. **29** Harry Cohn buys out Joseph Brandt and becomes president of Columbia pictures.

Births, Deaths, Marriages, and Divorces

JANUARY 5　Tom Mix is divorced from Mary Morgan. **22** Piper Laurie (Rosetta Jacobs) b.

FEBRUARY 15　Tom Mix m. Mabel Ward. **27** Elizabeth Taylor b.

MARCH 16　Joan Bennett m. Gene Markey.

APRIL 1　Debbie Reynolds (Mary Reynolds) b. **4** Anthony Perkins b. **10** Omar Sharif (Michael Shalhoub) b.

JUNE 11　Jean Arthur m. Frank Ross Jr. **19** Pier Angeli (Anna Maria Pierangeli), twin sister of Marisa Pavan, b.

JULY 2　Jean Harlow m. producer Paul Bern.

AUGUST 2　Peter O'Toole b. **8** Buster Keaton and Natalie Talmadge divorce.

Cortez reveals in *Modern Screen* that he is really Jacob Krantz, from Hester Street on New York's Lower East Side. • Joan Crawford tells a newspaper interviewer that she'll know when to retire: "I shall walk off at the climax. No, just before the climax. I want to do some really fine things to be remembered by, and then I shall say goodbye, thanks a lot, it was lovely." **3** Katharine Hepburn boards the "Super Chief" in Harmon, New York, for California, where she will make her first film, *A Bill of Divorcement*. Also on the train are Billie Burke, who will be in the same film, and her husband, Flo Ziegfeld. **5** "Warners is preparing to groom Dick Powell, stage m.c., as a film prominent," reports *Variety*. **31** John Gilbert's MGM contract ends. Contrary to legend, it appears to have been Louis B. Mayer's enmity toward Gilbert and not Gilbert's voice that forced him out.

SEPTEMBER • In "Mad, Merry Malibu," *Photoplay* describes "A row of houses on a sandy shore. Bound by Connie Bennett on the north and Wesley Ruggles on the south. With Louise Fazenda smack in the middle. The spray ground of the stars. Hollywood gone pajama. The gay, hysterical Hollywood of old, moved twenty miles north and twenty times goofier." **5** MGM producer Paul Bern, Jean Harlow's husband, commits suicide two months after their marriage. He leaves a note: "Dearest Dear: Unfortunately this is the only way to make good the frightful wrong I have done you and to wipe out my abject humiliation. You understand that last night was only a comedy." His precise motive for the act remains a mystery. **9** "Question about this chap, Dick Powell, is whether he will be star material right now," comments the *Los Angeles Times*, about the singer/actor who

was well received in his first film, *Blessed Event*. **12** The day after Paul Bern's funeral, Jean Harlow returns to work on *Red Dust*, but faints while working. Also today, the body of Dorothy Millette, Paul Bern's common-law wife at the time he married Jean Harlow, is discovered. Millette committed suicide, and many will conjecture that Bern's note was meant for her. **18** Lillian "Peg" Entwhistle, a stage actress unsuccessful in films, climbs to the top of the "H" in the HOLLYWOODLAND sign and leaps to her death. **28** James Cagney settles his salary dispute with Warners, netting himself a raise.

OCTOBER • Tom Mix retires his horse, Tony. **27** The "Hollywood on the Air" radio show begins to broadcast celebrity interviews from the Cocoanut Grove.

James Cagney. MGM bankrolled the Broadway stage version of Baum's play in order to secure the film rights. Despite Metro's publicity indicating that all was sweetness and light on the set, the leads were often unhappy with their parts and with each other. Director Goulding was often forced to play ringmaster. MGM will try to reproduce the spirit and profits of this film in 1945 with its less adept and successful *Weekend at the Waldorf*. **29** Joan Crawford stars in *Letty Lynton*, opening at the Capitol. Macy's sells thousands of knockoffs of the Gilbert Adrian ruffle-shouldered, white organdy dress she wears in the film.

MAY 19 Howard Hughes's *Scarface: The Shame of a Nation*, directed by Howard Hawks and starring Paul Muni, Karen Morely, George Raft, and Ann Dvorak, opens at the Rialto. The subtitle was added on January 3 at the insistence of Will Hays.

JULY 8 MGM's *Freaks*, directed by Tod Browning, opens at the Rialto. Browning, who directed *Dracula*, now exploits the shock value of real people with severe disabilities. Studio head Louis B. Mayer is appalled. Critics and moviegoers feel the same way, and the studio will withdraw it, releasing it later as *Nature's Mistakes*.

JULY 30 Walt Disney releases *Flowers and Trees*, his first color cartoon, and the first film in three-color Technicolor, to which Disney has negotiated exclusive animation rights for the next three years. The three-color process adds a third, blue negative to the red and green negatives used in the two-color variety. The result is richer, more accurate color.

AUGUST 10 *Horse Feathers*, starring the Marx Brothers, opens at the Rialto. **12** The Betty Boop cartoon series begins with the release of *Stopping the Show*.

Betty Boop
LC

FEBRUARY 2 A *Variety* headline reads: "Banned From Bathroom By Hays Office, Pictures Hop Into Pansy Stuff." But, cautions the newspaper, "Hays officials...say the industry won't stand for more than a dash of lavender."

MARCH 10 Paramount closes its Astoria, New York, studios.

MAY • Warners bans the Joyce-Selznick Agency from its lot for trying too aggres-

sively to boost client salaries. Fox will do the same thing in June. **1** Producers and screenwriters work out a labor code, but it will be poorly enforced. **19** New York's Roxy Theater is put in receivership. **21** The Senate Banking Committe, investigating the New York Stock Exchange, hears testimony that seems to indcate that the Warner brothers may have benefitted from inside information while trading stock in their own company. The brothers deny it.

• Rin Tin Tin d. **10** John Gilbert m. Virginia Bruce. **13** George Brent m. Ruth Chatterton, who was divorced from Ralph Forbes yesterday. **18** Bette Davis m. Oscar Nelson Jr.

SEPTEMBER 30 Angie Dickinson (Angeline Brown) b.

OCTOBER 4 Johnny Weissmuller and Bobbe Arnst divorce.

NOVEMBER 26 Don Ameche m. Honore Prendergast.

DECEMBER 7 Ellen Burstyn (Edna Rae Gillooly) b.

Also this year: • Jack Hawkins m. Jessica Tandy.

Personalities

NOVEMBER 18   The Academy Awards are given out at the Ambassador Hotel. Fredric March, co-winner of the Best Actor Award with Wallace Beery—the only time this ever happens—jokes about how strange it is that he and Beery have been honored for "best male performance of the year" when the two have each adopted children in 1932.

DECEMBER •   MGM executive Ben Piazza discovers Spangler Arlington Brugh in a Pomona College production of *Journey's End*. Piazza encourages him to take a screen test, but it will be another year and a half before the studio signs Brugh and changes his name to Robert Taylor. **2** Bob Hope and Bing Crosby appear together for the first time in the stage show accompanying the Paramount Theater opening of *The Mask of Fu Manchu*, starring Boris Karloff and Myrna Loy. But, the *New York Times* will report, the "heartiest applause" goes to the "Radio Rubes," a singing group. **6** *Variety* reports that college student Jackie Coogan "is understood to have a trust fund of more than a million dollars that he earned in pictures."

Movies

SEPTEMBER 23   Marlene Dietrich, Herbert Marshall, and Cary Grant star in *Blonde Venus*, premiering at the Paramount, where Ray Bolger headlines the stage show. **29** *A Bill of Divorcement*, premiering at the Mayfair, stars John Barrymore "with" twenty-four-year-old Katharine Hepburn in her film debut. *Variety* says the film leaves a "smash impression," but "It will take another role to test the future of the girl."

OCTOBER 12   *Rain*, opening at the Rivoli, stars Joan Crawford as Sadie Thompson.

NOVEMBER 4   Clark Gable, Jean Harlow, and Mary Astor star in *Red Dust*, opening at the Capitol. **8** Ernst Lubitsch's *Trouble in Paradise*, starring Miriam Hopkins, Kay Francis, and Herbert Marshall, opens at the Rivoli. **10** Paul Muni is on the run in *I Am a Fugitive from a Chain Gang*, premiering at the Strand. **17** Samuel Goldwyn's *The Kid from Spain*, starring Eddie Cantor and directed by Busby Berkeley, premieres at the Palace, where Cantor makes a personal appearance.

DECEMBER 2   *If I Had a Million* opens at the Rivoli. It's a Paramount all-star vehicle for Charles Laughton, Gary Cooper, George Raft, Charlie Ruggles, and others, and the first film in which W.C. Fields uses the phrase "my little chickadee." **8** *A Farewell to Arms*, starring Helen Hayes and Gary Cooper, premieres at the Criterion. **27** The Radio City Music Hall, "Showplace of the Nation," opens in New York with a two-a-day stage show but no film. Among the notables present is Amelia Earhart. Showman Samuel "Roxy" Rothapfel's creation is the world's biggest theater, although its seating capacity of 5,945 is second to the Roxy's 6,214. **30** Clark Gable and Carole Lombard star in *No Man of Her Own*, the only film they make together, opening at the Paramount.

Business and Society

JUNE •   Exhibitors, fearing that movie star appearances on the radio are competing with theaters, attack the studios for allowing it. They particularly object to the participation of personnel from several studios on RKO's "Hollywood on the Air." **11** Theodore Dreiser, unhappy at how Paramount has filmed his *An American Tragedy*, attacks the movie industry in *Liberty* magazine for its insensitivity to creativity.

SEPTEMBER •   Jesse Lasky resigns from Paramount, charging breach of contract in the studio's failure to pay the percentage due him on various business deals.

OCTOBER •   Columbia's Harry Cohn removes the phones from his writers' offices and forbids them to have visitors, hoping to get more productivity.

DECEMBER •   Several studios, appeasing theater owners who fear competition, ban the radio appearance of their stars. But it lasts only a few weeks. **26** MGM's Irving Thalberg has a heart attack that will keep him off the lot for seven months.

Births, Deaths, Marriages, and Divorces

*T*heaters open refreshment stands to sell what patrons had previously brought in from nearby stores. Programs of three to six cartoons begin to replace westerns at some children's matinees. Fred Astaire teams with Ginger Rogers, and King Kong with Fay Wray; but Doug and Mary split up. Fox signs four- (or is it five-?) year-old Shirley Temple, while Jack Benny turns thirty-nine (for real). "Who's Afraid of the Big Bad Wolf?" asks a hit song popularized in a cartoon. The answer is: the Paramount and RKO parent companies, which are placed in receivership.

- Number of releases: 644
- Number of theaters: 18,553 (wired for sound: 14,405)
- Capacity of first drive-in: 400 cars
- Average weekly theater attendance: 60,000,000
- Average ticket price: $.23
- Box office receipts: $482,000,000
- Fred Astaire's first screen dancing partner: Joan Crawford (in *Dancing Lady*)
- Height of the model ape used to film *King Kong*: 18 inches
- Clark Gable's salary: $2,500 per week
- Number of Hollywood stars billed only by their last names: 2—"Garbo" and "Karloff"
- Real age of new Fox contract player Shirley Temple: 5—not 4, as her birth certificate is altered to read
- Jack Benny's real age: 39

Top stars at the box office, based on a Quigley Publications poll of exhibitors:

1. Marie Dressler
2. Will Rogers
3. Janet Gaynor
4. Eddie Cantor
5. Wallace Beery
6. Jean Harlow
7. Clark Gable
8. Mae West
9. Norma Shearer
10. Joan Crawford

King Kong, with Fay Wray   LC

January	February	March	April	May	June
• Paramount and RKO in receivership		**10** Long Beach earthquake			**6** First drive-in
16 David O. Selznick moves to MGM		**19** United Artists buys out D.W. Griffith		• Studios accede to Nazi demands to exclude Jews from their German offices	

July	August	September	October	November	December
• Clark Gable's teeth pulled and replaced by dentures		**25** John Huston kills dancer in Sunset Blvd. auto accident		**22** Louis B. Mayer fires Lee Tracy	
	23 *Dinner at Eight*		**9** Screen Actors Guild breaks away from Actors' Equity		**21** Fox signs Shirley Temple

Personalities

JANUARY 9   Duncan Renaldo is sentenced to two years in federal prison for falsifying information on his passport. **24**   Silent screen star William Farnum files for bankruptcy. **25**   Testifying in a lawsuit, Tom Mix acknowledges that his stunts were done by doubles or faked. **26**   While dancing at the Cocoanut Grove, Australian writer and director John Farrow, engaged to Maureen O'Sullivan, is arrested for deportation as an illegal immigrant, Louis B. Mayer, pulling strings, will secure American citizenship for the future father of Mia Farrow. **26**   David O. Selznick approves the results of Fred Astaire's RKO screen test, "in spite of his enormous ears and bad chin line."

FEBRUARY • Vincente Minnelli becomes the costumer and, by May, will be the art director, for the Radio City Music Hall. **2**   MGM notifies Buster Keaton that it is terminating his contract because of his excessive drinking. Keaton has just finished filming *What, No Beer?* **14**   Jack Benny is thirty-nine today, an age he will claim for several decades.

MARCH • *Dinner at Eight* goes into production at MGM. Stars Wallace Beery and Jean Harlow feud. Beery, comparing his co-stars, says that if stranded on a desert island, "I'd pick Marie Dressler rather than Harlow." Harlow on Beery: "He's a mean old son-of-a-bitch, whose grave I'd love to piss on." **10**   A severe earthquake in Long Beach, forty miles south of Hollywood, forces MGM to cancel tonight's premiere of *Hell Below*. Busby Berkeley, directing the neon-lit violin number from *Gold Diggers of 1933*

at Warners in Burbank, calms 100 chorus girls, some high up on the rigging, when their instruments short-circuit and they are plunged into darkness. **28**   *Variety* reports that "Anna Sten, Sam Goldwyn's German find, has been in Hollywood a year now without doing anything except learning English and making tests." She will become known as "Goldwyn's Folly."

APRIL 3   The Marx Brothers incorporate, with Harpo as president. **19**   United Artists buys out D.W. Griffith, whose active career has ended. **20**   Silent screen star Blanche Sweet declares bankruptcy. **23**   The failure of the Guaranty Trust & Savings Bank wipes out the savings of many movie industry workers. **26**   "There's a newcomer just signed by Metro-Goldwyn-Mayer," reports The New York *Sun*. He's Nelson Eddy, "young baritone."

Movies

JANUARY 5   The Radio City Music Hall announces that next week it will shift to a movie and stage show policy. The stage show-only approach is not filling the huge hall. **5**   *Cavalcade*, starring Diana Wynyard and Clive Brook, premieres at the Gaiety Theater. **6**   Boris Karloff stars in *The Mummy*, opening at the Mayfair. **11**   Frank Capra's *The Bitter Tea of General Yen* is the first film to play the Radio City Music Hall. It stars Barbara Stanwyck and Nils Asther. Onstage is Ray Bolger. **12**   Charles Laughton, Bela Lugosi, and Richard Arlen

star in *Island of Lost Souls*, opening at the Rialto. It will be remade in 1977 as *The Island of Dr. Moreau*. **26**   *State Fair*, starring Will Rogers and Janet Gaynor, premieres at the Radio City Music Hall. Eleanor Powell heads the stage show. *State Fair* will be remade in 1945 and 1962.

FEBRUARY 9   Mae West and Cary Grant star in *She Done Him Wrong*, premiering at the Paramount. Mae's performance as "one of the finest women who ever walked the streets" is instrumental in creating a new demand for movie censorship.

MARCH 2   *King Kong*, starring Fay Wray,

Bruce Cabot, and Robert Armstrong in the first film heavily promoted on the radio, premieres at the Radio City Music Hall. Producer Merian C. Cooper had tried to interest Adolphe Zukor in the film, but Zukor said: "You know what a fifty-foot gorilla would see in a five-foot girl? His breakfast!" Max Steiner's score is probably the first to serve as a cinema explanation mark, echoing every strong feeling expressed in the film, including Kong's. Ads for the film read: "King Kong, of a former world, comes to destroy our world—all but the soft, white female thing he holds like a fluttering bird." Subsequent re-releases of *King Kong* will be cut, eliminating such

Business and Society

JANUARY • Henry J. Forman's *Our Movie-Made Children*, a study that claims to show the harmful effects of watching movies on young minds and character, raises demands for censorship. **26**   Paramount-Publix, parent company of Paramount Pictures, is placed in receivership. **27**   RKO is placed in receivership.

FEBRUARY • Jesse Lasky, now an independent producer at Fox, agrees to pay Preston Sturges an advance against royalties—an unprecedented deal for a screenwriter—for his *The Power and the Glory* screenplay. **14**   Merian C. Cooper becomes head of production at RKO. **16**   David O. Selznick becomes a vice president and producer at MGM.

MARCH 8   The studios institute an eight-week wage cut. **13**   Carpenters and

electricians protesting management's call for across-the-board wage cuts go on strike, shutting all studios. The one-day action is settled when the studios agree not to cut anyone making less than $50 a week and to reduce the pay of others on a sliding scale.

APRIL • The Screen Writers Guild is formed. **1**   The Fox Film Corporation is reorganized. **3**   Columbia restores its wage cuts. **12**   Paramount and Warners restore their wage cuts. **27**   Darryl Zanuck, who left

Births, Deaths, Marriages, and Divorces

JANUARY 4   Joan Blondell m. cameraman George Barnes. **8**   Buster Keaton m. Mae Scribbens, and then remarries on October 22 because his divorce from Natalie Talmadge was not final when he and

Scribbens first wed. **25**   Lewis J. Selznick d. **31**   Bela Lugosi m. Lillian Arch.

FEBRUARY 13   Kim Novak b.

MARCH 14   Michael Caine (Maurice Micklewhite) b.

APRIL 7   Janet Gaynor divorces Lydell Peck. **11**   Eleanor Boardman divorces King Vidor. **19**   Jayne Mansfield (Vera Jayne Palmer) b.

MAY 19 Marlene Dietrich, arriving in Paris, is threatened with arrest if she appears in public wearing men's clothing. **24** The *Los Angeles Times* reports: "It begins to look like a team of Norman Foster and Ginger Rogers will be created." They have just starred in *Professional Sweetheart*.

JUNE 1 Boris Karloff walks out of Universal and stays out for a month until he gains the right to make movies outside the studio. **5** A Chicago court declares Francis X. Bushman bankrupt.

JULY • Clark Gable, contracting gum disease, has most of his teeth pulled and replaced by dentures. • Robert Mitchum is sentenced to a Georgia chain gang for vagrancy, and then escapes. **2** The Hearst papers headline a Louella Parsons exclusive: PICKFORD AND FAIRBANKS SPLIT: PERFECT

COUPLE SEPARATE. • Writer Nathaniel West comes to Hollywood to write an original screenplay for Columbia, which will go unproduced. In 1939 he will write *Day of the Locust*, a biting portrait of Hollywood. **11** *Variety* reports that producer Walter Wanger would like to cast Jean Harlow and Guy Lombardo in a film because each represents "the spirit of young America." **16** The *New York Times* says that Ann Dvorak is thinking of changing her last name to D'Vorak. **21** Al Jolson punches Walter Winchell at fight night at the Hollywood Stadium. The singer feels that Winchell's screenplay for *Broadway through a Keyhole* caricatures Jolson's romance with Ruby Keeler. **31** Sylvia Sidney, saying that she's suffering from a glandular condition, leaves *The Way to Love*, co-starring Maurice Chevalier, after ten days of filming and returns to the East. She says that

Paramount's doctors have treated her like "a nobody, although I am somebody." A studio spokesperson accuses her of "professional anarchy." Ann Dvorak will replace her in the film.

AUGUST • Norma Jeane Mortenson (Marilyn Monroe), because of an incident in which a neighbor shoots her dog, leaves her foster parents for her mother's home. When her mother becomes mentally ill, Grace McKee, her mother's friend, will care for Norma Jeane. Grace thinks that the girl can be a movie star, like Jean Harlow. **1** Laurence Olivier arrives at MGM to rehearse with Greta Garbo for *Queen Christina*. There is no chemistry between them, and in a few days he will hear from the studio that he is "too young and inexperienced" for the role. **21** The *New York Times* reports: "Ida Lupino, a young English

---

scenes as the ape peeling away Fay Wray's clothing. They will be restored in the late 1960s. The film will be remade in 1976. **3** The W.C. Fields short, *The Fatal Glass of Beer*, is released. **8** Warner Baxter, Ruby Keeler, and Dick Powell star in *42nd Street*, choreographed by Busby Berkeley but directed by Lloyd Bacon, premiering at the Strand. **31** Walter Huston, Karen Morely, and Franchot Tone star in *Gabriel Over the White House*, a political fantasy, opening simultaneously in 100 cities.

APRIL 27 *Poor Fish* is released, the first of the ninety-eight shorts Leon Errol will make through 1951.

MAY 27 The release of Walt Disney's *Three Little Pigs* introduces the Depression-fighting song, "Who's Afraid of the Big Bad Wolf?" It becomes the most popular cartoon to-date.

JUNE 6 The first drive-in movie opens near Camden, New Jersey. It covers ten acres, has room for four hundred cars, and contains a forty-foot screen. Admission is $.25 per car and an additional quarter for each passenger. The first program, which draws about two hundred cars, is made up of shorts exclusively, but in a few days it will show its first feature: *Wife, Beware*.

JULY 14 With the release of Paramount's *Popeye the Sailor*, a Betty Boop cartoon, the muscular seaman makes his first appearance.

AUGUST 23 Jean Harlow, Wallace Beery, Marie Dressler, Lionel Barrymore, John Barrymore, and Billie Burke star in *Dinner at Eight*, premiering at the Astor.

SEPTEMBER 7 Frank Capra's *Lady for a Day*, starring May Robson, premieres at the Radio City Music Hall. Capra will remake it with Bette Davis in 1961 as *Pocketful of Miracles*.

OCTOBER 10 The release of *Riders of Destiny* marks the first of sixteen B westerns

---

Warner Bros. two weeks ago, announces the formation of Twentieth Century Pictures. He will be vice president in charge of production, and Joseph Schenck will be president. Providing capital are Nicholas Schenck, Joseph's brother, and Louis B. Mayer, whose son-in-law, William Goetz, becomes an executive at the new studio.

MAY • The studios begin to give in to Nazi demands that they exclude Jews from their German offices.

JUNE 30 The Screen Actors Guild is formed within Actors Equity, with Ralph Morgan president.

JULY 11 The Hays Office asks Paramount to remove from Mae West's *I'm No Angel*, the line: "When I'm good I'm very good, but when I'm bad I'm *better*." The studio refuses. **18** *Variety*'s headline, "Hitler Thing Deadly," refers to his film policies. **24** France's new film quota again restricts imports of American movies. **24** A

strike by members of the International Alliance of Theatrical Stage Employees hits eleven studios. The union is reacting to the studio's refusal to establish minimum wage scales for some job classifications and to studio support for the International Brotherhood of Electrical Workers in a jurisdictional dispute over sound men.

AUGUST 5 The producers recognize the International Brotherhood of Electrical Workers and bring them into the studio

---

MAY 12 Joan Crawford divorces Douglas Fairbanks Jr. **23** Joan Collins b.

JUNE 24 John Wayne m. Josephine Saenz. **29** Roscoe "Fatty" Arbuckle d.

APRIL 30 Katharine Hepburn divorces Ludlow Ogden Smith.

JULY 13 Fred Astaire m. Phyllis Potter.

AUGUST 10 Hedy Lamarr m. munitions manufacturer Fritz Mandl. **18** Carole Lombard divorces William Powell. • Director Roman Polanski b. **25** Tom Skerrit b.

SEPTEMBER 6 Director William Wellman is divorced from Helene Chadwick. **18** Jean Harlow m. cameraman Harold Rosson. **22** Sime Silverman, founder and publisher of *Variety*, d. **24** Hoot Gibson and Sally Eilers are divorced. **28** Greer Garson m. Edward Snelson, from whom she separates after five weeks.

Personalities

actress recently placed under contract by Paramount will arrive here Friday . . . en route to Hollywood for her first picture assignment." She is fifteen years old. **23** John Gilbert returns to MGM to begin work on *Queen Christina* with Greta Garbo. To Louis B. Mayer's chagrin—he hates Gilbert—she insists on Gilbert for the male lead or she won't work. **29** Spencer Tracy and his wife, Louise, announce their separation (they will later reconcile). He's rumored to be having an affair with Loretta Young.

SEPTEMBER 15 Clara Lou (Ann) Sheridan, a winner in Paramount's "Search for Beauty" contest, boards a train in Dallas to claim her prize: a trip to Hollywood and a part in a movie. **25** John Huston, driv-

Movies

John Wayne will make through 1935 for Lone Star/Monogram. In the series, Wayne, stuntman Yakima Canutt, and director Robert N. Bradbury perfect the choreographed fistfight. **12** Charles Laughton stars in *The Private Life of Henry VIII*, opening at the Radio City Music Hall. **13** Mae West and Cary Grant star in *I'm No Angel*, opening at the Paramount. West's line, "Beulah, peel me a grape," is from this film. **20** *Bombshell* (retitled *Blonde Bombshell* on November 6), starring Jean Harlow, Lee Tracy, and Franchot Tone, opens at the Capitol.

Little Women with Katharine Hepburn, Joan Bennett, Francis Dee, and Jean Parker   LC

NOVEMBER 16 Katharine Hepburn, Joan Bennett, Frances Dee, and Paul Lukas star in *Little Women*, premiering at the Radio City Music Hall. **17** *The Invisible Man* opens at the Roxy. *Variety*'s review does not mention star Claude Rains (appearing in his first film), except for the cast listing, although supporting actors are praised.

Business and Society

basic agreement on labor relations. **19** Irving Thalberg is back at MGM. **23** The National Labor Relations Board mediates an end to the IATSE strike, which has all but petered out with IATSE having to accept the jurisdictional victory of the the Electrical Workers.

SEPTEMBER 6 *Daily Variety*, published in Hollywood, the New York–based *Variety*'s answer to the *Hollywood Reporter*, begins publication. Today's issue reports that the head of Central Casting has ordered employees to stop giving preference to their relatives for movie roles. And again, someone has punched gossip columnist Walter Winchell. **16** According to *Daily Variety*, "Pinks Plan to Stalinize Studios."

OCTOBER 1 Future studio executive Dore Schary begins work at MGM as a screen-writer. **9** The Screen Actors Guild breaks away from Actors Equity to form an organization devoted solely to the interests of film actors. Eddie Cantor is now president; James Cagney, vice president; and Groucho Marx, treasurer.

NOVEMBER 29 The New Deal's Code of Fair Competition for the Movie Industry goes into effect. Theater giveaways, such as chinaware night, will be ruled unfair competition. The movie industry's attempt

Births, Deaths, Marriages, and Divorces

OCTOBER • Richard Harris b. **5** Renée Adorée d. **8** Lupe Velez and Johnny Weissmuller get married. **10** Louise Brooks m. manufacturer Deering Davis. **20** Joel McCrea m. Frances Dee. **24** Mae Murray divorces Prince David Mdivani.

DECEMBER 15 Gary Cooper m. Veronica Balfe.

Also this year: • Henry Fonda and Margaret Sullavan divorce.

ing on Sunset Boulevard, hits and kills dancer Tosca Roulien. An inquest (September 29) will clear Huston of any blame, and Louis B. Mayer, as a favor to Huston's father, Walter, gets the Hearst papers to downplay it.

OCTOBER 5 Jack Warner's memo directs Hal Wallis to have Joan Blondell wear a brassiere when she films. "Don't let those bulbs stick out," he cautions his production chief. **19** Joan Blondell tells Warners that she wants to be billed as Joan Barnes, her married name, an unprecedented request for a star. Jack Warner calls it "foolish." **20** Joan Blondell's Laurel Canyon home burns down. Her eyelashes are singed when she tries to douse the flames with a garden hose.

NOVEMBER 9 A Los Angeles Superior

Court judge orders that Mae Murray's opulent Playa del Rey estate be sold at auction to satisfy a judgment against her, and on January 31 she will file for bankruptcy. **18** Bob Hope opens on Broadway in the musical *Roberta*. Fred MacMurray, who plays the saxophone with the California Collegians, the show's band, and clowns a little, will be spotted by Paramount, which will sign him in March. **22** Louis B. Mayer fires Lee Tracy from the film *Viva Villa* and from his long-term contract with MGM. The actor was reported to have stood drunk and nude on his Mexico City hotel balcony a few days ago and urinated on a parade of army cadets in the street below. **30** *Los Angeles Times* movie reporter Edwin Schallert notes the favorable buzz about Fred Astaire in the not-yet-released *Flying down to Rio* and in *Dancing Lady*, which has only previewed in Holly-

wood. "Astaire is rated star material," he writes."Well, we'll see!" The paper also reports that Alice Faye, a singer on Rudy Vallee's radio show, is going to Hollywood to appear in her first film, *George White's Scandals*.

DECEMBER 13 George Raft knocks down Paramount producer Benjamin Glazer, who is sarcastic when Raft does not want to speak the line in *Bolero*, ". . . what a swell publicity stunt it would be to have some picture taken of him at his mother's grave." **21** Fox signs five-year-old Shirley Temple. At the behest of the studio, her birth certificate is altered to make it appear that she is four years old. **27** Dorothy Parker's putdown of Katharine Hepburn's performance in the play, *The Lake*, appears in the *New York Journal-American*: "She ran the gamut of emotion from A to B."

22 Ernst Lubitsch's *Design for Living*, starring Fredric March, Miriam Hopkins, and Gary Cooper premieres at the Criterion. **22** The Marx Brothers star in *Duck Soup*, opening at the Rivoli. **27** Eddie Cantor stars in Samuel Goldwyn's *Roman Scandals*, premiering at Grauman's Chinese Theater in Hollywood, where Will Rogers, Groucho Marx, Mary Pickford, Gloria Swanson, and Claudette Colbert are in the audience. **30** *Dancing Lady*, starring Clark Gable, Joan Crawford, Franchot Tone, and Fred Astaire playing himself in his film debut, premieres at the Capitol. In Crawford's fourth film with Clark Gable, she becomes Astaire's first screen dance partner. Her

romantic pairing with Tone reflects what is happening off the screen as well. Crawford has broken off with Gable, who is sleeping with Jean Harlow, among others.

DECEMBER 21 *Flying Down to Rio*, starring Dolores Del Rio and Gene Raymond "with"

Fred Astaire and Ginger Rogers in their first pairing, opens at the Radio City Music Hall. Astaire will write to his agent, Leland Hayward, that he doesn't mind working with Rogers, but "as for this team idea, it's *out*!" **26** Greta Garbo and John Gilbert star in *Queen Christina*, premiering at the Astor.

to cap salaries under the Code prompts a surge in unionizing activity. The Code implicitly recognizes the monopoly of the five major studios and accepts such practices as block booking.

Shirley Temple

MSN

1934

With the Hays Office now enforcing the Production Code, even married couples will move into separate beds. Clark Gable undercuts the undershirt market in *It Happened One Night*, Carole Lombard and John Barrymore are "screwballs" in *Twentieth Century*, and William Powell and Myrna Loy are sophisticates in *The Thin Man*. Mary Pickford's *Why Not Try God?* (ghostwritten by Hearst writer Adela Rogers St. John) becomes a bestseller, while screenwriter Joseph Mankiewicz is said to be the first Hollywood personality to try Benzedrine. On a warm night in Chicago, John Dillinger takes in a movie—his mistake.

- Number of releases: 662
- Number of theaters: 16,885 (wired for sound: 14,381)
- Average weekly attendance: 70,000,000
- Average ticket price: $.23
- Box office receipts: $518,000,000
- Jean Harlow's salary: $3,000 a week
- First film granted a Production Code seal: *The World Moves On*
- Number of films Boris Karloff and Bela Lugosi will make together, beginning with this year's *The Black Cat*: 8
- Film seen by John Dillinger just before he is gunned down outside a Chicago theater: *Manhattan Melodrama*, starring Clark Gable

Top stars at the box office, based on a Quigley Publications poll of exhibitors:
1. Will Rogers
2. Clark Gable
3. Janet Gaynor
4. Wallace Beery
5. Mae West
6. Joan Crawford
7. Bing Crosby
8. Shirley Temple
9. Marie Dressler
10. Norma Shearer

The Academy Awards (covering, for the first time, films opening over a period of an entire calendar year—1934—and presented February 27, 1935)
Best Picture: *It Happened One Night*
Actor: Clark Gable (*It Happened One Night*)
Actress: Claudette Colbert (*It Happened One Night*)
Director: Frank Capra (*It Happened One Night*)

Will Rogers, #1 box office star   *MSN*

January	February	March	April	May	June
26 Goldwyn buys rights to *The Wonderful Wizard of Oz*	**22** *It Happened One Night* premieres at Radio City	**30** Zeppo Marx leaves the Marx Brothers • Helen Kane sues Max Fleischer and Paramount over "Betty Boop" cartoons		**3** *Twentieth Century*	• Ida Lupino and cinematographer Hal Rosson contract polio in L.A. outbreak

July	August	September	October	November	December
6 Joseph Breen heads Production Code Administration—the "Hays Office"	**17** Cafe Trocadero opens in Hollywood	**5** "Hollywood Hotel" on the air	**14** Ginger Rogers m. Lew Ayres		**5** Fire causes more than $100,000 in damage at Warner Bros.

Personalities

JANUARY • Greta Garbo and director Rouben Mamoulian, traveling together, stir rumors of romance. • Jean Harlow's ten-week suspension at MGM ends when she and the studio compromise on a raise to $3,000 a week from the $1,500 she had been getting. **8** According to the *Los Angeles Times*, RKO is looking for a new first name for Ginger Rogers. • Rudy Vallee's estranged wife names Alice Faye a corespondent in her divorce suit. **26** Samuel Goldwyn buys the rights to L. Frank Baum's *The Wonderful Wizard of Oz* (published August 1, 1900).

FEBRUARY 6 Douglas Fairbanks is named as a co-respondent in Lord Ashley's divorce suit against Lady Ashley. **13** *Variety* re-

ports that RKO has slated *The Gay Divorcee* for Fred Astaire's first featured role, and it's "Practically set that Ginger Rogers will be his leading lady." **24** The Capitol goes to a six-shows-a-day policy to accommodate the thousands—mostly women—trying to get in this week to see Clark Gable in person. **28** Paramount signs Ray Milland, who has yet to star in a film, to a long-term contract. He's been working in a gas station to make ends meet.

MARCH 9 Paramount announces that George Raft has refused to play opposite Mae West in *It Ain't No Sin* because too many shots will be closeups of her, showing him from the back. **16** Academy

Awards for 1932–1933 are handed out at the Ambassador Hotel. Walt Disney, accepting a statuette for Best Cartoon, *The Three Little Pigs*, is the first winner to refer to the award as "Oscar." **30** Zeppo Marx leaves the Marx Brothers to become an agent.

APRIL • Helen Kane sues Max Fleischer and Paramount for $250,000, claiming that their "Betty Boop" cartoons have undermined her career by appropriating her singing style. The suit will be thrown out on May 5. **5** The Biltmore Bowl nightclub opens at Hollywood's Biltmore Hotel. **19** Joan Blondell allows herself to be pelted with tomatoes for twenty minutes in order to get a scene right in Warner Bros.'

Movies

FEBRUARY 22 Frank Capra's *It Happened One Night*, starring Clark Gable and Claudette Colbert, neither of whom wanted to make this picture, premieres at the Radio City Music Hall. Colbert had said on the first day of shooting on this picture, for which she will receive an Academy Award: "I'm just a stooge for Clark Gable." In the film, Gable performs a celebrated strip tease.

MARCH 14 *The House of Rothschild*, starring George Arliss, Loretta Young, and Boris

Clark Gable and Claudette Colbert in *It Happened One Night*   MSN

Business and Society

FEBRUARY 27 Members of the Russian aristocracy, claiming that they have been libeled by MGM's *Rasputin and the Empress*, sue the studio in an English court. After a trial of several weeks, they will win a large settlement, resulting in the disclaimer on future biographical films: "The events and characters in this film are fictional and any resemblance to characters living or dead is purely coincidental."

MARCH 28 President Roosevelt watches *Gabriel over the White House*, a political fantasy, for the second time in less than two weeks. He has watched eighty-three films since taking office.

MAY 5 The Hays Office prohibits movie stars from endorsing alcoholic beverages.

JUNE 8 Cardinal Dougherty of Philadelphia announces a boycott in his diocese of all movies, calling them "perhaps the greatest

Births, Deaths, Marriages, and Divorces

FEBRUARY 9 Cary Grant m. Virginia Cherrill. **12** Harry Langdon marries Mabel Sheldon. Langdon's Mexican divorce from his second wife, Helen Walton, is not recognized everywhere, so Langdon and

his new bride will tie the knot again, in the U.S., on December 12. They will divorce and remarry several times before his death in 1944. **13** George Segal b. **17** Alan Bates b. **19** Bob Hope m. Dolores Reade.

MARCH 26 Alan Arkin b.

APRIL 14 Norma Talmadge and producer Joseph Schenck divorce. **17** Laura La Plante divorces William Seiter. **23** Norma Talmadge m. George Jessel. **24** Shirley MacLaine (Shirley MacLean Beatty) b.

Dames. **29** Gilbert Roland, with Constance Bennett at a party at Samuel Goldwyn's house, takes exception to something Clark Gable says to Bennett. The two men are separated just as the punches are about to fly.

MAY 1 The parents of Mary Astor, who sued her on March 20 for support, claiming they were "broke," lose their case. She charged them with living extravagantly off her money. **29** *Variety* concludes its interview with Fred Astaire, departing for Hollywood to film *The Gay Divorcee:* "Nobody knows him in pictures yet, he says, but perhaps they will. At least they've come to accept him on stage without Adele."

JUNE • Ida Lupino and cinematographer Hal Rosson contract minor cases of polio during an outbreak in Los Angeles.

JULY 2 Silent screen director Marshall Neilan files for bankruptcy. **4** Fox's new contract with Shirley Temple raises her salary from $150 to $1,000 per week plus a $35,000 per film bonus held in trust till the contract ends in seven years, pays her mother $250 a week, stipulates that Shirley will not use an agent, and gives the studio control of all her public appearances. **22** John Dillinger comes out of hiding to take in a movie at Chicago's Biograph Theater. He sees Clark Gable, in *Manhattan Melodrama,* play a gangster who goes to the electric chair. "Die the way you live," Gable says on the screen. As Dillinger leaves the theater, he dies in a fusillade of police gunfire, betrayed by "the woman in red." **25** The *New York Times* reports that "Peter Lorre, European stage and screen actor . . . arrived in New York yesterday aboard the *Majestic* on his way to Hollywood to

begin work for Columbia Pictures."

AUGUST • Spencer Tracy disappears for ten days from the set of Fox's *Marie Galante.* • George Jessel, emceeing the stage show at the Oriental Theater in Chicago, changes the name of the Gumm Sisters to the Garland Sisters (the youngest, Frances, will later change her first name to Judy). **3** With Carole Lombard looking on, George Raft beats up a man with whom he has had words in the parking lot of a cafe near Hollywood and Vine.

SEPTEMBER 12 John Ford becomes a Lieutenant Commander in the naval reserve. **17** The Cafe Trocadero opens in Hollywood. • Olivia de Havilland, eighteen, makes her professional stage debut in *A Midsummer Night's Dream,* directed by Max Reinhardt at the Hollywood Bowl.

Karloff, premieres at the Astor Theater. **30** John Ford's *The Lost Patrol,* starring Victor McLaglen and Boris Karloff, opens at the Rialto.

APRIL 10 Wallace Beery stars in *Viva Villa,* with Leo Carillo and Fay Wray, premiering at the Criterion.

MAY 3 *Twentieth Century,* one of the first "screwball comedies," written by Ben Hecht and Charles MacArthur, directed by Howard Hawks, and starring John Barrymore and Carole Lombard, premieres at the Radio City Music Hall. **4** *Manhattan Melodrama,* premiering at the Capitol, resurrects

the career of William Powell and is his first teaming with Myrna Loy. Clark Gable also stars. Jack Benny heads the stage show. **5** With *Woman Haters,* Columbia releases the first of its 190 Three Stooges comedies. The series will run through 1959. **18** *The Black Cat,* premiering at the Roxy, is the first of eight films to costar Bela Lugosi and Boris Karloff. Karloff receives top billing as, simply, "KARLOFF"—a la MGM's crediting of GARBO—an honor Universal will accord him for the next two years. At the Paramount, opening today, is *Little Miss Marker,* starring Shirley Temple and Adolphe Menjou.

JUNE 9 Donald Duck makes his screen debut with the release of Walt Disney's *The Wise Little Hen.* **28** *Of Human Bondage* opens at the Radio City Music Hall, where the audience finds Bette Davis so good as the wicked Mildred that they applaud when she dies. The role makes Davis a star. Co-starring is Leslie Howard. **29** Opening at the Capitol are William Powell and Myrna Loy in *The Thin Man,* the first of six in the series they will do for MGM through 1947. Duke Ellington and his Orchestra are onstage.

The Thin Man, with William Powell, Myrna Loy, and Henry Wadsworth   LC

menace to faith and morals today." **17** A Cleveland rally of fifty thousand Catholics attacks indecent films and takes the pledge of the Catholic League of Decency to boycott them. **22** The Federal Council of the Churches of Christ in America recommends that Protestants support the Catholic League of Decency in its efforts to suppress immoral films. The Central Conference of American Rabbis calls for Jews to back the Catholic crusade.

JULY 6 In response to pressure from religious groups to "clean up" the movies, a frightened Motion Pictures Producers and Distributors Association appoints Joseph Breen as its official censor and head of its Production Code Administration—the "Hays Office." Its seal will designate compliance with the Association's motion picture code, until now not strictly enforced. The movies will maintain this self-censorship through the mid-1960s. **7** The Chicago Archdiocese begins to classify films as to their

MAY 25 John Gilbert and Virginia Bruce divorce.

JUNE 19 Gena Rowlands b.

JULY 17 Donald Sutherland b. **20** Van Heflin m. Esther Ralston. **28** Marie Dressler d.

AUGUST 14 Adolphe Menjou m. Veree Teasdale.

SEPTEMBER 20 Sophia Loren b.

AUGUST 1 Ronald Colman and Thelma Raye divorce.

OCTOBER 4 Ruth Chatterton divorces George Brent. **18** Inger Stevens (Inger Stensland) b.

NOVEMBER 7 Gloria Swanson divorces Michael Farmer. **14** Ginger Rogers m. Lew Ayres. **25** Margaret Sullavan m. William Wyler, her director in *The Good Fairy.*

Personalities

Warners's Hal Wallis sees her and decides to cast de Havilland in the movie version.

OCTOBER • Charles Laughton, playing Micawber in *David Copperfield*, backs out after a few days of filming and is replaced by W. C. Fields. **5** "Hollywood Hotel" goes on the air, with Dick Powell as emcee and Louella Parsons interviewing stars who appear to plug their films. **5** Cary Grant, despondent over his separation from Virginia Cherrill, calls the police to report that he has been poisoned. He's only drunk, but there is an unopened bottle of poison on the table when the police arrive. **10** Josef von Sternberg begins filming his last picture with Marlene Dietrich, *Capricio Espagnol*, later retitled *The Devil Is a Woman*. John Dos Passos, assigned the screenplay, is drunk much of the time in a Los Angeles hotel. Male lead Joel McCrea—Dietrich is already making passes at his wife—can't get along with von Sternberg and will be replaced by Cesar Romero. **24** Loretta Young tells reporters that she and Spencer Tracy—separated, temporarily, from his wife—cannot marry because both are Catholics. **25** Producer B.P. Schulberg says that his romance with Sylvia Sidney is "definitely at an end."

NOVEMBER 6 Lupe Velez, filming in London, shows up for work with a black eye and a split lip. Husband Johnny Weissmuller, the movies' Tarzan, says "It's nobody's business" how it happened. **21** "Errol Flynn, young Irishman recently signed by Warner Brothers and now on his way to the West Coast, will have featured parts in their forthcoming productions," reports the *New York Herald-Tribune*.

DECEMBER 25 Santa Anita racetrack, the successor to Agua Caliente as the playground of the stars, opens.

Movies

AUGUST 16 Cecil B. DeMille's *Cleopatra*, starring Claudette Colbert, premieres at the Paramount.

SEPTEMBER 6 Grace Moore stars in *One Night of Love*, opening at the Radio City Music Hall.

OCTOBER 2 King Vidor's *Our Daily Bread*, starring Karen Morely and Tom Keene in Hollywood's first serious drama about the Depression, premieres at the Rialto. Vidor made the film independently after MGM's Irving Thalberg got scared off by its positive view of communal action. **11** Ernest Lubitsch's *The Merry Widow*, starring Maurice Chevalier and Jeanette MacDonald, opens at the Astor.

NOVEMBER 3 Billie "Buckwheat" Thomas makes his first *Our Gang* appearance with the release of *Mama's Little Pirates*. **15** "Introducing on the screen 'The Continental,'" say the Radio City Music Hall ads for today's opening of Fred Astaire and Ginger Rogers in *The Gay Divorcee*. RKO has changed the title from the Broadway show's "The Gay Divorce" because the Hays Office doesn't want to imply that there's anything frivolous about ending a marriage. **23** *Imitation of Life*, based on Fannie Hurst's bestseller, starring Claudette Colbert and Louise Beavers, premieres at the Roxy. It will be remade in 1959.

DECEMBER 12 Laurel and Hardy are the stars of *Babes in Toyland*, opening at the Astor.

Business and Society

moral suitability. **15** Warners is the first studio to shut its Berlin distribution office in response to Nazi anti-Jewish policies.

AUGUST • The studios begin to pressure accredited fan magazine correspondents to tone down their stories.

SEPTEMBER 17 The *Hollywood Reporter* claims that at least four studios, fearing increased taxes and an antibusiness, socialistic administration, will close and move if the progressive novelist Upton Sinclair is elected governor of California. **28** Grauman's Chinese Theater in Hollywood goes into bankruptcy.

OCTOBER 6 Louis B. Mayer offers to help Frank Merriam, who is running for governor of California against radical Upton Sinclair. MGM is already producing anti-Sinclair "newsreels" and will suggest that theaters show them if they also want to show the studio's feature films. The studios are now pressuring their employees to contribute to Merriam's campaign, which in November will bring him the governor-ship. **31** William Randolph Hearst agrees to move his Cosmopolitan Pictures from the Metro lot to Warner Bros, as of January 1.

DECEMBER 5 Fire causes more than $100,000 in damage at Warner Bros.

Births, Deaths, Marriages, and Divorces

DECEMBER 28 Maggie Smith b. and Lowell Sherman d. **30** Russ Tamblyn b.

Also this year: • Rex Harrison m. Collette Thomas. • Fifteen-year-old Carole Landis has a three-week marriage to Irving Wheeler.

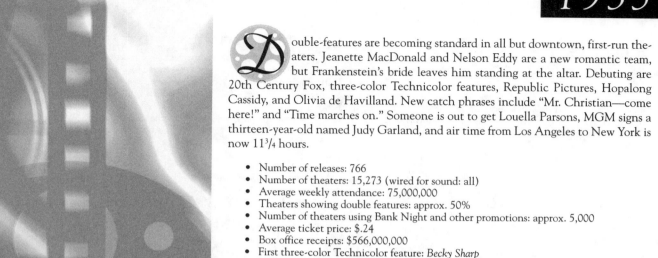

Double-features are becoming standard in all but downtown, first-run theaters. Jeanette MacDonald and Nelson Eddy are a new romantic team, but Frankenstein's bride leaves him standing at the altar. Debuting are 20th Century Fox, three-color Technicolor features, Republic Pictures, Hopalong Cassidy, and Olivia de Havilland. New catch phrases include "Mr. Christian—come here!" and "Time marches on." Someone is out to get Louella Parsons, MGM signs a thirteen-year-old named Judy Garland, and air time from Los Angeles to New York is now 11³/₄ hours.

- Number of releases: 766
- Number of theaters: 15,273 (wired for sound: all)
- Average weekly attendance: 75,000,000
- Theaters showing double features: approx. 50%
- Number of theaters using Bank Night and other promotions: approx. 5,000
- Average ticket price: $.24
- Box office receipts: $566,000,000
- First three-color Technicolor feature: *Becky Sharp*
- Time required to apply Boris Karloff's makeup for *The Bride of Frankenstein*: 7 hours
- Total weight of Karloff's makeup and costume: 62 pounds
- Gary Cooper's salary: $311,000 per year
- Katharine Hepburn's salary: $221,572 per year
- Fan letters per month received by Shirley Temple: 60,000

Top stars at the box office, based on a Quigley Publications poll of exhibitors:

1. Shirley Temple
2. Will Rogers
3. Clark Gable
4. Fred Astaire and Ginger Rogers
5. Joan Crawford
6. Claudette Colbert
7. Dick Powell
8. Wallace Beery
9. Joe E. Brown
10. James Cagney

The Academy Awards (presented March 5, 1936)
Best Picture: *Mutiny on the Bounty*
Actor: Victor McLaglen (*The Informer*)
Actress: Bette Davis (*Dangerous*)
Director: John Ford (*The Informer*)

The Bride of Frankenstein, with Elsa Lanchester and Boris Karloff   MOMA

January	February	March	April	May	June	
8 Elvis Presley b.	**4** Ernst Lubitsch becomes production chief at Paramount	**11** Spencer Tracy arrested on drunk and disorderly charge	**12** Monogram becomes part of the new Republic Pictures **27** 20th Century Fox formed		• W.C. Fields, seriously ill, temporarily gives up drinking	

July	August	September	October	November	December	
17 Variety front-page headline: STICKS NIX HICK PIX	**15** Will Rogers d. in plane crash	**8** Busby Berkeley kills three people in auto accident	**15** Selznick International Pictures incorporated	**8** *Mutiny on the Bounty*	**1** Woody Allen b.	

Personalities

• Throughout the year, *Variety* surveys eleven leading fan magazines and reports that the covers of every issue of each depict a female star. Claudette Colbert leads with eleven covers.

JANUARY • Hollywood fashion leader Loretta Young tells an interviewer: "I generally want breakfast in a sleeveless chartreuse negligee with an ensemble effect created by ample duchesse lace sleeves." **4** Creighton Chaney, son of Lon Chaney, announces that he's changing his name to Lon Chaney Jr. to jump-start his stalled film career. **27** The *New York Times* comments about a thirteen-year-old in the play *Fly Away Home*, which opened on Broadway on Janu-

ary 15: "Despite his inexperience, the boy has a natural histrionic instinct which, if he wants to stick to the theater, should take him very far." He is Montgomery Clift.

FEBRUARY 27 Five-year-old Shirley Temple chats with President Roosevelt in his White House office. **27** At Hollywood's Biltmore Hotel, the Academy Awards for 1934—eligible films are now those debuting in the previous twelve months—are held. Claudette Colbert, about to board the "20th Century" for New York, has to be rushed to the hotel from the train station to accept the award for Best Actress in *It Happened One Night*, the prospects of which she had given little thought.

MARCH 11 Spencer Tracy is arrested in Yuma, Arizona, for being drunk and disorderly. Police, called to the actor's hotel

room when he begins to throw things while on the phone to his wife, have to use force to subdue him. **14** Shirley Temple puts her prints in the cement outside Grauman's Chinese Theater. **18** Clark Gable cannot get off his plane in Dallas because several thousand women have overrun the arrival area trying to get near him. He has to take off again. **20** Lucille Ball signs with RKO.

APRIL 2 Fox releases Spencer Tracy from his contract, and he signs with MGM, where he will report for work on April 5. **13** The Marx Brothers open in Salt Lake City a one-hour stage version of their upcoming film, *A Night at the Opera*, as a dry run to see which jokes work.

MAY 4 Jackie Coogan survives, with broken ribs, a car crash near San Diego that kills his father and three of the actor's

Movies

JANUARY 18 *The Lives of a Bengal Lancer*, starring Gary Cooper and Franchot Tone, premieres at the Paramount. **18** *David Copperfield*, directed by George Cukor and starring Freddie Bartholomew, W.C. Fields, Lionel Barrymore, Maureen O'Sullivan, Basil Rathbone, Edna May Oliver, Madge Evans, and Roland Young, premieres at the Capitol.

FEBRUARY 1 The first *March of Time* "newsreel" premieres at the Capitol Theater in New York. The twenty-two-minute feature

follows the docudrama style of its radio counterpart, on the air since March 6, 1931. This *Time* magazine production mixes newsreel film with reenacted segments. Westbrook Van Voorhis provides dramatic narration, ending with "Time Marches On!" RKO will distribute it until 1942, after which it is handled as a short subject, not a newsreel, by 20th Century Fox. Production will end in 1951. **7** Leslie Howard and Merle Oberon star in *The Scarlet Pimpernel*, opening at the Radio City Music Hall. **23** *Beginner's Luck*, Carl "Alfalfa" Switzer's first *Our Gang* comedy, is released. And Mascot releases *The Phantom Empire*, a science-fiction western serial,

in which Gene Autry has his first starring role after brief appearances in two Ken Maynard films.

MARCH 6 *The Ruggles of Red Gap*, starring Charles Laughton, Mary Boland, and Charlie Ruggles opens at the Paramount. **21** Shirley Temple stars in *The Little Colonel*, with Lionel Barrymore and Bill "Bojangles" Robinson, opening at the Radio City Music Hall. **21** The U.S. premiere of Alfred Hitchcock's *The Man Who Knew Too Much*, starring Peter Lorre and Leslie Banks, takes place at the Mayfair. The director will remake it in 1956. **22** Jeanette MacDonald and Nelson Eddy

Business and Society

JANUARY 7 The U.S. Treasury Department approves the Commissioner of Customs' decision to ban the German film *Ecstasy*, starring Hedy Keisler (later Hedy Lamarr), because of nudity. **8** *Variety* reports that MGM has three undercover men at Santa Anita to catch employees who should be at work.

FEBRUARY 4 Ernst Lubitsch becomes production chief at Paramount, replacing Emmanuel Cohen. It is the first time a director has achieved this position at a major studio.

MARCH 4 The Supreme Court holds invalid William Fox's Movietone sound patents. **29** Herbert Yates starts Republic Pictures, which will include Monogram and Mascot Pictures.

MAY • The Museum of Modern Art film library is founded in New York. **27** Twentieth Century Pictures and the Fox Film Corporation announce their merger to form 20th Century Fox. Joseph Schenck will serve as chairman and Darryl Zanuck will head production. The Bank of America is a major investor.

JUNE 3 "Color Seen as a Defense Against Television," says a *Hollywood Reporter* headline. **12** Al Lichtman succeeds

Births, Deaths, Marriages, and Divorces

JANUARY 8 Elvis Presley b. **10** Douglas Fairbanks and Mary Pickford divorce. The New York *Evening Post* headlines it: "Mary Erases the Mark of Zorro."

MARCH 11 Jean Harlow divorces Harold Rosson. **26** Cary Grant and Virginia Cherrill divorce. **31** Richard Chamberlain (George Richard Chamberlain) b.

APRIL 5 Claude Rains divorces Beatrix Thomas. **8** Claude Rains marries Frances Propper. **12** Mary Astor and Dr. Franklin Thorpe divorce. **19** Dudley Moore b. **21** Charles Grodin b.

MAY 10 Dorothy Lamour m. orchestra leader Herbie Kaye.

friends, including former child star Junior Durkin. **9** According to the *Hollywood Reporter*, Fox wants to sign Henry Fonda to a contract, but "Fonda wants to see himself on the screen before committing himself." The same issue notes that "MGM has signed James Stewart, stage actor." **12** MGM orders Myrna Loy, who wants $3,000 per week rather than the $1,500 she's getting under her 1931 contract, to return to the studio instead of sailing for Europe tomorrow. She refuses. When she returns, in August, she will declare her contract broken. **18** "Nineteen-year-old Vivien Leigh, an unknown actress, leaped to fame in Ashley Dukes' 'The Mask of Virtue,'" a *New York Times* London dispatch reports of a theatrical event that happened a few days ago. Yesterday Alexander Korda signed her to a movie contract. **18** Samuel Goldwyn announces that he

and Anna Sten, the actress he brought over from Germany—"Goldwyn's Folly"—have mutually agreed to terminate her contract, ending his three-year effort to make her a star.

JUNE • W.C. Fields is seriously ill, sick enough to—temporarily—give up drinking. Over the next two years a variety of ailments, including pneumonia, will disrupt his career.

W.C. Fields   MSN

team for the first of their eight films together, *Naughty Marietta*, opening at the Capitol.

APRIL 10 *Black Fury*, starring Paul Muni and Karen Morely, opens at the Strand. "The screen may never take such a chance again!" brags the Warner Bros., but Warners' didn't take so many chances this time. The studio cut some scenes from this story of industrial strife in the coal mining industry for New York censors, who think that "some of the labor troubles . . . are inflammatory." **20** Premiering at the Rivoli is *Les Misérables*, starring Fredric March and Charles Laughton.

Joseph Schenck as president of United Artists. **27** David O. Selznick resigns from MGM to become an independent producer, but will stay at Metro long enough to finish *Anna Karenina* and *A Tale of Two Cities*.

JULY 1 Paramount emerges from bankruptcy. **16** The Writers Guild demands that the studios engage in collective bargaining, as specified in the new Wagner Act. **17** In a legendary front-page headline, *Variety* reports that Midwestern moviego-

ers are willing to pay to see sophisticated films: STICKS NIX HICK PIX. **18** Samuel Goldwyn buys the physical facilities of the United Artists Studio from Darryl Zanuck and Joseph Schenck.

AUGUST 23 David O. Selznick announces that he will sign the best available stars and ignore the studios' antiraiding pact. **31** "Communism in Studios," blares the front-page headline of the *Hollywood Reporter*, the first assault from the peri-

odical that will later lead the campaign to uncover moviemaking subversives.

SEPTEMBER • The Hays Office warns producers and screenwriters away from "bum," "lousy," "joint," "chippie," "floosey," and "goose." And there will be no more Bronx cheers. **13** Sam Briskin resigns as head of production at Columbia, which will now be handled by Harry Cohn. **23** Producer Merian C. Cooper leaves RKO for Jock Whitney's Pioneer Studio.

JUNE 11 Gene Wilder (Jerry Silberman) b. **19** Errol Flynn m. Lili Damita.

AUGUST 15 Will Rogers d. **30** Claudette Colbert divorces Norman Foster.

SEPTEMBER 4 Joan Blondell and George Barnes divorce.

OCTOBER 1 Sylvia Sidney m. publisher Bennett Cerf, a match that will last three months. Julie Andrews (Julia Welles) b. **8** Harriet Hilliard m. Ozzie Nelson. **9** Blanche Sweet m. Raymond Hackett. • John Barrymore and Dolores Costello divorce. **11** Joan Crawford m. Franchot Tone. • Dorothy Gish and James Rennie

divorce.

NOVEMBER 10 Roy Scheider b.

DECEMBER 1 Woody Allen (Allen Stewart Konigsberg) b. **14** Lee Remick b. **24** Claudette Colbert m. Dr. Joel Pressman. **30** Barbara Stanwyck divorces Frank Fay.

Personalities

11 Robert Donat, having withdrawn from the lead in *Captain Blood*, and Warners' other choices, Leslie Howard, Fredric March, Clark Gable, and Ronald Colman being unavailable, Hal Wallis asks Mervyn LeRoy to test contract players George Brent and Errol Flynn for the part. Flynn has yet to star in a movie. **16** Carole Lombard rents a whole amusement park in Los Angeles for the night and throws a party. Marlene Dietrich, who scratches her famous legs during the evening, goes down the chute-the-chute with Claudette Colbert. **17** At a play in London, Laurence Olivier is introduced to Vivien Leigh.

JULY 10 After a year at Fox with little to show for it, "Rita Cansino, 17, daughter of the Dancing Cansinos," is offered a featured part in *Ramona*, reports *Variety*. But the future Rita Hayworth will have to settle for a supporting role when Loretta Young is later cast in the lead. **14** Dr. Joseph Goebbels orders that no film credited to Herman J. Mankiewicz be shown in Germany because he has shown disrespect for Hitler. **20** The Mexican government bans gambling at Agua Caliente, ending an era of Hollywood junkets to its casino and track, and costing Joseph Schenck, who has invested in these establishments, several hundred thousand dollars.

AUGUST • An article in *New Theater* magazine denounces "Louella Parsons: Hearst's Hollywood Stooge." "Louella's chief function is to ballyhoo Marion Davies, the blond girl friend of her boss," writes "Joel Faith," whose real name many in Hollywood would like to know. **31** Reporters spot a large diamond on Jean Harlow's left hand but can't get her or William Powell, her boyfriend, to interpret its meaning. **31** George Cukor signs with David O. Selznick for $4,000 per week, making him the highest-paid contract director in Hollywood.

SEPTEMBER 1 Myrna Loy returns to the MGM lot after a four-month "strike" for higher wages. She also wanted less work than the twenty-three pictures she has made at Metro in the past four years. MGM's threatened litigation that could put her career in limbo for several years forced her return. **8** Busby Berkeley kills three people when his car crashes into theirs. He is charged with second-degree murder. **8** "The Hoboken Four," including nineteen-year-old Frank Sinatra, appear on

Movies

MAY 3 Josef von Sternberg's *The Devil Is a Woman*, starring Marlene Dietrich, Lionel Atwill and Cesar Romero, premieres at the Paramount. **9** "Slowly, hair grew on the palms of his hands!" says the newspaper ad for *Werewolf of London*, the first werewolf film, starring Henry Hull and Warner Oland, opening at the Rialto. Also today, John Ford's *The Informer*, starring Victor McLaglen, opens at the Radio City Music Hall. **9** Grauman's Chinese Theater begins to show double features. **10** *The Bride of Frankenstein*—"The Monster Talks!"—starring Boris Karloff and Elsa Lanchester (who screams when she sees him), premieres at the Roxy. Many critics will see it as a minor masterpiece for director James Whale. The film has beautiful black and white cinematography, despite cinematographer John Mescall's drinking binges.

JUNE 13 *Becky Sharp*, the first three-color Technicolor feature, opens at the Radio City Music Hall. It stars Miriam Hopkins and Nigel Bruce.

JULY 30 *Hop-A-Long Cassidy*, the first of sixty-six Hopalong Cassidy westerns that William Boyd will star in through 1948, is released.

AUGUST 9 Clark Gable, Jean Harlow, and Wallace Beery are the stars of MGM's *China Seas*, premiering at the Capitol. **15** *Alice Adams*, starring Katharine Hepburn and Fred MacMurray, opens at the Radio City Music Hall. **29** Fred Astaire and Ginger Rogers star in *Top Hat*, opening at the Radio City Music Hall. **30** Greta Garbo stars in *Anna Karenina*, with Fredric March, Basil Rathbone, and Freddie Bartholomew, premiering at the Capitol.

Business and Society

OCTOBER 3 Al Lichtman, after arguing with Samuel Goldwyn, resigns as president of United Artists. **10** Joseph Breen informs MGM that the plot of James Cain's *Double Indemnity*, which the studio wants to film, includes adultery and has a generally low moral tone and thus could not receive a seal of approval. **11** RCA sells half its share in RKO to Floyd Odlum's Atlas Corporation and Lehman Brothers, which have an option to buy the rest in two years. **15** Selznick International Pictures is incorporated, with John Hay "Jock" Whitney principal backer. **31** Spain threatens to bar Paramount's films from the country unless *The Devil Is a Woman* is withdrawn from worldwide distribution and the negative burned. The government objects to having a member of its Civil Guard depicted in a drinking scene. Adolph Zukor has assured the Spanish government that "we do not make movies with any idea of depicting real life."

NOVEMBER 11 Paramount placates Spain by moving up the booking dates for *The Devil Is a Woman* in order to hasten the end of its run and promises to withdraw it afterward. **14** Leo Spitz is RKO's new president.

DECEMBER 9 The International Association of Theatrical Stage Employees, agreeing to

Births, Deaths, Marriages, and Divorces

Also this year: • John Carradine m. Ardanelle Cosner. • Burt Lancaster m. fellow acrobat June Ernst—a union of short duration. • Tom Mix remarries Olive Stokes.

Major Bowes' "Amateur Hour" on CBS radio. This is the first big break for Sinatra and will lead to a $50-a-week job with the show. **13** Norma Jean Mortenson (Marilyn Monroe) is sent to the Los Angeles Orphans Home to live when the woman caring for her gets married. **23** Charles Bickford is hospitalized after a lion bites him on the neck during filming of *East of Java*. **27** Thirteen-year-old Judy Garland signs her first contract with MGM. Harriet Hilliard, singer with the Ozzie Nelson Band, signs with RKO. **30** After noticing all the velvet and lace on Errol Flynn's costumes in *Captain Blood*, Hal Wallis complains to director Michael Curtiz that he has Flynn looking like "a God damned faggot."

OCTOBER 1 Louella Parsons reports that after an absence from Hollywood of several years, Humphrey Bogart, "who not so long ago was appearing in juvenile roles," is returning to play a gangster in *The Petrified Forest*. **21** Buster Keaton is taken to a hospital in an alcoholic stupor. When he regains consciousness, he has to be restrained in a straightjacket.

NOVEMBER 29 Dr. Joel Pressman, fiancé of Claudette Colbert, smashes a news photographer's camera when the couple, traveling together as "Mr. and Mrs.," land in San Francisco and are pursued by journalists. In character, Colbert mutters, "It's all so silly."

DECEMBER 4 A drunken Spencer Tracy gets the worst of an exchange of punches with his friend, director William Wellman, and ends up prone on the dance floor of the Cafe Trocadero. Wellman is said to have provoked Tracy by disparaging Loretta Young. **14** Ida Lupino hosts a party given by her father at the Trocadero to honor popular actress Thelma Todd, who is later found dead in her car. A grand jury concludes that death was caused by carbon monoxide poisoning; beyond that, rumors and theories abound. **20** Louella Parsons reports that Jean Harlow will play only "good girls" from now on, and not as a platinum blonde. **27** Warners suspends James Cagney in a contract dispute. He cites an oral agreement requiring no more than four films a year, while the studio has been assigning him more. Warners has already announced him as the star of its *Robin Hood*.

SEPTEMBER • All but one Loews and one RKO theater in New York City abandon stage shows and a movie for double features. **5** Republic releases *Tumbling Tumbleweeds*, Gene Autry's first western feature, which cost $18,000 and will gross $1 million. **18** Jack Benny, Eleanor Powell, Robert Taylor, and Buddy Ebsen star in *Broadway Melody of 1936*, premiering at the Capitol. **27** *Powdersmoke Range's* release inaugurates the series of fifty-one Republic "Three Mesquiteers" westerns.

OCTOBER 9 Warners' *A Midsummer Night's Dream* premieres at the Hollywood Theater in New York. Stars include James Cagney, Mickey Rooney, Joe E. Brown, and Olivia de Havilland in her film debut.

NOVEMBER 8 *Mutiny on the Bounty*, starring Clark Gable, Charles Laughton, and Franchot Tone (with young David Niven as an extra) opens at the Capitol. It was not an easy voyage: Gable balked at the "pigtail and velvet knee pants and shoes with siver buckles!" Laughton, Captain Bligh, got seasick. But the film proves artistically and commercially successful and will be remade in 1962. **30** The release of *Our Gang Follies of 1936* marks Darla Hood's series debut.

DECEMBER 6 *A Night at the Opera*, starring the Marx Brothers, Margaret Dumont, Allan Jones, and Kitty Carlisle, opens at the Capitol. **25** *Captain Blood*, starring Errol Flynn, Olivia de Havilland, and Basil Rathbone, premieres at the Strand. *A Tale of Two Cities* stars Ronald Colman, Elizabeth Allan, Blanche Yurka, and Basil Rathbone, and premieres at the Capitol. **30** The premiere of *Magnificent Obsession*, which raises Robert Taylor to stardom, draws capacity crowds at the Radio City Music Hall despite frigid weather. Irene Dunne co-stars.

---

arbitration of its jurisdictional dispute with the International Brotherhood of Electrical Workers, is reinstated in the studio basic labor agreement. **18** Samuel J. Briskin becomes production head at RKO.

1936

Katharine Hepburn dresses as a boy in a movie and gets involved with Howard Hughes offscreen. Tyrone Power becomes a star, Lana Turner is discovered, and Sonja Henie is an Olympic skating champion. Margaret Mitchell sells the movie rights to her first novel, but Mary Astor's diary will be too hot for the screen. Warners and Bette Davis go to war, while David O. Selznick tries to imagine Tallulah Bankhead as Scarlett O'Hara.

- Number of releases: 735
- Number of theaters: 15,858
- Theaters showing double features: approx. 85%
- Average weekly attendance: 88,000,000
- Average ticket price: $.25
- Box office receipts: $626,000,000
- Number of takes required for Fred Astaire and Ginger Rogers to film "Never Gonna Dance" sequence from *Swing Time*: 47
- Length of the earthquake sequence in *San Francisco*: 20 minutes
- Production cost of *Flash Gordon* serial, most expensive to date: $350,000
- Price paid by David O. Selznick for movie (and TV) rights to *Gone With the Wind*: $50,000

Top stars at the box office, based on a Quigley Publications poll of exhibitors:
1. Shirley Temple
2. Clark Gable
3. Fred Astaire and Ginger Rogers
4. Robert Taylor
5. Joe E. Brown
6. Dick Powell
7. Joan Crawford
8. Claudette Colbert
9. Jeanette MacDonald
10. Gary Cooper

The New York Film Critics Circle Awards
Best Picture: *Mr. Deeds Goes to Town*

The Academy Awards (including, for the first time, Supporting Actor and Actress categories, and presented March 4, 1937)
Best Picture: *The Great Ziegfeld*
Actor: Paul Muni (*The Story of Louis Pasteur*)
Actress: Luise Rainer (*The Great Ziegfeld*)
Supporting Actor: Walter Brennan (*Come and Get It*)
Supporting Actress: Gale Sondergaard (*Anthony Adverse*)
Director: Frank Capra (*Mr. Deeds Goes to Town*)

January	February	March	April	May	June
	• Billy Wilkeson of the *Hollywood Reporter* discovers Lana Turner	**16** *Flash Gordon*	• Major studios begin payoffs to hoods George Browne and Willie Bioff	**17** Dennis Hopper b.	**13** Universal signs 13-year-old Edna Mae [Deanna] Durbin

July	August	September	October	November	December
	27 *Swing Time* / **9** Warner Bros. tells Bette Davis she's suspended	**9** Warners gets injunction against Bette Davis	**19** Bette Davis's contract with Warners declared valid by British court	**23** Bette Davis back at Warner Bros.	**18** Hollywood divorce rate reported as four times national average

Personalities

JANUARY • Billy Wilkerson, editor and publisher of the *Hollywood Reporter*, discovers sixteen-year-old Julia (Lana) Turner at the Top Hat Malt Shop at Sunset and Highland in Hollywood. **23** At the annual Mayfair Club Ball at the Victor Hugo restaurant in Beverly Hills, the ladies are dressed in white, as requested by hostess Carole Lombard, except for Norma Shearer, who arrives in scarlet. Lombard tells her off, provoking Clark Gable to criticize Lombard for being too sharp with Metro's reigning lady.

FEBRUARY 7 Samuel Goldwyn gives William Wyler a long-term contract. **11** Paramount suspends George Raft when he complains that cinematographer Ted Tetzlaff, assigned

to Raft's next film, *Concertina*, co-starring Carole Lombard, is her personal photographer and will give her "all the breaks." On February 13 Fred MacMurray will replace Raft. **15** Sonja Henie wins her third Olympic figure skating championship. **27** Shirley Temple receives a new 20th Century Fox contract, retroactive to September 9, paying over $50,000 per film.

MARCH 5 The votes for the Academy Awards, handed out at the Biltmore tonight, have been tabulated by Price-Waterhouse for the first time. Bette Davis receives the Best Actress award for *Dangerous*—clearly a consolation prize for not receiving an Oscar for *Of Human Bondage* the year before. **9** British stage actor Rex Harrison flunks a Warner Bros. screen test. **10** Jack Warner, looking at Errol Flynn's screen tests for *The Charge of the*

Light Brigade, suggests that Flynn "leave the moustache on." **16** James Cagney's suit against Warners fails on a technicality involving the four-films-per-year limit he claims was agreed to verbally. But the court releases him from his contract anyway because the studio did not give him the top billing in ads for *Ceiling Zero*, to which his contract entitled him. **17** The wall of wooden bricks burying Clark Gable in the earthquake scene in *San Francisco*, now shooting at MGM, is not fake enough, and he has to be treated for real cuts and bruises. **19** Margaret Sullavan falls and breaks her arm on the set of *Hotel Imperial*. Stu Erwin had been playfully chasing her off-camera with a seltzer bottle.

APRIL 1 Jimmy Fidler, radio personality and gossip columnist, begins appearing regularly in Fox-Movietone newsreels. **14** Warner

Movies

JANUARY 6 The release of Warner Bros.'s cartoon *Gold Diggers of '49* marks the debut of Porky Pig. **9** Katharine Hepburn, dressed as a boy, and Cary Grant, Brian Aherne, and Edmund Gwenn star in *Sylvia Scarlett*, opening at the Radio City Music Hall.

FEBRUARY 5 Charlie Chaplin's *Modern Times*, costarring Paulette Goddard, premieres at the Rivoli. The police riot squad is called out to control the crowds on Broadway trying to glimpse Douglas Fairbanks, Gloria Swanson, George Burns and Gracie

Allen, Ginger Rogers, Eddie Cantor, Edward G. Robinson, and Elsa Maxwell arriving for the premiere. **6** *The Petrified Forest* premieres at the Radio City Music

Hall. Warner Bros. wanted to use Edward G. Robinson as the gangster, Duke Mantee, but Leslie Howard would not do the film unless Humphrey Bogart, who created the role

Charlie Chaplin in *Modern Times*   MSN

Business and Society

JANUARY 2 A closed shop and jurisdiction over several categories of craft workers for IATSE takes effect. George Browne and Willie Bioff have risen to the top of this union in partnership with Frank "The Enforcer" Nitti of the Al Capone mob. **16** The Screen Directors Guild is incorporated, with King Vidor as president.

Births, Deaths, Marriages, and Divorces

JANUARY 9 John Gilbert d. **27** Troy Donahue (Merle Johnson Jr.) b. **28** Alan Alda b.

FEBRUARY 8 Frances Farmer m. Lief Erickson. **11** Burt Reynolds b. **17** Jim Brown,

football player and movie star, b.

MARCH 5 Dean Stockwell b. **6** Margaret Sullavan divorces William Wyler. **7** Douglas Fairbanks m. Lady Sylvia Ashley. **19** Ursula Andress b. **23** Randolph

Scott m. Mariana du Pont Somerville.

APRIL 9 Sylvia Sidney divorces Bennett Cerf.

MAY 9 Glenda Jackson and Albert Finney are born. **17** Dennis Hopper b. **27** Louis Gossett Jr. b. **30** Keir Dullea b.

Bros. signs Olivia de Havilland to a seven-year contract.

MAY • After seventeen years and 240 films, comedian Charlie Chase leaves the Hal Roach studio. **18** Rin Tin Tin Jr., Hollywood's wonder dog, who has just starred in a film in which he captures a whole gang of robbers single-handedly, sleeps soundly while thieves break into and rob the home of his master, Lee Duncan. **27** Olympic skating champion Sonja Henie signs a five-year contract with 20th Century Fox. **31** A mob of fifty to one-hundred people attack interior decorator and former MGM silent film star William Haines and several of his male companions near Haines's El Porto beach home in Los Angeles. Members of the group, some of whom call themselves "The White Legion," claim that a young boy was molested in Haines's home, and

they want him and his friends out. The police say there is no evidence of such molestation. Haines is not seriously injured.

JUNE 1 The Lux Radio Theater, a program of condensed versions of movies and plays, not always featuring their original casts, begins to broadcast from Hollywood, hosted by Cecil B. DeMille. Tonight's show is "The Legionnaire and the Lady," starring Clark Gable and Marlene Dietrich. Theater owners complain that it cuts attendance by ten percent. **13** Universal signs thirteen-year-old Edna Mae [Deanna] Durbin to a contract. MGM, which had her for six months, has nothing for her. **17** Loretta Young, filming *Ramona*, saves the life of a two-year-old actor by grabbing him and running when scenery catches fire. Her clothes ignite, but the fire is put out.

JULY 1 According to the *Hollywood Reporter*, Universal has changed Edna Mae Durbin's first name to "Dianna" [*sic*]. **1** Ann Sheridan signs with Warners for $75 per week, rising to a maximum of $750 per week by the contract's end, December 18, 1943. **9** Warner Bros., responding to Bette Davis's June 18 refusal to appear in *God's Country and the Woman* and her demand for more money, informs her that she has been off the payroll as of June 19. **13** Grand National announces the signing of James Cagney, who will make films for them with his own production company. **14** Mary Astor sues to regain custody of her daughter, charging she gave her up last year because her husband threatened to "scandalize" her if she didn't. **15** A coroner's jury in Los Angeles holds Howard Hughes blameless for the death of a man in an auto accident on July 11, and

on stage, got the part. Bette Davis also stars. **8** Paul Muni has the lead in *The Story of Louis Pasteur*, premiering at the Strand. It initiates a series of screen biographies of inventors, doctors, and scientists: *The Story of Alexander Graham Bell* (1939), *Young Tom Edison* (1940), *Edison the Man* (1940), *Dr. Ehrlich's Magic Bullet* (1940), and *Madam Curie* (1943). **19** *Trail of the Lonesome Pine*, the first outdoors, three-color Technicolor film, starring Henry Fonda, Sylvia Sydney, and Fred MacMurray, opens at the Paramount. Onstage is Eddy Duchin and his Orchestra. **20** Frigid weather does not keep twenty thousand customers from the Radio City Music Hall for Fred Astaire and

Ginger Rogers in *Follow the Fleet* on its opening day. The film introduces Irving Berlin's "Let's Face the Music and Dance."

MARCH 18 The first chapter of Universal's *Flash Gordon*, starring Buster Crabbe, is released. At $350,000 it's the most expensive serial to date.

APRIL 2 *Little Lord Fauntleroy*, starring Freddie Bartholomew, C. Aubrey Smith, Guy Kibbee, and Mickey Rooney, opens at the Radio City Music Hall. **8** William Powell has the title role in *The Great Ziegfeld*, premiering at the Astor. Myrna Loy plays Ziegfeld's second wife, Billie Burke,

who serves as a technical advisor on the film, although Fanny Brice and Ray Bolger play themselves. Luise Rainer also stars. **16** Frank Capra's *Mr. Deeds Goes to Town*, starring Gary Cooper and Jean Arthur, opens at the Radio City Music Hall. **18** Alexander Korda's *Things to Come*, starring Raymond Massey, Ralph Richardson, and Cedric Hardwicke, opens at the Rivoli.

MAY 10 Pare Lorentz's documentary on the plight of the dust-bowl farmer, *The Plow That Broke the Plains*, made for the New Deal's Resettlement Administration, premieres at an invitational showing at the Mayflower Hotel in Washington, D.C.

FEBRUARY 7 William LeBaron replaces Ernst Lubitsch as Paramount production head. **14** Independent producer Walter Wanger agrees to release his films through United Artists. **15** Sinclair Lewis charges that the Hays Office has "forbidden" MGM to film his antifascist novel, *It Can't Happen Here*, for fear of offending Germany and Italy. Louis B. Mayer replies that it was cost, not politics, that shut down the production, which was about to start shooting. **22** Screenwriter Sidney

Howard, who has scripted *It Can't Happen Here*, shows reporters a January 31 Hays Office memo to MGM describing the screenplay as "of so inflammatory a nature and so filled with dangerous material that only the greatest possible care will save it from being rejected on all sides."

MARCH 2 Walt Disney agrees to switch his distribution from United Artists to RKO. **5** Irving Thalberg signs a new ten-year pact with MGM. **14** Carl Laemmle

sells Universal to a group of investors. Charles R. Rogers is the new studio head, replacing Carl Laemmle Jr.

APRIL • For lack of sufficient funds, the Democratic Party abandons plans to conduct a media campaign through the making of film shorts to be shown in theaters. • The major studios begin payoffs of $50,000 a year to George Browne and Willie Bioff of IATSE to maintain labor peace. Smaller studios pay $25,000. Joseph

JUNE 4 Bruce Dern b. **20** Fred MacMurray m. Lillian Lamont. **27** Myrna Loy m. producer Arthur Hornblow Jr.; Corinne Griffith m. professional football team owner George Preston Marshall.

JULY 8 Thomas Meighan d.

AUGUST • Ann Sheridan m. S. Edward Norris.

SEPTEMBER 12 Maureen O'Sullivan m. director John Farrow. **14** Irving Thalberg d. **16** Henry Fonda m. Frances Brokaw. **19** Joan Blondell m. Dick Powell.

OCTOBER 1 Stella Stevens (Estelle Egglestone) b. **8** Van Heflin and Esther Ralston divorce. **14** Buster Keaton and Mae Scribbens divorce.

NOVEMBER 9 John Barrymore m. Elaine Jacobs. **16** Margaret Sullavan m. Leland Hayward.

Personalities

charges of negligent homicide are dropped. **28** Mary Astor's diary, written in lavender and detailing her affair with playwright George S. Kaufman, becomes an issue in her child custody suit. Newspapers will reprint the sensational material, including some that Astor maintains is faked.

AUGUST • Marlene Dietrich, filming *Knight without Armour* in Europe for Alexander Korda, begins an affair with Douglas Fairbanks Jr. CBS head William S. Paley is also courting her. **13** Mary Astor wins split custody of her daughter.

SEPTEMBER • Silent screen star Mae Murray, who was worth $3,000,000 in 1926, spends several nights sleeping on a park bench in New York. Silent screen personalities bankrupted by the Depression include William Farnum, Blanche Sweet, Francis X. Bushman and director Marshall "Mickey" Neilan. **9** Warners gets an injunction in a London court preventing Bette Davis from making films in England, where she has gone to work. **15** Lucille Ball, unbeknownst to her, is appointed to the State Central Committee of the Communist Party of California. **15** Attending fifteen-year-old Jackie Cooper's birthday party are eleven-year-old Donald O'Connor, Freddie Bartholomew, twelve, Judy Garland and Deanna Durbin, fourteen, and fifteen-year-old Mickey Rooney. **16** Attending a Hollywood preview of *Dodsworth*, in which she plays "the other woman," Mary Astor receives an ovation when her name appears on the screen. She cries, grateful for fan support after her bruising child-custody battle. **25** In his third trial, Busby Berkeley is found innocent of second-degree murder in the death of three people in an auto accident last year. Even so he settles a civil suit with the survivors for $95,000. **27** Claudette Colbert collapses on the set of *Maid of Salem*, as what appeared yesterday to have been a mere bump on the head from the auto collision she was in turns out to have been a concussion. She will be out three weeks.

OCTOBER 6 Dick Powell and Joan Blondell, arriving in New York aboard the ship on which they were married on September 19, are greeted by tooting tugboats and five planes circling overhead, one of them towing a banner: "Welcome, Joan and Dick." **14** Warners's lawyer refers to Bette Davis in a British court as "a very naughty young lady." **14** Actors Equity suspends Lionel

Movies

14 Irene Dunne, Helen Morgan, Paul Robeson, Allan Jones, and Joe E. Brown star in the second of three versions of *Show Boat*, opening at the Radio City Music Hall.

JUNE 5 Fritz Lang's *Fury*, starring Spencer Tracy and Sylvia Sydney, opens at the Capitol. **26** *San Francisco*, MGM's greatest financial success until *Gone With the Wind*, opens at the Capitol, starring Clark Gable, Jeanette MacDonald, and Spencer Tracy.

JULY 16 *The Green Pastures*, starring Rex Ingram and Eddie Anderson, opens at the Radio City Music Hall. **29** *Anthony Adverse*, starring Fredric March and Olivia de Havilland, premieres at the Carthay Circle in Hollywood.

AUGUST 20 *Romeo and Juliet*, premiering at the Astor, stars Norma Shearer, Leslie Howard, John Barrymore, and Basil Rathbone. "It is a momentous marriage," Walter Winchell writes, "this one of Irving Thalberg and William Shakespeare." **27** *Swing Time*, starring Fred Astaire and Ginger Rogers, opens at the Radio City Music Hall with two thousand people on line at 9 A.M. on a Thursday morning. The theater sells 27,821 tickets today, a new record for an opening day. The music is by Jerome Kern, the choreography by Hermes Pan, and for the only time on the screen, Astaire does a number, "Bojangles of Harlem," in blackface. Other songs include "Never Gonna Dance" (one of the picture's working titles), "Pick Yourself Up," "The Way You Look Tonight," and "A Fine Romance." **29** *Killer Dog*, the first of 209 MGM "Pete Smith Specialties" short subjects is released. Smith had been head of the studio's publicity department.

SEPTEMBER 13 Robert Donat and Madeleine Carroll are in *The 39 Steps*, released last year

Business and Society

Schenck, who has negotiated on behalf of the studios, is raking off some of this money for himself. **15** Hollywood movie stars are paying the new California state income tax for the first time and marking their forms "Paid Under Protest," at the suggestion of the studios. **16** Grand National, a new studio, is launched, with backing from Pathé.

JUNE 31 Jock Whitney's Pioneer Pictures merges with Selznick International.

JULY • RCA–NBC begins experimental TV transmissions from the Empire State Building. **2** Barney Balaban becomes president of Paramount. **2** Pope Pius XI issues an encyclical aimed primarily at the United States, calling for the banning of indecent films and urging the bishops to support a film classification system based on moral content. **8** The Bank of America's A.H. Giannini becomes president and chairman of the board of United Artists. **23** The Hollywood League Against Nazism (later the Hollywood Anti-Nazi League) is formed.

AUGUST • New York City begins to license "matrons," who will patrol specially designated children's sections of theaters. **6** W. Ray Johnston, president of Republic Pictures, resigns.

Births, Deaths, Marriages, and Divorces

DECEMBER 7 Bessie Love and William Hawks divorce.

Also this year: • Charlie Chaplin m. Paulette Goddard.

Barrymore, Rosalind Russell, and Jack Oakie for not joining the Screen Actors Guild, now Equity's sister organization. **19** Bette Davis's contract with Warners is declared valid by a British court, preventing her from working for anyone else but Warners. **28** The *London Daily Telegraph* reports that Merle Oberon has confirmed her engagement to David Niven (nothing comes of it).

NOVEMBER • Katharine Hepburn, on the rebound from losing Leland Hayward to Margaret Sullavan, whom he has just married, becomes involved with Howard Hughes. **19** A day after the second unit crew of *A Star Is Born* has filmed background scenes at Huntington Beach for the scene in which Norman Main (Fredric March) kills himself by walking into the sea, the body of actor John Bowers, a sui-

cide, washes up on the beach a mile away. **20** "Dorothy Lamour . . . who is she?" teases Paramount's trade paper ad containing a photo of her in a sarong, hyping *The Jungle Princess*, Lamour's first film. **23** Bette Davis is back on the Warners lot, ready for her next film, *Marked Woman*.

DECEMBER 5 A sailor on the aircraft carrier *Lexington* is arrested for threatening to kill Ginger Rogers unless she paid him $5,000. It's the first of several such incidents involving her. **13** Dave Chasen's Southern Pit Barbecue opens on Beverly Boulevard, specializing in chili. Over the next year it will develop a full menu and evolve into Chasen's restaurant, one of the film community's most popular eating places. **18** The Associated Press reports that the divorce rate in Hollywood is four times the national average.

Bette Davis is at war with Warners throughout 1936. *LC*

in Great Britain and opening at the Roxy today. The ads do not mention the director, not yet widely known in the U.S.: Alfred Hitchcock. **17** William Powell and Carole Lombard, ex-marrieds off the screen, star in the screwball comedy *My Man Godfrey*, opening at the Radio City Music Hall. **23** Samuel Goldwyn's *Dodsworth*, directed by William Wyler and starring Walter Huston, Mary Astor, and Ruth Chatterton, premieres at the Rivoli.

OCTOBER • MGM releases *Every Sunday*, a musical short featuring Deanna Durbin and Judy Garland.

NOVEMBER 19 *The Garden of Allah*, in

Technicolor and starring Marlene Dietrich and Charles Boyer, premieres at the Radio City Music Hall. Dietrich makes the cover of *Newsweek* (Nov. 21) and *Time* (Nov. 30). **25** Tyrone Power, Freddie Bartholomew, Madeleine Carroll, and George Sanders are the stars of *Lloyds of London*, premiering at the Astor.

DECEMBER 31 Sonja Henie makes her screen debut in *One in a Million*, opening at the Roxy.

SEPTEMBER • The Negro Improvement League attacks Warners' *The Green Pastures* as "insulting, degrading and malicious," and has similar criticism for other Hollywood films with racial themes. **16** MGM closes for the day in observance of the funeral of Irving Thalberg, who died two days ago.

NOVEMBER 17 Will H. Hays discusses the issue of morality in films in a private audience with the Pope.

With $1,300,000 compensation from MGM this year, Louis B. Mayer is the highest-salaried man in America. Hollywood unions, flexing their muscles, aim for something more modest. "Sneak Previews," a theater practice on the West Coast for several years, spreads to the East. Gene Autry is the movies' most popular cowboy. Deanna Durbin, Daffy Duck, and the Dead End Kids debut; Jean Harlow dies; Dietrich is through at Paramount; Lana Turner makes a sweater go a long way; and Warners signs an Iowa sports announcer named Reagan. In France, Jean Renoir's antiwar masterpiece, *Grand Illusion*, is released.

- Number of releases: 778
- Number of theaters: 18,192
- Average seating capacity of theaters in large cities: 1,021
- Average run of a feature film: 2 1/2 days
- Average weekly attendance: 85,000,000
- Average ticket price: $.23
- Box office receipts: $676,000,000
- Total industry employment: 294,000
- Louis B. Mayer's compensation from MGM: $1,300,000

Top stars at the box office, based on a Quigley Publications poll of exhibitors:

1. Shirley Temple
2. Clark Gable
3. Robert Taylor
4. Bing Crosby
5. William Powell
6. Jane Withers
7. Fred Astaire and Ginger Rogers
8. Sonja Henie
9. Gary Cooper
10. Myrna Loy

The New York Film Critics Circle Awards
Best Picture: *The Life of Emile Zola*

The Academy Awards (presented March 10, 1938)
Best Picture: *The Life of Emile Zola*
Actor: Spencer Tracy (*Captains Courageous*)
Actress: Louise Rainer (*The Good Earth*)
Supporting Actor: Joseph Schildkraut (*The Life of Emile Zola*)
Supporting Actress: Alice Brady (*In Old Chicago*)
Director: Leo McCarey (*The Awful Truth*)

Gene Autry, America's most popular cowboy LC

January	February	March	April	May	June	
	1 Judy Garland sings "You Made Me Love You" to Clark Gable at his 36th birthday party		**12** Hollywood unions begin to press the studios for collective bargaining and a closed shop			
29 *The Good Earth*		**19** Warren Beatty b.		**31** Ronald Reagan, driving from Des Moines, reaches Hollywood	**9** 10,000 throng Jean Harlow funeral	

July	August	September	October	November	December	
		8 Dustin Hoffman b.	**3** Anthony Quinn m. Katherine DeMille		**21** *Snow White and the Seven Dwarfs*	
7 Mae West forced to acknowledge husband in court suit		**27** Vittorio Mussolini rebuffed on quest for Hollywood production deal		**11** Mervyn LeRoy agrees to leave Warner Bros. for MGM		

Personalities

JANUARY 10   Under the heading "New Juvenile," The *New York Times* reports that 20th Century Fox has signed Tyrone Power to a seven-year contract. **20** "Warner Bros. is considering plans to star Humphrey Bogart," reports *Variety*. But it will be several more years before his name appears above the title. **30** Laurence Olivier is playing *Hamlet* at the Old Vic in London tonight with Michael Redgrave—whose wife has just given birth to daughter, Vanessa—as Laertes. Olivier makes a curtain speech: "Tonight, a lovely new actress has been born. Laertes has a daughter."

FEBRUARY • Independent producer Walter Wanger signs several members of The Group Theater, including Lee J. Cobb and Elia

Kazan. • Filming on Samuel Goldwyn's *Dead End* is scheduled to begin, but has to be put off until May when Sylvia Sidney, the female lead, at Elizabeth Arden to get a beauty treatment, falls against a table, breaking her nose and bruising the rest of her face. **1** Judy Garland sings "You Made Me Love You" to Clark Gable at his thirty-sixth birthday party on the MGM lot. Studio executives like it so much that they will have her sing it to a picture of Gable in *Broadway Melody of 1938* (during the filming of which she will begin to take Benzedrine to suppress her appetite and phenobarbital to come down from the uppers).

MARCH 4   Gable and Lombard and William Powell and Jean Harlow are at the Biltmore Bowl nightclub as couples, part of the audience to see the Academy Awards for 1936—for the first time including Best Supporting Actor and Actress. **20** The *New York Herald-Tribune* reports that "Rita Cansino, young Mexican dancer, has been signed by Columbia Pictures." In fact, the soon-to-be-Rita Hayworth is of Spanish descent.

APRIL 6   Errol Flynn, arriving in Paris from the Spanish Civil War front, says that the bump on his head was caused by falling plaster and not a bullet, as some reports had it. **22** Jack Nicholson is born. His mother is not sure who Jack's father is, and to keep up appearances, the boy will grow up thinking that his grandmother is his mother and that his mother is his sister.

MAY 5   The *New York Times* reports: "Ronald Regan [*sic*], sports announcer and baseball writer for the *Des Moines Register-Tribune*,

Movies

• Process—"special effects"—shots have improved and are more believable, as in *The Hurricane*. They cost less so they can now be used even in low budget films. *Captains Courageous* was almost completely shot on a set, whereas only a few years ago *Mutiny on the Bounty* had to be filmed on location.

JANUARY 13   Cecil B. DeMille's *The Plainsman*, starring Gary Cooper and Jean Arthur, opens at the Paramount. **22** Fifteen-year-old Deanna Durbin makes her feature film debut in *Three Smart Girls*, opening at

Marlene Dietrich   LC

"ravishing" because it suggests the verb "to ravish." • Selznick International Pictures moves onto the RKO-Pathé lot. **2** Nat

the Roxy. **22** Greta Garbo and Robert Taylor star in MGM's *Camille*, opening at the Capitol. **29** *The Good Earth*, starring Paul Muni and Louise Rainer, premieres at Hollywood's Carthay Circle Theater. Rainer, for her portrayal of O-lan, will receive her second consecutive Academy Award for best actress. The movie carries the tribute: "To the memory of Irving Grant Thalberg, we dedicate this picture—his last great achievement." It's Thalberg's first screen credit.

MARCH 3   *Lost Horizon*, directed by Frank Capra and starring Ronald Colman, Sam Jaffe, Jane Wyatt, Edward Everett Horton, and Thomas Mitchell, opens at the Globe.

Business and Society

JANUARY • A Hollywood flu epidemic, peaking in the middle of the month, delays over thirty productions and fells many of the top stars. **6** W. Ray Johnston, having left Republic, announces the revival of Monogram Pictures.

FEBRUARY • The Hays Office tells United Artists not to describe Marlene Dietrich as

Levine quits as president of Republic Pictures, leaving Herbert Yates to run it.

MARCH • By acquiring Warners' sound patent rights, RCA-Photophone completes its domination of movie sound reproduction. **12** *Hollywood Reporter* publisher H. R. Wilkerson advises the studios not to get upset because the new pictorial magazines such as *Life* and *Look* publish old and unusual photographs of stars instead of publicity stills. He explains that the fans

Births, Deaths, Marriages, and Divorces

JANUARY 8   Luise Rainer m. playwright Clifford Odets. **15** Margaret O'Brien (Angela O'Brien) b. **21** Silent screen actress Marie Prevost d. **30** Vanessa Redgrave b.

FEBRUARY 18   Mary Astor m. Manuel Del Campo. **25** Tom Courtenay b.

MARCH 30   Warren Beatty (Henry Beatty), brother of Shirley MacLaine, b.

APRIL 6   Billy Dee Williams b. **9** Arline Judge divorces Wesley Ruggles. **22** Jack Nicholson b. **27** Sandy Dennis b.

MAY 10   George Brent m. Constance Worth. It will last five weeks. **29** Rita Hayworth m. Edward Judson. **30** Martha Raye m. makeup man Bud Westmore.

Rita Hayworth   *LC*

has been signed by the Warners to become an actor." **11** Loretta Young adopts a baby girl, resurrecting speculation about an affair between her and Clark Gable at the beginning of 1935. The girl bears some resemblance to Young and Gable. **15** Peter Lorre has a nervous breakdown from overwork. **20** Western actor Charles Frederick Gebhard petitions Los Angeles Superior Court to change his name legally to the one he uses on the screen: Buck Jones. **28** At the Hollywood Shriners Auditorium, stars out to raise funds for Spanish Civil War aid include James Cagney, Lionel Stander, Frederic March, Sylvia Sidney, and George Gershwin. **31** Ronald Reagan, driving from Des Moines, reaches Hollywood. His Warner Bros. contract goes into effect tomorrow, and in a week he will be working in his first film, *Love Is on the Air*.

Four blocks south in Times Square, Benny Goodman is opening for the first time onstage at the Paramount, with *Maid of Salem* on the screen.

APRIL 10 *Collier's* magazine publishes two short stories from which movies will be made: "Bringing Up Baby" and "Stage to Lordsburg" (*Stagecoach*). **17** The release of Warner Bros.'s *Porky's Duck Hunt* cartoon is the debut of Daffy Duck. **27** David O. Selznick's *A Star Is Born*, starring Janet Gaynor, Fredric March, and Adolphe Menjou, premieres at Grauman's Chinese Theater in Hollywood. It will be remade with Judy Garland and James Mason in

---

find them interesting.

APRIL 12 The Supreme Court's validation of the Wagner Act ignites a drive by Hollywood unions to press the studios for collective bargaining and a closed shop, in which all workers must join the union. **30** The Federated Motion Picture Crafts, an amalgam of local crafts unions not in IATSE, chiefly painters, scenic artists, and makeup people, go on strike for a closed shop.

MAY 3 In inter-union strife, vandals damage Westmore's Salon of Beauty and IATSE headquarters. **7** The Commercial Artists and Designers Union begins what will be a five-month strike against the Fleischer Studio. Issues include a speed-up caused by a big demand for Popeye cartoons, higher salaries, and union recognition. **9** The producers agree to give the Screen Actors Guild a closed shop.

JUNE 1 20th Century Fox reports that its

radio advertising and publicity campaign for *Wake Up and Live* increased revenues by as much as twenty-five percent. Fox becomes the first studio to systematically exploit radio to promote movies. **10** The Federated Motion Picture Crafts strike ends when the striking unions achieve a closed shop.

JULY 14 *Variety* reports that Universal executives have met with Dr. Joseph Goebbels, German propaganda minister, and that he will allow *The Road Back*

JUNE 1 Morgan Freeman b. **3** Joan Bennett and Gene Markey divorce. **7** Jean Harlow d. **16** Jeanette MacDonald m. Gene Raymond, with thousands waiting outside the Wilshire Boulevard Church to see them emerge. Nelson Eddy sings "I Love You Truly." **26** Mary Pickford m. Buddy Rogers.

JULY 10 Ingrid Bergman m. Dr. Peter Lindstrom. **11** Composer George Gershwin d.

AUGUST 8 Dustin Hoffman b. **9** Humphrey Bogart and Mary Phillips divorce. **18** Robert Redford (Charles Robert Redford) b. **22** John Payne and Anne Shirley get married.

SEPTEMBER 4 Miriam Hopkins m. director Anatole Litvak. • Alice Faye m. singer Tony Martin. **21** Cornel Wilde m. Patricia Knight. **28** Martha Raye divorces Bud Westmore.

OCTOBER 3 Anthony Quinn m. Katherine DeMille, daughter of Cecil B. DeMille. **16** Francis Lederer m. actress Margo

Personalities

JUNE 7 Eleven-year-old Norma Jean Mortenson (Marilyn Monroe) leaves the Los Angeles Orphans Home to live again with Grace McKee, her mother's friend. When Grace's husband sexually attacks Norma Jean, she will be sent to live with relatives, where, allegedly, she will be sexually assaulted by her thirteen-year-old cousin, and then sent off to live with other relatives. **9** About ten thousand fans are outside Forest Lawn during Jean Harlow's funeral. At the service, Jeanette MacDonald sings "Indian Love Call," and Nelson Eddy, "Sweet Mystery of Life." William Powell, Harlow's lover, is in a state of near-collapse. Within weeks his health will deteriorate, and he will battle cancer for two years. **10** Despite Jean Harlow's

death, MGM decides to finish *Saratoga*, having already spent $300,000 on it. Mary Dees, Harlow's double, is used to complete her shots. **15** Jane Wyman, overcome when seeing herself in rushes for the first time in a feature at Warners, has a nervous collapse and has to be hospitalized. **17** 20th Century Fox announces that Alice Faye will have the female lead in *In Old Chicago*, which had been set for Jean Harlow. **18** Carole Lombard signs with David O. Selznick for three films a year for three years. **25** "Bob Hope, comedian" has signed to make movies at Paramount, according to the *Hollywood Reporter*.

JULY 1 Dolores Del Rio dives into her pool and saves the life of her two-year-old godchild, Dolores Ellsworth, who has fallen in. **1** "Believing that in James Stewart they have a property comparable to Gary Coo-

per, Metro is to launch him on a new career as one of the screen's strong and silent men," reports the *New York Times*. **7** Mae West, who denied for years that she ever married, is forced to acknowledge her husband in court in a suit that he has filed. Her age—forty-four—also becomes known. **11** The Beverly Hills Tennis Club opens, with Charlie Chaplin and Fred Perry beating Groucho Marx and Ellsworth Vines, 6-3, 9-7. **14** Having won a struggle with MGM over the profits due Irving Thalberg's estate from MGM's films, Norma Shearer signs a new contract with the studio. **22** Barbara Stanwyck, attending a preview with Robert Taylor of *Stella Dallas* at Warners' Hollywood Theater, is mistaken by a policeman for a fan trying to sneak in. He pushes and bruises her. Taylor threatens to punch the cop.

Movies

1954, and Barbra Streisand and Kris Kristofferson in 1976. Much of the bite in the dialogue in this year's version comes from writer Dorothy Parker. When the alcoholic, falling star husband, Norman Maine, played by March, walks into the sea to kill himself at the end, character actor Lionel Stander comments, "First drink of water he's had in twenty years, and then he had to get it by accident."

MAY 11 Spencer Tracy, Freddie Bartholomew, Lionel Barrymore, and Mickey Rooney star

in *Captains Courageous*, opening at the Astor.

JUNE 17 The Marx Brothers, Maureen O'Sullivan, and Margaret Dumont star in *A Day at the Races*, opening at the Capitol.

JULY 14 *They Won't Forget* opens at the Strand. In her first credited role, sixteen-year-old Lana Turner wears a tight sweater, earning her the nickname, "the sweater girl."

AUGUST 5 Barbara Stanwyck is the star of *Stella Dallas*, premiering at the Radio City Music Hall. Its success will generate the popular radio soap opera. Bette Midler will

remake the film in 1990. **11** "Mr." Paul Muni stars in *The Life of Emile Zola*, with Gale Sondergaard and Joseph Schildkraut, premiering at the Hollywood Theater in New York. **24** Samuel Goldwyn's *Dead End*, directed by William Wyler and starring Sylvia Sidney, Joel McCrea, Humphrey Bogart, Claire Trevor, and introducing the "Dead End Kids," (Leo Gorcey, Huntz Hall, Billy Halop, Gabriel Dell, Bobby Jordan, and Bernard Punsley—later "The Bowery Boys" and the "East Side Kids") premieres at the Rivoli.

SEPTEMBER 2 *The Prisoner of Zenda*, starring Ronald Colman, Raymond Massey,

Business and Society

(which premiered at the Globe on June 17), sequel to *All Is Quiet on the Western Front*, to be shown in Germany if the film's criticism of German militarism is deleted. The studio's executives deny meeting with Goebbels, but acknowledge altering the film—to play up the romantic angle, they say. The movie flops anyway.

SEPTEMBER 3 20th Century Fox takes control of New York's Roxy Theater, where it will premiere most of its major films. **25** Several talent agencies, including Charles K. Feldman, combine to form International Artists Corporation. **27** Vittorio Mussolini, son of the Italian dictator, arrives in Hollywood to make a production deal with his host, Hal Roach. But Luise Rainer, Fredric March, and others picket the Roach studio; the deal falls through and only Walt Disney and Gary Cooper want

to talk to young Mussolini.

OCTOBER 13 The five-month strike at the Fleischer cartoon studio ends with recognition of the union, a forty-hour week, and a wage increase. In September 1938, the studio will be moved from New York to Miami, partly to find a more antiunion climate.

NOVEMBER • IATSE official Willie Bioff, thinking that Louis B. Mayer has instigated the current California state investigation

Births, Deaths, Marriages, and Divorces

(Marie Marguerita Guadalupe Teresa Estela Bolado Castilla y O'Donnell)

NOVEMBER 20 Betty Grable m. Jackie Coogan.

DECEMBER 7 George Brent and Constance Worth divorce. **21** Jane Fonda, daughter of Henry Fonda, b. **31** Anthony Hopkins b.

Also this year: • Jane Wyman m. Myron Futterman. • Hedy Lamarr divorces Fritz Mandl.

AUGUST • Vaudeville comedian Red Skelton, in the stage show accompanying *Saratoga* at Loew's State in New York, announces from the stage that he has signed a movie contract with RKO. **20** The *Hollywood Reporter* says that MGM has picked the screen name "Ruth March" for recently signed Ruth Hussey.

SEPTEMBER • MGM classifies eighteen of its younger players as candidates for stardom, including Ilona Massey and Judy Garland. **1** Judy Canova breaks her engagement to Edgar Bergen. **3** Clara Bow opens her "It" cafe on Hollywood's Vine Street. **24** W.C. Fields calls the police twice to his home, claiming that his butler and his secretary, Carlotta Monti, have been arguing violently. But the police find nothing amiss.

SEPTEMBER 30 Greer Garson will soon report to MGM to begin work on a contract, "to which he [sic] was signed by Louis B. Mayer," claims the *Hollywood Reporter*, possibly copying a similar gaffe that appeared in the *New York Herald-Tribune* yesterday.

OCTOBER • Warner Bros.' *Jezebel* goes into production. Bette Davis and director William Wyler will became romantically involved during filming. Co-star Henry Fonda has to leave the set for the birth of daughter Jane. Fonda and Wyler have each been married to Margaret Sullavan, and each is a client of agent Leland Hayward, Sullavan's current husband. On November 4, Hal Wallis, concerned that Wyler seems to be demanding an excessive number of takes from Fonda, will write to Warners' producer Henry Blanke, "Do you think Wyler is mad at Henry Fonda or something

because of their past? . . . by-gones should be by-gones." **4** Hedy Lamarr, just renamed from Hedy Kiesler by MGM, checks into the Chateau Marmont and misspells her new name, "Lamar," in the registry. The *New York Times* will call her "Le Marr" and *Photoplay*, "LaMarr." **30** In Hollywood's first case of criminal plagiarism, a U.S. District Court convicts Groucho and Chico Marx of appropriating without compensation material used on an April 1, 1936 radio show. They will pay $1,000 in fines each plus a total $7,500 in civil penalties.

NOVEMBER 1 The *Saturday Evening Post* prints photos of model Edythe Marrener, soon to become Susan Hayward. **11** Mervyn LeRoy agrees to leave Warner Bros. to produce and direct at MGM. He will bring along teenager Lana Turner, who is under personal contract to him. **17** The *New*

Madeleine Carroll, Mary Astor, David Niven, and C. Aubrey Smith, premieres at the Radio City Music Hall. The theater sells 1,600 standing room tickets for the night's last show and there are 1,200 people still on line when the box office closes. There was a silent film version of *The Prisoner of Zenda*, and it will be remade in 1952 and 1979.

OCTOBER 7 *Stage Door*, directed by Gregory La Cava and starring Katharine Hepburn, Ginger Rogers, Lucille Ball, Eve Arden, Ann Miller, and Adolphe Menjou, opens at the Radio City Music Hall. Hepburn and Rogers, both romantically involved with

Howard Hughes, barely spoke during filming. **29** Pare Lorentz's documentary about the Mississippi, *The River*, premieres in New Orleans.

NOVEMBER 4 Cary Grant and Irene Dunne star in Leo McCarey's *The Awful Truth*, opening at the Radio City Music Hall. **5** Walt Disney releases *The Old Mill*, the first cartoon to use a multiplane camera, which photographs through several layers of celluloid drawings to add a feeling of depth. **9** John Ford's *The Hurricane*, opening at the Rivoli, stars Dorothy Lamour, Jon Hall, Mary Astor, Thomas Mitchell, and Raymond Massey. **25** David O.

Selznick's *Nothing Sacred*, directed by William Wellman and starring Carole Lombard and Fredric March, opens at the Radio City Music Hall. Screenwriter Ben Hecht, a former newspaper man, had no trouble concocting this comedy of the journalistic exploitation of a young woman's poignant—but fake—terminal illness. The Lombard character will be transposed in gender for Jerry Lewis in 1954 for *Living It Up*.

DECEMBER 21 The Hollywood premiere of Walt Disney's *Snow White and the Seven Dwarfs*, the first feature-length cartoon, is attended by, among others, Charlie Chaplin, Marlene Dietrich, and Shirley

---

of labor conditions, threatens Mayer's life. • Pandro Berman replaces Sam Brisken as vice president and production supervisor at RKO. **30** Nate Blumberg is named president of Universal.

Personalities

York Herald-Tribune reports that "Danny Kaye, vaudeville comic, has been signed by Educational Pictures to be featured in two-reel comedies."

DECEMBER 9   Clark Gable and Myrna Loy are crowned King and Queen of Hollywood at the El Capitan Theater. They won a poll conducted by columnist and radio correspondent Ed Sullivan. **12** Mae West's sexual suggestiveness in her "Adam and Eve" radio sketch with Don Ameche on tonight's *Chase and Sanborn Hour* will draw widespread criticism. **22** Paramount, worried about Marlene Dietrich's recent box office flops (*The Garden of Allah*, *Knight without Armour*, and *Angel*), buys out her contract.

Dustin Hoffman, born this year.   LC

Movies

Temple. The film has several catchy songs, including "Whistle While You Work" and "Some Day My Prince Will Come," but the Oscar for the best song this year will go to "Sweet Leilani," from *Waikiki Wedding*.

Business and Society

Births, Deaths, Marriages, and Divorces

*B*ringing Up Baby flops, and Katharine Hepburn is labeled "box office poison." Andy Hardy hits his stride, there's a new Charlie Chan, *Photoplay* causes a scandal with "Unmarried Husbands and Wives of Hollywood," and Vivien Leigh lands the role of the century. But as *The Wizard of Oz* and *Gone With the Wind* go into production, a government lawsuit filed this year threatens the breakup of the studio system, and just around the corner looms television. In the U.S.S.R., Sergei Eisenstein's *Alexander Nevsky* is released.

- Number of releases: 769
- Average number of shooting days per feature film: 22
- Average production cost per feature film: $275,000
- Number of theaters: 18,192
- Average weekly attendance: 85,000,000
- Average ticket price: $.23
- Box office receipts: $663,000,000
- Percentage of studio foreign profits coming from German-controlled markets: 30%
- Claudette Colbert's salary: $150,000 per year
- Ginger Roger's salary: $219,500 per year
- Salary of the dog, "Toto," in *The Wizard of Oz*: $125 a week
- Judy Garland's salary: $500 a week
- Alfred Hitchcock's fee for his first U.S. film: $50,000
- Players with term contracts at major studios: 554

Top stars at the box office, based on a Quigley Publications poll of exhibitors:

1. Shirley Temple
2. Clark Gable
3. Sonja Henie
4. Mickey Rooney
5. Spencer Tracy
6. Robert Taylor
7. Myrna Loy
8. Jane Withers
9. Alice Faye
10. Tyrone Power

The New York Film Critics Circle Awards
Best Picture: *The Citadel*

The Academy Awards (presented February 23, 1939)
Best Picture: *You Can't Take It with You*
Actor: Spencer Tracy (*Boys Town*)
Actress: Bette Davis (*Jezebel*)
Supporting Actor: Walter Brennan (*Kentucky*)
Supporting Actress: Fay Bainter (*Jezebel*)
Director: Frank Capra (*You Can't Take It with You*)

January	February	March	April	May	June	
3 James Cagney to return to Warner Bros.	**14** Hedda Hopper's first Hollywood gossip column	**3** *Bringing Up Baby*	• RKO buys out Howard Hawks's contract	**3** Katharine Hepburn buys out her RKO contract	• Victor Mature discovered at Pasadena Playhouse	

July	August	September	October	November	December	
20 *United States v. Paramount Pictures, Inc., et al.*	**30** *Boys Town* **8** Paramount announces investment in the Dumont television company		**12** *The Wizard of Oz* goes into production.	**17–18** Lana Turner tests for Scarlett O'Hara	**10** Filming begins on *Gone With the Wind*	

Personalities

JANUARY 3 James Cagney agrees to return to Warner Bros., ending his relationship with Grand National. **20** Errol Flynn buys a seventy-five-foot yacht and names it the "Sirocco."

FEBRUARY 3 Burlesque comedians Bud Abbott and Lou Costello reach the big time with an appearance on *The Kate Smith Hour* radio program. And Louella Parsons reports yesterday's signing of Paulette Goddard to a contract by David O. Selznick, "which, of course, only means that she will play Scarlett O'Hara." **13** Sixteen-year-old Linda Darnell arrives in Hollywood to take a screen test at 20th Century Fox. **14** Hedda Hopper's first Hollywood gossip column appears in the *Los Angeles*

Times. **24** *Variety* reports that MGM, which six days ago bought the film rights to *The Wizard of Oz* from Samuel Goldwyn, has cast Judy Garland as Dorothy Gale. Contract player Ray Bolger will play the Tin Woodman; Buddy Ebsen, the Scarecrow. (Bolger sees the Scarecrow offering better dance possibilities, and he and Ebsen will switch over the summer.) **25** Producer Arthur Freed sends a memo to Louis B. Mayer emphasizing that the emotional roots of *The Wizard of Oz* must be laid in the early Kansas sequences with music. The result will be Harold Arlen's "Over the Rainbow." Freed also reminds Mayer: "Get Judy a dog."

MARCH 10 The names of the Academy Awards winners, for the first time, have been kept secret until the presentation— this year at the Biltmore. An imposter ac-

cepts the Best Supporting Actress award for the absent Alice Brady and steals the statuette. The first Irving Thalberg Memorial Award goes to Darryl Zanuck. **17** A Memphis judge fines Western star Ken Maynard $50 for assaulting a woman backstage yesterday at the Memphis Theater. Maynard claims that she's been harrassing him. **17** Greta Garbo denies that she will marry conductor Leopold Stokowski, with whom she has been vacationing in Italy. **29** Warner Bros. suspends Bette Davis for refusing a role in *Comet Over Broadway*. She will stay out for a month until she agrees to return to work in *The Sisters*. She is getting over her affair with William Wyler and the abortion that was a consequence of it.

APRIL • RKO, unhappy with the commercial failure of Howard Hawks's *Bringing Up Baby*,

Movies

JANUARY 6 Alice Faye, starring with Tyrone Power and Don Ameche in *In Old Chicago*, attends the opening at the Astor in New York, wearing a fox cape.

MARCH 3 Howard Hawks's *Bringing Up Baby*, starring Katharine Hepburn and Cary Grant, opening at the Radio City Music Hall, does such poor business that it will be lifted a week early to make room for Bette Davis's *Jezebel*. **4** Republic releases *The Lone Ranger* serial, based on the radio program. The film will engender the King Feature's comic

strip. **9** Paramount's all-star *The Big Broadcast of 1938*, opening at the Paramount, is notable for Bob Hope's feature film debut and his introduction of the song, "Thanks for the Memory." Onstage is Cab Calloway. **10** *Jezebel*, which raises Bette Davis to the rank of top movie star, premieres at the Music Hall in a snowstorm. Also starring are Henry Fonda and George Brent. David O. Selznick has complained to Jack Warner that dialogue in *Jezebel* comes uncomfortably close to that in *Gone with the Wind*.

APRIL 20 *Under Western Skies*, featuring Roy Rogers in his first starring role in a Republic western, is released.

MAY 12 *The Adventures of Robin Hood*, in Technicolor and starring Errol Flynn, Olivia de Havilland, Claude Rains, and Basil Rathbone, premieres at the Radio City Music Hall. At $2 million it is Warner Bros.'s costliest film to date. Alan Hale, who plays Little John, had the same role in Douglas Fairbanks Sr.'s 1922 production. **25** *The Saint in New York* opens, the first of nine B movies, released through 1954, featuring detective Simon Templar, played at various times by Louis Hayward, George Sanders, and Hugh Sinclair.

JUNE 2 *Three Comrades* opens at the Capitol. Starring Robert Taylor, Margaret

Business and Society

JANUARY 27 At the behest of the German Consul in Los Angeles, the Hays Office's Joseph Breen gets MGM to water down *Three Comrades* so that it is not overtly anti-Nazi.

FEBRUARY 4 20th Century Fox bans agent Myron Selznick from its lot because studio executives think his attempts to boost his clients' contract demands are

ruining the industry. He's currently renegotiating Loretta Young's contract. **21** Grand National files for voluntary reorganization.

MARCH • Harry Warner will not permit The March of Time's "Inside Nazi Germany, 1938," to be shown in Warner Bros. theaters. He says it's pro-Nazi. The March of Time counters with endorsements of such people as Rabbi Stephen Wise. **28** San Fernando Valley municipal officials turn down a

request by members of the movie colony, led by Al Jolson, to restrict residence in the area of Studio City, Canoga Park, and Encino to whites only.

APRIL 1 A Federal judge dismisses the Knights of the Ku Klux Klan's patent infringement suit against Warners. The Klan protested the use of their insignia in *The Black Legion*. **19** RCA-NBC begins an experimental period of regular TV program transmissions, five hours a week, from the

Births, Deaths, Marriages, and Divorces

JANUARY 1 Stan Laurel m. Ivanova Shuvalova. **30** Victor Mature m. Frances Evans.

FEBRUARY 10 Louise Brooks and Deering Davis divorce. **13** Oliver Reed b.

24 James Farentino b.

MARCH 28 Arthur Kennedy marries Mary Cheffey.

APRIL 1 Ali MacGraw (Alice MacGraw) b.

MAY 22 Richard Benjamin b.

JUNE 2 Sally Kellerman b. **24** Genevieve Tobin marries director William Keighly.

JULY 10 Jon Hall m. Frances Langford **20** Natalie Wood (Natasha Gurdin) b. **27** Claire Trevor marries Clark Andrews.

buys out the director's contract for $40,000. **11** Twenty-three-year-old Jackie Coogan files a suit against his mother and stepfather to recoup some of the $4,000,000 he earned but never received as a child star. **18** Jackie Coogan's mother tells the court that she kept her son's earnings from him when he came of age because California law permits it and because "Jackie was a bad boy, a very bad 20-year-old boy." **21** A Los Angeles Superior Court ruling requires that at least half of all child star salaries must be placed in a trust fund. The ruling stems from the April 11 Jackie Coogan suit.

MAY 3 Refusing to do *Mother Carey's Chickens*, Katherine Hepburn buys her way out of her RKO contract. Also on this day, the Independent Exhibitors of America take out an ad in the Hollywood trade papers

DOUBLE HORROR SHOW

Dracula　　　　MSN

Frankenstein　　　　MSN

AUGUST 5 The Regina Theater in Los Angeles, on the edge of insolvency, tries a triple feature today: *Dracula*, *Frankenstein*, and *The Son of Kong*. Lines stretch for two blocks, and Bela Lugosi will be brought in for a personal appearance. Universal responds, rereleasing *Frankenstein* and *Dracula* as a double feature.

Sullavan, Franchot Tone, and Robert Young, it is the only film for which F. Scott Fitzgerald, co-screenwriter, ever receives screen credit.

JULY 8 *Marie Antoinette*, Norma Shearer's first film in several years, premieres at the Carthay Circle in Hollywood. Jimmy Stewart, hosting a broadcast from the theater over NBC radio, greets Norma Shearer, Tyrone Power, Clark Gable and Carole Lombard, Barbara Stanwyck and Robert Taylor, John Barrymore, and Hedy Lamarr. Afterwards they will party at the Trocadero. **14** *Algiers* premieres at the Radio City Music Hall. It stars Charles

Boyer and Hedy Lamarr, in her first American film, creating a new fashion fad with her white turban. **21** *Love Finds Andy Hardy*, opening at the Capitol, is one of eight movies Mickey Rooney makes for MGM this year. The Andy Hardy series, of which this is the fourth (but the first with

Andy's name in the title), will by 1958 include sixteen films. This is the first with an A budget, and co-stars teenagers Lana Turner and Judy Garland.

AUGUST 5 *Alexander's Ragtime Band* opens at the Roxy, where Cuban bandleader Desi

Empire State Building. **26** Murray Silverstone, Samuel Goldwyn's choice, becomes operating head of United Artists, replacing banker A. H. Giannini.

MAY 13 Hal Roach sells rights to *Our Gang* comedies to MGM; United Artists will distribute his feature films. **17** Sam Briskin returns to Columbia to head production. **18** Engineers are "amused at radio and film fears of television," reports *Variety*. The technical people say the new

medium is "ill-adapted" to showing movies. **19** Cliff Work moves over from RKO to head Universal, replacing Charles R. Rogers. **31** *The Return of the Scarlet Pimpernel* is the first feature film broadcast on television. NBC's telecast can be seen within a radius of forty miles from mid-Manhattan. According to the *New York Times*, the aim of the test is to see "if pictures of this type are good program material and if such shows will hold the attention of the audience for an hour and

Our Gang　　　　MSN

AUGUST 4 Silent screen serial heroine Pearl White d. **6** Warner Oland, "Charlie Chan," d. **8** Connie Stevens (Concetta Ann Ingolia) b. **13** Sylvia Sidney m. Luther Adler. **15** Johnny Weissmuller and Lupe Velez divorce. **20** Humphrey Bogart m. Mayo Methot. **29** Elliott Gould (Elliott Goldstein) b. **30** Max Factor d.

SEPTEMBER 10 Stewart Granger marries Elspeth March. **19** Pauline Frederick d. **30** Ronald Colman m. Benita Hume. • Keenan Wynn m. Eve Abbott.

OCTOBER 8 Martha Raye m. David Rose.

NOVEMBER 13 Jean Seberg b. **17** Ida Lupino m. Louis Hayward.

DECEMBER • Jane Wyman and Myron Futterman divorce. **6** Bette Davis and Ham Nelson divorce. **18** Karl Malden marries Mona Graham. **24** Vera Zorina m. George Balanchine. **27** Florence Lawrence, "the Biograph girl," the movies' first star, commits suicide. **29** Jon Voight b.

Personalities

naming as "box-office poison" Hepburn and Joan Crawford, Greta Garbo, Marlene Dietrich, and Fred Astaire. **4** Ending a walkout, Gene Autry returns to Republic, agreeing to an exclusive contract in return for a doubling of his former $5,000 per picture.

JUNE • Producer Charles R. Rogers discovers Victor Mature at the Pasadena Playhouse. **1** According to the *Hollywood Reporter*, Bette Davis will play a nun in Warners's *The Miracle*. **10** Hollywood Park—officially, the Hollywood Turf Club—opens. Shareholders include Ernest Lubitsch, Bing Crosby, Darryl Zanuck, and Ronald Colman. Among the horse owners whose steeds are active at the track are Barbara Stanwyck, Chico Marx, and Joe E. Brown.

Movies

Arnaz heads the stage show. Tyrone Power, Alice Faye, Don Ameche, and Ethel Merman star.

AUGUST 18 The premiere of *Four Daughters* at the Radio City Music Hall marks John Garfield's film debut. The *New York Times* calls him "a sweet relief from conventional screen types."

SEPTEMBER 1 Jean Arthur, Lionel Barrymore, and James Stewart star in Frank Capra's *You Can't Take It with You*, premiering at the Radio City Music Hall. **8** Spen-

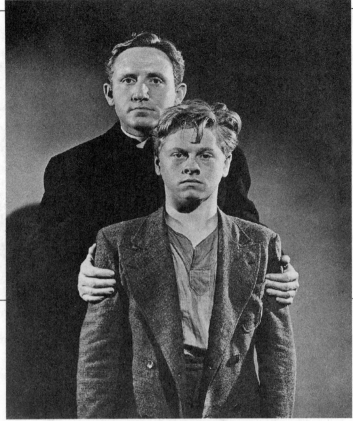

Spencer Tracy and Mickey Rooney in *Boys Town*   MOMA

cer Tracy is Father Flanagan in *Boys Town*, co-starring Mickey Rooney and opening at the Capitol. In 1941 a sequel, *Men of Boys Town*, will be made with the same leads.

OCTOBER 27 MGM's *Young Dr. Kildare*, starring Lew Ayres and Lionel Barrymore and premiering at the Radio City Music Hall, is the first of nine films in the Dr. Kildare series.

Business and Society

a half." **31** Macy's in New York begins to sell television sets.

JUNE • The Motion Picture Democratic Committee is organized by Melvyn Douglas, the first group of movie stars to work for a specific party. They help elect Culbert Olsen governor of California. **14** A group of blacks calls at the Hays

Office, demanding access to parts other than doormen, porters, and maids. **28** Anticipating government action against them for violating the antitrust laws, the heads of all the major studios, accompanied by Will Hays, call on President Roosevelt to suggest that they can regulate themselves better than Washington can.

JULY 5 *Variety* calls "revolutionary" a California theater owner's plans to build a two-auditorium theater, each showing a dif-

ferent film. **18** The Boston City Council unanimously requests that Mayor Tobin ban *Blockade*, a film about the Spanish Civil War, starring Henry Fonda, which the Knights of Columbus calls "leftist propaganda." He will refuse. **20** The U. S. Department of Justice sues the major motion picture companies (*United States v. Paramount Pictures, Inc., et al.*), charging that their domination of both production and distribution—partly through their ownership or control of 2,300 (mostly

Births, Deaths, Marriages, and Divorces

27 Constance Ockelman, now calling herself Connie Keane (not yet Veronica Lake), leaves upstate New York for California. Her promised MGM screen test will not materialize, but she will begin acting school in September.

JULY 7 Director William Wyler, in London to line up the cast for Samuel Goldwyn's production of *Wuthering Heights*, finds Laurence Olivier reluctant to sign on. Wyler discovers a replacement and cables Goldwyn: HAVE FOUND HEATHCLIFF AMAZING YOUNG ENGLISH ACTOR . . .MUCH BETTER THAN OLIVIER. But Goldwyn doesn't want Robert Newton for the role, and eventually Olivier comes around. **14** British director Alfred Hitchcock signs with David O. Selznick to make his first U.S. film, for $50,000. There are also options for four more pictures over a four-year period. **26** Kay

Brown, David O. Selznick story editor, after viewing the foreign version of *Intermezzo*, reports to her boss that Swedish actress Ingrid Bergman is both "absolutely enchanting" and "terribly ugly," depending on which part of the film you're watching.

AUGUST 17 Harry Langdon signs with Hal Roach to replace Stan Laurel as Oliver Hardy's partner. Laurel is being dropped because of a dispute over his contract.

SEPTEMBER 9 Bert Lahr signs to play the Cowardly Lion in *The Wizard of Oz*. **20** Margaret Sullavan, dozing off at poolside, is awakened by her dog barking in time for her to jump in and save her baby daughter, Brooke Hayward, who had fallen in. **22** Frank Morgan is picked to play the Wizard in MGM's *The Wizard of Oz*. **28** Stan Laurel is arrested for drunken driving.

OCTOBER • John Ford begins to film *Stagecoach* in Monument Valley, the first time he has worked there. Walter Wanger is producing the film because David O. Selznick won't touch it unless he can star Gary Cooper and Marlene Dietrich. **1** Bette Davis's new Warners contract, taking effect with *Dark Victory*, raises her to $3,500 per week and cancels the $5,000 in court costs she owed the studio from her 1936 attempt to break her contract. **1** Leo Singer of Singer's Midgets signs a contract to supply MGM with the lion's share of the 124 Munchkins it will need for *The Wizard of Oz*. None can be more than 4½ feet tall. **7** Warners closes the set of *They Made Me a Criminal* to reduce pressure on new star John Garfield, who has been giving six to eight interviews a day. **10** Margaret Hamilton is chosen over Gale Sondergaard for the Wicked Witch in *The Wizard of Oz*.

NOVEMBER 1 Capitalizing on the panic and publicity generated by Orson Welles's Halloween radio broadcast of "The War of the Worlds," Universal rushes into release *Mars Attacks the World* (also known as *The Deadly Ray from Mars*). It's a feature version of the serial *Flash Gordon's Trip to Mars*, with Buster Crabbe. **24** *Angels with Dirty Faces*, starring Humphrey Bogart, Jimmy Cagney, Pat O'Brien, the "Dead End Kids," and Ann Sheridan, premieres at Warners' Hollywood and Downtown Theaters in Los Angeles.

DECEMBER 21 *Blondie* opens at the Criterion, the first of a series of twenty-eight B

pictures, produced through 1950, based on the Chic Young comic strip (begun in 1930). They star Penny Singleton and Arthur Lake. **24** Alfred Hitchcock's *The Lady Vanishes*, starring Michael Redgrave, Margaret Lockwood, Dame Mae Whitty, and Paul Lukas, opens at the Globe.

first-run) theaters of the nation's total of 17,829—is a restraint of trade. **25** Motion picture spokesperson Will Hays asks President Roosevelt to intercede with the Justice Department to stop its antitrust suit against the movie industry. Roosevelt declines to interfere. **28** The Screen Writers Guild wins the certifying election to be the sole bargaining agent for writers at all studios.

AUGUST 2 The first concert devoted exclu-

sively to film music, called "Music of the Cinema," is held at the Hollywood Bowl. **8** Paramount announces its investment of $400,000 in the Allen B. Dumont Laboratories, a television company. **22** James B. Matthews, a former communist, testifies to the House Un-American Activities Committee that Shirley Temple, Clark Gable, James Cagney, Bette Davis, and Miriam Hopkins "unwittingly" serve the cause of communism.

SEPTEMBER 2 Union official William Bioff, accused of corruption, resigns from IATSE. **7** Studio craftsmen file a complaint with the National Labor Relations Board, charging that IATSE official William Bioff took a $100,000 bribe from Joseph Schenck, president of the Association of Motion Picture Producers, to ensure labor peace in the industry. They say that Bioff has been acting on behalf of the producers since July 2, 1936. On September 8, Schenck calls the charges "ridiculous." **22** MGM, in

Personalities

12 MGM's *The Wizard of Oz* goes into production, with Richard Thorpe directing. Of all the major actors in the film, only the dog, Toto, whose salary is $125 a week, is drawing less than Judy Garland's $500 per week. MGM pays Leo Singer $100 per day per Munchkin; he pays them $50. **14** Sidney Toler signs with 20th Century Fox to replace the deceased Warner Oland in the revived Charlie Chan series. He wins out over more than thirty actors tested, including Charles Coburn. **19** Buddy Ebsen is hospitalized, seriously ill from his Tin Woodman makeup on *The Wizard of Oz*. Work on the film can't be held up, and producer Mervyn LeRoy will replace him with Jack Haley. **25** Mervyn LeRoy, unhappy with director Richard Thorpe's work on The *Wizard of Oz*, brings in George Cukor as a temporary replacement. Working for only three days, Cukor has Judy Garland remove her blond wig and act more naturally.

NOVEMBER 3 Victor Fleming begins directing *The Wizard of Oz*. He will stay for four months, until MGM transfers him to *Gone with the Wind*. King Vidor will finish up for him on *The Wizard of Oz*. **5** The *Normandie* sails from Southampton, carrying both Laurence Olivier, headed for Hollywood to film *Wuthering Heights*, and Leslie Howard, bound for the same place, where in two months he will sign to appear in *Gone with the Wind*.

DECEMBER • The January issue of *Photoplay*, on sale now, contains an article that the Screen Actors Guild and the Hays Office deem offensive, perhaps libelous, for its implications of adultery. "Unmarried Husbands and Wives of Hollywood," describes the relationships of Clark Gable and Carole Lombard, Charlie Chaplin and Paulette Goddard, George Brent and Virginia Pine, Robert Taylor and Barbara Stanwyck, and Gilbert Roland and Constance Bennett. In the February issue the magazine will apologize and say that the article was referring only to "friendships." **5** Filming begins in California on *Wuthering Heights*. Within weeks Merle Oberon will complain that she is getting Laurence Olivier's spit in her face when he enunciates. He calls her an "amateur little bitch." **7** Stan Laurel sues Hal Roach for $700,000 for breach of contract. **11** Errol Flynn gets into two fights at a party at the home of Mrs. Jock Whitney. **23** Margaret Hamilton's costume and broom catch fire in the first scene she films for *The Wizard of Oz*, burning the skin on her right hand and singeing off her eyebrows.

Movies

A furious Louis B. Mayer hears that Mickey Rooney, eighteen, and Norma Shearer, thirty-six, have begun an affair. He calls them in and, according to Billy Wilder, who claims to have heard it, lectures Rooney: "You're Andy Hardy! You're the United States! You're a symbol! Behave yourself!" The affair ends.

Business and Society

response to the goverment's anti-trust moves, tells exhibitors they will not have to take the studio's short subjects with its feature films. **26** The Screen Actors Guild agrees to a pact calling for a forty-eight-hour work week. **27** A red-baiting Darryl Zanuck, addressing an American Legion convention, denounces Hollywood's "pink shirts."

OCTOBER 20 George Schaefer is brought over from United Artists by the Rockefellers to replace Leo Spitz as president of the RKO in hopes of boosting the studio's finances.

NOVEMBER 3 William LeBaron succeeds Paramount head Adolph Zukor, who will direct the studio's activities in Great Britain. **29** Leni Riefenstahl, Hitler's personal filmmaker, in Hollywood to publicize *Olympiad*, her movie on the 1936 Olympics, gets the cold shoulder—except from Walt Disney—when she attempts to see major studio executives.

DECEMBER • Warner Bros. submits to the Hays Office the script for *Confessions of a Nazi Spy*, based on a true story of Nazi spying in America. German-controlled markets still account for thirty percent of American movies' foreign profits, so the censors waffle. Warners decides to go ahead with it anyway.

Births, Deaths, Marriages, and Divorces

The Saga of Gone With the Wind

1926

Margaret Mitchell begins to write *Gone With the Wind*, whose lead character is "Pansy" (later Scarlett) O'Hara.

1936

MAY 24 David O. Selznick decides to pass on *Gone With the Wind*, despite urging by his story editor, Kay Brown, to buy it, because he has no one under contract who could play Scarlett.

JULY 30 Margaret Mitchell sells the movie and television rights—Selznick has his eye on the future—to *Gone With the Wind* for $50,000 to David O. Selznick, who has reconsidered his earlier rejection. Warner Bros. passed when Bette Davis was too miffed at her studio to even consider the role of Scarlett. A reader at Universal had recommended the book to her boss, Charles Rogers, but he responded: "I told you no costume pictures." Katharine Hepburn sees herself as Scarlett, but RKO sees it as too expensive. Irving Thalberg advises Louis B. Mayer: "Civil War pictures have never made a dime."

DECEMBER 22 Tallulah Bankhead tests for Scarlett O'Hara.

1937

MARCH 19 The *New York Times* reports "from a source close to the producer" that Miriam Hopkins will play Scarlett O'Hara and Janet Gaynor, Melanie, in *Gone With the Wind*.

DECEMBER 2 Edythe Marrener (Susan Hayward) tests for Scarlett O'Hara.

1938

FEBRUARY 9 Six days ago Louella Parsons reported David O. Selznick's signing of Paulette Goddard, "which, of course, only means that she will play Scarlett O'Hara." Today, Paulette Goddard takes the first of her several screen tests for the role of Scarlett.

JUNE 24 The *New York Times* reports that Norma Shearer will play Scarlett O'Hara.

JULY 31 Norma Shearer says she does not want to play Scarlett O'Hara because her fans think she is too old and ladylike for the role. Shearer jokes: "Scarlett is a thankless role; the one I'd like to play is Rhett."

AUGUST 24 Clark Gable, borrowed from MGM by David O. Selznick, signs to play Rhett Butler in *Gone With the Wind*. Gable is not sure that he can handle the role, given his public's high expectations,

The retreat from Atlanta

MSN

but Carole Lombard (and a bonus from MGM) reassure him. MGM's price for Gable and the co-financing of the film (to the tune of $1.25 million) is high; it will release the movie and get half the profits.

NOVEMBER 17–18 Lana Turner tests for Scarlett O'Hara, with Melvyn Douglas playing Ashley Wilkes.

DECEMBER 10 The filming of *Gone With the Wind* begins tonight on the Selznick lot with the burning of Atlanta, part of which is re-dressed sets from *King Kong* (the wall and gate leading to Kong's domain on Skull Island). Watching is Vivien Leigh, just arrived from London to visit Laurence Olivier (also on the set). She is introduced to David O. Selznick by his brother, Myron, her agent, who tells David that he is meeting his Scarlett. **17** Jean Arthur, who had once had an affair with David O. Selznick, tests for Scarlett O'Hara. **20** Joan Bennett tests for Scarlett. **21–22** Vivien Leigh tests for Scarlett. **25** Director George Cukor, at a Christmas party, tells Vivien Leigh that she will play Scarlett O'Hara in *Gone With the Wind*.

1939

JANUARY 3 JEAN ARTHUR TO BE SCARLETT headlines Hearst's *New York Journal-American*, which, on the basis of "exclusive information," can say that it is "virtually a certainty." **12** Leslie Howard signs to play Ashley Wilkes in *Gone With the Wind*. **13** Vivien Leigh signs to play Scarlett O'Hara. She will earn $30,000. Olivia de Havilland signs to play Melanie. **26** Principal filming begins on *Gone*

With the Wind. **31** Clark Gable is working on the set of *Gone With the Wind* for the first time. There is no great chemistry between him and Vivien Leigh. He thinks she's a bit too intellectual; she thinks he's a little dull and is annoyed by his bad breath, caused by his false teeth.

FEBRUARY 13 Director George Cukor is dismissed from *Gone With the Wind*, partly over conflicts with David O. Selznick at the slow pace of filming and partly at the behest of Clark Gable, who says "I won't be directed by a fairy." Gable appears to have had a sexual encounter with a man—possibly MGM silent star William Haines—some years ago and was recently reminded of it. Neither is the star happy that Cukor is Jewish as well as gay. **14** Victor Fleming, who has been directing *The Wizard of Oz*, replaces George Cukor on *Gone With the Wind*. The macho Fleming is known to be Gable's choice for director.

MAY 26 On the set of *Gone With the Wind*, Clark Gable has to carry Vivien Leigh up the stairs into the darkness to ravish her six times before they get a good take.

JUNE 27 Rhett Butler's farewell to Scarlett O'Hara is filmed. David O. Selznick adds "Frankly" at the last minute to "[Frankly] my dear, I don't give a damn." (Because of the censors, it's also filmed as "I just don't care.") This is the first use of "damn" in a film since 1933. The Hays Office will fine Selznick $5,000 for the word, but will give the film a Production Code seal. With principal photography completed, there's a "wrap" party tonight.

SEPTEMBER 9 At the Fox Theater in Riverside, California, where *Beau Geste* is about to follow its co-feature, *Hawaiian Nights*, the manager announces a sneak preview of a long film he will not identify. Anyone wishing to leave must do so now because the doors will be closed once the picture starts. When Margaret Mitchell's name appears on the screen, the audience breaks into cheers. David O. Selznick, sitting in the rear of the theater, is crying.

DECEMBER 14 At 3:30 P.M., Clark Gable and Carole Lombard land in Atlanta for tomorrow's premiere of *Gone With the Wind*. Along with Vivien Leigh, Olivia de Havilland, Ona Munson, Evelyn Keyes, Ann Rutherford, and Claudette Colbert (not in the cast but along for the ride), they travel in open cars via the Macon Highway to Peachtree Street, passing 300,000 people. Atlanta has begun a three-day public holiday in honor of the picture. **15** At a cocktail party in Atlanta this afternoon, Carole Lombard turns to a shy-looking woman and says: "Clark has been dying to meet you, Miss Mitchell." Tonight the world premiere of *Gone With the Wind* is held at Loew's Grand—the first premiere in which the ceremonies are televised. Six batteries of antiaircraft lights brighten the sky. A black choir, dressed in "plantation garb," according to the *New York Times*, serenades the spectators. When Gable arrives at 8:40, several women faint in the crush as the crowd surges forward. But the biggest cheers are for Margaret Mitchell. **16** GONE WITH THE WIND ENTHRALLS AUDIENCE WITH MAGNIFICENCE, reads the *Atlanta Constitution*'s banner front-page headline. "It is wonderful," begins the review. **19** Celebrities attending *Gone With the Wind*'s dual New York premieres, at the Astor and Capitol, include James Stewart, Olivia de Havilland, Constance Bennett, and Alice Faye. **21** Howard Rushmore quits as film reviewer for the Communist Party's newspaper, the *Daily Worker*, declining to follow the party line and savage *Gone With the Wind* for its glorification of slavery and the old South.

Gone with the Wind Atlanta premiere   MSN

26 President Roosevelt has *Gone With the Wind* screened at the White House. **28** Two blocks of searchlights along San Vicente Boulevard blaze the way to the Hollywood premiere of *Gone With the Wind* at the Carthay Circle, attended by Clark Gable, Carole Lombard, Vivien Leigh, and Laurence Olivier. During the film's run, patrons will complain that, relative to the duration of the intermission, the rest room facilities are insufficient.

1976

NOVEMBER 6 Olivia de Havilland has declined to host tonight's first network TV showing of *Gone With the Wind*—HBO showed the movie on June 11—because the film will be spread over two nights rather than be seen in one viewing. The broadcast is introduced by a voice-over calling it "the most eagerly awaited event in television history."

1977

NOVEMBER • The American Film Institute's poll of movie professionals ranks *Gone With the Wind* the greatest American film, followed by *Citizen Kane, Casablanca, The African Queen,* and *The Grapes of Wrath,* in that order.

1985

Hattie McDaniel and Clark Gable   MSN

MARCH • *Gone With the Wind* is released on video cassette.

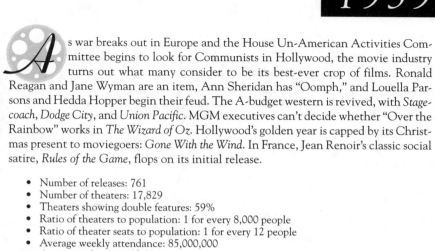

As war breaks out in Europe and the House Un-American Activities Committee begins to look for Communists in Hollywood, the movie industry turns out what many consider to be its best-ever crop of films. Ronald Reagan and Jane Wyman are an item, Ann Sheridan has "Oomph," and Louella Parsons and Hedda Hopper begin their feud. The A-budget western is revived, with *Stagecoach*, *Dodge City*, and *Union Pacific*. MGM executives can't decide whether "Over the Rainbow" works in *The Wizard of Oz*. Hollywood's golden year is capped by its Christmas present to moviegoers: *Gone With the Wind*. In France, Jean Renoir's classic social satire, *Rules of the Game*, flops on its initial release.

- Number of releases: 761
- Number of theaters: 17,829
- Theaters showing double features: 59%
- Ratio of theaters to population: 1 for every 8,000 people
- Ratio of theater seats to population: 1 for every 12 people
- Average weekly attendance: 85,000,000
- Average ticket price: $.23
- Box office receipts: $659,000,000
- Total industry employment: 300,000
- Number of trade and fan publications: 58
- Players with term contracts at major studios: 458
- Number of speaking roles for women in *The Women*: 135
- Running time of *Gone With the Wind*: 3 hours, 40 minutes
- Total number of actresses tested for Scarlett O'Hara (according to the official Selznick studio list): 31

Top stars at the box office, based on a Quigley Publications poll of exhibitors:

1. Mickey Rooney
2. Tyrone Power
3. Spencer Tracy
4. Clark Gable
5. Shirley Temple
6. Bette Davis
7. Alice Faye
8. Errol Flynn
9. James Cagney
10. Sonja Henie

The Harvard Lampoon's first "worst" awards (awarded in 1940):
Worst actor: Tyrone Power (*The Rains Came*)
Worst actress: Norma Shearer (*Idiot's Delight*)

The New York Film Critics Circle Awards
Best Picture: *Wuthering Heights*

The Academy Awards (presented February 29, 1940)
Best Picture: *Gone With the Wind*
Actor: Robert Donat (*Goodbye, Mr. Chips*)
Actress: Vivien Leigh (*Gone With the Wind*)
Supporting Actor: Thomas Mitchell (*Stagecoach*)
Supporting Actress: Hattie McDaniel (*Gone With the Wind*)
Director: Victor Fleming (*Gone With the Wind*)

January	February	March	April	May	June	
		13 Director George Cukor dismissed from *Gone With the Wind*	**11** Joan Crawford divorces Franchot Tone		**14** Barbara Stanwyck m. Robert Taylor	
	13 Vivien Leigh signs to play Scarlett O'Hara	**29** Clark Gable m. Carole Lombard				

July	August	September	October	November	December	
20 Orson Welles arrives in Hollywood to learn how to make movies		• Warner Bros. promotes Ann Sheridan as "The Oomph Girl"		**1** Engagement of Jane Wyman to Ronald Reagan announced		
	15 *The Wizard of Oz*		**29** Hedda Hopper/ Louella Parsons feud begins		**15** *Gone With the Wind*	

Personalities

JANUARY • Bela Lugosi, his career revived by renewed interest in horror films (*The Son of Frankenstein* is hot at the box office), signs again with Universal. **23** George Raft and Paramount agree to part when he refuses to play yet another gigolo, in *The Magnificent Fraud*. **31** George Burns is fined $8,000 and given a one-year suspended sentence on a charge of "smuggling." He could have received eighteen years for buying jewelry from smuggler Albert M. Chaperau. Jack Benny is under indictment for a similar crime.

FEBRUARY 19 "New Ingenue—Gene Tierney" reads the headline on the *New York Herald Tribune*'s drawing of the nineteen-year-old Connecticut debutante, who made her Broadway stage debut on February 8 in *Miss O'Brien Entertains*. The "motion picture companies are trying to lure her to Hollywood," says the paper. **23** The Motion Picture Academy thwarts a surreptitious attempt to broadcast the Academy Awards presentations at the Biltmore. Bette Davis, who like Margaret Sullavan has been nominated for Best Actress, arrives with William Wyler, Sullavan's ex-husband. Davis will win the award, too.

MARCH • The Hays Office objects to the current issue of *Screen Guide* and its article "Deanna Durbin Is a Woman," with its superimposition of her head on someone else's body dressed in a sexy gown. **14** The *Hollywood Reporter* notes Samuel Goldwyn's signing of "Dana Andrews, gas station attendant." **16** Principal filming is finished on *The Wizard of Oz*.

APRIL 4 Jack Benny pleads guilty to buying smuggled jewelry worth over $2,000. He's fined $10,000 and given a suspended year-and-a-day sentence. **8** Stan Laurel settles his dispute with Hal Roach, and he and Oliver Hardy sign a one-year contract to continue with the Roach studio. **13** At an alimony hearing, the estranged wife of Stan Laurel claims he threatened to bury her alive in their backyard. She also claims he invited his first wife on their honeymoon. **20** On the fourth day of filming *Golden Boy*, his first film, William Holden, experiencing a bad case of nerves, leaves the set. Co-star Barbara Stanwyck coaxes him back and restores his confidence. **20** Newly signed Ingrid Bergman arrives in New York to no accompanying publicity, as ordered by David O. Selznick, who fears that Americans are tiring of new foreign stars with puffed-up reputations. He also wants to

Movies

JANUARY 13 Tyrone Power and Henry Fonda star in *Jesse James*, premiering at the Roxy. **26** *Gunga Din*, starring Cary Grant, Victor McLaglen, Douglas Fairbanks Jr., and Sam Jaffe, premieres at the Radio City Music Hall.

FEBRUARY 3 Warners's *Wings of the Navy* premieres in New York, Washington, San Diego, Pensacola, and aboard the USS *Lexington*. The military is approaching stagecenter as the war clouds gather. **11** As part of its "Americanism" program, with which the American Legion cooperates, Warners releases "Lincoln in the White House," a short. Other studios are also picking up this theme in response to the turmoil in Europe.

MARCH 2 John Ford's *Stagecoach*, which finally brings stardom to John Wayne, opens at the Radio City Music Hall. Claire Trevor and Thomas Mitchell also star. **24** Basil Rathbone and Nigel Bruce make their first of fourteen appearances as Sherlock Holmes and Dr. Watson in *The Hound of the Baskervilles*, opening at the Roxy. The first two films are from 20th Century Fox; the rest, through 1946, are from Universal.

APRIL 1 Warner Bros. has transported 350 people by train, including Errol Flynn, Ann Sheridan, and Humphrey Bogart, to Dodge City, Kansas, for today's premiere of *Dodge City*, starring Flynn, Sheridan, and Olivia de Havilland. **13** Samuel Goldwyn's *Wuthering Heights*, directed by William Wyler and starring Laurence Olivier, Merle Oberon, and David Niven, premieres at the Hollywood Pantages. Goldwyn, who wants credit for the film, has seen to it that director Wyler is kept out of the spotlight, and it is Goldwyn who escorts Merle Oberon and Eleanor Roosevelt into the theater. It opens simultaneously at the Rivoli in New York. **20** Bette Davis co-stars for the

Business and Society

JANUARY • The Motion Picture Research Project, funded by the Carnegie Corporation and directed by Leo Rosten, begins a sociological study of Hollywood that will lead to his 1941 book, *Hollywood: The Movie Colony, The Movie Makers*. **3** President Roosevelt's son James begins work as a vice president at the Samuel Goldwyn studio. Goldwyn wants him for his connections and the prestige he lends the studio.

FEBRUARY 1 20th Century Fox's Darryl Zanuck bans radio appearances by Tyrone Power, and on February 21 he will buy up Alice Faye's radio contract to keep her from competing with entertainment offered in theaters. **13** The Supreme Court rules that distributors cannot prevent theaters from showing a film as part of a double feature.

MARCH 19 Violence provoked by intra-union battles breaks out at a meeting of IATSE dissidents at Hollywood Legion Stadium.

APRIL 5 Employees of Loew's theaters are attaching paper panties to the pictures of two infants on ten thousand posters, heralding the phrase "twin features" as a synonym for double features. A Brooklyn judge ordered the cover-up. **21** A trade paper ad urging exhibitors to book the soon-

Births, Deaths, Marriages, and Divorces

JANUARY 2 Robert Walker m. Phyllis Isely (not yet Jennifer Jones) **5** Constance Talmadge divorces Townsend Netcher. **10** Sal Mineo and Yvette Mimieux are born. **19** Nelson Eddy m. Ann Franklin. **24** In one of Hollywood's shortest marriages, Priscilla Lane separates from Orin Haglund, whom she married yesterday.

FEBRUARY 4 Frank Sinatra m. Nancy Barbato. **23** Peter Fonda, son of Henry and brother of Jane Fonda, b.

MARCH 4 Hedy Lamarr m. Gene Markey, ex-husband of Joan Bennett. **7** Clark Gable and Rhea Langham divorce. **26** James Caan b. **29** Clark Gable and Carole Lombard marry. Louella Parsons is hurt because she didn't get the scoop.

APRIL 7 Director Francis Ford Coppola b. **11** Joan Crawford divorces Franchot

change her name because it sounds too German, but she refuses. **26** Conductor Arturo Toscanini is knocked down and almost trampled when one thousand women recognize Spencer Tracy at London's Waterloo train station.

MAY 25 Paramount decides not to renew its option on Betty Grable and drops Donald O'Connor, child actor. **29** David O. Selznick fires William Wyler as director of *Intermezzo* because he's working too slowly. Gregory Ratoff will take over on June 5th.

JUNE • Joan Crawford clicks her knitting needles on the set of *The Women*, disrupting Norma Shearer's attempt to rehearse a scene from the film. Director George Cukor sends Crawford home, and the two stars never speak again. **2** "The Ingrid Bergman

gal must have something," notes the *Hollywood Reporter*, "with everyone talking about her expressive hands and Leslie Howard saying, 'she looks like a sexy virgin.'" **3** Alfred Hitchcock and David O. Selznick have their first confrontation. Selznick is "shocked beyond words" at the director's screen treatment for *Rebecca*, and then proceeds to explain why in a memo of several thousand words. **5** Deanna Durbin signs a new five-year contract with Universal, which will pay her $195,000 a year. **6** Greta Garbo is on a set for the first time in two years as the cameras roll for *Ninotchka*. **10** David O. Selznick, dissatisfied with how cinematographer Harry Stradling is photographing Ingrid Bergman in *Intermezzo*, replaces him with Gregg Toland. **14** The U.S. government requires that Marlene Dietrich, sailing for Europe today, leave behind $100,000

worth of jewelry against the $284,000 in back taxes it says she owes. **15** *Daily Variety* reports that Robert Stack, "USC polo star," will debut in the upcoming Deanna Durbin film, *First Love*. In it, he will give Durbin her first screen kiss.

JULY 5 *Variety*, under the headline "H'wood's New Recruits," reports that "Two strangers to Hollywood, Maureen O'Hara and Edmond O'Brien" will star with Charles Laughton in RKO's *The Hunchback of Notre Dame*. **13** George Raft signs a long-term pact with Warner Bros. **18** After tonight's Los Angeles preview of *The Wizard of Oz*, MGM executives will remove "Over the Rainbow," then put it back, then take it out and put it in again several times before the movie opens. **20** Arriving in Hollywood, Orson Welles registers at the Chateau Marmont, home

seventh time with George Brent—and had an on-set romance with him for the first time— in *Dark Victory*, opening at the Radio City Music Hall. Humphrey Bogart plays a stablehand with what is supposed to be an Irish accent. **25** *Juarez*, starring Paul Muni and Bette Davis, premieres at Warner's Hollywood Theater. **28** *Union Pacific* premieres in Omaha. A Paramount contingent, including Cecil B. DeMille and Barbara Stanwyck, arrived by old-style train yesterday and were driven into town by horse-drawn carriages. **28** Edward G. Robinson stars in *Confessions of a Nazi Spy*, opening at the Strand, accompanied by a stage show with Fred Waring and his Pennsylvanians.

to-be-released *Confessions of a Nazi Spy* proclaims: "It was *Warner's* American Duty to make it! It is your American Privilege to show it!"

MAY 21 The Screen Directors Guild ratifies its pact with the producers, providing for better working conditions and a closed shop.

JUNE 1 With European markets closing, the studios begin a campaign to increase their

"WE'RE OFF TO SEE THE WIZARD"

The Wizard of Oz   MSN

AUGUST 15 *The Wizard of Oz* premieres in Hollywood at Grauman's Chinese Theater. Thousands of spectators watch the arrival of celebrities such as Hedy Lamarr, Wallace Beery, Orson Welles, and Eddie Cantor—but not Judy Garland, who's in a stage show, working her way up the East Coast toward the movie's New York opening on August 17th. **17** *The Wizard*

of Oz opens in New York at Loew's Capitol, with Judy Garland and Mickey Rooney onstage. There are fifteen thousand people in line when the box office opens at 8 A.M. this morning. The theater sells thirty-seven thousand tickets to the seven showings on the first day. Garland will appear live for the run of the film, through September 6.

Tone. **22** Douglas Fairbanks Jr. m. Mary Eppling. **23** Tyrone Power m. Annabella (Ann Carpentier).

MAY 1 Wallace Beery and Rita Gilman divorce, as do Dorothy Lamour and Herbie Kaye. **14** Barbara Stanwyck m. Robert Taylor. **22** Richard Benjamin b.

JUNE 3 Merle Oberon m. director Alexander Korda.

JULY 30 Director Peter Bogdanovich b.

AUGUST 11 Norma Talmadge divorces George Jessel. **12** George Hamilton b. **14** Janet Gaynor m. costume designer

Gilbert Adrian. **20** Joan Fontaine m. Brian Aherne. • Johnny Weissmuller m. Beryl Scott.

SEPTEMBER 1 Lily Tomlin (Mary Jean Tomlin) b. **18** Frankie Avalon (Francis Avallone) b. **24** Universal founder Carl Laemmle d.

Personalities

to many stars, ready to learn how to make movies. **26** Warner Bros. informs Notre Dame that it prefers to use James Cagney and not Pat O'Brien, the University's choice, in *Knute Rockne—All American*, because O'Brien isn't popular enough and starring him would be a "risky gamble." **31** "Ronald Reagan and Jane Wyman holding hands at the Derby, still denying that they're elopmental," gossips the *Hollywood Reporter*.

AUGUST 9 Errol Flynn, boarding a friend's yacht in New York for a trip, discovers someone else in the cabin assigned to him. When Flynn doesn't get a satisfactory explanation for the man's presence, he beats him up. **16** A Los Angeles Superior Court

judge awards Jackie Coogan $126,000 in his suit against his mother and stepfather for the $4,000,000 the actor claims he earned while a minor. **18** David O. Selznick cables Vivien Leigh and Laurence Olivier, advising that he's decided against having Leigh play opposite her husband in *Rebecca*. Olivier will take out his unhappiness on Joan Fontaine, who lands the role. **21** Orson Welles signs a two-film contract with RKO. **23** Louella Parsons breaks the story of the Norma Shearer–George Raft romance.

SEPTEMBER • Warner Bros. promotes Ann Sheridan as "The Oomph Girl." **3** Laurence Olivier, on a yacht off Catalina with David Niven, Douglas Fairbanks Jr., and Vivien Leigh, gets drunk when he hears that Britain is at war. He rows from boat to boat, warning everyone

that they are "Doomed!" **10** Irene Dunne withdraws from the role of Hildy in *His Girl Friday*, Howard Hawks's remake of *The Front Page*, leaving Jean Arthur the favorite for the part. **15** RKO head George Schaefer warns Orson Welles that with the beginning of war and the diminishing of European markets, Welles's plans for an art film based on Joseph Conrad's *Heart of Darkness* will not do. **25** Production begins on Howard Hawks's *His Girl Friday*, with Rosalind Russell in the female lead, a replacement for Jean Arthur, who refused the role and has been suspended by Columbia.

OCTOBER • Lana Turner is the first Hollywood star reported wearing nylons. **17** Bing Crosby, now filming *The Road to Singapore*, the first "Road" film with Bob Hope and Dorothy Lamour, shows up for

Movies

MAY 16 Robert Donat and Greer Garson star in *Goodbye, Mr. Chips*, opening at the Astor. It will be remade in 1969 with Peter O'Toole. **30** Henry Fonda is *Young Mr. Lincoln*, premiering at the Fox-Lincoln Theater in Springfield, Illinois, where Marian Anderson sings before the first showing.

JULY 18 *Beau Geste*, starring Gary Cooper, Ray Milland, Robert Preston, and Brian Donlevy, premieres at the Carthay Circle in Hollywood. NBC broadcasts the arrival

of Cooper, Milland, Cecil B. DeMille, Loretta Young, and David Niven. **28** *The Old Maid*, starring Bette Davis and Miriam Hopkins, who feuded during production, premieres at Warners' Beverly Hills Theater in Beverly Hills.

AUGUST 31 George Cukor's *The Women*, from the Claire Boothe play, premieres in Hollywood at Grauman's Chinese Theater. The cast includes Norma Shearer, Joan Crawford, Rosalind Russell, Joan Fontaine, Paulette Goddard, and Mary Boland. Norma Shearer agreed to waive the clause in her contract forbidding co-star credit to any other actress on her films so that MGM

could give joint billing to Joan Crawford. Shearer did the same for Rosalind Russell, although Russell's name had to appear in a type size smaller than Shearer's.

SEPTEMBER 7 *Golden Boy*, starring William Holden and Barbara Stanwyck, opens at the Radio City Music Hall. Holden is playing the role that John Garfield originated on the stage in the Group Theater's production of this Clifford Odets boxing drama.

OCTOBER 5 David O. Selznick's *Intermezzo* premieres at the Radio City Music Hall, introducing Americans to Ingrid Bergman. Leslie Howard also stars. **10** *Babes in*

Business and Society

film rentals in South America. **6** A Securities and Exchange Commission report says that the studios are making a net profit of 8.3 percent.

AUGUST • James Cagney, Humphrey Bogart, Fredric March, and screenwriter Philip Dunne tell the House Un-American Activities Committee at its San Francisco

hearings that they are not communists. **2** The *New York Times* reports that IATSE executive Willie Bioff had connections to the Al Capone mob. *Daily Variety*'s investigative reporting has turned up much of the information that will now surface about this connection. **14** Special Assistant U. S. Attorney Charles H. Carr begins investigating movie producers' payoffs to union leaders and related income tax liabilities. A prime target is Joseph M. Schenck and 20th Century Fox. **18** The federal

government rejects as still a violation of the antitrust laws a code proposed by the movie industry that would modify its practice of block-booking.

SEPTEMBER 3 All movie houses close in Britain as war brings the threat of enemy attack. They gradually reopen over the next three weeks. By 1941, bombs have knocked out 170 theaters; they will shut a total of 330 by 1945. **3** Alfred Hitchcock reshoots the ending of *Foreign Correspondent*,

Births, Deaths, Marriages, and Divorces

OCTOBER 11 Betty Grable divorces Jackie Coogan. • Miriam Hopkins divorces Anatole Litvak. **12** Douglas Fairbanks d. **27** John Cleese b. **28** Jane Alexander (Jane Quigley) b.

NOVEMBER 13 Lois Weber, the first woman to direct feature films, d.

DECEMBER 13 Fay Wray divorces John Monk Saunders (who will hang himself on March 10).

Also this year: • Randolph Scott and Mariana du Pont Sommerville divorce. • Victor Mature's marriage to Frances Evans is annulled. • Tom Mix and Olive Stokes divorce for the second time.

His Girl Friday, with Cary Grant and Rosalind Russell LC

lunch at Hollywood's Cafe Continental wearing a sarong. **25** Betty Grable signs with 20th Century Fox. **29** Hedda Hopper scoops Louella Parsons on the divorce of James Roosevelt, beginning the feud between the two Hollywood gossip columnists.

NOVEMBER 1 The engagement of Jane Wyman to Ronald Reagan is announced. **6** James Cagney's new contract with Warners raises him from $5,000 to $12,500 per week, but he does not get the script approval he demanded. **18** Louella Parson's stage revue, "Hollywood Stars of 1940 on Parade," with Jane Wyman, Ronald Reagan, and Susan Hayward, begins its national tour in San Francisco.

Arms premieres at Grauman's Chinese Theater. Judy Garland leaves her handprints and footprints in the cement outside, and inside joins Clark Gable, Carole Lombard, Cary Grant, Lana Turner, and Edward G. Robinson to see the first of four Busby Berkeley musicals with Garland and Mickey Rooney. **19** Frank Capra's *Mr. Smith Goes to Washington* premieres at the Radio

City Music Hall. It stars James Stewart, Jean Arthur, Claude Rains, and Edward Arnold.

NOVEMBER 9 "Garbo Laughs" in Ernst Lubitsch's *Ninotchka*, also starring Melvyn Douglas, Ina Claire, and Bela Lugosi, premiering at the Radio City Music Hall. **10** Raoul Walsh's *The Roaring '20s* stars James Cagney and Humphrey Bogart,

opening at the Strand, where the stage show led by Bob Crosby includes ventriloquist Paul Winchell and his dummy, Jerry Mahoney. **23** *Flying Deuces*, starring Laurel and Hardy, opens at the Rialto. **29** *Destry Rides Again*, Marlene Dietrich's comeback film, with James Stewart, premieres at the Rivoli. She introduces the song, "See What the Boys in the Back Room Will Have."

DECEMBER 30 *The Hunchback of Notre Dame*, starring Charles Laughton, Maureen O'Hara, Cedric Hardwicke, and Thomas Mitchell, opens at the Radio City Music Hall.

quickly rewritten by Ben Hecht to include the anticipated bombing of London.

NOVEMBER 2 Grand National files for bankruptcy. **3** House Un-American Activities Committee chairman Martin Dies offers as the reason to continue his committee's work the need to investigate communism in Hollywood.

DECEMBER 8 James Roosevelt, the President's son, is elected president of

Samuel Goldwyn Pictures. **16** Pandro Berman leaves RKO and, in April, will join MGM as a producer.

Warner Bros.' highest weekly salaries, by gender, as of December 1, 1939:	
James Cagney	$12,500
Paul Muni	11,500
Edward G. Robinson	8,500
Bette Davis	$4,000
Olivia de Havilland	1,250
Geraldine Fitzgerald	1,250

*F*acing cash-flow problems, several studios turn to independent producers, who finance their own films, producing them on the studios' lots. A few agents, such as Berg-Allenberg, are beginning to "package" films, putting together creative talent and story material and taking a percentage of the profits. Stereophonic sound and pancake makeup are new, as are Bugs Bunny, Woody Woodpecker, Carmen Miranda, and Hope, Crosby, and Lamour in a "road" movie. Lana Turner marries Artie Shaw on their first date. And hanging over everything is the war abroad.

- Number of releases: 673
- Average production cost of a feature film: $300,000
- Number of theaters: 19,042
- Average weekly attendance: 80,000,000
- Average ticket price: $.24
- Box office receipts: $735,000,000
- Total industry employment: 282,000
- Number of Hollywood correspondents and staff photographers: 395
- Number of "road" films made by Bob Hope, Bing Crosby, and Dorothy Lamour, beginning with this year's *Road to Singapore*: 7
- Most paid this year for screen rights to a Broadway play : $275,000 (*The Man Who Came to Dinner*)
- Most paid for a novel: $150,000 (*For Whom the Bell Tolls*)
- Amount that Katharine Hepburn paid playwright Philip Barry for the screen rights to *The Philadelphia Story*: $25,000
- Amount that MGM pays Katharine Hepburn for the screen rights to *The Philadelphia Story*: $175,000—plus $75,000 for her appearance in the film, in which she has the right to approve the director and her co-stars and supervise the script
- Katharine Hepburn's first choice for the male lead in *The Philadelphia Story*: Spencer Tracy, whom she has never met (he's unavailable)

Top billing in Hollywood films, according to *The Guinness Book of Movie Facts and Feats*:
men: 68%
women: 32%

Top stars at the box office, based on a Quigley Publications poll of exhibitors:

1. Mickey Rooney
2. Spencer Tracy
3. Clark Gable
4. Gene Autry
5. Tyrone Power
6. James Cagney
7. Bing Crosby
8. Wallace Beery
9. Bette Davis
10. Judy Garland

The New York Film Critics Circle Awards
Best Picture: *The Grapes of Wrath*

The Academy Awards (presented February 27, 1941, with the winners' names in sealed envelopes for the first time)
Best Picture: *Rebecca*
Actor: James Stewart (*The Philadelphia Story*)
Actress: Ginger Rogers (*Kitty Foyle*)
Supporting Actor: Walter Brennan (*The Westerner*)
Supporting Actress: Jane Darwell (*The Grapes of Wrath*)
Director: John Ford (*The Grapes of Wrath*)

January	February	March	April	May	June	
	13 Lana Turner m. Artie Shaw on first date		• Laurel and Hardy leave Hal Roach	**16** Lana Turner has "nervous collapse"	**20** Stereophonic sound demonstrated	
	24 *The Grapes of Wrath*					

July	August	September	October	November	December	
	• Germany bans MGM and 20th Century Fox films	**1** Laurence Olivier m. Vivien Leigh	**12** Tom Mix killed in auto accident		**26** *The Philadelphia Story*	
29 Orson Welles starts filming *Citizen Kane*			**20** Consent decree allows studios temporarily to retain theaters			

Personalities

JANUARY 25 Clark Gable signs a new MGM contract, raising him from $4,000 to $7,500 a week. **28** Constance Bennett and Anita Louise are robbed of $33,000 in jewelry in Chicago when their car is forced to the curb and their chauffeur is beaten. **31** Ciro's opens in Hollywood. In February, on a typical Saturday night, Loretta Young, Cesar Romero, Robert Young, Myrna Loy, Joan Bennett, Humphrey Bogart, Joan Crawford, Robert Taylor, Barbara Stanwyck, and Claudette Colbert will be found on its celebrity-populated dance floor.

FEBRUARY 13 Lana Turner marries band leader Artie Shaw on their first date. Betty Grable tells reporters that she received a love letter from him only yesterday. Judy Garland is devastated that the romance she fantasized between herself and Shaw will never be. **29** The winners' names have already appeared in the *Los Angeles Times* by the time the Oscar banquet, the first hosted by Bob Hope, begins tonight at the Cocoanut Grove.

MARCH 1 A New York court approves 20th Century Fox's long-term contract with sixteen-year-old Anne Baxter. **5** Ann Sheridan calls the editors of the *Harvard Lampoon*, who named her the actress "least likely to succeed," "bozos." **27** MGM signs Vincente Minnelli as an advisor for its musicals.

APRIL • Laurel and Hardy leave Hal Roach to work independently. **11** Greta Garbo makes a rare public appearance, at Ciro's. **28** Louella Parsons predicts: "If Lana Turner will behave herself and not go completely berserk she is headed for a top spot in motion pictures."

MAY • Errol Flynn, playing a galley slave, threatens to walk off the set of *The Sea Hawk* when a whip comes too close, pulling off his wig and stinging him. **7** Darryl Zanuck says that twelve-year-old Shirley Temple (the public thinks she's eleven)—now an "aging" star—will probably make no more films for 20th Century Fox. **9** Sterling Hayden, sometime model and twenty-three-year-old captain of a brigantine sailing out of Gloucester, Massachusetts, leaves for Hollywood and work at Paramount Pictures, where he will be billed at first as Stirling Hayden. **9** With long lines just down the street waiting to see *Rebecca* at the Radio City Music Hall, Laurence Olivier opens with Vivien Leigh

Movies

JANUARY 11 Howard Hawks's *His Girl Friday*, a remake of *The Front Page*, starring Cary Grant, Rosalind Russell, and Ralph Bellamy, premieres at the Radio City Music Hall. **19** The Three Stooges's *You Nazty Spy* is released, featuring Moe as a Hitler-like dictator of "Moronica," nine months before the opening of *The Great Dictator*, in which Charlie Chaplin's tyrant rules "Ptomania." **24** John Ford's *The Grapes of Wrath*, starring Henry Fonda, Jane Darwell, and John Carradine, premieres at the Rivoli. **25** Ernst Lubitsch's *The Shop Around the Corner*, starring James Stewart and Margaret Sullavan, opens at the Radio City Music Hall.

FEBRUARY 7 Walt Disney's *Pinocchio* premieres at the Center Theater in Rockefeller Center. **10** The release of MGM's *Puss Gets the Boot* is the debut of the Tom and Jerry characters, although in this film Tom is called Jasper and Jerry remains anonymous.

MARCH 13 *The Road to Singapore*, the first of Bob Hope and Bing Crosby's seven "road" films, co-starring Dorothy Lamour,

Business and Society

JANUARY 8 The Screen Writers Guild forbids members to take ads in Hollywood trade publications because of their red-baiting of the union. **26** A reorganized RKO leaves receivership.

FEBRUARY • House Un-American Activities Committee chairman Martin Dies, in "The Reds in Hollywood" in *Liberty* magazine,

The Grapes of Wrath   MSN

Births, Deaths, Marriages, and Divorces

JANUARY 3 Danny Kaye m. Sylvia Fine. **5** William Powell m. Diana Lewis. **12** Joan Bennett m. producer Walter Wanger. **22** John Hurt b. **26** Ronald Reagan m. Jane Wyman. **29** Laurence Olivier and Jill Esmond divorce.

FEBRUARY 13 Lana Turner m. band leader Artie Shaw.

MARCH 9 Raul Julia b. **10** Chuck Norris b. **13** Ginger Rogers and Lew Ayres divorce. **22** Alice Faye divorces Tony Martin.

APRIL 25 Al Pacino b.

MAY 14 Luise Rainer divorces playwright Clifford Odets. **17** Anita Louise m. producer Buddy Adler. Martha Raye divorces David Rose. **29** Buster Keaton m. Eleanor Norris.

in a stage production of *Romeo and Juliet*. The play is a flop, but the performance of Cornel Wilde, also serving as fencing instructor for the cast, will earn him a Hollywood contract. **16** Lana Turner is hospitalized for a "nervous collapse."

JUNE 5 Mexican artist Diego Rivera, arriving by plane in Los Angeles with Paulette Goddard, tells reporters that she saved his life. Neither will elaborate. (Goddard had been posing for him and warned Rivera when she saw police surrounding his house, allowing him to escape. They apparently were going to blame him for a recent attempt on the life of the exiled Leon Trotsky.) **12** Charlie Chaplin gets a court injunction forcing *Life* to remove a photo of him, dressed as a dictator, from a million copies of the magazine now on the presses. The release of the image, from his upcoming *The*

Great Dictator, was unauthorized. **13** In a review of Columbia's *Babies for Sale*, a B movie, *The Hollywood Reporter* notes that Glenn Ford "is a personable young actor and should go a long way." **20** Radio gossip columnist Jimmy Fidler says he's not pro-Nazi but that the movies should not be used "to rouse people of this country to a blind war fever."

JULY 18 With three years left on his contract, Paul Muni and Warners part company because of conflicts over his choice of roles and desire to change story material, especially on *High Sierra*, which the studio reassigns to Humphrey Bogart. **29** Orson Welles films the first scene of *Citizen Kane*: "News on the March."

AUGUST 26 American newspapers carry British producer Michael Balcon's criticism

of his countrymen who remain safely abroad while Britain is under attack. He singles out Alfred Hitchcock, who, in reply, compares Balcon to Donald Duck. **28** Judy Garland signs a new MGM contract, raising her to $2,000 a week.

SEPTEMBER 5 As shooting begins on *Mr. and Mrs. Smith*, Carole Lombard, teasing Alfred Hitchcock for calling actors "cattle," brings three heifers on the set, each tagged with the name of an actor in the film. **16** John Barrymore preserves his left profile in the cement outside Grauman's Chinese Theater. **18** Hal Wallis urges Jack Warner to bill Ida Lupino's name above Humphrey Bogart's in *High Sierra* because Bogart has been making mostly B movies and his name won't sell the film. Warner agrees. **18** Charles Laughton, in Chicago, is informed that a German dive bomber has

---

opens at the Paramount. Onstage: Tommy Dorsey and his orchestra with vocalist Frank Sinatra. Extra added attraction: Red Skelton. **27** Alfred Hitchcock's *Rebecca*, starring Laurence Olivier, Joan Fontaine, George Sanders, and Judith Anderson, premieres at the Four Star Theater in Los Angeles.

MAY 4 Irene Dunne, Randolph Scott, and producer Leo McCarey are at the Rialto Theater in Louisville, Dunne's hometown, for the premiere of *My Favorite Wife*, also starring Cary Grant. **16** *Waterloo Bridge*, starring Robert Taylor and Vivien Leigh, opens at the Capitol.

JULY 27 Bugs Bunny, who has been evolving through several Warner Bros. cartoons, is fully recognizable for the first time with the release of *A Wild Hare*.

AUGUST 8 Greer Garson, Laurence Olivier, Mary Boland, Edna May Oliver, Maureen O'Sullivan, and Ann Rutherford star in *Pride and Prejudice*, opening at the Radio City Music Hall. **9** With the Battle of Britain beginning, *The Sea Hawk*, about patriotic pirates who save Britain from a foreign foe, opens at the Strand. Directed by Michael Curtiz, it stars Errol Flynn, Flora Robson, Claude Rains, and Brenda Marshall. **10** "Darn That Dream," the first "soundie,"

is copyrighted. Soundies, brief movie musicals played on jukebox-like machines, will be produced through 1946 and then sold as home movies. **14** Preston Sturges's first film as a director, *The Great McGinty*, starring Brian Donlevy, opens at the Paramount, with Cab Calloway and his Cotton Club Orchestra heading the stage show. **27** Alfred Hitchcock's *Foreign Correspondent*, starring Joel McCrea, Laraine Day, and Herbert Marshall, premieres at the Rivoli.

SEPTEMBER 19 In Ft. Worth, Texas, 100,000 see Gary Cooper, Walter Brennan, Bob Hope, Edward Arnold, and George Raft parade by in the rain at the premiere of

---

charges that Communists have powerful positions in the industry. The *Hollywood Reporter* (February 10) and *Variety* (February 21) attack his article. **12** Globe-Mills Productions, which will install jukebox-type machines with small screens in restaurants and bars to play "soundies," three-minute musical films, is launched. James Roosevelt, son of the President, is a partner.

MARCH 1 The Gallup Poll begins a private

survey for RKO of audience reaction to the studio's stars and potential picture titles.

APRIL 3 Max Factor's ad in the *Hollywood Reporter* proclaims: "New! Revolutionary! Never before has there been anything like PAN-CAKE. It makes greasepaint forever obsolete…"

JUNE 1 20th Century Fox has settled its differences with agent Myron Selznick, who was banned from the lot two years ago.

20 Electrical Research Products and Bell Labs demonstrate stereophonic sound to an audience of movie people at Hollywood's Pantages Theater. "Just what commercial value this new, projected sound development has to the picture business is something that hasn't yet been determined," says the *Hollywood Reporter*.

JULY • The Hays Office establishes the Motion Picture Committee Cooperating for National Defense, which fosters production

---

JUNE 20 Charlie Chase d.

JULY 1 Ben Turpin d. **10** Francis Lederer and Margo divorce. **31** Loretta Young m. Thomas Lewis.

AUGUST 3 Martin Sheen (Ramon Estevez) b. **19** Jill St. John (Jill Oppenheimer) b.

SEPTEMBER 1 Laurence Olivier and Vivien Leigh are married. **5** Raquel Welch (Raquel Tejada) b. **11** Director Brian De Palma b. **12** Lana Turner divorces Artie Shaw. **21** David Niven m. Primula Rollo. **27** Hedy Lamarr divorces Gene Markey.

OCTOBER 2 Dean Martin m. Elizabeth MacDonald. **12** Tom Mix is killed in an auto accident.

NOVEMBER 14 Constance Bennett divorces the Marquis de la Falaise de la Coudraye. **27** John Barrymore and Elaine Jacobs divorce. **30** Lucille Ball m. Desi Arnaz.

Personalities

crashed into his London home.

OCTOBER 6　Fifteen-year-old Sidney Lumet, former "Dead End Kid," plays the boy Jesus in Maxwell Anderson's play *Journey to Jerusalem*, opening on Broadway tonight. **31**　The Hollywood Palladium opens with Tommy Dorsey and Frank Sinatra.

NOVEMBER •　Bugsy Siegel, awaiting trial for the Murder, Inc., rubout of Harry (Big Greenie) Greenberg, and supposedly confined to a Los Angeles jail, is seen dining with actress Wendy Barrie and a deputy sheriff at a Wilshire Boulevard restaurant. **10**　Walt Disney agrees to spy on Hollywood subversives for the FBI. **21**　The Hollywood District Attorney's office says

that a cancelled check made out to George Raft was found in the papers of Bugsy Siegel. Raft says it was a repayment of a loan.

DECEMBER 4　Joan Crawford is mobbed when she shops in New York for Christmas presents for her newly adopted daughter, Christina. A reporter, whom the actress has invited along, notes the frequency with which Crawford stops to buy presents for children who come up to her. **12**　On Warners' promotional train trip bound for Santa Fe for the premiere of *The Santa Fe Trail*, Olivia de Havilland has an attack of appendicitis. She's taken off at Albuquerque and flown back to Hollywood. **13**　Unable to resolve their differences, Howard Hughes removes Howard Hawks from *The Outlaw* and will direct it himself. **19**　Mike Romanoff, with the financial

backing of Cary Grant, Jock Whitney, Jack Warner, Robert Benchley, and Darryl Zanuck, opens Romanoff's, which will become a celebrity favorite, on Rodeo Drive in Beverly Hills. **21**　Jane Russell, an "unknown," begins work on Howard Hughes's *The Outlaw*.

Movies

Samuel Goldwyn's *The Westerner*.

OCTOBER 4　Pat O'Brien and Ronald Reagan attend the premiere of *Knute Rockne—All-American* in South Bend, Indiana. Tomorrow they will see a Notre Dame football game, where Kate Smith will sing "God Bless America" at halftime. **15**　Charlie Chaplin's *The Great Dictator*, co-starring Jack Oakie and Paulette Goddard, premieres at the Astor and Capitol theaters. Chaplin is knocked to the ground at the Capitol by the surging crowd.

Then he and Goddard join H.G. Wells, Fannie Hurst, and Charles Laughton inside for the film. **17**　*Down Argentine Way*, opening at the Roxy, is Betty Grable's first Technicolor musical, which catapults her to stardom. It's also Carmen Miranda's U.S. film debut.

NOVEMBER 13　The last reel of Walt Disney's *Fantasia* arrives by air from California four hours before the premiere tonight at the Broadway Theater. It is the first film with stereophonic sound ("Fantasound"), but the process is expensive and will be dropped after the film goes into general release. **22**　*The Letter*, starring Bette Davis, Herbert

Marshall, and Gale Sondergaard, opens at the Strand. The stage show features Ozzie and Harriet Nelson. **25**　Woody Woodpecker debuts with the release of Walter Lanz's Andy Panda cartoon, *Knock Knock*.

DECEMBER 5　*The Thief of Baghdad*, a Technicolor special-effects extravaganza starring Sabu and Conrad Veidt, opens at the Radio City Music Hall. **19**　Abbott and Costello debut, in supporting roles, in *One Night in the Tropics*, opening at the Roxy. **26**　Katharine Hepburn, Cary Grant, and James Stewart star in *The Philadelphia Story*, opening at the Radio City Music Hall.

Business and Society

of shorts backing the defense effort. • Paramount is filming two versions of *Arise, My Love*, about a correspondent in the Spanish Civil War, with Claudette Colbert and Ray Milland. One version goes lightly on the Nazis to make it more marketable in neutral and occupied countries. **1**　A federal tax of \$.02 on theater tickets, to bolster government defense programs, takes effect.

AUGUST 14　Germany bans all MGM films, claiming they are anti-German—and, later in the week, also bans movies from 20th Century Fox—in territory it controls. **20**　Congressman Martin Dies, holding HUAC hearings in San Francisco, clears James Cagney, Irene Dunne, Humphrey Bogart, and Fredric March of involvement with communism.

SEPTEMBER 26　The Screen Writers Guild ratifies its first contract with the producers.

NOVEMBER 1　Studio facilities are placed at the disposal of the government for the making of armed forces training films. **20**　In a consent decree in the government's monopoly case against the movie industry, the studios are temporarily allowed to retain ownership of theaters. The industry is required to screen films in advance for buyers and may sell pictures in blocks of five.

Births, Deaths, Marriages, and Divorces

DECEMBER 1　Richard Pryor b. **28**　Ruby Keeler divorces Al Jolson.

Also this year: • Seventeen-year-old Dorothy Dandridge m. Harold Nicholas, one

of the Nicholas Brothers. • Seventeen-year-old Rhonda Fleming m. Thomas Lane. • Jack Hawkins and Jessica Tandy divorce.

al Wallis renames *Everybody Comes to Rick's*, calling it *Casablanca*. Humphrey Bogart becomes a star, as do Abbott and Costello. Citizen William Randolph Hearst tries to squelch *Citizen Kane*, John Huston's directorial career begins with *The Maltese Falcon*, and the Marx Brothers split up, but Elizabeth Taylor arrives. Shirley Temple is a confused teenager, Broadway chorus girl June Allyson gets her big break, and Katharine Hepburn meets Spencer Tracy. And Hollywood goes to war; the conflict is already beginning to boost movie attendance.

- Number of releases: 598
- Average production cost of a feature film: $330,000
- Number of theaters: 19,750, of which 75 are drive-ins
- Number of theaters showing films released by the War Activities Committee: 12,000
- Average weekly attendance: 85,000,000
- Average ticket price: $.25
- Box office receipts: $809,000,000
- Total industry employment: 193,600
- Players at major studios with term contracts: 545
- Joan Crawford's salary: $195,673 per year
- Bette Davis's salary: $252,333 per year
- Jeanette MacDonald's salary: $300,000 per year
- Sidney Greenstreet's weight while filming *The Maltese Falcon*: 285 pounds
- Number of times *The Maltese Falcon* has been filmed before: twice—in 1931, under the same title, and in 1936 as *Satan Met a Lady*
- Size of William Randolph Hearst's San Simeon estate, model for "Xanadu" in *Citizen Kane*: 240,000 acres, with 50 miles of California coastline

Top stars at the box office, based on a Quigley Publications poll of exhibitors:
1. Mickey Rooney
2. Clark Gable
3. Abbott & Costello
4. Bob Hope
5. Spencer Tracy
6. Gene Autry
7. Gary Cooper
8. Bette Davis
9. James Cagney
10. Judy Garland

The "stars of tomorrow," based on a Quigley Publications poll of exhibitors:
1. Laraine Day
2. Rita Hayworth
3. Ruth Hussey
4. Robert Preston
5. Ronald Reagan
6. John Payne
7. Jeffrey Lynn
8. Ann Rutherford
9. Dennis Morgan
10. Jackie Cooper

The New York Film Critics Circle Awards
Best Picture: *Citizen Kane*

The Academy Awards (presented February 26, 1942)
Best Picture: *How Green Was My Valley*
Actor: Gary Cooper (*Sergeant York*)
Actress: Joan Fontaine (*Suspicion*)
Supporting Actor: Donald Crisp (*How Green Was My Valley*)
Supporting Actress: Mary Astor (*The Great Lie*)
Director: John Ford (*How Green Was My Valley*)

January	February	March	April	May	June	
	8 Nick Nolte b.	**22** James Stewart enlists		**1** *Citizen Kane*		
14 Faye Dunaway b.			**10** Marx Brothers split up		**6** George Raft turns down *The Maltese Falcon*	

July	August	September	October	November	December	
	11 *Life* publishes Rita Hayworth pin-up		**3** *The Maltese Falcon*	• War economy boosts movie attendance		
1 Harpo Marx speaks in summer stock		**9** Senate hearings on Hollywood war propaganda			**7** Paramount baseball team beats LA Nippons	

Personalities

JANUARY 3 The Mocambo opens on the Sunset Strip. **4** Jane Wyman and Ronald Reagan have their first child. Says Reagan: "We were so sure it would be a boy that we haven't got a name for it—I mean for her." They name her Maureen. **23** Danny Kaye, in his Broadway stage debut in *Lady in the Dark*, sings the "Tchaikowsky" song, rattling off the names of fifty Russian composers in forty-three seconds. **26** Editors of the *Harvard Lampoon* designate Miriam Hopkins as their "least desirable companion on a desert island" and Mickey Rooney and Jane Withers as "most objectionable movie children."

FEBRUARY 9 Ronald Reagan's draft notice arrives. Jack Warner will get him a tempo-

Movies

JANUARY 8 Ginger Rogers and Dennis Morgan star in *Kitty Foyle*, opening at the Rivoli. **24** *High Sierra* opens at the Strand. Humphrey Bogart finally becomes a star. Ida Lupino co-stars in this film, directed by Raoul Walsh.

FEBRUARY 13 Abbott and Costello have their first starring roles in *Buck Privates*, opening at Loew's State. **25** Preston Sturges's *The Lady Eve*, starring Barbara Stanwyck, Henry Fonda, and Charles Coburn, opens at the Paramount.

rary deferment. **15** Katharine Hepburn, in an emotional speech in Philadelphia following the final curtain of her national tour of the play *The Philadelphia Story*, cites the drama as a career-saver when "most people considered me a has-been." **27** President Roosevelt addresses the Academy Award ceremonies at the Biltmore via radio, thanking the industry for its defense preparedness work. For the first time, the win-

The famous Marx Brothers announce in April they are splitting up.   *MSN*

ners' names are in sealed envelopes. It's a memorable evening for Carole Landis, whose slip drops to her ankles as she attempts a grand entrance.

MARCH 14 Ann Sheridan ends her six-month strike against Warner Bros., returning to work at the $600 per week she had been earning rather than the $2,000 she wanted. **21** *Look* reports

Business and Society

JANUARY 13 Isolationist Senator Burton K. Wheeler warns Will Hays that Hollywood films are "propaganda for war," and that Congress will act if this doesn't stop.

FEBRUARY 4 Buddy De Sylva becomes Paramount production head, replacing William LeBaron.

MARCH 11 Samuel Goldwyn ends his association with United Artists. He will distribute through RKO.

APRIL 17 20th Century Fox chairman Joseph Schenck is convicted of income tax fraud, for which he will serve four months in prison. **17** The Hays Office asks Universal to make sure that in W.C. Field's *The Great Man* (retitled *Never Give a Sucker an Even Break*), J. Franklin Pangborn not act "in any way suggestive of a 'pansy,'"

although a "fussbudget" would be okay. The censors are also unhappy with Field's line to a lady: "Did you ever gondola?" **24** Joseph Breen resigns as the Hays Office's chief censor.

MAY • The Hays Office grants a seal of approval to Howard Hughes's *The Outlaw*, but specifies that he must submit the film's ads for inspection. **28** Cartoonists strike the Disney studios.

Births, Deaths, Marriages, and Divorces

JANUARY 14 Faye Dunaway b. **17** Dolores Del Rio divorces Cedric Gibbons.

FEBRUARY 8 Nick Nolte b. **12** James Mason m. Pamela Kellino. **19** Edmond O'Brien m. actress Nancy Kelly.

MARCH • Doris Day m. Al Jordan.

APRIL 14 Julie Christie b. **18** Deanna Durbin m. Vaughn Paul. **20** Constance Bennett m. Gilbert Roland. • Ryan O'Neal b.

28 Ann-Margret b. **30** Pioneer director Edwin S. Porter d.

MAY 12 Alice Faye m. bandleader Phil Harris. • Greer Garson divorces Edward Snelson. **21** Gordon McRae m. Sheila Stevens.

that Jackie Cooper and Bonita Granville "are going steady." **22** James Stewart enlists in the Armed Forces. Stewart, who was classified too skinny for military service in November, appealed and was then reclassified 1-A.

APRIL • Among the new contract players at work on the Warners lot is Jackie Gleason. Universal gives nine-year-old Elizabeth Taylor her first movie contract, although the casting director says that "Her eyes are too old, she doesn't have the face of a child." **10** Following the completion of *The Big Store*, the Marx Brothers announce that they are splitting up. **21** Thomas Mitchell, filming *The Devil and Daniel Webster*, suffers a brain concussion when the horse-drawn buggy he's riding in overturns. **23** Shirley Temple, thirteen, who thinks this is her twelfth birthday, is informed that

25 Chester Morris plays the detective in *Meet Boston Blackie*, the first of fourteen in a series of B films extending through 1949, opening at the Rialto.

MARCH 12 Frank Capra's *Meet John Doe* premieres simultaneously in New York and at the Warners Theater in Hollywood, where Capra, Gary Cooper, Barbara Stanwyck, Robert Taylor, and Edward Arnold attend. **21** *The Sea Wolf*, starring Edward G. Robinson, John Garfield, and Ida Lupino, premieres aboard the S.S. *America* off the California coast. At the ceremonies Ronald Reagan introduces Garfield, Mary Astor, and Robinson, who wears an ID badge that

JUNE 23 Joseph Breen becomes general manager and executive vice president in charge of production at RKO.

JULY • Dore Schary becomes an executive producer at MGM. **1** NBC is the first major commercial television station to go on the air, telecasting the Brooklyn Dodgers–Philadelphia Phillies game and a 1935 movie, *Death from a Distance*, a mystery with Lola Lane. **2** In an ad appearing in *Variety* and the *Hollywood Reporter*, Walt

JUNE 1 Gene Tierney m. Count Oleg Cassini. **2** Stacy Keach b. **18** Victor Mature m. Martha Stephenson Kemp, widow of bandleader Hal Kemp.

JULY 13 William Holden m. Brenda Marshall. **28** Judy Garland m. David Rose, former husband of Martha Raye.

her birth certificate was altered when she signed with Fox in 1933 to make her appear even younger than she was. "I don't want you entering your teens without even knowing it," her mother tells her. **26** George Raft and Edward G. Robinson, rehearsing a scene from *Manpower*, get into a fight. A photographer from *Life* captures it, and the photo will make the May 12 issue.

MAY 6 Bob Hope makes his first radio broadcast from a military base: the Army's March Field, in Riverside, California. **12** A witness at a Hollywood trial involving a morals charge identifies the Malibu house of actor Lionel Atwill as the location of an orgy last December. **19** Betty Hutton, down with the measles, can't go on tonight in the Broadway musical *Panama Hattie*. Chorus girl June Allyson, her understudy, has her big chance. A Hollywood

agent will spot her, resulting in a movie career for Allyson. **28** Orson Welles's draft board classifies him "1-B," available for limited service, because of bronchial asthma.

JUNE 8 The first Hollywood "camp show," featuring Laurel and Hardy and Chico Marx, is staged at California's Camp Roberts before twenty thousand soldiers. **10** "The Donna Reed that you will see in MGM's preview of *The Get-Away* today is a young kid that MGM plucked from the USC campus and this is her first picture," advises the *Hollywood Reporter*. **23** Katharine Hepburn signs with MGM to appear in *Woman of the Year*. She has been seeing George Stevens, who will direct the film, but that will soon end. A few weeks ago she was introduced to her co-star, Spencer Tracy.

ORSON WELLES'S MASTERPIECE: CITIZEN KANE

Citizen Kane   MSN

JANUARY 8 William Randolph Hearst instructs his newspapers not to take any ads from RKO in retaliation for its impending release of Orson Welles's *Citizen Kane*. The film is widely understood to be a thinly veiled portrait of Hearst. **9** RKO screens *Citizen Kane* for Hearst columnist Louella Parsons and two people she says are reporters from the Hearst press. Actually, they are Hearst lawyers. Later today, she calls RKO president George Schaefer, demanding that he withdraw the film.

MAY 1 *Citizen Kane*, remarkable for, among many things, Gregg Toland's deep-focus photography, premieres at the RKO Palace (the Radio City Music Hall de-

clined to show it). Director and star Orson Welles, who also co-wrote the screenplay with Herman J. Mankiewicz, attends with Dolores Del Rio. Joseph Cotten and Everett Sloane have featured roles, as well. Reviews of the film have been appearing since March. The *New York Times* tomorrow will say that it "comes close to being the most sensational film ever made in Hollywood." On March 1, Welles threatened to sue both William Randolph Hearst if the press baron was successful in his efforts to have *Citizen Kane* suppressed, and RKO, if it did not finally release it. The picture will lose $160,000 on its initial release. It will go down in film history, however, as one of the best movies of all time.

Personalities

JULY 28 Harpo Marx speaks before an audience for the first time in twenty-five years when he opens as "Banjo" in *The Man Who Came to Dinner*, at the Bucks County Playhouse in Pennsylvania. His first line is: "I can feel the hot blood pounding through your varicose veins."

AUGUST 1 "Ava Gardner, photographer's model of Wilson, North Carolina, has been contracted by MGM," notes the *Hollywood Reporter*. **11** *Life* publishes a photo of Rita Hayworth in a negligee, which will be one of World War II's prime pinups.

SEPTEMBER • In *Modern Screen*'s article "Call Me 'Dutch': Ronnie Reagan Blackens That Boy Scout Reputation of His," Reagan com-

plains that "There's something about the name Ronald that tickets me as a nice boy even before people know me." The magazine notes that Reagan "has never been known to turn down a part." **5** Pat O'Brien and Ralph Bellamy help lifeguards save a drowning man off Del Mar, California. In July, while swimming with Ronald Reagan, O'Brien saved his own daughters from being dragged out by the undertow. **5** B-movie actress Phyllis Walker takes a screen test for David O. Selznick. He finds her name "undistinguished" and will later change it to Jennifer Jones. **21** Errol Flynn, encountering radio columnist Jimmy Fidler at the Mocambo, hits him. Flynn has long been at odds with Fidler.

OCTOBER • George Raft's inability to secure a divorce leads to the end of his romance with Norma Shearer. • Maurice Cheva-

lier, in occupied Paris, says that French-German "collaboration" might be a good idea. There follows a controversy over what he meant by the word. **16** Universal suspends Deanna Durbin for refusing to begin work on *They Lived Alone*. The reason for the dispute is not revealed, although she is said to be upset that her husband of six months, assistant director Vaughn Paul, has not been getting work from the studio.

NOVEMBER 10 Rita Hayworth is on the cover of *Time*, which calls her Fred Astaire's "best" dance partner. **14** Warners' general counsel Roy Obringer writes to Hal Wallis, complaining about the studio's buying B. Traven's *Treasure of the Sierra Madre*. He says "the deal is with some sort of spook in Mexico, as Traven apparently will not sign any documents but wants it all done through a Power of Attorney."

Movies

reads: "Shirley Temple." **28** The first episode of Republic's serial, *The Adventures of Captain Marvel*, is released. It's the first screen appearance of a comic strip or comic book superhero.

MAY 22 Tyrone Power, Rita Hayworth, and Linda Darnell star in *Blood and Sand*, premiering at the Roxy.

JULY 2 *Sergeant York*, starring Gary Cooper, premieres at the Astor Theater in New York. Present are Cooper, Sgt. Alvin York,

Eleanor Roosevelt, General John J. Pershing, Henry Luce, and the head of Selective Service, Gen. Lewis B. Hershey. **23** Carol Reed's *The Stars Look Down*, based on A. J. Cronin's novel about Welsh coal miners, opens at the Criterion. This uncompromising look at lives that are difficult and dangerous, starring Michael Redgrave, Margaret Lockwood, and Emlyn Williams is, according to the *New York Times*, "a film to be remembered in this or any other season."

AUGUST 7 *Here Comes Mr. Jordan*, starring Robert Montgomery and Claude Rains, opens at the Radio City Music Hall.

21 Bette Davis, Herbert Marshall, and Teresa Wright star in *The Little Foxes*, premiering at the Radio City Music Hall.

SEPTEMBER 25 Tyrone Power and Betty Grable are at Grauman's Chinese Theater for the gala premiere of their *A Yank in the R.A.F.* Also on hand are Irving Berlin, Claudette Colbert, Ann Sothern, Victor Mature, Merle Oberon, Pat O'Brien, and Cesar Romero.

OCTOBER 3 *The Maltese Falcon*, "the stuff that dreams are made of," opens at the Strand. John Huston's first film as a director—he "gives promise of becoming one of the smartest directors in the field," says the

Business and Society

Disney suggests that communists are behind the current strike at his studio. **29** The Disney studio strike ends. The Screen Cartoon Guild wins bargaining rights and a pay raise for the animators.

SEPTEMBER 9 A Senate subcommittee investigating Hollywood war propaganda opens hearings in Washington.

OCTOBER 4 David O. Selznick becomes a partner at United Artists.

NOVEMBER • The growth of defense jobs and cutbacks in the production of luxury goods that have become scarce and more expensive begins to bring higher movie attendance. • Bette Davis is the first woman elected president of the Motion Picture Academy of Arts and Sciences. **6** IATSE officials George Browne and Willie Bioff are convicted of extortion.

Browne is sentenced to eight years; Bioff, to ten.

DECEMBER 7 Neighborhood movie business is down by as much as fifty percent on this Sunday as people stay home to hear the radio bulletins about Pearl Harbor. **12** The War Activities Committee (WAC) replaces the Motion Picture Committee Cooperating for National Defense. **18** President Roosevelt names journalist Lowell Mellet to act as liaison to the movie

Births, Deaths, Marriages, and Divorces

SEPTEMBER 21 Joanne Marshall (later Joanne Dru) m. Dick Haymes. **22** Gene Kelly m. Betsy Blair.

OCTOBER 8 Franchot Tone m. Jean Wallace. **25** Rosalind Russell m. producer Frederick Brisson.

DECEMBER • Lena Horne m. musician Lennie Hayton. **9** Beau Bridges (Lloyd Bridges III), son of Lloyd Bridges, b. **31** Bette Davis m. Arthur Farnsworth. • Sarah Miles b.

Also this year: Bruce Lee b. • Lassie b.

DECEMBER 7 The Paramount baseball team is playing the Japanese-American LA Nippons. The bombing of Pearl Harbor is announced in the third inning, but the game continues, with Paramount winning, 6–3. Bob Hope is listening to a football game when he hears the bulletin. Alfred Hitchcock is at Universal, working on storyboards for *Saboteur*. Frank Sinatra, Linda Darnell, and Susan Hayward are at a party at Lana Turner's home. Movietone newsreel cameraman Al Brick is at Pearl Harbor, filming a documentary on the fleet. He gets vivid footage of the Japanese attack, much of which is not shown in theaters because it is too graphic and demoralizing. **11** Stephen Karnot, a reader in the story department at Warner Bros., submits to producer Hal Wallis a one-page synopsis of an unproduced play, *Everybody Comes to Rick's*, suggesting Humphrey Bogart, George Raft, or James Cagney for Rick, and Mary Astor for the female lead in the film version. **21** Col. Darryl Zanuck—commissioned a lieutenant colonel in the U. S. Signal Corps reserve in January—breaks his nose playing polo. **22** The Screen Actors Division of the Hollywood Victory Committee, which will engage in defense and morale-building work, meets at the Beverly Wilshire Hotel. Clark Gable heads the group that will send stars such as his wife, Carole Lombard, on bond drives. **23** Cary Grant donates his salary from *Arsenic and Old Lace* to the American Red Cross, the USO, and British War Relief. **24** Warner Bros. production head Hal Wallis informs his casting director that he's trying to get Irene Dunne, Norma Shearer, or Ginger Rogers interested in starring in *Now, Voyager*, in what will become one of Bette Davis's greatest roles. **31** Hal Wallis notifies all Warner Bros. personnel that *Everybody Comes to Rick's* will now be called *Casablanca*.

New York Times—stars Humphrey Bogart, Mary Astor, Sidney Greenstreet, Peter Lorre, and Elisha Cook Jr. On June 6, George Raft, scheduled by Warners to play Sam Spade, complained to Jack Warner that it's "not an important picture" and he shouldn't have to do it. He was suspended, and the part fell to Bogart, whose name is above the title for the first time. **23** Walt Disney's feature-length cartoon, *Dumbo*, about the baby elephant who can fly, opens at the Broadway Theater. It has pink elephants and a veritable pyramid of pachyderms. **28** John Ford's *How Green Was My Valley* premieres at the Rivoli. It stars Walter Pidgeon, Maureen O'Hara, Roddy McDowall, and Donald Crisp. Pidgeon, Crisp, and Darryl Zanuck attend the gala opening. This second film about coal mining in Wales to open in the U. S. in the last two months—*The Stars Look Down* arrived in July—is a career-maker for young Roddy McDowall.

NOVEMBER 20 Alfred Hitchcock's *Suspicion*, starring Cary Grant, Joan Fontaine, and Nigel Bruce, opens at the Radio City Music Hall. **20** Raoul Walsh's *They Died with Their Boots On*, starring Errol Flynn, Olivia de Havilland, and Arthur Kennedy, opens at the Strand. Woody Herman and his orchestra are onstage.

DECEMBER 5 The release of Columbia's *The Fox and the Grapes* introduces the Fox and the Crow cartoon characters.

industry in the war effort and tells him to minimize censorship. **24** After two months as president of the Motion Picture Academy, Bette Davis resigns because she doesn't have the time or the stamina to handle it. Walter Wanger will replace her.

onald Reagan asks " . . . where's the rest of me?" Carole Lombard dies, and Barbra Streisand is born. The stars are selling War Bonds; Orson Welles's brief, brilliant film career is already getting sidetracked; and many male stars are going off to war. Rationing hits Hollywood, the bright lights are dimmed, Washington proposes censorship, and the question in the air is "Will this picture help win the war?"

- Number of releases: 533
- Average production cost of a feature film: $336,600
- Number of theaters: 20,380, of which 99 are drive-ins
- Average weekly attendance: 85,000,000
- Average ticket price: $.27 (from now through 1953, this figure includes the federal amusement tax)
- Box office receipts: $1,022,000,000
- Total industry employment: 200,000
- Players at major studios with term contracts: 550
- Humphrey Bogart's salary: $114,125
- Abbott & Costello's combined salary: $786,628
- Number of films Katharine Hepburn and Spencer Tracy will make together, beginning with this year's *Woman of the Year*: 9
- Number of times James Cagney will appear on the screen as George M. Cohan: twice—in this year's *Yankee Doodle Dandy* and in 1955 in *The Seven Little Foys*
- Value of war bonds sold at premiere of *Yankee Doodle Dandy*: almost $6,000,000
- Value of war bonds sold by Dorothy Lamour on an eight-week tour: $25,000,000

Top box office stars, based on a Quigley publications poll of exhibitors:

1. Abbott & Costello
2. Clark Gable
3. Gary Cooper
4. Mickey Rooney
5. Bob Hope
6. James Cagney
7. Gene Autry
8. Betty Grable
9. Greer Garson
10. Spencer Tracy

The "stars of tomorrow," based on a Quigley Publications poll of exhibitors:

1. Van Heflin
2. Eddie Bracken
3. Jane Wyman
4. John Carroll
5. Alan Ladd
6. Lynn Bari
7. Nancy Kelly
8. Donna Reed
9. Betty Hutton
10. Teresa Wright

The New York Film Critics Circle Awards
Best Picture: *In Which We Serve*

The Academy Awards (presented March 4, 1943)
Best Picture: *Mrs. Miniver*
Actor: James Cagney (*Yankee Doodle Dandy*)
Actress: Greer Garson (*Mrs. Miniver*)
Supporting Actor: Van Heflin (*Johnny Eager*)
Supporting Actress: Teresa Wright (*Mrs. Miniver*)
Director: William Wyler (*Mrs. Miniver*)

January	February	March	April	May	June	
16 Carole Lombard killed in plane crash	**14** Major Frank Capra on active duty	**30** Lew Ayres's C. O. status causes ruffle	**30** Hollywood Victory Caravan begins fund-raising tour	**13** *This Gun for Hire*	**19** Norma Jean Mortenson (Marilyn Monroe) m. James E. Dougherty	

July	August	September	October	November	December	
1 RKO orders Orson Welles's Mercury Productions off the lot	**12** Private Clark Gable enters army	**19** Frank Sinatra leaves Tommy Dorsey band **3** Hollywood Canteen opens		**26** *Casablanca*	**17** Government's Lowell Mellet calls for censorship	

Personalities

• Model Lauren Bacall is named "Miss Greenwich Village." • Marlene Dietrich, no longer with Erich Maria Remarque, has a new lover: Jean Gabin. Jealous of the bisexual Dietrich's dalliances with Edith Piaf and General James Gavin, he will beat her.

JANUARY 1 Corporal James Stewart is promoted to Second Lieutenant. **1** Dorothy Lamour begins an eight-week tour in which she will sell $25,000,000 worth of war bonds. **12** Carole Lombard leaves Los Angeles by train for a war bond rally in Indianapolis. In a hurry to return to Clark Gable, she will fly back. **17** Hollywood is stunned to learn of the death of Carole Lombard, one of its most beloved figures, in yesterday's plane crash near Las Vegas.

18 Jack Benny, shaken by the death of Carole Lombard, his friend and co-star in *To Be or Not to Be*, does not appear on his Sunday night radio show. **30** Deanna Durbin is reinstated at Universal with the right to approve her directors and stories but not the option she wanted of doing outside work.

FEBRUARY 5 Orson Welles leaves for Brazil to make *It's All True*, a semidocumentary and thus a film intended to be only partly true. **14** Major Frank Capra goes on active duty in the Army Signal Corps. **26** Oscar night at the Biltmore Bowl—a "dinner" rather than a "banquet," toned down because there's a war on—is enlivened by competition between sisters Olivia de Havilland and Joan Fontaine, each nominated for Best Actress. Fontaine wins.

MARCH 4 Joan Fontaine and Hedda Hopper almost come to blows at the Brown Derby over Hopper's bad-mouthing of the star. **17** At a preview of *The Magnificent Ambersons* in Pomona, California, many in the audience laugh inappropriately and leave. Orson Welles intends to direct the re-editing and additional filming from Brazil. **30** *Dr. Kildare's Victory* is pulled from some theaters when the news breaks that star Lew Ayres has been sent to a conscientious-objectors camp. But over the next few days, the controversy ends when the public learns that Ayres has volunteered for noncombatant service.

APRIL 10 "Bogart Replaces Reagan as Lead in 'Casablanca,'" says a *Hollywood Reporter* headline. **19** Ronald Reagan enters the U.S. Army as a Second Lieutenant. **24** Warners signs Ingrid Bergman for

Movies

FEBRUARY 2 *Kings Row*, in which Ronald Reagan asks, ". . . where's the rest of me?" premieres at the Astor. It also stars Ann Sheridan and Robert Cummings. **5** *Woman of the Year*, premiering at the Radio City Music Hall, is the first of nine films starring Katharine Hepburn and Spencer Tracy.

MARCH 5 *The Invaders* (later retitled *49th Parallel*), starring Leslie Howard, Laurence Olivier, Eric Portman, Anton Walbrook, and Raymond Massey, opens at the Capitol. Howard and Olivier address the audi-

Business and Society

JANUARY • Paramount takes over the Fleischer cartoon studio, to which it has lent $1,000,000. • The war brings a growing shortage of male stars, the closing of Santa Anita race track, and a cutback on location shooting because the police don't want anything done that will draw crowds. **5** The Senate subcommittee investigating Hollywood war propaganda is

Spencer Tracy and Katharine Hepburn　　　　　*MSN*

Births, Deaths, Marriages, and Divorces

JANUARY 1 Shelley Winters m. Paul Mayer. **5** George Brent m. Ann Sheridan. **10** Mickey Rooney m. Ava Gardner. **16** Carole Lombard d. **29** Katherine Ross b.

FEBRUARY 2 Edmond O'Brien and Nancy Kelly divorce. **14** Sterling Hayden m. Madeleine Carroll. **19** Anne Shirley divorces John Payne.

MARCH 14 Rita Tushingham b. **15** Alan Ladd m. his agent, Sue Carol. **27** Michael York b. **31** Errol Flynn and Lili Damita divorce.

APRIL 3 Marjorie Daw divorces Myron Selznick. • Marsha Mason b. **5** Richard Widmark m. Jean Hazlewood. **23** Sandra

Casablanca. She's being loaned out by David O. Selznick, who will get Olivia de Havilland in return, for one film. **29** Silent screen star Ramon Novarro is fined for drunken driving in Los Angeles, given a suspended jail term, and has his license temporarily revoked. **30** In Washington, the Hollywood Victory Caravan, an all-star variety show, begins a thirteen-city tour of one-night stands to raise money for the Army and Navy Relief Funds. The group includes Groucho Marx, Claudette Colbert, Laurel and Hardy, Spencer Tracy, Charles Boyer, James Cagney, Pat O'Brien, Merle Oberon, Olivia de Havilland, and Desi Arnaz.

MAY • The *Chicago Tribune*—New York *News* Syndicate picks up Hedda Hopper's column, tripling her circulation to just under 6,000,000 (Louella Parsons has 17,000,000).

16 Katharine Hepburn, appearing in Pittsburgh in a stage production of *Without Love,* breaks a photographer's camera when he takes her picture after saying he wouldn't. **25** Filming on *Casablanca* must begin at Warner Bros. today because Ingrid Bergman will soon have to fulfill

Veronica Lake, *This Gun for Hire*   MSN

other commitments. But the screenplay is not finished. Bergman complains that she will find it hard to give a good performance when she does not know with whom she is really in love, Humphrey Bogart's Rick Blaine or Paul Henreid's Victor Laszlo. MGM contract player Conrad Veidt, who plays Major Strasser, is costing Warner Bros. $5,000 per week, more than they pay anyone else in the film. Max Steiner, who will do the score, argues against the use of "As Time Goes By" because it is too simple. The song, written by Herman Hupfeld, first appeared in a Broadway show called *Everybody's Welcome,* but does not become widely played until the release of this movie. And Bogart is distracted by his deteriorating marriage to Mayo Methot, who threatens to kill him if he gets involved off-screen with Bergman.

ence via phone hookup from London. **6** Ernst Lubitsch's *To Be or Not to Be,* starring Jack Benny and, in her final role, Carole Lombard, opens at the Rivoli. It will be remade in 1983. **21** *Secret Agent of Japan,* the first film to incorporate Pearl Harbor into its plot, starring Preston Foster and Lynn Bari, opens at the Globe.

MAY 7 Alfred Hitchcock's *Saboteur,* starring Robert Cummings, Prisiclla Lane, and Otto Kruger, opens at the Radio City Music Hall. **13** *This Gun for Hire* opens at the Paramount, making a major star of Alan Ladd and boosting the career of Veronica Lake. Woody Herman and the Ink Spots

head the stage show. **29** The price of admission to the premiere of *Yankee Doodle Dandy* at the Hollywood Theater in New York is purchase of a war bond, with almost $6,000,000 worth sold. James Cagney is at one of his own premieres for the first time.

JUNE 4 *Mrs. Miniver* premieres at the Radio City Music Hall, where it will play for a record ten weeks before giving way to *Bambi.* It stars Walter Pidgeon and Greer Garson, whose romance with Richard Ney, who plays her son in the film, threatens a publicity disaster. Louis B. Mayer made her promise not to marry him before the film's release.

JULY 1 Without director Orson Welles seeing the final print, *The Magnificent Ambersons* premieres in Hollywood. It stars Joseph Cotten, Tim Holt, Dolores Costello, and Agnes Moorehead. In general release, RKO will distribute it as the lower half of a double feature with *Mexican Spitfire Sees a*

dissolved. **14** Warners announces that Hal Wallis has stepped down as production supervisor to head his own production unit.

FEBRUARY 5 The Treasury Department begins to censor all films entering or leaving the U.S. under the 1917 "Trading With The Enemy Act." **8** Gen. Lewis B. Hershey, director of Selective Service, declares the movies to be an "essential" activity and permits draft boards to defer movie personnel when they cannot be replaced. **9** The Screen Actors Guild Board of Directors rejects the idea of special draft treatment for actors.

APRIL • Nelson Poynter heads the new Hollywood Office of the Office of War Information Motion Picture Bureau. "Will this picture help win the war?" will be its guiding slogan. **9** Spyros Skouras becomes president of 20th Century Fox, replacing Sidney Kent, who died on March

19. Wendell Willkie becomes chairman of the board. **29** Times Square movie marquees are blacked out.

MAY 6 The War Production Board sets a $5,000 ceiling on new construction for each film, encouraging greater use of process shots and miniatures. It hurts independent producers the most because, unlike the studios, they do not have a stockpile of material and equipment. **7** Charles W. Koerner replaces Joseph Breen as head of

Dee (Alexandra Zuck) b. **24** Barbra Streisand b.

MAY 16 Van Heflin marries Frances Neal. **29** John Barrymore d.

JUNE 1 Myrna Loy divorces Arthur Hornblow Jr. **4** Charlie Chaplin and

Paulette Goddard divorce. **6** Myrna Loy m. John D. Hertz Jr. **12** Frances Farmer and Leif Erickson divorce. **19** Norma Jean Mortenson (Marilyn Monroe) m. James E. Dougherty

JULY 1 Karen Black (Karen Ziegler) b. **8** Cary Grant m. Barbara Hutton.

13 Harrison Ford b. **17** Lana Turner m. Stephan Crane. **21** Joan Crawford m. Phillip Terry at midnight. **23** Mae West and Frank Wallace divorce.

AUGUST 23 Fay Wray m. screenwriter Robert Riskin.

Personalities

JUNE • Bob Hope completes a ten-week, fifty-thousand-mile tour of 100 army camps, during which he entertained two million members of the armed forces. **10** Warners clarifies the status of Lieut. Ronald Reagan who, according to the studio, is on "detached service with the Army Air Corps at Burbank, California." **18** Joseph Breen of the Hays Office cautions Warner Bros. not even to hint in *Casablanca* that Rick and Ilsa had a sexual relationship in Paris. **19** Norma Jean Mortenson (Marilyn Monroe) marries James E. Dougherty at the behest of her guardian, Sadie McKee, who is moving away and would otherwise have to return the sixteen-year-old to the Los Angeles Orphans Home. **26** Cary Grant becomes an American citizen.

JULY 1 RKO head Charles Koerner orders Orson Welles's Mercury Productions to vacate its offices on the lot and disclaims any further responsibility for the mounting debts Welles is piling up in Brazil while filming *It's All True*. **17** "It's torrid romance between 17-year-old Donald O'Connor and 15-year-old Gloria Jean," gossips the *Hollywood Reporter*. **26** Gene Autry is sworn in as a member of the Army Air Corps on the air on his radio program.

AUGUST 8 Universal removes director Jean Renoir from the latest Deanna Durbin film, *Forever Yours*, becuse he's working too slowly. **12** Refusing an immediate commission, Clark Gable enters the army as a private and is assigned to the Army Air Force Officer's Candidate School, where, on August 17, he will shave off his moustache. **19** Orson Welles returns to the U.S. from Brazil. **22** Norma Shearer holds a press conference to announce a rare prenuptial property agreement with her fiancé, Martin Arrouge. **24** Henry Fonda enlists in the Navy; Tyrone Power, in the Marines.

HOLLYWOOD IS A WAR PLANT!

In a memo to officers in the Army's Film Production Section, Major Frank Capra writes: "This is total war, fought with every conceivable weapon. Your weapon is film! Your bombs are ideas! Hollywood is a war plant!"

August 8, 1942

Movies

Ghost. **15** Samuel Goldwyn's *Pride of the Yankees*, with Gary Cooper as Lou Gehrig, opens simultaneously in forty New York neighborhood theaters and at the Astor, all on a reserved-seat basis for this one day. Babe Ruth attends at the Astor.

AUGUST 4 *Holiday Inn*, in which Bing Crosby introduces Irving Berlin's "White Christmas" and Fred Astaire co-stars, premieres at the Paramount. The song is not an immediate hit. In fact, many moviegoers are more partial to the film's "Be Careful, It's My Heart." But requests over Armed Forces Radio will build the popularity of "White Christmas" and in the next decade, Crosby's recording will sell nine million copies. **13** Walt Disney's *Bambi* premieres at the Radio City Music Hall. **29** Proceeds from tonight's premiere of *The Talk of the Town* in Hollywood at the Four Star Theater and dinner-dance at Ciro's go toward The Hollywood Canteen. The film stars Ronald Colman, Jean Arthur, and Cary Grant.

SEPTEMBER 1 *Wake Island*, Hollywood's first major World War II film, starring Brian Donlevy, William Bendix, and Robert Preston, premieres at the Rivoli.

OCTOBER 16 Mighty Mouse debuts with the release of Terrytoon's *The Mouse of Tomorrow*. **21** *For Me and My Gal*, starring Judy Garland, with her name above the title for the first time, and Gene Kelly, in his film debut, opens at the Astor. It contains a scene in which Kelly intentionally injures his hand to avoid the World War I draft. **22** Bette Davis, Paul Henreid, and Claude Rains star in *Now, Voyager*, opening at the Hollywood Theater in New York.

NOVEMBER 11 The Bob Hope-Bing Crosby-Dorothy Lamour *Road to Morocco* is rushed into the Paramount for today's

Business and Society

production at RKO. Breen will return to the Hays Office.

JUNE • Wartime cloth rationing is applied to movie costumes (historical pictures excepted): no pleats or cuffed trousers. **25** Peter Rathvon becomes president of the parent company of RKO Pictures.

AUGUST 20 The entire Pacific Coast is ordered dimmed out: no more klieg-lit Hollywood premieres. **30** 20th Century Fox announces that Col. Darryl Zanuck will take a leave of absence to devote full-time to the Army Signal Corps. William Goetz will fill in while he's away.

SEPTEMBER 17 The War Production Board reduces film stock use by each studio by about twenty-five percent. **27** The film industry dedicates The Motion Picture Relief Fund Country House for indigent, aged, and infirm movie personnel.

OCTOBER • Movie theaters run scrap drives for the war effort, rewarding contributions with free passes.

NOVEMBER • Studio founder William Fox begins to serve a one-year prison sentence for trying to bribe a judge in a bankruptcy case.

Births, Deaths, Marriages, and Divorces

SEPTEMBER 27 Hume Cronyn m. Jessica Tandy. **29** Madeleine Kahn b.

OCTOBER • Gregory Peck m. Greta Konen. **13** Pamela Tiffin b. **22** Annette Funicello b. **26** Bob Hoskins b.

NOVEMBER 17 Director Martin Scorsese b. **30** Buck Jones dies of burns sustained in the Cocoanut Grove fire in Boston two days ago.

DECEMBER 14 Mary Astor divorces Manuel Del Campo.

Also this year: • Dan Dailey m. Elizabeth Hofert. • Rex Harrison and Collette Thomas divorce, as do Betty Furness and Johnny Green.

SEPTEMBER 19 Frank Sinatra leaves the Tommy Dorsey band. Legend has it that gangster Willie Moretti held a gun to Dorsey's head to convince him to let the singer out of his contract—source material for *The Godfather*, the novel on which the 1972 film will be based. **22** Paul Robeson says he won't make another Hollywood film until there are roles for blacks besides "plantation hallelujah shouters."

OCTOBER 3 The Hollywood Canteen opens on Cahuenga, near Sunset. John Garfield and Bette Davis initiated the project, in which service personnel mingle with Hollywood's elite—all volunteers. Duke Ellington, Kay Kyser, and Rudy Vallee are on the bandstand tonight. In shifts of several hundred at a time, service personnel rub elbows with Eddie Cantor, Abbott and Costello, Marlene Dietrich, Greer Garson, and many

others. **15** Lionel Atwill pleads guilty to perjury and receives five years probation for lying to a grand jury when he said that "lewd" films were not shown at his house. Atwill called them travelogues, but others present identified them as "The Plumber's Daughter" and "The Daisy Chain." **19** Frances Farmer, on her way to a party at Deanna Durbin's house, is stopped in Santa Monica for driving through a wartime dimout area with her lights on. She left her license home and gets nasty with the policeman, who arrests her. The judge imposes a fine. **28** Clark Gable has earned his commission today as a Second Lieutenant.

NOVEMBER 11 George Raft buys out his Warner Bros. contract. **28** A fire at Boston's Cocoanut Grove nightclub kills several New England film distributors and fatally injures Buck Jones (he dies Novem-

ber 30), who is being honored there with a testimonial dinner.

DECEMBER 19–20 Warner Bros. executives caution Bette Davis and Miriam Hopkins on the set of *Old Acquaintance* to stop their feuding, a carryover from their clashes while making *The Old Maid* in 1939. Davis and Gig Young, also in the film, are having an affair.

CASABLANCA HURRIED INTO RELEASE

NOVEMBER 26 Warner Bros. hurries *Casablanca* into the Hollywood Theater in Manhattan to exploit the prominence of North Africa in the war news. It stars Humphrey Bogart, Ingrid Bergman, Claude Rains, Sidney Greenstreet, Paul Henreid, Conrad Veidt, Dooley Wilson, and Peter Lorre. The studio has no inkling of the film's future status, and advertises it as part of a joint ad with Errol Flynn's *Gentlemen Jim*, also debuting today. *Casablanca* will enter general release in January, coinciding with a meeting in Casablanca of Roosevelt, Churchill, and de Gaulle. Photos courtesy MOMA / © Warner Brothers.

opening to take advantage of publicity generated by the landing of Allied troops in North Africa four days ago.

DECEMBER 3 *You Were Never Lovelier*, starring Fred Astaire and Rita Hayworth, opens at the Radio City Music Hall. **17** *Random Harvest* premieres at the Radio City Music Hall, where it does even better than *Mrs. Miniver*, playing for eleven weeks. Ronald Colman and Greer Garson star. **23** Noel Coward's *In Which We Serve*, David Lean's directing debut, starring Coward, John Mills, and Celia Johnson, opens at the Capitol.

DECEMBER 1 Gas rationing begins on the West Coast, curbing the use of location shots. **17** Studio heads receive a letter from Lowell Mellet asking to see scripts and rough cuts of films in advance so that his office may "recommend the deletion of any material which may be harmful to the war effort." Initially, movie executives are very unhappy with this de facto censorship.

mericans are spending on movies more than $.25 out of every dollar they devote to recreation. Never again will movies take so large a slice of the pie. 20th Century Fox begins to distribute—mostly to servicemen—the first of five million pin-up shots of Betty Grable. Batman makes his first screen appearance, and Elizabeth Taylor begins her MGM career, as Joan Crawford leaves the studio. Roy Rogers supplants Gene Autry as the movies' most popular cowboy.

- Number of releases: 427
- Average production cost of a feature film: $395,000
- Number of theaters: 20,293, of which 97 are drive-ins
- Theaters showing War Activities Committee films: 16,463
- Scrap metal collected at theaters for the War effort: 1,000 tons
- Average weekly attendance: 85,000,000
- Average ticket price: $.29
- Box office receipts: $1,275,000,000
- Industry employment: 204,000
- Players with term contracts at major studios: 725
- Elizabeth Taylor's salary: $100 a week
- Industry personnel in the Armed Forces: 36,500
- Artists participating in Hollywood Victory Committee events: 1,562
- Third War Loan bond sales by the movie industry: $1,909,889,196
- Theaters in U.S. Army camps: 1,158, charging $.15 admission
- Real first name of Tuesday Weld, born this year: Susan

Top stars at the box office, based on a Quigley Publications poll of exhibitors:

1. Betty Grable
2. Bob Hope
3. Abbott & Costello
4. Bing Crosby
5. Gary Cooper
6. Greer Garson
7. Humphrey Bogart
8. James Cagney
9. Mickey Rooney
10. Clark Gable

The "stars of tomorrow," based on a Quigley Publications poll:

1. William Bendix
2. Philip Dorn
3. Susan Peters
4. Donald O'Connor
5. Anne Baxter
6. Van Johnson
7. Gene Kelly
8. Diana Barrymore
9. Gig Young
10. Alexis Smith

The New York Film Critics Circle Awards
Best Picture: *Watch on the Rhine*

The Golden Globe Awards
Best Picture: *The Song of Bernadette*

The Academy Awards (presented March 2, 1944)
Best Picture: *Casablanca*
Actor: Paul Lukas (*Watch on the Rhine*)
Actress: Jennifer Jones (*The Song of Bernadette*)
Supporting Actor: Charles Coburn (*The More the Merrier*)
Supporting Actress: Katina Paxinou (*For Whom the Bell Tolls*)
Director: Michael Curtiz (*Casablanca*)

January	February	March	April	May	June	
5 Elizabeth Taylor signs first long-term MGM contract	**20** Studios agree to informal censorship	**30** Van Johnson in near-fatal auto accident • Howard Hughes suspends Jane Russell			**27** *Cabin in the Sky* **29** Joan Crawford buys out MGM contract	

July	August	September	October	November	December	
	10 Bob Hope begins first war zone tour **14** *For Whom the Bell Tolls*	**7** Rita Hayworth m. Orson Welles	**4** Capt. Clark Gable awarded Air Medal	**2** Kirk Douglas m. Diana Dill	**31** *Destination Tokyo*	

Personalities

JANUARY 3 Fire all but destroys Bing Crosby's North Hollywood home. **5** Elizabeth Taylor signs her first long-term MGM contract, starting her at $100 a week. **14** The Hollywood Democratic Committee is launched to carry on the work of the now moribund Motion Picture Democratic Committee. Activists include Edward G. Robinson, James Cagney, Eddie Cantor, and Orson Welles. **14** Francis Farmer this morning slaps a hairdresser on the set, dislocating her jaw. Later in the day the actress, who hasn't paid her fine for her October 19 arrest, is arrested again; and, when she refuses to get dressed, the officers forcibly dress her and take her to jail, where she will create a commotion and be placed under psychiatric observation. **20** A Los

Frances Farmer is placed in a sanitorium in January.   *LC*

Angeles judge orders Francis Farmer placed in a sanitorium—where she will be given electroshock therapy—because of her bizarre behavior.

FEBRUARY • Model Lauren Bacall appears in *Harper's Bazaar*. Howard Hawks's wife will spot her, leading to a screen test for Bacall. **6** Errol Flynn is acquitted on charges of the statutory rape of two teenage girls. **15** Betty Grable leaves the imprint of one of her legs in the cement outside Grauman's Chinese Theater.

MARCH • With only two films to her credit, Betty Hutton is already getting 4,000 fan letters per week, many from servicemen. **3** Lou Costello, diagnosed with rheumatic fever, will be away from the cameras for almost a year. **4** Carole Landis, back from entertaining servicemen in North

Movies

JANUARY 12 Joseph Cotten, who co-stars with Teresa Wright in Alfred Hitchcock's *Shadow of a Doubt*, is at the Rivoli for its premiere. **14** *Hitler's Children*, with Bonita Granville and Tim Holt, premiering in Cincinnati, turns out to be the sleeper of the year for RKO. **28** Paramount's *Star-Spangled Rhythm* opens in Hollywood. It is the first of the World War II all-star, plotless, patriotic entertainments.

FEBRUARY 4 Howard Hawks's *Air Force*, starring John Garfield, Gig Young, and

Arthur Kennedy, opens at the Hollywood Theater in New York. **5** *The Outlaw* premieres at the Geary Theater in San Francisco. Howard Hughes flies the Hollywood press corps up to see it.

MARCH 20 The Droopy Dog cartoon character debuts with the release of MGM's *Dumb Hounded*.

APRIL 29 Warner Bros. previews *Mission to Moscow* at Washington's Earle Theater for congressmen, diplomats, and journalists, who acclaim this sugary view of our ally, Joseph Stalin, and his purge trials. With no irony, the *Hollywood Reporter*, which will

be a leading force in the post-war Red scare and witch hunt, proclaims the occasion "a red letter day in Washington for the motion picture industry." Critic James Agee will term the film "canned borscht."

MAY 8 William Wellman's *The Ox-Bow Incident*, starring Henry Fonda, Anthony Quinn, and Dana Andrews, opens at the Rivoli. **13** Frank Capra's *Prelude to War*, the first in the government's "Why We Fight" series, is theatrically released. **13** George Stevens's *The More the Merrier*, starring Jean Arthur, Joel McCrea, and Charles Coburn, premieres at the Radio City Music Hall. **27** *Cabin in the Sky*,

Business and Society

FEBRUARY 20 Studio executives agree to the informal censorship proposed in December by Lowell Mellet of the Office of War Information.

MARCH • With war movies proliferating, government limits on the use of textiles causes

a shortage of Nazi uniforms in Hollywood.

APRIL • MGM is the first studio to start a victory garden, growing vegetables on two acres in Culver City. **3** The U.S. Senate's Truman Committee, investigating the military commissions that have been given to Frank Capra, Hal Roach, Arthur Loew, and Anatole Litvak — the so-called "Hollywood Colonels" — today focuses on

Col. Darryl Zanuck. "Why don't you send him to school and make a real officer out of him?" Sen. Harry Truman challenges the Army. **5** Paramount informs its players that because of textile shortages, they will not, as is usually the case, be permitted to buy the costumes they wear in their films. **19** MGM announces the completion of its seven air raid shelters, capable of holding 6,000 people. **25** Will Hays tells

Births, Deaths, Marriages, and Divorces

JANUARY 5 Ann Sheridan divorces George Brent. **16** Ginger Rogers m. Jack Briggs. **25** Rex Harrison m. Lilli Palmer.

FEBRUARY 4 Lana Turner, pregnant with daughter Cheryl, gets an annulment of her marriage to Stephan Crane on the grounds

that his divorce was not final when they wed. **9** Joe Pesci b. **10** Victor Mature and Martha Kemp divorce.

MARCH 3 Evelyn Keyes m. director Charles Vidor. Lynn Redgrave, daughter of Michael and sister of Vanessa Redgrave, b.

31 Christopher Walken b.

APRIL 3 Conrad Veidt d. **18** Linda Darnell m. cinematographer Peverell Marley. **24** Jane Russell m. football player Bob Waterfield.

MAY 21 Ava Gardner divorces Mickey Rooney. **23** Ann Sothern m. Robert Sterling. **27** Hedy Lamarr m. John Loder.

Africa with Martha Raye, Kay Francis, and Mitzi Mayfair, says that the boys were "starved for civilization," so she wore a sweater onstage. They will portray their experiences in the 1944 film *Four Jills in a Jeep*. **4** Privates Tyrone Power and Alan Ladd troop the colors at the Cocoanut Grove to open the Academy Awards ceremonies. **11** After a head-on collision in Beverly Hills with a car driven by the wife of Ira Gershwin, Joseph Mankiewicz is charged with drunken driving. The Hearst press, unhappy with his co-authorship of the screenplay for *Citizen Kane*, plays up the incident. **30** Van Johnson is in critical condition after a near-fatal auto accident in which Keenan Wynn is also shaken up.

APRIL • Jane Russell walks out on her personal-services contract with Howard

Hughes, who suspends her for two years. • Learning that MGM is not going to make its $750,000 war bond quota this month, Norma Shearer buys $100,000 worth to put Metro over the top. **23** A judge in Hollywood allows Lionel Atwill to change his plea of guilty of showing lewd films to not guilty, and then dismisses the case, freeing him from probation. **26** A *Hollywood Reporter* headline announces: "Peck Gets Starring Role in First Film." The working title of Gregory Peck's debut vehicle, "This Is Russia," will be changed to *Days of Glory*.

MAY 31 Col. Darryl Zanuck, at his request, is placed on inactive duty.

JUNE 2 Tyrone Power is commissioned a second lieutenant in the Marines. **7** Teenager Peter Lawford signs his first MGM contract. **10** Judy Garland turns

twenty-one, and having gotten over a brief romance with Tyrone Power, is about to fall in love with Joseph Mankiewicz. **11** Sabu joins the U.S. Army. Universal slates Turhan Bey to replace him in the films he's been making with Jon Hall and Maria Montez. **27** Fire guts Ciro's. **29** Joan Crawford agrees to pay MGM $100,000 to release her from her contract, and on July 1 she signs with Warner Bros.

JULY 14 James Stewart is promoted to Captain.

AUGUST • In *Photoplay* this month: "Breakup—The Truth About Rita Hayworth and Victor Mature." • Louis B. Mayer, enraged that writer Joseph L. Mankiewicz has been having an affair with Judy Garland, assigns his contract to 20th Century Fox. **10** Bob Hope, in his first

Cabin in the Sky   MOMA

producers to keep "zoot suits" out of the movies.

MAY 7 Joseph Schenck, out of prison, re-

Vincente Minnelli's first film as director, opening at the Criterion, stars Ethel Waters, Lena Horne, Eddie "Rochester" Anderson, and Louis Armstrong.

JULY 14 Gary Cooper, Ingrid Bergman, and Katina Paxinou star in *For Whom the Bell Tolls*, premiering at the Rivoli. **16** Columbia releases *Batman*, the serial, the character's first screen appearance. **21** *Stormy Weather* has a joint premiere at the Roxy and the Alhambra Theater in Harlem. It stars Lena Horne, Bill "Bojangles" Robinson, Cab Calloway, and Fats Waller. **28** Warners' all-star *This Is the Army* debuts at the Hollywood

joins 20th Century Fox as a top studio executive. **11** The War Production Board replaces the $5,000-per-picture limit on set construction with quarterly allocations, which studios may apply as they wish.

JUNE 23 The War Shipping Administration announces that it will use Warners' *Action in the North Atlantic* as a merchant marine training film. **30** The Senate cuts funds

Theater in New York in the first klieg-lit premiere since the war began. Jeeps and anti-aircraft guns are on display in Times Square. Irving Berlin, Kate Smith, Al Jolson, and Jack Warner attend.

SEPTEMBER 15 Bert Brecht and Thomas Mann attend the Hollywood premiere of *Watch on the Rhine*, starring Bette Davis and Paul Henried, at Warners' Hollywood Theater.

OCTOBER 7 *Lassie Come Home*, the first Lassie film, premieres at the Radio City Music Hall. The ads feature stars Roddy McDowall, Donald Crisp, Dame Mae

to the Office of War Information's film bureau, severely limiting its activities. **30** William Goetz and Leo Spitz announce the formation of International Pictures.

JULY • The wartime manpower shortage forces the Radio City Music Hall to hire its first female ushers. **6** Darryl Zanuck returns to 20th Century Fox.

JUNE 2 Leslie Howard dies in a plane crash. **15** Malcolm McDowell b. **16** Charlie Chaplin m. Oona O'Neill, daughter of playwright Eugene O'Neill.

JULY 5 Betty Grable m. trumpeter Harry James. **13** Maria Montez m. Jean-Pierre Aumont. **24** Greer Garson m. Richard Ney, who played her son in *Mrs. Miniver*. **25** Lana Turner remarries Stephan Crane.

BOB HOPE ON VERONICA'S HAIRSTYLE

Star Spangled Rhythm has plenty of topical allusions to Paramount's stars. In one exchange, the peekaboo hair style of a prominent leading lady is the butt of a joke:

Victor Moore: "I'm putting on a show for the sailors tonight and I wanted to get you to help me out."

Bob Hope: "Oh, I can't make it tonight. No, not tonight. Veronica Lake's going to show me her other eye tonight."

Personalities

war zone tour, arrives in Algiers.

SEPTEMBER • A trade paper ad for *So Proudly We Hail* states: "Watch for Sonny Tufts, Paramount's sensational new Star find—a great man in a fight or in love—...especially in the clinches!" Tufts is one of many men studios are promoting to replace their male stars who are in the service. **2** Francis Farmer is released from a sanitorium in her mother's custody. But, in the next eight years, she will spend most of her time back in such institutions and in trouble with the police. **5** NBC radio gossiper Jimmy Fidler apologizes on the air to Gene Tierney for saying in a broadcast last November that she smokes cigars. 20th Century Fox has held its contract employ-

ees off the network until the retraction. **7** The stars of the Hollywood Bond Caravan, including Greer Garson, Fred Astaire, Olivia de Havilland, Judy Garland, Dick Powell, and Mickey Rooney, arrive in Washington to begin a fifteen-city tour. **8** Wartime factory production helps to create the first bad smog day in Los Angeles, forcing the movement of some exterior shots for *Since You Went Away* indoors. Jennifer Jones's eyes have been tearing, but for another reason: strain from having to play love scenes with Robert Walker, her estranged husband. **12** Gossip columnist Jimmy Fidler denounces the Army's practice of keeping actors out of combat.

OCTOBER • Tallulah Bankhead endears herself to the crew of Alfred Hitchcock's *Lifeboat*, now filming, when she stops wearing underwear. The cast has to climb a ladder

to get into the boat, which is in a tank. **4** The Army Air Force announces that Captain Clark Gable has been awarded the Air Medal for his five combat missions.

NOVEMBER 4 Lou Costello's year-old son drowns in the family pool. Costello, who was set to return to his radio program tonight for the first time since he took ill last spring, decides to go on. At the end of the show, Bud Abbott tells the audience what happened and pays tribute to his partner's courage. **30** Jack Warner threatens to sue Hal Wallis if he doesn't stop claiming total producer's credit for *This Is the Army* and several other films on which Warner says he did most of the work.

DECEMBER • *Photoplay* proclaims Cheryl Crane, Lana Turner's infant daughter, "Hollywood's Newest Pin-up Girl."

Movies

Whitty, Edmund Gwenn, and the dog (a male playing a female), but do not mention Elizabeth Taylor, in her MGM debut.

NOVEMBER 4 Samuel Goldwyn's *The North Star*, starring Dana Andrews, Ann Baxter, and Walter Huston, premieres at the Palace and Victoria theaters. *Life* calls this celebration of Soviet bravery the "Movie of the Year." **10** *Guadalcanal Diary* premieres at Grauman's Chinese Theater, with William Bendix, Lloyd Nolan, and Richard Jaeckel (in his screen debut) from

the cast present, as well as D.W. Griffith and Mary Pickford.

DECEMBER 15 In the most gala Hollywood premiere since Pearl Harbor, *Madame Curie*, starring Greer Garson and Walter Pidgeon, debuts at Grauman's Chinese Theater. Arc lights again search the sky, heralding the arrival of Garson, Claudette Colbert, Judy Garland, Lana Turner, George Raft, Hedy Lamarr, Cary Grant, Loretta Young, Jack Benny, Irene Dunne, Charles Boyer, Paulette Goddard, Dorothy Lamour, and many more. **31** Cary Grant and John Garfield star in *Destination Tokyo*, opening at the Strand in New

York, where Charlie Barnet and his orchestra head the stage show.

Business and Society

AUGUST 13 Olivia de Havilland, claiming that her contract has run out, refuses to report to Warners for another film and is suspended. **23** After six suspensions (the latest on August 13), Olivia de Havilland asks the Superior Court of California to terminate her seven-year contract

with Warner Bros. She bases her suit on the state's antipeonage laws, limiting contracted employment to seven years. With her suspensions added on, she says, she's over the limit.

SEPTEMBER 8 In thousands of theaters this evening films are interrupted for the live broadcast of President Roosevelt's war bond appeal.

NOVEMBER 1 The marquee lights go back on in Hollywood, but restrictions keep them slightly dimmed. **5** Dore Schary, who has risen from writer to executive producer at MGM, quits to freelance.

DECEMBER 13 The War Production Board stipulates that to conserve fuel, marquee lights should be dimmed by 10 P.M.

Births, Deaths, Marriages, and Divorces

AUGUST • Errol Flynn m. Nora Eddington, a courthouse worker he met while on trial for statutory rape. **17** Robert DeNiro b. **27** Tuesday Weld (Susan Weld) b.

SEPTEMBER 7 Rita Hayworth, who divorced Edward Judson earlier this year, m. Orson

Welles. **30** Mickey Rooney m. Betty Jane Rase.

OCTOBER 24 Glenn Ford and Eleanor Powell marry.

NOVEMBER 2 Kirk Douglas m. Diana Dill.

DECEMBER 2 Jane Greer m. Rudy Vallee. **5** Dinah Shore m. George Montgomery. **14** Deanna Durbin and Vaughn Paul divorce. **31** Ben Kingsley (Krishna Banji) b.

Also this year: • Doris Day and Al Jordon divorce.

*T*he government renews its anti-monopoly case against the studios, and a Los Angeles court frees Olivia de Havilland from her Warners' contract, breaking the power of studios to control players indefinitely by adding on suspension time to a contract's term. Meanwhile, some stars, such as Bing Crosby and Fred MacMurray, are forming their own production companies to decrease their tax bite. Danny Kaye and Lauren Bacall make their film debuts, but *Our Gang* comedies end. And Charlie Chaplin fights a paternity suit and indictment under the Mann Act.

- Number of releases: 442
- Average number of shooting days per feature film: 31
- Number of theaters: 20,375, of which 96 are drive-ins
- Average weekly attendance: 85,000,000
- Average ticket price: $.32
- Box office receipts: $1,341,000,000
- Average production cost per feature film: $462,150
- Players with term contracts at major studios: 800

Top stars at the box office, based on a Quigley publications poll of exhibitors:
1. Bing Crosby
2. Gary Cooper
3. Bob Hope
4. Betty Grable
5. Spencer Tracy
6. Greer Garson
7. Humphrey Bogart
8. Abbott & Costello
9. Cary Grant
10. Bette Davis

The "stars of tomorrow," based on a Quigley Publications poll of exhibitors:
1. Sonny Tufts
2. James Craig
3. Gloria DeHaven
4. Roddy McDowall
5. June Allyson
6. Barry Fitzgerald
7. Marsha Hunt
8. Sydney Greenstreet
9. Turhan Bey
10. Helmut Dantine

The New York Film Critics Circle Awards
Best Picture: *Going My Way*

The Golden Globe Awards
Best Picture: *Going My Way*

The Academy Awards (presented March 15, 1945)
Best Picture: *Going My Way*
Actor: Bing Crosby (*Going My Way*)
Actress: Ingrid Bergman (*Gaslight*)
Supporting Actor: Barry Fitzgerald (*Going My Way*)
Supporting Actress: Ethel Barrymore (*None but the Lonely Heart*)
Director: Leo McCarey (*Going My Way*)

January	February	March	April	May	June	
15 Irene Dunne christens Liberty Ship S. S. *Carole Lombard*	**4** Motion Picture Alliance for the Preservation of American Ideals formed	**14** Court rules studios cannot add suspension time to contracts	**4** Charlie Chaplin not guilty of violating the Mann Act	• James Cagney leaves Warners	**2** Joan Fontaine divorces Brian Aherne	

July	August	September	October	November	December	
31 Darryl Zanuck says 20th Century Fox musicals will be in Technicolor	**7** Government renews antimonopoly case against studios	**6** *Double Indemnity*	**12** Frank Sinatra, at Paramount Theater, touches off bobbysoxer hysteria	**17** Danny DeVito b.	**18** "Humphrey Bogart and Lauren Bacall cheek-to-cheeking," says the *Hollywood Reporter*	

Personalities

JANUARY 15 Irene Dunne christens the Liberty Ship S.S. *Carole Lombard*. At the launching are Louis B. Mayer, Lt. Commander Robert Montgomery, and Capt. Clark Gable, who is openly weeping. **27** Captain James Stewart, bombardier pilot, is promoted to Major. **31** Margaret O'Brien, who has come down with a cold, is spirited off to Arizona by her aunt to recover, shutting down production on *Meet Me in St. Louis* for over a week. Judy Garland's lateness and her physical and emotional ailments and Mary Astor's pneumonia have also held up filming.

FEBRUARY 10 Charlie Chaplin, already being sued for support as the father of actress Joan Barry's child, is indicted under the Mann Act for having her unwillingly transported across state lines to have sex with him. **14** Humphrey Bogart is back in Hollywood after entertaining the troops for three months in North Africa and Italy.

MARCH 2 Jack Benny is the master of ceremonies when, for the first time, the Oscars are handed out as part of a variety show, staged at Grauman's Chinese Theater. NBC does not think its network audience would be interested in such a program, so the first broadcast of an Oscar ceremony is carried by two Los Angeles stations. **15** Barry Fitzgerald, who plays a lovable priest in *Going My Way*, opening in May, is arrested on suspicion of manslaughter in an auto accident on Hollywood Boulevard in which an eighty-seven-year-old woman is killed and her daughter critically injured.

APRIL 2 The *New York Times* reports that Howard Hawks is getting the desired huskiness in Lauren Bacall's voice for *To Have and Have Not* by having her spend part of each day screaming herself hoarse. Andy Williams, hired to dub her singing voice, will not have to be used. **4** A Los Angeles jury finds Charlie Chaplin not guilty of violating the Mann Act. **11** Marlene Dietrich does her first overseas show for GIs, playing the musical saw at a base in Algiers. By war's end she will have put in more time at the front than any other entertainer. **15** Busby Berkeley and Warner Bros. mutually agree to terminate his contract. **18** A jury declares that Charlie Chaplin did father Joan Barry's child.

MAY • Fred Astaire and Gene Kelly rehearse and film their dance number for MGM's *Ziegfeld Follies*. It is the only time they will

Movies

JANUARY 12 Alfred Hitchcock's *Lifeboat*, starring Tallulah Bankhead, William Bendix, and Walter Slezak, premieres at the Astor. **19** Laird Cregar, starring as Jack the Ripper in *The Lodger*, appears onstage when it opens at the Roxy. George Sanders and Merle Oberon are also in the film. **26** *The Song of Bernadette*, opening at the Rivoli, stars Jennifer Jones in her first major film role. 20th Century Fox, seeking to give her a virginal image, keeps under wraps her marriage to Robert Walker. Unbilled Linda Darnell is the Virgin Mary.

Jennifer Jones in *The Song of Bernadette*   LC

FEBRUARY 14 The release of *Charlie Chan in the Secret Service* marks the first of Monogram's Chan films, starring Sidney Toler. **17** *Up in Arms*, Danny Kaye's first film, premieres at the Radio City Music Hall.

MARCH 8 *The Purple Heart*, starring Dana Andrews, Farley Granger, and Richard Conte, opens at the Roxy, with Count Basie onstage. **30** *Cover Girl*, with Rita Hayworth and Gene Kelly, opens at the Music Hall.

APRIL 13 William Wyler's *Memphis Belle*, a documentary about a bomber, opens in Hollywood. **29** *Dancing Romeo*, the final *Our Gang* comedy, is released.

Business and Society

FEBRUARY • The government eases restraints on Hollywood's depiction of Japanese brutality. The restrictions stemmed from fears that such portrayals might prompt reprisals against American P.O.W.s, but recent reports have shown that captured G.I.s are treated brutally anyway. **2** A *Hollywood Reporter* headline, "Lack of Jap Types Cramps War Pix," speaks of the problem Central Casting may face as attention shifts to the war in the Pacific. Many Japanese villains are being played by actors of Chinese extraction. **4** The Motion Picture Alliance for the Preservation of American Ideals is formed to counter Hollywood liberals and radicals, and to speak "for the vast, silent majority of our fellow workers." Sam Wood, King Vidor, and Walt Disney are founders. Gary Cooper, John Wayne, Ward Bond, Robert Taylor, Ayn Rand, and Hedda Hopper will become active in the organization.

MARCH 14 A Los Angeles Superior Court judge, in a precedent-setting decision, rules that Warner Bros. had no claims on the services of Olivia de Havilland after the

Births, Deaths, Marriages, and Divorces

MARCH 17 Charlton Heston m. Lydia Clarke. **21** Timothy Dalton b. **23** Myron Selznick d.

APRIL 29 Cinematographer Billy Bitzer d. **30** Jill Clayburgh b.

MAY 21 Paulette Goddard m. Burgess Meredith.

JUNE 2 Joan Fontaine divorces Brian Aherne. • Composer Marvin Hamlisch b.

18 Alexis Smith m. Craig Stevens. **29** Gary Busey b.

JULY 14 Joan Blondell divorces Dick Powell. **23** Susan Hayward m. Jess Barker. **27** Jane Greer and Rudy Vallee divorce. **31** Geraldine Chaplin, daughter of Charlie Chaplin and granddaughter of Eugene O'Neill, b.

dance together in a feature film. • James Cagney leaves Warners to make films with his own company, Cagney Productions. **11** Paulette Goddard is back from a thirty-eight-thousand-mile tour of Army bases in China, India, and Burma. **13** Captain Clark Gable is promoted to major. **25** Police raiding a Hollywood apartment and arresting Bugsy Siegel for bookmaking find George Raft there, too. **30** Zasu Pitts, while visiting wounded veterans, is booed out of a ward at a Galesburg, Illinois, hospital when she attacks President Roosevelt for breaking his promise to avoid a war.

JUNE • Louis B. Mayer leaves his wife, Margaret, who has attempted suicide several times, and is now courting Ann Miller.

JULY 26 "Perry Como, singer, and Jackie Gleason, comedian, are headed for a buildup as a song-and-comedy team in both films and on the air (a la Bing Crosby and Bob Hope)," notes *Variety*. Como is onstage at the New York Paramount and Gleason is about to make his first film.

AUGUST 5 Jon Hall's nose is severely damaged—by whom it is not clear—in a brawl at Tommy Dorsey's home when the band leader, who has been drinking, thinks that the actor is getting too familiar with Mrs. Dorsey.

SEPTEMBER 16 Lana Turner, her current boyfriend Turhan Bey, and Turner's ex-husband Stephan Crane show up at the same party. Crane takes loud exception to Turner still wearing her wedding ring, a Crane family heirloom. Bey gives Crane a black eye, and Turner throws away the ring in disgust.

20 Leading Hollywood Republicans, headed by Ginger Rogers and Lionel Barrymore, endorse the presidential candidacy of Thomas Dewey. Others signing today's trade paper ad are Cecil B. DeMille, Walt Disney, Fred MacMurray, Joel McCrea, and Rosalind Russell.

OCTOBER 2 The names of Hollywood's prominent Democrats appear in a trade paper ad backing the reelection of President Roosevelt—about four times as many names as in the Republican ad of September 20. Included are Katharine Hepburn, Lucille Ball, Humphrey Bogart, James Cagney, Judy Garland, Rita Hayworth, Lana Turner, and Edward G. Robinson. Screenwriter Ben Hecht's name appears in both ads. **3** Seaman Jackie Cooper is acquitted on an August charge of contributing to the delinquency of two teenage

MAY 3 *Going My Way*, starring Bing Crosby and Barry Fitzgerald, shown in a "Fighting Front Premiere" in Army camps on April 27, has its theatrical premiere at the Paramount. **4** *Gaslight*, starring Charles Boyer, Ingrid Bergman, Joseph Cotten, and introducing Angela Lansbury, premieres at the Capitol. **25** *Mr. Skeffington*, starring Bette Davis and Claude Rains, premieres at Warners' Hollywood Theater in New York.

JUNE 19 MGM's *The White Cliffs of Dover*, starring Irene Dunne, premieres at Hollywood's Egyptian Theater. Tomorrow, with this movie, the studio begins a new policy of "showcasing" first-run films im-

mediately following the premiere in several of its Los Angeles theaters—the Egyptian, the Fox Ritz, and the Los Angeles. **27** *Bathing Beauty*, the first film in which Esther Williams swims, premieres at the Astor.

JULY 20 David O. Selznick's *Since You Went Away*, starring Jennifer Jones, Claudette Colbert, Joseph Cotten, Shirley Temple, and Robert Walker, premieres at the Capitol, where drummer and band leader Gene Krupa heads the stage show.

AUGUST • John Huston's *The Battle of San Pietro*, screened for a roomful of generals,

is found too harsh and antiwar, and the Army only releases it to the troops when General George C. Marshall intervenes. **9** Preston Sturges's *Hail the Conquering Hero*, starring Eddie Bracken, Ella Raines, and William Demarest, opens at the Paramount. Vaughn Monroe is onstage.

SEPTEMBER 1 Frank Capra's *Arsenic and Old Lace*, starring Cary Grant, Raymond Massey, and Peter Lorre, opens at the Strand. **6** Billy Wilder's *Double Indemnity*, starring Barbara Stanwyck, Fred MacMurray, and Edward G. Robinson, opens at the Paramount. The stage show features the Andrews Sisters.

BETTE ON BEAUTY

CLAUDE RAINS: *"A woman is beautiful only when she is loved."*

BETTE DAVIS: *"A woman is beautiful if she has eight hours of sleep and goes to the beauty parlor every day. And bone structure has a lot to do with it."*

from *Mr. Skeffington* premiere
May 25, 1944

May 5 expiration of her contract, regardless of how much time she spent on suspension. The California State Supreme Court will uphold it. **22** Paramount runs the first TV ad for a film in a thirty-minute promotional program about *The Miracle of Morgan's Creek*, narrated by the director-writer, Preston Sturges, on the studio's Los Angeles station.

APRIL 4 Claiming that producer Hal Wallis has been talking to other studios about

working for them, Warners abrogates his contract. **14** United Artists buys out Alexander Korda.

MAY 25 Hal Wallis Productions affiliates with Paramount.

JUNE 6 Theater attendance is down by as much as fifty percent on D-Day.

JULY 6 On "free movie" day more than half the theaters in America charge no admis-

AUGUST 13 John Carradine m. Sonia Sorrel. Inability to meet alimony payments to his first wife will send Carradine to jail for a week this year.

SEPTEMBER 6 Yul Brynner m. Virginia Gilmore. **9** Larry Parks m. Betty Garrett. **13** Jacqueline Bisset b. **5** Michael Douglas b.

OCTOBER 3 Jerry Lewis m. Patti Palmer. **8** Chevy Chase (Cornelius Chase) b.

NOVEMBER • John Wayne and Josephine Saenz divorce. **17** Danny DeVito (Daniel Michaeli) b.

DECEMBER 3 Faye Emerson m. Elliott Roosevelt, son of the President. **14** Lupe Velez commits suicide. **17** Veronica Lake m. director André

Personalities

girls in South Bend, Indiana. His latest film is *Where Are Your Children?*, about juvenile delinquency. **8** "Ex-Model Gets Featured Role With Bogart in First Picture," headlines the New York *Herald Tribune* concerning Lauren Bacall. *To Have and Have Not* is about to open. **12** Frank Sinatra's appearance at the Paramount, heading the stageshow accompanying *Our Hearts Were Young and Gay*, draws thousands of bobbysoxers to Times Square. They smash the glass in the box office and injure some of the two hundred police officers trying to contain them. **15** Lucille Ball is granted an interlocutory decree of divorce from Desi Arnaz, but they are still co-habiting. **15** "Gregory Peck is the hottest thing in town," writes Hedda Hopper. "Some say he

is a second Gary Cooper." **19** Marlon Brando makes his Broadway stage debut in *I Remember Mama*.

NOVEMBER • The Boston archdiocese criticizes Bob Hope for making GI audiences "laugh at the wrong things." **8** Helen Gahagan Douglas, actress and wife of Melvyn Douglas, is elected to Congress; and Albert Dekker, to the California state assembly. **27** Lucille Ball and Desi Arnaz say they will let their interlocutory decree of divorce lapse.

DECEMBER • Director Michael Curtiz clashes with Joan Crawford on the set of *Mildred Pierce*. Claiming that her inappropriate attempts to add glamour to her role, such as using shoulder pads, are ruining the picture, he asks that she be fired and replaced by Barbara Stanwyck. Producer Jerry Wald

plays peacemaker. **18** "Humphrey Bogart and Lauren Bacall cheek-to-cheeking," gossips the *Hollywood Reporter*. **26** Humphrey Bogart delays production on *The Big Sleep* when a hangover keeps him from the set. Bogart has moved out of the home he shared with wife Mayo Methot and into the Beverly Wilshire Hotel. **31** Jack Benny's New Year's Eve party guests include Bing Crosby, Clark Gable, Joan Crawford, Gene Tierney, Ginger Rogers, Ray Milland, Judy Garland, Robert Taylor, Barbara Stanwyck, Claudette Colbert, Dorothy Lamour, and Van Johnson.

Movies

OCTOBER 11 Otto Preminger's *Laura*, starring Gene Tierney, Clifton Webb, and Dana Andrews, opens at the Roxy. **11** Humphrey Bogart, Walter Brennan, and Lauren Bacall in her screen debut, star in Howard Hawks's *To Have and Have Not*, opening at the Hollywood Theater in New York.

NOVEMBER 15 Spencer Tracy, Van Johnson, and Robert Walker star in *Thirty Seconds over Tokyo*, premiering at the Capitol. Onstage: Jimmy Dorsey and comedian

Henny Youngman. Admission today is by purchase of a war bond. **22** *Meet Me in St. Louis* premieres in its namesake city. "Have Yourself a Merry Little Christmas," "The Boy Next Door," and "The Trolley Song" were written for the film. Judy Garland, Margaret O'Brien, and Mary Astor star.

DECEMBER 14 *National Velvet* premieres at the Radio City Music Hall. Elizabeth Taylor's fifth film, at age twelve, makes her a star, although she takes second billing to Mickey Rooney.

Fred McMurray and Barbara Stanwyck in *Double Indemnity*　　*MSN*

Business and Society

sion to anyone buying a war bond. **31** Darryl Zanuck announces that all 20th Century Fox musicals in the future will be made in Technicolor.

AUGUST 7 The government renews its anti-monopoly case against the movie studios, seeking again to have them divest themselves of their theater interests.

27 Louis B. Mayer sustains a broken pelvis in a fall from a horse, keeping him away from MGM until Christmas.

SEPTEMBER • Buddy De Sylva steps down as Paramount production head to produce independently. • Hollywood studios, at the request of the government, begin supplying films to be used to reeducate German prisoners of war held in the U.S. Included are *The Life of Emile Zola*, *Union Pacific*, and *Abe Lincoln in Illinois*.

OCTOBER 6 Painters and set decorators strike the studios in a jurisdictional dispute. **12** The War Labor Board forces striking set decorators and painters back to work.

NOVEMBER 21 Henry Ginsberg is made production head at Paramount.

Births, Deaths, Marriages, and Divorces

DeToth. **22** Harry Langdon d. **28** John Payne m. Gloria De Haven.

Also this year: • Myrna Loy and John D. Hertz Jr. divorce. • Lana Turner and Stephan Crane divorce.

"*P*sychological Murder Yarns Getting Big Play at Studios" reads a March *Hollywood Reporter* headline, heralding what will later (1955) be termed "film *noir*." "A post-war enterprise that looks promising is the production of television commercials," the same publication comments in passing on July 13, about possible new opportunities for the film industry. Audie Murphy wins the Medal of Honor. Lauren Bacall marries Humphrey Bogart, and Judy Garland marries Vincente Minnelli. The rationing of film stock ends, and violence breaks out on the Hollywood picket lines. In war-torn Italy, Roberto Rossellini films *Open City*, shooting where he can amid the debris and using nonprofessionals when trained actors are unavailable. The gritty look and feel of his film gives birth to Italian neorealism.

- Number of releases: 377
- Number of theaters: 20,457, of which 102 are drive-ins
- Theaters showing double features: 60%
- Average weekly attendance: 90,000,000
- Average ticket price: $.35
- Box office receipts: $1,450,000,000

Top stars at the box office, based on a Quigley Publications poll of exhibitors:

1. Bing Crosby
2. Van Johnson
3. Greer Garson
4. Betty Grable
5. Spencer Tracy
6. Humphrey Bogart and Gary Cooper (tie)
7. Bob Hope
8. Judy Garland
9. Margaret O'Brien
10. Roy Rogers

The "stars of tomorrow," based on a Quigley Publications poll of exhibitors:

1. Dane Clark
2. Jeanne Crain
3. Keenan Wynn
4. Peggy Ann Garner
5. Cornel Wilde
6. Tom Drake
7. Lon McCallister
8. Diana Lynn
9. Marilyn Maxwell
10. William Eythe

The New York Film Critics Circle Awards
Best Picture: *The Lost Weekend*

The Golden Globe Awards
Best Picture: *The Lost Weekend*

The Academy Awards (presented March 7, 1946)
Best Picture: *The Lost Weekend*
Actor: Ray Milland (*The Lost Weekend*)
Actress: Joan Crawford (*Mildred Pierce*)
Supporting Actor: James Dunn (*A Tree Grows in Brooklyn*)
Supporting Actress: Anne Revere (*National Velvet*)
Director: Billy Wilder (*The Lost Weekend*)

January	February	March	April	May	June
15 Fuel shortage to "brown out" marquee lights					**2** Lieut. Audie Murphy awarded Medal of Honor
		12 Beginning of studio strike			
	9 Mia Farrow b.		**29** Errol Flynn and John Huston fight at a party		**21** Humphrey Bogart m. Lauren Bacall

July	August	September	October	November	December
	19 June Allyson m. Dick Powell			**22** Hollywood Canteen closes	
• Humphrey Bogart and Elsa Maxwell feud		**28** *Mildred Pierce*			
			24 Studio strike ends	**19** The *Hollywood Reporter* calls Joan Crawford new "queen of the lot at Warners"	

Personalities

JANUARY 1 Susan Peters, shot in a hunting accident, is paralyzed. **3** "The New Year kiss implanted upon Olivia de Havilland by Maj. John Huston should have been photographed in Technicolor," says the *Hollywood Reporter*. **9** Barry Fitzgerald is found not guilty of manslaughter in the auto accident of last March 15, and the judge says that he should never have been charged with the crime.

MARCH 11 Keenan Wynn suffers a broken jaw and back injury in a Hollywood motorcycle accident. **15** The Paramount publicity department drags a reluctant Bing Crosby off a golf course at the last minute to attend the Academy Awards ceremonies at Grauman's Chinese Theater. He's a winner.

25 Joan, the youngest of the Bennett sisters, admitting to thirty-five, remarks on a radio program that lately Constance and Barbara Bennett "have been knocking off the years so much that I'm becoming the older sister." Constance is displeased. **28** Swerving to avoid a car driving on the wrong side of the street, Clark Gable hits a tree and will spend two days in a hospital.

APRIL 8 Ann Blyth breaks her back tobogganing. **29** Errol Flynn and John Huston get into a fight at a party over Flynn's remarks about Olivia de Havilland. Huston sustains a broken nose; Flynn, broken ribs. Both end up in the hospital.

MAY 22 Alan Ladd and John Garfield enter the armed forces and are almost immediately discharged by the new order exempting men over thirty. Garfield spends a

total of three hours in the Navy.

JUNE 2 Army Lieutenant Audie Murphy is awarded the Congressional Medal of Honor. **13** Shirley Temple, an aging Hollywood veteran, graduates from the Westlake School for Girls. **14** According to the *Hollywood Reporter*, Paramount has given a screen test to "Syd Charris." Previously in films in bit parts under the name Lily Norwood, dancer Cyd Charisse will sign with MGM next year.

JULY • Humphrey Bogart and Elsa Maxwell feud over her put-down of Lauren Bacall's acting. **27** Bing Crosby, Frank Sinatra, and Claudette Colbert are mingling with the men and women in uniform at the Hollywood Canteen tonight as the War draws close to its end.

Movies

FEBRUARY 7 Ray Milland stars in Fritz Lang's *Ministry of Fear*, opening at the Paramount. **28** Elia Kazan's *A Tree Grows in Brooklyn*, starring Peggy Ann Garner, Dorothy McGuire, James Dunn, Lloyd Nolan, and Joan Blondell, premieres at the Roxy. Victor Borge heads the stage show.

MARCH 8 *Murder, My Sweet*, in which musical comedy star Dick Powell, as hard-boiled private eye Philip Marlowe, changes his screen persona, opens at the

RKO Palace. Raymond Chandler's *Farewell, My Lovely*, on which this movie was based, was filmed before as part of The Falcon series of B movies, *The Falcon Takes Over* (1942). Robert Mitchum will do another version in 1975.

MAY 2 *Blood on the Sun*, with James Cagney and Sylvia Sidney, premieres at the United Artist Theater in San Francisco.

JUNE 19 Republic releases Roy Rogers's most popular Western, *The Bells of Rosarita*, with Wild Bill Elliot, Rocky Lane, Red Barry, and Sunset Carson. **20** The opening of *The Naughty Nineties* is notable

for Abbott and Costello's legendary "Who's On First" routine, which they have done on the stage and radio and now bring to the screen.

JULY 12 Burgess Meredith and Robert Mitchum are in *The Story of G.I. Joe* premiering in Albuquerque, hometown of cartoonist Ernie Pyle. **19** *Anchors Away*, in which Gene Kelly dances with Jerry, the cartoon mouse of "Tom and Jerry," premieres at the Capitol. It also stars Frank Sinatra and Kathryn Grayson.

AUGUST 8 *Pride of the Marines*, starring John Garfield, premieres in Philadelphia, home-

Business and Society

JANUARY 15 The War Production Board orders outdoor display lights "browned out" as of February 1 because of the fuel shortage. By the end of the month the shortage will temporarily close more than one hundred theaters in the Northeast.

MARCH 12 The Screen Set Designers, Decorators, and Illustrators union strikes most

of the studios, supported by some of the other craft unions in the Conference of Studio Unions, headed by Herbert Sorrell. They are in a jurisdictional dispute with IATSE over who will represent the set dressers. The War Labor Relations Board has already ruled in favor of the Screen Set Designers, but IATSE had threatened to strike if that decision took effect. Neither the producers nor the WLB had moved to enforce the decision. **21** The National War Labor Board orders the strikers back to work, but they refuse.

APRIL 4 The major studios fire thirty-six hundred striking workers, and tomorrow will hand the jobs to members of IATSE. **14** Most of the nation's movie theaters remain closed until 6 P.M. as part of the national day of mourning for President Roosevelt, who died two days ago. **26** *Harper's* magazine goes on sale with a story quoting State Department official Frances C. De Wolfe offering the studios help in marketing their films abroad if they give a favorable impression of America.

Births, Deaths, Marriages, and Divorces

JANUARY 29 Gloria Swanson m. William Davey. **•** Tom Selleck b.

FEBRUARY 9 Mia Farrow (Maria de Lourdes Villiers Farrow), daughter of Maureen O'

Sullivan and director John Farrow, b. Her godmother is Louella Parsons.

MAY 10 Humphrey Bogart and Mayo Methot divorce. **11** Ida Lupino and

Louis Hayward divorce. **21** Humphrey Bogart m. Lauren Bacall.

JUNE • Judy Garland and David Rose divorce. **4** Merle Oberon and Alexander Korda divorce. **15** Judy Garland m. director Vincente Minnelli. Louis B. Mayer gives the bride away.

AUGUST 10 King Vidor, disgusted with producer David O. Selznick's meddling, quits as director of *Duel in the Sun*. Second-unit directors Josef von Sternberg and William Dieterle will finish the picture. **13** Orson Welles remains at the microphones of Warners' radio station KFWB all night, broadcasting the news of Japan's surrender. Handing him bulletins from the teletype machines are Rita Hayworth and Marlene Dietrich. **14** Carmen Miranda, trapped in the traffic jam created at Hollywood and Vine by a crowd celebrating news of the Japanese capitulation, stands up on the seat of her convertible to rhumba. **15** With the War over, the mood is especially light at the Hollywood Canteen tonight. In a sketch with Robert Alda, Bette Davis takes two pies in her face (cherry and custard). **22** Paramount suspends Alan Ladd for refusing a role in *California*. He

town of Al Schmid, the subject of the film, who was blinded at Guadalcanal.

SEPTEMBER 12 John Wayne and Anthony Quinn star in *Back to Bataan*, opening at the RKO Palace. **26** Twentieth Century Fox's *The House on 92nd Street* opens at the Roxy. On August 12, six days after Hiroshima was bombed, Darryl Zanuck revealed that this movie was about German attempts to steal the atomic bomb secrets. This plot detail was kept even from the actors, among whom are Leo G. Carroll, Lloyd Nolan, Signe Hasso, William Eythe, and Gene Lockhart. During production the "secrets" were designated as a mysterious

Humphrey Bogart and Lauren Bacall marry—May 21, 1945   *LC*

MAY 1 Pathé newsreel footage of the liberated concentration camps is released. The Radio City Music Hall will declare it "too gruesome to be shown at a family theater." **9** Midnight curfews for theaters and the brownout of display lights are cancelled.

JUNE 9 The government ends the export/import censorship of movies instituted at the beginning of the war.

AUGUST 9 Inspired by recent headlines,

Paramount advertises *Incendiary Blonde* in the trade papers as its "newest ATOMIC BOMB." **15** All studios remain closed today to celebrate the end of World War II. **20** The government announces the end of raw film stock allocations.

SEPTEMBER 19 Eric A. Johnston, former president of the U.S. Chamber of Commerce, succeeds Will Hays as president of the Motion Picture Producers and Distributors Association.

OCTOBER 5 Violent confrontations occur between members of the Conference of Studio Unions picketing Warner Bros. and workers crossing their picket line. **8** Violence flares again at Warners when labor goons attack strikers and the studio turns hoses on picketers. **12** An IATSE trade paper ad attacks the Conference of Studio Unions as communist-dominated. **23** At Paramount, renewed violence in the Conference of Studio Unions strike injures fifty. **24** The eight-month Con-

13 Deanna Durbin m. Felix Jackson. • Constance Bennett divorces Gilbert Roland. **20** Jennifer Jones and Robert Walker divorce. **26** Merle Oberon m. cinematographer Lucien K. Ballard.

JULY 13 Alla Nazimova d.

AUGUST 18 Steve Martin b. **19** June Allyson m. Dick Powell. Louis B. Mayer gives the bride away. **30** Cary Grant and Barbara Hutton divorce.

SEPTEMBER 3 Betty Hutton m. Theodore Brisken. **19** Shirley Temple m. John Agar.

NOVEMBER 11 Jerome Kern d. **21** Goldie Hawn b. **25** Esther Williams m. radio personality Benjamin Gage. **28** Deborah Kerr m. Anthony Bartley. **30** Bette Davis m. William Sherry.

DECEMBER 1 Bette Midler b. **5** Eddie Albert m. actress Margo, ex-wife of Francis

Personalities

wants more money. **30** Bob Hope returns to Los Angeles following his sixth overseas trip to entertain the troops.

SEPTEMBER • The OSS reveals that Capt. John Hamilton (Hollywood's Sterling Hayden) carried out secret and dangerous operations for it along the Greek and Yugoslav coasts during the war. **1** Frank Capra pays RKO $10,000 for the rights to *The Greatest Gift*, from which Dalton Trumbo, Marc Connelly, and Clifford Odets have failed to produce an acceptable screenplay. It will become *It's a Wonderful Life*. **8** Among those attending Sonja Henie's tent party tonight are Lana Turner, Joan Crawford, Frank Sinatra, Claudette Colbert, Cary Grant, Van Heflin, Charles

Boyer, Joan Fontaine, and Clark Gable. **23** The Hollywood Victory Committee announces that during the War 4,012 stars made 53,056 appearances at a total of 7,336 events, covering 5,000,000 miles in the process. **27** Captain John Ford is awarded the Legion of Merit.

OCTOBER 15 William Faulkner, asking that he be released from his 1942 Warners contract, writes to Jack Warner: "I feel that I have made a bust at moving picture writing and therefore have mis-spent and will continue to mis-spend time which at my age I cannot afford." But Warners won't budge. **24** John Garfield signs with RKO to do a picture a year for five years.

NOVEMBER 13 William Boyd buys the rights to the "Hopalong Cassidy" character, making him a wealthy man when he

later sells the series to TV. **22** The Hollywood Canteen closes, after serving more than three million members of the Armed Forces.

DECEMBER • The French government rules that Maurice Chevalier's wartime tours of French POW camps in Germany and a forced meeting with Hermann Goering did not constitute collaboration. **19** The *Hollywood Reporter* says that Joan Crawford is the new "queen of the lot at Warners," dethroning Bette Davis. **26** Bugsy Siegel's Flamingo Hotel in Las Vegas opens. Siegel pals George Raft, Charles Coburn, and George Sanders are on hand.

Movies

"Process 97." The movie was filmed in secret, with the cooperation of the FBI, some agents of which appear in it. **28** *Mildred Pierce*, starring Joan Crawford, Ann Blyth, Jack Carson, Zachary Scott, and Eve Arden, opens at the Strand. The stage show features The Three Stooges. Dr. Spock's *Baby and Child Care* book has only recently been published, but Eve Arden, in *Mildred Pierce*, offers some decidedly unprogressive thoughts on parenting: "Personally, I think alligators have the right idea. They eat their young."

NOVEMBER 1 Alfred Hitchcock's *Spellbound*, starring Gregory Peck and Ingrid Bergman, opens at New York's Astor Theater. Composer Miklos Rozsa's use of the theremin to produce an eerie sound is probably the first use of electronic music in film. **16** Casper makes his cartoon debut with the release of Paramount's *The Friendly Ghost*. **30** *Detour*, starring Tom Neal, about a hitchhiker who picks up the wrong woman, directed by Edgar G. Ulmer, is released by Producers Releasing Corporation. It will become a cult favorite.

DECEMBER 1 Billy Wilder's *The Lost Weekend*, which flopped at its Santa Barbara pre-

view and was almost shelved by Paramount, opens at the Rivoli, where the critics and public turn it into a huge success. (Some liquor industry figures have been reported trying to buy the negative of this film about an alcoholic to destroy it.) Ray Milland and Jane Wyman star. **15** *The Enchanted Forest* opens at the Victoria. Its relatively inexpensive Cinecolor process will afterwards be used by other independent studios through the mid-1950s. **20** John Ford's *They Were Expendable*, starring Robert Montgomery and John Wayne, premieres at the Capitol, accompanied by a stage show featuring Tommy Dorsey.

Business and Society

ference of Studio Unions strike ends. The Conference has triumphed over IATSE on the jurisdictional issue concerning set decorators; all striking workers will return to their jobs; and remaining issues will be settled by arbitration.

NOVEMBER 27 Universal Studios, International Pictures, and J. Arthur Rank

announce that they will cooperate on producing and distributing films in the U.S. and in Britain.

DECEMBER 12 The Motion Picture Producers and Distributors of America changes its name to the Motion Picture Association of America.

Births, Deaths, Marriages, and Divorces

Lederer. **11** Teri Garr b. **24** Mary Astor m. Thomas Wheelock.

Also this year: • Miriam Hopkins m. Ray Brock. • Angela Lansbury m. Richard

Cromwell, a match that will not last a year. • Dorothy Dandridge and Harold Nicholas divorce. • Evelyn Keyes divorces Charles Vidor.

*N*ow at its peak, the movie industry, with 0.5 percent of the national income and employing the same percentage of the labor force, earns 1.5 percent of all corporate profits. Kirk Douglas and Burt Lancaster debut, Norma Shearer discovers Janet Leigh, Dean Martin and Jerry Lewis begin a partnership, and 20th Century Fox signs Norma Jean Dougherty, whose name is changed to Marilyn Monroe. Ads for *The Outlaw* make no reference to Jane Russell's acting ability, and Ronald Reagan is on the defensive about his lack of combat service in the war.

- Number of releases: 467
- Average production cost per feature film: $665,863
- Number of theaters: 19,019, of which 300 are drive-ins
- Number of theaters showing serials: 8,000
- Average weekly attendance: 90,000,000
- Average ticket price: $.40
- Box office receipts: $1,692,000,000
- Percentage of all corporate profits earned by the movie industry: 1.5%
- Judy Garland's salary: $5,600 a week
- Marilyn Monroe's salary: $125 per week
- Actors with term contracts at major studios: 598

Top stars at the box office, based on a Quigley publications poll of exhibitors:

1. Bing Crosby
2. Ingrid Bergman
3. Van Johnson
4. Gary Cooper
5. Bob Hope
6. Humphrey Bogart
7. Greer Garson
8. Margaret O'Brien
9. Betty Grable
10. Roy Rogers

The "stars of tomorrow, based on a Quigley Publications poll of exhibitors:

1. Joan Leslie
2. Jackie "Butch" Jenkins
3. Zachary Scott
4. Don Defore
5. Mark Stevens
6. Eve Arden
7. Lizabeth Scott
8. Dan Duryea
9. Yvonne De Carlo
10. Robert Mitchum

The New York Film Critics Circle Awards
Best Picture: *The Best Years of Our Lives*

The Golden Globe Awards
Best Picture: *The Best Years of Our Lives*

The Cannes Film Festival
Grand Prize: *La Bataille du Rail*, *Symphonie Pastorale*, *The Lost Weekend*, *Brief Encounter*, *Open City*, *Maria Candelaria*, and *The Last Chance*

The Academy Awards (presented March 13, 1947)
Best Picture: *The Best Years of Our Lives*
Actor: Fredric March (*The Best Years of Our lives*)
Actress: Olivia de Havilland (*To Each His Own*)
Supporting Actor: Harold Russell (*The Best Years of Our Lives*)
Supporting Actress: Anne Baxter (*The Razor's Edge*)
Director: William Wyler (*The Best Years of Our Lives*)

January	February	March	April	May	June	
5 Diane Keaton b. • Ads for *The Outlaw* emphasize Jane Russell's breasts		**14** *Gilda*	**24** San Francisco police seize print of *The Outlaw*	**20** Cher b.	**11** Court orders studios to change block booking practice	

July	August	September	October	November	December	
1 Atom bomb decorated with Rita Hayworth's picture	**24** Norma Jean Dougherty (Marilyn Monroe) signs first film contract	**8** *The Outlaw* loses MPAA seal	**4** Susan Sarandon b.	**27** NAACP says Walt Disney's *Song of the South* romanticizes slavery	**21** *It's a Wonderful Life*	

Personalities

JANUARY 8 Hal Wallis's ad in the trade papers touts for "stardom in 1946," stage actor Kirk Douglas, now filming *The Strange Love of Martha Ivers*. **18** MGM's new contract with Elizabeth Taylor raises her to $750 a week. **23** Twenty-eight-year-old nightclub singer Dean Martin files for bankruptcy.

FEBRUARY • Howard Hughes begins advertising *The Outlaw*, emphasizing Jane Russell's breasts with lurid drawings and lines such as: "What are the two great reasons for Jane Russell's rise to stardom?" **4** Two days ago the cast and staff of the play *Born Yesterday* took out an ad in the *New York Times* to scotch rumors that Jean Arthur had withdrawn from the lead for

Jane Russell in *The Outlaw*   MSN

anything but health reasons. Tonight the play opens on Broadway, creating a new star: Judy Holliday. **12** Gossip columnist Louella Parsons raves: "Not in a long time have I heard so much talk about a child as about Dean Stockwell, the cute little 10-year-old who played Kathryn Grayson's brother in 'Anchors Aweigh.'" **14** Howard Hughes pilots the first TWA Constellation flight from Los Angeles to New York. Aboard are Cary Grant, Lana Turner, Alfred Hitchcock, Bugsy Siegel, Edward G. Robinson, and Paulette Goddard.

MARCH 7 Ann Blyth, with a broken back, is at Grauman's Chinese Theater for the Academy Awards ceremonies. **22** "Introducing Another New Hal Wallis Personality," proclaims a trade paper ad about Burt Lancaster, signed by Wallis two days ago.

Movies

JANUARY 4 The release of Terrytoon's *The Talking Magpies* cartoon introduces the characters Heckle and Jeckle.

MARCH 14 Rita Hayworth, Glenn Ford, and George Macready star in *Gilda*, premiering at the Radio City Music Hall. "If I were a ranch, they would have named me the 'Bar Nothing,'" says Rita Hayworth in the film. A test atomic bomb dubbed "Gilda" will go off with her picture on it this year.

APRIL 8 The Hollywood premiere of *Ziegfeld*

Follies at Grauman's Egyptian is the first gala opening since the end of the War. At the theater are Edward Arnold, Jimmy Durante, Glen Ford, Maureen O'Hara, Mickey Rooney, Agnes Moorehead, and Peter Lawford. **15** Universal's *So Goes My Love*, with Myrna Loy and Don Ameche, premieres on a Pan-American Clipper flight between New York and London, the first feature to open in this way.

MAY 2 *The Postman Always Rings Twice*, starring Lana Turner and John Garfield, opens at the Capitol, with a stage show headed by Guy Lombardo. James Cain's novel was filmed in France in 1939 and as Luchino

Visconti's 1942 *Ossessione* (not released in the U.S. until 1977), and will be remade in 1981 with Jack Nicholson and Jessica Lange.

JUNE 17 Laurence Olivier's *Henry V* has its U.S. premiere at New York's City Center, where it will play for forty-six weeks. In the audience are Olivier, Vivien Leigh, Alexander Korda, and Trygvie Lie, Secretary General of the new United Nations.

JULY 2 *The Stranger*, directed by Orson Welles and starring Welles, Edward G. Robinson, and Loretta Young, premieres in Hollywood. **24** Kirk Douglas makes his film debut in *The Strange Love of Martha*

Business and Society

FEBRUARY 6 RKO announces that its president, N. Peter Rathvon, will take over as production chief, following the death, on February 2, of Charles Koerner.

MARCH 3 The Screen Extras Guild is certified as the bargaining agent for all extras.

APRIL 24 Eagle-Lion Films is formed to

make B movies and to act as U.S. distributor for the British J. Arthur Rank company. **•** San Francisco police seize the print of *The Outlaw* being shown at the United Artists Theater and arrest the manager.

JUNE 11 The U.S. Statutory Court rules that the major studios are violating the antitrust laws with practices such as block booking, which will have to change. But it does not order the studios to divest themselves of their theaters. The government will appeal.

JULY 2 A two-day strike over wages and jurisdiction by the Conference of Studio Unions stops production.

AUGUST 8 Paramount announces that its earnings for the first six months are up 100% over last year's. The studio's ownership of many theaters, which hurt during the Depression, is beneficial now that attendance is way up.

SEPTEMBER • A revised Motion Picture Code permits the showing of drug trafficking, but

Births, Deaths, Marriages, and Divorces

JANUARY 3 Myrna Loy m. Gene Markey, former husband of Joan Bennett and Heddy Lamarr. **•** Florence Vidor and Jascha Heifitz divorce. **5** Diane Keaton b. **17** John Wayne m. Esperanza "Chata" Baur. **20** Director David Lynch b.

FEBRUARY 5 George Arliss d.

MARCH 12 Liza Minnelli is born to Judy Garland and Vincente Minnelli. Liza will be the only child of Oscar winners to win

an Oscar. **30** Doris Day m. George Weidler.

APRIL 1 Noah Beery d. **18** Hayley Mills, daughter of John Mills, b. **25** Joan Crawford divorces Phillip Terry. **•** Talia Shire (Talia Coppola), sister of Francis Ford Coppola, b.

MAY Paulette Goddard and her husband, Burgess Meredith, are steaming over *Time's* claim that she wears falsies. And RKO repossess from Orson Welles all footage of *It's All True*. **20** David Niven's wife, Primula, is fatally hurt in an accident at Tyrone Power's home. Playing a party hide-and-seek game in the dark, she mistakes the basement door for a closet entrance and falls down the stairs.

JULY 1 The atom bomb tested today at Bikini Atoll in the Marshall Islands has been named "Gilda" and is decorated with Rita Hayworth's picture. She is not pleased. **7** Howard Hughes is seriously injured when a plane he is test-flying crashes near Beverly Hills. **14** Elizabeth Taylor makes her first appearance on the cover of *Life*. **18** Busby Berkeley is released from a Los Angeles hospital after treatment for

self-inflicted slash wounds. **19** Norma Jean Dougherty (Marilyn Monroe) takes a screen test at 20th Century Fox. **25** Dean Martin and Jerry Lewis perform together for the first time, at the 500 Club in Atlantic City. **29** Hedda Hopper is the first gossip columnist to mention Norma Jean Dougherty (Marilyn Monroe), declaring that Howard Hughes would like to sign her.

AUGUST 13 Ronald Reagan, in a letter to the editor of the *Hollywood Reporter*, denies the paper's claim that the American Veterans Committee is a red front. **20** A letter in the *Hollywood Reporter* signed "A Wounded Marine," replying to Ronald Reagan's letter of August 13, recalls how the actor, "as a Cutting Room Commando at Fort Roach [the Hal Roach studio, used by the Army to make training films during

the War], so bravely fought the war from the polished night club floors of Hollywood...." **21** MGM announces that it will cast Norma Shearer's discovery, nineteen-year-old Janet Leigh, who has never acted, as the female lead in its upcoming Van Johnson film, *The Romance of Rosy Ridge*. **22** A letter in the *Hollywood Reporter* from a group of stars, including Melvyn Douglas and Medal of Honor winner Audie Murphy, defends Ronald Reagan, pointing out that his poor eyesight kept him from the overseas assignment he had requested. **24** Norma Jean Dougherty signs her first contract with 20th Century Fox. Told that she needs to change her name, she chooses her mother's maiden name, "Monroe." Ben Lyon, star of *Hell's Angels* and now a Fox executive, picks "Marilyn" for her first name, after stage star Marilyn Miller.

Ivers, also starring Barbara Stanwyck, Van Heflin, and Lizabeth Scott. Dinah Shore heads the stage show at the Paramount, where the film premieres.

AUGUST 15 Cary Grant, Ingrid Bergman, and Claude Rains are the stars of Alfred Hitchcock's *Notorious*, premiering at the Radio City Music Hall. **23** Humphrey Bogart and Lauren Bacall star in Howard Hawks's *The Big Sleep*, opening at the Strand. **24** David Lean's *Brief Encounter*, starring Celia Johnson and Trevor Howard, has its U.S. premiere at the Little Carnegie. **28** *The Killers*, starring Edmond O'Brien, Ava Gardner, and introducing Burt

Lancaster, premieres at the Winter Garden.

OCTOBER 10 *The Jolson Story*, starring Larry Parks (with Al Jolson dubbing the songs), premieres at the Radio City Music Hall. **16** John Ford's *My Darling Clementine*, starring Henry Fonda, Victor Mature, and Linda Darnell, premieres at the Fox Theater in San Francisco.

NOVEMBER 12 Walt Disney's *Song of the South*, based on the Uncle Remus stories, premieres at the Fox Theater in Atlanta. One of its songs, "Zip-A-Dee Doo Dah," becomes a hit. **19** *The Razor's Edge*, with Tyrone Power, Ann Baxter, and

Gene Tierney premieres at the Roxy. **21** Samuel Goldwyn's *The Best Years of Our Lives* premieres at the Astor, where TV cameras catch the arriving celebrities. Directed by William Wyler, it stars Dana Andrews, Fredric March, Myrna Loy, Harold Russell (a nonprofessional actor and disabled veteran), Teresa Wright, Cathy O'Donnell, Hoagy Carmichael, and Virginia Mayo.

DECEMBER 18 *The Yearling* premieres at Hollywood's Carthay Circle Theater. The film's stars, Gregory Peck, Jane Wyman, and Claude Jarman Jr. attend. **21** Frank Capra's *It's a Wonderful Life*, starring James Stewart, Donna Reed, Lionel Barrymore,

---

not enough to "stimulate curiosity." **8** The Motion Picture Association of America withdraws its seal of approval from Howard Hughes's *The Outlaw* because Hughes has broken his promise to submit ads for the film for MPAA approval. **20** The first Cannes Film Festival opens on the French Riviera. Its debut, scheduled for September 1939, was delayed by World War II. **26** The Conference of Studio Unions again strikes the studios, claiming that they are stalling on signing contracts. The stu-

dios say that this is a jurisdictional dispute over which unions should do which jobs. For the most part, production of films continues.

OCTOBER • California exhibitors report an increase in the number of suburban theaters showing first-run films. **8** The Screen Actors Guild votes by five to one not to back the Conference of Studio Unions strike. **9** The *Hollywood Reporter* gossip column cautions: "If you have a membership card in the Communist Party under your mattress,

or certain interested parties are sure you have, begin getting nervous and sleeping in your pants, because (and how they do it is a big secret) you've got a surprise coming...."

NOVEMBER 12 Universal merges with International Pictures. The latter's William Goetz and Leo Spitz will head production at Universal–International. **27** The NAACP criticizes Walt Disney's *Song of the South* for romanticizing slavery in its depiction of the "Uncle Remus" stories.

MAY 2 Joan Fontaine m. RKO producer William Dozier. **8** Madeleine Carroll divorces Sterling Hayden. **•** Candice Bergen, daughter of ventriloquist Edgar Bergen, b. **20** Cher (Cherilyn Sarkisian), b.

JUNE 22 Constance Bennett m. John Coulter. **23** William S. Hart d.

JULY 2 Ron Silver (Ron Zimelman) b. **6** Sylvester Stallone b. **7** Anne Baxter m. John Hodiak. **12** Sue Lyon b. **23** John Huston m. Evelyn Keyes.

AUGUST 10 Kitty Carlisle m. Moss Hart. **26** Olivia de Havilland m. Marcus Goodrich.

SEPTEMBER 13 Marilyn Monroe and James Dougherty divorce. **15** Tommy Lee

Jones and director Oliver Stone are born.

OCTOBER 4 Susan Sarandon (Susan Tomalin) b. **13** Jeff Chandler m. Marjorie Hoshelle.

NOVEMBER 6 Sally Field b.

DECEMBER 25 W.C. Fields dies, at Las Encinas Sanitorium, on the holiday he despised.

Personalities

SEPTEMBER 11 *Variety* headlines: "James Mason Hot with Bobbysoxers." **23** Tyrone Power and Cesar Romero, on a goodwill trip to Latin America, have lunch with Eva Perón in Buenos Aires.

OCTOBER 1 The *Hollywood Reporter* prints in full an editorial from a labor paper by AF of L vice president Matthew Woll, accusing several stars, including Myrna Loy and Orson Welles, of being part of a Hollywood "Communist Fifth Column." **4** Myrna Loy sues the *Hollywood Reporter* for libel for its October 1 reprint of the Woll editorial. **9** Lawrence Tierney, movie tough guy and star of *Dillinger*, is sentenced by a Hollywood Municipal Court judge to five days in jail for repeated drunkenness.

21 The *Hollywood Reporter* clears Myrna Loy of the Communist taint smeared on her in its October 1 article. On October 28 it will print a similar retraction about Orson Welles.

NOVEMBER 1 Scores of people are injured as Londoners crowd around the Empire Theater where the first Royal Command Performance involving Hollywood figures is taking place. Among those appearing are Pat O'Brien, Ray Milland, and Joan Bennett. **21** MGM gives Judy Garland a new contract and a raise to $5,600 a week. **29** Five-year-old Ann-Margret arrives in the U.S. from her native Sweden.

DECEMBER • Judy Garland prerecords her songs for *The Pirate*. Her emotional problems—paranoia, hysteria, and pill addiction—will fully surface for the first

time in the production of this picture, which will be filmed into the middle of next year. **9** In his unsuccessful suit to break his contract with Columbia, director Charles Vidor testifies to the verbal abuse he had to take from studio head Harry Cohn. This is the beginning of public knowledge of Cohn's legendary foul mouth. **21** Ava Gardner's new MGM contract raises her from $350 per week to $1,250 a week, following her success on a loanout to Universal for *The Killers*.

Movies

Henry Travers, Beulah Bondi, and Thomas Mitchell, premieres at the Globe. **25** Joan Crawford and John Garfield star in *Humoresque*, opening at the Hollywood Theater in New York. Garfield as a boy is played by Bobby (Robert) Blake, who has played Little Beaver in Republic's Red Ryder series, appeared in Our Gang comedies, and will be TV's "Barreta." **30** David O. Selznick's *Duel in the Sun* premieres at the Egyptian Theater in Hollywood. "Lust in the Dust" took longer to make and will cost more—seven million

dollars, including publicity—than any film before it. Cast members Gregory Peck, Lionel Barrymore, and Jennifer Jones are

here tonight, as are Alfred Hitchcock and John Huston. The post-premiere party is at the Mocambo.

Gregory Peck, Jennifer Jones, Joseph Cotten in *Duel in the Sun*   LC

Business and Society

DECEMBER 3 Members of the House Committee on Un-American Activities, after meeting in closed session in Los Angeles and hearing testimony from Hollywood labor leaders, decide that the full Committee will reconvene here next spring to look into Communism in the film industry. **11** David O. Selznick announces that he will release his films himself rather than

through United Artists. **5** Lew Wasserman becomes president of MCA. **31** U.S. Statutory Court orders the major studios to take

various actions to increase competition in the distribution of their films, but still does not order them to get rid of their theaters.

Births, Deaths, Marriages, and Divorces

28 Burt Lancaster m. Norma Anderson.

Also this year: • Sylvia Sidney divorces Luther Adler.

*T*he price of candy bars at lobby refreshment stands rises from five to six cents. Chaplin is back on the *star* screen after seven years, MGM introduces Deborah Kerr ("rhymes with *star*"), newcomer Richard Widmark pushes a woman in a wheelchair down the stairs, and there are long lines for *Forever Amber*. Elsa Maxwell finds baby Liza Minnelli "enchanting," while Judy Garland has her first major nervous breakdown. The Actors Studio is set up, and 20th Century Fox prematurely gives up on starlet Marilyn Monroe. And in Washington, the House Committee on Un-American Activities (HUAC) begins to cast a pall over Hollywood.

- Number of releases: 486
- Number of theaters: 18,607, of which 548 are drive-ins
- Average weekly attendance: 90,000,000
- Average ticket price: $.40
- Price of a candy bar at lobby refreshment stands: $.06
- Average production cost per feature film: $732,449
- Box office receipts: $1,594,000,000
- Players with term contracts at major studios: 487
- Number of people thanked by Olivia de Havilland while receiving an Oscar for Best Actress for last year's *To Each His Own*: 27

Top stars at the box office, based on a Quigley Publications poll of exhibitors:

1. Bing Crosby
2. Betty Grable
3. Ingrid Bergman
4. Gary Cooper
5. Humphrey Bogart
6. Bob Hope
7. Clark Gable
8. Gregory Peck
9. Claudette Colbert
10. Alan Ladd

Top rental earnings, based on figures reported in *Variety* (these and subsequent figures in this category have been rounded off to the nearest $50,000):

1. *The Best Years of Our Lives* $11,500,000
2. *Duel in the Sun*   10,750,000
3. *Forever Amber*   8,000,000
4. *The Jolson Story*   8,000,000
5. *Unconquered*   7,500,000

The New York Film Critics Circle Awards
Best Picture: *Gentleman's Agreement*

The Golden Globe Awards
Best Picture: *Gentlemen's Agreement*

The Cannes Film Festival
Grand Prize: *Antoine et Antoinette*, *Les Maudits*, *Crossfire*, *Dumbo*, and *Ziegfeld Follies*

The Academy Awards (presented March 20, 1948)
Best Picture: *Gentlemen's Agreement*
Actor: Ronald Colman (*A Double Life*)
Actress: Loretta Young (*The Farmer's Daughter*)
Supporting Actor: Edmund Gwenn (*Miracle on 34th Street*)
Supporting Actress: Celeste Holm (*Gentlemen's Agreement*)
Director: Elia Kazan (*Gentlemen's Agreement*)

January	February	March	April	May	June
21 Laraine Day m. Leo Durocher	**27** Louis B. Mayer's racehorses auctioned	**10** Ronald Reagan pres. of SAG	**10** SAG president Ronald Reagan agrees to inform for the FBI	**22** *Great Expectations*	**20** Bugsy Siegel murdered in Beverly Hills

July	August	September	October	November	December
30 Arnold Schwarzenegger b.	**7** British import duty on American films • The Actors Studio created		**20** HUAC opens hearings into communism in Hollywood	**11** *Gentlemen's Agreement*	**31** Roy Rogers m. Dale Evans

Personalities

JANUARY • James Stewart and Frank Capra are in New York to do some much needed publicizing of *It's a Wonderful Life*, which has been fading at the box office.

FEBRUARY 12 Columnist Jimmy Fidler admits that while he was sick in December, his assistant, over Fidler's byline, gave a glowing review to *Duel in the Sun* based not on his having seen the film but on a press release from David O. Selznick. Fidler says he has now seen the movie and finds it "not conducive to good morals." **27** Louis B. Mayer's sixty racehorses are auctioned off at Santa Anita. Successful bidders include Harry M. Warner, Raoul Walsh, Harry James, and George Brent.

MARCH • Marilyn Monroe films her first movie scene—a second or two in 20th Century Fox's *Scudda-Hoo! Scudda-Hay!* She's walking behind eight-year-old Natalie Wood. **7** The first Fred Astaire dance studio opens, in New York. **13** The Motion Picture Academy gives a special Oscar to disabled veteran Harold Russell at tonight's awards ceremony at the Shrine Auditorium because they felt that, as a non-professional, he had no chance of winning on his own. They were wrong, and he takes a second award for Best Supporting Actor in *The Best Years of Our Lives*.

APRIL 8 Frank Sinatra, at Ciro's, punches syndicated columnist Lee Mortimer, who, says Sinatra, "called me a Dago." Arrested for his action tomorrow, he will settle Mortimer's subsequent lawsuit for $9,000.

MAY • Elsa Maxwell writes in *Photoplay* that baby Liza Minnelli "is enchanting." **9** Big-band singer Doris Day signs with Warners.

JUNE 20 Benjamin "Bugsy" Siegel, gangster and Hollywood socialite since 1936, is murdered in Beverly Hills. **26** Gene Autry leaves Republic Pictures.

JULY • Judy Garland finishes her role in *The Pirate* and enters a sanitorium. **8** Laurence Olivier is knighted.

AUGUST • 20th Century Fox drops Marilyn Monroe.

SEPTEMBER • The Actors Studio, proponent of "method acting," is set up in New York by Cheryl Crawford, Bob Lewis, and Elia Kazan. **1** With a goodbye kiss from

Movies

MARCH 5 Elia Kazan's *Boomerang*, starring Dana Andrews, Jane Wyatt, and Lee J. Cobb opens at the Roxy, where Ed Sullivan emcees a variety show onstage, featuring, "direct from the Copa," Sid Caesar. **6** The Three Stooges's *Fright Night*, in which Shemp Howard replaces Jerry "Curly" Howard, is released. **21** A gala premiere at Hollywood's Carthay Circle Theater launches *The Egg and I*, starring Claudette Colbert and Fred MacMurray, and Marjorie Main and Percy Kilbride as Ma and Pa Kettle, characters they will play in a series of films.

APRIL 11 Charlie Chaplin's first film since 1940, *Monsieur Verdoux*, also starring Martha Raye, opens at the Broadway theater. **23** Carol Reed's *Odd Man Out*, starring James Mason and Robert Newton, opens at the Criterion.

MAY 3 In several Warner Bros. cartoons, a bird has already uttered the classic, "I tawt I taw a putty tat." But in *Tweetie Pie*, released today, the "putty tat," for the first time, is Sylvester. **22** David Lean's *Great Expectations*, starring John Mills, Valerie Hobson, Alec Guinness, and Jean Simmons, opens at the Radio City Music Hall.

JUNE 4 *Miracle on 34th Street* stars Maureen O'Hara, John Payne, Emund Gwenn, and Natalie Wood, opening today at the Roxy.

JULY 15 *The Hucksters* opens today at MGM's showcase theaters in Los Angeles. "Gable's New Star Is Deborah Kerr (Rhymes with Star)," say the ads. **22** RKO's *Crossfire* premieres at the Rivoli. A story about homophobia has become a film about anti-Semitism, with Robert Ryan as the soldier and bigot. The Army will show it only at its U.S. bases, and the Navy won't show it at all. **24** Cary Grant, Myrna Loy, Shirley Temple, and Rudy Vallee star

Business and Society

JANUARY 1 Dore Schary becomes head of RKO. **23** The Crest, a Fox West Coast theater, opens in Long Beach, California. Prefabricated, with a spun glass curtain and seats that slide back, it is called "the theater of the future."

FEBRUARY 21 David O. Selznick sells his stock in United Artists and will release his

films himself.

MARCH Msgr. Fulton Sheen, Dr. Harry Emerson Fosdick, and Rabbi Sidney Goldstein, writing in *Motion Picture Magazine*, condemn the threat to the American home posed by Hollywood's high divorce rate. **2** Conference of Studio Unions strike leader Herbert Sorrell is found beaten and bound a hundred miles from Los Angeles. **10** Ronald Reagan becomes president of the Screen Actors Guild.

APRIL 10 Screen Actors Guild president Ronald Reagan agrees to inform the FBI of any communist activity in SAG.

MAY 29 According to the *Hollywood Reporter*, the film industry is "poised for a leap from psychology to politics—both national and international—for its next cycle . . . ." The paper cites such upcoming titles as *A Foreign Affair*, *State of the Union* and *All the King's Men*.

Births, Deaths, Marriages, and Divorces

JANUARY 21 Laraine Day m. baseball manager Leo Durocher and will remarry him next year, because of a problem with her divorce from her previous husband. **25** Keenan Wynn and Eve Abbott divorce, and four hours later she m. Van

Johnson, her ex-husband's best friend.

FEBRUARY 24 Edward James Olmos b.

MARCH 14 Billy Crystal b. **19** Glenn Close b.

APRIL 18 James Woods b. **25** Sterling Hayden m. Betty De Noon. **28** Louis B. Mayer and his wife, Margaret, are divorced.

JULY 5 Joan Blondell m. producer Mike Todd. **6** Virginia Mayo m. Michael O'Shea. **17** Hedy Lamarr divorces John Loder. **22** Danny Glover is born, as is Albert Brooks (Albert Einstein), son of

Lana Turner, Tyrone Power takes off from Hollywood, flying his own plane, for a tour of Africa and Europe. In Ethiopia he will meet Emperor Haile Selassie. In Rome he will meet Linda Christian, putting an end to his affair with Turner. **13** MGM grants an emotionally shaky Robert Walker a leave without pay to pull himself together. **25** Producer Mike Todd is declared bankrupt. **29** In the *Hollywood Reporter,* Joan Crawford quotes her daughter Christina, who wrote from camp: "Mummy dearest—I got the candy. It was beautiful. I love you."

OCTOBER • Claudette Colbert backs out of *State of the Union* because the script reveals that it's going to be Spencer Tracy's film, not hers. Katharine Hepburn will replace her. **11** Gene Kelly breaks his ankle, forcing him out of *Easter Parade,* now in

in *The Bachelor and the Bobby-Soxer,* opening at the Radio City Music Hall.

AUGUST 27 *Kiss of Death* opens at the Mayfair. It introduces Richard Widmark, who giggles and pushes a woman in a wheelchair down a flight of stairs.

SEPTEMBER 11 Howard Hughes's *The Outlaw* finally opens in New York, at the Broadway Theater.

OCTOBER 22 *Forever Amber* sets a new house record for opening days at the Roxy, grossing over $25,000. Linda Darnell can go back to being a brunette from the

A WESTERN TRIO IS BORN

Western star Roy Rogers marries Dale Evans on December 31, 1947. Roy, Dale, and Trigger will be one of Hollywood's most beloved and famous trios.   *LC*

bleached blonde she has hated but has been contractually required to keep until the picture's release. Cardinal Spellman cites *Forever Amber,* already rated "condemned" by the Legion of Decency, as a "glorifica-

tion of immorality and licentiousness." On December 4, 20th Century Fox president Spyros Skouras says that the studio will re-edit *Forever Amber* to attain Legion of Decency approval.

JUNE 18 "Stix Still Nix British Pix," says a *Variety* headline.

JULY 2 "Weighty Social Themes Give Hywd. Films New Adult Slant" headlines the *Hollywood Reporter.* **30** The motion picture advertising code is revised to forbid the ridiculing of anyone's race. **31** Grad Sears is named president of United Artists.

AUGUST 7 Britain places a seventy-five

percent import duty on American films. **8** U.S. film companies retaliate against the new British tax with a boycott of the British market. **16** PRC (Producers Releasing Corporation) is merged with Eagle-Lion Films. PRC will continue to produce films under the name "Mutual." **18** The federal government brings an antitrust case against Technicolor and Eastman for monopolizing access to color film technology.

OCTOBER 16 The Gallup Poll organization reveals that it helped Samuel Goldwyn choose the title of *The Best Years of Our Lives* and the casting of Fredric March in a lead role.

NOVEMBER • Although the Conference of Studio Unions strike is still on, only the carpenters remain out. Most of the painters and decorators have been replaced and do not have the muscle to get their jobs back. **27** Pressure from the Catholic

radio comedian "Parkyakarkus" (Harry Einstein). **30** Arnold Schwarzenegger b.

SEPTEMBER 26 Greer Garson divorces Richard Ney.

OCTOBER 5 Choreographer Gower Champion m. Marge Belcher, dancer and half-

sister of silent film star Lina Basquette, creating the Marge and Gower Champion partnership. **24** Kevin Kline b. **29** Richard Dreyfuss b.

NOVEMBER 13 Joe Mantegna b. **30** Director Ernst Lubitsch d.

DECEMBER 17 George Brent m. Janet Michaels. **18** Director Steven Spielberg b. **31** Roy Rogers m. Dale Evans.

Personalities

rehearsals, and setting the stage for Fred Astaire to emerge from "retirement."

DECEMBER 3 Marlon Brando is recognized as one of America's foremost actors when he opens on Broadway in Tennessee William's play, *A Streetcar Named Desire*. **14** Ronald Reagan and Jane Wyman separate.

Movies

NOVEMBER 8 John Garfield stars in *Body and Soul*, opening at the Globe. **11** Darryl Zanuck's expose of anti-Semitism, *Gentlemen's Agreement*, starring Gregory Peck, Dorothy McGuire, and John Garfield, premieres at the Mayfair. **25** *Out of the Past*, starring Robert Mitchum, Jane Greer, Kirk Douglas, and Rhonda Fleming, premieres at the Palace.

OPEN-AIR "FLICKERIES" ON ROMANCE PATROL

The October 1 Variety *reports:* "With the boom in drive-ins in full swing, operators of the open-air flickeries are now ganging up to put a crimp in necking and other boy-girl antics."

October 1, 1947

Business and Society

War Veterans appears to have influenced the decision of Loew's Theaters to cancel its bookings of Chaplin's *Monsieur Verdoux*.

Births, Deaths, Marriages, and Divorces

Also this year: • Sylvia Sidney m. agent Carleton Alsop. • Rhonda Fleming and Thomas Lane divorce.

HUAC HITS HOLLYWOOD

Screen actor Adolphe Menjou (right) named names of people he believed to be Communist sympathizers. HUAC used this information to help compile subpeona lists for its 1947 fall hearings. The hearings were held over several days. At the October 23 hearing, Gary Cooper (left)—along with Robert Montgomery, George Murphy, and Ronald Reagan—testified on communism in their industry.   *Photos LC*

MAY 14 The House Un-American Activities Committee (HUAC), conducting ten days of closed hearings in Los Angeles, hears Robert Taylor and Leila Rogers, mother of Ginger Rogers, testify to the threat of communism in Hollywood. **15** Jack Warner and Adolphe Menjou name names that HUAC will use to compile subpoena lists for its coming fall hearings.

JULY 30 Congressman Richard Nixon says that the upcoming HUAC hearings "will be sensational" but kept "on a high plane and very factual."

SEPTEMBER 12 The Screen Actors Guild adopts a voluntary loyalty oath.

OCTOBER 20 The House Un-American Activities Committee opens Washington hearings into communism in Hollywood. Jack Warner and Louis B. Mayer say that the industry has controlled communism in its ranks. **21** Adolphe Menjou tells HUAC that "Hollywood is one of the main centers of Communist activity in America." **22** Robert Taylor names Howard da Silva and Karen Morley as communist sympathizers. **22** *Variety* editorializes: "Hollywood is being slapped across its glamorous visage with a red herring that may well result in a tragic shutdown on all chance-taking, new ideas and free expression." **23** Gary Cooper, Robert Montgomery, George Murphy, and Ronald Reagan testify at the HUAC hearings on communism in their industry. John Garfield,

at a press conference, attacks the hearings. **25** Motion Picture Association of America president Eric Johnston calls for better protection of the civil liberties of those being accused at the current hearings into communism in Hollywood. Walt Disney retracts the testimony he gave yesterday describing The League of Women Voters as a "communist front." **26** The Committee for the First Amendment sponsors a network radio broadcast attacking the HUAC hearings and sends a chartered plane from Hollywood to Washington carrying Humphrey Bogart, Lauren Bacall, Danny Kaye, John Huston, Sterling Hayden, Gene Kelly, Ira Gershwin, and others to protest the hearings. **30** With the end of the hearings, the Committee has charged with contempt all of the men who will become known as the Hollywood Ten. The ten writers, producers, and directors, who in the past few days have refused to cooperate with the inquiry, include Ring Lardner Jr., Lester Cole, John Howard Lawson, Alvah Bessie, Dalton Trumbo, Albert Maltz, Samuel Ornitz, Herbert Biberman, Edward Dmytryk, and Adrian Scott.

NOVEMBER 19 Anticommunists are elected to top posts in the Screen Writers Guild. **24** The House of Representatives cites the Hollywood Ten for contempt of Congress. **25** Ending a two-day conference at the Waldorf Astoria in New York, industry leaders announce that the Hollywood Ten will be fired or suspended without pay. The

executives aim to "eliminate any subversives in the industry," while safeguarding free speech. It is the beginning of the "blacklist."

DECEMBER • A federal grand jury indicts the Hollywood Ten for contempt of Congress. **2** Humphrey Bogart issues a statement calling his participation in the plane trip to Washington to protest HUAC "ill-advised and even foolish."

1948

JANUARY 14 The Screen Writers Guild votes to limit its support for the Hollywood Ten to friend-of-the-court briefs in their suits to gain reinstatement at the studios.

APRIL 19 John Howard Lawson is the first of the Hollywood Ten to be convicted of contempt of Congress.

1950

JUNE 9 John Howard Lawson and Dalton Trumbo are the first of the Hollywood Ten to go to prison. **29** The eight remaining members of the Hollywood Ten are convicted of contempt of Congress.

1951

MARCH 26 The Supreme Court refuses to review a lower-court decision upholding the firing of Hollywood Ten writer Lester Cole based on the "morals clause" in his contract.

Photo opposite: Marlon Brando in *The Wild One*, courtesy MSN /© COLUMBIA PICTURES

The Age of the Independents

1948–The Present

RKO's announcement that it will divest itself of its theater interests is the beginning of the end of the studio system, in which vertical control of production and distribution created a predictable environment for the factory-like making and marketing of movies. Combined with the weakening of control over contract players, it points the studios toward their future role as backers and distributors of films made by independent producers. Meanwhile, in Hollywood, ticket sales are off, production is down, and layoffs are spreading. In its first TV-related survey, the Gallup Poll reveals that TV owners decrease their moviegoing by ten percent. In Italy, Vittorio De Sica's neorealist classic *The Bicycle Thief* is released.

- Number of releases: 459
- Number of theaters: 18,395, of which 820 are drive-ins
- Average weekly attendance: 90,000,000
- Average ticket price: $.40
- Box office receipts: $1,506,000,000
- Average production cost per feature film: $1,028,240
- Number of TV sets in use: approx. 1,000,000
- Players with term contracts at major studios: 449
- Bette Davis's salary: $365,000
- The 15-year-old winner of the Miss Burbank contest: Debbie Reynolds
- Flight time between New York and Los Angeles: 10 hours

Top stars at the box office, based on a Quigley Publications poll of exhibitors:
1. Bing Crosby
2. Betty Grable
3. Abbott & Costello
4. Gary Cooper
5. Bob Hope
6. Humphrey Bogart
7. Clark Gable
8. Cary Grant
9. Spencer Tracy
10. Ingrid Bergman

Top rental earnings, based on figures reported in *Variety*
1. *The Road to Rio* $4,500,000
2. *Easter Parade*   4,200,000
3. *Red River*   4,150,000
4. *Johnny Belinda*   4,100,000
5. *The Three Musketeers* 4,100,000

The New York Film Critics Circle Awards
Best Picture: *The Treasure of the Sierra Madre*

The Golden Globe Awards:
Best Picture: *The Treasure of the Sierra Madre*

The Cannes Film Festival: not held

The Academy Awards (presented March 24, 1949)
Best Picture: *Hamlet*
Actor: Laurence Olivier (*Hamlet*)
Actress: Jane Wyman (*Johnny Belinda*)
Supporting Actor: Walter Huston (*The Treasure of the Sierra Madre*)
Supporting Actress: Claire Trevor (*Key Largo*)
Director: John Huston (*The Treasure of the Sierra Madre*)

January	February	March	April	May	June
23 *The Treasure of the Sierra Madre*	**11** Britain and American movie industry end conflict		**19** John Howard Lawson is first of Hollywood Ten convicted		**9** *The Lady from Shanghai*
5 Barbara Hershey b.				**10** Howard Hughes gains control of RKO	

July	August	September	October	November	December
5 Ida Lupino m. producer Collier Young			**30** RKO is first major studio to announce sale of theaters		• Hal Roach leaves films for TV production
1 Dore Schary agrees to head production at MGM	**21** Milton Berle's success begins TV challenge to movies			• Rita Hayworth divorces Orson Welles	

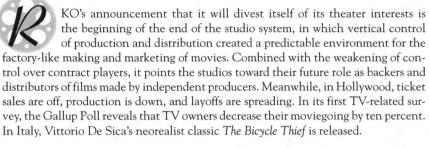

Personalities

JANUARY • Warner Bros. is looking for B. Traven, mysterious author of *The Treasure of the Sierra Madre*, thought to be in Mexico. They would like him to attend the opening of the film.

FEBRUARY • Frank Sinatra makes *Who's Who* for the first time. **23** Ronald Reagan is elected to the national board of Americans for Democratic Action. **24** "Debra Paget, the beautiful fourteen-year-old redhead signed by 20th Fox, isn't reporting to the studio until June, when she finishes school," says the *Hollywood Reporter*.

MARCH 9 Marilyn Monroe begins a six-month contract at Columbia. Fox's Joseph Schenck, with whom Monroe has had an affair, introduced her to Columbia's Harry Cohn. **14** Danny Kaye concludes six weeks of personal appearances at the London Palladium, where he has played to 250,000 people. **16** Mary Pickford meets with the FBI, at her request, to discuss subversives in Hollywood (possibly with emphasis on Charlie Chap-lin). **16** Hedda Hopper and Louella Parsons call a temporary truce in their feud to lunch together at Romanoff's. **21** Joan Crawford arrives for the Academy Awards ceremonies at the Shrine Auditorium dressed in an all-white gown covered with silver beads and topped by a white mink stole.

APRIL 3 Practicing riding for the western *Yellow Sky*, Gregory Peck breaks his leg when his horse falls on him. **22** Lon Chaney Jr. attempts suicide by swallowing sleeping tablets.

JUNE 8 "Vera-Ellen and good-looking Rock Hudson, currently toiling at Warners, are making with the dates," observes the *Hollywood Reporter*. **17** A plane crash in Pennsylvania kills producer and showman Earl Carroll and his actress wife, Beryl Wallace. Jack Oakie missed the flight because of retakes on a film.

JULY • Sixteen-year-old Elizabeth Taylor is having her first romance, with Army football star Glenn Davis. Rex Harrison testifies at the inquest into the suicide of Carole Landis, with whom he was having an affair; reconciles with his wife, Lilli Palmer; and starts a new affair with Martine Carol. • Cartoonist Walter Lantz and his studio are basking in the glow of "The Woody Woodpecker Song," which has become a top-selling record. **6** "I can't go on being sexy and sultry forever. It's not a solid

Movies

JANUARY 23 John Huston's *The Treasure of the Sierra Madre*, staring Humphrey Bogart, Walter Huston, Tim Holt, and Bruce Bennett, opens at the Strand, with a stage show headed by Lionel Hampton.

FEBRUARY 24 *Sitting Pretty*, in which Clifton Webb creates the character "Mr. Belvedere," genius babysitter, premieres at the Lincoln Theater in Miami.

MARCH 3 *The Naked City*, starring Barry Fitzgerald, Don Taylor, and Howard Duff,

HALF THE FUN IS IN READING THE ADS

"Bud and Lou are in a stew when they tangle with the titans of terror!"—Abbott & Costello Meet Frankenstein

"Where love and murder meet!"—Key Largo

"Men turned tyrant and women sold their souls to possess the gold in a mighty mountain of malice!—Treasure of the Sierra Madre

Business and Society

JANUARY 10 The Pantages Theater in Hollywood is the first major movie house to show theater TV — races from Santa Anita —as part of its regular show.

FEBRUARY • Republic's Truecolor begins to compete with Cinecolor and Technicolor. Warners and 20th Century Fox are testing Eastman Color. **17** The House Labor Subcommittee begins hearings into Hollywood's long-running jurisdictional strike, in which producers will deny they conspired with IATSE to fire Conference of Studio Unions carpenters and the CSU denies it is communist-led.

MARCH • Writers and directors working on campaign films for progressive presidential candidate Henry Wallace ask to remain anonymous for fear of retribution in Hollywood. **11** The British government and the American movie industry negotiate an end to their conflict in which last August's seventy-five-percent tax was met by an American boycott.

APRIL • WPIX TV in New York buys from Alexander Korda the rights to show twenty-four of his films—the first quality films to be shown on TV. **18** The Motion Picture Country Hospital, a facility for those in the industry who cannot afford to care for themselves, is dedicated.

Births, Deaths, Marriages, and Divorces

JANUARY 4 Judy Holliday m. David Oppenheim. **14** David Niven m. Hjoerdis Tersmeden. **26** Tyrone Power and Annabella divorce. **29** Johnny Weissmuller is divorced from Beryl Scott and m. golfer Allene Gates.

FEBRUARY 5 Barbara Hershey (Barbara Herzstein) b. **28** Victor Mature m. Dorothy Berry.

MARCH 5 Eli Wallach m. Anne Jackson.

APRIL 26 Lana Turner m. millionaire Bob Topping, one of Arline Judge's ex-husbands. **28** Margaret Sullavan divorces Leland Hayward.

MAY 7 Jason Robards Jr. m. Eleanor Pittman. **9** Cyd Charisse m. Tony Martin, ex-husband of Alice Faye.

career," says Lauren Bacall in *Look* magazine. In *Key Largo*, she declares, she will play it straight, "without tricks." **19** Eve Arden's radio program, "Our Miss Brooks," premieres on CBS. It features the acerbic wit she has developed in her film roles. **19** MGM informs Judy Garland, due to work in the upcoming *The Barkleys of Broadway*, that, as of July 12, she has been suspended until she is emotionally capable of working. **28** All major studios observe a three-minute period of silence during the funeral of D. W. Griffith, who died five days ago. Honorary pallbearers at the service include Lionel Barrymore, Richard Barthelmess, Charlie Chaplin, Cecil B. DeMille, John Ford, Samuel Goldwyn, Sid Grauman, Will Hayes, Jesse Lasky, Louis B. Mayer, Hal Roach, Joseph Schenck, Mack Sennett, Erich von Stroheim, and Adolph Zukor.

AUGUST 8 MGM starts filming *The Barkleys of Broadway*, with Ginger Rogers replacing Judy Garland and working again with Fred Astaire. Garland has to be escorted off the set when she shows up during the first weeks of shooting and harasses Rogers. **19** Threatened with a Howard Hughes lawsuit, Howard Hawks agrees to cut a scene from *Red River* that Hughes claims was lifted from *The Outlaw*.

SEPTEMBER 1 Robert Mitchum is arrested in a raid on a cottage where people are smoking marijuana. The thirty-one-year-old actor speculates that it may be "the bitter end" of his career. Within a month, the Mayan Theater in Los Angeles will run a double feature: *Marijuana* and *Devil Smoke*, advertised as "Ripped From Today's Headlines!" **9** Columbia does not renew Marilyn Monroe's contract.

OCTOBER 26 With Harry Truman looking like a sure loser in his campaign against Tomas Dewey, the *Hollywood Reporter* comments: "The Man in the White House would certainly like to get his name on a ballot like the one Ronald Reagan, as incumbent, has on the Screen Actor's Guild Ticket." Reagan is running unopposed. **29** James Dean plays Frankenstein in his high school Halloween Carnival play, *Goon with the Wind*.

NOVEMBER 6–7 At a Mexico City hotel, Rita Hayworth and Prince Aly Khan keep at bay a pack of photographers, who have Hollywood's hottest romance surrounded. **18** Arriving for the opening on Broadway of Ingrid Bergman in the play, *Joan of Lorraine*, Charles Boyer is pulled from his limousine by bobby-soxers, Myrna Loy's mink coat is yanked off her shoulders, and Paulette Goddard is greeted by excited shouts of "Evelyn Keyes!"

---

opens at the Capitol. Director Jules Dassin has used location shots exclusively. The basis for the later TV show, the film ends with a voice-over: "There are eight million stories in the naked city. This has been one of them." Onstage: Dean Martin and Jerry Lewis.

MAY 20 Vincente Minnelli's *The Pirate*, starring Judy Garland, Gene Kelly, and Walter Slezak, opens at the Radio City Music Hall, which has just raised evening prices from $1.25 to $1.40.

JUNE 9 Orson Welles's *The Lady from Shanghai*, opening at the Criterion, stars Welles, Rita Hayworth, and Everett Sloane.

24 John Ford's *Fort Apache*, the beginning of his cavalry trilogy, stars John Wayne, Henry Fonda, Shirley Temple, Pedro Armendariz, and John Agar. Lena Horne heads the stage show at the Capitol, where it opens today. **30** *Easter Parade*, starring Judy Garland and Fred Astaire, premieres at Loew's State. **30** Marlene Dietrich, Jean Arthur, and John Lund star in Billy Wilder's *A Foreign Affair*, premiering at the Paramount, where singer Jo Stafford heads the stage show.

JULY 15 Columbia's *Superman* serial, starring Kirk Alyn, is released. **16** Humphrey Bogart, Edward G. Robinson, Lauren

Bacall, Clair Trevor, and Thomas Gomez star in John Huston's *Key Largo*, opening at the Strand, where Count Basie and Billie Holiday are onstage. **28** *Abbott and Costello Meet Frankenstein*, with Bela Lugosi, Lon Chaney Jr., and Glenn Strange, opens at the Criterion. When Lon Chaney Jr. (son of the legendary horror-film star) explains that he becomes a wolf when the moon is full, Costello quips, "You and twenty million other guys." Chaney will later say that Abbott and Costello "ruined the horror films; they made buffoons out of the monsters." Bela Lugosi is playing Dracula on the screen for only the second time. Glenn Strange, this movie's Franken-

---

MAY 3 The Supreme Court tells the U.S. District Court to reconsider the possibility of ordering the studios to divest themselves of all their movie theaters. **10** Howard Hughes gains control of RKO.

JULY 1 Dore Schary, who resigned from RKO yesterday, agrees to become head of production at a floundering MGM. **23** After clashing with Howard Hughes, RKO production head N. Peter Rathvon resigns.

> In 1920, sixty thousand acres in the U.S. were planted in seed for popcorn; this year it will be 300,000. (Popcorn has a high markup and the salt makes people thirsty, boosting soft drink sales.)

AUGUST 25 *Variety* reports that Paramount newsreels are presenting more feature stories because they can't compete with TV's prompt delivery of the news.

SEPTEMBER • The studios are announcing plans to expand into TV. **21** On this Tuesday night, Milton Berle becomes the permanent host of the *Texaco Star Theater* on NBC TV, beginning an entertainment revolution that will almost topple the movies.

---

28 Mickey Rooney and Betty Jane Rase divorce.

JUNE 28 Jane Wyman divorces Ronald Reagan. • Kathy Bates b.

JULY 5 Rex Harrison discovers the body of Carole Landis, his former lover, who has committed suicide with sleeping pills.

8 Silent screen star King Baggot d. **9** Robert Walker m. Barbara Ford, daughter of director John Ford. **23** D.W. Griffith d.

AUGUST 5 Ida Lupino m. producer Collier Young. **23** Franchot Tone and Jean Wallace divorce. **29** Rory Calhoun m. Lita Baron.

SEPTEMBER 19 Jeremy Irons b. **28** Cinematographer Gregg Toland d.

OCTOBER 17 Margot Kidder b.

NOVEMBER • Rita Hayworth divorces Orson Welles.

Personalities

DECEMBER • MGM's *Words and Music* opens at Loew's State in Memphis with two numbers by Lena Horne deleted. The theater's racial policy also dictates that her name be removed from all ads. **6** On the cover of *Life*, illustrating the story "New Male Movie Stars," is Montgomery Clift. **6** Robert Walker goes berserk at a police station in Topeka, Kansas, after his arrest for fighting a cab driver in front of a local hotel. Walker, also arrested for drunkenness in Los Angeles six weeks ago, is under treatment at the Menninger Clinic. **7** Errol Flynn, arrested in a 2 A.M. dispute with New York police over a cab ride, kicks one of the officers.

Olivia de Havilland, star of *The Snake Pit*   *LC*

Movies

stein, will be Sam the bartender in TV's *Gunsmoke*. The film is a critical and financial success, re-establishing Abbott and Costello among the top draws at the box office.

AUGUST 26 *Rope*, starring James Stewart, Farley Granger, and John Dall, opens at the Globe. Alfred Hitchcock's first color film, it is notable for his use of extended takes.

SEPTEMBER 29 Laurence Olivier's *Hamlet* opens at the Park Avenue Cinema. **30** John Wayne and Montgomery Clift

star in Howard Hawks's *Red River*, opening at the Capitol.

OCTOBER 1 *Johnny Belinda*, starring Jane Wyman, Lew Ayres, Charles Bickford, and Agnes Moorehead opens at the Strand. Onstage, "Merve" Griffin sings with the Freddy Martin Orchestra. **22** Moira Shearer and Anton Walbrook star in *The Red Shoes*, opening at the Bijou.

NOVEMBER 4 *The Snake Pit*, starring Olivia de Havilland in a film about mental asylums, premieres at the Rivoli. The film prompts many states to review their treatment of mental illness.

DECEMBER 15 *The Paleface*, opening at the Paramount, stars Bob Hope and Jane Russell and features the song, "Buttons and Bows." Benny Goodman heads the stage show.

Business and Society

OCTOBER 30 RKO becomes the first major studio to announce that it will separate its ownership of theaters from its production facilities.

NOVEMBER 24 Eastman signs a consent decree in the government's antitrust case against it, opening its color film processing patents to everyone.

DECEMBER • Hal Roach leaves films for TV production.

Births, Deaths, Marriages, and Divorces

DECEMBER 4 Louis B. Mayer m. Lorena Danker. **9** Ossie Davis m. Ruby Dee. **16** Robert Walker and Barbara Ford divorce. **28** Gloria Swanson and William Davey divorce.

Also this year: • Marrying are Corinne Calvet and John Bromfield, Gloria Grahame and director Nicholas Ray, and Walter Matthau and Grace Johnson. • Shelley Winters and Paul Mayer divorce.

*P*roducers are beginning to shoot abroad, where labor is cheaper and they can use currency earned but not exportable. Acetate-based film is replacing nitrate stock. On the screen, Dean Martin and Jerry Lewis debut, and Fred and Ginger are together again. Gene Kelly discovers Leslie Caron, and Marilyn Monroe poses for a calendar. Bette Davis and Warners divorce, Rita Hayworth marries a prince, and Ingrid Bergman is a fallen woman. In this year's class at Hollywood's Panaieff Ballet Center are eight-year-old Stephanie Powers, nine-year-old Jill St. John, and eleven-year-old Natalie Wood. In Washington and Hollywood, the witch hunt goes on.

- Number of releases: 470
- Number of theaters: 18,570, of which 1,203 are drive-ins
- Average weekly attendance: 87,500,000
- Average ticket price: $.46
- Box office receipts: $1,451,000,000
- Number of TV sets in use: approx. 4,000,000
- Number of films Dean Martin and Jerry Lewis will make together, beginning with this year's *My Friend Irma*: 12
- Number of roles played by Alec Guinness in *Kind Hearts and Coronets*: 8
- Marilyn Monroe's pay for posing nude for a calendar: $50

Top stars at the box office, based on a Quigley Publications poll of exhibitors:

1. Bob Hope
2. Bing Crosby
3. Abbott & Costello
4. John Wayne
5. Gary Cooper
6. Cary Grant
7. Betty Grable
8. Esther Williams
9. Humphrey Bogart
10. Clark Gable

Top Rental Earnings

1. *Jolson Sings Again* — $5,500,000
2. *Pinky* — 4,200,000
3. *I Was a Male War Bride* — 4,100,000
4. *Joan of Arc* — 4,100,000
5. *The Snake Pit* — 4,100,000

The New York Film Critics Circle Awards
Best Picture: *All the King's Men*

The Golden Globe Awards
Best Picture: *All the King's Men*

The Cannes Film Festival
Grand Prize: *The Third Man*

The Academy Awards (presented March 23, 1950)
Best Picture: *All the King's Men*
Actor: Broderick Crawford (*All the King's Men*)
Actress: Olivia de Havilland (*The Heiress*)
Supporting Actor: Dean Jagger (*12 O'Clock High*)
Supporting Actress: Mercedes McCambridge (*All the King's Men*)
Director: Joseph L. Mankiewicz (*A Letter to Three Wives*)

January	February	March	April	May	June	
10 Robert Mitchum gets two months on marijuana charge			**2** George Sanders m. Zsa Zsa Gabor		**22** Meryl Streep b.	
	25 Government says Paramount has signed consent decree	• Motion Picture Industry Council formed to keep Hollywood free of Communists			**27** Marilyn Monroe poses nude for calendar	

July	August	September	October	November	December	
13 Jennifer Jones m. David O. Selznick		• Humphrey Bogart banned from El Morocco			**12** Louella Parsons breaks story of Ingrid Bergman's pregnancy by Roberto Rossellini	
	31 Richard Gere b.		**10** Marilyn Monroe's first appearance in *Life*	**8** *All the King's Men*		

Personalities

JANUARY 10   Robert Mitchum is found guilty of smoking marijuana and is sentenced to two months in jail. He will serve forty-nine days and be released March 29.

FEBRUARY 10   "Ingrid Bergman is trying to get her medico husband [Dr. Peter Lindstrom] to take three months away from his practice to be with her in Italy for the shooting of the Rossellini picture," the *Hollywood Reporter* notes. **10** MGM celebrates its twenty-fifth anniversary by assembling fifty-eight of its biggest stars for a group portrait, which will be published in *Life* on February 28.

MARCH 1   James Cagney, who left Warner Bros. in 1942, agrees to return to make films both as a contract player and an independent producer. **18** Montgomery Clift has turned down the lead role in *Sunset Boulevard*, and today Paramount announces that William Holden will play it. **24** The Academy Awards are given out this year in the 950-seat Academy Theater. The studio's most attractive female stars have been assigned the task of handing out the statuettes, including statuesque Ava Gardner and Elizabeth Taylor, seventeen, who walks out to the strains of "Did You Ever See a Dream Walking?" **28** MGM begins shooting *On the Town* at the Brooklyn Navy Yard. It sets a precedent for the outdoor, on-location filming of musicals.

APRIL • Leslie Caron debuts with Les Ballets des Champs-Elysées in Paris, where she will be spotted by Gene Kelly, who will get her an MGM screen test. **9** James Dean finishes first in the Indiana state competition of the National Forensic League contest with a reading from Dickens's *Pickwick Papers*: "The Madman." Dean begins by screaming, which gets the judges' attention. **13** The first public mention of an affair between Ingrid Bergman and Roberto Rossellini appears in Igor Cassini's "Cholly Knickerbocker" column in the New York *Journal-American*. **28** "The Hollywood she-wolves are drooling for one Tony Curtis, U-I [Universal-International] player, who is young, dark, good-looking, and what's more important—single," says the *Hollywood Reporter*.

MAY 1   MGM, which has warned Judy Garland about her lateness on *Annie Get Your Gun*, removes her from the film when she refuses to return to the set after lunch today, and will replace her (May 19) with Betty

Movies

JANUARY 19   *So Dear to My Heart*, opening today in 150 Midwestern theaters, is the first Disney feature with very limited animation—just twelve minutes. It includes the hit song, "Lavender Blue." **20** Joseph Mankiewicz's *A Letter to Three Wives*, starring Jeanne Crain, Linda Darnell, Ann Sothern, Kirk Douglas, and Paul Douglas, with the voice of Celeste Holm as "Addie," premieres at the Radio City Music Hall.

MARCH 24   *Ma and Pa Kettle* premieres at three Kansas City theaters, with stars Marjorie Main and Percy Kilbride on hand. It's the first of a series of movies based on characters that appeared in *The Egg and I*. **29** With the opening of *The Set-Up* at the Criterion, a boxing film starring Robert Ryan, RKO has beaten to the punch Stanley Kramer's *Champion*, another fight film, scheduled to open in April. Howard Hughes is in court, claiming *Champion* has story elements too close to *The Set-Up*.

APRIL 10   Kirk Douglas stars in *Champion*, with Arthur Kennedy and Marilyn Maxwell, opening at the Globe. On May 20 the producers will settle Howard Hughes's suit claiming that this movie copies from his boxing film, *The Set-Up*, and agree to delete a minute of action and several words from the soundtrack. The re-edited *Champion* will be re-released in June.

MAY 4   Ten years after *The Story of Vernon and Irene Castle*, Fred Astaire and Ginger Rogers are together for a tenth and final time in *The Barkleys of Broadway*, premiering at Loew's State. **12** *Home of the Brave*, starring James Edwards, Jeff Corey, Lloyd Bridges, and Frank Lovejoy, premieres at the Victoria. It's the story of prejudice experienced by a black soldier.

Business and Society

JANUARY 18   Eastman Kodak announces reduced prices for acetate-based "safety" film stock, which has replaced the inflammable nitrate stock in about twenty-five percent of current releases.

FEBRUARY 25   The Justice Department announces that Paramount has signed a consent decree, agreeing to divorce its production from its distribution activity.

MARCH • The Motion Picture Industry Council is formed to keep Hollywood free of Communists. Active in it are Roy Brewer (head of IATSE), Ronald Reagan, Dore Schary, and Cecil B. DeMille.

APRIL 30   Joseph Schenck resigns from 20th Century Fox because the government will not let him retain his theater interests *and* serve as an executive at the studio.

JUNE 8   An FBI informant in a secret report revealed at a spy trial names as Communists or sympathizers John Garfield, Paul Muni, Sylvia Sidney, Fredric March, Edward G. Robinson, and Melvyn Douglas. **8** The California State Senate Committee on Un-American Activities links many in Hollywood, including Charlie Chaplin, Katharine Hepburn, Danny Kaye, Gene Kelly, Gregory Peck, Frank Sinatra, and Orson Welles to the Communist Party line.

Births, Deaths, Marriages, and Divorces

JANUARY 6   Director Victor Fleming d. **11** Keenan Wynn m. Betty Walker. **27** Tyrone Power m. Linda Christian.

FEBRUARY 5   Richard Burton m. Sybil Williams. **8** Audie Murphy m. Wanda Hendrix.

MARCH 14   Jean Arthur divorces Frank Ross Jr.

APRIL 2   George Sanders m. Zsa Zsa Gabor. **15** Wallace Beery d. **20** Jessica Lange b.

MAY 27   Rita Hayworth m. Prince Aly Khan. **31** Doris Day divorces George Weidler.

JUNE 3   Mickey Rooney m. Martha Vickers. **6** Paulette Goddard divorces Burgess

Hutton. Garland has been receiving shock treatment for depression. **20** Peter Lorre files for bankruptcy. **27** For $50, Marilyn Monroe poses nude for history's most famous calendar. **27** Louella Parsons writes from Cannes on the marriage today of Rita Hayworth to Prince Aly Khan: "The Arabian Nights wedding…glittered to its storybook climax when the bridegroom knelt and kissed the foot of his tired but beautiful bride from the sidewalks of New York." **29** Judy Garland enters a Boston Hospital to recover from a nervous collapse.

JUNE 19 Ronald Reagan breaks his leg while sliding at a charity baseball game in Chicago.

AUGUST 1 Bob Hope, filming a scene from *Fancy Pants* with Lucille Ball, falls off a wooden horse and is hospitalized with a back injury. **4** Bette Davis announces

Marilyn Monroe poses this year for history's most famous calendar   *LC*

that, after eighteen years, she and Warner Bros. have signed a "professional divorce." Her last day on the lot will be August 9. She is now filming *Beyond the Forest*, which she later characterizes as "horseshit." On her final day, in a dubbing session, she will speak the line, "I can't stand it here anymore." **24** Stage actor Marlon Brando signs to make his film debut in Stanley Kramer's *The Men.*

SEPTEMBER • Humphrey Bogart is banned from El Morocco in New York when, having had too much to drink, he gets into an argument and tussle with a woman over possession of a stuffed animal. **5** Critic James Agee's article on "Comedy's Greatest Era," a celebration of silent screen comics in today's *Life* will draw a huge response and begin to revive the reputations of Harold Lloyd, Buster Keaton, and Harry

JUNE 7 Republic releases its *King of the Rocketmen* serial, a source for *The Rocketeer* (1991).

JULY 26 *Mighty Joe Young*, starring Terry Moore, Ben Johnson, and Robert Armstrong, with special effects by Willis O'Brien, creator of *King Kong*, opens at the Criterion and proves so popular that the theater is put on a nine A.M. to three A.M. schedule.

AUGUST 26 Cary Grant and Ann Sheridan star in Howard Hawks's *I Was a Male War Bride*, opening at the Roxy.

SEPTEMBER 2 James Cagney stars as the murderous mama's boy Cody Jarrett ("Made it, Ma. Top of the world!") in *White Heat*, directed by Raoul Walsh, opening at the Strand. **8** Mr. Magoo, the nearsighted old man with the voice of actor Jim Backus, debuts with the release of UPA's *Ragtime Bear* cartoon. **16** Road Runner makes his cartoon debut with the release of Warner Bros.'s *Fast and Furry-ous.* **28** *My Friend Irma*, the first of twelve films Dean Martin and Jerry Lewis will make together, premieres at the Paramount. Martin and Lewis head the stage show. **29** Elia Kazan's *Pinky*, starring Ethel Waters, Ethel Barrymore, and Jeanne Crain, a white

woman playing a light-skinned black woman who passes for white, opens at the Rivoli in New York.

OCTOBER 6 *The Heiress*, starring Olivia de Havilland, Montgomery Clift, and Ralph Richardson, premieres at the Radio City Music Hall and at Grauman's Chinese Theater in Hollywood, where Clift attends with Elizabeth Taylor, whom he has just met and has decided to call "Bessie Mae." **11** *Intruder in the Dust*, with Juano Hernandez and Claude Jarman Jr., one of several films this year with a racial theme, premieres in Oxford, Mississippi, near where it was filmed.

JULY • Warner Bros. is the first major studio to open a division to license its cartoon characters to children's clothing manufacturers. Walt Disney is already in the field. **20** The *Hollywood Reporter* says teenagers are calling drive-ins the "passion pit." **25** A federal statutory court order directs 20th Century Fox, Warner Bros., and Loew's (MGM) to divest themselves of their theater holdings.

AUGUST 30 *Variety* notes that drive-ins in many parts of the South are the only un-

segregated theaters and are building up a substantial black patronage.

SEPTEMBER 12 Motion Picture Associaton head Eric Johnston announces that in the past year foreign markets accounted for thirty-eight percent of U.S. film rentals, second highest ever.

OCTOBER 25 "…Seems I can't get a job," writes B.P. Schulberg in a full-page ad in the trade papers asking for work. The

one-time head of production at Paramount wonders, "must we always wait until a productive pioneer is found dead in some 'obscure Hollywood hotel room' to feel sympathetic?"

NOVEMBER 30 *Variety* headlines on the front page: "$20,000,000 Boxoffice Payoff for H'wood Negro-Tolerance Pix."

DECEMBER 12 All sectors of the industry unite in a Conference of Motion Picture

Meredith. **22** Meryl Streep (Mary Louise Streep) b. **28** Joanne Dru and Dick Haymes divorce.

JULY 7 Errol Flynn and Nora Eddington divorce. • Shelley Duvall b. **13** Jennifer Jones m. David O. Selznick. **15** Greer Garson m. Texas oil man E.E. Fogelson. **31** Guy Madison m. Gail Russell.

AUGUST 7 Joanne Dru m. John Ireland. **9** James Stewart m. Gloria McLean. **10** Viveca Lindfors m. director Don Siegel. **12** Angela Lansbury m. agent Peter Shaw. **24** Dean Martin and Elizabeth MacDonald divorce. **31** Richard Gere b.

SEPTEMBER 1 Dean Martin m. Jeanne Beigger. **2** Ernest Borgnine m. Rhoda Kemins. **6** Ginger Rogers divorces Jack Briggs. **20** Richard Dix d.

OCTOBER 4 Armand Assante b. **8** Sigourney Weaver (Susan Weaver) b. **27** Deanna Durbin divorces Felix Jackson.

Personalities

Langdon. On the magazine's cover is a photograph of Ben Turpin.

OCTOBER • Marlon Brando lives in a hospital for paralyzed veterans and uses a wheelchair for a month to prepare for his role in *The Men*. **10** Marilyn Monroe appears in *Life* for the first time, one of eight starlets in a photo essay. **19** Warner Bros. suspends Lauren Bacall, for the sixth time, for refusing a role in *Storm Center*, and issues a statement denouncing her. **31** "The Nancy Davis now under contract to MGM is not the Nancy Davis frequently identified with the party-liners," writes the *Hollywood Reporter*. Mervyn LeRoy had asked SAG president Ronald Reagan to clear her of any Communist taint. Reagan then begins to socialize with her.

NOVEMBER • Several distributors blame Shirley Temple's announcement that she will divorce John Agar for the poor showing of her *Seabiscuit* and *Kiss for Corliss*. They say the public won't accept her as *that* kind of grownup.

DECEMBER 8 Ava Gardner's romance with Frank Sinatra begins when the two renew an old acquaintance at the Broadway opening night of *Gentlemen Prefer Blondes*. **12** Louella Parsons breaks the story of Ingrid Bergman's pregnancy by Roberto Rossellini, to whom she is not married. Howard Hughes, who knew and was sworn to secrecy, has told Parsons, thinking it will help to jump-start *Stromboli* at the box office.

Movies

NOVEMBER 8 *All the King's Men*, starring Broderick Crawford, Mercedes McCambridge, Joanne Dru, John Ireland, and John Derek, opens at the Victoria. **11** *Battleground*, starring Van Johnson, John Hodiak, and Ricardo Montalban, premieres at the Astor. **17** John Ford's *She Wore a Yellow Ribbon*, opening at the Capitol, stars John Wayne, Joanne Dru, John Agar, Ben Johnson, Harry Carey Jr., and Victor McLaglen.

DECEMBER 8 *On the Town*, starring Frank Sinatra and Gene Kelly, opens at the Radio City Music Hall. **14** *Sands of Iwo Jima*, starring John Wayne, premieres at the Fox Theater in San Francisco. **25** Spencer Tracy, Katharine Hepburn, Judy Holliday, and Tom Ewell star in *Adam's Rib*, opening at the Capitol, which has a stage show featuring Eddie Duchin.

Meryl Streep, born this year   *LC*
© *UNITED ARTISTS*

Business and Society

Organizations (COMPO) to work on better public relations for the movies. **21** Warner Bros. announces that it will sell its theaters. **23** Under threat of a libel suit, *Counterattack*, an anti-Communist newsletter, retracts charges that Fredric March and his wife, actress Florence Eldridge, are Communist, or fellow-travelers. The accusations have kept the Marches from working. **28** 20th Century Fox announces that it will produce TV programs. **31** Paramount Pictures divests itself of its movie houses, spinning off United Paramount Theaters.

Births, Deaths, Marriages, and Divorces

NOVEMBER 6 Brad Davis b. **13** Whoopi Goldberg (Caryn Johnson) b.

DECEMBER • Paul Newman m. Jackie Witte. **4** Jeff Bridges, brother of Beau and son of Lloyd Bridges, b. **5** Shirley Temple divorces John Agar. **20** Clark Gable m. Sylvia Ashley, Douglas Fairbanks's widow. **25** Cary Grant m. Betsy Drake. • Sissy Spacek (Mary Elizabeth Spacek) b.

Also this year: • John Belushi b. • Merle Oberon and Lucien K. Ballard divorce.

*F*ilm attendance is beginning to plummet as the studios try to find ways they can make money from television, and the Hollywood Ten begin to go to prison. Elizabeth Taylor's wedding just before the opening of *Father of the Bride* is a publicity coup for MGM. Norma Desmond is ready for her closeup in *Sunset Boulevard*, and *All About Eve* is everything but a "bumpy night" for Bette Davis. Ingrid Bergman, having played a nun and a saint, gives birth to a baby out of wedlock; Marlon Brando comes to the screen; Charlton Heston is the first movie star from TV; and Rosetta Jacobs becomes Piper Laurie.

- Number of releases: 622
- Number of theaters: 19,106, of which 2,202 are drive-ins
- Theaters selling popcorn: 95%
- Average weekly attendance: 60,000,000
- Average ticket price: $.53
- Box office receipts: $1,376,000,000
- Average production cost per feature film: $1,100,000
- Number of TV sets in use: approx. 11,000,000
- Players with term contracts at major studios: 315
- Number of Oscar nominations earned by *All About Eve*: a record 14 (wins 6)

Top billing by gender in Hollywood films, according to *The Guinness Book of Movie Facts and Feats*:
men: 72%
women: 28%

Top stars at the box office, based on a Quigley publications poll of exhibitors:
1. John Wayne
2. Bob Hope
3. Bing Crosby
4. Betty Grable
5. James Stewart
6. Abbott & Costello
7. Clifton Webb
8. Esther Williams
9. Spencer Tracy
10. Randolph Scott

Top rental earnings, based on figures reported in *Variety*:
1. *Samson and Delilah* $11,000,000
2. *Battleground*   4,550,400
3. *King Solomon's Mines*   4,400,000
4. *Cheaper by the Dozen*   4,325,000
5. *Annie Get Your Gun*   4,200,000

The New York Film Critics Circle Awards
Best Picture: *All About Eve*

The Golden Globe Awards
Best Picture: *Sunset Boulevard*

The Academy Awards (presented March 29, 1951)
Best Picture: *All About Eve*
Actor: Jose Ferrer (*Cyrano de Bergerac*)
Actress: Judy Holliday (*Born Yesterday*)
Supporting Actor: George Sanders (*All About Eve*)
Supporting Actress: Josephine Hull (*Harvey*)
Director: Joseph L. Mankiewicz (*All About Eve*)

January	February	March	April	May	June
	14 Joan Bennett ad ridicules Hedda Hopper	**20** William Hurt b.		**6** Elizabeth Taylor m. Nicky Hilton	**9** First of Hollywood Ten go to prison
	17 Faye Emerson divorces Elliott Roosevelt		• Gene Autry is first film star to announce appearance in TV series		

July	August	September	October	November	December
20 *Broken Arrow*		**28** Judy Garland leaves MGM		• Patent Office upholds Motion Picture Academy exclusive right to phrase "Academy Awards"	
	10 *Sunset Boulevard*		**22** Screen Directors Guild battle over loyalty oath		**17** Elizabeth Taylor and Nicky Hilton separate

Personalities

JANUARY 2 Stage actor Walter Matthau places his first bet on a horse, a habit that will cost him more than $3 million over the next few decades. **6** In an interview with Bob Thomas in the *Los Angeles Mirror*, Ronald Reagan complains about the quality of the roles being offered to him. "Well, I can always go back to being a sports announcer," he says. **11** Brian Donlevy is able to walk away from his plane after he crashes into a hillside near Solvang, California. **22** Rosetta Jacobs, signed in the fall to a Universal contract, graduates from high school and in three weeks will be playing Ronald Reagan's daughter in her first film, *Louisa*. She will also have a new name: Piper Laurie. **25** John Wayne becomes the 125th star to leave his hand- and footprints outside Grauman's Chinese Theater.

FEBRUARY 2 Ingrid Bergman gives birth to Roberto Rossellini's child, offending U.S. religious groups. RKO is reconsidering plans to re-release *The Bells of St. Mary's*, in which she plays a nun, and is worried about the upcoming general release of *Joan of Arc*, in which she plays a saint. **14** Joan Bennett takes a full page ad in the *Hollywood Reporter* to ridicule Hedda Hopper, with whom she has been feuding. Bennett also sends the columnist a skunk for Valentine's Day, which Hopper names "Joan." **14** Nancy Sinatra, having discovered her husband Frank's romance with Ava Gardner, orders him out of the house. **18** At New York's Stork Club, director André De Toth, Veronica Lake's husband, beats up a man who tries to touch her hair.

MARCH 23 The Academy Awards ceremonies have moved to the Hollywood Pantages Theater this year. Paul Douglas, emceeing tonight, introduces Anne Baxter and John Hodiak, commenting on their "really handsome marriage," which, in fact, has only three more years to go before a divorce.

APRIL • Gene Autry is the first major film star to announce that he will appear in a sponsored TV series. **1** The *New York Times* reports that "Charlton Heston, a recruit from Broadway and East Coast television, will take over the role previously announced for Burt Lancaster in 'Dark City,'" making Heston the first major film star to come to the movies from TV. **15** Bette Davis, protected by a bodyguard against threats from her estranged husband, William Sherry, begins work in San Francisco

Movies

FEBRUARY 2 Carol Reed's *The Third Man*, starring Joseph Cotten, Orson Welles, Alida Valli, and Trevor Howard, opens at the Victoria. **8** *Francis*, the first of a series of films about a talking mule, starring Donald O'Connor, premieres in New Orleans. **15** *Stromboli*, the Rossellini/Bergman film, does well on this first day of its national release, but will quickly fade at the box office (except at the drive-ins). Howard Hughes has re-edited the film without Rossellini's permission and is advertising it with images of spurting volcanoes. **22** Walt Disney's *Cinderella* opens at the Mayfair.

MAY 17 Humphrey Bogart and Gloria Grahame are *In a Lonely Place*, opening at the Paramount, where Frankie Laine and Patti Page head the stage show. **18** Vincente Minnelli's *Father of the Bride*, starring Spencer Tracy, Joan Bennett, and Elizabeth Taylor, opens at the Radio City Music Hall. MGM integrates Elizabeth Taylor's May 6th marriage, to Nicky Hilton, into publicity for the film.

JUNE 7 *Winchester 73*, opening at the Paramount, is the first of several James Stewart films directed by Anthony Mann and the beginning of a cycle of 1950s "adult" westerns, including *High Noon* and *Shane*. **8** Sterling Hayden, Louis Calhern, Sam Jaffe, and Marilyn Monroe are in John Huston's *The Asphalt Jungle*, opening at the Capitol. **27** George Pal's *Destination Moon*, the first major film in a cycle of 1950s science-fiction movies dealing with outer space and other worlds (the low-budget *Rocketship XM* opened May 26), premieres at the Mayfair.

JULY 20 *Broken Arrow*, starring James Stewart, Jeff Chandler, and Debra Paget, premieres at the Roxy. Onstage are the Andrews Sisters. **20** Marlon Brando makes his

Business and Society

JANUARY • MGM is trying to placate exhibitors, who are furious at Lana Turner's recent statement to the Associated Press that she has given up moviegoing to watch TV.

FEBRUARY 8 In its final decree (upheld by the Supreme Court on June 5), the Federal statutory court hearing the antitrust case against the studios orders 20th Century Fox, Loew's, and Warners to get rid of their theater interests. **28** The anti-monopoly consent decree signed by Technicolor and approved today in Federal court provides that the company will license its patents to other companies.

MARCH 14 Colorado Sen. Edwin Johnson, chairman of the Senate Interstate Commerce Committee, attacks the morals of the movie industry in general and Ingrid Bergman in particular and says that the government should license movie actors.

APRIL 4 The Screen Producers Guild is founded.

JUNE 21 The Motion Picture Association bans movie ads that refer to the misconduct of a film's stars.

JULY 12 Paul McNutt, representing an investment syndicate, takes over and becomes chairman of the board of United Artists,

Births, Deaths, Marriages, and Divorces

JANUARY 17 Faye Emerson divorces Elliott Roosevelt.

FEBRUARY 8 Kirk Douglas and Diana Dill divorce. **9** Gloria De Haven divorces John Payne. **10** Evelyn Keyes and John Huston divorce. **18** Cybill Shepherd b.

MARCH 20 William Hurt b.

APRIL 4 Christine Lahti b. **7** Walter Huston d. **14** Wanda Hendrix divorces Audie Murphy.

MAY 6 Vera Jayne Palmer m. Paul Mansfield and becomes Jayne Mansfield. **6** Elizabeth Taylor m. Nicky Hilton. **7** Jack Lemmon m. Cynthia Stone. **31** Tom Berenger b.

on *All About Eve*. She and co-star Gary Merrill are soon having an affair. **23** Lucille Ball and Desi Arnaz announce the creation of Desilu Productions.

MAY 1 Frank Sinatra leaves MGM. **6** Eighteen-year-old Elizabeth Taylor marries Nicky Hilton at the Church of the Good Shepherd in Beverly Hills, where the six hundred guests include people with names like Astaire, Rogers, Tracy, Garson, etc. MGM has provided her white satin negligee for tonight. Her seventeen trunks are packed for the honeymoon trip on the *Queen Mary*, where she and her hotel-heir husband will dine with the Duke and Duchess of Windsor. "I just love everything about getting married," says Elizabeth. (They will separate on December 17.) **8** Bing Crosby's lawyer says that "strained relations" characterize the marriage of the

singer/actor and his wife, Dixie. **19** Alice Faye leaves 20th Century Fox.

JUNE • *Modern Screen* tells about Janet Leigh's two teenage marriages, "—the story of a girl who grew up too soon, married too soon and suffered before her time." **19** Two days after MGM suspended Judy Garland for missing rehearsals for *Royal Wedding*, she makes a halfhearted attempt at suicide, running the edge of a broken bottle across her throat after locking the bathroom door—but first calling out her intentions to her husband, Vincente Minnelli.

JULY • *Christian Life*, a fundamentalist magazine, reports that Jane Russell and Roy Rogers are born-again Christians. One reader will respond: "I didn't know there were Hollywood Christians." **10** After

six suspensions in as many years, Warners announces the termination of Lauren Bacall's contract by mutual agreement.

AUGUST 16 "Cecil B. DeMille is very eager to sign up Gina Lollobridgida, the Italian actress Howard Hughes flew in for an RKO test two weeks ago," says the *Hollywood Reporter*. Hughes will sign her to a seven-year contract, but then does not use her. **19** Danny Kaye gives a gala party at the Beverly Hills Hotel for Laurence Olivier and Vivien Leigh. Guests include Louis B. Mayer, Ginger Rogers, Lana Turner, Rosalind Russell, Van Johnson, and Montgomery Clift.

SEPTEMBER 17 Dean Martin and Jerry Lewis debut on TV's *The Colgate Comedy Hour*, with a skit satirizing the effect of TV on the movies. **22** Dean Martin and Jerry

Jeff Chandler and James Stewart in *Broken Arrow*   MOMA

and Frank L. McNamee is now its president. **17** Y. Frank Freeman takes over as Paramount production chief. **19** John Wayne, president of the Motion Picture Alliance, announces that his organization has asked the Los Angeles City Council to require the registration of all local Communists.

screen debut in *The Men*, directed by Fred Zinnemann, with a screenplay by Carl Foreman, opening at the Radio City Music Hall.

AUGUST 4 Elia Kazan's *Panic in the Streets*, opening at the Roxy, stars Richard Widmark, Paul Douglas, Jack Palance, Zero Mostel, and Barbara Bel Geddes. **10** Billy Wilder's *Sunset Boulevard*, starring William Holden, Gloria Swanson, and Erich von Stroheim, premieres at the Radio City Music Hall. It includes a clip from *Queen Kelly*, the uncompleted 1920s film in which von Stroheim directed Swanson. At its Hollywood preview for industry figures, Louis B. Mayer reportedly gave it an instant

AUGUST • Due to insufficient interest, Walter Reade Theaters cancels an experiment at its Woodbridge, New Jersey, drive-in, where it had set up customer charge accounts. **3** The Defense Department classifies film as an essential industry for purposes of determining draft classifications. **8** *Daily Variety* reveals that subsidiaries of Universal, 20th Century Fox, Columbia, and RKO have been making commercials for TV, the medium with which the studios are supposedly locked in

review. "You bastard, you have disgraced the industry that made you and fed you," he shouted at Wilder. "You should be tarred and feathered and run out of Hollywood." Wilder replied, "Fuck you."

OCTOBER 13 Joseph Mankiewicz's *All About Eve*, starring Bette Davis, Ann Baxter, Celeste Holm, Thelma Ritter, Gary Merrill, George Sanders, and (in a small but memorable appearance at a party) Marilyn Monroe, opens at the Roxy. It earns a record fourteen Oscar nominations.

NOVEMBER 1 John Ford's *Rio Grande* premieres at the Majestic Theater in San An-

mortal combat. **13** RKO signs Jerry Wald and Norman Krasna to the biggest contract yet given independent producers by a major studio—a potential sixty pictures over five-and-a-half years.

SEPTEMBER 1 Harry Warner addresses all employees at Warner Bros. about the dangers of Communism.

OCTOBER 3 After losing a certifying election on September 13, Carpenters Local

JUNE 8 Joan Blondell divorces Mike Todd.

JULY 3 Bette Davis divorces William Sherry. **28** Bette Davis m. Gary Merrill, who divorced his previous wife this morning.

AUGUST • Myrna Loy and Gene Markey divorce. **30** Margaret Sullavan m.

Kenneth Wagg. **31** Director-screenwriter-actor John Sayles b.

SEPTEMBER 21 Bill Murray b.

OCTOBER 1 Randy Quaid b. **23** Al Jolson d. **30** Errol Flynn m. Patrice Wymore. **31** John Candy b.

NOVEMBER 28 Ed Harris b.

DECEMBER 7 Robert Montgomery and Elizabeth Allen divorce. **9** Robert Montgomery m. Elizabeth Harkness. **12** Faye Emerson m. orchestra leader Skitch Henderson. **16** Shirley Temple m. Charles Black. **21** Stewart Granger m.

Personalities

Lewis publicly apologize to irate movie-theater owners for ridiculing the industry in their September 17 TV appearance. **23** In the first Hollywood show for soldiers wounded in Korea, Donald O'Connor, Shelly Winters, Keenan Wynn, Janet Leigh, and Debbie Reynolds entertain at a northern California air base. **26** Alfred Hitchcock fires Raymond Chandler from *Strangers on a Train*. **28** Judy Garland and MGM agree jointly to cancel her contract, and she leaves Metro after being there a few days short of fifteen years.

OCTOBER • Bob Hope entertains American troops in Korea. **5** Groucho Marx, his movie career winding down, brings radio's "You Bet Your Life" to TV. His theme music is "Hooray for Captain Spaulding," from *Animal Crackers* (1930).

NOVEMBER • Montgomery Clift begins to see a psychiatrist for his drinking problem.

DECEMBER 13 James Dean begins his professional career with an appearance in a Pepsi commercial in which he, Nick Adams—another aspiring actor—and other teenagers sing the Pepsi jingle while dancing around a jukebox. **15** The joint statement by Barbara Stanwyck and Robert Taylor that they will divorce surprises many in Hollywood, where they were considered one of the most happily married couples. **25** A woman who says she wanted to beat up Errol Flynn ransacks his Los Angeles home while he's on his honeymoon with Patrice Wymore.

Movies

tonio, with personal appearances by Ford, John Wayne, and Maureen O'Hara, who lay a wreath at the Alamo. **9** *King Solomon's Mines*, starring Stewart Granger and Deborah Kerr, premieres at the Radio City Music Hall. **16** *Cyrano de Bergerac*, starring Jose Ferrer, opens at the Bijou Theater.

DECEMBER 20 The Astor in New York hosts the premiere of *Harvey*, starring James Stewart. **26** *Born Yesterday*, opening at the Victoria, stars Judy Holliday, William Holden, and Broderick Crawford.

Gloria Swanson and William Holden in *Sunset Boulevard*   MSN
© PARAMOUNT PICTURES

Business and Society

946 removes the picket line it first put up in front of the studios on September 23, 1946. IATSE has won out as bargaining agent for studio carpenters. **16** *Hollywood the Dream Factory*, by Hortense Powdermaker, the first anthropological study of the movie industry, is published. **22** At a Screen Directors Guild Meeting, Cecil B. DeMille and other conservative members of the board of directors fail in their attempt to recall the group's president, Joseph Mankiewicz, because he opposes a mandatory loyalty oath (to the U.S.). DeMille and his allies then resign. **26** Joseph Mankiewicz asks Screen Directors Guild members to voluntarily sign a loyalty oath.

NOVEMBER • The U.S. Patent Office upholds the Academy of Motion Picture Arts and Science's exclusive right to the use of the phrase "Academy Awards." **20** RKO announces that it has divested itself of its theaters in order to comply with the antitrust consent decree.

Births, Deaths, Marriages, and Divorces

Jean Simmons. • Deanna Durbin m. director Charles Henri-David. **28** Henry Fonda m. Susan Blanchard, Oscar Hammerstein II's stepdaughter.

Also this year: • Gabriel Byrne and Steven Seagal are born. • Edna McRae (Ellen Burstyn) m. William Alexander. • Barbara Rush m. Jeffrey Hunter.

7he House Committee on Un-American Activities opens another round of hearings focused on Hollywood, with Sterling Hayden and Edward Dmytryk naming names. The first movie theater in a shopping center is built in Framingham, Massachusetts, and Hollywood tries to fight TV with color, not yet available on the tube. The use of the unstable cellulose nitrate as a film stock ends, but not before the deterioration process has set in that will destroy almost half the films made so far in America. Director Akira Kurosawa's *Rashomon*, released last year, wins the Grand Prize at the Venice Film Festival, leading to the rebirth of the Japanese film industry.

- Number of releases: 654
- Number of theaters: 18,980, of which 2,830 are drive-ins
- Average weekly attendance: 54,000,000
- Average ticket price: $.53
- Box office receipts: $1,310,000,000
- Average production cost per feature: $1,100,000
- Number of TV sets in use: approx. 16,700,000
- Players with term contracts at major studios: 318
- Mario Lanza's salary: $800,000 per year
- Elizabeth Taylor's salary: $1,500 per week
- Number of costumes used in *Quo Vadis*: 32,000
- Cost of the eighteen-minute ballet sequence in *An American in Paris*: $542,000

Top stars at the box office, based on a Quigley Publications poll of exhibitors:

1. John Wayne
2. Dean Martin & Jerry Lewis
3. Betty Grable
4. Abbott & Costello
5. Bing Crosby
6. Bob Hope
7. Randolph Scott
8. Gary Cooper
9. Doris Day
10. Spencer Tracy

Top rental earnings, based on figures reported in *Variety*

1.	*David and Bathsheba*	$7,000,000
2.	*Show Boat*	5,200,000
3.	*An American in Paris*	4,500,000
4.	*The Great Caruso*	4,500,000
5.	*A Streetcar Named Desire*	4,250,000

The New York Film Critics Circle Awards
Best Picture: *A Streetcar Named Desire*

The Golden Globe Awards
Best Picture (Drama): *A Place in the Sun*
Best Picture (Musical/Comedy): *An American in Paris*

The Cannes Film Festival
Grand Prize: *Miracle in Milan* and *Miss Julie*

The Academy Awards (presented March 20, 1952)
Best Picture: *An American in Paris*
Actor: Humphrey Bogart (*The African Queen*)
Actress: Vivien Leigh (*A Streetcar Named Desire*)
Supporting Actor: Karl Malden (*A Streetcar Named Desire*)
Supporting Actress: Kim Hunter (*A Streetcar Named Desire*)
Director: George Stevens (*A Place in the Sun*)

January	February	March	April	May	June	
29 Elizabeth Taylor divorces Nicky Hilton	**15** *Bedtime for Bonzo*	**8** HUAC begins more hearings into communism in Hollywood	• Veronica Lake files for bankruptcy	**11** Marilyn Monroe begins long-term contract with 20th Century Fox	**4** Tony Curtis m. Janet Leigh	

July	August	September	October	November	December	
	16 Dore Schary gains full power to run MGM **14** *A Place in the Sun*	**18** *A Streetcar Named Desire*	**16** Judy Garland opens at the Palace		• Marilyn Monroe calendar a bestseller **7** Ava Gardner m. Frank Sinatra	

Personalities

JANUARY 7   Ten-year-old Peter Fonda accidentally shoots himself in the stomach while his father, Henry, is on his honeymoon with his third wife. The boy is hospitalized in "fair" condition.

FEBRUARY 1   At a preview of John Huston's *The Red Badge of Courage*, the audience laughs and many walk out before the two-hour, fifteen-minute film ends. Huston, who is about to leave the country to film *The African Queen*, entrusts the picture to MGM to cut, which it does, with a vengeance, removing much of its antiwar sentiments. The film will be released on the lower half of a double feature and loses money. **7**   The *Hollywood Reporter* gossips: "Ronald Reagan won't say a thing but Nancy Davis insists there'll be no wedding." **9**   Greta Garbo, wearing a black veil, becomes an American citizen.

MARCH 24   Elizabeth Taylor and director Stanley Donen make a quick exit from the Mocambo when Taylor's ex-husband, Nicky Hilton, walks in with Gloria De Haven. **27**   "Harlow, Russell and Now Domergue," is *Look* magazine's cover story on Howard Hughes's latest star project, Faith Domergue. **29**   At the Pantages Theater, Marilyn Monroe makes her only appearance at an Academy Awards ceremony, giving out the Oscar for Sound Recording.

APRIL •   Veronica Lake files for bankruptcy. •   Maurice Chevalier is denied a visa to come to the U.S. because he allegedly supports Communist-front groups in France. **12**   Greer Garson becomes an American citizen.

MAY •   Louella Parsons, in a *Modern Screen* article titled "The Truth about My Feuds," trashes Orson Welles, James Mason, Gene Tierney, and Rex Harrison. Then she writes: "As I grow older, I realize you only hurt yourself by holding grudges and enmity against others." **8**   Mary Astor unsuccessfully attempts suicide. **11**   Marilyn Monroe begins a long-term contract with 20th Century Fox, starting at $500 a week. **16**   Sandra Shaw announces that she and husband Gary Cooper have separated—a parting that will last three years. Cooper's romance with Patricia Neal is a factor.

JUNE •   Darryl Zanuck and his wife meet Bella Wegeir, who will become the producer's protégé, Bella Darvi. The screen name of the Polish-born woman, who becomes like a "niece" to Mrs. Zanuck, will be made from the first names of the producer and his wife,

Movies

JANUARY 25   UPA releases *Gerald McBoing Boing*, a cartoon about a boy who goes "boing" when he tries to speak.

FEBRUARY 15   *Bedtime for Bonzo*, starring Ronald Reagan as a monkey's father, premieres at the Circle Theater in Indianapolis. Bonzo the chimp is there, but his co-star isn't.

MARCH 8   *Royal Wedding*, starring Fred Astaire and Jane Powell, opens at the Radio City Music Hall.

Bedtime for Bonzo   MOMA

APRIL 19   Warners' *I Was a Communist for the FBI*, starring Frank Lovejoy, premieres at the Stanley Theater in Pittsburgh, the city where the film's true story took place. **27**   MGM's *The Great Caruso*, which catapults concert tenor Mario Lanza to a brief stardom, premieres in Cincinnati.

MAY 2   Howard Hawks's production of *The Thing from Another World* opens at the Criterion in New York. In this first film to combine horror with science fiction, the monster (played by James Arness), says Walter Winchell, "makes Dracula look like a petunia."

Business and Society

JANUARY 1   A test is begun in Chicago in which three hundred families can receive new feature films without commercials on TV for $1 per showing. It is the first test of movies on "pay" TV. Warner Bros.' *April Showers*, released in 1948, is the first film made available for the test.

FEBRUARY 7   Lawyers Arthur B. Krim and Robert S. Benjamin agree to take control of the faltering United Artists. **16**   New York State bans the showing of Roberto Rossellini's *The Miracle* because it is "sacrilegious." It will become a censorship test case for the Supreme Court.

MARCH 14   *Daily Variety* reports that Ward Bond has convinced the California Teacher's Association not to make its planned award to Jose Ferrer for *Cyrano de Bergerac* because of Ferrer's "subversive" connections.

27   The Movie Production Code is changed to once again totally ban narcotics as a film subject. Abortion, for the first time, is also explicitly placed off limits. **29**   The FCC suggests to the major Hollywood studios that it will prevent them from investing in the lucrative TV business if they continue to restrict the availability of their stars to TV and keep their movies off the home screen.

APRIL •   Forty-one Technicolor films are in production, about double the number this

Births, Deaths, Marriages, and Divorces

JANUARY 16   Betty Hutton and Theodore Brisken divorce. **25**   Joan Fontaine divorces William Dozier. **29**   Elizabeth Taylor divorces Nicky Hilton.

FEBRUARY 9   Terry Moore m. football star Glenn Davis, Elizabeth Taylor's first boyfriend. **19**   Linda Darnell divorces Peverell Marley. **21**   Barbara Stanwyck and Robert Taylor divorce.

MARCH 4   Bonzo, the chimp who costarred with Ronald Reagan in *Bedtime for Bonzo*, dies in a Hollywood fire. **17**   Kurt Russell b. **22**   Judy Garland divorces Vincente Minnelli.

APRIL 3   Doris Day m. producer Martin Melcher, ex-husband of Patti Andrews of

Virginia. Darvi and Zanuck almost immediately begin an affair. **5** Hedy Lamarr is furious with *Look* magazine's publication today of a still from a nude scene in the 1933 *Ecstasy*, which she would just as soon forget. **12** Prince Aly Khan, estranged husband of Rita Hayworth, threatens violence against photographers in Paris if they try to snap him dancing with Joan Fontaine.

JULY • *Modern Screen* runs a photograph of Joan Crawford romping with daughter Christina and her other children. The caption reads: "Vacations with her children are the high spots in Joan's life." **17** Filming in the jungle on *The African Queen* is finished. While Katharine Hepburn has been away, Spencer Tracy has been repeatedly flirting with Joan Fontaine in London.

AUGUST • Anita Ekberg, Miss Sweden, comes to America to begin a movie career, but fails to land anything. She will be more successful when she returns next year. **5** Hedda Hopper reports that "Dan Dailey, Hollywood's best all-around actor, is back in circulation again after five months stay at the Menninger Clinic in Topeka, Kas." Dailey says that he "cracked."

SEPTEMBER 8 *Collier's* magazine carries the first major feature story on Marilyn Monroe. **14** B movie actor Tom Neal beats Franchot Tone into unconsciousness in front of the Hollywood Hills home of Barbara Payton, the actress whom they both want to marry. Neal, a former golden gloves boxer, gives Tone a concussion, fractured cheek, and broken nose. Payton gets a black eye from a stray punch. **16** Barbara Payton, who was to marry Tom Neal, says

"yes" to Franchot Tone's hospital bedside proposal. She also says "That Neal is a brute." **28** Franchot Tone, his eyes still blackened from the September 14 beating administered by Tom Neal, marries Barbara Payton, whom they both wanted. Neal says: "I hope they'll both be happy." The marriage will last seven weeks. **30** After their car collides with another on La Cienga Boulevard, Judy Garland and Sid Luft, her manager and lover, get into a fistfight with bystanders. Garland makes a quick exit, and Luft is arrested for drunken driving.

OCTOBER 9 "They've had to insist that Marilyn Monroe don panties over at RKO. That tight skirt she wears with nothing underneath has caused too many work delays on the lot...," notes the *Hollywood Reporter*. Monroe is at RKO on a loanout from Fox. **16** The marquee of New

---

JUNE 14 Billy Wilder's *Ace in the Hole* (later retitled *The Big Carnival*) premieres at three theaters in Albuquerque. Stars Kirk Douglas and Jan Sterling are on hand.

JULY 3 Alfred Hitchcock's *Strangers on a Train*, starring Farley Granger and Robert Walker, opens at the Warner Theater (formerly the Strand). **17** MGM's *Show Boat*, starring Kathryn Grayson, Ava Gardner, Howard Keel, and William Warfield, premieres at the Egyptian in Hollywood. Ava Gardner arrives with Frank Sinatra, the first time they've taken their romance public. **28** Walt Disney's animated feature *Alice in Wonderland* opens at

the Criterion. **30** David Lean's *Oliver Twist*, starring Robert Newton and Alec Guinness, released in Britain in 1948 but held up in the U.S. because of charges that it is anti-Semitic, opens at the Park Avenue Theater with some footage deleted.

AUGUST 14 George Stevens's *A Place in the Sun*, starring Montgomery Clift, Shelly Winters, and Elizabeth Taylor in the movie that makes her an adult star, premieres at the Fine Arts in Los Angeles. Gary Cooper, Barbara Stanwyck, William Holden, Lucille Ball, Desi Arnaz, Bob Hope, and Jerry Lewis attend. Paramount has removed from ads the name of actress Anne Revere,

who has not cooperated with the House Un-American Activities Committee.

SEPTEMBER 18 *A Streetcar Named Desire*, starring Marlon Brando—who becomes a star with this film—Vivien Leigh, and Karl Malden, opens at Warners' Beverly Theater in Beverly Hills. Elia Kazan is furious with cuts Warners' made in the film, without consulting him, to avoid a "condemned" rating from the Legion of Decency. They include the words "on the mouth" in "I would like to kiss you softly and sweetly on the mouth." **18** Robert Wise's *The Day the Earth Stood Still*, starring Michael Rennie and Patricia Neal,

---

time last year. **8** The government removes the film industry from the list of "essential" occupations with regard to the draft.

MAY 21 The results of the Phonevision test, begun in Chicago in January, are revealed. The 300 families spent an average of $22.50 per month on pay TV movies. But it will be years before the FCC decides if pay TV is in the public interest.

JUNE 1 20th Century Fox agrees to a consent

decree under which the studio will divest itself of its theaters. **3** The *New York Times* reports that more hours of film are now being shot in Hollywood for TV than for feature films. **25** MGM announces that Louis B. Mayer has resigned.

JULY 16 Producer Dore Schary gains full power to run MGM.

AUGUST-SEPTEMBER *Films in Review* charges that New York University screened a "de-

generate" film for students: avant-garde filmmaker Gregory Markopoulos's *Trilogy*.

AUGUST • A Gallup Poll shows that the percentage of the public familiar with films before they are released has declined from twenty percent in 1946 to eleven percent now. **1** "Trend in Filmdom Toward Musicals," reads a *New York Times* headline. **8** "Old Celluloid Fades Away," says the *Variety* headline in a story alerting readers to the deterioration of old films. The Museum of Modern Art now has the only known print of *Morocco*.

The Andrews Sisters. **16** Arlene Dahl m. Lex Barker.

MAY 7 Warner Baxter d.

JUNE 2 Myrna Loy m. Howland Sargeant. **4** Tony Curtis and Janet Leigh marry. **12** Hedy Lamarr m. Ted Stauffer.

JULY 8 Anjelica Huston, daughter of John and granddaughter of Walter Huston, b.

AUGUST 28 Robert Walker dies, from a reaction to a physician-administered sedative, sodium amytal. **30** Cornel Wilde and Patricia Knight divorce. • Timothy Bottoms b. (1950 is also cited as his birth year). **31** George C. Scott m. Carolyn Hughes.

SEPTEMBER 4 Cornel Wilde m. Jean Wallace, former wife of Franchot Tone. **9** Michael Keaton (Michael Douglas) b. **15** Peter Sellers m. Anne Hayes. **23** Leslie Caron weds meat-packing heir George Hormel II. **25** Mickey Rooney and Martha Vickers divorce. **28** Franchot Tone m. Barbara Payton.

Personalities

York's Palace Theater reads, simply: JUDY. In the audience are Dietrich, Swanson, Durante, and Benny. Also present are Sophie Tucker, Billy Rose, and Irving Berlin to see Judy Garland open the first of her three engagements—two performances a day—at the theater. **31** The government attaches Mickey Rooney's property for back taxes.

NOVEMBER 24 Audrey Hepburn makes her Broadway stage debut in *Gigi*. The *Times*'s Brooks Atkinson finds her "a young actress of charm, honesty and talent . . . ."

DECEMBER • In an effort to exploit the sensational Franchot Tone–Barbara Payton–Tom Neal love triangle, some neighborhood theaters in New York are double-featuring *Bride of the Gorilla*, with Barbara Payton, and *The Dalton Woman*, with Tom Neal. • A 1952 calendar with a nude photo of Marilyn Monroe is a bestseller. **12** "Rock Hudson shed narry a tear when he and Vera-Ellen stopped being serious," gossips the *Hollywood Reporter*. **13** In a Beverly Hills parking lot, producer Walter Wanger shoots agent Jennings Lang, who, Wanger believes, has become involved with his wife, actress Joan Bennett. She is speaking to Lang when her husband, who will serve four months in jail, fires the nonfatal shots. **18** For the second time this week, Rita Hayworth has refused to report to Columbia to film *Affair in Trinidad* because she wants to see more of the script first. (What she really wants is to leave Columbia.)

> **Alien phrase that controls the robot in The Day the Earth Stood Still: "Klaatu barada nikto."**

Movies

opens at the Mayfair. **27** MGM's *An American in Paris*, a musical based on George Gershwin's music, with Gene Kelly and Leslie Caron, premieres on the composer's birthday in five cities.

OCTOBER 15 From Britain's Ealing Studios comes *The Lavender Hill Mob*, starring Alec Guinness, having its U.S. premiere at the Fine Arts. **17** *The Desert Fox*, starring James Mason as General Irwin Rommel, opens at the Globe. **18** John Huston's *The Red Badge of Courage* opens at the Trans-Lux in New York. Audie Murphy stars. **24** *The Detective Story* stars Kirk Douglas, William Bendix, and Eleanor Parker, premiering at the Fox Wilshire in Los Angeles.

NOVEMBER 8 MGM's much ballyhooed and expensive epic *Quo Vadis* premieres at the Capitol and Astor Theaters in New York. It stars Robert Taylor, Deborah Kerr, and, in his first American film, Peter Ustinov.

Business and Society

Vivien Leigh and Marlon Brando in *A Streetcar Named Desire*   MOMA/© WARNER BROS.

Births, Deaths, Marriages, and Divorces

OCTOBER 20 Ida Lupino divorces Collier Young **21** Ida Lupino m. Howard Duff. **31** Marion Davies m. Horace Brown. Her mentor and lover, William Randolph Hearst, died two months ago.

NOVEMBER 1 Frank Sinatra and Nancy Barbato divorce. **7** Ava Gardner m. Frank Sinatra.

DECEMBER 1 Treat Williams b.

Also this year: • Dan Dailey and Elizabeth Hofert divorce. • Miriam Hopkins and Ray Brock divorce. • Sylvia Sidney divorces Carleton Alsop.

THE WITCH HUNT RESUMES, 1951–1956

Last year, Senator Joseph McCarthy's speech charging that the State Department was infested with Communists touched off a new era of Washington politicians hunting for subversives. The House Committee on Un-American Activities, picking up the torch, now attempts to smoke out more Communists in Hollywood. This round of hearings will be characterized by HUAC's efforts to get individuals with past ties to Communism to "name names"—to clear themselves by giving the Committee the names of others who were members or "fellow-travelers" of the Communist Party.

1951

JANUARY 10 The House Committee on Un-American Activities issues a report clearing Edward G. Robinson after he testifies in secret at his own request.

MARCH 8 The House Un-American Activities Committee begins another series of hearings into communism in Hollywood. **21** Howard da Silva and Gale Sondergaard, wife of Hollywood Ten writer Herbert Biberman, take the Fifth Amendment before HUAC. Actor Larry Parks (*The Jolson Story*) admits past membership in the Party but refuses to name others who joined.

APRIL 4 HUAC issues a list of film figures it claims have ties to Communist front organizations. Included are Judy Holliday and Jose Ferrer, who won Oscars last week, Marlon Brando, and Lee J. Cobb. **10** Sterling Hayden admits to HUAC that he was a Communist for six months in 1946 and gives the Committee a list of Hollywood figures he suspects of being Communists. SAG president Ronald Reagan commends his "honesty and frankness." **13** Screenwriters Waldo Salt and Paul Jarrico refuse to answer HUAC's questions about their politics. **23** John Garfield tells HUAC: "I am no red. I am no 'pink.' I am no fellow traveler. I am a Democrat by politics, a liberal by inclination, and a loyal citizen of this country by every act of my life." **25** Director Edward Dmytryk, the only one of the Hollywood Ten to retestify, after serving a prison term, clears himself before HUAC by naming names. He will work again in Hollywood. Director-screenwriter Abraham Polonsky also testifies, but as an unfriendly witness.

MAY 17–18 Roy Brewer, International Alliance of Theatrical Stage Employees official in Hollywood, testifies to HUAC about subversives in the trade unions. **22** Jose Ferrer tells HUAC that he's never been a Communist. Although he can't remember particulars about ties to front organizations, he assumes that "the charges against me are true." **23** Screenwriter Budd Schulberg acknowledges to the House Committee on Un-American Activities his former involvement with the Communist Party.

JUNE 25 Director Robert Rossen tells HUAC that he is not a member of the Communist Party now, but also takes the Fifth Amendment on whether he was in the past.

SEPTEMBER 19 Screenwriter Martin Berkeley, a former member of the Communist Party, gives the House Un-American Activities Committee the names of more than 120 "subversives" in closed session. **24** Screenwriter and producer Carl Foreman appears as an unfriendly witness before the House Un-American Activities Committee.

1952

FEBRUARY 16 HUAC issues a report that says Hollywood is not doing enough to rid itself of Communists.

APRIL 8 The *Hollywood Reporter*, mistaking writer Garson Kanin for director Elia Kazan, reports that Kanin has told HUAC in closed session that he was once a Communist. They will be forced to print a front-page retraction on April 10. **12** Director Elia Kazan, appearing before HUAC, says he was a member of the Communist Party, as was Clifford Odets. **30** Edward G. Robinson concedes the accuracy of HUAC Chairman Frances Walter's characterization of him as "a number one choice sucker" for the Communists.

MAY 19 Clifford Odets tells HUAC that he was once briefly a Communist, but John Garfield never was. (Garfield will be dead of a heart attack in three days.) **21** Screenwriter and playwright Lillian Hellman refuses to tell HUAC whether she ever belonged to the Communist Party because doing so might hurt others as well as herself. "I cannot and will not cut my conscience to fit this year's fashions," she says.

Arthur Miller and wife Marilyn Monroe *LC*

"I am no red," actor John Garfield tells HUAC. *LC*

1953

MAY 6 Lionel Stander tells HUAC how he as been blacklisted because of allegations of subversion. In response to the Committee's questions, he takes the Fifth Amendment. **7** Robert Rossen, now a cooperative witness before HUAC, admits his former membership in the Communist Party and names other members.

SEPTEMBER 11 HUAC publicizes Lucille Ball's closed session testimony in which she acknowledged her brush with Communism in 1936. **29** HUAC makes public Lee J. Cobb's testimony about having been a member of the Communist Party.

1955

OCTOBER 14 Zero Mostel describes to the House Un-American Activities Committee how he was blacklisted after being named by others as a subversive.

1956

JUNE 21 Arthur Miller acknowledges working with communist-related groups but pleads political ignorance and naivete in testimony to HUAC. Congressman Walter suggests that Miller can save himself a contempt citation if Walter can be photographed with Marilyn Monroe, but Miller refuses.

ollywood throws Cinerama and 3-D into the battle with TV. The Supreme Court says that films express free speech, the big studios begin to pull out of B movies, and Decca buys Universal-International. Propelled by her calendar and 20th Century Fox publicity, Marilyn Monroe is on her way to becoming a national icon. Jimmy Stewart sets a profit-sharing precedent for other stars, Katharine Hepburn and Humphrey Bogart are alone in a boat, Frank Sinatra is apparently washed up, and now it's Rock Hudson and Piper Laurie.

- Number of releases: 463
- Number of 3-D releases: 1
- Number of TV sets in use: approx. 21,000,000
- Number of theaters: 18,623, of which 3,276 are drive-ins
- Average weekly attendance: 51,000,000
- Average ticket price: $.60
- Box office receipts: $1,246,000,000
- Total industry employment: 200,000
- Players with term contracts at major studios: 283

Top stars at the box office, based on a Quigley Publications poll of exhibitors:
1. Dean Martin & Jerry Lewis
2. Gary Cooper
3. John Wayne
4. Bing Crosby
5. Bob Hope
6. James Stewart
7. Doris Day
8. Gregory Peck
9. Susan Hayward
10. Randolph Scott

Top rental earnings, based on figures reported in *Variety*:
1. *The Greatest Show on Earth* $12,000,000
2. *Quo Vadis*   10,500,000
3. *Ivanhoe*   7,000,000
4. *The Snows of Kilimanjaro*   6,500,000
5. *Sailor Beware*   4,300,000

The New York Film Critics Circle Awards
Best Picture: *High Noon*

The Golden Globe Awards
Best Picture (Drama): *The Greatest Show on Earth*
Best Picture (Musical/Comedy): *With a Song in My Heart*

The Cannes Film Festival
Grand Prize: *Othello* and *Two Cents Worth of Hope*

The Academy Awards (presented March 19, 1953, and televised for the first time)
Best Picture: *The Greatest Show on Earth*
Actor: Gary Cooper (*High Noon*)
Actress: Shirley Booth (*Come Back, Little Sheba*)
Supporting Actor: Anthony Quinn (*Viva Zapata*)
Supporting Actress: Gloria Grahame (*The Bad and the Beautiful*)
Director: John Ford (*The Quiet Man*)

January	February	March	April	May	June	
	21 Elizabeth Taylor m. Michael Wilding		**7** Marilyn Monroe's first appearance on cover of *Life*			
19 Three Stooges's Curly Howard d.	**27** *Singin' in the Rain*			**26** Supreme Court says films are expression of free speech	**10** Darryl Zanuck says 20th Century Fox will abandon B movies	

July	August	September	October	November	December	
24 *High Noon*	**20** MGM sues Mario Lanza		**15** Arlene Dahl divorces Lex Barker		**21** Paramount announces it will produce TV programs	
	14 Gloria Grahame divorces director Nicholas Ray		**12** Joan Fontaine m. Collier Young, Ida Lupino's ex			

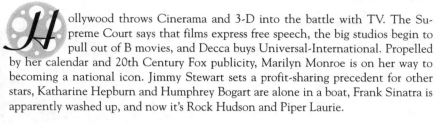

Personalities

JANUARY 8   Mickey Rooney and MGM sign an agreement that will sever his relations with the studio after one more film. **23**   James Stewart's participation in the profits of *Bend of the River*, premiering at the Broadway Theater in Portland, Oregon, tonight, is a precedent-setting deal that other stars will emulate.

FEBRUARY •   Marilyn Monroe begins to date Joe DiMaggio. **24**   Judy Garland closes her engagement at the Palace. She and Sid Luft are planning to produce a remake of the 1937 *A Star is Born*, hoping to co-star Cary Grant. Warners, which will release it, wants to use Humphrey Bogart.

MARCH 13   In a Los Angeles *Herald-Exam-*

Movies

JANUARY 10   Cecil B. DeMille's *The Greatest Show on Earth*, starring Charlton Heston, Betty Hutton, James Stewart, and Cornel Wilde, premieres at the Radio City Music Hall.

FEBRUARY 7   Elia Kazan's *Viva Zapata*, starring Marlon Brando, Jean Peters, and Anthony Quinn, opens at the Rivoli. Kazan had an affair with Marilyn Monroe while filming it at the Fox ranch in California. **20**   John Huston's *The African Queen*, starring Humphrey Bogart and Katharine

Gene Kelly in *Singin' in the Rain*   LC/© MGM

Business and Society

JANUARY 28   The Justice Department announces that it has agreed on the terms of a consent decree with Loew's for the company's divestment of its theaters.

FEBRUARY 12   SAG negotiates the first contract providing residual payments to actors for films sold to TV. **28**   A federal judge rules that corporations set up to make one

film and then folded are valid for the purpose of securing the twenty-five percent capital gains tax rate.

MARCH 26   Judy Holliday tells the Senate Subcommittee on Internal Security in closed session that she is not a Communist.

APRIL 6   Howard Hughes temporarily suspends production at RKO to—he claims—ferret out Communists at his studio. **13**   Edward R. Murrow's "See It Now" TV

program is the first to show a movie being made: Samuel Goldwyn's *Hans Christian Andersen*.

MAY •   The studios are calling in for interviews more than 200 actors, directors, and other employees named by the American Legion as Communists or sympathizers. **16**   Fire causes $1.5 million in damage at Warner Bros. Burbank studios. **26**   The U.S. Supreme Court, classifying films as an expression of free speech, overturns a New

Births, Deaths, Marriages, and Divorces

JANUARY 19   Curly Howard of the Three Stooges d.

FEBRUARY 5   Lee Marvin m. Betty Edeling.

21   Elizabeth Taylor m. Michael Wilding. **28**   Gene Tierney divorces Count Oleg Cassini.

MARCH 4   Ronald Reagan m. Nancy Davis, with William Holden and Brenda Marshall attending them. **15**   Vera Ralston m. Republic Studio head Herbert Yates. **17**   Hedy Lamarr divorces Ted Stauffer. **18**   Betty Hutton m. Charles O'Curran. **25**   Bonnie Bedelia (Bonnie Culkin) b.

iner exclusive, Marilyn Monroe confirms that she is the nude on the bestselling calendar. **13** In her first public, post-Aly Khan date, Rita Hayworth is at Ciro's with Kirk Douglas. **20** Ronald Reagan escorts fiancée Nancy Davis to the RKO Pantages Theater on Oscar night. **26** In a joint interview with reporters, James and Pamela Mason complain about Hollywood's cliqueishness. "I guess we're not chi-chi enough to make that smart, ultra-British set, the type that plays games and toasts each other at parties," Pamela says. "This includes Ronald Colman, Brian Aherne, Joan Fontaine, Richard Green, the Charles Boyers. The set's leader is Douglas Fairbanks Jr."

APRIL 7 "Marilyn Monroe: The Talk of Hollywood," marks the new star's first appearance on the cover of *Life*. Inside, the

magazine reprints the famous calendar photo. **18** "Doris Day wants her husband referred to as MARTIN Melcher," says the *Hollywood Reporter*, of the man who will dissipate her considerable fortune. **22** Producer Walter Wanger is sentenced to four months in jail for the December 13 shooting of agent Jennings Lang.

JUNE • Elizabeth Taylor, who married actor Michael Wilding on February 21, tells reporters she wants to be called "Mrs. Wilding," not "Miss Taylor." **6** Ronald Reagan emcees a Presidential Ball honoring Harry Truman in Springfield, Missouri. **8** As called for in the script of *Ruby Gentry*, Jennifer Jones strikes Charlton Heston. But breaking her hand was unscripted. **16** The debut of TV's *My Little Margie* returns to prominence silent screen and early talkie actor Charles Farrell, who was

a leading romantic star when paired with Janet Gaynor in the late 20s and early 30s. He plays Gale Storm's father on the show. **24** Jean Simmons, testifying in a law suit, says that she didn't know that J. Arthur Rank had sold part of her contract to Howard Hughes until she read about it in the papers.

JULY 7 On the cover and inside *Life*, Arlene Dahl, who once modeled girdles for the Sears Roebuck catalog, wears the lingerie she has designed and is about to market.

AUGUST 4 The movies' censorship office informs Columbia that Burt Lancaster and Deborah Kerr should wear bathrobes in their on-the-beach lovemaking scene in *From Here to Eternity*. Columbia ignores the suggestion. **18** *Life* publishes "A Tribute to Mama [Marlene Dietrich] From Papa

Hepburn, opens at the Capitol. **28** *Royal Journey*, a documentary opening at the Guild, is the first film in Eastman Color, which needs less light and costs less to process than Technicolor, which it will gradually displace.

MARCH 6 Fritz Lang's *Rancho Notorious*, starring Marlene Dietrich, premieres at Chicago's State-Lake Theater, with Dietrich appearing onstage for today's shows. **27** *Singin' in the Rain*, starring Gene Kelly, Debbie Reynolds, Donald O'Connor, and Jean Hagen, premieres at the Radio City Music Hall.

Gary Cooper and Grace Kelly in *High Noon*, opening July 24. *LC*/© MGM

York court's decision to ban the showing of Roberto Rossellini's *The Miracle* on the grounds that it was "sacrilegious." The Supreme Court is also reversing its own 1915 decision classifying movies as the product of a "business pure and simple" and not eligible for constitutional protection.

JUNE 10 Darryl Zanuck announces that 20th Century Fox will abandon B movies, concentrating on quality films. **11** Jack Warner says that Warner Bros. will stop

APRIL 1 Terry Moore divorces Glenn Davis. **21** Clark Gable and Sylvia Ashley divorce. **28** Shelley Winters m. Vittorio Gassman.

MAY 8 Studio founder William Fox d. **19** Franchot Tone and Barbara Payton di-

vorce. He says that she had assignations in their home with Tom Neal, who beat up Tone last September 14. **21** John Garfield d.

JUNE 2 Veronica Lake divorces André De-Toth. **7** Liam Neeson b. **8** Judy

Garland m. Sid Luft, former husband of Lynn Bari. **18** Carol Kane b. **20** John Goodman b.

JULY 1 Dan Aykroyd b. **21** Robin Williams b.

Personalities

Hemingway." According to the writer, with her voice alone "she could break your heart," and she knows "more about love than anyone."

SEPTEMBER • William Bendix, Mickey Rooney, and William Holden visit U.S. forces in Korea. **10** Columnist Sheilah Graham reports that screen newcomer Tab Hunter, twenty-two, is in love with a fourteen-year-old girl. **20** MGM, which suspended Mario Lanza on August 25 for his failure to appear for the filming of *The Student Prince*, sues him for $5,000,000.

OCTOBER 5 Earl Wilson's syndicated column is accompanied by a photo of the author spanking Corrine Calvet, who has told

him that her husband, John Bromfield, does it to her. "Women need a good spanking from time to time," she says. **8** MGM announces that the Lana Turner–Fernando Lamas engagement is off. **19** Police are called to the Palm Springs home of Frank Sinatra, where he is creating a disturbance over the belief that his wife, Ava Gardner, and guest Lana Turner have been bad-mouthing him.

NOVEMBER • Ava Gardner is stricken by a tropical disease while filming *Mogambo* in Africa and must be flown to London for recuperation. **6** Broderick Crawford is arrested in Los Angeles for drunken driving after he hits two parked cars. He will be fined $250. **12** Joan Fontaine marries producer Collier Young. Fontaine tells reporters that last week she and Young stood godparents to the daughter of his ex-

wife, Ida Lupino, at the child's christening. Young says of his present and past wives, Fontaine and Lupino: "The two girls exchanged girlish confidences throughout our romance." Fontaine says she would like to make a film with Lupino. Next year she will: *The Bigamist*, directed by Lupino, starring her and Fontaine and produced by Young, about a man married to two women. **25** The name "Woody Allen" (chosen for himself a few months ago by Allen Stewart Konigsberg) appears in print for the first time when columnist Earl Wilson relates a joke Allen sent to *The New York Post*: "Woody Allen figured out what OPS [Office of Price Stabilization] prices are—[Prices] Over People's Salaries."

DECEMBER • Frank Sinatra's recording contract with Columbia expires, and neither they nor anyone else is anxious to offer him

Movies

APRIL 4 Susan Hayward plays 1940s singer Jane Froman, disabled in a plane crash, in *With a Song in My Heart*, opening at the Roxy.

JUNE 20 Spencer Tracy and Katharine Hepburn star in *Pat and Mike*, opening at the Capitol.

JULY 24 *High Noon*, directed by Fred Zinnemann and starring Gary Cooper, Grace Kelly, Katy Jurado, Thomas Mitchell, and Lee van Cleef, with Tex Ritter

singing the title song, opens at the Mayfair. **31** *Ivanhoe*, starring Robert Taylor, Elizabeth Taylor, George Sanders, and Joan Fontaine, has its U.S. premiere at the Radio City Music Hall.

AUGUST 21 John Ford's *The Quiet Man* stars John Wayne, Victor McLaglen, and Maureen O'Hara, who attend its U.S. premiere at the Capitol.

SEPTEMBER 30 *This Is Cinerama*, the first film in that process, premieres at the Broadway Theater, where it will run for 122 weeks. Cinerama uses three synchronized cameras to project a wide image on a curved

screen. The film, a travelogue, includes a you-are-in-the-middle-of-it ride on Coney Island's steepest roller coaster. *Variety*'s October 8 headline: "Hail Cinerama's B.O. [Box Office] Promise: Compare It to Birth of Sound," is unduly hopeful. The expensive process limits showings to eleven cities.

NOVEMBER 24 Producer Samuel Goldwyn and star Danny Kaye attend the premiere of *Hans Christian Andersen* at the Criterion. **26** The first modern 3-D movie, *Bwana Devil*, viewed with special glasses, premieres at the Hollywood and Downtown Paramount Theaters in Los Angeles. Reviewers pan the film—starring Robert Stack and

Business and Society

making B films.

JULY 22 The Justice Department sues the movie studios to compel them to release their films to TV, which the film companies still regard as competitors.

SEPTEMBER 23 Howard Hughes agrees to sell RKO to an unnamed five-man invest-

ment syndicate. **27** 20th Century Fox divests itself of its theaters, which become National Theaters, Inc.

OCTOBER 16 The *Wall Street Journal* reveals that three members of the investment group to whom Howard Hughes has sold his share of RKO Pictures are gangsters. **28** Jerry Wald, who yesterday left RKO, becomes head of production at Columbia.

DECEMBER 21 Paramount announces that

it will begin to produce TV programs. **23** Jose Ferrer denounces Paul Robeson for accepting the Stalin Peace Prize.

Births, Deaths, Marriages, and Divorces

AUGUST 14 Gloria Grahame divorces director Nicholas Ray. **26** Olivia de Havilland divorces Marcus Goodrich on their sixth wedding anniversary.

SEPTEMBER 25 Christopher Reeve b.

OCTOBER 15 Arlene Dahl divorces Lex Barker. **22** Jeff Goldblum b. **26** Hattie McDaniel d.

NOVEMBER 2 Jane Wyman m. Fred Karger. **12** Joan Fontaine m. producer Collier Young. **18** Mickey Rooney m. Elaine Mahnken.

DECEMBER 15 Lana Turner divorces Bob Topping.

a new one. His career is dead in the water, unless his November 20 Columbia screen test for a role in *From Here to Eternity* bears fruit. • Judy Garland, back on pills and in a postpartum depression after the birth of daughter Lorna, cuts her throat in an unsuccessful suicide attempt. **3** James Dean debuts on Broadway in the play *See the Jaguar*, about a boy whose crazy mother keeps him locked in an ice house. The play closes after five nights, but he receives good reviews. **19** "Rock Hudson with Piper Laurie. They meet every evening," writes Sheilah Graham in her column, smelling a romance. **28** Hedda Hopper assures her readers that they will like Richard Burton, Welsh actor, about to make his U.S. film debut in *My Cousin Rachel*.

Lana Turner and Kirk Douglas in *The Bad and the Beautiful*　　LC

Barbara Britton, and advertised as "A Lion in Your Lap!"—but long lines requiring police to keep order have all studios planning 3-D pictures.

DECEMBER 23 John Huston's *Moulin Rouge*, starring Jose Ferrer, receives a gala premiere in Beverly Hills at the Fox Wilshire. Humphrey Bogart and Lauren Bacall, among the many celebrities attending, are seen arguing in the lobby. Edith Piaf will sing at the party later at the Mocambo. **23** Burt Lancaster and Shirley Booth star in *Come Back, Little Sheba*, directed by Daniel Mann, opening at the Victoria. **25** *The Bad and the Beautiful*, about a ruth- less Hollywood producer, starring Kirk Douglas, Lana Turner, Gloria Grahame, and Dick Powell, premieres at Hollywood's Vogue Theater and at the United Artists Downtown in Los Angeles. Thinking it's about him, David O. Selznick contemplates suing.

Also this year: • Angeline Brown m. Gene Dickinson, becoming Angie Dickinson.

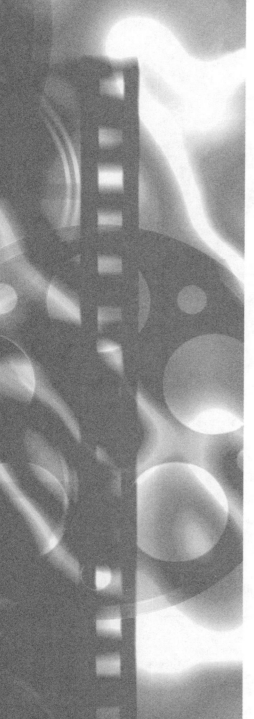

Seven-year contracts are being replaced by either the single-film deal or one for a number of films. Location shooting is widespread, and the year sees continued heavy use of color as well as the new 3-D and wide-screen formats, with CinemaScope making its debut. But, hedging their bets, the studios are also moving into TV production. Hollywood moguls can now fly coast-to-coast nonstop.

- Number of releases: 534
- Number of 3-D releases: 23
- First CinemaScope release: *The Robe*
- Number of theaters: 17,965, of which 3,791 are drive-ins
- Average weekly attendance: 46,000,000
- Average ticket price: $.60
- Box office receipts: $1,187,000,000
- Total industry employment: 147,000
- Players with term contracts at major studios: 179
- Marilyn Monroe's salary: $1,200 per week
- Frank Sinatra's fee for *From Here to Eternity*: $8,000

Top stars at the box office, based on a Quigley Publications poll of exhibitors:

1. Gary Cooper
2. Dean Martin & Jerry Lewis
3. John Wayne
4. Alan Ladd
5. Bing Crosby
6. Marilyn Monroe
7. James Stewart
8. Bob Hope
9. Susan Hayward
10. Randolph Scott

Top rental earnings, based on figures reported in *Variety*:

1.	*The Robe*	$20–30,000,000
2.	*From Here to Eternity*	12,500,000
3.	*Shane*	8,000,000
4.	*How to Marry a Millionaire*	7,500,000
5.	*Peter Pan*	7,000,000

The New York Film Critics Circle Awards
Best Picture: *From Here to Eternity*

The Golden Globe Awards
Best Picture (Drama): *The Robe*
Best Picture (Musical or Comedy): no award

The Cannes Film Festival
Grand Prize: *Wages of Fear*

The Academy Awards (presented March 25, 1954)
Best Picture: *From Here to Eternity*
Actor: William Holden (*Stalag 17*)
Actress: Audrey Hepburn (*Roman Holiday*)
Supporting Actor: Frank Sinatra (*From Here to Eternity*)
Supporting Actress: Donna Reed (*From Here to Eternity*)
Director: Fred Zinnemann (*From Here to Eternity*)

January	February	March	April	May	June
26 Rita Hayworth divorces Prince Aly Khan	**7** Ginger Rogers m. Jacques Bergerac	**4** Dan Dailey punches photographer at Cocoanut Grove	**27** Army Archerd takes over *Daily Variety*'s "Just For Variety" column	**11** MGM settles Mario Lanza suit	• Betty Grable leaves 20th Century Fox

July	August	September	October	November	December
7 Jose Ferrer m. Rosemary Clooney	**5** *From Here to Eternity*	**16** First CinemaScope film	**19** First nonstop air service between L.A. and N.Y.	**21** Monogram becomes Allied Artists	**30** *The Wild One*

Personalities

JANUARY • Marilyn Monroe is consistently late arriving on the set of *Gentlemen Prefer Blondes*. • *Modern Screen* predicts "Heartbreak Ahead" for Ava Gardner, whose noisy quarrels with husband Frank Sinatra do not let up. **19** Columbia Pictures announces the signing of Frank Sinatra to play the role of Maggio in *From Here to Eternity*.

FEBRUARY 9 Tab Hunter escorts Debbie Reynolds to the *Photoplay* awards dinner. Rock Hudson arrives with Mamie Van Doren. Marilyn Monroe is with columnist Sidney Skolsky. Joan Crawford will denounce Monroe for attending in a skimpy dress. Crawford says that movie fans still want "to know that underneath it all the actresses are ladies." **19** "One more film

and I will have made my pile," says Marlon Brando to reporters. **19** Paul Newman's performance in the play *Picnic*, opening tonight on Broadway, will earn him a movie contract. Understudying the female lead roles is Joanne Woodward, who falls in love with the already married actor.

MARCH 4 At the Cocoanut Grove, Dan Dailey punches photographer Murray Garrett for snapping a picture of him with Donald O'Connor's estranged wife, Gwen. O'Connor is across town attending the premiere of *Call Me Madam* at the Fox Ritz. **14** Laurence Olivier is en route from Italy to Hollywood to be with Vivien Leigh, who has had a nervous breakdown. At Idlewild Airport in New York he is strip-searched by a "customs agent," who then removes his disguise to reveal Danny Kaye, playing a joke on Olivier, with whom he has had a

sexual relationship. **19** The Academy Awards ceremonies at the RKO Pantages Theater are televised for the first time. The first statuette handed out on TV goes to Gloria Grahame for Best Supporting Actress in *The Bad and the Beautiful*.

APRIL 2 The *Hollywood Reporter* quotes a "Midwest critic," who writes: "I've seen Piper Laurie, Ella Raines, Rhonda Fleming, and Yvonne DeCarlo in various movies but can never remember what they look like after I leave the theater." **15** Clark Gable drives Grace Kelly to London's Heathrow airport. Their filming of, and affair during, *Mogambo* is over. **15** The U.S. government announces that Charlie Chaplin, living in Switzerland, has given up the reentry permit that would enable him to return to this country. When he left last September, the Attorney General said

Movies

JANUARY 21 *Niagara*, starring Marilyn Monroe and Joseph Cotten, opens at the Roxy.

FEBRUARY 11 Walt Disney's *Peter Pan* premieres at the Roxy and at the State-Lake Theater in Chicago.

MARCH 10 *Lili*, starring Leslie Caron and Mel Ferrer, premieres at the Trans-Lux 52nd St. It will play for ninety weeks and make a hit of the song, "Hi Lili, Hi Lo."

APRIL 9 Warners's *House of Wax*, the first 3-D film from a major studio, premieres at the Paramount. Stars Vincent Price, Phyllis Kirk, and Frank Lovejoy attend the opening. Eddie Fisher heads the stage show. **23** Alan Ladd, Jean Arthur, Van Heflin, Brandon De Wilde, and Jack Palance star in George Stevens's *Shane*, premiering at the Radio City Music Hall.

MAY 13 *Law and Order*, a Ronald Reagan western, opens in Los Angeles on a double feature with *Abbott and Costello Go to Mars*. **26** *It Came from Outer Space*, the first 3-D science fiction film, starring Richard Carlson, premieres at the RKO Hillstreet

and Pantages Theaters in Los Angeles. **28** Walt Disney releases *Melody*, the first 3-D cartoon.

JUNE 4 *Julius Caesar*, directed by Joseph L. Mankiewicz and starring Marlon Brando, James Mason, Louis Calhern, Greer Garson, Edmond O'Brien, and Deborah Kerr, has its U.S. premiere at the Booth Theater, a Broadway house usually used for plays. **24** *Beast from 20,000 Fathoms*, first of the 1950s cycle of movies about monsters stirred up by atomic weapons tests, opens at the Paramount.

JULY 1 Billy Wilder's *Stalag 17*, starring

Business and Society

JANUARY 23 IATSE head Roy Brewer, worried about his membership losing work, attacks the increasing tendency of U.S. stars to make pictures abroad—the so-called "runaway productions." The stars want to take advantage of the 1951 tax law that exempts income made during any sojourn outside the country of seventeen out of eighteen months. Gene Kelly, Alan Ladd,

Gregory Peck, Clark Gable, and Gene Tierney are among those exploiting this tax loophole.

FEBRUARY 12 Howard Hughes's sale of his shares in RKO Pictures is cancelled. **28** Warner Bros. sells its theaters to the Stanley Warner Corporation.

MARCH 7 Violent harassment by some Silver City, New Mexico, residents forces the crew filming *The Salt of the Earth*, the story

of a miners' strike, to depart for the Coast to finish up. HUAC, crafts union head Roy Brewer, and Howard Hughes have used their influence to create the uproar and thus keep blacklisted director Herbert J. Biberman and producer Paul Jarrico from finishing the film.

APRIL 22 The Screen Writers Guild rescinds its January 8, 1940 resolution forbidding members to advertise in trade publications. It also agrees to let producers remove screen

Births, Deaths, Marriages, and Divorces

JANUARY 26 Rita Hayworth divorces Prince Aly Khan. **27** Anne Baxter divorces John Hodiak.

FEBRUARY 7 Ginger Rogers m. Jacques Bergerac. **29** Director Don Siegel divorces Vivica Lindfors.

JUNE 5 Silent screen star William Farnum d. **29** Keenan Wynn and Betty Walker divorce.

JULY 2 Patricia Neal m. author Roald Dahl. **7** Jose Ferrer m. singer Rosemary Clooney. **17** Bela Lugosi and Lillian Arch divorce.

he would be investigated for immoral conduct and communism if he tried to come back. **27** Army Archerd takes over *Daily Variety*'s "Just For Variety" gossip column from Sheilah Graham and will still be writing it in the 1990s. Today he reports that Marilyn Monroe is not impressed with how CinemaScope looks on the small screen in Darryl Zanuck's private projection room. Archerd, also this year, becomes the first TV reporter to cover the entertainment beat—on KNXT-TV in Los Angeles.

MAY 11 MGM settles its lawsuit of last year with Mario Lanza, who agrees to have recordings of his voice used on the soundtrack of *The Student Prince*.

JUNE • Betty Grable leaves 20th Century Fox after a series of suspensions. **26** Marilyn Monroe and Jane Russell place their handprints in the cement outside Grauman's Chinese Theater.

JULY 17 Susan Hayward and husband Jess Barker argue violently. He beats her and throws her into their pool.

AUGUST 6 Singer-actor Dick Haymes is arrested while driving on Sunset Boulevard and held for deportation. The government charges that the Argentine-born Haymes reentered the country illegally after a June trip to Hawaii to visit Rita Hayworth. It questions his right to citizenship because he claimed draft exemption in World War II as the citizen of a foreign country. Haymes says it's a plot. **27** Tuesday Weld is ten years old, and beginning to drink.

SEPTEMBER 13 Ava Gardner, appearing as a mystery guest on TV's "What's My Line,"

is asked by blindfolded panelist Arlene Francis: "Are you married?" "Yes," replies Gardner. "Are you glad?" asks Francis, which is met by an embarrassing silence. The public knows about Gardner's marital problems with Frank Sinatra. **24** At the Hollywood premiere of *The Robe* at Grauman's Chinese Theater, Joan Crawford is introduced as "the greatest star in Hollywood." But when she discovers that a snafu has put someone else in the seat reserved for her, she stalks out without seeing the movie.

OCTOBER • At the divorce trial of John Wayne and Esperanza "Chata" Baur, she accuses him of beating her and having an affair with actress Gail Russell, while he says that she had Nicky Hilton as a house guest while he was away. **11** Bing Crosby hits another car with his Mercedes on Wilshire

---

William Holden, Peter Graves, Don Taylor, and Otto Preminger, opens at the Astor. **8** Otto Preminger's *The Moon Is Blue*, starring David Niven, William Holden, and Maggie McNamara, opening at the Victoria and Sutton Theaters, creates a sensation with its use of words such as "virgin," "pregnant," and "mistress." **9** *The Band Wagon*, directed by Vincente Minnelli and starring Fred Astaire, Cyd Charisse, Oscar Levant, Nanette Fabray, and Jack Buchanan, premieres at the Radio City Music Hall. **15** Howard Hawks's *Gentlemen Prefer Blondes*, starring "two little girls from Little Rock," Jane Russell and Marilyn Monroe, opens at the Roxy.

credit for any writer connected to Communism.

MAY 5 Columbia, charged with "offending public morals" with its billboard at Fairfax and Wilshire depicting Rita Hayworth in *Salome*, says it will come down.

JUNE 11 The Walt Disney studio announces that it will expand into TV production.

SEPTEMBER 7 Lana Turner m. Lex Barker, former husband of Arlene Dahl. **10** Amy Irving b. **11** Lewis Stone d. **24** Rita Hayworth m. Dick Haymes, ex-husband of Joanne Dru. **27** John Payne m. Alexandra Crowell Curtis.

OCTOBER 8 Nigel Bruce dies. **28** John

AUGUST 5 *From Here to Eternity*, the film that resurrects the career of Frank Sinatra, premieres at the Capitol. Burt Lancaster, Deborah Kerr, Montgomery Clift, Donna Reed, and Ernest Borgnine also star. Reed and Kerr are signing autographs in the Capitol's lobby. Tomorrow, Clift and Sinatra will slip into the Capitol's balcony

unannounced to catch the film. **13** George Pal's *The War of the Worlds*, opening at the Mayfair, stars Gene Barry. **27** Audrey Hepburn achieves stardom with the opening at the Radio City Music Hall of William Wyler's *Roman Holiday*, co-starring Gregory Peck and Eddie Albert.

Deborah Kerr and Burt Lancaster in their steamy beach scene in *From Here to Eternity*   LC
© *COLUMBIA PICTURES*

Personalities

Boulevard, seriously injuring three people. Crosby, coming from a dinner honoring Claudette Colbert, says that the four scotches and champagne he had during the evening did not leave him drunk. He will settle out of court for $100,000. **12** Judy Garland is using Bette Davis's old dressing room at Warners as filming begins on *A Star Is Born*. **29** MGM, without informing Frank Sinatra, announces that Ava Gardner's marriage to him has failed.

NOVEMBER • Joan Crawford, rumored to have been feuding with Mercedes McCambridge on the set of *Johnny Guitar*, poses with her for a photo at a party, smiling and hugging. McCambridge will later say she did it because Crawford said it would

be needed to dispel the rumors and sell the picture. **7** "Brando Will Star In Local Pier Film," reports the *New York Times* of the movie that will become *On the Waterfront*. **18** *Variety* reports SAG president Ronald Reagan's complaint that actors doing benefits compete unfairly with other actors playing club dates. According to Reagan, it's getting out of hand. "We take care of our own through the Motion Picture Fund," he says, "and never ask anyone else for anything."

DECEMBER • Marilyn Monroe is on the cover and in the centerfold of *Playboy's* first issue. • Robert Montgomery becomes a consultant to President Eisenhower on his TV appearances. **15** Marlene Dietrich, "the world's most glamorous grandmother," begins her U.S. cabaret career with a three-week engagement at the Sahara in Las Ve-

gas, where she has also begun an affair with Eddie Fisher. Dietrich, wearing next to nothing, sings "See What the Boys in the Back Room Will Have," "Lili Marlene," and "Falling in Love Again." **24** Frank Sinatra flies to Madrid to effect what will be a temporary reconciliation with Ava Gardner.

MGM announces on October 29 that Ava Gardner's marriage to Frank Sinatra has failed.
LC

Movies

SEPTEMBER 16 CinemaScope debuts at the Roxy with the premiere of *The Robe*. The Roxy marquee proclaims: "The Modern Entertainment Miracle You See Without the Use of Glasses." The film, which begins with a newly augmented 20th Century Fox fanfare, stars Richard Burton, Jean Simmons, and Victor Mature. Several Broadway movie theaters blink their marquee lights in code, spelling out "good luck." Their owners hope they have the antidote to TV's capture of movie audiences.

OCTOBER 1 John Huston's *Mogambo*, starring Clark Gable, Grace Kelly, and Ava Gardner, premieres at the Radio City Music Hall, with Gardner and Frank Sinatra present. **14** Fritz Lang's *The Big Heat*, starring Glenn Ford, Gloria Grahame, and Lee Marvin, opens at the Criterion.

NOVEMBER 10 Walt Disney's *Toot, Whistle, Pluck and Boom*, the first CinemaScope cartoon, is released.

DECEMBER 23 *Miss Sadie Thompson*, the 3-D remake of *Rain*, starring Rita Hayworth—"She's the only dame with a kiss of flame"—and Jose Ferrer, premieres

at the Capitol. **30** *The Wild One*, starring Marlon Brando and Lee Marvin, opens at the Palace in New York. It will be banned in Britain.

Business and Society

AUGUST 3 Congress repeals all but $20,000 of the tax exemption for residing abroad, effective January 1, cutting down on the motivation for stars to film abroad rather than in Hollywood. **21** Roy Brewer resigns as local head of IATSE.

OCTOBER 19 TWA inaugurates the first nonstop coast-to-coast service between Los

Angeles and New York.

NOVEMBER 6 Howard Hughes sells his RKO Theaters stock, complying with court instructions to separate ownership of studios from ownership of theaters. **21** After producing movies under its new name for several months, Monogram, a producer of B movies since 1930, officially becomes Allied Artists.

DECEMBER 17 The FCC approves RCA's

black-and-white-compatible color TV broadcast system, clearing the way for the use of color broadcasting, another reason for consumers to spend their dollars on home, rather than theater entertainment.

Births, Deaths, Marriages, and Divorces

Wayne and Esperanza "Chata" Baur divorce.

DECEMBER 6 Tom Hulce b. **8** Kim Basinger (Kamilia Basinger) b. **9** John

Malkovich b. **19** Clint Eastwood m. Maggie Johnson. **22** Hedy Lamarr m. Texas oilman Howard Lee.

Also this year: • Mary Steenburgen b.

1954

VistaVision is ascendant and other kinds of wide-screen processes are debuting as 3-D dies, and the old Hollywood that is beginning to disappear is celebrated in the second version of *A Star Is Born*. Kim Novak and James Dean are the new faces in town. Marilyn Monroe marries Joe DiMaggio, goes to Korea, and divorces Joe DiMaggio. Debbie Reynolds and Eddie Fisher are courting; and Peter Lawford marries Pat Kennedy, sister of the senator from Massachusetts. Frank Sinatra begins to wear a toupee, and Piper Laurie is dating Pfc. G. David Schine, a central figure in the Senate's investigation into the activities of Senator Joseph McCarthy. A Los Angeles court upholds the blacklist. Federico Fellini's *La Strada*, blending romance, fantasy, and exotic imagery, is released in Italy.

- Number of releases: 427
- 3-D releases: 13
- CinemaScope releases: 34
- Number of theaters: 19,101, of which 4,062 are drive-ins and 226 are art theaters
- Average weekly attendance: 49,000,000
- Average ticket price: $.45
- Box office receipts: $1,228,000,000
- Players with term contracts at major studios: 209

Top box office stars, based on a Quigley Publications poll of exhibitors:
1. John Wayne
2. Dean Martin & Jerry Lewis
3. Gary Cooper
4. James Stewart
5. Marilyn Monroe
6. Alan Ladd
7. William Holden
8. Bing Crosby
9. Jane Wyman
10. Marlon Brando

Top rental earnings, based on figures reported in *Variety*:
1. *White Christmas* — $12,000,000
2. *The Caine Mutiny* — 8,700,000
3. *The Glenn Miller Story* — 7,000,000
4. *The Egyptian* — 6,000,000
5. *Rear Window* — 5,300,000

The New York Film Critics Circle Awards
Best Picture: *On the Waterfront*

The Golden Globe Awards
Best Picture (Drama): *On the Waterfront*
Best Picture (Musical/Comedy): *Carmen Jones*

The Cannes Film Festival
Grand Prize: *Gate of Hell*

The Academy Awards (presented March 30, 1955)
Best Picture: *On the Waterfront*
Actor: Marlon Brando (*On the Waterfront*)
Actress: Grace Kelly (*The Country Girl*)
Supporting Actor: Edmond O'Brien (*The Barefoot Contessa*)
Supporting Actress: Eva Marie Saint (*On the Waterfront*)
Director: Elia Kazan (*On the Waterfront*)

January	February	March	April	May	June
14 Marilyn Monroe m. Joe DiMaggio	• Marilyn Monroe entertains troops in Korea	**31** Howard Hughes becomes the only person to own completely a major studio	**21** Danny Kaye UNICEF's "Ambassador-at-Large"		• Charles Buchinsky now "Charles Bronson"; **26** "3-D Looks Dead in United States," says *Variety*

July	August	September	October	November	December
28 *On the Waterfront*	• Judy Garland has nervous breakdown while on vacation	**25** Audrey Hepburn m. Mel Ferrer; **15** *The Country Girl*		**15** Lionel Barrymore d.	**9** Frank Sinatra punches press agent at Sunset Strip nightclub

Personalities

JANUARY 18 At a party at Ciro's, Darryl Zanuck, slightly drunk, strips to the waist and swings on a trapeze bar as a *Life* magazine photographer records it. **26** 20th Century Fox suspends Marilyn Monroe for a second time for failure to report for *Pink Tights*.

FEBRUARY 2 Joanne Dru calls off the deputy sheriffs besieging the New York hotel room of Dick Haymes, her former husband, who is behind in his alimony payments. Haymes and his current wife, Rita Hayworth, had locked themselves in for almost twenty-four hours. **5** Elia Kazan wires Jack Warner: "FOUND NEW BOY THAT I MOST ENTHUSIASTIC ABOUT AND WHO, COULD MAKE PICTURE THIS SPRING…." The picture is *East of Eden*, and the "new boy" is James Dean. **9** In "Call

Me Mamie," *Look* magazine quotes Universal's starlet Mamie Van Doren, one of several buxom blondes in Hollywood who are being promoted as Marilyn Monroe clones: "I'm *me*, not Marilyn." **16** 20th Century Fox, ignoring the telegram from Marlon Brando's psychiatrist describing him as "a very sick and mentally confused boy," sues the actor for his February 1 failure to report for the filming of *The Egyptian*, in which he agreed to star. **16** Marilyn Monroe begins four days of entertaining U. S. troops in Korea.

MARCH • Sheree North, 20th Century Fox starlet, has a brush with scandal when it is revealed that she danced in a bikini in an eight millimeter "nudie" film. **3** Samuel Goldwyn pays $1,000,000 plus ten percent of the profits in an auction for film rights to *Guys and Dolls*, the most ever paid for

story material. **19** Errol Flynn ends his association with Warner Bros. **25** For Columbia starlet Kim Novak, Oscar night at the RKO Pantages Theater is a coming-out party, as she meets the photographers.

APRIL 1 Darryl Zanuck announces that 20th Century Fox has cancelled its suit against Marlon Brando for walking out on *The Egyptian*. Brando will atone by paying a reported $75,000 for delaying that film and by appearing in the studio's *Desiree*. **8** 20th Century Fox cancels Marilyn Monroe's January 26th suspension and signs her to a new seven-year contract. **10** William Holden reveals that Billy Wilder had picked Charlton Heston to star in *Stalag 17*, but then changed his mind and offered it to Holden as a second thought. **21** Danny Kaye is appointed UNICEF's "Ambassador-at-Large" and will make a

Movies

JANUARY 19 *The Glenn Miller Story*, starring James Stewart and June Allyson, premieres in Miami.

FEBRUARY 18 Don Siegel's *Riot in Cell Block 11*, starring Neville Brand, premieres at the Mayfair (it previewed at Folsom Prison on February 4).

MARCH 12 John Huston's *Beat the Devil*, starring Humphrey Bogart, Robert Morely, Peter Lorre, Jennifer Jones, and Gina Lollobrigida, opens at seventy New York theaters.

The Creature from the Black Lagoon　　　LC

APRIL 15 *Executive Suite* premieres at the Egyptian in Hollywood. Stars Barbara Stanwyck, Walter Pidgeon, June Allyson and Louie Calhern attend. **27** *White Christmas*, Paramount's first film in VistaVision, its wide-screen process, opens at the Radio City Music Hall. It stars Bing Crosby and Danny Kaye. **30** *The Creature from the Black Lagoon*, in 3-D, starring Richard Denning, Julie Adams, and Richard Carlson, opens at the Paramount.

MAY 5 Joan Crawford, Mercedes McCambridge, and Sterling Hayden star in *Johnny Guitar*, premiering in ten Los Angeles theaters. **27** William Wellman's *The*

Business and Society

JANUARY 4 The Supreme Court upholds the right of distributors to confine first-run film engagements to downtown theaters. **6** The Motion Picture Association fines RKO $25,000 for opening *The French Line* (in St. Louis, on December 29) without a Production Code seal—apparently a Howard Hughes ploy to generate publicity. **13** Ronald Reagan, testifying in

a suit, says that he was threatened in 1946 when as SAG president he urged actors to cross the Conference of Studio Unions picket lines. He says that he carried a gun for protection. **18** In a move that somewhat widens the freedom of filmmakers, the Supreme Court throws out New York's ban on *La Ronde* on the grounds of "immorality," and Ohio's prohibition of the film M because it could incite crime. But it does not say that films can never be censored.

FEBRUARY 10 Drive-in theater owners at a trade meeting express anxiety about the trend toward tinted car windows. **14** Ed Sullivan's TV tribute to MGM's thirtieth birthday infuriates Louis B. Mayer and David O. Selznick, who hear only the name of Dore Schary, the studio's present head, mentioned.

MARCH 31 By buying all outstanding shares of RKO stock, Howard Hughes becomes the only individual to ever completely own a major studio.

Births, Deaths, Marriages, and Divorces

JANUARY 8 Keenan Wynn m. Sharley Hudson. **12** Edie Adams marries Ernie Kovacs. **14** Marilyn Monroe m. Joe DiMaggio. **18** Sidney Greenstreet d.

FEBRUARY 18 John Travolta b.

25 Linda Darnell m. Philip Liebmann.

MARCH 1 Ron Howard b. **7** Movie "czar" Will Hays d. **17** Corrine Calvet divorces John Bromfield. **31** George Hormel II divorces Leslie Caron.

APRIL 1 Zsa Zsa Gabor divorces George Sanders. **9** Dennis Quaid b. **24** Peter Lawford m. Patricia Kennedy, sister of John, Robert, and Edward Kennedy.

MAY 29 Jean Peters m. Stuart Cramer III. **29** Kirk Douglas m. Anne Buydens.

forty-thousand-mile good-will trip, which will result in the short: *Assignment Children*. **26** Three days after a judge ordered Rita Hayworth's two daughters be taken from her because of parental neglect, they are restored to her under court supervision. Hayworth, mobbed by teenagers when she arrives for the hearing, begs them, "Please, please, go away, leave me alone." **26** At Warner Bros. to film *East of Eden*, James Dean writes to an old friend: "Wow. Am I fucked up. I got no motorcycle, I got no girl." He signs it "Jim (Brando Clift) Dean."

MAY 6 Bing Crosby is upset with photographers at the Mocambo, who snap him while he's dancing, toupee-less, with Grace Kelly. **12** Clark Gable signs a multi-picture deal with 20th Century Fox, including profit participation, which MGM would not give him. He was making $300,000 a year when

he left Metro after twenty-three years. **15** Carol Haney of the Broadway show *The Pajama Game* broke her ankle this afternoon during the matinee. Tonight, understudy Shirley MacLaine replaces her, going out a chorus girl and coming back a star. Film producer Hal Wallis will see MacLaine and sign her to a movie contract in August. **21** Marilyn Monroe, driving on Sunset Boulevard, hits another car from behind. She will settle out of court. **27** Filming begins on *East of Eden*, James Dean's first movie.

JUNE • Jack Nicholson graduates from Manasquan High School in New Jersey and heads for California, where he will work in the MGM cartoon department mail room. • John Wayne, Susan Hayward, Dick Powell, Agnes Moorehead, and Pedro Armendariz film *The Conqueror* in a windy Utah desert, near the government atom

bomb testing area. When years later they all die of cancer, it will be alleged that the radiation they absorbed on location is the cause. • Charles Buchinsky, who has already made ten films, begins to use the professional name "Charles Bronson." **9** MGM suspends Ava Gardner for turning down *Love Me or Leave Me*. **16** Debbie Reynolds and Eddie Fisher are on their first date—a dinner party at Dinah Shore's home. **28** *Hollywood Reporter* columnist Mike Connolly writes: "Shame on Gloria Grahame for bringing her five-year-old David to the preview of Universal-International's *Naked Alibi* wherein Gloria drinks and carouses and gets mauled and slugged. Tot kept whining, 'Let's go home!'" **27** In her Las Vegas debut, Mae West opens a new act at the Sahara, in which she's surrounded by strong men.

High and the Mighty, starring John Wayne, premieres at the Paramount in San Francisco and the Egyptian Theater in Hollywood. **28** Alfred Hitchcock's *Dial M for Murder*, starring Ray Milland, Grace Kelly, and Robert Cummings, opens at the Paramount. Although filmed in 3-D, Warners has dropped the requirement that first-run houses show it that way.

JUNE 16 *Them!*, a science-fiction thriller about giant ants starring James Arness, James Whitmore, and Edmund Gwenn, opens at the Paramount. **24** Humphrey Bogart, Van Johnson, Fred MacMurray, Jose Ferrer, Robert Francis, and E.G. Marshall

are the stars of *The Caine Mutiny*, premiering at the Capitol.

JULY 15 *Magnificent Obsession*, a remake of the 1935 Irene Dunne–Robert Taylor film, stars Rock Hudson and Jane Wyman this time and premieres at the RKO Palace in Cleveland. Wyman and Agnes Moorehead attend. **15** The MGM musical *Seven Brides for Seven Brothers*, featuring Howard Keel, Jane Powell, and Russ Tamblyn, premieres at Loew's State in Houston. **28** Elia Kazan's *On the Waterfront*, starring Marlon Brando, Karl Malden, Lee J. Cobb, Rod Steiger, and "introducing" Eva Marie Saint—in a part turned down by

Grace Kelly, who opted for *Rear Window* instead—opens at the Astor.

AUGUST 4 Alfred Hitchcock's *Rear Window*, starring James Stewart, Grace Kelly and Raymond Burr, has a gala premiere at the Rivoli. **20** *Dragnet*, the first feature film generated by a TV show, premieres in Chicago, New York, and Atlantic City.

SEPTEMBER 21 William Holden is present from the cast of *Sabrina*, also starring Audrey Hepburn and Humphrey Bogart, as it premieres tonight at the Criterion. In the movie, Humphrey Bogart wins Hepburn, but off the set, reportedly, she had an affair

Howard Hughes *LC*

APRIL 2 The Motion Picture Alliance attacks Samuel Goldwyn's purchase of the movie rights to *Guys and Dolls*, questioning the patriotism of the show's co-author, Abe Burrows. **2** The federal tax on theater admissions drops from twenty to ten percent.

MAY 26 "3-D Looks Dead in United States," says a *Variety* headline.

JULY 12 A Superior Court judge in Los Angeles upholds the movie industry's

blacklist, in which companies will not hire people with any kind of connection to radical movements, present or past.

AUGUST 12 New York's Censor Board lifts its ban on Walt Disney's *The Vanishing Prairie* nature film, despite the scene showing the birth of a buffalo. It will open August 16 at the Fine Arts.

SEPTEMBER 1 Loew's Theaters split off from Loew's, Inc., parent company of MGM.

JUNE 15 Jim Belushi b. **19** Kathleen Turner b. **25** Arlene Dahl m. Fernando Lamas. **29** Fred MacMurray m. June Haver.

AUGUST 15 Gloria Grahame marries Cy Howard. **17** Susan Hayward divorces Jess Barker. **18** Patrick Swayze b.

SEPTEMBER 17 Shirley MacLaine, future proponent of New Age ideas, is married to producer Steve Parker by Rev. Norman Vincent Peale, the apostle of "the power of positive thinking." **25** Audrey Hepburn m. Mel Ferrer.

OCTOBER 7 Guy Madison and Gail Russell

Personalities

AUGUST • On vacation on the French Riviera, Judy Garland has a nervous breakdown.

SEPTEMBER 15 A blast of air from a vent at 51st St. and Lexington Avenue in Manhattan lifts Marilyn Monroe's dress while she's filming a scene from *The Seven Year Itch*. This infuriates Joe DiMaggio, who finds it immodest, and later this evening he will reportedly beat her for it. **21** Gene Tierney has a nervous breakdown when Prince Aly Khan will not marry her after a two-year romance. **26** Ronald Reagan begins hosting the "General Electric Theater" on TV.

OCTOBER 5 The newspaper headlines report that Marilyn Monroe has filed for a divorce from Joe DiMaggio, whom she married less than nine months ago. **19** MGM announces the engagement of Debbie Reynolds to Eddie Fisher.

NOVEMBER 5 Joe DiMaggio, trying to find out whether Marilyn Monroe has been sleeping with anyone else, but mistaking where she is staying, recruits several men to raid the wrong apartment in Los Angeles. Along for the ride is Frank Sinatra. **19** Sammy Davis Jr. loses his left eye in an auto accident. **29** Roger Corman sits in the director's chair for the first time as *Five Guns West* begins filming in Monument Valley.

DECEMBER 7 Newspapers nationwide carry the UPI story of silent screen comedian Chester Conklin, discovered working as a Santa Claus at J. W. Robinson's department store in Los Angeles. **9** Frank Sinatra mistakes press agent Jim Byron for a reporter or private detective and exchanges punches with him at the Crescendo Club on Sunset Strip while Judy Garland waits in the singer's Cadillac.

Grace Kelly and William Holden in *The Country Girl* MSN/© PARAMOUNT PICTURES

Movies

with Holden. **29** *The Barefoot Contessa* premieres at the Capitol. Judy Garland, in Hollywood awaiting tonight's premiere of *A Star Is Born*, wires *Contessa* star Ava Gardner in New York: "Good luck. Hope you're not as nervous as I." In Hollywood, with 250 celebrities due for the premiere of *A Star Is Born*, including stars Judy Garland and James Mason, traffic has been rerouted on Hollywood Boulevard to provide a clear path for limousines to the klieg-lit, red-carpeted entrance of the RKO Pantages Theater. Thousands of fans fill the nearby streets. NBC TV and ABC radio broadcast the proceedings to the entire country, with hookups to many foreign countries. The postpicture party is at the Cocoanut Grove.

OCTOBER 15 *The Country Girl* premieres at the Criterion. The *New York Times* says that Bing Crosby's portrayal of an actor dragged down by drink "hits the audience right between the eyes." But it is co-star Grace Kelly, playing his wife, who will win an Oscar. William Holden is also in this adaptation of a Clifford Odets play. **28** *Carmen Jones*, starring Dorothy Dandridge, Harry Belafonte, and Pearl Bailey, premieres at the Rivoli.

DECEMBER 23 *20,000 Leagues Under the Sea*, starring Kirk Douglas, James Mason, Paul Lukas, and Peter Lorre, premieres at the Astor. **25** *Vera Cruz*, the first film in SuperScope, RKO's answer to CinemaScope, starring Gary Cooper and Burt Lancaster, opens at the Capitol. Exhibitors can use the SuperScope projector lens to show films in Paramount's VistaVision as well.

Business and Society

20 Walt Disney Productions announces that it is ending its two-decade relationship with RKO and will release its own films through its Buena Vista Film Distributing Company, formed last year.

OCTOBER 14 Joseph Breen, administrator of the Production Code office since 1934, retires, to be replaced by Geoffrey Shurlock.

19 The Supreme Court, setting a precedent, upholds a lower court decision that Republic can sell the feature films of Gene Autry and Roy Rogers to TV. The cowboy stars sued to prevent the sale on the grounds that their contracts didn't allow their films to be exploited for advertising.

NOVEMBER 24 *Variety* quotes James Nicholson, head of the recently formed American Releasing Corporation (renamed American International Pictures in 1956):

"We are not interested in Academy awards, only in pictures which the exhibitor can play with the assurance that he will make a profit."

Births, Deaths, Marriages, and Divorces

divorce. **27** Marilyn Monroe divorces Joe DiMaggio.

NOVEMBER 1 John Wayne m. Pilar Palette. **15** Lionel Barrymore d. **24** Pier Angeli m. Vic Damone as James Dean, Angeli's former boyfriend, restlessly guns his motorcycle motor across the street.

DECEMBER 7 Jane Wyman divorces Fred Karger. **28** Denzel Washington b. **29** Gregory Peck and Greta Konen divorce.

31 Gregory Peck m. Veronique Pasani.

Also this year: • Geraldine Page m. violinist Alexander Schneider of the Budapest Quartet. • George Peppard m. Helen Davies. • George C. Scott and Carolyn Hughes divorce, and Scott m. Patricia Reed. • Shelley Winters divorces Vittorio Gassman.

*T*he studios begin to sell their film libraries to TV. Brando sings in *Guys and Dolls*; *The Man with the Golden Arm* is daring in its treatment of drug addiction; and on the soundtrack of *Blackboard Jungle* is something new: rock 'n' roll. James Dean and Shirley MacLaine debut in featured roles, while Jack Lemmon has his first major screen role in *Mr. Roberts*, William Powell's last film. Marilyn Monroe studies with Lee Strasberg at the Actors Studio and begins her relationship with Arthur Miller while still seeing Joe DiMaggio. She's also becoming addicted to sleeping pills. And Grace Kelly meets Prince Rainier.

- Number of releases: 392
- 3-D releases: 1
- CinemaScope releases: 72
- Number of theaters: 19,200, of which 4,587 are drive-ins
- Average weekly attendance: 46,000,000
- Average ticket price: $.50
- Box office receipts: $1,326,000,000
- State in which *Oklahoma!* is filmed: Arizona
- Number of *Rebel Without a Cause* cast members who will die violently: 4—James Dean, in an auto accident this year; Nick Adams, from a drug overdose; Sal Mineo, murdered in 1968; and Natalie Wood, by drowning, in 1981

Top box office stars, based on a Quigley Publications poll of exhibitors:

1. James Stewart
2. Grace Kelly
3. John Wayne
4. William Holden
5. Gary Cooper
6. Marlon Brando
7. Dean Martin & Jerry Lewis
8. Humphrey Bogart
9. June Allyson
10. Clark Gable

Top rental earnings, based on figures reported in *Variety*:

1. *Cinerama Holiday* $10,000,000
2. *Mister Roberts*   8,500,000
3. *Battle Cry*   8,000,000
4. *20,000 Leagues Under the Sea* 8,000,000
5. *Not as a Stranger*   7,100,000

The New York Film Critics Circle Awards
Best Picture: *Marty*

The Golden Globe Awards
Best Picture (Drama): *East of Eden*
Best Picture (Musical/Comedy): *Guys and Dolls*

The Cannes Film Festival
Palme d'Or: *Marty*

The Academy Awards (presented March 21, 1956)
Best Picture: *Marty*
Actor: Ernest Borgnine (*Marty*)
Actress: Anna Magnani (*The Rose Tattoo*)
Supporting Actor: Jack Lemmon (*Mister Roberts*)
Supporting Actress: Jo Van Fleet (*East of Eden*)
Director: Delbert Mann (*Marty*)

January	February	March	April	May	June	
	28 Charlie Chaplin no longer connected to United Artists	**7** Theda Bara d.			**1** *The Seven Year Itch*	
5 Warners signs 18-year-old Dennis Hopper	**14** *Hollywood Reporter* says Brando and Dean see same psychiatrist			**6** Grace Kelly meets Prince Rainier		

July	August	September	October	November	December	
	5 Carmen Miranda d.			**4** Willie Bioff killed by car bomb		
17 Disneyland opens		**30** James Dean killed in car crash			**26** RKO first major studio to announce sale of film library to TV	
		26 *Rebel Without a Cause*				

Personalities

JANUARY 5 Eighteen-year-old Dennis Hopper plays an epileptic in an episode of TV's *Medic*. Warner Bros. likes what it sees and will sign him (January 12). **7** Marilyn Monroe, dressed in ermine and white silk, tells a press conference that she would like to play in *The Brothers Karamazov*. She also claims that the seven-year contract she signed with 20th Century Fox in 1951 is no longer valid since she and the studio have been trying to renegotiate it—an interpretation rejected by Fox. **9** "The star system is dead," says Ronald Reagan, quoted in Sheila Graham's column. **12** Robert Mitchum is fired from *Blood Alley*, allegedly for a prank in which he pushed a crew member into San Francisco Bay. He is replaced in the part by

John Wayne on January 17. **14** 20th Century Fox suspends Marilyn Monroe, who has not shown up to film *How to Be Very, Very Popular*. **29** Rumors of Alan Ladd's romance with June Allyson on the set of *The McConnell Story* lead to a temporary separation of the actor from his wife, agent Sue Carol.

FEBRUARY 25 Pier Angeli sustains a broken pelvis when the plane she's on hits turbulence. She will collect $45,000 from the airline in 1957 in settlement of her lawsuit. **28** United Artists announces that Charlie Chaplin has sold his remaining interests in it back to the company.

MARCH 30 Fans outside the Pantages Theater on Oscar night see Marlon Brando in a tuxedo—a rare Hollywood sight. **30** At the opening night benefit perfor-

mance of the Ringling Brothers circus at Madison Square Garden, Marilyn Monroe enters the ring riding a pink elephant.

APRIL 1 The *Hollywood Reporter* says that Walter Matthau, "a leading TV dramatic actor," has been signed for *The Indian Fighter*, his first film. Diana Douglas, ex-wife of Kirk Douglas, the picture's star and producer, will also be in it. The casting director, Ann Douglas, his current spouse, approves. **2** Nevada denies George Raft permission to buy into the Flamingo Hotel, built by his friend, Bugsy Siegel. **5** The New Frontier Hotel in Las Vegas cancels Mario Lanza's $100,000, two-week engagement because he did not show up for opening night yesterday, remaining in his room and claiming he had a cold. Jimmy Durante steps in for him. **6** Brian Donlevy is fined for drunken driving for a

Movies

JANUARY 20 *The Bridges at Toko-Ri*, starring William Holden and Grace Kelly, opens at the Radio City Music Hall and the Hollywood Paramount.

FEBRUARY 1 *Bad Day at Black Rock*, starring Spencer Tracy, Lee Marvin, Ernest Borgnine, Robert Ryan, and Anne Francis, opens at the Rivoli.

MARCH 19 *Blackboard Jungle* premieres at Loew's State. Glenn Ford, Sidney Poitier, Anne Francis, Vic Morrow, Louis Calhern,

and Richard Kiley star. The film's soundtrack include's Billy Haley's "Rock Around the Clock." Clare Booth Luce, U.S. Ambassador to Italy, will refuse to attend the Venice Film Festival if this film is shown, contending that it presents a derogatory image of the U.S. The festival's sponsors will withdraw the film on August 26.

APRIL 11 *Marty*, starring Ernest Borgnine and Betsy Palmer, premieres at the Sutton. This is the first American film to be chosen Best Picture at Cannes since the Festival introduced this award. The film is based on the NBC Television Playhouse production of May 27, 1953, which starred Rod Steiger.

MAY 26 *Love Me or Leave Me*, starring Doris Day and James Cagney, opens at the Radio City Music Hall.

JUNE 1 *The Seven Year Itch*, starring Marilyn Monroe and Tom Ewell, is set to "premiere" on June 3, but tonight's "sneak preview" at Loew's State is attended with great fanfare by Monroe. Klieg lights and cameras catch her arriving with Joe DiMaggio. Henry Fonda, Judy Holliday, Gene Kelly, and Eddie Fisher are also there. DiMaggio throws a post "preview" surprise twenty-ninth birthday party for Marilyn at Toots Shor's. The fifty-two-foot billboard picture above the theater of Monroe, her skirt

Business and Society

MARCH 8 MGM, joining other studios making deals with independent producers, agrees to distribute Samuel Goldwyn's *Guys and Dolls*. It is Goldwyn's first deal with MGM since Metro was founded.

APRIL • Los Angeles smog regulations are now being applied to fires used in movies. *Invasion of the Body Snatchers* is one of the

first films to fall under these regulations. **20** Samuel Goldwyn outbids Mary Pickford for the old United Artists studio.

JULY 17 Disneyland opens in Anaheim. **18** Howard Hughes sells RKO-Radio Pictures to the General Tire and Rubber Company's General Teleradio. **27** Sen. Estes Kefauver's Senate Juvenile Delinquency Subcommittee issues a report warning the movie industry to "police itself," especially with regard to violence in films,

or else the government will do the job.

AUGUST 15 The Motion Picture Association upholds the denial of a Production Code seal to *I Am a Camera* because it has "racy dialogue, a discussion of abortion, and portrayed promiscuity without punishment."

SEPTEMBER 12 Republic, in response to the federal government's 1952 suit, which is about to go to trial, signs a consent decree

Births, Deaths, Marriages, and Divorces

JANUARY 8 Danny Aiello m. Sandy Cohen. **18** Kevin Costner b.

FEBRUARY 5 Dan Dailey m. Gwen O'Connor, ex-wife of Donald O'Connor. **•** Omar Sharif m. Faten Hamama.

21 Betty Hutton divorces Charles O'Curran.

MARCH 8 Betty Hutton m. Alan Livingston. **19** Bruce Willis b.

APRIL 2 Olivia de Havilland m. Pierre Galante.

7 Theda Bara d. **16** Ellen Barkin b.

MAY 3 Tyrone Power and Linda Christian divorce. **16** Critic James Agee d. **17** Debra Winger b.

JULY 11 Clark Gable m. Kay Spreckles. **22** Willem Dafoe (William Dafoe II) b.

March 11 incident in which his car jumped the curb on a Hollywood street and hit a parked car. **8** Disc jockey and some-time-movie actor Alan Freed opens his first live rock 'n roll show in a movie theater—the Brooklyn Paramount. Teenagers dance in the aisles and hear the Penguins sing "Earth Angel." On the screen is *The Americano*, with Glenn Ford. **20** Alfred Hitchcock becomes an American citizen. **21** Bela Lugosi commits himself to a hospital for treatment of drug addiction. **26** Susan Hayward is hospitalized after taking an overdose of sleeping pills.

MAY • Tab Hunter's bylined article in *Photoplay* declares: "I'm in Love with a Wonderful Mom." In the same issue, a feature on Richard Burton reports that he's a flirt and sometimes can't remember his wife Sybil's name. • *Confidential* magazine reveals the

blown upward, has been toned down in response to complaints that the image pushes the limits of modesty. **21** Katharine Hepburn and Rossano Brazzi are in David Lean's *Summertime*, premiering in the U.S. at the Astor. **23** Walt Disney's *Lady and the Tramp*, the first animated feature in CinemaScope, featuring the voice of Peggy Lee in multiple roles, opens at the Roxy.

JULY 14 *Mister Roberts*, starring Henry Fonda, James Cagney, Jack Lemmon, and William Powell in his final screen role, opens at the Radio City Music Hall. **26** In Des Moines, fifty thousand turn out to see a motorcade carrying Charles Laughton,

to release its films to TV three years after they play in theaters.

OCTOBER 24 Otto Preminger sends a telegram to Bureau of Narcotics head Harry J. Anslinger protesting his criticism of *The Man with the Golden Arm*, not yet released. **24** The Supreme Court strikes down the Kansas censorship law used to ban the film *The Moon Is Blue* because the law is too vague and broad.

JAMES DEAN, TEEN IDOL

Rebel Without a Cause   MSN

MARCH 7 *Life* magazine's article, "Moody New Star," is on James Dean. **9** James Dean debuts in *East of Eden*, directed by Elia Kazan and also starring Raymond Massey, Jo Van Fleet, and Burl Ives, premiering at the Astor Theater in a benefit for the Actor's Studio. Author John Steinbeck attends. Marilyn Monroe and Marlene Dietrich work as ushers. TV's *Tonight Show*, with Steve Allen, broadcasts live from the postpremiere party at the Astor Hotel. **14** According to today's *Hollywood Reporter*, Marlon Brando and James Dean are seeing the same psychiatrist. **28** Filming begins on *Rebel Without a Cause*. Dennis Hopper later says that both he and director Nicholas Ray had affairs with Natalie Wood during its production.

APRIL 22 James Dean, filming a scene in a police station for *Rebel Without a Cause*, pounds a desk so hard that he has to be taken to a hospital for treatment of bruises on his hand.

MAY 21 James Dean, filming a knife fight with Nick Adams for *Rebel Without a Cause*, is bloodied, and director Nicholas Ray yells "Cut." Dean yells at him: "Can't you see I'm having a *real* moment? Don't you *ever* cut a scene when I'm having a real moment. What the fuck do you think I'm here for?"

SEPTEMBER 17 James Dean films a TV commercial for the National Highway Safety Committee, urging viewers to "drive safely." **22** James Dean films his final scene in *Giant*. **30** Carroll Baker, Rock Hudson, and director George Stevens are viewing rushes from *Giant* when the phone rings. Stevens takes it, turns pale, and says: "There's been a crash. Jimmy Dean has been killed." The actor died in his new Porsche, bought with his salary from this, his third major film. In 1978, Richard Thomas will star in *September 30, 1955*, about the effect of Dean's death on a young man.

OCTOBER 1 The "Daily Production and Progress Report" from *Giant*, reads: "Elizabeth Taylor grief stricken reported on set 11:45 A.M.," and "Miss Taylor unable to work, Co. dismissed at 5:00 P.M." **26** James Dean in *Rebel Without a Cause* opens at the Astor. Also starring are Natalie Wood, Sal Mineo, Dennis Hopper, Jim Backus, and Nick Adams.

NOVEMBER • Some Americans abroad, including George Jessel, urge Warners to withdraw *Rebel Without a Cause* because of its downbeat portrayal of American life.

NOVEMBER 4 Former IATSE officer Willie Bioff is killed by a car bomb.

DECEMBER 7 United Artists withdraws from the Motion Picture Association of America

when the organization refuses to grant a production seal to the company's *The Man with the Golden Arm*. The film deals with drug addiction, a subject forbidden by the Production Code. The action will lead to

AUGUST 5 Carmen Miranda d. **23** Jon Hall and Frances Langford divorce. **25** Bela Lugosi m. Hope Lininger. **26** Sterling Hayden and Betty De Noon divorce. **29** Mamie Van Doren m. musician Ray Anthony. **31** Mary Astor divorces Thomas Wheelock.

SEPTEMBER 26 Debbie Reynolds m. singer Eddie Fisher. **30** James Dean d.

OCTOBER 19 John Hodiak d.

NOVEMBER 8 Victor Mature and Dorothy Stanford Berry divorce. **9** Rock Hudson m. Phyllis Gates.

DECEMBER • Linda Darnell and Philip Liebmann divorce. **12** Rita Hayworth divorces Dick Haymes. **18** Ray Liotta b.

Also this year: • Woody Allen m. Harlene Rosson. • Ellen McRae (Ellen Burstyn) is divorced from William Alexander.

Personalities

youthful Rory Calhoun's arrest record and jail time for theft and burglary. **6** In Cannes for the film festival, Grace Kelly drives to nearby Monaco to be photographed for *Paris Match*. She meets Prince Rainier, finding him a "nice man." **31** Abbott and Costello leave Universal. They will make one more film together, as independents: *Dance with Me, Henry* (1956).

JUNE • Asked by *Woman's Home Companion* what she least likes about show business, Debbie Reynolds says: "Your private life is not too private." **17** Hedy Lamarr finds in her house the $50,000 in jewelry she reported stolen last month. Everyone else in her household passed a lie detector test, but the results of hers were "inconclusive." **25** Spencer Tracy, who has been

disappearing from the set of *Tribute to a Bad Man* for days at a time—he says he can't deal with the high-altitude Rockies location—is fired from the picture, effectively ending his career at MGM.

JULY 25 The U.S. government drops its two-year attempt to deport Dick Haymes, following a May 31 federal judge ruling in Haymes's favor.

AUGUST 27 The *New York Times* reports: "Kim Novak, who is being groomed for stardom by Columbia, will be loaned out for Otto Preminger's independent production, *The Man with the Golden Arm*." **29** 20th Century Fox sues Frank Sinatra for $1,000,000 for walking out of *Carousel* and replaces him with Gordon McRae. Sinatra contends that the shooting of the picture in both CinemaScope 55—which

uses a larger negative for greater resolution—and 35mm CinemaScope means that he is making two movies but being paid for only one. In a few weeks Fox will decide to film it only with the larger negative, and they will drop the suit.

SEPTEMBER • *Confidential* reports that on October 14, 1950, Tab Hunter was arrested in Los Angeles under his real name, Arthur Gelein, at a "limp-wrist pajama party." **24** Judy Garland, up and down like a yo-yo, on Dexedrine and Seconal, makes her live TV debut on CBS's first color "special."

OCTOBER 2 *Alfred Hitchcock Presents* debuts on TV with "Revenge," starring Vera Miles, one of the few programs actually directed by Hitchcock. **3** *Life*'s cover story is "Rock Hudson, Hollywood's Most Handsome Bachelor." **13** George Axelrod's

Movies

Agnes Moorehead, and Cesar Romero to the Paramount for the premiere of *The Night of the Hunter*, with a screenplay by James Agee, the only film Laughton directs. It stars Robert Mitchum, Shelley Winters, and Lillian Gish.

AUGUST 2 Alfred Hitchcock's *To Catch a Thief*, whose stars, Cary Grant and Grace Kelly, are present, premieres at the Trans-Lux in Philadelphia. **17** *To Hell and Back*, in which Audie Murphy plays himself as a war hero, premieres at San

Antonio's Majestic Theater and proves to be Universal's biggest money-maker to date. **18** *Love Is a Many Splendored Thing*, starring Jennifer Jones and William Holden, opens at the Roxy. The Four Aces's recording of the title song reaches #1 on the pop charts. **31** Gene Kelly, Dan Daily, and Cyd Charisse star in MGM's *It's Always Fair Weather*, directed by Kelly, premiering at the Orpheum in Denver and in several Los Angeles theaters.

SEPTEMBER 12 Orson Welles's *Othello* premieres at the Paris. **30** Alfred Hitchcock's *The Trouble with Harry*, Shirley MacLaine's film debut, premieres at the

Paramount in Barre, Vermont, near where it was filmed, with Hitchcock and MacLaine in attendance.

OCTOBER 5 William Wyler's *The Desperate Hours*, starring Fredric March and Humphrey Bogart, premieres at the Criterion. Bogart and Bacall, in for the World Series, are at the theater. **13** *Oklahoma!*, filmed in the new 65mm Todd-AO process, starring Gordon McRae, Gloria Grahame, Eddie Albert, and Rod Steiger, premieres at the Rivoli. At the premiere are newlyweds Debbie Reynolds and Eddie Fisher. **25** Robert Aldrich's *The Big Knife*, a look at Hollywood's dark, cutthroat side, star-

Business and Society

modification of the Code. **14** Arthur Loew, son of Marcus Loew, becomes president of the company his father founded, Loew's, Inc. Nicholas Schenck moves up to Chairman of the Board. **26** RKO is the first major studio to announce the sale of its film library to TV. C. & C. Super Corporation purchases the studio's output of 740 features for $15,200,000. RKO can

delay the televising of any film until at least three years after its theatrical release. **30** Columbia is the first studio to lease, not sell its films to TV. Through its subsidiary, Screen Gems, the company will lease 104 of its features, retaining residual rights. All of the films predate 1948 and thus do not involve residual rights for performers.

HOLLYWOOD'S MOST HANDSOME BACHELOR

The October 3 *LIFE* magazine features Rock Hudson on its cover, calling him "Hollywood's most handsome Bachelor."
Photo courtesy LC

Births, Deaths, Marriages, and Divorces

play *Will Success Spoil Rock Hunter?*, a thinly veiled portrait of Marilyn Monroe, opens on Broadway, making a star of Jayne Mansfield. Her co-star is Walter Matthau, just beginning to make films this year, who meets his future wife, Carol Marcus Saroyan, in the cast.

NOVEMBER 4 Susan Hayward fights with actress Jill Jarmyn when Jarmyn discovers Hayward in pajamas, in the bedroom of Jarmyn's friend, actor Don "Red" Barry. **9** A Los Angeles court approves Walt Disney Production's contract with twelve-year-old Annette Funicello.

DECEMBER 14 B-movie actress Barbara Payton, former wife of Franchot Tone and the focal point of the 1951 fight between Tone and Tom Neal that put Tone in the hospital, pleads guilty to passing bad checks.

ring Jack Palance, Ida Lupino, Rod Steiger, and Shelley Winters, premieres at the Hollywood Paramount. Local civic and business leaders have already called it a "gross misrepresentation of the motion picture industry."

NOVEMBER 3 Samuel Goldwyn's *Guys and Dolls*, starring Marlon Brando, Frank Sinatra, Jean Simmons, and Vivian Blaine, premieres at the Capitol.

DECEMBER 8 American Releasing Corporation, soon to become American International Pictures, premieres its first double feature, *The Day the World Ended*—"See!

Marilyn Monroe   LC

Personalities

31 Marilyn Monroe signs a new contract with 20th Century Fox, ending her suspension and giving her more freedom to do outside films.

Susan Hayward stars in *I'll Cry Tomorrow*, premiering December 22.   *LC*

Movies

The Horrible 'Mutant' Who Seeks a Mate!"—and *The Phantom from 10,000 Leagues*, at the Fox Theater in Detroit. Samuel Z. Arkoff, cofounder of AIP with James H. Nicholson, later says: "I look upon my movies as being merchandise, just as Woolworth's has a line of merchandise." **12** The premiere, at the Astor, of *The Rose Tattoo*, a benefit for the Actor's Studio, sees Marilyn Monroe, Jayne Mansfield, and Joan Crawford working the aisles as "usherettes." The film stars Anna Magnani and Burt Lancaster. **15** Otto Preminger's film about drug addiction, *The Man with the Golden Arm*, starring Frank Sinatra, Eleanor Parker, and Kim Novak, premieres at the Victoria. Elmer Bernstein's jazzy theme music for the picture becomes popular. **22** The premiere of *I'll Cry Tomorrow* at the Four Star Theater in Hollywood is attended by star Susan Hayward and by the film's subject, Lillian Roth, 1920s and 30s singer and actress whose career was overshadowed by alcoholism.

Business and Society

Births, Deaths, Marriages, and Divorces

lack-and-white shooting increases, as the obsession with color abates. The industry is becoming intensely conscious of the teenage audience. Humphrey Bogart's film career ends, and Elvis Presley's begins. Ingrid Bergman returns triumphantly in *Anastasia*, Otto Preminger discovers Jean Seberg, and Montgomery Clift is scarred in an auto accident. Dean Martin and Jerry Lewis split up, as do Abbott and Costello. Marilyn Monroe marries a playwright; Grace Kelly, a prince; and Natalie Wood begins to date Robert Wagner.

- Number of releases: 479
- CinemaScope releases: 56
- Number of theaters: 19,003, of which 4,494 are drive-ins
- Average weekly attendance: 47,000,000
- Average ticket price: $.50
- Box office receipts: $1,394,000,000
- Annual theater revenue from popcorn sales: $126,000,000
- Players with term contracts at major studios: 253
- Steve McQueen's pay as an extra in *Somebody Up There Likes Me*: $19 per day
- Columbia's fee to permit Otto Preminger to use Kim Novak in *The Man with the Golden Arm*: $100,000
- Kim Novak's salary from Columbia: $100 per week
- Length of Anthony Quinn's Oscar-winning role (Best Supporting Actor) in *Lust for Life*: 8 minutes
- Length of billboard advertising the New York premiere of *Baby Doll*: 135 feet
- Number of buffalo used in *Around the World in 80 Days*: 2,448 (8,552 animals used, all told)

Top stars at the box office, based on a Quigley Publications poll of exhibitors:

1. William Holden
2. John Wayne
3. James Stewart
4. Burt Lancaster
5. Glenn Ford
6. Dean Martin & Jerry Lewis
7. Gary Cooper
8. Marilyn Monroe
9. Kim Novak
10. Frank Sinatra

The New York Film Critics Circle Awards
Best Picture: *Around the World in 80 Days*

The Golden Globe Awards
Best Picture (Drama): *Around the World in 80 Days*
Best Picture (Musical/Comedy): *The King and I*

The Cannes Film Festival
Palme d'Or: *World of Silence*

The Academy Awards (presented March 27, 1957)
Best Picture: *Around the World in 80 Days*
Actor: Yul Brynner (*The King and I*)
Actress: Ingrid Bergman (*Anastasia*)
Supporting Actor: Anthony Quinn (*Lust for Life*)
Supporting Actress: Dorothy Malone (*Written on the Wind*)
Director: George Stevens (*Giant*)

January	February	March	April	May	June	
30 The 5-day Hollywood work week takes effect	**5** Darryl Zanuck leaving 20th Century Fox		**18-19** Grace Kelly m. Prince Rainier	**3** Jayne Mansfield signs with 20th Century Fox		
		20 Director Spike Lee b.			**29** Marilyn Monroe m. Arthur Miller	

July	August	September	October	November	December	
	16 Bela Lugosi d.		**21** Otto Preminger picks Jean Seberg for *Saint Joan*		**11** Hays Code liberalized	
11 Warner Bros. bought by syndicate		**15** Jean Seberg auditions for *Saint Joan*		**8** *The Ten Commandments*		

Personalities

FEBRUARY 8 After twenty-five years in Hollywood, Edward G. Robinson returns to Broadway in *The Middle of the Night*, co-starring Gena Rowlands. **9** One of two straps holding up Marilyn Monroe's dress snaps at a Plaza Hotel press conference in New York, held to announce that she will film *The Prince and the Show Girl* with Laurence Olivier. Monroe arranged the "accident." **10** Jack Lemmon, rehearsing the role of John Wilkes Booth for the TV play *The Day Lincoln Was Shot*, sprains his ankle leaping from the theater balcony after "shooting" the president—the same thing that happened to Booth.

MARCH 2 "Unknown Opposite Monroe in *Bus Stop*," reads a *Hollywood Reporter*

headline. He's Don Murray. **5** *Life's* cover story on Kim Novak tells of "The Trials of a New Movie Star." She's "lonely." **8** The greatest array of movie stars yet to appear on TV are on CBS's "The Louella Parsons Story." Teresa Wright plays Parsons, and "supporting" players include Ginger Rogers, John Wayne, Susan Hayward, Lana Turner, and Charles Boyer. **21** Princess-to-be Grace Kelly is the center of attention at the RKO Pantages Theater on Oscar night.

APRIL 18–19 Grace Kelly marries Prince Rainier of Monaco, in a civil ceremony on the 18th and in church the next day, becoming "Her Serene Highness, Princess Grace of Monaco." *Variety* notes, typically, "Bride is film star; groom non-pro." **23** Opening at the New Frontier Hotel in Las Vegas, as an "Extra Added Attrac-

tion" with Shecky Greene, is "The Atomic Powered Singer," Elvis Presley, who has just signed a movie contract with Hal Wallis.

MAY • *Confidential* explains "Why Frank Sinatra Is the Tarzan of the Boudoir." He eats Wheaties. **3** Jayne Mansfield signs a long-term contract with 20th Century Fox. **9** With the opening of *The Harder They Fall* at the Astor, Humphrey Bogart's film career ends. **13** Driving home from a dinner party given by Elizabeth Taylor, with whom he is filming *Raintree County*, Montgomery Clift is seriously hurt in an auto accident that scars his face. He will not be able to work for nine weeks.

JUNE 6 A jealous Mae West holds a press conference to dismiss one of the strong men in her nightclub act, Mickey Hargitay (Mr. Universe), who's carrying on a romance

Movies

FEBRUARY 16 *Carousel*, in CinemaScope 55, starring Gordon McRae and Shirley Jones, premieres at the Roxy and at Grauman's Chinese Theater in Hollywood. **16** William Holden and Kim Novak star in *Picnic*, opening at the Radio City Music Hall.

MARCH 11 In a first, Laurence Olivier's *Richard III* has its U.S. premiere on NBC TV at 2:30 P.M., and at the Bijou Theater this evening. **27** *Patterns*, based on Rod Serling's TV play, premieres at the Mayfair. It stars Van Heflin, Everett Sloane, and Ed Begley.

APRIL 27 "People Turned into Loveless Pod Creatures" say the ads for Don Siegel's *Invasion of the Body Snatchers*, starring Kevin McCarthy and Dana Wynter, opening on a double feature with *World Without End* in New York theaters. According to Siegel, the title, *Invasion of the Body Snatchers*, was "created by the pods that ran Allied Artists"; he wanted to call it *Sleep No More*. He also wanted a more pessimistic ending, but has been overruled. Siegel and McCarthy will have bit roles in the 1978 remake.

MAY 3 MGM's *Forbidden Planet*, starring Walter Pidgeon, Anne Francis, Leslie Nielsen, and Robby the Robot opens at the

Globe. **16** John Ford's *The Searchers*, starring John Wayne, Natalie Wood, and Jeffrey Hunter, premieres at the Chicago Theater in Chicago, with a personal appearance by Wayne and Ward Bond. **16** Alfred Hitchcock's remake of his 1934 *The Man Who Knew Too Much* opens at the Paramount. It stars James Stewart and Doris Day, who sings "Que Sera, Sera." **19** Sterling Hayden stars in *The Killing*, opening at the Mayfair, the film that establishes the reputation of director Stanley Kubrick. *Time* compares him to Orson Welles. **29** Burt Lancaster, Tony Curtis, and Gina Lollobrigida star in *Trapeze*, which premieres at the Fox Wilshire in Beverly Hills.

Business and Society

JANUARY 30 The five-day Hollywood work week, agreed to last October 21 by management, takes effect.

FEBRUARY 5 Darryl Zanuck announces that he is leaving 20th Century Fox to produce independently. Buddy Adler will replace him as head of production. **23** Mary Pickford has sold her stock in United Art-

ists, it is announced.

MARCH • Hollywood is relying more on pre-sold material, the Production Code Office Reports. Only fifty-five percent of the films it approved in 1955 were based on original screenplays, compared with seventy-three percent in 1950. **1** Warner Bros. sells all the rights to its pre-1950 films to P.R.M., Inc., an investment group.

APRIL 4 The *Hollywood Reporter* quotes

Ronald Reagan, now working for General Electric, on the commercializing of celebrity names and images: " . . . my kind of an association with a big business firm not only adds half or better to the economic value of my name, but provides a degree of security entirely foreign to the movie business. . . ." **11** *Daily Variety* reports that some exhibitors are worried about booking the just-released *Rock Around the Clock*, the first rock 'n' roll film, featuring disc jockey Alan Freed, because they fear the new music

Births, Deaths, Marriages, and Divorces

JANUARY 1 Gene Hackman m. Fay Maltese. **1** Terry Moore m. Eugene McGrath. **3** Mel Gibson b. **21** Robby Benson (Robert Segal) b. **23** Director Alexander Korda d.

FEBRUARY 14 Russ Tamblyn m. Venetia Stevenson.

MARCH 20 Director Spike Lee (Shelton Lee) b. **25** Robert Newton d.

APRIL 12 Andy Garcia (Andres Arturo Garcia Mendez) b. **18** Eric Roberts b. **18–19** Grace Kelly m. Prince Rainier of Monaco. **26** Edward Arnold d.

MAY • Claude Rains is divorced from Frances Propper. **2** Henry Fonda and Susan Blanchard divorce. **10** Joan

with Jayne Mansfield. When Hargitay shows up unannounced to quit, he tussles with another of the star's muscle men, who gives Hargitay a black eye. **6** The New York *Daily News* reports that "Steven McQueen, an Actor's Studio and Neighborhood Playhouse grad, will replace Ben Gazzara July 2 in *A Hatful of Rain*. It will be McQueen's first Broadway role." He has yet to make a film. **17** Vincent Price wins $32,000 on the TV quiz show *The $64,000 Challenge* by answering questions on art. **18** Dean Martin and Jerry Lewis announce that they are splitting up. **20** Diana Dors, yet another starlet bearing some resemblance to Marilyn Monroe, leaves Britain for Hollywood and a role in *I Married a Woman*, with George Gobel. **29** Marilyn Monroe marries Arthur Miller. Earlier in the day an overzealous reporter is killed in a crash as he speeds to

JULY 4 A quarrel between Joanne Dru and her husband, John Ireland, begun at a party at the home of director Mark Stevens, turns violent, sending Dru to the hospital with two black eyes and a broken nose. **6** John Ireland, at his wife's hospital bedside, remorseful about hitting her on July 4, takes an overdose of sleeping pills and ends up in the same hospital. **7** Paul Newman, arrested at 2 A.M. on Long Island for ramming his car into a hydrant and running a red light, struggles with the police, who arrest him. When shown to a cell, he says "Don't lock the door on me, I have claustrophobia." **13** Marilyn Monroe leaves for London to film *The Prince and the Show Girl* with Laurence Olivier. She

keep up with the Millers along a twisting Connecticut road. Monroe and Miller stop to help, but it's too late.

will find him condescending and intimidating, and he will call her "a thoroughly ill-mannered and rude girl." **20** Robert Wagner asks Natalie Wood for their first date on her eighteenth birthday.

AUGUST • 20th Century Fox changes the title of Elvis Presley's first film, now in production, from *The Reno Brothers* to *Love Me Tender*, after RCA announces that it already has orders for 400,000 copies of the yet-to-be recorded song of the same title. **13** Production begins in the Bronx on *Rock, Rock, Rock*, starring disc jockey Alan Freed, twelve-year-old Tuesday Weld in her first film (Connie Francis dubs her singing), Chuck Berry, and Frankie Lymon and the Teenagers. **16** Bela Lugosi dies. As he wished, he will be buried in his Dracula cape, made up to look like the Count. His wife says of the man whose career was en-

---

JUNE 28 *The King and I*, starring Yul Brynner and Deborah Kerr, premieres at the Roxy and at Grauman's Chinese Theater in Hollywood.

JULY 5 Achieving stardom in a role earmarked for James Dean, Paul Newman stars, with Pier Angeli, in *Somebody Up There Likes Me*, opening at Loew's State.

AUGUST 1 *High Society*, the musical remake of *The Philadelphia Story*, starring Bing Crosby, Grace Kelly (in her final film), Frank Sinatra, and Louis Armstrong, premieres at the RKO Pantages Theater in Hollywood. Over one million copies of

"True Love," sung by Crosby and Kelly, will be sold, giving him his twentieth gold record and Grace Kelly her first. **14** *Bus Stop*, starring Marilyn Monroe and Don Murray, premieres in Atlantic City. **21** King Vidor's *War and Peace*, a Paramount–Dino De Laurentiis co-production, starring Henry Fonda, Audrey Hepburn, and Mel Ferrer, premieres at the Capitol. Alexandra Tolstoy, the author's daughter, is in the theater.

SEPTEMBER 17 *Lust for Life*, starring Kirk Douglas as Vincent Van Gogh, premieres at the Plaza. **27** Vincente Minnelli's *Tea and Sympathy*, with Deborah Kerr and

John Kerr (no relation) premieres at the Radio City Music Hall. The stage play's theme of homosexuality has disappeared in the screen version.

OCTOBER 10 *Giant*, starring Rock Hudson, Elizabeth Taylor, James Dean, and Carroll Baker premieres at the Roxy, with Hudson, Mercedes McCambridge, Dennis Hopper, and Natalie Wood in attendance. **17** Mike Todd's *Around the World in 80 Days*, in Todd-AO, starring David Niven, Cantinflas, Shirley MacLaine, and Robert Newton, premieres at the Rivoli. It also features cameo appearances by scores of stars, including Frank Sinatra and Marlene

---

will stir up "teenage antics." **18** Motion Picture Association head Eric Johnston says that the 90,000,000 per week paid admissions in 1946, a figure often cited to show Hollywood at its peak, was based on unscientific samplings of several kinds of data.

JUNE • Schwab's Drug Store on Sunset Boulevard, the legendary hangout of Hollywood celebrities, undergoing renovation, auctions off its old fixtures, including the soda fountain, for $57. **5** The *New*

York Times's panning of *Trapeze*—story and direction are "dismally obvious and monotonous"—prompts United Artists to temporarily withdraw ads from the paper. **20** Loew's, Inc.'s board of directors votes to expedite the sale of MGM films to TV and to get the company into TV broadcasting and production. **24** The Fund for the Republic, a foundation studying threats to American liberty, issues a report on widespread blacklisting in the entertainment industry, written by John

Cogley. Cogley is a former editor of *Commonweal*.

JULY 11 Warner Bros. announces that a syndicate led by Serge Semenenko has purchased a controlling interest in the company, including the shares of Harry and Albert Warner. Jack Warner keeps his holdings and becomes president.

AUGUST 14 MGM leases 725 of its movies to Los Angeles TV station KTTV and at

---

Crawford m. Pepsi-Cola president Alfred Steele. **22** Anita Ekberg m. Anthony Steel.

JUNE 2 Jean Hersholt dies. **29** Marilyn Monroe m. Arthur Miller.

JULY 9 Tom Hanks b.

AUGUST 5 Shirley Jones m. singer Jack Cassidy. **6** Leslie Caron m. director Peter Hall. • Edward G. Robinson and Gladys Lord divorce. **16** Bela Lugosi d. • Christopher Plummer m. Tammy Grimes. **17** James Garner m. actress Lois Clarke.

OCTOBER 21 Carrie Fisher is born to Debbie Reynolds and Eddie Fisher.

NOVEMBER 2 Steve McQueen m. Neile Adams. **6** Paul Kelly d. **20** Bo Derek (Cathleen Collins) b.

Personalities

twined with the undead that "He was just terrified of death." **23** American International Pictures's entry into the cycle of rock films, *Shake, Rattle and Rock*, with Touch (Mike) Connors, Fats Domino, and Joe Turner, begins filming.

SEPTEMBER 15 Seventeen-year-old Jean Seberg, whose experience consists of one season of summer stock, auditions for the lead role in Otto Preminger's *Saint Joan*. Preminger has said he wanted a new face and has undertaken a much-publicized talent search for one.

OCTOBER 8 When Margaret Sullavan does not show up for tonight's CBS "Studio One" show, the network broadcasts a film

of an old show. Under stress and feeling not up to it, she "disappears" for a few days to a rest home. **21** Otto Preminger announces that he has chosen Jean Seberg to star in *Saint Joan*. **29** Marilyn Monroe is presented to Queen Elizabeth at a Royal command performance.

NOVEMBER • Norma Shearer spots Robert Evans, a garment industry executive, at a Beverly Hills pool. Struck by his resemblance to her late husband, Irving Thalberg, she gets him a screen test to play Thalberg in *Man of a Thousand Faces*, leading to an acting and studio executive career for Evans. • Piper Laurie, sick of making what she calls "sex and sand sagas with Tony Curtis," gets her release from Universal. **3** *The Wizard of Oz* is being given its first TV showing, on CBS. Judy Garland, playing the Palace on this Saturday night, can-

not introduce the film, so Bert Lahr and ten-year-old Liza Minnelli stand in for her.

DECEMBER • *Photoplay* this month includes: "Frank and Intimate—Natalie Wood's Diary," "*First Report*: Elvis Presley in Hollywood Plus Pinups In Full Color," "The Men In Kim Novak's 'Lavender Life,'" and "Win A Date With Sal Mineo." • Chesterfield cigarettes dealers are handing out four million Kim Novak calendars. • Abbott and Costello split up. **8** Elizabeth Taylor has an operation for the crushed disc she sustained in a November boating accident. It will cause a chronic pain condition requiring extensive medication. **15** John Ireland is arrested for ignoring a Debtor's Court subpoena. He tells the judge: "I don't know who is going to pay my next month's rent." **29** Dana Andrews is arrested in North Hollywood

Movies

Dietrich. The film is the first for which tickets may be purchased with a credit card, Diners Club. **25** *The Solid Gold Cadillac*, starring Judy Holliday and Paul Douglas, opens at the Victoria.

NOVEMBER 1 Gary Cooper, Anthony Perkins, and Dorothy McGuire star in William Wyler's *Friendly Persuasion*, opening at the Music Hall. Pat Boone sings the title song. Screen credit for writer Michael Wilson has been omitted because he refused to cooperate with the House Un-American

Business and Society

the same time acquires twenty-five percent of the station's stock. **23** The Warner-Pathé newsreel is discontinued.

OCTOBER 3 Arthur Loew resigns as president of Loew's and will be succeeded on October 18 by Joseph Vogel.

NOVEMBER 28 Loew's announces that it

Charlton Heston as Moses in *The Ten Commandments*　　LC/© PARAMOUNT PICTURES

Births, Deaths, Marriages, and Divorces

DECEMBER 23 Keefe Brasselle m. Arlene DeMarco of the DeMarco Sisters. **28** Gig Young m. Elizabeth Montgomery.

Also this year: • Evelyn Keyes m. Artie Shaw, former husband of Lana Turner and Ava Gardner. • Jack Lemmon and Cynthia Stone divorce.

for drunken driving after his car plows into the rear of another. He will plead guilty and pay a fine. **30** Reviewing the year, Louella Parsons writes: "The 'Bundle of Joy' arrived all over town, including the nursery of Debbie Reynolds and Eddie Fisher, who completed their movie *Bundle of Joy* just in time for Debbie to welcome Carrie Frances."

Carroll Baker in *Baby Doll*, condemned by The National Legion of Decency
LC/© WARNER BROTHERS

Activities Committee. **8** Cecil B. DeMille's remake of his 1923 film, *The Ten Commandments*, premieres at the Criterion, which is selling souvenir pencils, each inscribed with a Commandment. Charlton Heston, Yul Brynner, Anne Baxter, Edward G. Robinson, Yvonne De Carlo, Debra Paget, Vincent Price, and John Derek star with a cast of thousands. Meanwhile, in the Middle East, Israelis are fighting Egyptians following the invasion of Egypt several days ago by Israel, Britain, and France. **15** *Love Me Tender*, Elvis Presley's first film, opens at the Paramount. Tomorrow a reviewer for the New York *Herald Tribune* will complain that the screams of teenage girls at the 10:30 A.M. show drowned out some of the dialogue. **20** Marlon Brando, Glenn Ford, and Machiko Kyo star in *Teahouse of the August Moon*, premiering at the Pantages in Hollywood.

DECEMBER 13 *Anastasia*, starring Ingrid Bergman and Yul Brynner, premieres at the Roxy and at the Academy Award Theater in Hollywood. **18** Marlon Brando and Marilyn Monroe are ushers at the Actors Studio benefit premiere of Elia Kazan's *Baby Doll*, starring Carroll Baker, at the Victoria. Stretching for a block above the Victoria and Astor Theaters in Times Square is the longest movie billboard ever, showing a 135-foot-long Carroll Baker in a crib, sucking her thumb—Kazan's idea. On December 16, Cardinal Spellman, at a rare appearance in the pulpit at St. Patrick's Cathedral, warned that Catholics who see the film, already condemned by The National Legion of Decency, are committing a sin. **22** Alfred Hitchcock's *The Wrong Man*, starring Henry Fonda, premieres at the Paramount. On December 28 a pipe bomb, planted by George Metesky, New York's "Mad Bomber," is discovered in the theater. Hitchcock will call him "a man with a diabolical sense of humor."

has fired MGM's head of production, Dore Schary. Schary's activities on behalf of the Democratic Party are thought to have played a role in the decision.

DECEMBER 11 The movie industry eases its "Hays Code," permitting references to drugs, abortion, prostitution, and kidnapping under certain circumstances and strengthening its ban on racial epithets. It is the first major revision since the Code's 1930 formulation. **27** California grants landmark status to the barn used by Cecil B. DeMille while making *The Squaw Man* in 1913. It is the first film-related landmark so designated.

H umphrey Bogart and Louis B. Mayer are dead, and RKO and Republic are out of the movie business. Anthony Perkins has his first role as a kook, Jerry Lewis goes solo, and Michael Landon is a teenage werewolf. Peter Cushing and Christopher Lee are a new horror film pairing, and the people of Peyton Place are on the screen. America gets a good look at "sex kitten" Brigitte Bardot when *And God Created Woman* opens in October. Hollywood finally gets *Confidential* magazine off its back and urges the public: "Get More Out of Life...Go to a Movie."

- Number of releases: 533
- CinemaScope releases: 64
- Number of theaters: 19,003, of which 4,500 are drive-ins
- Average weekly attendance: 45,000,000
- Average ticket price: $.51
- Box office receipts: $1,126,000,000
- Players with term contracts at major studios: 196
- Marlene Dietrich's fee for a night's work playing a prostitute in *Touch of Evil*: $7,500

Top stars at the box office, based on a Quigley Publications poll of exhibitors:

1.	Rock Hudson	6.	Gary Cooper
2.	John Wayne	7.	William Holden
3.	Pat Boone	8.	James Stewart
4.	Elvis Presley	9.	Jerry Lewis
5.	Frank Sinatra	10.	Yul Brynner

Top rental earnings, based on figures reported in *Variety*:

1.	*The Ten Commandments*	$18,500,000
2.	*Around the World in 80 Days*	16,200,000
3.	*Giant*	12,000,000
4.	*Pal Joey*	6,700,000
5.	*Seven Wonders of the World*	6,500,000

The New York Film Critics Circle Awards
Best Picture: *The Bridge on the River Kwai*

The Golden Globe Awards
Best Picture (Drama): *The Bridge on the River Kwai*
Best Picture (Musical/Comedy): *Les Girls*

The Cannes Film Festival
Palme d'Or: *Friendly Persuasion*

The Academy Awards (presented March 26, 1958)
Best Picture: *The Bridge on the River Kwai*
Actor: Alec Guinness (*The Bridge on the River Kwai*)
Actress: Joanne Woodward (*The Three Faces of Eve*)
Supporting Actor: Red Buttons (*Sayonara*)
Supporting Actress: Miyoshi Umeki (*Sayonara*)
Director: David Lean (*The Bridge on the River Kwai*)

January	February	March	April	May	June	
			• Tab Hunter's "Young Love" tops charts		**23** Rex Harrison m. Kay Kendall	
	22 *The Incredible Shrinking Man*					
14 Humphrey Bogart d.			• Republic switching from feature films to TV		**12** Erich von Stroheim d.	

July	August	September	October	November	December	
		1 • Mirisch Co. multipicture deal with United Artists			**18** *The Bridge on the River Kwai*	
5 Ava Gardner divorces Frank Sinatra	**13** Joanne Dru files for bankruptcy		**19** Louella Parsons shocked at Rock Hudson marital rift			
				7 *Confidential* agrees to halt exposés about movie stars		

Personalities

JANUARY 19   Ingrid Bergman, back in public favor, returns to the United States.

FEBRUARY • Production begins on Orson Welles's *Touch of Evil*. Janet Leigh reports with her arm in a sling, broken on January 31 while she filmed a TV show. Her injury will affect how she's photographed throughout the film. Mercedes McCambridge, black shoe polish in her hair, films her role as the gang leader the same day that Welles asks her to be in the movie. Marlene Dietrich's prostitute role isn't written into the script until she agrees to a night's work for $7,500.   **5**   Errol Flynn wins $30,000 on the TV quiz show *The Big Surprise*, answering questions on "The Sea and Ships."   **21**   Jean Seberg's hands and feet

"If You Need Anything, Just Whistle"

JANUARY 17   All studios observe a minute of silence during Humphrey Bogart's Los Angeles funeral. In front of the church altar is a model of his sailboat. John Huston delivers the eulogy before Hollywood's elite, including Lauren Bacall, Gary Cooper, Spencer Tracy, Katharine Hepburn, William Wyler, Marlene Dietrich, Danny Kaye, Gregory Peck, David O. Selznick, Billy Wilder, and Dick Powell. Placed with Bogart's ashes at Forest Lawn is a whistle inscribed: "If you need anything, just whistle."   Photo courtesy MOMA

Movies

JANUARY 1   Jose Ferrer directs and stars in *The Great Man*, premiering at the Sutton.

FEBRUARY 21   James Stewart plays Charles Lindbergh in *The Spirit of St. Louis*, premiering at the Radio City Music Hall, with Stewart present.   **22**   *The Incredible Shrinking Man*, directed by Jack Arnold and starring Grant Williams, opens at the Globe.

MARCH 14   Deborah Kerr and Robert Mitchum star in *Heaven Knows, Mr.*

Allison, premiering at Grauman's Chinese Theater in Hollywood and at the Roxy.   **20**   *Fear Strikes Out*, opening at Loew's State, establishes the offbeat screen persona of Anthony Perkins.   **28** Funny Face, starring Fred Astaire and Audrey Hepburn, premieres at the Radio City Music Hall.

APRIL 9   Don Murray and Carolyn Jones star in *Bachelor Party*, based on a Paddy Chayefsky TV play, premiering at the Victoria.   **11**   Ronald Reagan and Nancy Davis attend the premiere of their *Hellcats of the Navy* at the Spreckles Theater in San Diego.   **13**   Sidney Lumet's *12 Angry*

Men, starring Henry Fonda, Lee J. Cobb, Ed Begley, E.G. Marshall, and Jack Warden, opens at the Capitol.

MAY 15   Spencer Tracy, Katharine Hepburn, Joan Blondell, and Gig Young star in *Desk Set*, a comedy about an efficiency expert, opening at the Roxy, where Tommy Sands, another ersatz Elvis, is appearing on stage.   **25**   *The Delicate Delinquent*, Jerry Lewis's first solo film, premieres at the Plaza Theater in Palm Springs.   **28**   Elia Kazan's *A Face in the Crowd*, starring Andy Griffith, Patricia Neal, Walter Matthau, Lee Remick, and Anthony Franciosa, premieres at the Globe.   **29**   Burt Lancaster

Business and Society

JANUARY 24   RKO, folding its feature-film business, announces that it will hand over domestic distribution of its films to Universal as of February 1 and that its Gower Street studio in Hollywood will be taken over by its parent company, General Tire and Rubber.

FEBRUARY • Louis B. Mayer is part of a group trying, unsuccessfully, to gain control of

Loew's board of directors.   **6**   The Academy of Motion Picture Arts and Sciences changes its bylaws to exclude blacklisted people from Oscar consideration (protested by the Writers Guild on February 20).   **15**   Paramount News, the studio's newsreel, is discontinued.   **26**   The Motion Picture Academy of Arts and Sciences announces the establishment of a Jean Hersholt Humanitarian Award.

MARCH 10   Columbia announces the signing of blacklisted Carl Foreman to a writer-producer contract. The studio says he testified last August before HUAC in executive session without taking the Fifth Amendment, thus making him politically acceptable.

APRIL 2   Republic Studios head Herbert J. Yates tells stockholders that the company is switching from feature films to TV production.   **9**   Hollywood Ten screen-

Births, Deaths, Marriages, and Divorces

JANUARY 12   Howard Hughes m. Jean Peters.   **14**   Humphrey Bogart d.   **21**   Geena Davis (Virginia Davis) b.   **31**   Elizabeth Taylor divorces Michael Wilding.

FEBRUARY 2   Elizabeth Taylor m. producer Mike Todd, ex-husband of Joan Blondell.   **6**   Rex Harrison and Lilli Palmer divorce.   **7**   Ginger Rogers and Jacques Bergerac divorce.   **8**   Susan Hayward m. Floyd Chalkley.   **28**   John Turturro b.

MARCH 1   Judy Holliday divorces David Oppenheim.   **3**   Linda Darnell m. Merle Robertson.   **9**   Henry Fonda m. Baroness Afdera Franchetti.   **15**   Alan Alda m. Arlene Weiss.

APRIL 1   Russ Tamblyn and Venetia Stevenson divorce.   **3**   Gene Kelly and

are burned when a gas jet malfunctions during filming of the execution of Joan of Arc at the stake for *Saint Joan* in a London studio. The actor playing her executioner helps rescue Seberg. **21** June Allyson and Dick Powell announce their separation, which will last less than six months.

MARCH • Tab Hunter's recording of "Young Love" tops many of the pop charts. **1** Stavros Niarchos, Greek shipping magnate, buys much of Edward G. Robinson's art collection, which the actor must sell to pay for a divorce settlement. **7** Laurence Olivier, who was to direct and star in *Separate Tables*, and Vivien Leigh, who was also set for a role in the film, withdraw because of differences between them and Hecht-Hill-Lancaster on Terence Rattigan's screenplay. **19** David O. Selznick writes an angry memo to director John Huston,

telling him to stop trying to change the script of *A Farewell to Arms*. Huston's response, on March 22, is to pack up and leave Italy, where it's being filmed. On April 6, Jennifer Jones, in tears that she does not explain to reporters, will arrive in Rome for a flight back to the U.S. **27** Maureen O'Hara gets the surprise of her life when she arrives at the Pantages Theater for the Academy Awards ceremonies. Waiting for her is Ralph Edwards of TV's *This Is Your Life* to inform her that she is the subject of his show tonight.

APRIL 19 Anthony Franciosa kicks a photographer's camera and assaults him when he tries to grab a shot of the actor and fiancée Shelley Winters. Franciosa will draw ten days in jail for it. **21** *Casablanca*'s first showing at the Brattle Theater in Cambridge, Massachusetts, be-

gins the Humphrey Bogart revival and cult.

MAY 5 "At Last He's Himself, Not Brando or Dean," headlines the *New York Times* in a feature about the brief career of thirty-two-year-old Paul Newman.

JUNE 19 Columnist Sheila Graham reports that Joan Fontaine has received racist hate mail for her role in *Island in the Sun*, in which she kisses Harry Belafonte—probably the first time a white woman has kissed a black man in an American film. **22** Jackie Cooper leads police on a chase through the Mohave Desert at 145 miles per hour, for which he will be fined and given a suspended jail sentence.

JULY • *Movie and TV Album* magazine features the story: "Doris Day: Did You Ever See a Dream Perking?" **4** A drunk Gail

and Kirk Douglas star in *Gunfight at OK Corral*, opening at the Capitol.

JUNE 6 *Tammy and the Bachelor*, starring Debbie Reynolds and Leslie Nielsen, premieres at the Joy Theater in New Orleans. Reynolds's recording of the title tune will be a hit. **12** Darryl Zanuck's first independent production, *Island in the Sun*, starring Harry Belafonte, Joan Fontaine, and James Mason, premieres at the Roxy. **13** Laurence Olivier directs and, with Marilyn Monroe, stars in *The Prince and the Show Girl*, premiering at the Radio City Music Hall. **21** *Love in the Afternoon*, starring Gary Cooper and Audrey Hepburn,

premieres in Los Angeles at the Egyptian and RKO Hillstreet Theaters. **27** *Sweet Smell of Success*, starring Burt Lancaster and Tony Curtis, premieres at Loew's State.

JULY 11 *An Affair to Remember*, starring Cary Grant and Deborah Kerr, premieres on the SS *Constitution*, where part of it was filmed, in New York harbor, and will open at the Roxy on July 19. **17** Eva Marie Saint and Don Murray star in *A Hatful of Rain*, premiering at the Victoria. **18** *Silk Stockings* has Fred Astaire and Cyd Charisse in a musical remake of *Ninotchka*, opening at the Radio City Music Hall. **19** American International Pictures releases *I Was a*

Teenage Werewolf, Michael Landon's first feature film. Made in six days for a modest $82,000, it appears on a typical AIP double feature with *Invasion of the Saucer Men*. "See Teenagers vs. Monsters," say the ads. **19** AIP will also produce *Teenage Frankenstein* and *Teenage Caveman* films.

AUGUST 7 Hammer Films' *The Curse of Frankenstein* opens at the Paramount, introducing American audiences to the British horror team of Peter Cushing and Christopher Lee. **13** James Cagney and Jane Greer, stars of *Man of a Thousand Faces*, a biography of Lon Chaney, attend its premiere at the Palace. Dorothy Malone also

writer Dalton Trumbo tells a TV interviewer that he was nominated for an Oscar for work done under a pseudonym while being blacklisted.

AUGUST 4 Universal–International leases its old films to TV, including the Karloff and Lugosi horror films.

SEPTEMBER 1 The newly founded Mirisch Company agrees to a multipicture distribution deal with United Artists, running

through 1974. The films will include *The Magnificent Seven* (1960), *West Side Story* (1961), and *In The Heat of the Night* (1967).

OCTOBER 4 Irene Dunne, appointed U.S. alternate representative to the U.N. by President Eisenhower, addresses the General Assembly on the refugee problem.

NOVEMBER 16 U.S. Roman Catholic bishops launch a crusade against obscenity in the movies and other media.

> *The movie industry begins to use the advertising slogan, "Get More Out of Life…Go to a Movie."*
>
> November, 1957

Betsy Blair divorce. **29** Michelle Pfeiffer b.

MAY • John Carradine and Sonia Sorrel divorce, and later this year he will marry Doris Rich. **5** Shelley Winters m. Anthony Franciosa. **12** Erich von Stroheim d. **16** Joanne Dru and John Ireland divorce. **23** Jill St. John m. Neil Dubin.

JUNE 23 Rex Harrison m. Kay Kendall.

JULY 5 Ava Gardner divorces Frank Sinatra. **8** Broderick Crawford and Kay Griffith are divorced. **9** Kelly McGillis b. **22** Lana Turner divorces Lex Barker.

AUGUST • Laurence Harvey m. Margaret Leighton. **3** Lee Remick m. William A.

Colleran. **7** Oliver Hardy d. **9** Melanie Griffith, daughter of Tippi Hedrin, b.

SEPTEMBER 27 Sophia Loren m. producer Carlo Ponti.

OCTOBER 11 Marlon Brando m. Anna Kashfi. **24** Bing Crosby m. Kathy Grant. **24** Inger Stevens, who though that

Personalities

Russell crashes her car into a Los Angeles restaraunt, breaking a man's leg. She will receive a thirty-day suspended sentence for it.

AUGUST • The *Confidential* magazine criminal libel trial begins in Hollywood. • Ethel Merman and Fernando Lamas, appearing on Broadway in *Happy Hunting,* have been feuding. "He has upstaged me since the play opened," says Merman. Lamas has been wiping off her stage kiss in front of the audience. To preserve the peace, the producers replace the kiss with a hug. **13** Joanne Dru files for bankruptcy, blaming her plight on financial mismanagement by husbands Dick Haymes and John Ireland. **26** Calling Arlene Dahl "hypersensitive," a New

York judge throws out her $1,000,000 suit against Columbia. She had charged that the studio's sexually suggestive promotion of *Wicked as They Come,* in which she stars, is "obscene, degrading and offensive."

SEPTEMBER 6 Jack Palance, in court for divorce proceedings, throws a notebook at a photographer who snaps his picture when warned not to. **7** The jury in the *Confidential* magazine libel trial (begun August 2) visits Grauman's Chinese Theater to see the seats where Maureen O'Hara allegedly had such a steamy necking session with a "Latin lover" in 1953 that she was asked to leave. **17** Rod Steiger, Inger Stevens, and twenty crew members of the film *Cry Terror* are overcome by carbon monoxide fumes and collapse in a tunnel under the Hudson River. Police are called to rescue and revive them. **22** In Washington,

D.C., for an engagement at the Capitol Theater, Judy Garland slashes her wrists in her hotel room. James Garner debuts as "Maverick" on ABC TV.

OCTOBER 17 Mike Todd, producer of *Around the World in Eighty Days,* throws a birthday party for himself in New York's Madison Square Garden. Millions attend via CBS TV, and eighteen thousand guests are there in person. His wife, Elizabeth Taylor, cuts the huge cake. **19** Louella Parsons reports: "One of the biggest surprises to hit Hollywood in a long time came yesterday when Rock Hudson moved into the Hotel Beverly Hills under an assumed name." His marriage to Phyllis Gates is over. **27** Truman Capote's profile of Marlon Brando, "The Duke in His Domain," appears in *The New Yorker.* Based on an interview in which Capote had gotten Brando

Movies

stars in the film. **23** Tyrone Power, Ava Gardner, Errol Flynn, and Mel Ferrer star in *The Sun Also Rises* opening at the Roxy. Henry King directs this film based on the Ernest Hemingway novel.

SEPTEMBER 18 *The Three Faces of Eve,* starring Joanne Woodward, premieres at the Miller Theater in Augusta, Georgia.

OCTOBER 2 Elizabeth Taylor, Eva Marie Saint, and Lee Marvin are in Louisville at the Brown Theater for the premiere of

Raintree County, MGM's first film in Panavision, also starring Montgomery Clift. **3** *Les Girls,* starring Gene Kelly, Kay Kendall, Taina Elg, and Mitzi Gaynor, opens at the Radio City Music Hall. **21** *And God Created Woman,* a French import starring Brigitte Bardot, opens at the Paris, a New York City art theater, where long lines form during the next week. This pouting "sex kitten" comes to epitomize the erotic allure of foreign stars for American filmgoers. **25** *Pal Joey* stars Frank Sinatra, Rita Hayworth, and Kim Novak, and premieres today in New York, Chicago, and Hollywood.

> *Frank Sinatra denounces rock 'n' roll as "sung, played and written for the most part by cretinous goons."*
>
> October 28, 1957

DECEMBER 5 Radio City Music Hall hosts the premiere of *Sayonara,* starring Marlon Brando, Miyoshi Umeki, and Red Buttons. **11** *Peyton Place* premieres in Camden, Maine, where much of it was filmed. Star-

Business and Society

DECEMBER • The San Francisco Film Festival is the first such international event held in the U.S.

Births, Deaths, Marriages, and Divorces

she had a lock on Crosby, will later describe herself as in "a state of shock" at the news of this marriage. **29** Louis B. Mayer d.

NOVEMBER Gloria Grahame divorces Cy Howard. **29** Composer Erich Wolfgang

Korngold d.

DECEMBER 24 Norma Talmadge d. **28** Natalie Wood m. Robert Wagner

Also This Year: • John Derek m. Ursula Andress. • Ellen McRae (Ellen Burstyn) m. Paul Roberts. • Cliff Robertson m. Cynthia Stone, ex-wife of Jack Lemmon. • Michael Caine and Patricia Haines, Paul Newman and Jackie Witte, and Geraldine Page and Alexander Schneider divorce.

drunk, it is a portrait of a boor.

NOVEMBER 4 "Ellen McRae, a newcomer to the Broadway stage, is a picture of loveliness," says the *New York Times* review of *Fair Game*, which opened last night with the actress who will become Ellen Burstyn. **7** Following a criminal libel trial that resulted in a hung jury, the California State Attorney General announces that *Confidential* magazine has agreed to stop publishing exposés about movie stars.

DECEMBER 10 After first rejecting a role in *Porgy and Bess* for fear that it would show blacks in a bad light, Sidney Poitier announces that Samuel Goldwyn and director Rouben Mamoulian have reassured him, and he has signed to do it, although he has not received the script approval he demanded. **18** Audrey Hepburn, at-

tending the premiere in Hollywood of *A Farewell to Arms*, faints while watching a scene in which Jennifer Jones experiences a difficult childbirth, and has to be taken home by husband Mel Ferrer. **24** The *New York Times* reports (with a December 23 dateline): "Connie Stevens, 19-year-old actress from Brooklyn, today received court approval of a contract with Paramount Pictures that gives her a starting salary of $600 a week." **27** Elvis Presley receives a temporary draft deferment so that he can finish *King Creole*. **31** Ciro's closes.

ring Lana Turner, Diane Varsi, Hope Lange, Arthur Kennedy, and Lloyd Nolan, the movie will open tomorrow at the Roxy. **18** David Lean's *The Bridge on the River Kwai*, starring William Holden, Alec Guinness, Jack Hawkins, and Sessue Hayakawa, after opening in Great Britain, has its U.S. premiere at the Palace. **20** Stanley Kubrick's *Paths of Glory*, starring Kirk Douglas, Ralph Meeker, and Adolpe Menjou, premieres at the Fine Arts in Los Angeles.

JAYNE MEETS THE QUEEN

Jayne Mansfield meets Queen Elizabeth. "You are so beautiful," says Jayne to the Queen. "So are you," replies Her Majesty. *LC*

November 4, 1957

The movie industry, beset by financial woes, begins to anticipate the baby boomers as ticket buyers. Drive-ins and 1950s horror and science fiction films are at their peak, with William Castle giving away free life insurance to patrons of his *Macabre*, Steve McQueen battling a blob, and Vincent Price dealing with a strange but personable fly. Meanwhile, Elvis goes into the Army, Cheryl Crane stabs Johnny Stompanato, Kim Novak dates a Dominican general, and Eddie Fisher leaves Debbie Reynolds for Elizabeth Taylor. Paul Newman marries Joanne Woodward, and Janet Leigh gives birth to daughter Jamie Lee Curtis.

- Number of releases: 507
- CinemaScope releases: 62
- Number of theaters: 16,000, of which 4,700 are drive-ins
- Average weekly attendance: 40,000,000
- Average ticket price: $.51
- Box office receipts: $992,000,000
- Total industry employment: 141,500
- Players with term contracts at major studios: 133
- Elizabeth Taylor's fee for *Cat on a Hot Tin Roof*: $500,000
- Steve McQueen's pay for *The Blob*: $3,000

Top stars at the box office, based on a Quigley Publications poll of exhibitors:

1. Glenn Ford	6. William Holden
2. Elizabeth Taylor	7. Brigitte Bardot
3. Jerry Lewis	8. Yul Brynner
4. Marlon Brando	9. James Stewart
5. Rock Hudson	10. Frank Sinatra

Top Rental Earnings:

1.	*The Bridge on the River Kwai*	$18,000,000
2.	*Peyton Place*	12,000,000
3.	*Sayonara*	10,500,000
4.	*No Time for Sergeants*	7,200,000
5.	*The Vikings*	7,000,000

The New York Film Critics Circle Awards
The Defiant Ones

The Golden Globe Awards
Best Picture (Drama): *The Defiant Ones*
Best Picture (Comedy): *Auntie Mame*
Best Picture (Musical): *Gigi*

The Cannes Film Festival
Palme d'Or: *The Cranes Are Flying*

The Academy Awards (presented April 6, 1959)
Best Picture: *Gigi*
Actor: David Niven (*Separate Tables*)
Actress: Susan Hayward (*I Want to Live!*)
Supporting Actor: Burl Ives (*The Big Country*)
Supporting Actress: Wendy Hiller (*Separate Tables*)
Director: Vincente Minnelli (*Gigi*)

January	February	March	April	May	June	
	29 Paul Newman m. Joanne Woodward	**24** Elvis Presley enters Army • Paramount is last major studio to sell TV rights to pre-1948 films	**4** Cheryl Crane, Lana Turner's daughter, kills mother's lover	**15** *Gigi*	**9** Robert Donat d.	

July	August	September	October	November	December	
2 Fire destroys *Porgy and Bess* sets **8** *The Defiant Ones*		• Eddie Fisher romancing Elizabeth Taylor	**5** Irene Dunne's support of anti-labor laws draws fire	**15** Tyrone Power d. **16** MCA buys Universal's back lot		

Personalities

JANUARY 16 Henry Fonda opens on Broadway in the play *Two for the See-Saw. New York Times* critic Brooks Atkinson describes Fonda's co-star as "an attractive young actress unknown to this department until this evening, but sure to be known to thousands of theatergoers before this season is over." Her name is Anne Bancroft. **21** The Menninger Psychiatric Clinic acknowledges that Gene Tierney is a patient. She will stay for eight months. **22** Hedda Hopper has the exclusive: Charlton Heston gets the lead role in *Ben-Hur*.

MARCH 11 Pressed by reporters, Lauren Bacall will neither confirm nor deny that she will marry Frank Sinatra. **12** Paramount assigns to contract player—and future best-

selling novelist—Tom Tryon the lead role in *I Married a Monster from Outer Space*. **19** Elizabeth Taylor becomes ill and will not be able to accompany her husband,

Elvis Presley enters the army on March 24. *LC*

Mike Todd, on his flight to New York for a Friars testimonial in his honor. **22** Producer Mike Todd is killed in the New Mexico crash of his plane, the "Lucky Liz." Debbie Reynolds cares for her friend Elizabeth Taylor's children while Taylor is incapacitated by the news of the death of her husband. **24** Elvis Presley enters the U.S. Army. **25** At Mike Todd's funeral in Chicago, thousands of fans besiege the cemetery, trying to get a look at the widow. A suggestion to erect a nine-foot reproduction of the "Oscar" statuette at the grave brings the threat of a lawsuit by the Motion Picture Academy. **26** The Oscars are handed out at the RKO Pantages Theater, where Rock Hudson and Mae West team up to sing "Baby, It's Cold Outside."

APRIL 2 United Artists, in a full-page trade paper ad, touts Yul Brynner as Spartacus in

Movies

FEBRUARY 20 *The Brothers Karamazov*, starring Yul Brynner, Maria Schell, Claire Bloom, and Lee J. Cobb, opens at the Radio City Music Hall.

MARCH 13 *The Long Hot Summer*, starring Paul Newman, Joanne Woodward, Anthony Franciosa, and Orson Welles, premieres in Baton Rouge, Louisiana. **19** Natalie Wood and Gene Kelly star in *Marjorie Morningstar*, premiering at the Beach Theater in Miami Beach. **27** *Run Silent, Run Deep*, starring Clark Gable and Burt

Lancaster, opens at the Victoria.

APRIL 2 *The Young Lions*, starring Marlon Brando, Montgomery Clift, and Dean Martin, opens at the Paramount, where Clift, attending with 1920s torch singer Libby Holman, and Hope Lange make personal appearances. **16** William Castle's *Macabre*, with Jim Backus, premieres at the Paramount and Fenway theaters in Boston. Producer-director Castle has long been associated with B films and has a flair for exploitation. All patrons for this film, except those with heart conditions, are insured by Lloyds of London for $1,000 against death by fright. "Nurses" are stationed in the lobby

of some theaters. Other Castle gimmick films include *The House on Haunted Hill* (1959), in *Emergo*, in which a skeleton comes out of a box next to the screen and swings over the audience, and *The Tingler* (1959) for which some theater seats will be wired to deliver a mild shock at the right moment. Each stars Vincent Price.

MAY 15 MGM's *Gigi*, starring Leslie Caron, Maurice Chevalier, Louis Jourdan, and Hermione Gingold, premieres at the Royale, a Broadway theater. Attending the opening are Chevalier, director Vincente Minnelli, Mary Martin, Noel Coward, and Kate Smith. **21** Universal thinks so little of Orson

Business and Society

JANUARY 17 In Hollywood, a closed meeting of exhibitors and heads of crafts unions is given a secret report detailing the decline in theater attendance since quality films began appearing in large numbers on TV last year. **27** Ronald Reagan tells the House Ways and Means Committee that high corporate and individual income tax rates are hurting the movie industry.

FEBRUARY • Theater owners worry about the poor popcorn crop, which is driving prices higher. • Paramount sells TV rights to its pre-1948 films to MCA. It is the last of the major studios to make such a sale.

MARCH • The Dallas police prevent the showing in a black neighborhood of *And God Created Women* starring Brigitte Bardot, although they allowed it to play in white areas. According to *Variety*, the police think the film is "too exciting for col-

ored folks." **3** The Supreme Court rules against twenty-three Hollywood figures who say their rights are violated by the industry's blacklist. **5** Amid the financial gloom in the movie business, *Variety* headlines: "Film 'Future': GI Baby Boom."

APRIL 14 Paramount makes its full facilities available to independents who wish to film on the lot and use studio services, right down to props and wardrobes. **16** Sam Briskin is named to run Columbia Pictures.

Births, Deaths, Marriages, and Divorces

JANUARY 7 Faye Emerson and Skitch Henderson divorce. **13** Jesse Lasky d. **10** Sammy Davis Jr. m. Loray White. **13** Jayne and Paul Mansfield divorce. **13** Jayne Mansfield m.

Mickey Hargitay. **16** Edward G. Robinson m. Jane Adler. **29** Paul Newman m. Joanne Woodward.

FEBRUARY 2 Rita Hayworth m. producer

James Hill. **25** Paulette Goddard m. novelist Erich Maria Remarque. **27** Columbia Pictures founder Harry Cohn d.

MARCH 19 John Cassavetes and Gena Rowlands marry. **20** Holly Hunter b. **21** Gary Oldman b.

The Gladiators, a film that will be cancelled when Kirk Douglas gets to the subject first. **4** Fourteen-year-old Cheryl Crane, Lana Turner's daughter, stabs to death Johnny Stompanato, her mother's hoodlum boyfriend, when he threatens to disfigure Turner. An inquest will find it "justifiable homicide." **8** The police are called to the home of Shelley Winters and Anthony Franciosa, where she has thrown a perfume bottle at him, hitting him in the head. **12** Gary Cooper has a face lift. **15** In Rome, Charlton Heston begins practicing chariot driving for *Ben-Hur* with master stunt man Yakima Canutt.

MAY • General Rafael "Ramfis" Trujillo Jr., son of the Dominican dictator, is romancing Kim Novak. When Columbia, Novak's studio, learns that he's married, they order her to end it. It will be over by July. **4** Louella

Parsons reports on actresses' reaction to the "sack" dress. Says Joanne Woodward: "I'm a firm believer in a woman dressing to please her husband—and my husband hates sacks." **4** *New York Herald-Tribune* drama critic Walter Kerr celebrates a new Shakespearean actor, the "imperious, disdainful, delightfully cold-blooded young player named George C. Scott…one of the finds of the year." Scott's features are distinguished by a nose broken several times in barroom fights. **20** William Wyler begins filming *Ben-Hur*. **31** John Huston meets with Jean-Paul Sartre and convinces the French existentialist to write the screenplay for *Freud*, which proves to be hopelessly long.

JUNE 2 San Simeon, William Randolph Hearst's estate, where the publisher hosted the movies' most famous stars, and which

served as a model for Xanadu in *Citizen Kane*, is opened to the public. **7** Deborah Kerr's husband, Anthony Bartley, accuses screenwriter Peter Viertel of trying to "entice" away his wife. Viertel, once linked romantically to Ava Gardner, denies it.

JULY 2 Charlton Heston films the scene in which he wins the chariot race in *Ben-Hur*. **2** A 4 A.M. fire destroys sets, costumes, and props for Samuel Goldwyn's *Porgy and Bess*, which had been set to begin filming in a few days. **8** *Confidential* settles the $1 million suit filed against it by Errol Flynn for its March 1955 article, "The Greatest Show on Earth: Errol Flynn and His Two-Way Mirror." **8** Marilyn Monroe arrives in Los Angeles to make her first Hollywood movie in two years: *Some Like It Hot*. Her constant demands for retakes will irk director Billy Wilder, Jack Lemmon, and

Welles's *Touch of Evil*, also starring Charlton Heston and Janet Leigh, that it opens the movie at New York neighborhood houses today on a double feature with *The Unholy Wife*, with Diana Dors and Rod Steiger. *Touch of Evil*, which crosses the border in more ways than one, opens with a famous tracking shot that crosses the border between Mexico and the U.S. **28** Alfred Hitchcock's *Vertigo*, starring James Stewart and Kim Novak, opens at the Capitol.

JUNE 11 Kirk Douglas, Tony Curtis, and Janet Leigh make personal appearances at the Astor and Victoria Theaters for the premiere of *The Vikings*, in which they all

have starring roles. **13** *The Bravados*, starring Gregory Peck, Joan Collins, and Stephen Boyd, premieres at the RKO Pantages in Hollywood. **26** Cary Grant and Ingrid Bergman star in *Indiscreet*, premiering at the Radio City Music Hall.

AUGUST 13 *The Defiant Ones*, starring Sidney Poitier and Tony Curtis as prison escapees—one black, the other white, chained together—premieres at the Roosevelt Theater in Chicago. **29** *The Fly*, starring David Hedison, Patricia Owens,

Sidney Poitier and Tony Curtis in *The Defiant Ones*   MSN/© UA

22 Sol C. Siegel becomes chief of production at MGM.

MAY 2 According to the *Hollywood Reporter*, Pentagon cooperation on films about World War II will no longer be forthcoming if there is a reference to "Japs" rather than "the enemy."

JUNE 6 Warner Bros. decides to move some of its corporate offices from New York to its California studios, the first of the major film companies to do so.

APRIL 3 Alec Baldwin b. **8** Esther Williams and Benjamin Gage divorce. **29** Daniel Day-Lewis b.

MAY • Mickey Rooney and Elaine Mahnken divorce. **7** Tyrone Power m. Deborah Minardos. **19** Ronald Colman d.

JUNE 3 Jill St. John divorces Neil Dubin. **9** Robert Donat d.

JULY 8 Kevin Bacon b.

AUGUST 13 Rock Hudson and Phyllis Gates divorce. **16** Madonna Ciccone b. **26** Ernest Borgnine and Rhoda Kemins

divorce. **28** Director Sidney Lumet m. Gloria Vanderbilt.

SEPTEMBER 5 Jean Seberg m. François Moreuil. **12** Robert Redford m. Lola Wagenen.

OCTOBER 16 Tim Robbins b.

Personalities

Tony Curtis. Curtis compares his love scenes with her to kissing Hitler. **17** The *Hollywood Reporter* notes that the equipment specified on today's call sheet for *Gidget*, a teen romance with Sandra Dee and James Darren, includes "ice machine, wind machine, and rain machine, also Coke machine." **27** Samuel Goldwyn fires Rouben Mamoulian, with whom he is continually clashing, as director of *Porgy and Bess* and replaces him with Otto Preminger. Mamoulian then fires his agent, Irving "Swifty" Lazar.

AUGUST • On the cover of *Mademoiselle* and guest-editing this month is model Ali MacGraw, about to enter her junior year at Wellesley. **8** Sidney Poitier and other

Movies

Vincent Price, and Herbert Marshall, opens in RKO neighborhood theaters in New York. It will be remade in 1986.

SEPTEMBER 18 Paul Newman, Elizabeth Taylor, and Burl Ives, star in *Cat on a Hot Tin Roof*, opening at the Radio City Music Hall. **19** *Damn Yankees*, starring Gwen Verdon, Tab Hunter, and Ray Walston, premieres at the Center Theater in Denver, where the Yankees' top minor-league farm club plays.

LOVERS BOTH ON- AND OFFSCREEN

Paul Newman and Joanne Woodward are lovers on the screen in *The Long Hot Summer* (above). But they are also in love offscreen and will marry on January 29, a few weeks before this film premieres. *LC/© 20TH CENTURY FOX*

OCTOBER 7 Spencer Tracy stars in *The Old Man and the Sea*, directed by John Sturges, premiering at the Criterion.

NOVEMBER 6 "Steven" McQueen, as he is billed in his first film, stars in *The Blob*, opening at the Mayfair, the title song from which is the first from a science fiction film

to become a hit. **18** *I Want to Live!*, starring Susan Hayward, Simon Oakland, and Theodore Bikel, opens at the Victoria.

DECEMBER 4 *Auntie Mame* premieres at the Radio City Music Hall, with an appearance by its star, Rosalind Russell. **18** Burt Lancaster, Rita Hayworth, Deborah Kerr,

Business and Society

OCTOBER 24 At the National Theater Owners of America convention, producer Jerry Wald attacks American International Pictures' exploitation films. AIP executive Samuel Z. Arkoff snaps back that his company's movies are cleaner than Wald's *Peyton Place*, and that AIP "monsters do not drink, smoke or lust."

NOVEMBER 14 The American Congress of Exhibitors is formed to better coordinate industry policies with respect to movies and television and the relationship between the film industry and government.

DECEMBER 2 Fire scorches more than half of Malibu Canyon Ranch, where 20th Century Fox makes westerns, and destroys the nearby home of Lew Ayres. **16** MCA buys Universal's back lot.

Births, Deaths, Marriages, and Divorces

NOVEMBER 15 Tyrone Power dies of a heart attack after filming an arduous sword fight with George Sanders for *Solomon and Sheba*. **17** Mary Elizabeth Mastrantonio b.

22 Jaime Lee Curtis is born to Janet Leigh and Tony Curtis.

DECEMBER • Mickey Rooney m. Barbara Thomason. **17** Sheree North m.

her psychiatrist, Dr. Gerhardt Sommer. **18** Pier Angeli divorces Vic Damone.

Also this year: • Chuck Norris m. Diane Holechek. • Divorces include Corinne Griffith and George Preston Marshall, Betty Hutton and Alan Livingston, Walter Matthau and Grace Johnson, and Jason Robards Jr. and Eleanor Pittman.

members of the cast of *Porgy and Bess* defend Otto Preminger against charges by disgruntled cast member Leigh Whipper that the new director is unsympathetic to blacks. The Screen Directors Guild abandons its boycott of Goldwyn, which it announced on August 3 in response to Goldwyn's firing of Rouben Mamoulian and replacing him with Preminger. **26** Mike Wallace's interview with Sidney Poitier in the *New York Post* is headlined, "Can a Negro Be a Film Star?"

SEPTEMBER 9 Eddie Fisher returns to California and Debbie Reynolds after two weeks of romancing Elizabeth Taylor in New York, including a highly visible Labor Day weekend at Grossinger's in the Catskills, where Fisher and Reynolds were married. After an explosive argument, the Fishers separate.

OCTOBER 5 Eleanor Roosevelt criticizes Irene Dunne for supporting antilabor "right-to-work" laws. **9** Stanley Kubrick and James B. Harris, producers of *Lolita*, attack Cary Grant, who has told an interviewer that he turned down the movie because he has "too much respect for the movie industry to do a picture like that." Kubrick and Harris say that Grant wasn't offered the film.

NOVEMBER 4 Producer Sam Zimbalist suffers a fatal heart attack on the set of *Ben-Hur*. **20** Marlon Brando takes over as director of *One-Eyed Jacks*, replacing Stanley Kubrick. It's Brando's first time in the director's chair.

DECEMBER 4 Debbie Reynolds sues Eddie Fisher for divorce. **28** Dan Dailey is arrested in Hollywood for drunken driving after crashing his car into another. Dailey has to be subdued and handcuffed. **29** The IRS announces that Charlie Chaplin's payment of $425,000 ends the government's claims against him. **31** The co-author of the screenplay for *The Defiant Ones*, "Nathan Douglas," reveals himself to be blacklisted Nedrick Young.

David Niven, and Wendy Hiller star in *Separate Tables*, opening at the Astor and Trans-Lux Normandie theaters. **18** Vincente Minnelli's *Some Came Running*, with Shirley MacLaine, Frank Sinatra, and Dean Martin, premieres at the Hollywood Paramount Theater.

*J*et service begins between New York and Los Angeles, and Soviet Premier Khrushchev visits Hollywood. *Room at the Top* is the first of a spate of successful British films dealing with class. French directors François Truffaut and Claude Chabrol ignite the New Wave (*la Nouvelle Vague*) with their films, *The 400 Blows* and *The Cousins*. Marcel Camus's *Black Orpheus*, Louis Malle's *The Lovers*, and Alain Resnais's *Hiroshima Mon Amour* augment this year's renaissance of French cinema. Jean-Luc Godard dedicates *Breathless* to Monogram, the American B-pictures studio. And Janus, a company distributing "art" films, achieves major success in America with the movies of Swedish director Ingmar Bergman, including *Wild Strawberries* (1957) and *The Magician* (1958).

- Number of releases: 439
- CinemaScope releases: 56
- Number of theaters: 16,103, of which 4,768 are drive-ins
- Average weekly attendance: 42,000,000
- Average ticket price: $.51
- Box office receipts: $958,000,000
- Total industry employment: 183,000
- Players with term contracts at major studios: 139
- Most takes required for a scene by Marilyn Monroe in *Some Like It Hot*: 59
- Number of horses used in the chariot race in *Ben Hur*: 78
- Oscars won by *Ben-Hur*: 11
- Year prophesied in *On the Beach* for the outbreak of nuclear war: 1964
- Film that jump-starts the U.S. soft-core porno film industry this year: Russ Meyer's *The Immoral Mr. Teas*

Top stars at the box office, based on a Quigley Publications poll of exhibitors:
1. Rock Hudson
2. Cary Grant
3. James Stewart
4. Doris Day
5. Debbie Reynolds
6. Glenn Ford
7. Frank Sinatra
8. John Wayne
9. Jerry Lewis
10. Susan Hayward

The New York Film Critics Circle Awards
Best Picture: *Ben Hur*

The Golden Globe Awards
Best Picture (Drama): *Ben Hur*
Best Picture (Comedy): *Some Like It Hot*
Best Picture (Musical): *Porgy and Bess*

The Cannes Film Festival
Palme d'Or: *Black Orpheus*

The Academy Awards (April 4, 1960)
Best Picture: *Ben Hur*
Actor: Charlton Heston (*Ben Hur*)
Actress: Simone Signoret (*Room at the Top*)
Supporting Actor: Hugh Griffith (*Ben Hur*)
Supporting Actress: Shelley Winters (*The Diary of Anne Frank*)
Director: William Wyler (*Ben Hur*)

January	February	March	April	May	June
25 Jet service between L.A. and N.Y. begins	**19** Debbie Reynolds divorces Eddie Fisher	**17** Diane Varsi walks out of her 20th Century Fox contract	**22** Marlon Brando and Anna Kashfi divorced — **12** Elizabeth Taylor m. Eddie Fisher		**7** Paramount to pay Jerry Lewis $10,000,000 for fourteen films

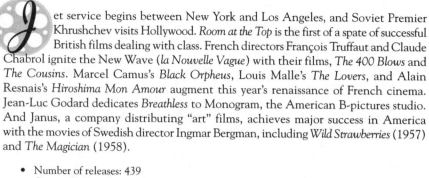

July	August	September	October	November	December
• *North by Northwest*	**6** Writer-director Preston Sturges d. — **19** Nikita Khrushchev visits Hollywood		**14** Errol Flynn d.	**18** *Ben Hur*	**7** 20th Century Fox suspends Joan Collins

Personalities

JANUARY 3 Silent screen idol Ramon Novarro is arrested for drunken driving in Hollywood. Inger Stevens, who is found unconscious in her New York apartment after swallowing poison, will survive. **7** Suzanne Pleshette's first film, Jerry Lewis's *The Geisha Boy*, opens at the Brooklyn Paramount, where her father is the manager and she spent much of her childhood. **16** Blacklisted Hollywood Ten writer Dalton Trumbo reveals that "Robert Rich," awarded the Oscar for Best Motion Picture Story in 1956, was a pseudonym for himself. **17** Defying a court order secured by his ex-wife, Sterling Hayden sets sail with his children for the South Pacific, and will not return until November 15. **28** Audrey Hepburn, while filming *The*

Unforgiven in Durango, falls off a horse and fractures several vertebrae.

FEBRUARY 4 *Photoplay* announces that Debbie Reynolds has edged out Elizabeth Taylor in the magazine's poll for "most popular actress of 1958." **8** Overenthusiastic fans in Rio react to Jayne Mansfield's impromptu shimmy at the Copacabana by grabbing at the flower decorations on her dress, stripping her to the waist. **16** Eight days into the production of *Spartacus*, Stanley Kubrick replaces Anthony Mann as director, who has been fired by producer and star Kirk Douglas. **24** Warner Bros. ends Natalie Wood's seven-month suspension, giving her the right to do outside films.

MARCH 9 Lana Turner leaves *Anatomy of a Murder* because of "Mr. Preminger's unpre-

dictable temper." Director Otto Preminger says: "I'll get an unknown and make her a new Lana Turner." He will get Lee Remick. **11** For the third successive year, *The Harvard Lampoon* votes Kirk Douglas "worst actor" (for *The Vikings*). **17** With six years to go on her contract, Diane Varsi tells 20th Century Fox that she's quitting the movie business. She finds acting "destructive" and says it's making her "miserable."

APRIL • Seventeen-year-old starlet Carol Lynley tells an interviewer that the word "teenager," because of the bad associations it has taken on, should be dropped in favor of "people in their teens." **6** The Oscar ceremonies at the RKO Pantages Theater tonight run short, and with twenty minutes of TV air time to fill, Jerry Lewis suggests the possibility of showing Three Stooges shorts—he's kidding. **20** Columnist Joe

Movies

FEBRUARY 11 Gary Cooper, Maria Schell, Karl Malden, and George C. Scott, in his first film, star in *The Hanging Tree*, opening at the Roxy. **17** Walt Disney's *Sleeping Beauty*, in Technirama 70, opens at the Criterion.

MARCH 18 *The Diary of Anne Frank*, starring Millie Perkins as Anne, opens at the Palace. Howard Hawks's *Rio Bravo*, starring John Wayne, Dean Martin, and Angie Dickinson, opens at the Roxy. **28** Billy Wilder's *Some Like It Hot* premieres at Loew's State, with Marilyn Monroe, Harry

Belafonte, and Prince Aly Khan in the audience. The theater has just been reduced from 3,316 to 1,885 seats, in keeping with the trend toward more intimate houses. **30** *Room at the Top*, directed by Jack Clayton and starring Laurence Harvey and Simone Signoret, opens at the Fine Arts.

APRIL 1 Orson Welles, Dean Stockwell, Bradford Dillman, and Diane Varsi star in *Compulsion*, premiering at the Rivoli.

JUNE 18 *The Nun's Story*, starring Audrey Hepburn, opens at the Radio City Music Hall. **24** James Cagney and Don Murray star in *Shake Hands with the Devil*, bypassing

Broadway's first-run houses to open in New York neighborhood theaters. **24** Samuel Goldwyn's *Porgy and Bess*, in Todd-AO, starring Sidney Poitier, Dorothy Dandridge, Brock Peters, and Sammy Davis Jr., premieres at the Warner Theater. Goldwyn, Davis, and Dandridge attend.

JULY 1 Otto Preminger's *Anatomy of a Murder*, starring James Stewart, Lee Remick, Ben Gazzara, Arthur O'Connell, Eve Arden, George C. Scott, and Joseph Welch (the real-life lawyer who sparred with Senator Joseph McCarthy) premieres at the United Artists Theater in Detroit. Preminger, Remick, Scott, O'Connell, and

Business and Society

JANUARY 13 The Academy of Motion Picture Arts and Sciences abandons the exclusion of blacklisted people from Oscar consideration. **25** American Airlines inaugurates the first jet service between Los Angeles and New York. **30** Almena Lomax, editor of the *L.A. Tribune*, a black newspaper, having seen a press preview of *Imitation of Life*, announces that the paper

will not accept ads for the film, which she calls a "libel on the Negro race."

FEBRUARY 28 The anti-Communist Motion Picture Industry Council votes to suspend its activities as of July 1.

MARCH 17 Egypt bans Elizabeth Taylor's films because she has helped to raise money for Israel.

APRIL • The government of Panama, hav-

ing discovered a $500,000 payment from John Wayne to rebel leader Roberto Arias, accuses Wayne of involvement in Panamanian politics. Wayne says the money was for a business deal involving shrimps.

MAY • Congress compels the U.S. Information Agency to give it a list of films that it keeps off the screens of Third World countries. On the list are *All Quiet on the Western Front*, *Blackboard Jungle*, and Samuel Fuller's *House of Bamboo*.

Births, Deaths, Marriages, and Divorces

JANUARY 21 Cecil B. DeMille d. **•** Carl "Alfalfa" Switzer of the *Our Gang* comedies is shot and killed in a dispute over a $50 debt. **22** Linda Blair b.

FEBRUARY 10 George Sanders m. Benita Hume, widow of Ronald Colman. **19** Debbie Reynolds divorces Eddie Fisher, charging that "another woman" has broken up their marriage.

MARCH 3 Lou Costello d. **8** Aidan Quinn b. **22** Matthew Modine b.

APRIL 15 Emma Thompson b. **22** Marlon Brando and Anna Kashfi divorce. **29** Sammy Davis Jr. and Loray White divorce.

Hyams, in the *New York Herald Tribune*, says that Cary Grant has been seeing a psychiatrist and using LSD. Grant told him in an interview: "Now I know that I hurt every woman I loved. I was an utter fake, a self-opinionated boor...." **21** Louella Parsons reports that Cary Grant called her twice to deny ever being interviewed by Joe Hyams. Grant appears to have sold an "exclusive" story about his use of LSD to *Look* magazine, which Hyams's piece yesterday upstaged. **27** The *New York Herald Tribune* prints a photograph of Joe Hyams interviewing Cary Grant during the filming of *Operation Petticoat* in February.

MAY 15 Cary Grant and Kim Novak, who were mobbed last night when they arrived for a screening at the Cannes Film Festival, dance all night, adding fuel to rumors of romance.

JUNE 7 In probably the most expensive contract ever signed with a performer, Paramount agrees to pay Jerry Lewis $10,000,000 for fourteen films. **9** Pier Angeli announces that she and Vic Damone, whom she divorced in December, have reconciled. On April 14 she flew to London with their son, defying a court order not to take him out of the country, and Damone asked that she be arrested. The reconciliation will last till August 22, when Damone announces that it's over for good. **12** Rhoda Borgnine, trying to have her divorce decree set aside, tells a court that her husband Ernest's beatings left her with "swollen lips, blackened eyes and other marks and bruises so noticeable that when I wanted to attend the Oscar awards in 1956 my low neck dress had to be altered to conceal the bruises." For his part, Borgnine says that he has a much more satisfactory sex

life since taking up with Katy Jurado. **22** Warners announces that Henry Fonda's twenty-one-year-old daughter, Jane, will make her film debut in *Tall Story*.

JULY • The long-standing feud between Joan Crawford and Arlene Dahl flares up when Crawford, according to Dahl, disparages Dahl's mental stability. She says of Dahl, who has been filming *Journey to the Center of the Earth*: "Those Carlsbad Caverns bats must have followed dear Miss Dahl back from location." Dahl says the feud goes back to 1947 and her first Hollywood party, at which she told Crawford: "You've always been a favorite of mine—and my mother's, too." Crawford says she hardly knows Dahl. **2** Columnist Joe Hyams sues Cary Grant for slander for denying that Hyams interviewed him for his April newspaper series on the star. It may be the first time a writer

Welch attend. • Alfred Hitchcock and Eva Marie Saint attend the premiere of *North by Northwest*, starring Saint, Cary Grant, and James Mason, at the United Artists Theater in Chicago.

AUGUST 5 *Have Rocket, Will Travel*, the Three Stooges' first feature film, premieres at the Twin Drive-In in Cincinnati.

OCTOBER 6 *Pillow Talk* premieres at the Palace and Murray Hill theaters. Rock Hudson and Doris Day are starring in the first of their three films together. **22** *A Summer Place*, starring Troy Donahue, Sandra Dee, Richard Egan, Arthur

19 Warner Bros. announces the sale of its 2,800-acre Calabassas Ranch, which it used for filming, to be subdivided for housing. **25** The Screen Directors Guild and the East Coast Screen Directors International Guild merge. **25** Developer William Zeckendorf dedicates Century City on the 20th Century Fox back lot.

JULY • Joseph E. Levine, through his Embassy Pictures, imports from Italy *Hercules*, with Steve Reeves. Levine has it dubbed into English

Cary Grant in *North by Northwest*   MSN/©MGM

and is spending more than $1,000,000 promoting it. It will lead to a spate of made-in-Italy epics that do well at the box office. **1** Herbert Yates leaves Republic Pictures.

SEPTEMBER 16 SAG drafts Ronald Reagan to become its president again. **19** Soviet Premier Nikita Khrushchev is given a luncheon at 20th Century Fox with luminar-

MAY 8 Raquel Tejada m. James Welch, becoming Raquel Welch. **10** Julie Andrews m. Tony Walton. **12** Elizabeth Taylor m. Eddie Fisher. **14** Anita Ekberg divorces Anthony Steel.

JUNE 18 Ethel Barrymore d. **22** Dorothy Dandridge m. Jack Denison. **28** Dorothy

Malone m. Jacques Bergerac, formerly married to Ginger Rogers. • Terry Moore m. Stuart Cramer III, ex-husband of Jean Peters. **29** Jeff Chandler and Marjorie Hoshelle divorce.

JULY 9 Deborah Kerr and Anthony Bartley divorce.

AUGUST 6 Preston Sturges d. **10** Rosanna Arquette, granddaughter of Cliff Arquette (TV's "Charlie Weaver"), b. **21** Walter Matthau m. Carol Marcus, former wife of William Saroyan.

SEPTEMBER 11 Paul Douglas d. **13** Costume designer Gilbert Adrian d.

Personalities

has done this to a celebrity. Grant will settle out of court. **2** Keenan Wynn acknowledges beating his wife, Sharley, at their Malibu home, claiming she kept him up late when he had to get up early to go to work. **16** The Senate confirms the promotion of James Stewart from Colonel to Brigadier General in the Air Force Reserve. At the insistence of Sen. Margaret Chase Smith, in event of war he will do public relations and not be given a command. **26** A photo in "Tuesday Weld: New Girl in Hollywood" in the Sunday supplement *American Weekly*, is captioned: "Tuesday is reading the works of Dr. Freud because, she says, she's a puzzle to herself and wants to find out why, with her bright future, she still chews her fingernails."

TRUFFAUT IGNITES FRENCH "NEW WAVE"

The 400 Blows   LC/JANUS FILMS

Francois Truffaut's realistic film about childhood loneliness was based in part on his own childhood. The low-budget feature remains a landmark film that continues to inspire other directors.

Movies

Kennedy, and Dorothy McGuire, with theme music that will become a hit, opens at the Radio City Music Hall.

NOVEMBER 18 *Ben Hur*, directed by William Wyler and starring Charlton Heston, Stephen Boyd, Jack Hawkins, Haya Harareet, and Hugh Griffith, premieres at Loew's State. In keeping with the religious theme of the picture, there are no searchlights outside or celebrity interviews in the lobby. For the same reason, this is the first time that Leo, MGM's symbol, does not

roar to start a film. The eighteen-acre arena, filled with forty-thousand tons of sand, in which the famed chariot race was filmed, is said to be the largest movie set ever.

DECEMBER 3 Cary Grant and Tony Curtis star in *Operation Petticoat*, opening at the Radio City Music Hall. **8** *Behind the Great Wall*, a documentary on China produced by Sidney Kaufman in Aroma Rama, a process involving seventy-two odors

pumped into and out of the theater to match what's on the screen—"You must breathe it to believe it!"—premieres at the DeMille Theater (formerly the Mayfair). Aroma Rama is barely around long enough to leave a scent. **17** Stanley Kramer's *On the Beach*, about the aftermath of a nuclear war, starring Gregory Peck, Ava Gardner, Fred Astaire, and Anthony Perkins, and including the haunting strains of "Waltzing Matilda" on the soundtrack,

Business and Society

ies from all studios present. Ronald Reagan and several others refuse to attend. Khruschev watches the filming of a cancan dance, featuring Shirley MacLaine and Juliet Prowse, from the movie *Can-Can*. Later he suggests it was in poor taste.

OCTOBER 10 The Writers Guild of America strikes independent film producers over the

issue of residuals from post-1948 films sold to TV.

NOVEMBER 9 *Happy Anniversary*, with David Niven, opens with a line added at the last minute to secure a Production Code seal: "I was wrong. I never should have taken Alice to that hotel room before we were married. What could I have been thinking of?" **10** *Marty* becomes the first new American feature to be shown in the U.S.S.R. since World War II

when it opens in Moscow as part of a cultural exchange program. Gary Cooper and Edward G. Robinson are at the showing. **12** *Daily Variety* reports that movie profit margins have declined from 1949's five to ten percent to the present three percent.

Births, Deaths, Marriages, and Divorces

19 Claire Bloom m. Rod Steiger.
27 Victor Mature m. Joy Urwick.

OCTOBER 7 Mario Lanza d. **14** Errol Flynn d.

NOVEMBER 7 Victor McLaglen d.
20 Sean Young b. **23** Glenn Ford and Eleanor Powell divorce.

DECEMBER 19 Yvette Mimieux m. Evan

Harland. **31** Ernest Borgnine m. Katy Jurado. • Val Kilmer b.

Also this year: • Peter O'Toole m. actress Sian Phillips. • Jason Robards m. Rachel Taylor. • Angie and Gene Dickinson divorce. • Ellen McRae (Ellen Burstyn) and Paul Roberts divorce. • Lassie d.

AUGUST • Columbia contract player Jean Seberg is loaned out to Iberia films for a movie to be directed by Jean-Luc Godard. The film is *Breathless*.

SEPTEMBER 1 Elizabeth Taylor agrees to make *Cleopatra* for 20th Century Fox for $1 million. **16** Beverly Aadland, Errol Flynn's "protégée" (she's either seventeen or twenty-two, according to conflicting accounts), exchanges punches with Nora Haymes, one of Flynn's ex-wives, at a Hollywood party after Flynn leaves. Haymes objected to Aadland calling Flynn "elderly."

NOVEMBER 29 William Inge's play, *A Loss of Roses*, opens and flops on Broadway. But critics' praise for a supporting player, TV actor Warren Beatty, will win him a movie contract. **30** Alfred Hitchcock's *Psycho* goes into production. Paramount is worried

not about the detailed depiction of Janet Leigh being slashed in the shower by a maniac, but rather about a toilet being flushed on screen.

DECEMBER 7 20th Century Fox suspends Joan Collins for refusing a role in *Sons and Lovers*. Collins complains that she didn't get the script changes she was promised. **29** Hedda Hopper denounces Charlton Heston, who is caught in the middle of her feud with Ed Sullivan over her wanting stars to appear on her network TV special for free while Sullivan pays them substantial amounts for being on his show. Heston has pulled out of the Hopper special because she won't pay him. **31** A New Year's eve brawl lands former Golden Gloves boxer Ryan O'Neal in jail for almost two months.

premieres in eighteen cities worldwide. **22** Tennessee Williams's *Suddenly, Last Summer*, directed by Joseph Mankiewicz and starring Elizabeth Taylor, Katharine Hepburn, and Montgomery Clift, premieres at the Criterion and Sutton theaters. Hepburn, furious with how Mankiewicz treated her during the production, spat in his face on the last day of filming.

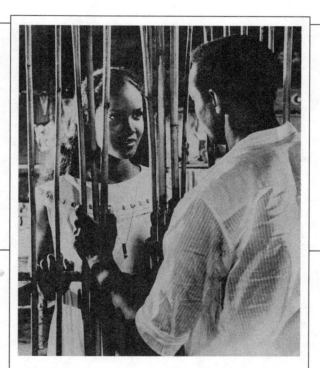

Black Orpheus, starring Marpessa Dawn (Eurydice) and Breno Mello (Orfeo) and directed by Marcel Camus, wins the Palm d'Or at the Cannes Film Festival this year. American audiences for foreign films are growing, and Janus Films becomes a main U.S. distributor of them. *LC/JANUS FILMS*

1960

The Hollywood Walk of Fame is dedicated. Shower curtains and mother love take a beating in *Psycho*. Elizabeth Taylor is a prostitute in *Butterfield 8* and a queen in *Cleopatra*, the filming of which gets off to a rocky start. *The Misfits* is also a troubled, star-crossed shoot. Frank Sinatra denies the existence of "The Clan," and Christina Crawford denies that she's feuding with her mother, Joan. Clark Gable is buried next to Carole Lombard, and Sandra Dee marries Bobby Darin. In Italy, Michelangelo Antonioni's *L'Avventura* uses the camera-scanned physical environment to express its characters' emotions.

- Number of releases: 387
- CinemaScope releases: 42
- Number of theaters: 16,999, of which 4,700 are drive-ins
- Average weekly attendance: 40,000,000
- Average ticket price: $.69
- Box office receipts: $951,000,000
- Players with term contracts: 230
- Substance "bled" by Janet Leigh in the shower scene in Psycho: chocolate sauce
- Number of shots required for *Psycho* shower scene: 78 (a week of filming for 45 seconds of screen time)
- Length of time required to shoot Roger Corman's *Little Shop of Horrors*: 2 ½ days

Top billing by gender, according to *The Guinness Book of Movie Facts and Feats*:
men: 81%
women: 19%

Top stars at the box office, based on a Quigley Publications poll of exhibitors:

1. Doris Day
2. Rock Hudson
3. Cary Grant
4. Elizabeth Taylor
5. Debbie Reynolds
6. Tony Curtis
7. Sandra Dee
8. Frank Sinatra
9. Jack Lemmon
10. John Wayne

The New York Film Critics Circle Awards
Best Picture (tie vote): *The Apartment* and *Sons and Lovers*

The Golden Globe Awards
Best Picture (Drama): *Spartacus*
Best Picture (Comedy): *The Apartment*
Best Picture (Musical): *Song Without End*

The Cannes Film Festival
Palme d'Or: *La Dolce Vita*

The Academy Awards (presented April 17, 1961)
Best Picture: *The Apartment*
Actor: Burt Lancaster (*Elmer Gantry*)
Actress: Elizabeth Taylor (*Butterfield 8*)
Supporting Actor: Peter Ustinov (*Spartacus*)
Supporting Actress: Shirley Jones (*Elmer Gantry*)
Director: Billy Wilder (*The Apartment*)

January	February	March	April	May	June	
25 *101 Dalmations*			• Marilyn Monroe affair with Yves Montand	• Montgomery Clift has hepatitis		
	18 First Smell-O-Vision film	**5** Elvis Presley out of Army			**16** Hitchcock's *Psycho*	

July	August	September	October	November	December	
	24 Frank Sinatra denies existence of "The Clan"			**23** Hollywood Walk of Fame dedicated	**11** "My mother and I are not feuding," says Christina Crawford	
6 Bette Davis divorces Gary Merrill		• Shooting begins on *Cleopatra*	**6** *Spartacus*			

Personalities

JANUARY • Stella Stevens appears nude in *Playboy*. **5** Judy Garland leaves a New York hospital, where she almost died from a diseased liver ravaged by pills and alcohol. **7** Sterling Hayden receives a five-day suspended sentence for defying a court order last year when he sailed to the South Pacific with his children. **9** John Wayne, who has just finished filming *The Alamo*, attacks *Suddenly, Last Summer* (he hasn't seen it) for dealing with "distasteful" subject matter, *They Came to Cordura* for "degrading the Medal of Honor," and *On the Beach* for its "defeatist attitude." **26** The sign outside the Sands Hotel in Las Vegas announces the opening of Frank Sinatra, Dean Martin, Sammy Davis Jr., Peter Lawford, and Joey Bishop. The "Clan" will appear for the next three weeks while they film *Ocean's Eleven*. Sinatra will introduce John F. Kennedy to mob moll Judith Campbell here somewhere around February 7.

FEBRUARY • The International Swimming Pool Corporation is attributing its bankruptcy to unreasonably high payments to Esther Williams for promoting their product. **18** According to the *Hollywood Reporter*, director David Lean and producer Sam Spiegel have chosen the lead for *Lawrence of Arabia*: Marlon Brando. **22** Jane Fonda makes the cover of *Life*, with her debut in *Tall Story*.

MARCH 5 Elvis Presley is released from the Army. On April 21 he will begin filming *G.I. Blues*. **17** Dick Haymes files for bankruptcy.

APRIL • Richard Burton turns down *The King of Kings* when producer Samuel Bronston won't give him equal billing with the film's title. • Marilyn Monroe, deeply unhappy in her marriage to Arthur Miller, begins a brief affair with Yves Montand, with whom she's filming *Let's Make Love*. Rex Harrison begins an affair with Tammy Grimes. **4** With the Screen Actors Guild on strike as the Oscars are awarded tonight, Bob Hope opens the ceremonies at the RKO Pantages with a quip about SAG's president: "I never thought I'd live to see the day when Ronald Reagan was the only actor working." **23** With his brother-in-law, John F. Kennedy, running for president, Peter Lawford becomes an American citizen. Sisters-in-law Joan and Ethel Kennedy wire him: "Congratulations and welcome to America."

MAY • Montgomery Clift is hospitalized for alcoholic hepatitis. **2** Marlon Brando and Shirley MacLaine have been among those protesting the imminent execution of Caryl Chessman. Today they lose their battle, as the state of California takes his

Movies

JANUARY 25 Walt Disney releases *One Hundred and One Dalmatians*.

MARCH 28 *Jazz on a Summer's Day*, arguably the best documentary jazz film ever, premieres at two New York theaters. Bert Stern's documentary of the 1958 Newport Jazz Festival features performers such as Thelonious Monk, Gerry Mulligan, and Louis Armstrong. **29** With the last showing of *The Wind Cannot Read*, New York's Roxy Theater closes, to be demolished this summer.

APRIL 6 John Huston's *The Unforgiven*, starring Burt Lancaster and Audrey Hepburn, opens at the Capitol.

JUNE 15 Billy Wilder's *The Apartment*, starring Jack Lemmon, Shirley MacLaine, and Fred MacMurray, opens at the Astor and Plaza Theaters. Filming was difficult for the cast, script-wise. Wilder, who co-authored the screenplay, maintained freshness in the last scenes by feeding his players their lines on the set, less than half an hour before rolling the cameras They had no idea beforehand how the film would conclude. **16** Alfred Hitchcock's *Psycho*, starring Anthony Perkins and Janet Leigh, opens

Director Alfred Hitchcock   LC

Business and Society

JANUARY • The studios are stuffing the Hollywood trade papers as never before with ads promoting their Oscar hopefuls. **1** The Screen Directors Guild merges with the Radio and TV Directors Guild to become the Directors Guild of America. **1** Herbert Kalmus retires as president of Technicolor. **5** Senator Wallace Bennett of the Senate Atomic Energy Committee attacks *On the Beach* as "unscientific, unrealistic and dangerously misleading." **16** The Writers Guild strikes the major studios over the issue of residual payments for films released to TV. **19** Producer-Director Otto Preminger says he will credit Hollywood Ten writer Dalton Trumbo as author of the screenplay for *Exodus*. Other blacklisted writers have worked under pseudonyms, but Trumbo will be the first to receive screen credit.

Births, Deaths, Marriages, and Divorces

JANUARY 1 Margaret Sullavan dies, possibly a suicide, from a pill overdose.

FEBRUARY 7 James Spader b. **14** Meg Tilly b.

MARCH 24 Jill St. John m. Lance Reventlow, son of Woolworth heiress Barbara Hutton. **26** Yul Brynner and Virginia Gilmore divorce. **28** Debra Paget m. director Bud Boetticher, whom she will leave after three weeks. **31** Yul Brynner m. Doris Kleiner.

APRIL • Christopher Plummer and Tammy Grimes divorce. **15** Dean Stockwell m. Millie Perkins. **22** Hedy Lamarr divorces W. Howard Lee.

life. **14** Frank Sinatra wears women's Native American garb to a costume benefit party, where he belligerently confronts John Wayne, who criticized him for hiring blacklisted screenwriter Albert Maltz. Wayne backs off. **30** Silent screen star Ramon Novarro's arrest for drunken driving will get him jail time in Van Nuys, California.

JUNE • Ft. Lauderdale sends out special coconut-trimming teams to make sure that the cast of *Where the Boys Are*, now filming, doesn't get beaned by falling fruit. **6** Sammy Davis Jr. and May Britt announce plans to wed. The interracial couple stirs up controversy with their decision. **29** Fred May, Lana Turner's boyfriend, upset that *Hollywood Reporter* gossip columnist Mike Connolly has criticized Turner's upbringing of her daughter, Cheryl, picks a fight with Connolly at a party at Romanoff's. Connolly's rival, *Daily Variety*

gossip columnist Army Archerd, comes to his rescue.

JULY 7 Dore Schary finishes the filming of *Sunrise at Campobello*, about Franklin D. Roosevelt, and begins to work to draft Adlai Stevenson for the Democratic presidential nomination. **18** Filming begins on *The Misfits*, Clark Gable's last picture and the last film that Marilyn Monroe will finish. Monroe and husband Arthur Miller, whose screenplay for the film reflects much of Marilyn's life, are barely speaking. He will fall in love with Inge Morath, a still photographer working on the set.

AUGUST • Sidney Poitier, alleging that discrimination has stymied his attempts to rent a house in Hollywood while making the film *A Raisin in the Sun*, takes an apartment in the Chateau Marmont. **8** Filming begins on *West Side Story* in New York. Natalie Wood's scenes will be filmed later

in Hollywood instead of on location because she is still working on *Splendor in the Grass*. **9** John Carradine files for bankruptcy. **24** Frank Sinatra, in a prepared statement, says that there is no such thing as the "Clan." **25** *The Misfits* shuts down for a week because John Huston's gambling losses have created a cash flow problem. Marilyn Monroe has been suffering from exhaustion and has not had the "breakdown" that some press reports allege has caused the production delay.

SEPTEMBER • Shooting begins in London on *Cleopatra*, with Stephen Boyd set to play Mark Antony and Peter Finch, Julius Caesar. They will be replaced by Richard Burton and Rex Harrison. Elizabeth Taylor has a sore throat, and the hairdressers are on strike. **26** At a nightclub on the Via Veneto in Rome, Cornel Wilde exchanges punches with a man who insists on dancing with the actor's wife. **27** Director

at the DeMille and Baronet Theaters. No one will be admitted once the film starts. **18** American International Pictures' *House of Usher*, starring Vincent Price, premieres at the Plaza Theater in Palm Springs. It's the first of a series of eight AIP color films based on the work of Edgar Allen Poe that Roger Corman will direct between now and 1964. **29** *Elmer Gantry*, starring Burt Lancaster and Jean Simmons, premieres at the Hollywood Paramount Theater, where children under sixteen will need parental accompaniment. Four days ago, police stopped United Artists from hiring college students to picket nearby with signs reading: "Sinners—Elmer Gantry Is Coming."

JULY 21 Spencer Tracy, Fredric March, and Gene Kelly star in *Inherit the Wind*, the story of the Scopes monkey trial. There is one show only at the U.S. premiere in Dayton, Tennessee, at the Dayton Drive-In Theater (the world premiere was in London on July 6), with general release in November. John Scopes, the man who insisted on teaching evolution in the 1920s in a state where fundamentalist beliefs predominated, will do a promotional tour for the film. **22** George Pal's *The Time Machine*, starring Rod Taylor, Alan Young, and Yvette Mimieux, opens in Chicago with saturation booking.

Mike Todd's Scent of Mystery, *in* Smell-O-Vision, *the first and last dramatic "smellie," starring Denholm Elliott, Peter Lorre, and Paul Lukas, opens at the Warner Theater. Ads proclaim: "First (1893) They Moved / Then (1927) They Talked / Now (1959) They Smell."*

February 18, 1960

FEBRUARY • The Telemeter company begins pay-TV service in Toronto. **1** Britain lifts restrictions on the amount of earnings that American film companies may take out of the country. **24** Universal–International agrees to pay SAG members residuals on films sold to TV.

MARCH 7 SAG strikes the major studios over the issue of residual payments for films

sold to TV. Layoffs begin in Hollywood.

APRIL 8 SAG settles its strike against the major studios, gaining the residuals for TV sales of films that it had demanded. **8** Frank Sinatra, bowing to pressure from the American Legion and the Hearst Press, fires blacklisted Albert Maltz, who he had hired to write the screenplay for *The Execution of Private Slovik*.

JUNE 1 A National Council of Churches report assails sex and violence in the movies. **7** Ronald Reagan resigns as president of the Screen Actors Guild because he is now a TV producer. **12** The Writers Guild of America settles its strike against the producers by gaining the residual payments for films released to TV that it had demanded. **12** The *New York Times* headlines: "Hollywood New Look: Major

MAY 4 Lucille Ball divorces Desi Arnaz. **13** Gloria Grahame m. Tony Ray, her stepson from her marriage to director Nicholas Ray. **28** James Franciscus m. Kathleen Wellman, daughter of director William Wellman. **31** Myrna Loy divorces Howland Sargeant.

JUNE • Marlon Brando m. Movita. **14** Laraine Day divorces Leo Durocher.

JULY 6 Bette Davis divorces Gary Merrill. **11** Gene Tierney m. W. Howard Lee, former husband of Hedy Lamarr. **22** Gene Wilder m. Mary Mercier. **23** Deborah

Kerr m. screenwriter Peter Viertel. **26** Art director Cedric Gibbons d.

AUGUST • Arlene Dahl divorces Fernando Lamas. **6** Gene Kelly m. Jeanne Coyne. **12** Jean Simmons divorces Stewart Granger. **16** Timothy Hutton b. **17** Sean Penn b.

Personalities

Stanley Kubrick says that he has chosen fourteen-year-old Sue Lyon, a model and TV actress he saw on "The Loretta Young Show," to play the nymphet in *Lolita*. **28** Rachel Robards sues husband Jason Robards Jr. for divorce, naming Lauren Bacall as "the other woman." **29** Fred MacMurray begins a twelve-year run on TV in "My Three Sons."

OCTOBER • Writer Ben Hecht claims in *Playboy* that the September 5, 1932, suicide of Jean Harlow's husband, Paul Bern, was really a case of murder by another woman. He says MGM wanted to cover it up to minimize damage to Harlow's career. **3** Jason Robards Jr. is arrested near Central Park in New York for drunken driving after hitting a parked car belonging to a policeman. He will have his license revoked and pay a $100 fine. Robards says he will not drive again. **25** A Glendale, California, jury acquits Tab Hunter of charges, brought by his neighbors, that he beat his dog.

NOVEMBER • Peter O'Toole, Shakespearean actor, tests in London for the tile role in *Lawrence of Arabia*, ending a long search for someone to play it. **4** Filming is completed on *The Misfits*. Marilyn Monroe tells John Huston she will not be able to appear in his *Freud* because her analyst says that Anna Freud did not want such a picture made. **6** Elizabeth Taylor's agent says that despite rumors, she will appear in Walter Mirisch's *Irma la Douce*, although probably not in *Two for the Seesaw*. But Mirisch claims she has reneged on commitments to both films and that he has already signed Shirley MacLaine for them. **6** Clark Gable has a heart attack. **9** Elizabeth Taylor, in the grip of an infection, is taken to a London hospital by ambulance for the second time in two weeks, resulting in the suspension of production on *Cleopatra* on November 20. **11** Marilyn Monroe and Arthur Miller announce that they will divorce. **21** Steve McQueen and his neighbor, who has complained about the actor's "reckless driving" and big dog, which runs loose, exchange punches. **23** The Hollywood Walk of Fame, on Hollywood Boulevard and Vine Street, is dedicated. Stars need to have a sponsor who contributes

Movies

AUGUST 2　*Sons and Lovers*, starring Trevor Howard, Dean Stockwell, and Wendy Hiller, opens at the Victoria and Beekman Theaters.

SEPTEMBER 28　*Sunrise at Campobello*, starring Ralph Bellamy and Greer Garson, premieres at the Palace Theater.

OCTOBER 2　*The Entertainer*, starring Laurence Olivier, premieres in the U.S. at the Sutton. **6** *Spartacus*, produced by Kirk Douglas, directed by Stanley Kubrick, and starring Douglas, Tony Curtis, Jean

Business and Society

Studios Losing Grip to Stars, Agencies, Independent Producers." **13** 20th Century Fox withdraws from the Motion Picture Association. Studio president Spyros Skouras charges "cannibalism," claiming that other studios have been stealing its ideas. **14** Replying to Skouras's charge

Kirk Douglas in *Spartacus*　　　　　　　　LC

Births, Deaths, Marriages, and Divorces

SEPTEMBER 21　Jean Seberg divorces François Moreuil.

OCTOBER 15　Arlene Dahl m. Christian Holmes, Fleischmann Yeast heir. **15** Silent-films star Clara Kimball Young d. **20** Joseph Cotten m. Patricia Medina.

NOVEMBER 1　Jean Simmons m. director Richard Brooks. **5** Mack Sennett d. **13** Sammy Davis Jr. m. May Britt. **16** Clark Gable d. He will be buried next to Carole Lombard at Forest Lawn. **18** Shelley Winters divorces Anthony Franciosa. **25** Debbie Reynolds m. Harry Karl. **27** Lana Turner m. department-store heir Fred May, ex-husband of Ann Rutherford.

$3,000, and honorees must appear when their star is unveiled. **30** On behalf of Elizabeth Taylor and Eddie Fisher, lawyer Louis Nizer sues a group of fan magazines for malicious libel for stories such as: "Liz-Eddie-Debbie: Are They Planning to Live Together?"

DECEMBER 1 Production begins in Tahiti on MGM's remake of *Mutiny on the Bounty*, starring Marlon Brando. **2** Darryl Zanuck announces that, for $175,000, he has acquired the film rights to *The Longest Day*, which he calls "the most ambitious undertaking since *Gone With the Wind* and *Birth of a Nation*." **11** "My mother and I are not feuding," Christina Crawford, Joan's daughter, tells *Parade* magazine. **31** Ernest Borgnine and Katy Jurado celebrate their first anniversary with a fistfight.

FELLINI'S *LA DOLCE VITA*

Anita Ekberg in *La Dolce Vita*   LC/JANUS FILMS

Actress Anita Ekberg and Italian director Frederico Fellini begin to become household names among film audiences every-where with the success of Fellini's *La Dolce Vita*, which wins the Palme d'Or at Cannes this year.

Simmons, Peter Ustinov, Laurence Olivier, and Charles Laughton, premieres at the DeMille. The audience tonight includes Douglas, Cary Grant, and Doris Day. **12** *The Magnificent Seven*, starring Yul Brynner, Steve McQueen, Eli Wallach, James Coburn, Horst Buchholz, Robert Vaughn, and Charles Bronson, opens in saturation booking throughout the South. **24** *The Alamo*, produced and directed by John Wayne, and starring Wayne, Laurence Harvey, Richard Widmark, Richard Boone, Linda Cristal, and Frankie Avalon, premieres at the Woodlawn Theater in San Antonio, where a three-day holiday has been declared. Wayne, Widmark, Harvey,

Avalon, Boone, and Cristal attend. After the opening Wayne will cut thirty-seven minutes out of the three-hour, nineteen-minute film.

NOVEMBER 10 John Wayne, Stewart Granger, Fabian, Capucine, and Ernie Kovacs star in *North to Alaska*, opening at the Paramount, where this afternoon, rock 'n roll singer Fabian will appear in the lobby to host an "After-School Coke Party." **16** Elizabeth Taylor, Laurence Harvey, and Eddie Fisher star in *Butterfield 8*, opening at the Capitol. Taylor, a call girl, puts it in a nutshell: "Mama, face it: I was the slut of all time."

DECEMBER 8 Deborah Kerr, Robert Mitchum, and Peter Ustinov star in *The Sundowners*, premiering at the Radio City Music Hall. **15** Otto Preminger's *Exodus*, starring Paul Newman, Eva Marie Saint, Peter Lawford, Lee J. Cobb, and Sal Mineo, premieres at the Warner Theater. Preminger, Lawford, and Mineo attend. **21** *Where the Boys Are*, starring Dolores Hart, George Hamilton, Paula Prentiss, Yvette Mimieux, Connie Francis, Jim Hutton, and Barbara Nichols, premieres at the Gateway Theater in Ft. Lauderdale.

of "cannibalism," producer Albert Broccoli says that "Skouras himself is the arch-cannibal." **29** The government loses its suit against Universal and Columbia, in which it charged them with fixing the prices of films sold to TV.

JULY • The Motion Picture Association of America reports that almost half of the films receiving Production Code seals of

approval since January have been made abroad. **9** Blacks picket two whites-only theaters in Kansas City, Missouri. They gain admission to one, where they see *Huckleberry Finn*. **12** 20th Century Fox executive producer Buddy Adler dies, and will be replaced by Robert Goldstein.

DECEMBER 1 Sandra Dee m. Bobby Darin. **10** Kenneth Branagh b. **24** Betty Hutton m. trumpeter Pete Candoli. **30** Carol Lynley m. Michael Selsman.

Also this year: • Darryl Hannah b. • Karen Ziegler becomes Karen Black on her marriage to Charles Black. • Peter

Falk m. Alice Mayo. • Ellen McRae m. Neil Burstyn, becoming Ellen Burstyn. • George C. Scott m. Colleen Dewhurst. • Woody Allen and Harlene Rosson divorce.

*T*he major studios are increasingly becoming financiers and distributors of foreign-made films and independently produced domestic pictures. Even much of Hollywood's own output is now shot abroad. In-flight movies begin. Marilyn Monroe divorces Arthur Miller, has a nightmarish encounter with a mental hospital, and then meets President Kennedy. United Artists announces a series of films based on the Ian Fleming character, James Bond. And Alain Resnais's dense, enigmatic *Last Year at Marienbad* opens in Paris to rave reviews.

- Number of releases: 462
- CinemaScope releases: 35
- Number of theaters: 21,000, of which 6,000 are drive-ins
- Average weekly attendance: 42,000,000
- Average ticket price: $.69
- Box office receipts: $921,000,000
- Players with term contracts at major studios: 164
- Hollywood's first on-screen French kiss: Natalie Wood and Warren Beatty in *Splendor in the Grass*

Top stars at the box office, based on a Quigley Publications poll of exhibitors:

1.	Elizabeth Taylor	**6.**	Sandra Dee
2.	Rock Hudson	**7.**	Jerry Lewis
3.	Doris Day	**8.**	William Holden
4.	John Wayne	**9.**	Tony Curtis
5.	Cary Grant	**10.**	Elvis Presley

Top rental earnings, based on figures reported in *Variety*:

1.	*The Guns of Navarone*	$8,600,000
2.	*The Absent-Minded Professor*	8,200,000
3.	*The Parent Trap*	8,000,000
4.	*Swiss Family Robinson*	7,500,000
5.	*Exodus*	7,350,000

The New York Film Critics Circle Awards
Best Picture: *West Side Story*

The Golden Globe Awards
Best Picture (Drama): *The Guns of Navarone*
Best Picture (Comedy): *A Majority of One*
Best Picture (Musical): *West Side Story*

The Cannes Film Festival
Palme d'Or: *Viridiana* and *Une Aussi Longue Absence*

The Academy Awards (presented April 9, 1962)
Best Picture: *West Side Story*
Actor: Maximilian Schell (*Judgment at Nuremberg*)
Actress: Sophia Loren (*Two Women*)
Supporting Actor: George Chakiris (*West Side Story*)
Supporting Actress: Rita Moreno (*West Side Story*)
Director: Robert Wise and Jerome Robbins (*West Side Story*)

January	February	March	April	May	June	
24 Marilyn Monroe divorces Arthur Miller	**27** Carol Reed fired from *Mutiny on the Bounty*	**17** Laurence Olivier m. Joan Plowright	**3** Eddie Murphy b.		**28** United Artists announces James Bond films	
					13 Gary Cooper d.	

July	August	September	October	November	December
	23 Joan Collins calls off engagement to Warren Beatty	**26** *The Hustler*		**28** NAACP threatens to picket theaters	**1** Lucille Ball m. Gary Morton
	19 TWA starts in-flight movies		**5** *Breakfast at Tiffany's*		

Personalities

JANUARY 19   Rouben Mamoulian resigns as director of *Cleopatra*. On January 27 Joseph Mankiewicz will replace him. **27**   *Life* runs a seven-page spread on Ann-Margret's successful January 13 screen test at 20th Century Fox. **31**   A tearful June Allyson obtains an interlocutory decree of divorce from Dick Powell. Charging that he came home late for dinner and criticized her constantly, she says of his behavior: "It made me cry all the time." They will reconcile.

FEBRUARY •   Bad weather in Tahiti forces the *Mutiny on the Bounty* production back to Hollywood for four months. **4**   In a *TV Guide* interview, "Rawhide" star Clint Eastwood says "I'd sort of like to branch out a bit, do other things. I don't figure 'Raw-hide' will last forever...." **5**   A depressed Marilyn Monroe, on her psychiatrists' advice, checks herself into New York's Payne Whitney Clinic, where she becomes distraught when they place her in a padded cell. Joe DiMaggio will get her out by threatening to tear the place apart and has her transferred to Columbia-Presbyterian for a month's stay. **17**   Lloyd's of London, which has insured *Cleopatra*, wants Elizabeth Taylor replaced by Marilyn Monroe, Kim Novak, or Shirley MacLaine. Says producer Walter Wanger: "No Liz—No Cleo." **19**   After an argument in a Rome nightclub, Ernest Borgnine chases Katy Jurado out onto the Via Veneto, and she ends up lying in the street—although no one will say whether he knocked her down. **27**   Carol Reed is fired as director of *Mutiny on the Bounty* when he clashes with MGM over production matters. Lewis Milestone will replace him.

MARCH 1   Nineteen-forties star John Payne, hit by a car while crossing Madison Avenue in Manhattan, suffers a fractured skull and broken leg. He requires six hours of surgery, 150 stitches, and the care of a plastic surgeon. **4**   Suffering from a severe case of the flu, Elizabeth Taylor stops breathing. An emergency tracheotomy saves her life. Work on *Cleopatra* is at a standstill. **5**   Marilyn Monroe, emerging from New York's Columbia-Presbyterian Medical Center, is almost overwhelmed by photographers. **27**   In a Hollywood trade press ad, John Wayne disowns the recent ads of Chill Wills, one of his *Alamo* co-stars, which read: "We of the Alamo cast are praying harder—than the real Texans prayed for their lives in the Alamo—for Chill Wills to win the Oscar."

APRIL •   Teenage girls in *Ingenue* magazine's poll of their favorite male stars rate Troy

Movies

JANUARY 31   Montgomery Clift escorts Marilyn Monroe to the premiere of *The Misfits* at the Capitol. It also stars Clark Gable, Eli Wallach, and Thelma Ritter.

FEBRUARY 28   Don Murray stars in *The Hoodlum Priest*, premiering at Loew's State in St. Louis.

MARCH 21   *Shadows*, the first film directed by John Cassavetes, has its U.S. premiere at the Embassy. **29**   *A Raisin in the Sun*, starring Sidney Poitier, Claudia McNeil, and Ruby Dee, premieres at the Forum and Trans-Lux 52nd St. Theaters. **30**   Marlon Brando directs and stars in *One-Eyed Jacks*, also featuring Karl Malden and Katy Jurado, opening at the Capitol.

APRIL 3   Albert Finney stars in *Saturday Night and Sunday Morning*, premiering in the U.S. at the Baronet.

JUNE 22   *The Guns of Navarone* premieres in the U.S. at the Criterion (the world premiere was in London on April 27). Gregory Peck, Anthony Quinn, David Niven, and Irene Papas star.

SEPTEMBER 26   Robert Rossen's *The Hustler*, starring Paul Newman, Jackie Gleason, George C. Scott, and Piper Laurie, opens at the Paramount.

OCTOBER 5   *Breakfast at Tiffany's*, starring Audrey Hepburn, George Peppard, Patricia Neal, Buddy Ebsen, Martin Balsam, Mickey Rooney, and featuring Henry Mancini's "Moon River," opens at the Radio City Music Hall. **10**   *Splendor in the Grass*, starring Natalie Wood and Warren Beatty in his screen debut, opens at the Victoria and Trans-Lux 52nd St. Theaters. Warner Bros. test-previewed it in key cities to gauge public reaction to the steamy love scenes.

Business and Society

JANUARY •   Muslims riot in Tunis over use of a mosque in the filming of Joseph E. Levine's *The Wonders of Aladdin*. **3**   Under pressure from the Fair Employment Practices Commission, Central Casting begins the policy of having blacks call in daily for work, as do whites. Previously, a "colored casting director" would phone blacks when they were needed. **23**   The Supreme Court rules that cities and states have a right to censor films before they are shown to the public.

MARCH •   The success of two of its theaters that are in shopping centers has the Stanley Warner company developing plans for others.

MAY •   Fox puts Peter G. Levathes, head of its TV division, in charge of production of feature films and begins a policy of "fewer but better pictures." He will also close the studio's commissary to save money.

JULY 19   TWA becomes the first airline to offer in-flight movies regularly—in first class only. The opening attraction is *By Love Possessed*. **31**   The Production Code Administration issues seals to *The Man with the Golden Arm* and *The Moon Is Blue*, now deemed acceptable.

AUGUST 16   William Wyler says that the Production Code Office has warned him

Births, Deaths, Marriages, and Divorces

JANUARY 3   Joan Fontaine divorces Collier Young. **4**   Barry Fitzgerald d. **24**   Marilyn Monroe divorces Arthur Miller.

FEBRUARY 17   Silent-screen star Nita Naldi d.

MARCH •   Jane Wyman remarries Fred Karger. **16**   Ginger Rogers m. William Marshall, ex-husband of actress Michele Morgan. **17**   Laurence Olivier m. Joan Plowright.

APRIL 3   Eddie Murphy b.

MAY 4   Silent-screen star Anita Stewart d. **13**   Gary Cooper d. **22**   Jason Robards Jr. and Rachel Taylor divorce.

JUNE 9   Michael J. Fox b. **17**   Jeff Chandler d.

Donahue tops, followed by Frankie Avalon and Fabian. • Stanley Kramer shoots the courtroom scenes for *Judgment at Nuremberg* as Adolf Eichmann is tried for genocide in Jerusalem. Montgomery Clift's characterization of a man shattered by the Nazis is lent realism by his drinking openly on the set and his emotional collapse offscreen as well as onscreen. **17** John Wayne's trade magazine mega-campaign nets none of the top Academy Awards for *The Alamo* tonight. The Oscars are given out at the Santa Monica Civic Auditorium.

JUNE 7 Marilyn Monroe, Elizabeth Taylor, and Eddie Fisher are among guests at a birthday party in Las Vegas for Dean Martin given by Frank Sinatra, who is having an affair with Monroe. **28** United Artists announces that it will release seven films based on Ian Fleming's James Bond novels, to be produced by Albert Broccoli and Harry Saltzman, who have begun a search for someone to play the lead role.

JULY 6 20th Century Fox announces that production on *Cleopatra* will continue, but in Italy and Egypt rather than in Britain, where shooting had begun.

AUGUST 23 Joan Collins announces the end of her engagement to Warren Beatty, who has taken up with Natalie Wood during the filming of *Splendor in the Grass*. Collins has been dating Robert Wagner, Wood's estranged husband.

SEPTEMBER 11 John Huston begins filming *Freud*, during which he will harass and belittle his star, Montgomery Clift, who will develop cataracts during the production. **25** In its three-paragraph obituary of Marion Davies, the *Hollywood Reporter* never mentions her lover and mentor, William Randolph Hearst, whose relationship with her was fictionally depicted in *Citizen Kane*. **25** Shooting resumes in Rome on *Cleopatra*. **25** With the Cold War heating up and fears of a nuclear war increasing, a large fallout shelter opens at the Beverly Hills end of the Sunset Strip. Groucho Marx, who lives nearby, had lobbied for it. Jane Powell and Glenn Ford have built their own, with his doubling as a wine cellar.

OCTOBER • Marilyn Monroe and President Kennedy meet for the first time at a party at Pat and Peter Lawford's home in Santa Monica, at which Janet Leigh, Kim Novak, and Angie Dickinson are also present. **2** Columnist Joe Hyams reports that several days ago, MGM head Sol Siegel

Audrey Hepburn *in Breakfast at Tiffany's*

MOMA
© *PARAMOUNT PICTURES*

The results show, says the studio, that the public wants "frankness." **11** Nicholas Ray's *King of Kings*, starring Jeffrey Hunter as Jesus and narrated by Orson Welles, premieres at Loew's State. The National Legion of Decency says it's "theologically, historically and scripturally inaccurate." **18** Robert Wise and Jerome Robbins's *West Side Story*, starring Natalie Wood, Richard Beymer, George Chakiris, Russ Tamblyn, and Rita Moreno premieres at the Rivoli. Wood (with Warren Beatty), Moreno, Chakiris, Wise, and Robbins are in the audience at the gala opening.

NOVEMBER 15 *Summer and Smoke*, starring

that *The Children's Hour* may be rejected for a seal because it deals with lesbianism. **30** Los Angeles police report that thirty-five nudie movies have been shot in the city in the past three months. The success of *Not Tonight, Henry*, a low-budget, softcore film, has spurred this production.

SEPTEMBER 7 The Screen Actors Guild rescinds its permission to MCA (granted in 1952) to function as both a talent agent and producer. **21** Under the headline

JULY 4 Lauren Bacall m. Jason Robards Jr. **8** James Caan m. Dee Jay Mattis. **18** Elizabeth McGovern b.

AUGUST 24 Debra Paget divorces Bud Boetticher. **29** Rebecca De Mornay (Rebecca George) b. **30** Charles Coburn d.

SEPTEMBER 7 Rita Hayworth divorces James Hill. **22** Marion Davies d.

OCTOBER 8 Peter Fonda m. Susan Brewer. **11** Chico Marx d. **20** Producer Joseph M. Schenck d.

NOVEMBER 20 Lucille Ball m. Gary Morton.

DECEMBER 23 Martin and Janet Sheen marry. **31** Anthony Franciosa m. Judy Balaban, daughter of Paramount president Barney Balaban.

Also this year: • Eric Stoltz b. • Richard Benjamin m. Paula Prentiss. • Henry Fonda and Baroness Afdera Franchetti

Personalities

accused Marlon Brando of not giving his all on *Mutiny on the Bounty* because he wasn't getting his way on the script. **15** Hollywood correspondent Florabel Muir describes Warren Beatty as "the hottest new star since Marlon Brando made the torn undershirt a symbol of virility." **16** The "Hollywood's Answer to Communism" rally at the Hollywood Bowl features Roy Rogers, Walt Disney, John Ford, Rock Hudson, Ozzie and Harriet, Ronald Reagan, Donna Reed, Jane Russell, James Stewart, and John Wayne leading the pledge of allegiance **18** Bobby Driscoll, Walt Disney child star of the 1940s and 50s, is committed to Chino State Hospital in California as a drug addict. His body will be discovered in a rubble pile in March

Movies

Geraldine Page, Laurence Harvey, Una Merkle, and "introducing" Pamela Tiffin, premieres at the DeMille. Tennessee Williams, Page, and Tiffin are at the opening.

DECEMBER 14 *El Cid*, starring Charlton Heston and Sophia Loren, has its U.S. premiere at the Warner Theater. It opened in London on December 6. **19** William Wyler's *The Children's Hour*, starring Audrey Hepburn, Shirley MacLaine, James Garner, and Miriam Hopkins, who was in the bowdlerized 1936 version, *These Three*, premieres

Sean Connery is chosen this year to play a character named James Bond.   *LC*

Business and Society

"Code Okays Homo Angle," *Daily Variety* reports that Otto Preminger has been told that he can deal with homosexuality in *Advise and Consent* as long as it's in good taste. **23** NBC inaugurates *Saturday Night at the Movies* with *How to Marry a Millionaire*, the beginning of regularly scheduled showings of recent Hollywood films.

OCTOBER 2 Sol Schwartz replaces Sam Briskin as production head at Columbia. **3** The Motion Picture Production Code is changed to permit the portrayal of "sexual aberration" (homosexuality).

NOVEMBER 5 Edward R. Murrow, director of the U.S. Information Agency, urges the film industry to convey a positive image of America, making movies a "strategic commodity." **28** The NAACP threatens to picket theaters unless blacks gain

access to more movie industry jobs and films begin to treat black characters with more dignity. **30** The Motion Picture Academy appeals to "the good conscience" of Oscar nominees to reign in "vulgar" campaigning for awards via trade paper ads.

DECEMBER • The major studios put only three films into production in Hollywood this month. **1** A Congressional subcommittee begins two days of hearings into "runaway" productions—U.S. films made abroad.

Births, Deaths, Marriages, and Divorces

divorce. • Laurence Harvey and Margaret Leighton divorce.

1968, but not be identified until 1969. **21** Barbra Streisand makes her first stage appearance in the off-Broadway revue, *Another Evening With Harry Stoones*, which will close after this evening. She beat out Louise Lasser and Linda Lavin for the job.

NOVEMBER 6 Los Angeles's worst fire hits the Hollywood Hills, destroying the homes of Zsa Zsa Gabor, Burt Lancaster, Joe E. Brown, and Joan Fontaine, and damaging those of Vincent Price, Fred MacMurray, Alfred Hitchcock, John Cassavetes, Kim Novak, and James Garner. **14** Production begins at Columbia on *Twist Around the Clock*, starring Chubby Checker and Dion (who sings "The Wanderer" and "Runaround Sue"). Finished in a week it is released mid-December to exploit the new dance craze. Several other twist films are also being rushed to completion. **17** A

trade paper ad calling for negotiated nuclear disarmament is signed by Martin Balsam, Marlon Brando, John Cassavetes, Richard Conte, Sammy Davis, Jr., John Forsythe, Rita Hayworth, Gary Merrill, Rita Moreno, Don Murray, Kim Novak, Cliff Robertson, Jean Simmons, and Shelley Winters. **30** Reviewing last night's opening of the Broadway play, *Sunday in New York*, the *New York Times* critic says of Robert Redford, in his first lead role, that he "will be a matinee idol, if he doesn't look out." **22** Producers Albert Broccoli and Harry Saltzman announce an expensive publicity campaign to make a star of Sean Connery, their choice for James Bond.

DECEMBER 28 In Santa Monica Superior Court for a child-custody hearing, Marlon Brando's ex-wife, Anna Kashfi, smacks him.

at the Fox Wilshire in Los Angeles. Hepburn, Garner, and MacLaine attend. **19** Stanley Kramer's *Judgment at Nuremberg*, starring Spencer Tracy, Burt Lancaster, Richard Widmark, Marlene Dietrich, Maximilian Schell, Judy Garland (making her third comeback), and Montgomery Clift, has its American premiere in New York at the Palace. Five days earlier it opened in Berlin. Marlene Dietrich arrives with Adlai Stevenson. Schell, Widmark, and Kramer are also at the theater. **21** Billy Wilder's *One, Two, Three*, starring James Cagney, Horst Buchholz, and Pamela Tiffin, opens at the Astor and Fine Arts. Cagney retires after this film. *One,*

Two, Three is notable for it's rapid-fire dialogue, especially propelled by the energy of James Cagney. Horst Bucholtz is also given the opportunity to spout some of Billy Wilder's witticisms, aided by co-writer I.A.L. Diamond. In the film, Bucholtz is an East German Communist and Cagney works for Coca-Cola in West Berlin:

Horst Bucholtz: "I spit on your money. I spit on Ft. Knox. I spit on Wall Street."
James Cagney: "Unsanitary little jerk, isn't he."
Bucholtz: "Capitalism is like a dead herring in the moonlight: It shines, but it stinks."

Gary Cooper dies this year, after a long and distinguished career.   *MSN*

*M*CA takes over Universal–International. It's the end of the road for the Hope-Crosby-Lamour team, but just the beginning for Elizabeth Taylor and Richard Burton, who turn the off-camera activity on *Cleopatra* into an epic within an epic. Meanwhile, *The Longest Day* helps to save 20th Century Fox, now controlled by the Zanucks, from financial disaster. Marilyn Monroe dies, Tony Curtis and Janet Leigh split up, George C. Scott turns down an Oscar nomination, and bitter enemies Joan Crawford and Bette Davis keep from shedding one another's blood on the set of *Whatever Happened to Baby Jane*. The September *McCall's* runs Judith Krantz's story, "The Night They Invented Troy Donahue."

- Number of releases: 427
- CinemaScope releases: 30
- Number of theaters: 21,000, of which 6,000 are drive-ins
- Average weekly attendance: 43,000,000
- Average ticket price: $.70
- Box office receipts: $903,000,000
- Total industry employment: 174,000
- Players with term contracts at major studios: 207
- Marlon Brando's total compensation for *Mutiny on the Bounty*: $1,250,000
- Original budget and shooting schedule for *Lawrence of Arabia*: $2,500,000 and four months
- Actual production cost and shooting schedule of *Lawrence of Arabia*: $13,000,000 and two years

Top stars at the box office, based on a Quigley Publications poll of exhibitors:

1. Doris Day
2. Rock Hudson
3. Cary Grant
4. John Wayne
5. Elvis Presley
6. Elizabeth Taylor
7. Jerry Lewis
8. Frank Sinatra
9. Sandra Dee
10. Burt Lancaster

The New York Film Critics Circle Awards
Best Picture: No Awards

The Golden Globe Awards
Best Picture (Drama): *Lawrence of Arabia*
Best Picture (Comedy): *That Touch of Mink*
Best Picture (Musical): *The Music Man*

The Cannes Film Festival
Palme d'Or: *The Given Word*

The Academy Awards (presented April 8, 1963)
Best Picture: *Lawrence of Arabia*
Actor: Gregory Peck (*To Kill a Mockingbird*)
Actress: Anne Bancroft (*The Miracle Worker*)
Supporting Actor: Ed Begley (*Sweet Bird of Youth*)
Supporting Actress: Patty Duke (*The Miracle Worker*)
Director: David Lean (*Lawrence of Arabia*)

January	February	March	April	May	June
3 Dick Powell and June Allyson call off the divorce		**5** George C. Scott spurns Oscar nomination for *The Hustler*		**19** Marilyn Monroe sings "Happy Birthday" to Pres. Kennedy	
	5 Jennifer Jason Leigh b.		**29** Vanessa Redgrave m. director Tony Richardson		**19** MCA merges with Universal–International–Decca

July	August	September	October	November	December
11 Janet Leigh divorces Tony Curtis		**5** Marilyn Monroe found dead of barbiturates overdose	**23** Darryl Zanuck fires *Cleopatra* director Joseph Mankiewicz	**14** Jodie Foster b.	
		21 Bette Davis "SITUATIONS WANTED" ad		**16** *Lawrence of Arabia*	

Personalities

JANUARY 3 Dick Powell and June Allyson tell their attorneys to call off their divorce. **22** Elizabeth Taylor and Richard Burton are together before the cameras for the first time on *Cleopatra*. **26** *Cleopatra* director Joseph Mankiewicz confides to producer Walter Wanger: "Liz and Burton are not just *playing* Antony and Cleopatra."

FEBRUARY 19 Richard Burton denounces "uncontrolled rumors" of a romance between himself and *Cleopatra* co-star Elizabeth Taylor. **20** Silent-screen star Ramon Novarro is arrested again for drunken driving, in Los Angeles, for which he will draw a two-week jail term. **22** Frank Sinatra and dancer-actress Juliet Prowse announce that their careers prevent them from marrying.

Richard Burton and Elizabeth Taylor in *Cleopatra*
LC/20TH CENTURY FOX

MARCH 5 George C. Scott turns down an Oscar nomination for Best Supporting Actor in *The Hustler* to protest the campaigning for awards that has become an annual practice. It is the first time anyone has ever declined an Oscar nomination or award, but the Academy says that the nomination stands. **17** Tony Curtis and Janet Leigh announce their separation, which Louella Parsons finds "a shocking bit of news." **19** Princess Grace (Kelly) of Monaco will star in Alfred Hitchcock's *Marnie*, it is announced. **22** The *New York Post* reveals that 1940s star Veronica Lake, wearing her hair pulled back, is a barmaid at the Martha Washington Hotel in New York City. **24** President Kennedy is staying with Bing Crosby in Palm Springs for the weekend. Marilyn Monroe is also staying at Crosby's home, and tonight will be the only time, according to Monroe, that she ever slept with Kennedy.

Movies

FEBRUARY 5 *The Victim*, a British film starring Dirk Bogarde that has been denied a Production Code seal because it is about a homosexual lawyer, premieres in the U.S. at the Forum and Murray Hill theaters.

MARCH 23 *Sweet Bird of Youth*, starring Paul Newman and Geraldine Page, premieres at the Egyptian in Hollywood.

APRIL 12 *Cape Fear*, starring Robert Mitchum, Gregory Peck, and Polly Bergen, premieres at four Miami theaters. It will be remade in 1991 by Martin Scorsese starring Robert DeNiro, Nick Nolte, and Jessica Lange. **30** Rita Tushingham stars in Tony Richardson's *A Taste of Honey*, premiering in the U.S. at the Paris Theater.

MAY 23 John Ford's *The Man Who Shot Liberty Valence*—"When the legend becomes the fact, print the legend"—starring John Wayne, James Stewart, and Lee Marvin, opens at the Capitol. **23** Patty Duke and Anne Bancroft star in *The Miracle Worker*, based on the life of Helen Keller and opening at several United Artist theaters in New York. **24** *Lonely Are the Brave*, directed by David Miller from a Dalton Trumbo screenplay, starring Kirk Douglas, Gena Rowlands, and Walter Matthau, premieres in seven Texas cities. Highly praised by critics, it will not do well at the box office.

JUNE 5 Otto Preminger's *Advise and Consent* premieres at the Criterion. The film's stars, Henry Fonda, Walter Pidgeon, Franchot Tone, and Burgess Meredith are there, as are Myrna Loy and Zsa Zsa Gabor. **13** "How did they ever make a movie out of *Lolita*?" tease the ads for the film starring James Mason, Sue Lyon, Shelley Winters, and Peter Sellers, premiering at Loew's State. Author Vladimir Nabakov and di-

Business and Society

JANUARY 3 Sol Siegel resigns as MGM production chief, to be replaced by Robert Weitman. **27** According to the *Hollywood Reporter*, original screenplays account for only fifteen percent of major films begun in the past year. **30** Producer Robert L. Lippert, the "King of the Bs," says he will produce only four second-features in Hollywood this year. They are now made more cheaply abroad.

FEBRUARY 19 Producer Charles Feldman cancels tomorrow night's New Orleans premiere of *A Walk on the Wild Side*—with its themes of prostitution and lesbianism—and switches it to New York on the 21st because the city has warned it will have agents present to determine if it is obscene. **27** SAG, in its publication *Screen Actor*, says it will penalize actors who impede production by showing up late, drinking, or through other misbehavior.

MARCH 27 A scene in *Judgment at Nuremberg* exposed the Nazi past of a current West German judge, Hermann Markl, and the resulting student demonstrations force him to resign today.

APRIL 13 Director Anthony Mann charges that "stars have ruined our business" with high salary demands.

MAY 26 Hollywood craft unions, protesting star William Holden's constant work

Births, Deaths, Marriages, and Divorces

JANUARY 1 Celebrity lawyer Jerry Giesler d. **11** Rhonda Fleming divorces Lang Jeffries. **13** Ernie Kovacs dies in a Beverly Hills car crash. **21** Piper Laurie m. movie critic Joseph Morgenstern

FEBRUARY 5 Jennifer Jason-Leigh b.

MARCH 21 Rex Harrison m. Rachel Roberts. • Matthew Broderick b. **25** Edmund Purdom m. Linda Christian, ex-wife of Tyrone Power

APRIL 10 Director Michael Curtiz d. **17** Silent screen star Louise Fazenda d. **19** Debra Paget m. Houston oilman Ling Chieh Kung, a nephew of Madame Chiang Kai-Shek. **29** Vanessa Redgrave m. director Tony Richardson.

MAY 9 Dinah Shore divorces George Montgomery. **12** Emilio Estevez, son of

APRIL 2 Elizabeth Taylor and Eddie Fisher announce the end of their three-year marriage. **4** The Vatican, responding to the Taylor-Fisher-Burton story, regrets that "many people seem to consider marriage as a game which can be started and ended with the capricious whims of children." Burton calls his wife from Rome to reassure her that there's no romance between Taylor and himself. **9** Louella Parsons misses her first Oscar night since the awards were invented; she's sick. But Natalie Wood and Warren Beatty are there together at the Santa Monica Civic Auditorium. **11** Marilyn Monroe films her first scene in her last movie, *Something's Got to Give*, a remake of the 1940 *My Favorite Wife*, co-starring Dean Martin. She will be fired before it is completed. **24** Burt Lancaster, taping Mike Wallace's TV show *PM* to publicize *Birdman of Alcatraz*, walks out when

Wallace violates the ground rules and begins to ask personal questions—about the quarrel between Lancaster and Maximilian Schell during filming of *Judgment at Nuremberg*, and about Lancaster's temper.

MAY 9 Bette Davis and Joan Crawford sign to appear in *Whatever Happened to Baby Jane*, to be directed by Robert Aldrich. At the signing ceremony, the two feuding stars jockey for the best position in front of the news photographers. Davis is to get top billing and more up-front money, Crawford a bigger percentage of the profits. Before agreeing to do the film, Davis had to be reassured by Aldrich that he had never slept with Crawford. **10** UCLA graduate student Francis Ford Coppola is awarded first prize in the Samuel Goldwyn Foundation Creative Writing Contest for a story called "Pilm Pilma." Coppola is supporting him-

self by working for director Roger Corman as a dialogue coach. **9** Marilyn Monroe sings a sexy "Happy Birthday" to President Kennedy at a Madison Square Garden party. **12** Burt Lancaster, in Rome to film *The Leopard*, and out with starlet Beatrice Altariba, punches and kicks one of the paparazzi trying to photograph him. **19** *The New Yorker* carries an interview with Barbra Streisand, "Coming Star." She's just opened on Broadway in *I Can Get It for You Wholesale*. Streisand says that she shops mostly in thrift shops and, "I suppose I'm going to be famous."

JUNE 6 At the behest of her subjects, Princess Grace of Monaco withdraws from Alfred Hitchcock's *Marnie*. **7** 20th Century Fox drops Marilyn Monroe from *Something's Got to Give* for repeated absences from the set and sues her. Monroe's replacement, Lee Remick, tells reporters:

rector Stanley Kubrick attend, as do Mason, Lyon, and Winters. **19** *The Music Man* is "previewed" for the press (actually a premiere) in Mason City, Iowa, home of its composer, Meredith Wilson. Arthur Godfrey emcees the ceremonies, which include stars Robert Preston and Shirley Jones in a parade that draws 125,000, possibly the biggest crowd ever in Iowa. The formal premiere will be in Denver on July 6. **20** Sam Peckinpah's *Ride the High Country*, Randolph Scott's last film, also stars Joel McCrea, Mariette Hartley, and Edgar Buchanan. A film whose reputation will grow with time, it opens in New York neighborhood theaters as the lower half of

a double feature with *The Tartars*, starring Orson Welles and Victor Mature. **27** With *The Road to Hong Kong*, the last Bob Hope–Bing Crosby–Dorothy Lamour "road" picture, United Artists begins its "premiere showcase" policy in New York, opening films simultaneously in neighborhood as well as Broadway houses. The practice has been in effect in Los Angeles for some time. The film premiered in San Francisco on May 23.

OCTOBER 4 At the Warner Theater, Cardinal Spellman and General Omar Bradley attend the U.S. premiere of Darryl Zanuck's *The Longest Day*, the profits from

which will help to save 20th Century Fox. John Wayne, Robert Ryan, and Henry Fonda are a few of the many stars in the film, which opened in Paris last month with a military parade. **8** Tom Courtenay stars in the British production, *The Loneliness of the Long Distance Runner*, directed by Tony Richardson and premiering in the U.S. at the Baronet. **24** John Frankenheimer's *The Manchurian Candidate*, starring Frank Sinatra, Laurence Harvey, Janet Leigh, and Angela Lansbury—at thirty-six, playing the totally evil mother of thirty-three-year-old Laurence Harvey—opens at United Artists Premiere Showcase Theaters in New York. This Cold War tale of the enemy within,

abroad, picket the DeMille Theater in New York, which is playing *The Counterfeit Traitor*.

JUNE 19 MCA merges with Universal-International-Decca.

JULY 23 MCA goes out of the agency business. **25** Darryl Zanuck becomes president of 20th Century Fox, which is sinking under the weight of *Cleopatra*. Former president Spyros Skouras became chairman of the board on June 27.

AUGUST • United Artists sends a print of *The Manchurian Candidate* to the White House at President Kennedy's request. **29** Darryl Zanuck shuts down 20th Century Fox for a retooling.

SEPTEMBER 18 The Justice Department permits the merger of MCA-Universal-International-Decca under tight antitrust guidelines. **19** Construction begins in the San Fernando Valley on the new Universal City.

OCTOBER 2 The *New York Times* has refused ads for Shirley Clarke's *The Connection*, about junkies, which today becomes the first film to open in New York without a state license, required since 1921. The State Board of Regents gets an injunction that also closes it today. **8** Richard Zanuck becomes head of production at 20th Century Fox. **18** MCA signs a consent decree in which it agrees to leave the talent agency business.

Martin Sheen (Ramon Estevez), b.

JUNE 13 Ally Sheedy (Alexandra Sheedy) b. **17** Jack Nicholson m. Sandra Knight.

JULY 3 Tom Cruise (Thomas Mapother IV) b. **13** Producer Jerry Wald d. **11** Janet

Leigh divorces Tony Curtis. **30** Millie Perkins divorces Dean Stockwell.

AUGUST 5 Marilyn Monroe is found dead. **13** Cary Grant and Betsy Drake are divorced. **17** Jack Lemmon m. Felicia Farr in Paris. He's filming *Irma La Douce* and has to be on location tomorrow morning

at five A.M. to be thrown into the Seine. **23** Hoot Gibson d. **24** Dan Dailey and Gwen O'Connor are divorced.

SEPTEMBER • Elizabeth Ashley m. James Farentino. **1** Billy Wilkerson, founder and publisher of the *Hollywood Reporter*, d.

Personalities

"I don't believe actors should be allowed to get away with that kind of behavior." **11** Walter Wanger, producer of *Cleopatra*, is taken off salary by 20th Century Fox. They can't fire him because he owns a piece of the film. **11** 20th Century Fox closes down *Something's Got to Give* when Dean Martin, exercising his right of approval over his leading lady, and in support of his friend, Marilyn Monroe, will not continue with her replacement, Lee Remick.

JULY 15 Marilyn Monroe and columnist Sidney Skolsky meet with Jean Harlow's mother and receive her permission to film the life of her daughter, to star Marilyn and be produced by Skolsky. **23** As filming begins on *Whatever Happened to Baby Jane?*,

BETTE DAVIS: WANTS EMPLOYMENT

LC

SEPTEMBER 21 Page five of the *Hollywood Reporter* this morning contains this ad: "SITUATIONS WANTED, WOMEN/ARTISTS. MOTHER OF THREE—10, 11 & 15—DIVORCÉE. AMERICAN. THIRTY YEARS EXPERIENCE AS AN ACTRESS IN MOTION PICTURES. MOBILE STILL AND MORE AFFABLE THAN RUMOR WOULD HAVE IT. WANTS STEADY EMPLOYMENT IN HOLLYWOOD (HAS HAD BROADWAY)." Accompanying it is a photo of a demure Bette Davis, her name, and the address of her agent.

Movies

with Laurence Harvey as a POW returned from Korea and programmed to kill on command, is controversial and unsuccessful on its intitial release. Critical reappraisal, however, enhances its reputation, and it will fare better in a 1987 rerelease. **30** *Billy Budd*, directed by Peter Ustinov and starring him, Robert Ryan, Melvyn Douglas, and introducing Terence Stamp, has its American premiere at the Cinemas I and II.

NOVEMBER 1 *Gypsy*, starring Rosalind Russell, Natalie Wood, and Karl Malden,

opens at the Radio City Music Hall. **6** *What Ever Happened to Baby Jane?* Stars Joan Crawford and Bette Davis, who appears today at seven of the RKO neighborhood theaters where the film is opening in New York and will make personal appearances as others throughout the week. **8** *Mutiny on the Bounty*, starring Marlon Brando, Trevor Howard, and Richard Harris, premieres at Loew's State. Brando, Tarita (Brando's onscreen and offscreen lover), and a descendant of Fletcher Christian attend, as do Jane Fonda, Peter Ustinov, Zsa Zsa Gabor, Paul Newman and Joanne Woodward, and Toots Shor. **21** Shirley MacLaine is making personal appearances

at United Artists Premiere Showcase Theaters in New York, where *Two for the Seesaw*, co-starring Robert Mitchum, opens today.

DECEMBER 12 John Huston's *Freud*, starring Montgomery Clift, Susannah York, and Larry Parks, premieres at Cinemas I and II. **25** Gregory Peck stars and Robert Duvall debuts in *To Kill a Mockingbird*, premiering at the Fox Wilshire in Los Angeles. **26** *David and Lisa*, starring Keir Dullea and Janet Margolin, opens at the Plaza Theater. **26** Jack Lemmon and Lee Remick star in *Days of Wine and Roses*, premiering at Hollywood's Vogue Theater.

Business and Society

NOVEMBER 1 The New York State Court of Appeals, overruling a censorship decision of the state's Board of Regents for the first time, orders that a license be granted to *The Connection*. **5** The Supreme Court rules that studios selling their old films to TV in blocks (block booking) violate antitrust laws. **6** The Theater Owners of America report an increase in

theater building, much of it of smaller houses and in shopping centers. **12** To prevent "runaway productions," SAG decides not to seek higher wages.

DECEMBER 10 *Daily Variety* reports that only 138 Hollywood movies—some filmed elsewhere—have gone into production so far this year. It's an all-time low and a drop-off of twenty-six percent from last year. But box office receipts are up. **19** Real estate developers announce that the Fox Theater,

in San Francisco, the largest movie house in the West, will be replaced by a skyscraper.

Births, Deaths, Marriages, and Divorces

OCTOBER 11 Joan Cusack b. **16** Jean Seberg m. novelist Romain Gary. Lana Turner divorces Fred May. **26** Louise Beavers d.

NOVEMBER 11 Demi Moore (Demi Guynes) b. **14** Jodie Foster (Alicia Foster) b. **30** Sean Connery m. Diane Cilento.

DECEMBER 15 Charles Laughton d. **17** Thomas Mitchell d.

Also this year: • Divorces include Dorothy Dandridge and Jack Denison, Ginger Rogers and William Marshall, Johnny Weissmuller and Allene Gates, and Natalie Wood and Robert Wagner.

the "cat fight" that the Hollywood press had been freely predicting does not occur. Says Joan Crawford about herself and Bette Davis: "Maybe they should put us in cages when they promote the picture." **26** In Rome to accept an award, Jayne Mansfield is scratched, kicked, and wrestled to the floor by a deranged woman at the ceremony.

AUGUST 5 Marilyn Monroe is found dead in her California home, of an overdose of barbiturates. She had recently come to an agreement with Fox to go back to work on *Something's Got to Give* and planned to remarry Joe DiMaggio on August 8. **15** Former Darryl Zanuck protégée Bella Darvi, having lost close to $2,000,000 at baccarat over the past few years and pawned many of her possessions, unsuccessfully attempts suicide. **23** Rita Hayworth, declaring herself "too

weak physically and emotionally," pulls out of *Step on a Crack*, which was to have been her Broadway stage debut.

SEPTEMBER 10 "MGM Inks 11-Yr.-Old," headlines *Daily Variety*, about the signing of Kurt Russell for Elvis Presley's next film, *It Happened at the World's Fair*.

OCTOBER 2 Katy Jurado, in court in an unsuccessful attempt to get alimony from Ernest Borgnine, sobs: "He hit me all the time. I love him very much." **23** Darryl Zanuck fires *Cleopatra* director Joseph Mankiewicz, who wanted to control the picture's editing. By December, however, Zanuck will agree to let Mankiewicz do the job, but he reserves the final cut for himself.

NOVEMBER 1 Alan Ladd accidentally shoots himself, according to what he will later tell the police.

DECEMBER 4 Shirley MacLaine sues Hal Wallis to void her contract with him, charging that to complete it would violate the California labor code, forcing her to work for him for more than seven years. He will describe her as "the most difficult and unpleasant star" he's worked with. **31** Mike Romanoff closes his Beverly Hills restaurant and retires.

"IT'S NO JOY BEING A SYMBOL"

MSN

OCTOBER 29 Sidney Poitier, testifying before Congressman Adam Clayton Powell's House Committee on Education and Labor, states: "I'm probably the only Negro actor who makes a living in the motion picture industry, which employs 13,000 performers. It's no joy to me to be a symbol."

"THE FINEST PICTURE EVER MADE"

Lawrence of Arabia

LC/© COLUMBIA PICTURES

DECEMBER 16 "Two months before its release, *Lawrence of Arabia* has already been described as the finest picture ever made," *Time* reported on October 19. Today, David Lean's 70mm epic, starring Peter O'Toole, Alec Guinness, Omar Sharif, Anthony Quinn, and Jack Hawkins, has its American premiere at the Criterion. Lean and O'Toole attend. Peter O'Toole (above) plays Lawrence.

ritic Andrew Sarris dedicates the Spring issue of *Film Culture* "to the notion of direction as the dominant artistic gesture of the cinema"—the *auteur* theory of *Cahiers du Cinéma*, now reaching America. Panavision is becoming the leading wide-screen process. Sean Connery debuts as James Bond, *Cleopatra* finally makes it to the screen, and Frankie Avalon and Annette Funicello get their feet wet in the first of the beach films. The success of *Mondo Cane*, an Italian documentary that roams the world for things shocking and bizarre, will set off a cycle of "Mondo" films, both here and abroad.

- Number of releases: 420
- CinemaScope releases: 11
- Number of theaters: 12,800, of which 3,550 are drive-ins
- Average weekly attendance: 44,000,000
- Average ticket price: $.85
- Box office receipts: $904,000,000
- Number of films in which Sean Connery will play James Bond, beginning with this year's *Dr. No*: 7
- Number of costumes worn by Elizabeth Taylor in *Cleopatra*: 65
- Running time of *Cleopatra*: 4 hours, 3 minutes
- Running time of Andy Warhol's *Sleep*: 6 hours, 30 minutes

Top stars at the box office, based on a Quigley publications poll of exhibitors:

1. Doris Day
2. John Wayne
3. Rock Hudson
4. Jack Lemmon
5. Cary Grant
6. Elizabeth Taylor
7. Elvis Presley
8. Sandra Dee
9. Paul Newman
10. Jerry Lewis

Top rental earnings, based on figures reported in *Variety*:

1. *Cleopatra* — $15,700,000
2. *The Longest Day* — 12,750,000
3. *Irma La Douce* — 9,250,000
4. *Lawrence of Arabia* — 9,000,000
5. *How the West Was Won* — 8,000,000

The New York Film Critics Circle Awards
Best Picture: *Tom Jones*

The Golden Globe Awards
Best Picture (Drama): *The Cardinal*
Best Picture (Musical/Comedy): *Tom Jones*

The Cannes Film Festival
Palme d'Or: *The Leopard*

The Academy Awards (presented April 13, 1964)
Best Picture: *Tom Jones*
Actor: Sidney Poitier (*Lilies of the Field*)
Actress: Patricia Neal (*Hud*)
Supporting Actor: Melvyn Douglas (*Hud*)
Supporting Actress: Margaret Rutherford (*The V.I.P.'s*)
Director: Tony Richardson (*Tom Jones*)

January	February	March	April	May	June
• Mirisch Co. sues Peter Ustinov over *The Pink Panther*	• Tony Curtis m. Christine Kaufmann **16** Mercedes McCambridge attempts suicide		**17** Paramount reports first loss in twenty-seven years	**29** *Hud*	**12** *Cleopatra*

July	August	September	October	November	December
12 Marlon Brando calls for boycott of racist filmmakers	**28** Brando, Heston, and others at March on Washington	**13** Barbra Streisand m. Elliott Gould	**30** Jill St. John divorces Lance Reventlow	**22** Lee Harvey Oswald captured in theater	**16** Richard and Sybil Burton divorce

Personalities

JANUARY • The Mirisch Company sues Peter Ustinov for cancelling out of *The Pink Panther*, now in production in Rome with his replacement, Peter Sellers. **14** Mamie Van Doren backs out of the film *Promise Her Anything* when the producer goes back on his promise of paying her the same amount as co-star Jayne Mansfield.

FEBRUARY 14 Judy Garland, hospitalized when she collapses from exhaustion dur ing an engagement at Lake Tahoe, is replaced by Mickey Rooney. **21** According to the *Hollywood Reporter*, "TV star and former Michigan State all-around athlete" James Caan will appear in his first film, *Lady in a Cage*. (In fact, he has a bit part in the up-coming *Irma La Douce*.)

Movies

FEBRUARY 20 Orson Welles's *The Trial*, starring Anthony Perkins, has its American premiere at the new RKO 23rd St. Theater. **20** The American premiere of *How the West Was Won* is held in Hollywood at the Warner Cinerama Theater; the New York opening is being delayed by a newspaper strike. Several of the film's many stars attend, including John Wayne, Walter Brennan, Debbie Reynolds, James Stewart, Karl Malden, Carolyn Jones, Lee J. Cobb, Carroll Baker, George Peppard, and Russ Tamblyn.

MARCH 16 Mercedes McCambridge un-successfully attempts suicide with sleeping pills.

APRIL 2 Sybil Burton announces her separation from her husband, Richard. **2** Liza Minnelli begins her show-business

Richard Burton   *LC/20TH CENTURY FOX*

MARCH 28 Alfred Hitchcock's *The Birds*, starring Rod Taylor, Tippi Hedren (in her film debut), Jessica Tandy, and Suzanne Pleshette, premieres at the Palace.

APRIL 4 *Bye Bye Birdie*, starring Dick Van Dyke, Janet Leigh, Ann-Margret, Paul

career, off-Broadway, in *Best Foot Forward*. Not wanting to make her daughter nervous, Judy Garland declines to claim the ticket left for her. **8** On Oscar night at the Santa Monica Civic Auditorium, a diamond-studded Joan Crawford is "thrilled" that Best Actress nominee Bette Davis loses—according to Davis. **19** Marlon Brando, on the *Today* show, strikes out at the press, which has "attacked, distorted, and maligned him." **19** *Life's* cover story is: "*Cleopatra*: Most Talked About Movie Ever Made." **23** Stanley Kubrick reports that a broken ankle will limit Peter Sellers to only three of the four roles he was to play in *Dr. Strangelove*— the fourth, the nuclear bomber pilot, will be taken by Slim Pickens. **25** Dorothy Dandridge files for bankruptcy.

JUNE 5 A Los Angeles judge bans Richard Chamberlain from the freeways for two

Lynde, and Bobby Rydell, opens at the Radio City Music Hall.

MAY 29 Paul Newman stars in Martin Ritt's *Hud*, with Patricia Neal, Melvyn Douglas, and Brandon De Wilde, opening at the Paramount. Also opening today, at United artists Premiere Showcase Theaters, is the first James Bond film, *Dr. No*, starring Sean Connery and Ursula Andress. *Daily Variety* calls it "the first of a series which should be both popular and profitable."

JUNE 5 Billy Wilder's *Irma La Douce*, starring Shirley MacLaine and Jack Lemmon, premieres at the DeMille and

Business and Society

JANUARY 9 Robert H. O'Brien succeeds Joseph Vogel as president of Loew's.

APRIL 17 Paramount reports its first annual loss in twenty-seven years.

JUNE 6 Cinerama demonstrates a single-lens projector system. **12** United Artists sells its Santa Monica Boulevard lot for use

as a shopping center. **25** The NAACP threatens legal and economic action unless the movies cease their demeaning stereo-types of black people and Hollywood craft unions stop discriminating against blacks.

AUGUST 4 The auction of the contents of the Hal Roach Studio is completed. The studio will be demolished to make way for a shopping center. **7** The landlord of the 3,340-seat, gold-leaf-lined Capitol

Theater, the largest in Washington D.C., announces that it will be demolished and replaced by an office building. **20** The Screen Producers Guild meets with the NAACP to explore ways of improving the image of blacks in film. **22** Eric Johnston, head of the Motion Picture Association of America, dies. Ralph Hetzel will become acting head of the organization. Among those discussed as a permanent replacement: Richard Nixon.

Births, Deaths, Marriages, and Divorces

JANUARY • Gig Young and Elizabeth Montgomery divorce. **2** Dick Powell and Jack Carson die.

FEBRUARY 8 Tony Curtis m. Christine Kaufmann.

MARCH 7 Peter Sellers divorces Anne Hayes.

APRIL 3 Ryan O'Neal m. Joanna Moore. **20** Bradford Dillman m. model and actress Suzy Parker. **30** Jayne Mansfield

divorces Mickey Hargitay.

MAY 11 Natasha Richardson, daughter of Vanessa Redgrave and director Tony Richardson, and granddaughter of Michael Redgrave, b. **27** Joan Collins m. Anthony Newly.

Doris Day, #1 at the box office this year   LC

months because of his recent convictions for speeding. **10** Shirley MacLaine, furious at *Hollywood Reporter* gossip columnist Mike Connolly for writing that she is giving in to Hal Wallis in her lawsuit to get out of her contract with the producer, drives to the paper's office and punches Connolly. **12** Dolores Hart abandons Hollywood and enters a convent. **14** Anthony Quinn acknowledges that he is the father of a baby born to Yolande Addolari, an Italian woman. Quinn is married to Katherine DeMille.

JULY • Filming a scene from *Move Over, Darling*, James Garner grabs Doris Day by the waist, lifts her, and cracks her rib. The film is a reworking of *Something's Got to Give*, from which Marilyn Monroe was fired just before she died last year. **12** *Life* magazine features: "Steve McQueen: Problem Kid Becomes a Star" **12** Marlon

Baronet Theaters. **12** *Cleopatra* premieres at the Rivoli. Elizabeth Taylor and Richard Burton are in London, but the ten thousand people outside the theater in arc-light-lit Times Square see Rex Harrison, Helen Hayes, Darryl Zanuck, Paul Anka, Joan Fontaine, Roddy MacDowall, and Leonard Bernstein arrive. Before the film's general release later this month, twenty-two minutes will be cut from its elephantine four hours.

JULY 3 *The Great Escape* premieres in the U.S. at Los Angeles area theaters. It stars Steve McQueen, Richard Attenborough, James Garner, Charles Bronson, James

SEPTEMBER 10 The first New York Film Festival opens with the showing of Luis Buñuel's *The Exterminating Angel*. **15** Motion Picture Code administrator Geoffrey Shurlock says that "treatment" and not "subject matter" is now the only criterion for awarding a seal.

NOVEMBER 22 Lee Harvey Oswald, alleged assassin of President Kennedy, is captured in the Texas theater in Dallas, which is showing *War Is Hell* and *Cry of*

Battle. **25** All studios close for President Kennedy's funeral.

DECEMBER • Panavision's new single-lens reflex, 30-pound, 70mm camera is being used in the filming of *Lord Jim*.

JUNE 3 Ernest Borgnine and Katy Jurado divorce. **7** ZaSu Pitts d. **9** Johnny Depp b. **28** Burt Reynolds m. Judy Carne.

JULY 21 Robert Wagner m. Marian Donen, former wife of director Stanley Donen.

AUGUST 17 Richard Barthelmess d. **24** Sidney Lumet and Gloria Vanderbilt divorce.

SEPTEMBER 13 Barbra Streisand m. Elliott Gould.

OCTOBER 12 June Allyson m. Alfred Glenn Maxwell, Dick Powell's barber. **29** Adolphe Menjou d. **30** Jill St. John divorces Lance Reventlow.

NOVEMBER 5 Tatum O'Neal, daughter of Ryan O'Neal and Joanna Moore, b. **23** Sidney Lumet m. Gail Jones, Lena

Personalities

Brando calls upon stars to boycott filmmakers who discriminate against blacks. **15** Hal Wallis and Shirley MacLaine make public their out-of-court settlement of her suit. She will make one more movie for him, with script approval.

AUGUST 9 Alfred Hitchcock's birthday present for Melanie Griffith, six-year-old daughter of Tippi Hedren, star of *The Birds*, is a doll resembling her mother—in a miniature, coffinlike pine box. **22** Marlon Brando, Paul Newman, and Anthony Franciosa attend rallies in Alabama to support civil-rights workers. **25** Police say that director Sidney Lumet, apparently in reaction to his divorce from Gloria Vanderbilt, has taken an overdose of sleep-

ing pills. Lumet says it was only "seven vodkas, a Miltown, and idiocy." **28** Burt Lancaster, Sammy Davis Jr., Marlon Brando, and Charlton Heston are among the many celebrities joining the civil rights March on Washington.

SEPTEMBER • In a *Playboy* interview, Richard Burton says that he has not been unfaithful to his wife, Sybil Burton. "What I have done is to move outside the accepted idea of monogamy without physically investing the other person with anything that makes me feel guilty," he explains. "So that I remain inviolate, untouched." **25** B-movie actress Barbara Payton, former wife of Franchot Tone, over whom Tone fought with, and was severely beaten by actor Tom Neal in 1951, is arrested in Los Angeles for prostitution.

OCTOBER 7 Frank Sinatra, under investigation by the Nevada gaming control board because of his association with hood Sammy "Momo" Giancana, announces that he will leave the casino gambling business in the state. **28** John Huston, on location in Mexico to film *Night of the Iguana*, presents Richard Burton, Deborah Kerr, Ava Gardner, and Sue Lyon with gold-plated derringers, each loaded with bullets bearing the names of the other stars. Elizabeth Taylor is on location to make sure it stays professional between Burton, her husband, and Gardner.

NOVEMBER 6 Ann-Margret, in London for the premiere of *Bye Bye Birdie*, tells reporters about Elvis Presley: "I'm going steady with him and I guess I'm in love."

DECEMBER 8 Frank Sinatra Jr. is kidnapped in Lake Tahoe. **11** Frank Sinatra Jr. is returned safely to his family.

Movies

Coburn, David McCallum, and Donald Pleasance.

AUGUST 19 Peter Brook's *Lord of the Flies*, starring James Aubrey and Tom Chapin, premieres at Loew's Tower East.

SEPTEMBER 25 "When 10,000 kids meet on 5,000 blankets, something's got to happen!" What happens is *Beach Party*, with Frankie Avalon and Annette Funicello, opening in New York area theaters. It's the first wave of '60s beach films.

OCTOBER 1 Sidney Poitier stars in *Lilies of the Field*, opening at the Murray Hill. **7** Tony Richardson's *Tom Jones*, starring Albert Finney, Susannah York, and Hugh Griffith, premieres in the U.S. at the Cinema I.

NOVEMBER 7 *It's a Mad, Mad, Mad, Mad World* premieres at the opening of the Hollywood Cinerama Dome, at Sunset and Vine. Spencer Tracy, Milton Berle, Sid Caesar, Buddy Hackett, Ethel Merman, Mickey Rooney, Phil Silvers, Jonathan Winters, and Jimmy Durante are a few of its stars.

DECEMBER 5 Audrey Hepburn, Cary

Grant, and Walter Matthau star in *Charade*, opening at the Radio City Music Hall. **11** Tom Tryon stars in Otto Preminger's *The Cardinal*, premiering at Boston's Saxon Theater. It's the first film in Panavision 70, a process in which 35mm film is enlarged to 70mm and shown on a wide screen.

Business and Society

Births, Deaths, Marriages, and Divorces

Horne's daughter. **28** Linda Darnell divorces Merle Robertson.

DECEMBER 2 Sabu d. **16** Richard and Sybil Burton divorce. **22** Sue Lyon m. Hampton Fancher III.

Also this year: • Wesley Snipes b. • Geraldine Page m. Rip Torn. • Edmund Purdom and Linda Christian divorce.

r. Strangelove and *Seven Days in May*, opening less than a month apart, and *Fail-Safe*, premiering later in the year, show the American military establishment in an unfavorable light. Peter Sellers is in the first Pink Panther film and also draws fire for his criticism of Hollywoood. The Beatles make a movie, Judy Garland is treated for "minor injuries to her wrists," Alan Ladd dies, and Clint Eastwood becomes a movie star, but only in Italy. Made-for-TV movies are here to stay, and Universal City Studio Tours begin.

- Number of releases: 502
- CinemaScope releases: 11
- TV owners with color sets: 3%
- Number of theaters: 13,750, of which 4,100 are drive-ins
- Average weekly attendance: 43,500,000
- Average ticket price: $.93
- Box office receipts: $913,000,000
- Number of letters in the adjective coined in *Mary Poppins*: 34— "supercalifragilisticexpialidocious"
- Julie Andrews's fee for *Mary Poppins*: $125,000
- Clint Eastwood's pay for *A Fistful of Dollars*: $15,000
- Number of roles played by Peter Sellers in *Dr. Strangelove*: 3
- Singer dubbing Audrey Hepburn's songs in *My Fair Lady*: Marni Nixon
- Car used by James Bond in *Goldfinger*: an Aston Martin DB5

Top rental earnings, based on figures reported in *Variety*:
1. *The Carpetbaggers* $13,000,000
2. *It's a Mad, Mad, Mad, Mad World*   10,000,000
3. *The Unsinkable Molly Brown*   7,500,000
4. *Charade*   6,150,000
5. *The Cardinal*   5,275,000

The New York Film Critics Circle Awards
Best Picture: *My Fair Lady*

The Golden Globe Awards
Best Picture (Drama): *Becket*
Best Picture (Musical/Comedy): *My Fair Lady*

The Cannes Film Festival
Palme d'Or: *The Umbrellas of Cherbourg*

The Academy Awards (presented April 5, 1965)
Best Picture: *My Fair Lady*
Actor: Rex Harrison (*My Fair Lady*)
Actress: Julie Andrews (*Mary Poppins*)
Supporting Actress: Lila Kedrova (*Zorba the Greek*)
Supporting Actor: Peter Ustinov (*Topkapi*)
Director: George Cukor (*My Fair Lady*)

January	February	March	April	May	June
	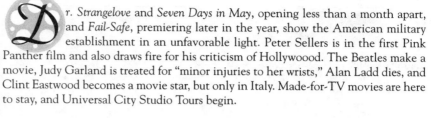 **19** Peter Sellers m. Britt Ekland		**8** *From Russia with Love*		**30** *Night of the Iguana*
	29 *Dr. Strangelove*		• Elizabeth Taylor divorces Eddie Fisher and m. Richard Burton	**7** Charlton Heston returns salary for Major Dundee	

July	August	September	October	November	December
15 Universal City Studio Tours begin		**8** Suzanne Pleshette divorces Troy Donahue	**30** Frank Sinatra romances 18-year-old Mia Farrow		**17** Zorba the Greek
	• Anne Bancroft m. Mel Brooks		**7** NBC broadcasts first regularly scheduled made-for-TV movie		

Personalities

JANUARY • William Holden, recently separated from his wife, Brenda Marshall, is now seeing Italian film star Capucine. **18** Marlon Brando comes out publicly for Indian rights for the first time at a National Congress of American Indians meeting. **29** Alan Ladd is dead. The coroner will report: "Accident due to a reaction to combination of Depressant and Ethanol."

MARCH 10 Peter O'Toole, exhausted from filming *Lord Jim* and having to fly from its Asian location to New York for the premiere of *Beckett*, collapses during a commercial break while appearing on Johnny Carson's *Tonight* show. **25** *Variety*'s review of the club act of twenty-four-year-old "colored comedian" Richard Pryor finds

him "still in the coffeehouse stages," too "intellectual," and not yet ready for the big time. He is four years away from his first film. **30** TV actress Mia Farrow flies to Britain to make her film debut as a replacement for Britt Ekland, who has quit *Guns at Batasi*.

APRIL 6 Peter Sellers has a heart attack. **13** Leslie Caron is on Warren Beatty's arm this year, as the Oscars are given out at the Santa Monica Civic Auditorium.

MAY 1 Elizabeth Taylor and Richard Burton make a grand entrance at Sammy Davis Jr.'s Copacabana opening in New York, walking past Eddie Fisher and his date and taking their seats at a front table fifteen minutes after Davis has begun his act. **7** Charlton Heston announces that he's returning his salary for *Major Dundee* to

Ray Walston and Kim Novak in *Kiss Me Stupid*. Walston was a last-minute replacement for the ailing Sellers. *LC*

Movies

JANUARY 17 *The Incredible Mr. Limpet*, the first of several films to feature the perpetually nervous Don Knotts, premieres in Weeki Wachee Springs, Florida. **29** Stanley Kubrick's *Dr. Strangelove* premieres in New York, Toronto, and London. Peter Sellers (in three roles), George C. Scott, Sterling Hayden, Keenan Wynn, and Slim Pickens star. The *New York Times* fears that it shows "contempt for our whole military establishment." The *Washington Post* calls it "anti-American."

Peter Sellers in *Dr. Strangelove*   *LC*/ © COLUMBIA PICTURES

Business and Society

MARCH 2 The American Federation of Labor criticizes the Johnson administration's opposition to legislation requiring the labeling of films by country of origin. **3** *Village Voice* critic and film-maker Jonas Mekas is arrested for showing at a New York theater *Flaming Creatures*, an avant-garde film the police consider obscene. **16** The same day that the Ford Foundation

Births, Deaths, Marriages, and Divorces

JANUARY 4 Troy Donahue m. Suzanne Pleshette. **7** Nicolas Cage (Nicholas Coppola) b. **27** Joan Fontaine m. Alfred Wright Jr., editor of *Sports Illustrated*. **29** Alan Ladd is dead.

FEBRUARY 18 Matt Dillon b. **19** Peter Sellers m. Britt Ekland.

MARCH 5 Elizabeth Taylor and Eddie Fisher divorce. **15** Elizabeth Taylor m. Richard

Burton. **17** Rob Lowe b. **23** Peter Lorre d.

APRIL 28 Screenwriter Ben Hecht d. • Carol Lynley divorces Michael Selsman.

JUNE 16 Alan Arkin m. Barbara Dana. **27** Ernest Borgnine m. Ethel Merman. It will last six loud weeks.

Columbia because he helped to push it over budget. **22** On the cover of *Life*: "Great New Star, Barbra Streisand, Her Success and Her Precarious Love Story." Inside the magazine says that women now want the "Streisand look." **25** Twenty-four-year-old Martin Sheen has his breakthrough role in the play *The Subject Was Roses*, opening on Broadway tonight. **29** Judy Garland, hospitalized in Hong Kong for a drug overdose last night, is mistakenly declared dead.

JUNE • British director Peter Hall sues Leslie Caron for divorce, naming Warren Beatty as corespondent. **20** The *Los Angeles Times* reports that in response to Peter Sellers's harsh criticism of Hollywood, Dean Martin, Kim Novak, and Billy Wilder, who were working with Sellers on *Kiss Me, Stupid* before his heart attack, have cabled him: "Talk about unprofessional rat finks."

JULY 2 Peter Sellers's "open letter" in the *Hollywood Reporter* and *Daily Variety*, states: "I have no criticism of Hollywood as a place, but only as a place to work in. The atmosphere is wrong for me." **2** Joan Crawford's viral pneumonia shuts down production of *Hush…Hush, Sweet Charlotte* for most of the next two months. Many people involved with the film feel that she's just unhappy playing second fiddle to Bette Davis. When first told by director Robert Aldrich that Crawford would be in the film, Davis is reported to have said, "I wouldn't piss on Joan Crawford if she were on fire." **9** Jack Palance and his family, in Tuscaloosa, Alabama, visiting relatives, take in a movie in a theater that's just been desegregated. A rumor starts that Palance is there to make a social statement, and police have to rescue him from a mob that forms outside the movie house. **20** Judy

Garland is treated at a London hospital for what is described as "minor injuries to her wrists."

AUGUST • Burt Lancaster co-chairs a committee of performing artists working to defeat the rescinding of California's fair housing law.

SEPTEMBER 9 Production resumes on *Hush…Hush, Sweet Charlotte*, with Olivia de Havilland in the role abandoned by Joan Crawford. In a pointed reference to Crawford's position as a director of Pepsi-Cola, Davis and de Havilland toast the renewal of filming with Coke. **2** Peter O'Toole is arrested in Rome for hitting paparazzi trying to photograph the married actor with actress Barbara Steele.

OCTOBER 14 Vic Damone is arrested and

FEBRUARY 19 *Seven Days in May*, starring Kirk Douglas, Burt Lancaster, Ava Gardner, Fredric March, and Edmund O'Brien, opens at the Criterion and Sutton Theaters.

MARCH 11 Richard Burton and Peter O'Toole star in *Beckett*, premiering at Loew's State, with O'Toole, Hal Wallis, Joan Bennett, Tallulah Bankhead, Leonard Bernstein, Lillian and Dorothy Gish, Jack Dempsey, June Havoc, Mike Nichols, and Jonathan Winters attending. **16** Joseph Losey's *The Servant*, starring Dirk Bogarde, James Fox, and Sarah Miles, is premiering in the U.S. at the Little Carnegie.

APRIL 5 *The Best Man*, starring Henry Fonda, Cliff Robertson, and Lee Tracy, premieres at the Coronet. **8** Sean Connery, Robert Shaw, Lotte Lenya, and Pedro Armendariz star in the second James Bond film, *From Russsia with Love*, opening at RKO showcase theaters. In the first five days it will set a record for showcase openings, grossing more than $400,000. **9** Joseph E. Levine's *The Carpetbaggers*, Alan Ladd's last film, premieres at the Paramount in Denver. Present are stars George Peppard, Robert Cummings, Martha Hyer, and Carroll Baker, wearing a diamond-studded evening gown. **23** *The Pink Panther*, starring Peter Sellers, follows another Sellers's film,

The World of Henry Orient, which closed yesterday at the Radio City Music Hall.

JUNE 30 John Huston's *Night of the Iguana* opens in a special preview at the new Lincoln Center in New York City, with stars Richard Burton, Ava Gardner, Deborah Kerr, and Sue Lyon attending.

AUGUST 5 New York City's palatial Paramount Theater closes as a first-run house with the final showing of *The Carpetbaggers*. It will reopen for one more first-run engagement—*Thunderball*—on December 21, 1965, and for some stage shows and second-run films. **11** The Beatles star in *A Hard*

---

announces a $10,000 grant to avant-garde filmmaker Kenneth Anger, the Hollywood Vice Squad seizes his *Scorpio Rising* from the Cinema Theater and arrests its manager for obscenity. **18** Martin Ransohoff, MGM's leading producer, calls for an end to the ban on nudity in Hollywood films after he's forced to remove some topless scenes from *The Americanization of Emily* to get a Production Code seal. **26** 20th Century Fox, recovered from *Cleopatra*, announces record earnings for last year.

APRIL 1 The Association of Motion Picture Producers and the Alliance of Television Film Producers merge to form the Association of Motion Picture and Television Producers.

JUNE 2 George Weltner replaces Barney Balaban as president of Paramount.

JULY 15 Universal City Studio Tours begin.

SEPTEMBER • President Johnson awards Walt

Disney the civilian Medal of Honor for creating "an American folklore." **22** Toronto-based Seven Arts Productions sets up Seven Arts Pictures with the aim of becoming a major film distributor. **25** In a deal announced today, the Mirisch Company will produce forty-eight films over the next ten years for distribution by United Artists.

OCTOBER 7 NBC broadcasts *See How They Run*, with John Forsythe and Senta Berger, the first regularly scheduled made-for-TV movie.

JULY 15 Margaret Leighton, formerly married to Laurence Harvey, m. Michael Wilding, ex-husband of Elizabeth Taylor.

AUGUST • Anne Bancroft m. Mel Brooks. **27** Gracie Allen d. **31** James Mason and Pamela Kellino divorce.

SEPTEMBER 8 Suzanne Pleshette divorces Troy Donahue. **24** Jayne Mansfield m. Matt Cimber. **28** Harpo Marx d.

OCTOBER 10 Eddie Cantor d. **13** Arlene Dahl divorces Christian Holmes.

NOVEMBER 18 Ethel Merman divorces Ernest Borgnine.

DECEMBER 8 Sue Lyon divorces Hampton Fancher III. • Dorothy Malone divorces Jacques Bergerac. **14** William Bendix d. **23** Arlene Dahl m. wine merchant Alexis Lichine. **24** Janet Gaynor m. producer Paul Gregory. **31** Robert Duvall m. Barbara Benjamin.

Personalities

held three hours on the complaint of his ex-wife, Pier Angeli, that he kidnapped their son. **23** The premiere in Cleveland of *Rio Conchos* marks the screen debut of former Cleveland Browns football star Jim Brown.

NOVEMBER 3 Former film star George Murphy is elected U.S. Senator from California. **8** Judy Garland and Liza Minnelli play the London Palladium. Garland has just introduced Liza to her future husband, musician Peter Allen. **30** "Frank Sinatra and eighteen-year-old Mia Farrow are the maddest, merriest romance of the year," writes gossip columnist Sheila Graham.

DECEMBER 7 After a week of filming, producer Martin Ransohoff fires director Sam Peckinpah from *The Cincinnati Kid*, for shooting unscheduled nude scenes and replaces him with Norman Jewison. Two weeks ago, Spencer Tracy, displeased with the script, dropped out and was replaced by Edward G. Robinson. • Marlon Brando's ex-wife, Anna Kashfi, goes berserk, injuring several people, including police officers, after taking their son Christian from her ex-husband's house. **29** John Wayne, a five-pack-a-day smoker, acknowledges that his September operation was for cancer. **29** Nine months of filming on *Dr. Zhivago* begins. Julie Christie will have a hard time with director David Lean's browbeating, Omar Sharif's low opinion of her, and Rod Steiger's return of her slap in one scene, which was not in the script.

Movies

Day's Night, opening at Premier Showcase Theaters. **27** Walt Disney's *Mary Poppins*, starring Julie Andrews and Dick Van Dyke, who are present, premieres at Grauman's Chinese Theater, the first Disney gala premiere since *Snow White* in 1937.

SEPTEMBER 17 *Topkapi*, starring Melina Mercouri, Peter Ustinov, Maximilian Schell, and Robert Morely, premieres in the U.S. at the Astor and Trans-Lux East Theaters.

OCTOBER 7 Sidney Lumet's *Fail-Safe*, starring Henry Fonda, Walter Matthau, and Larry Hagman in a drama about nuclear war, opens in New York area theaters after a September 15 premiere at the New York Film Festival. **21** Stars Audrey Hepburn, Rex Harrison, and Stanley Holloway, director George Cukor, and Jack Warner are present for the premiere of *My Fair Lady* at the Criterion. Warner Brothers paid a record $5.5 million to CBS for the movie rights to the hit Broadway show. **27** *The Americanization of Emily*, starring James Garner and Julie Andrews, premieres at Loew's State.

DECEMBER • *A Fistful of Dollars* makes Clint Eastwood a star in Italy, but it won't be released in the U.S. until 1967. **17** *Zorba the Greek*, starring Anthony Quinn, Alan Bates, Irene Papas, and Lila Kedrova, opens at the Sutton. **18** The Pink Panther cartoon character gets his own cartoon series with the release of *The Pink Phink*. **21** Sean Connery stars in *Goldfinger*, the third and most-popular-yet James Bond movie, opening at the DeMille and Coronet, where it breaks house records. Shirley Bassey sings the title song. The picture features a character named "Oddjob," who has the deadly habit of doffing his cap to people he does not like. *Goldfinger* is banned in Israel because Gert Frobe, who plays the villain, was a Nazi Party member.

Business and Society

DECEMBER 1 The RKO Hillstreet Theater, the largest in downtown Los Angeles, will be demolished and replaced by a garage, a developer announces. **3** The Legion of Decency attacks the increasing number of Hollywood's "morally objectionable films."

Births, Deaths, Marriages, and Divorces

Also this year: • Annabella Sciorra b. • George Peppard and Helen Davies divorce, as do Raquel and James Welch.

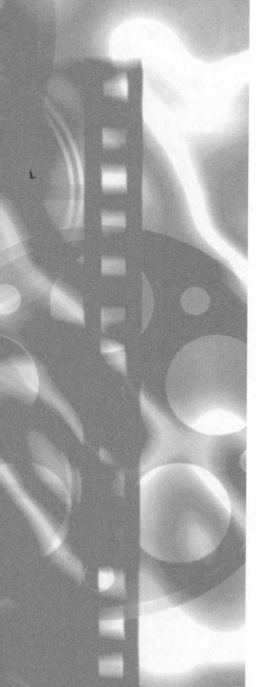

*N*udity in mainstream American films begins with *The Pawnbroker*, and Hollywood begins to recognize that there is a black audience for films. The French honor Jerry Lewis, and Sandra Dee becomes the last star to be under exclusive contract to a major studio. Eighteen-year-old Arnold Schwarzenegger wins his first bodybuilding title, Louella Parsons retires, and David O. Selznick is dead.

- Number of releases: 452
- CinemaScope releases: 11
- Number of theaters: 14,000, of which 4,150 are drive-ins
- Average weekly attendance: 44,000,000
- Average ticket price: $1.01
- Box office receipts: $927,000,000

Top stars at the box office, based on a Quigley Publications poll of exhibitors:

1. Sean Connery
2. John Wayne
3. Doris Day
4. Julie Andrews
5. Jack Lemmon
6. Elvis Presley
7. Cary Grant
8. James Stewart
9. Elizabeth Taylor
10. Richard Burton

The "stars of tomorrow," based on a Quigley Publications poll of exhibitors:

1. Rosemary Forsyth
2. Michael Anderson Jr.
3. Michael Parks
4. Michael Caine
5. Mary Anne Mobley
6. Jocelyn Lane
7. Mia Farrow
8. Julie Christie
9. Richard Johnson
10. Senta Berger

Top rental earnings, based on figures reported by *Variety*:

1. *Mary Poppins* $28,500,000
2. *The Sound of Music*   20,000,000
3. *Goldfinger*   19,700,000
4. *My Fair Lady*   19,000,000
5. *What's New Pussycat?*   7,150,000

The New York Film Critics Circle Awards
Best Picture: *Darling*

The Golden Globe Awards
Best Picture (Drama): *Doctor Zhivago*
Best Picture (Musical/Comedy): *The Sound of Music*

The Cannes Film Festival
Palme d'Or: *The Knack*

The Academy Awards (presented April 18, 1966)
Best Picture: *The Sound of Music*
Actor: Lee Marvin (*Cat Ballou*)
Actress: Julie Christie (*Darling*)
Supporting Actor: Martin Balsam (*A Thousand Clowns*)
Supporting Actress: Shelley Winters (*A Patch of Blue*)
Director: Robert Wise (*The Sound of Music*)

January	February	March	April	May	June	
• Columbia begins marketing to blacks	**17** Patricia Neal has several strokes	**28** First Production Code seal for film with nudity	**20** *The Pawnbroker*	**15** Angie Dickinson m. Burt Bacharach	**22** David O. Selznick d.	

July	August	September	October	November	December	
12 Publication of Jean Harlow's novel, *Today Is Tonight*	**14** Jane Fonda m. director Roger Vadim	**28** IRS fines George Raft; **30** Arnold Schwarzenegger wins first body-building title at 18	**8** Gossip columnist Dorothy Kilgallen d.	**22** *Doctor Zhivago*		

Personalities

JANUARY 7 In her child-custody suit against Vic Damone, Pier Angeli acknowledges that he did not beat her many times as she previously said, but only once, in 1960, when he knocked her down, kicked her, and threatened: "I'm going to kill you, you…." **28** Arthur Miller's play, *A View from the Bridge*, starring the little-known Robert Duvall, Jon Voight, and Susan Anspach, opens off-Broadway. Unknown Dustin Hoffman is the assistant director. **28** The *New York Times* runs an article headlined "Old Bogart Films Packing Them In," commenting on the cult status achieved by Humphrey Bogart. Bogart retrospectives got their start a few years ago when the Brattle Theater near Harvard began to feature his films. The article quotes one college student

on her fascination with Bogey: "He always has the jump on everybody, and he does good things without being goody. Besides, I'm tired of those Italian films where everybody just sits around and has boring parties."

FEBRUARY 17 Patricia Neal suffers several strokes and undergoes brain surgery, from which she will recover.

MARCH • French film critics name Jerry Lewis the best director of 1964 for *The Nutty Professor*. • Carol Lynley appears nude in Playboy, for which she will be chastised by Louella Parsons. **1** A lie detector test clears Peter Fonda of any involvement in the February 3 murder of his closest friend, Eugene McDonald, Zenith Radio heir. **10** Walter Matthau achieves stardom with his role in the Broadway play, *The Odd Couple*, co-starring Art Carney,

opening tonight. It will lead to Matthau's first starring role in a movie, *The Fortune Cookie*, which he will begin filming in November. **24** Ginger Rogers replaces Eleanor Parker, who yesterday replaced Judy Garland as Jean Harlow's mother in the "Electronovision" biography of Harlow. Money disputes in this film with an eight-day shooting schedule are causing the turmoil. (Rogers's paycheck will bounce.)

APRIL 1 B-movie actor Tom Neal, who sent Franchot Tone to the hospital in 1951 in a fight over the affections of Barbara Payton, is arrested for the murder of his estranged wife, Gail, for which he will go to prison. **5** Hedda Hopper is peeved that no American takes an Oscar for acting tonight at the Santa Monica Civic Auditorium, where the awards are given out.

Movies

FEBRUARY 15 *The Greatest Story Ever Told*, with an all-star cast that includes Charlton Heston, Max von Sydow, Carroll Baker, and John Wayne presiding over the crucifixion, premieres at the Warner Cinerama Theater, with Lady Bird Johnson, accompanied by Adlai Stevenson, in the audience. After initial engagements the film's running time will be cut from 225 to 198 minutes.

MARCH 2 *The Sound of Music*, starring Julie Andrews and Christopher Plummer, premieres at the Rivoli. **3** *Hush…Hush, Sweet*

Charlotte opens at New York showcase theaters, with stars Bette Davis and Olivia de Havilland appearing live at twenty of them in the first week. **17** Burt Lancaster and Paul Scofield star in *The Train*, having its U.S. premiere at the Astor and Plaza theaters.

APRIL 20 Rod Steiger is the star of Sidney Lumet's *The Pawnbroker*, premiering at three New York theaters. It is notable for its display of bare female breasts, the beginning of nudity in 1960s mainline American films.

MAY 7 *Cat Ballou* premieres at the Centre Theater in Denver, with stars Jane Fonda and Lee Marvin attending. **12** The

"Electronovision"—filmed with TV cameras—version of *Harlow*, starring Carol Lynley, opens across the country. Joseph E. Levine, producer of a rival Harlow film, takes out newspaper ads in key cities, beginning "Let there be no confusion…."

JUNE 16 *Those Magnificent Men in Their Flying Machines*, starring Stuart Whitman, Sarah Miles, James Fox, and Terry-Thomas, has its American premiere at the DeMille, with Cardinal Spellman and Darryl Zanuck in attendance. **23** Frank Sinatra and Trevor Howard star in *Von Ryan's Express*, premiering at Loew's State. **23** *The Sons of Katie Elder*, a western starring John

Business and Society

JANUARY • Columbia Pictures begins a program of marketing its releases to black audiences. **1** The Theater Owners of America merge with the Allied States Association of Motion Picture Exhibitors to form the National Association of Theater Owners (NATO).

MARCH • Supreme Court decisions on

March 1 and 15, ruling invalid provisions of the film-censorship laws in Maryland and New York, respectively, increase demands for a movie rating system. **10** The project to build a Hollywood Museum, lacking funds and coordination, suspends activities. **28** *The Pawnbroker*, starring Rod Steiger, receives a Production Code seal, the first for a film containing nudity.

APRIL 7 Ralph Hetzel, acting president of the Motion Picture Association of

America, says that the movies' morality code is being revised.

MAY • Increased competition to create blockbuster films by buying the rights to bestselling novels is ratcheted up a notch when Twentieth Century Fox pays close to $1 million to Irving Wallace for two unpublished novels—bought solely on the basis of brief outlines. **17** The Vatican denounces James Bond as a man of "violence, vulgarity, sadism and sex." **31** The

Births, Deaths, Marriages, and Divorces

JANUARY 14 Jeanette MacDonald d. **21** Anthony Quinn and Katherine DeMille divorce.

FEBRUARY 5 Leslie Caron is divorced by Peter Hall, and co-respondent Warren

Beatty is ordered to pay court costs. **23** Stan Laurel d.

MARCH 9 Jane Wyman and Fred Karger divorce a second time. **15** Kim Novak m. Richard Johnson. **23** Silent-screen star

Mae Murray d.

APRIL 10 Linda Darnell dies of injuries sustained yesterday in a fire. **20** June Allyson divorces Alfred Glenn Maxwell.

MAY 15 Angie Dickinson m. composer Burt Bacharach. **19** Judy Garland and Sid Luft divorce. **31** Brooke Shields b.

MAY • With the election of Donald O'Connor, Debbie Reynolds ends eight years as president of the Thalians, the entertainment industry charitable organization. • Louella Parsons begins to share her by-line with daughter Harriet and Dorothy Manners. **17** Four-and-a-half-year-old Timothy Hutton debuts before the cameras in Warners' *Never Too Late*, which co-stars his father, Jim. **28** Yul Brynner, who held dual U.S.-Swiss citizenship, renounces his U.S. citizenship to make it easier to be with his wife and daughter, who are Swiss.

JUNE • Warren Beatty is telling interviewers that he will marry Leslie Caron. **19** The *New York Times* reports: "The screen is about to have what is believed to be its first Negro detective hero. Sidney Poitier, who won an Academy award two years ago for "Lilies of the Field," will play the detective of John

Ball's novel, "In the Heat of the Night."

JULY 12 Taking advantage of publicity generated by two Harlow films, Grove Press publishes Jean Harlow's novel, *Today Is Tonight*.

AUGUST 12 Frank Sinatra's yacht docks in Manhattan, his romantic cruise with nineteen-year-old Mia Farrow shortened by the drowning of a crewman. Coincidentally, Montgomery Clift arrives to board his boat and, when urged by a photographer to pose, punches him. **12** The Hollywood Overseas Committee begins to mobilize entertainment for U.S. soldiers in Vietnam. **14** Sonny and Cher's "I Got You Babe" reaches number one on *Billboard*'s record chart, beginning Cher's career. **20** Sandra Dee, the last major star to be under exclusive contract to a big studio, ends that relationship with Universal–International

when *A Man Could Get Killed* is wrapped.

SEPTEMBER 28 George Raft is fined $2,500 for income-tax evasion.

> *Hedda Hopper reports that Hollywood producers want to star Sonny and Cher in a movie. "Sonny and who?" Hopper writes.*
>
> September 30, 1965

OCTOBER 1 Anna Kashfi is awarded custody of Christian Brando, her son by Marlon Brando. **30** While AWOL from the Austrian Army, eighteen-year-old Arnold

---

Wayne and Dean Martin, premieres at the Roosevelt Theater in Chicago. **29** Richard Lester's *The Knack...and How to Get It*, a British import starring Rita Tushingham, premieres in the U.S. at the Plaza.

JULY 15 "The Shadow of Your Smile" is the theme music and Elizabeth Taylor and Richard Burton are the stars of *The Sandpiper*, which grosses a house record of $30,000 when it opens today at the Radio City Music Hall. **21** Joseph E. Levine's *Harlow*, starring Carroll Baker, opens at the Palace and RKO 58th St. Theaters. **28** Stanley Kramer's *Ship of Fools*, starring Vivien Leigh, Simone Signoret, Jose Ferrer,

Lee Marvin, and Oscar Werner, premieres at the Victoria and Sutton Theaters.

AUGUST 2 Michael Caine stars in *The Ipcress File*, in its U.S. premiere at the Coronet. **3** Julie Christie achieves stardom in *Darling*, premiering at the Lincoln Art and Loew's Tower East theaters.

OCTOBER 11 *The Loved One*, "The motion picture with something to offend everyone!", with Robert Morse and Jonathan Winters heading an all-star cast, premieres at Cinema I. **15** "Tonight 8:15 P.M. Hollywood Stars On Stage In Person" reads the marquee on the Saenger Theater in New Orleans, where

The Cincinnati Kid is premiering. Steve McQueen had to cancel, but Edward G. Robinson, Karl Malden, Ann-Margret, and Tuesday Weld, on their way to the theater in limousines, parade past seventy thousand fans.

DECEMBER 10 In *A Patch of Blue*, Shelley Winters is the mother of a blind woman, Elizabeth Hartman, who loves a black man, Sidney Poitier. Premiering at the Crest in the Westwood neighborhood of Los Angeles today, it will be shown in the South with a kissing scene between Poitier and Hartman deleted. **13** Jason Robards stars as the eccentric in *A Thousand Clowns*, premiering at the Trans-Lux East. **21** Sean

---

Motion Picture Association of America reveals that it has settled out of court the December 30, 1960, suit by twelve actors, writers, and directors who charged that they were blacklisted. The Association, however, does not acknowledge the existence of the blacklist.

JUNE 9 The National League of Decency condemns film nudity.

JULY • Hollywood studios, which only re-

cently were being underutilized, are suddenly heavily booked as the trend toward producing overseas diminishes. Increased shooting costs in Europe have contributed to the resurgence in domestic production.

NOVEMBER 29 The Legion of Decency becomes the National Catholic Office of Motion Pictures.

JUNE • Sandy Dennis m. jazz saxophonist Gerry Mulligan. **7** Judy Holliday d. **22** David O. Selznick d. • Lana Turner m. Robert Eaton.

JULY • George C. Scott and Colleen Dewhurst divorce. **22** Cary Grant m. Dyan Cannon. **25** Constance Bennett d.

AUGUST 14 Jane Fonda m. director Roger Vadim, former husband of Brigitte Bardot.

SEPTEMBER 3 Charlie Sheen (Carlos Estevez), brother of Emilio Estevez and son of Martin Sheen, b. **8** Dorothy Dandridge commits suicide by drug overdose, a conclusion the coroner will not

reach until November 17 after first calling it an embolism. **27** Clara Bow d.

OCTOBER • Rhonda Fleming m. director-producer Hall Bartlett. **7** Betty Grable and Harry James divorce.

Personalities

Schwarzenegger wins his first body-building title, "Jr. Mr. Europe," and then spends time in jail for his trouble.

NOVEMBER 11 Faye Dunaway's acclaimed performance in the off-Broadway *Hogan's Goat*, opening tonight, will bring her a movie contract.

DECEMBER • A drunken George C. Scott, arguing with Ava Gardner at London's Savoy Hotel, is arrested and will be fined. The two have been romantically linked. **1** Dorothy Manners takes over Louella Parsons's Hearst newspaper column, with "A Tribute to 'Miss P.'" **20** Brigitte Bardot, publicizing *Viva Maria*, makes her first visit to Hollywood.

Movies

Connery is James Bond in *Thunderball*, opening at New York Premier Showcase theaters and at the Paramount, where it plays around the clock. **22** David Lean's *Doctor Zhivago* premieres at the Capitol. Attending the gala are Lean, producer Carlo Ponti, and stars Omar Sharif, Julie Christie, Geraldine Chaplin, Rod Steiger, Tom Courtenay, and Rita Tushingham. **23** *The Spy Who Came in from the Cold*, which stars Richard Burton, Claire Bloom, and Oscar Werner, opens at the DeMille and Coronet Theaters.

Julie Christie in *Doctor Zhivago*   *LC*/© MGM

Business and Society

Births, Deaths, Marriages, and Divorces

NOVEMBER 8 Hearst gossip columnist Dorothy Kilgallen dies from a combination of alcohol and barbiturates. **14** Judy Garland m. Mark Herron.

DECEMBER • Joan Bennett and Walter Wanger divorce. **2** Henry Fonda m. Shirlee Adams.

Also this year: • Elizabeth Ashley and James Farentino divorce.

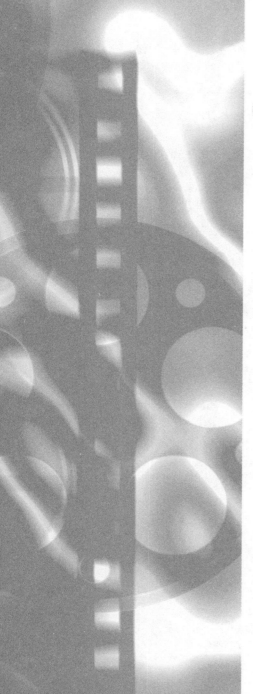

Gulf & Western takes over Paramount, the Production Code is revised, Jack Valenti is named head of the Motion Picture Association, and New York City begins a drive to lure feature-film production away from Hollywood. Hollywood is increasingly playing it safe, with remakes, such as *Stagecoach* and *Goodbye, Mr. Chips*; sequels, as in *Return of the Seven* (following *The Magnificent Seven*); and films generated from TV series, such as *Batman*, starring Adam West. Rona Barrett makes her debut as a video Hollywood gossip reporter on KABC TV in Los Angeles.

- Number of releases: 451
- CinemaScope releases: 7
- TV owners with color sets: 10%
- Number of theaters: 14,350, of which 4,200 are drive-ins
- Average weekly attendance: 38,000,000
- Average ticket price: $1.09
- Box office receipts: $964,000,000

Top stars at the box office, based on a Quigley Publications poll of exhibitors:

1. Julie Andrews
2. Sean Connery
3. Elizabeth Taylor
4. Jack Lemmon
5. Richard Burton
6. Cary Grant
7. John Wayne
8. Doris Day
9. Paul Newman
10. Elvis Presley

Top rental earnings, based on figures reported by *Variety*:

1.	*Thunderball*	$26,000,000
2.	*Doctor Zhivago*	15,000,000
3.	*Who's Afraid of Virginia Woolf?*	10,300,000
4.	*That Darn Cat*	9,200,000
5.	*The Russians Are Coming, The Russians Are Coming*	7,750,000

The New York Film Critics Circle Awards
Best Picture: *A Man for All Seasons*

The Golden Globe Awards
Best Picture (Drama): *A Man for All Seasons*
Best Picture (Musical/Comedy): *The Russians Are Coming, The Russians Are Coming*

The Cannes Film Festival
Palme d'Or: *A Man and a Woman* and *The Birds, the Bees and the Italians*

The Academy Awards (presented April 10, 1967)
Best Picture: *A Man for All Seasons*
Actor: Paul Scofield (*A Man for All Seasons*)
Actress: Elizabeth Taylor (*Who's Afraid of Virginia Woolf?*)
Supporting Actor: Walter Matthau (*The Fortune Cookie*)
Supporting Actress: Sandy Dennis (*Who's Afraid of Virginia Woolf?*)
Director: Fred Zinnemann (*A Man for All Seasons*)

January	February	March	April	May	June	
2 Anthony Quinn m. Yolande Addolari	• First-ever Ronald Reagan film festival **28** Glenn Ford m. Kathryn Hayes		**25** Jack Valenti heads MPAA	**26** Kim Novak divorces Richard Johnson	**22** *Who's Afraid of Virginia Woolf?*	

July	August	September	October	November	December	
	• Marlon Brando buys coral atoll near Tahiti **23** Montgomery Clift d.	**20** Major revision of Production Code	**19** Paramount bought by Gulf & Western	**8** Ronald Reagan elected governor of California	**18** *Blow-Up*	

Personalities

JANUARY 7 Director Otto Preminger and agent Irving (Swifty) Lazar argue at the 21 Club in New York over the movie rights to Truman Capote's *In Cold Blood*. When Preminger makes a remark about Lazar's wife, the agent hits him on the head with a goblet, leaving cuts that require fifty stitches to close. **27** Hedy Lamarr is arrested for shoplifting in a Wilshire Boulevard store.

FEBRUARY • The Hub Theater on San Francisco's Market Street, a third-run house, holds what it claims to be the first-ever Ronald Reagan film festival, featuring *Hellcats of the Navy*, *The Killers*, *Cavalry Charge*, and *Bombs over China*. **3** Hedy Lamarr, who had replaced Gene Tierney in

Picture Mommy Dead, is fired when she doesn't show up for the first day of shooting. Zsa Zsa Gabor replaces her. **21** Jack Palance rejects the role of the psycho in *The Dirty Dozen*—which will go to Telly Savalas—because he would be portraying a "Negro-baiter." Palance has been active in the civil rights movement.

APRIL 18 On Oscar night at the Santa Monica Civic Auditorium, Julie Andrews tells disbelieving reporters that "it's almost a relief not to win again." **25** Production begins on *The Dirty Dozen*. It will be delayed occasionally by Lee Marvin's heavy drinking. **26** A Los Angeles jury acquits Hedy Lamarr on a January 27 charge of shoplifting. **29** Filming a scene from *The Defectors*, Montgomery Clift, in the Danube, is swept away by the current and has to be rescued by a German patrol boat.

MAY 8 Hollywood columnist Florabel Muir predicts: "Just past her 18th birthday, Barbara Hershey, a product of Hollywood High School, is a pretty fair bet to make it to stardom as an actress in one leap."

JUNE 8 Frank Sinatra is with Dean Martin, celebrating Martin's birthday at the Polo Lounge in Beverly Hills, when a man drinking nearby says something objectionable and ends up with a skull fracture. No one will say how it happened. **8** Edward G. Robinson crashes his car when he falls asleep at the wheel in Beverly Hills. Four hours of surgery saves his life.

JULY 19 Jerry Lewis and several others escape in a raft when his yacht springs a leak and breaks up off Monterey. **26** William Holden escapes injury when his car collides with another in Italy, between Florence and

Movies

FEBRUARY 18 Dean Martin and Stella Stevens star in *The Silencers*, the first of several secret agent Matt Helm films, premiering at the Chicago Theater in Chicago.

APRIL 23 The craze over the campy *Batman* TV program with Adam West (first aired January 12) brings the rerelease of the 1943 Columbia serial with the same title. Republic has also brought back *The Adventures of Captain Marvel*.

MAY 25 Alan Arkin (in his first film), Carl Reiner, and Eva Marie Saint star in *The Russians Are Coming, The Russians Are Coming*, opening at three New York theaters.

JUNE 22 The premiere of *Who's Afraid of Virginia Woolf?*, directed by Mike Nichols, photographed by Haskell Wexler, and starring Elizabeth Taylor, Richard Burton, Sandy Dennis, and George Segal, is held at the Pantages Theater in Hollywood. Edward Albee, on whose play the film is based, had suggested Bette Davis and Henry Fonda for the lead roles.

JULY 30 *Batman*, a movie starring Adam West and Burt Ward, based on the popu-

lar, campy TV show, premieres at the Paramount in Austin, Texas. Burgess Meredith plays the Penguin; Cesar Romero, the Joker; and Lee Meriwether, the Catwoman.

AUGUST 16 *Fantastic Voyage*, a science-fiction film in which Raquel Welch is shrunk to microscopic size, premieres at Grauman's Chinese Theater. **24** Michael Caine achieves stardom in *Alfie*, premiering in the U.S. at the Coronet and at the New Embassy theater, where early birds in line are served tea and crumpets. The movie is so popular that the New Embassy has to go on a round-the-clock schedule. The Burt Bacharach–Hal David title song is a hit.

Business and Society

JANUARY 19 A New York State Supreme Court judge rules that Otto Preminger can't prevent *Anatomy of a Murder* from being edited for TV and interrupted by commercials.

FEBRUARY 7 Last year American studios financed eighty percent of the movies made in Britain, it is announced by British filmmakers.

APRIL 25 Jack Valenti, an aide to President Lyndon Johnson, becomes head of the Motion Picture Association of America.

JUNE 10 *Who's Afraid of Virginia Woolf?*, is the first film to receive a Production Code seal despite the presence of four-letter words. Warner Bros.'s promise to limit admission to those over eighteen helps. **20** Bell Telephone Laboratories demonstrates computer-animated movies.

JULY 14 The U.S. Court of Appeals voids the Directors Guild of America loyalty oath as "inherently vague."

AUGUST 2 *Alfie* receives a Production Code seal even though it contains the strictly forbidden word "abortion."

SEPTEMBER 20 In a major revision of its Production Code, the movie industry drops several specific prohibitions and will label certain films "recommended for mature

Births, Deaths, Marriages, and Divorces

JANUARY 2 Anthony Quinn m. Yolande Addolari. **22** Herbert Marshall d.

FEBRUARY 1 Buster Keaton and Hedda Hopper die. • Peter Lawford and Patricia Kennedy divorce. **2** Woody Allen m.

Louise Lasser. **10** Laura Dern, daughter of Bruce Dern and Diane Ladd, b. **25** Brian Donlevy m. Lillian Lugosi, ex-wife of Bela Lugosi.

MARCH 28 Glenn Ford m. Kathryn Hayes.

APRIL 1 June Allyson rem. Alfred Glenn Maxwell. **17** George Peppard m. Elizabeth Ashley, ex-wife of James Farentino.

MAY 26 Kim Novak divorces Richard Johnson. • Helena Bonham-Carter b.

JUNE 28 John Cusack, brother of Joan Cusack, b.

> *A sniper's bullet strikes the ground thirty feet from where John Wayne is signing autographs for soldiers in Vietnam. "Hell, I didn't even know we were being fired at until I saw the marines running for cover," he says later.*
>
> *June 21, 1966*

Pisa, but the other driver is killed. **29** Lauren Bacall is on the cover of *Time*, illustrating the story, "The Pleasures and Perils of Middle Age."

AUGUST • Marlon Brando buys Tetiarora, a coral atoll twenty-five miles north of Tahiti. *Playboy* runs photographs of a seminude Jane Fonda taken by a photographer hiding on the set of her film, *La Curée*, which she is making under the direction of her husband, Roger Vadim. **21** Jason Robards Jr. is arrested in Malibu for running drunk through the backyard of former screen star Jon Hall. Hall later drops the charges, calling it a "misunderstanding."

OCTOBER • George Hamilton, who is dating Lynda Bird Johnson, the President's daughter, comes under fire for being draft-deferred as the sole support for his mother and brothers. By the time he's reclassified 1A in March, he will be twenty-seven, too old by a year for the draft. **4** Filming begins on *Bonnie and Clyde*. Warren Beatty's girlfriend, Leslie Caron, takes credit for urging him to

buy the screenplay. His decision, as producer, not to cast Caron in the female lead role embitters her. Newcomer Faye Dunaway was Beatty's fourth choice after Tuesday Weld, Jane Fonda, and Sue Lyon rejected it. Arthur Penn, Beatty's third choice for director after Truffaut and Godard passed, eliminated from the screenplay the homosexual attraction between Clyde and the member of his gang played in the film by Michael Pollard. **26** George Sanders files for bankruptcy, claiming he has been "swindled" by other investors in a British sausage company.

NOVEMBER 8 Former movie star Ronald Reagan is elected governor of California. **15** Betty Hutton tells police that her husband, jazz trumpeter Pete Candoli, has threatened to kill her.

OCTOBER 17 *Georgy Girl*, starring Lynn Redgrave, Alan Bates, and James Mason, premieres in the U.S. at the Fine Arts. "It's the wildest thing to hit the world since the mini-skirt!," say the ads. It's also the first film to be labeled "suggested for mature audiences only." The title song will become a hit. **19** Billy Wilder's *The Fortune Cookie*, starring Jack Lemmon and Walter Matthau, premieres at several New York theaters.

DECEMBER 1 Andy Warhol's *Chelsea Girls*, the first underground film to make it to a midtown art house, opens at the Cinema Rendezvous. **12** *A Man for All Seasons*, starring Paul Scofield, Wendy Hiller, Leo

audiences." The new code relies on general admonitions, calling for "restraint" in portraying violence and for no "undue exposure of the human body."

OCTOBER 5 Shirley Temple Black resigns as a director of the San Francisco Film Festival, objecting to its scheduling of *Night Games*, a sexually explicit Swedish film. **19** Paramount Pictures is absorbed by Gulf & Western Industries, Inc.

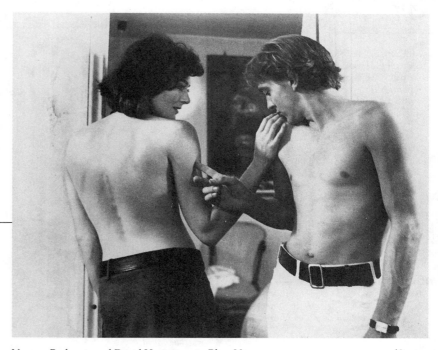

Vanessa Redgrave and David Hemmings in *Blow-Up*   LC/© MGM

JULY 19 Mia Farrow m. Frank Sinatra. **23** Montgomery Clift d.

AUGUST 6 Donald Sutherland m. Shirley Douglas, whose father, Tommy, heads Canada's New Democratic party. **23** Francis X. Bushman d.

SEPTEMBER 10 Mickey Rooney m. Margaret Lane. This one lasts only three months.

OCTOBER 25 Burt Reynolds and Judy Carne divorce.

DECEMBER 15 Walt Disney d. **21** Kiefer Sutherland, son of Donald Sutherland and

Shirley Douglas, b. • Cliff Robertson m. Dina Merrill. **31** Martha Hyer m. Hal Wallis.

Also this year: • Divorced are Ursula Andress and John Derek, James Caan and Dee Jay Mattis, and Jayne Mansfield and Matt Cimber.

Personalities

DECEMBER 27 In an unprecedented action, ABC secures TV broadcast rights to *The Man with the Golden Arm* by promising to show it uncut. It also grants producer Otto Preminger the right to choose where the film will be interrupted for commercials.

Frank Sinatra, 50, marries 21-year-old Mia Farrow on July 19, 1966.   *LC*

Movies

McKern, Robert Shaw, and Orson Welles, opens at the Fine Arts. **18** Michelangelo Antonioni's *Blow-Up*, his first English-language film, premieres at the Coronet without a Production Code seal. The film's distributor, MGM, in refusing to make the cuts demanded by the Production Code office, is defying that body for the first time. **20** *The Sand Pebbles*, starring Steve McQueen, Richard Attenborough, Richard Crenna, and Candice Bergen, premieres at the Rivoli.

Business and Society

NOVEMBER 9 Paramount announces that Robert Evans will become its new production chief. **14** Jack Warner announces that he has sold his shares in Warner Bros. to Seven Arts.

Montgomery Clift dies on July 23, 1966, at the age of forty-five. He will be remembered for his intense, often harrowing performances in films including *A Place in the Sun, Judgment at Nuremburg,* and *The Misfits.*   *LC*

Births, Deaths, Marriages, and Divorces

*T*ransamerica takes over United Artists, and Seven Arts gains control of Warner Bros. Clint Eastwood, nameless in Sergio Leone's first "spaghetti western," *A Fistful of Dollars*, begins to make a name for himself with American movie fans. Arthur Penn's *Bonnie and Clyde* is a landmark American film. The Tracy-Hepburn partnership ends with their last film and his death. With the opening of *The Graduate*, Dustin Hoffman becomes a new star. A Los Angeles draft board classifies Richard Dreyfuss as a conscientious objector and sends him to Los Angeles General Hospital for two years of alternative service. And Sandra Dee divorces Bobby Darin.

- Number of releases: 462
- CinemaScope releases: 2
- Number of theaters: 13,490, of which 3,670 are drive-ins (figures, beginning this year, are based on those issued by Motion Picture Association of America—previous year's figures were from *Film Daily Yearbook*)
- Average weekly attendance: 17,800,000
- Average ticket price: $1.20
- Box office receipts: $989,000,000
- Approximate popcorn sales: $265,200,000
- Approximate number of people employed in movie industry: 190,000
- Director Mike Nichols's compensation for *The Graduate*: about $1,000,000
- Dustin Hoffman's pay for *The Graduate*: $17,000
- Dustin Hoffman's age when making *The Graduate*: 30
- Age of Anne Bancroft when she plays Mrs. Robinson in *The Graduate*: 35
- Spencer Tracy's fee for *Guess Who's Coming to Dinner*: $300,000
- Total number of takes ordered by Arthur Penn in the shooting of *Bonnie and Clyde*: a reported 125,000

Top stars at the box office, based on a Quigley Publications poll of exhibitors:

1. Julie Andrews
2. Lee Marvin
3. Paul Newman
4. Dean Martin
5. Sean Connery
6. Elizabeth Taylor
7. Sidney Poitier
8. John Wayne
9. Richard Burton
10. Steve McQueen

The New York Film Critics Circle Awards
Best Picture: *In the Heat of the Night*

The Golden Globes Awards
Best Picture (Drama): *In the Heat of the Night*
Best Picture (Musical/Comedy): *The Graduate*

The Cannes Film Festival
Palme d'Or: *Blow-Up*

The Academy Awards (presented April 10, 1968)
Best Picture: *In the Heat of the Night*
Actor: Rod Steiger (*In the Heat of the Night*)
Actress: Katharine Hepburn (*Guess Who's Coming to Dinner*)
Supporting Actor: George Kennedy (*Cool Hand Luke*)
Supporting Actress: Estelle Parsons (*Bonnie and Clyde*)
Director: Mike Nichols (*The Graduate*)

January	February	March	April	May	June	
	28 Ryan O'Neal m. Leigh-Taylor Young		**20** Dummies of Sonny and Cher unveiled at Hollywood Wax Museum		
18 *A Fistful of Dollars*		**18** UCLA awards Master of Fine Arts to Francis Ford Coppola	**11** Transamerica takes over United Artists	**23** Sidney Poitier is 154th star and first black to place prints at Grauman's Chinese Theater	

July	August	September	October	November	December	
		16 Susan Tomalin m. Chris Sarandon, becoming Susan Sarandon			**21** *The Graduate*
14 Seven Arts Ltd. takes over Warner Bros.			**26** William Holden gets fine and suspended sentence for fatal car crash	• Bette Midler has replacement role in *Fiddler on the Roof*	
	13 *Bonnie and Clyde*				

Personalities

JANUARY 3 Naval Reserve Commander Glenn Ford is called to active duty to make a documentary in Vietnam publicizing the Marines. **6** In London, where it had its world premiere last night, the critics turn thumbs down on Charlie Chaplin's *A Countess from Hong Kong*. Chaplin calls them "bloody idiots." **11** Director Mike Nichols announces a search for a male, 19 to 23, to play opposite Anne Bancroft (a role turned down by Doris Day) in a film called *The Graduate*. In four weeks Nichols will come up with 30-year-old stage actor Dustin Hoffman. Nichols will later recall his conversation with Robert Redford, who read for the part of Benjamin in *The Graduate*: "What I said to Redford was that he could not at that point in his life play a loser, because nobody would ever buy it. He didn't understand, and I said, 'Well, let me put it to you another way: Have you ever struck out with a girl?' And he said, 'What do you mean?' It made my point."

FEBRUARY 24 George Raft is prevented from entering Great Britain, where he is the host at the George Raft Colony Club (a London gambling establishment) because his presence "would not be conducive to the public good."

MARCH 18 UCLA awards a Master of Fine Arts degree to Francis Ford Coppola, whose thesis was the film, *You're a Big Boy Now*, released this year as a feature film.

APRIL 10 Best Actor nominee Richard Burton comes up a loser for the fifth time on Oscar night at the Santa Monica Civic Auditorium. **27** Sophia Loren and Carlo Ponti win their ten-year battle to quash bigamy charges based on their 1967 Mexican wedding by proxy.

MAY 3 The Italian-American Anti-Defamation League announces that it has chosen Frank Sinatra to lead it. **4** Susan Hayward replaces Judy Garland in *Valley of the Dolls*. Garland, fired last week, was unable to memorize lines or show up when filming was scheduled. **20** Dummies of Sonny and Cher are unveiled at the Hollywood Wax Museum, coinciding with the local opening of their film, *Good Times*. **26** Filming ends on *Guess Who's Coming to Dinner*, Spencer Tracy and Katharine Hepburn's ninth picture together. Tracy will be dead in less than three weeks.

JUNE • Danny Aiello, after working for ten

Movies

JANUARY 18 Sergio Leone's *A Fistful of Dollars* premieres in the U.S. at the Hollywood Pantages. Clint Eastwood begins his rise to superstardom in this first "spaghetti western," which opened in Italy in 1964. A January 19 ad in the *Los Angeles Times* says: "It's the first motion picture of its kind. It won't be the last." The paper's reviewer calls the movie "sadistic," a "freak affair."

MARCH 20 Martin Ritt's *Hombre*, starring Paul Newman, Fredric March, and Richard Boone, premieres at the Astor.

APRIL 27 Audrey Hepburn and Albert Finney are *Two for the Road*, opening at the Radio City Music Hall.

MAY 25 *Barefoot in the Park*, starring Jane Fonda and Robert Redford, opens at the Radio City Music Hall.

JUNE 13 Sean Connery is James Bond in *You Only Live Twice*, opening at many theaters. **14** *To Sir, With Love*, starring Sidney Poitier, opens at the Cinema I. **15** Robert Aldrich's *The Dirty Dozen*, starring Ernest Borgnine, Charles Bronson, Jim Brown, John Cassavetes, George Kennedy, Lee Marvin, Telly Savalas, and Donald Sutherland, premieres at the Capitol, with all except Sutherland present.

AUGUST 2 *In the Heat of the Night*, starring Sidney Poitier and Rod Steiger, opens at the Capitol and 86th St. East Theaters. **30** John Boorman's revenge drama, *Point Blank*, starring Lee Marvin and Angie Dickinson, premieres at San Francisco's Northpoint Theater.

OCTOBER 26 *Wait until Dark*, starring Audrey Hepburn, Alan Arkin, and Richard Crenna, opens at the Radio City Music Hall.

Business and Society

FEBRUARY 23 The Screen Producers Guild becomes the Producers Guild of America.

APRIL 11 United Artists becomes a subsidiary of Transamerica, the Bank America conglomerate.

MAY 15 Martin S. Davis becomes Paramount's CEO. **15** A fire at Universal destroys $1 million worth of sets but does not disrupt production or the studio tour.

JUNE 5 The American Film Institute is created.

JULY 10 Robert M. Weitman resigns as MGM production head to take the same spot at Columbia, beginning in January. **14** Seven Arts Ltd. takes control of Warner Bros. when it buys Jack Warner's shares in the studio. **24** Jack Warner resigns as head of production at Warner Bros.–Seven Arts and is succeeded, on August 7, by Kenneth Hyman.

AUGUST • The *Los Angeles Times* will not permit an American International Pictures ad for *The Trip* to quote a reviewer's references to LSD, even though the review is the paper's own. **5** Gregory Peck is picked to chair the American Film Institute, which was founded on June 5.

NOVEMBER 24 Robert Vaughn and James

Births, Deaths, Marriages, and Divorces

JANUARY • James Earl Jones m. Julienne Marie. **4** Lee Marvin is divorced from Betty Edeling. **21** Ann Sheridan d. **27** Bridget Fonda, daughter of Peter, niece of Jane, and granddaughter of Henry Fonda, b.

FEBRUARY • Connie Stevens m. Eddie Fisher. **14** A miniskirted Raquel Welch m. her manager, Patrick Curtis. **24** Composer Franz Waxman d. **28** A few days after his divorce from Joanna Moore, Ryan O'Neal m. Leigh-Taylor Young.

MARCH 3 Liza Minnelli m. Peter Allen. **6** Nelson Eddy d. **7** Sandra Dee divorces Bobby Darin.

APRIL 11 Judy Garland and Mark Herron divorce. **15** Gordon and Sheila McRae divorce. **28** Vanessa Redgrave divorces Tony Richardson.

years at the Greyhound terminal in New York and becoming president of Local 1202 of the Amalgamated Transit Union, loses his job following a wildcat strike. **23** Sidney Poitier puts his hand and footprints in Grauman's Chinese Theater forecourt, the 154th star and the first black to do so.

JULY • George Hamilton's romance with Lynda Bird Johnson ends. **26** Richard Pryor is arrested for assaulting the desk clerk at his apartment house in West Hollywood. Pryor will be fined, placed on probation, and have to pay as much as $100,000 in an out-of-court settlement of a civil suit.

AUGUST 3 "A third generation Huston moves into the limelight," writes *Daily Variety* columnist Army Archerd about John Huston's plans to star his sixteen-year-old

daughter, Anjelica, in *A Walk with Love and Death.* **21** Filming begins on *Rosemary's Baby.* Mia Farrow will be served with divorce papers from husband Frank Sinatra on the set. **29** Shirley Temple Black, a conservative Republican, declares herself a candidate for Congress in California's 12th congressional district. "I've been in public life for 36 of my 39 years," she says. She will lose.

SEPTEMBER 11 Frank Sinatra, enraged that the Sands Hotel in Las Vegas will not extend him gambling credit, throws his chips in the face of Hotel V.P. Carl Cohen, who then punches the singer-actor, breaking two of his teeth. Sinatra had been set to shift his performances from the Sands to Caesar's Palace anyway.

OCTOBER 25 Columnist Sheila Graham reports that Shirley MacLaine, concerned that the public is linking her to Maharishi Mahesh Yogi, characterizes the Beatles' and Mia Farrow's attraction to him as "all a bit adolescent." **26** William Holden is fined $80,000 by an Italian court and given an eight-month suspended jail term for manslaughter for his involvement in last July's car crash in which a person was killed.

NOVEMBER • Hawaiian-born singer Bette Midler, who says she was the only Jewish girl in a Samoan neighborhood, takes over the role of Tzeitel in the Broadway production of *Fiddler on the Roof.* **9** Jennifer Jones is discovered unconscious in the surf off Malibu, where she either leaped or fell partway down a cliff after trying to kill herself with an overdose of Seconal.

NOVEMBER 1 Paul Newman stars in *Cool Hand Luke,* opening at Loew's State.

DECEMBER 11 Stanley Kramer's *Guess Who's Coming to Dinner,* about an interracial romance, starring Spencer Tracy in his last film, Katharine Hepburn, Sidney Poitier, and Katharine Houghton (Hepburn's niece), premieres at the Victoria Theater. **14** *In Cold Blood* opens at the Cinema I. It stars Robert Blake and Scott Wilson. **15** *Valley of the Dolls* premieres at the Criterion and Festival theaters. Based on the Jacqueline Susann bestseller, it is a hit and an instant camp classic. Among the stars are Sharon Tate and Susan Hayward. Richard Dreyfuss,

A NEW KIND OF GANGSTER FILM

Warren Beatty and Faye Dunaway in *Bonnie and Clyde*   MSN
© WARNER BROTHERS

Garner, on Los Angeles TV, debate the role of the actor in politics. Vaughn calls for involvement, but Garner relates that when TV personality Steve Allen was thinking of running for Congress, the Republicans asked Garner to oppose him simply to come up with another famous name. "Reagan running for president is even more dangerous," adds Garner.

DECEMBER 11 The American Film Institute announces a film archive and restoration

MAY 1 Elvis Presley m. Priscilla Beaulieu. **8** Ann-Margret m. Roger Smith. **30** Claude Rains d.

JUNE 10 Spencer Tracy d. **16** Betty Hutton divorces Pete Candoli. **29** Jayne Mansfield dies in an auto accident.

AUGUST 13 Arthur Penn's *Bonnie and Clyde,* starring Warren Beatty, Faye Dunaway, Gene Hackman, Estelle Parsons, Michael Pollard, and Gene Wilder in his screen debut, has its theatrical premiere at the Forum and Murray Hill Theaters after a showing a few days ago at the Montreal Film Festival. The *New York Times* (August 14) decries "the blending of farce with brutal killings." Pauline Kael writes in *The New Yorker* (October 21):

"How do you make a good movie in this country without being jumped on?" *Time's* December 8 cover story "The New Cinema: Violence...Sex...Art..." sees the picture as the U.S. counterpart of the work of European directors such as Antonioni. The costumes influence clothing styles, especially Dunaway's beret. Flatt and Scruggs recording of "Foggy Mountain Breakdown" from the film becomes popular.

JULY 4 George C. Scott and Colleen Dewhurst remarry. **8** Vivien Leigh d. **21** Basil Rathbone d.

AUGUST 25 Paul Muni d.

SEPTEMBER • Sondra Locke m. Gordon Anderson. **16** Susan Tomalin becomes

Personalities

29 20th Century Fox announces that in *The Detective* Jacqueline Bisset will replace Mia Farrow, who last week announced her separation from Frank Sinatra, the picture's star. **30** Columnist Sheilah Graham reports that Barbra Streisand's dates with Omar Sharif, with whom she's now filming *Funny Girl*, are beginning to bother Elliott Gould. He says that his wife is "naive…just a little girl from Brooklyn…" Last month he told an interviewer that "She's a vulnerable, fragile girl. She needs taking care of."

DECEMBER 6 Filming a scene from *Isadora* in a theater filled with extras, Vanessa Redgrave duplicates an incident in Isadora Duncan's life by ripping off the top of her

Barbra Streisand is "Just a little girl from Brooklyn," according to her husband Elliot Gould.   *LC*

dress and dancing bare-breasted. The extras, who were not told she would do this, provide the audience-aghast reaction shots desired by director Karl Reisz.

Movies

in his film debut, has a bit part, as does author Susann. **20** "Mrs. Robinson, you're trying to seduce me. Aren't you?" says Dustin Hoffman to Anne Bancroft, starring with Katherine Ross in Mike Nichols's *The Graduate*, premiering at the Coronet. The title song, "Here's to You, Mrs. Robinson," is sung by Simon and Garfunkel. With this film, Hoffman becomes a star. **22** Walt Disney's *The Jungle Book* opens in New York area theaters.

Business and Society

project. **21** Construction of the Ziegfeld, midtown Manhattan's first new movie theater in thirty years, to be the most automated in the country, is announced by the Walter Reade organization. **21** Universal Newsreel, the last service supplying newsreels to theaters, announces that it has ceased production. **31** Bosley Crowther, the *New York Times* movie critic for twenty-

seven years, steps down and is replaced by Renata Adler.

Births, Deaths, Marriages, and Divorces

Susan Sarandon with her marriage to Chris Sarandon.

OCTOBER 14 Jill St. John m. singer Jack Jones. **22** Morgan Freeman m. Jeanette

Bradshaw. **27** Gene Wilder m. Mary Schutz.

Also this year: • Julia Roberts b. • Esther Williams m. Fernando Lamas, ex-

husband of Arlene Dahl. • Divorced are Jose Ferrer and Rosemary Clooney, Dennis Hopper and Brooke Hayward, and Jack Nicholson and Sandra Knight. • Marlon Brando's marriage to Movita is annulled.

The movie rating system is introduced. Cinemobiles, film studios on wheels, begin to lower the cost of on-location filming. Film studies on campuses burgeon, with sixty thousand students enrolled in courses, doubling 1967's figures. Woody Allen begins a new career as a director, and Barbra Streisand becomes a major movie star. Charles Bronson moves to Europe, where he will become a star. Future superagent Michael Ovitz begins working in the mail room at the William Morris Agency. UCLA student Steve Martin is hired to write for the Smothers Brothers TV show, and Cybill Shepherd is Model of the Year.

- Number of releases: 454
- TV owners with color sets: 24%
- Number of theaters: 13,1200, of which 3,700 are drive-ins
- Average weekly attendance: 18,800,000
- Average ticket price: $1.31
- Box office receipts: $1,045,000,000
- Barbra Streisand's fee for *Funny Girl*: $200,000
- Production cost of *Night of the Living Dead*: $114,000
- Worldwide rentals from *Night of the Living Dead*: $12,000,000
- Cost of makeup for *Planet of the Apes*: $1,000,000
- Running time of credits in *Once Upon a Time in the West*: 12 minutes
- Source of "HAL," the name of the computer in *2001: A Space Odyssey*: each letter of the name directly precedes in the alphabet the corresponding letters in IBM.

Top rental earnings, based on figures reported in *Variety*:
1. *The Graduate* — $39,000,000
2. *Guess Who's Coming to Dinner* — 25,100,000
3. *Gone With the Wind* (re-release) — 23,000,000
4. *The Valley of the Dolls* — 20,000,000
5. *The Odd Couple* — 18,500,000

The New York Film Critics Circle Awards
Best Picture: *The Lion in Winter*

The Golden Globe Awards
Best Picture (Drama): *The Lion in Winter*
Best Picture (Musical/Comedy): *Oliver!*

The Cannes Film Festival
no award

The Academy Awards (presented for the first time at the Dorothy Chandler Pavilion, April 14, 1969)
Best Picture: *Oliver!*
Actor: Cliff Robertson (*Charly*)
Actress: Katharine Hepburn (*The Lion in Winter*)
Supporting Actor: Jack Albertson (*The Subject Was Roses*)
Supporting Actress: Ruth Gordon (*Rosemary's Baby*)
Director: Carol Reed (*Oliver!*)

January	February	March	April	May	June	
4 Dana Andrews hospitalized for skull fracture in fall		**21** Dyan Cannon divorces Cary Grant **18** *Planet of the Apes*	**2** *2001: A Space Odyssey*	**5** Avco purchase of Embassy Pictures creates Avco-Embassy	**17** Woody Allen begins directing career	

July	August	September	October	November	December	
30 Jane Russell divorces Bob Waterfield	• Shirley MacLaine a delegate to Democratic Convention	**18** *Funny Girl*	**30** *The Lion in Winter*	**20** Audrey Hepburn and Mel Ferrer divorce	**5** Marlon Brando, mistaken for a terrorist, is removed from plane	

Personalities

• Glenn Ford sees a few weeks of duty as a briefing officer in Vietnam. • Nineteen-year-old Sissy Spacek, an aspiring singer who has been told she sounds like Loretta Lynn, records, under the name Rainbow, the song "John, You've Gone Too Far This Time," about John Lennon.

JANUARY 4 Dana Andrews is hospitalized for a fractured skull, suffered when he fell in a hotel bathroom. **12** Anne Francis, whose role in *Funny Girl* was substantially cut, says in a *Hollywood Reporter* interview that Barbra Streisand wanted to "run the whole show." **12** *Bonnie and Clyde*'s influence on clothing styles is echoed in *Life* magazine's cover story: "Faye Dunaway in a 30's Revival: Bonnie Fashion's New

Darling." **17** Jill Clayburgh and Al Pacino, who met last year at the Charles Playhouse in Boston, have moved in together and open tonight in an off-Broadway double bill. She's in *It's Called the Sugar Plum*, and he's in *The Indian Wants the Bronx* (co-starring John Cazale, who will play Pacino's older brother, Fredo, in *The Godfather*). They are each making $56 a week. **19** Carroll Baker wins a $200,000 judgment against Paramount and Embassy Pictures for not giving her work—other than *Harlow*— under a contract that began on May 19, 1966. Disgusted with Hollywood, Baker will move to Europe. **21** Paul Newman and Barbra Streisand appear at "Broadway for Peace" to raise money for antiwar political candidates. **22** Warner Bros.–Seven Arts and the Coppola Co. announce that twenty-three-year-old USC student George Lucas will write and direct

a film for them titled *THX 1138 4EB*, later released as *THX 1138*. **28** Goldie Hawn joins the cast of the new TV program *Laugh In*. **29** The *Times of India* reports that Mia Farrow, separated from Frank Sinatra and in India to meditate with the Maharishi Mahesh Yogi, hit a photographer trying to snap her picture at her New Delhi hotel.

FEBRUARY 6 Nick Adams, who was in *Rebel Without a Cause*, dies of what the coroner calls "Paraldehyde intoxication"—an overdose of the drug used to treat alcoholism. **14** Katy Jurado unsuccessfully attempts suicide with an overdose of sleeping pills. **16** In an article on student films at USC, the *Hollywood Reporter* praises an eight-minute movie by John Milius, the future screenwriter and director, called *Marcello— I'm So Bored*.

Movies

FEBRUARY 8 *Planet of the Apes*, the first of five in a simian series, starring Charlton Heston and, in monkey makeup, Roddy McDowall, Kim Hunter, and Maurice Evans, premieres at the Capitol.

MARCH 18 Zero Mostel and Gene Wilder star in Mel Brooks's *The Producers*, opening at the Fine Arts. **29** *Madigan*, starring Richard Widmark and Henry Fonda, opens at the DeMille. It will lead to a TV series, debuting September 20, 1972.

Business and Society

JANUARY • MGM apologizes to theater owners for mistakenly releasing to TV *Welcome to Hard Times* only seven months after it opened theatrically. The gap between theatrical exhibition and appearance on TV has been narrowing, in some cases, to as little as a year.

FEBRUARY 28 Warners announces that for

Charlton Heston, captive in *Planet of the Apes*   LC

Births, Deaths, Marriages, and Divorces

JANUARY 8 Director Roman Polanski m. Sharon Tate.

FEBRUARY 13 Silent-screen star Mae Marsh d. **18** Molly Ringwald b.

MARCH 16 Suzanne Pleshette m. Thomas Gallagher III. **21** Dyan Cannon divorces Cary Grant, charging that he went crazy when he used LSD. **27** Michael York m. Patricia McCallum.

APRIL 16 Tony Curtis divorces Christine Kaufmann. **20** Tony Curtis m. Leslie Allen.

MAY 5 Albert Dekker d. **7** Julie Andrews divorces Tony Walton.

JUNE 4 Dorothy Gish d. **7** Dan Duryea d.

MARCH 4 Using water-resistant dyes, the Warners makeup department takes nine hours to cover Rod Steiger with "tatoos" for his role, beginning tomorrow, in *The Illustrated Man*. **9** Praising Lily Tomlin, the star of *Photofinish*, a revue that just opened at New York's Upstairs at the Downstairs, the *New York Times* says that she "may well be headed for the big time." **29** Warner Bros. announces that Gordon Parks will become the first black to direct a major feature film: *The Learning Tree*.

APRIL • Paul Newman campaigns for Sen. Eugene McCarthy in the Indiana presidential primary. Marlon Brando gives up the lead role in *The Arrangement* to work in the civil-rights movement, but then confirms his commitment to appear in Gillo Pontecorvo's *Burn*, about British imperialism in the Caribbean. **10** The

Academy Awards ceremonies at the Santa Monica Civic Auditorium, originally scheduled for April 8, have been postponed for two days because of the assassination of Dr. Martin Luther King. Warren Beatty arrives with Julie Christie this year. **26** Sidney Pollack grabs a camera and shoots whatever he can when the castle set in Yugoslavia on which he is filming *Castle Keep*, starring Burt Lancaster, blows up and accidentally burns down.

MAY • Jack Lemmon pledges half his salary from his next film for the civil-rights Poor People's Campaign. **5** Albert Dekker, who appeared in some thirty films from the 1930s through the 1950s, is found dead in his bathroom, handcuffs on one wrist, a rope around his neck, obscenities written on his body, and hyperdermic marks on his skin. "This is certainly a strange death," says

L. A. Deputy Coroner Herbert McRoy, who calls it "accidental." **20** A Manhattan court fines Elliott Gould $795 for the sixty-three traffic summonses he's ignored. **25** Judy Garland fails to show up for her scheduled show at Boston's Back Bay Theater.

JUNE 17 Woody Allen begins his directing career with the start of filming on *Take the Money and Run*.

JULY 23 Stepin Fetchit (Lincoln Perry), a black man who portrayed shuffling, comic Uncle Toms in many 1930s films, angrily responds to a negative depiction of his career in a TV documentary on black history: "It was not Martin Luther King who emancipated the modern Negro, but Stepin Fetchit." **25** Columnist Sheila Graham reports that Michael Caine's new girlfriend, Bianca, a twenty-year-old Nicaraguan, is

APRIL 2 A year before men walk on the moon, Stanley Kubrick's *2001: A Space Odyssey*, in 70mm wide-screen and starring Keir Dullea, premieres at the Uptown Theater in Washington, D.C. It introduces advances in special effects that will be used and refined by many science-fiction films in the future. The film's effective use of the theme from Richard Strauss's "Thus Spake Zarathustra" in its opening sequence virtually makes a hit of the piece. The 1984 sequel, *2010*, will be directed by Peter Hyams. **10** Charlton Heston is *Will Penny*, opening at Paramount Presentation Showcase Theaters.

MAY 2 Jack Lemmon and Walter Matthau are

The Odd Couple, opening at the Radio City Music Hall. **28** Frank Sinatra and Lee Remick star in *The Detective*, premiering at the Forum.

JUNE 12 Roman Polanski's *Rosemary's Baby*, starring Mia Farrow, John Cassavetes, Ruth Gordon, and Ralph Bellamy, premieres at the Criterion. **19** *The Thomas Crown Affair*, starring Steve McQueen and Faye Dunaway, premieres at the Music Hall in Boston.

AUGUST 13 Peter Bogdanovich's first film, *Targets*, about a sniper, with Boris Karloff in his final role playing an aging horror-film star, premieres at the New Embassy Theater.

John Wayne stars in *The Green Berets*, premiering at the Warner Theater. Tomorrow's *New York Times* review will call it "so unspeakable, so stupid, so rotten and false…"

June 19, 1968

SEPTEMBER 18 The Criterion hosts the gala premiere of *Funny Girl*. Barbra Streisand, Omar Sharif, and Walter Pidgeon star. The arrival of Streisand with husband Elliott Gould, according to the *New York Times*, is greeted by "agonized screams, frenzied waving and

the first time it will rent out space at its Burbank studio.

MARCH 28 According to the *Hollywood Reporter*, fifty percent of films earning Production Code seals in the first two months of the year are "suggested for mature audiences," compared with fifteen percent for the same period last year.

APRIL 5 Columbia Pictures orders deleted from all prints of *Guess Who's Coming to*

Dinner a joke referring to Dr. Martin Luther King, who was assassinated yesterday.

MAY 5 The Avco Corp., a conglomerate, announces its purchase of Joseph Levine's Embassy Pictures, resulting in Avco-Embassy.

AUGUST 22 The Soviet invasion of Czechoslovakia causes the cast and crew of David Wolper's *The Bridge at Remagen*, filming at a bridge in that country, to abandon their equipment and flee for the border. Every-

one gets out and they will finish at a replica of the bridge near Rome.

INDUSTRY INTRODUCES RATING SYSTEM

In response to charges that violence and nudity are running rampant in its product, the movie industry announces that it has set up a rating system for films. The ratings are: "G," for general audiences; "M," for mature audiences; "R," no one under age 16 admitted without an accompanying adult; and "X," for those 16 and older, without exception.

October 7, 1968

JULY 30 Jane Russell divorces Bob Waterfield.

AUGUST 16 Mia Farrow divorces Frank Sinatra. **25** Jane Russell m. Roger Barrett. **27** Kay Francis d.

SEPTEMBER 16 Sally Field m. Steve Craig. **18** Franchot Tone d.

OCTOBER 30 Silent-screen star Ramon Novarro is beaten to death in his Hollywood home by two young men in the course of a robbery.

NOVEMBER 8 Producer Walter Wanger d. **20** Audrey Hepburn and Mel Ferrer divorce. **23** Lee Remick divorces William Colleran.

Personalities

"studying the scene in London." The future Mrs. Jagger says she wants to be a psychoanalyst.

AUGUST • Shirley MacLaine is a delegate, and Robert Ryan, one of the founding members, of SANE, an alternate delegate to the Democratic Convention. **5** John Wayne tells the Republican Convention in Miami that while his daughter will never have to fight for her country, he wants her to respect those who do. **13** According to today's *Hollywood Reporter*, the final title for the movie about General George Patton, starring George C. Scott, is *Patton, Blood and Guts*.

SEPTEMBER 24 Burt Lancaster is arrested

Movies

hysterical pushing." And premiering at the Vogue Theater in Los Angeles is *Pretty Poison*, starring Tuesday Weld and Anthony Perkins. **23** Cliff Robertson and Claire Bloom star in *Charly*, premiering at the Baronet.

OCTOBER • The press releases for Universal's *Colossus*, a science-fiction film about computers, are the first from a Hollywood studio to be printed by a computer. **8** Franco Zeffirelli's *Romeo & Juliet*, starring Olivia Hussey and Leonard Whiting, premieres in the U.S. at the Paris Theater.

Business and Society

SEPTEMBER • Beverly Hills High School begins to offer its first film studies course. **18** J. Edgar Hoover tells a government commission investigating violence in America that "seemingly limitless excess of sex, sadism, degeneracy and violence is only too apparent in the offerings of the motion picture industry."

and spends a night in jail for refusing to sign a speeding ticket issued to him near Malibu.

OCTOBER 3 James Earl Jones becomes a star with the opening of the Broadway play *The Great White Hope*. **25** Joan Crawford, working for scale, replaces her daughter Christina for four episodes of the TV soap opera *The Secret Storm*, beginning today. Christina is recovering from surgery, and Crawford didn't want her to lose the role.

Jane Fonda in *Barbarella*   LC

Christina says "it was fantastic that she would care that much." **28** Elliott Gould roughs up a photographer trying to take pictures of him and his wife, Barbra Streisand, at a Hollywood preview of *Bullitt*.

NOVEMBER 10 Mia Farrow, out late with friends at London's Cavendish Hotel, gets involved in a fracas with police who try to arrest one of her party for drunkenness. Although not charged herself, she uses a "very naughty four-letter word" with the officers, according to the British press.

DECEMBER 5 A pigtailed, bearded Marlon Brando, boarding a flight to Miami in Los Angeles, jokes with a stewardess: "Is this the flight to Cuba?" Mistaking him for a hippie terrorist, she has him removed from the craft. After finally being recognized, Brando refuses to reboard the plane.

11 Jane Fonda stars in *Barbarella*, opening at several New York theaters. **17** Steve McQueen is the star of *Bullitt*, the car chase of which is copied in many other films, opening at the Radio City Music Hall. **30** Peter O'Toole attends the premiere at the Lincoln Art Theater of *The Lion in Winter*, in which he and Katharine Hepburn star.

DECEMBER • George Romero's low-budget *Night of the Living Dead*, showing up most often on the lower half of double features, is beginning to acquire a cult following. **11** *Oliver!*, starring Mark Lester and Oliver Reed, opens at Loew's State I.

OCTOBER 2 A small private plane crashes into the administration building at the 20th Century Fox studio, missing Darryl Zanuck's office by thirty feet (he's out). The pilot is killed.

NOVEMBER 26 The U.S. Court of Appeals rules that the sexually explicit Swedish film *I Am Curious (Yellow)* is not obscene.

DECEMBER 10 Louis F. Polk becomes president of MGM.

Births, Deaths, Marriages, and Divorces

DECEMBER 18 Peter Sellers and Britt Ekland divorce. **19** Sammy Davis Jr. and May Britt divorce. **30** Leslie Caron m. producer Michael Laughlin.

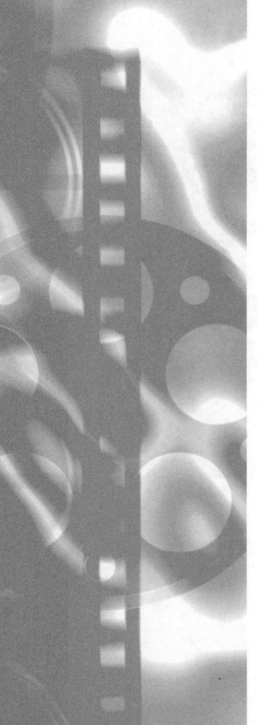

irk Kerkorian takes control of MGM. *Midnight Cowboy* is the first major X-rated film, *The Wild Bunch* explores the aesthetics of violence, *Easy Rider* embodies '60s values, and *Butch Cassidy and the Sundance Kid* is the quintessential buddy film. Judy Garland dies, and Sharon Tate is massacred by the Manson "family." Twenty-four-year-old Michael Douglas, Kirk's son, is making his first movie; Tommy Lee Jones, football player and Al Gore's roomate at Harvard, graduates; and six-year-old Jodie Foster is appearing on TV in *Mayberry, R.F.D.*

- Number of releases: 412
- Number of theaters: 13,500, of which 3,700 are drive-ins
- Average weekly attendance: 17,500,000
- Average ticket price: $1.42
- Box office receipts: $1,099,000,000
- Dustin Hoffman's fee for *Midnight Cowboy*: $250,000
- Pseudonym chosen by Director's Guild for directors who want their real names removed from a film: "Allen Smithee"
- Total number of minutes of music in *Butch Cassidy and the Sundance Kid*, including "Raindrops Keep Falling on My Head": 12

Top stars at the box office, based on a Quigley Publications poll of exhibitors:

1. Paul Newman
2. John Wayne
3. Steve McQueen
4. Dustin Hoffman
5. Clint Eastwood
6. Sidney Poitier
7. Lee Marvin
8. Jack Lemmon
9. Katharine Hepburn
10. Barbra Streisand

Top rental earnings, based on figures reported by *Variety*:

1. *The Love Bug*	$17,000,000
2. *Funny Girl*	16,500,000
3. *Bullitt*	16,400,000
4. *Butch Cassidy and the Sundance Kid*	15,000,000
5. *Romeo and Juliet*	14,500,000

The New York Film Critics Circle Awards
Best Picture: *Z*

The Golden Globe Awards
Best Picture (Drama): *Anne of the Thousand Days*
Best Picture (Musical/Comedy): *The Secret of Santa Vittoria*

The Cannes Film Festival
Palme d'Or: *If...*

The Academy Awards (presented April 7, 1970)
Best Picture: *Midnight Cowboy*
Actor: John Wayne (*True Grit*)
Actress: Maggie Smith (*The Prime of Miss Jean Brodie*)
Supporting Actor: Gig Young (*They Shoot Horses, Don't They?*)
Supporting Actress: Goldie Hawn (*Cactus Flower*)
Director: John Schlesinger (*Midnight Cowboy*)

January	February	March	April	May	June	
	2 Boris Karloff d.		• Hollywood's Carthay Circle Theater closes		**22** Judy Garland found dead of accidental drug overdose	
• Faye Dunaway begins romance with Marcello Mastroianni		**12** Kinney National Service merges with Warner Bros.–Seven Arts			**25** *Midnight Cowboy,* first major X-rated film	

July	August	September	October	November	December	
• Reformed alcoholic Mercedes McCambridge testifies at Senate hearing	**9** Sharon Tate massacred by Manson "family"	**23** *Butch Cassidy and the Sundance Kid*	**21** Kirk Kerkorian takes control of MGM	**14** Francis Ford Coppola incorporates American Zoetrope	**1** Barbra Streisand rejected for Park Avenue apartment	

Personalities

JANUARY • Faye Dunaway has begun a two-year romance with Marcello Mastroianni. **4** Jim Brown is fined $300 for resisting arrest on June 9, 1968 when police responded to reports that the actor had assaulted a woman—a charge since dropped.

FEBRUARY • Production begins on *Patton*. John Wayne wanted the lead role but didn't get it, and Robert Mitchum, Burt Lancaster, and Lee Marvin rejected it before it went to George C. Scott. Three thousand Spanish soldiers portray both German and American soldiers in the movie. **5** Los Angeles declares Charlie Chaplin's studio on La Brea Avenue an historic landmark. **12** Woody Allen opens in his only Broadway stage role, starring in his *Play It Again,*

Movies

FEBRUARY 11 *Sweet Charity* premieres in Boston at the Music Hall and Saxon Theaters. Stars Shirley MacLaine, Chita Rivera, and Ricardo Montalban motorcade to the ceremonies through the snow-clogged city.

MARCH 2 *The Prime of Miss Jean Brodie*, starring Maggie Smith, premieres in the U.S. at the Baronet. **9** British director Lindsay Anderson's *If...*, starring Malcolm McDowell, has its U.S. premiere at the Plaza. **10** *I Am Curious (Yellow)*, a Swedish film

Dustin Hoffman and Jon Voight in *Midnight Cowboy*   *LC*/© *UNITED ARTISTS*

opening in New York, creates a sensation with its nudity and frank depiction of sex.

APRIL 3 *Goodbye Columbus*, opening at the Forum and Loew's Tower East, features Richard Benjamin and Ali McGraw in their first starring roles.

MAY 7 The film *Young Americans*, which won an Oscar for best documentary last

Business and Society

JANUARY 14 The Adult Film Association of America, a trade group for makers of sexually explicit movies, is founded.

FEBRUARY 29 Robert Aldrich's *The Killing of Sister George*, which has a lesbian theme and stars Beryl Reid and Susannah York, is banned in Boston.

MARCH 12 Kinney National Service, headed by Steven J. Ross, merges with Warner Bros.–Seven Arts. **13** The Equal Employment Opportunities Commission warns the movie industry that it must end racial discrimination or face Justice Department lawsuits.

APRIL • Hollywood's Carthay Circle Theater, where many premieres have been held, closes, to be replaced by an office building. **3** Herbert F. Solow becomes head of production at MGM. **9** Clifford Alexander,

head of the Equal Employment Opportunity Commission, resigns when the Nixon administration will not move against film-industry racial discrimination. **10** The American Civil Liberties Union attacks the new rating system, particularly the "X" rating, as an infringement of First Amendment freedoms.

MAY 5 ABC announces that twenty-seven-year-old Barry Diller will head its feature films division. **26** Edgar Bronfman be-

Births, Deaths, Marriages, and Divorces

JANUARY 9 Judy Garland m. Mickey Deans in a Catholic ceremony, (and again, on March 15, in a civil ceremony). **18** Audrey Hepburn m. Dr. Andrea Dotti.

FEBRUARY 2 Boris Karloff d. **5** Thelma Ritter d. **9** George "Gabby" Hayes d.

MARCH 3 Executive Nicholas Schenck d.

APRIL 2 Lana Turner divorces Robert Eaton. **12** Mickey Rooney m. Carolyn Hockett—in Mexico, because his divorce from Margaret Lane will not come through until December.

MAY 4 Dustin Hoffman m. Anne Byrne. **8** Lana Turner m. hypnotist Ronald Dante,

Sam, with Diane Keaton and Tony Roberts. His 1972 film with the same title will be based on this play.

MARCH • Director Sidney Pollack works as a cameraman in the filming of the marathon dance sequence in his *They Shoot Horses, Don't They?* To make his cast, including Jane Fonda and Michael Sarrazin, look and feel genuinely bedraggled, he makes them run around the set before shooting. One of the extras in the audience watching the marathon is famed producer and director Mervyn LeRoy. **26** Motion Picture Academy president Gregory Peck defends the granting of membership to Barbra Streisand while she was making her first movie, *Funny Girl*, even though she had not yet starred in three films or been nominated for an Oscar, requirements for membership. Peck says that her status as a

Broadway star and not politics caused the Academy to use its discretionary judgment. **31** London police say that Peter Sellers talked a man out of jumping off a bridge by talking about his movie career.

APRIL • The stunt person for twenty-four-year-old Michael Douglas, son of Kirk Douglas, in *Hail Hero*, his first film, is Deidre Flynn, daughter of Errol Flynn. **14** This year, the Academy Awards ceremonies have moved from the Santa Monica Civic Auditorium to the Dorothy Chandler Pavilion. Martha Raye receives the Jean Hersholt Humanitarian Award—the first female winner—for entertaining American troops in Vietnam.

MAY 11 MGM lifts its longstanding ban against the televising of clips from Greta Garbo's films. **18** Ali MacGraw tells a

reporter about the character she plays in the recently opened *Goodbye Columbus*: "Only when I discovered there's a little of Brenda in every honest woman, could I even start to play her. You know what I mean: that certain arrogance, a high-handedness that makes you feel good while others have to crawl, the cruel flirtiness, that certain tease, tease, tease, and then stop." **19** Six-year-old Jodie Foster makes her first dramatic appearance, on the TV program *Mayberry, R.F.D.*, which stars her brother, Buddy.

JUNE • Marlon Brando forces the production of Gillo Pontecorvo's *Burn* to move from Colombia to Morocco because, after seven months of location work in South America, Brando can no longer stand the climate. • Tommy Lee Jones, all-Ivy offensive guard, graduates *cum laude* from Harvard,

month, is disqualified when it is learned that it opened in October 1967, and was thus ineligible. This is the first time a film has been disqualified. **25** Dustin Hoffman and Jon Voight star in John Schlesinger's *Midnight Cowboy*, premiering with the "X" rating it received five days ago—the first major, commercial film to be so rated and the only such film to ever win an Oscar—at the Coronet. On the soundtrack Harry Nilsson sings "Everybody's Talking," which becomes a hit.

JUNE 10 *Last Summer*, starring Barbara Hershey, Richard Thomas, and Cathy Burns, premieres at Cinema I. Barbara Hershey

John Wayne in *True Grit*   MSN
© PARAMOUNT PICTURES

says that she feels the spirit of the bird she accidentally killed while making the film and for a few years will change her last name to "Seagull." **11** Premiering at Grauman's Chinese Theater in Hollywood is *True Grit*, starring John Wayne, Kim Darby, and Glen Campbell. **25** Sam Peckinpah's *The Wild Bunch* opens at the Trans-Lux East and West Theaters. Starring William Holden, Robert Ryan, Ernest Borgnine, Edmond O'Brien, Warren Oates, and Ben Johnson, it pushes bloodshed-as-ballet to a new extreme.

JULY 10 Robert Downey's *Putney Swope* opens at the Cinema II. **14** Peter Fonda,

comes chairman of the board at MGM.

JUNE 12 20th Century Fox rebuts Congressional critics who say that the company's *Tora! Tora! Tora!* will favor the Japanese viewpoint on the Pearl Harbor attack.

JULY 18 A *Daily Variety* headline identifies as "PANSIES" those in San Francisco who are picketing the film *The Gay Deceivers* for its homophobia.

AUGUST • Las Vegas hotel magnate Kirk Kerkorian becomes MGM's biggest shareholder, surpassing Edgar Bronfman. **28** Darryl Zanuck is named chairman of the board and CEO of 20th Century Fox, and Richard Zanuck becomes president.

SEPTEMBER 11 Jack Warner severs all connections to Warner Bros. **29** Jerry Lewis announces the formation of the Jerry Lewis Cinema Corporation to market movie houses in which much of the tasks involved in showing the films are automated.

OCTOBER 21 Kirk Kerkorian takes control of MGM and has James T. Aubrey Jr., formerly president of CBS, named the studio's third president in ten months. Drastic cutbacks in feature-film production and diver-

her eighth husband. **16** Goldie Hawn m. Gus Trikonis. **27** Jeffrey Hunter d. **30** Natalie Wood m. Richard Gregson.

JUNE 2 Leo Gorcey d. **8** Robert Taylor d. **12** Connie Stevens divorces Eddie Fisher. **22** Judy Garland dies—of an accidental drug overdose. **27** Glenn Ford and

Kathryn Hayes divorce, as do Burt Lancaster and Norma Anderson.

AUGUST 18 Christian Slater b.

SEPTEMBER 10 Lauren Bacall and Jason Robards Jr. divorce.

OCTOBER • Charles Bronson m. Jill Ireland. **12** Sonja Henie d. **15** Silent-screen star Rod La Rocque d. **21** Loretta Young divorces Thomas Lewis. **24** Ali MacGraw m. producer Robert Evans.

NOVEMBER 13 Julie Andrews m. director Blake Edwards.

Personalities

where he roomed with Al Gore, son of the senator from Tennessee. **11** California Governor Ronald Reagan delivers the eulogy at Robert Taylor's Forest Lawn funeral. **11** Sidney Poitier, Barbra Streisand, and Paul Newman incorporate First Artists Productions to finance and release their films. **17** Lana Turner's husband, Ronald Dante, is arrested for theft on a year-old warrant. **27** Since yesterday, twenty thousand people have filed past the body of Judy Garland at a Manhattan funeral home. She died on June 22.

JULY • Mercedes McCambridge testifies as a reformed alcoholic before the Senate Subcommittee on Alcoholism and Narcotics. **2** A Dublin court fines Peter O'Toole for punching a pub owner who wouldn't serve the actor a drink at 3:30 A.M. **18** Paul Newman and Joanne Woodward take out a half-page ad in the *Los Angeles Times* to ridicule columnist Joyce Haber's report of the breakup of their marriage.

AUGUST • Residents of Braintree, Massachusetts are upset that Otto Preminger is filming Liza Minnelli's nude scenes from *Tell Me That You Love Me, Junie Moon* in a cemetery. **5** Jim Brown is arrested for assaulting his girlfriend and the police officer investigating her complaint. He's also arrested this month for assaulting a driver after their autos collide. **9** A massacre in the Bel-Air home of actress Sharon Tate takes her life and those of four others. Tate, the wife of director Roman Polanski, was eight months pregnant. Charles Manson and his "family" will be convicted of the crime.

SEPTEMBER 18 Henry Fonda, completing filming of *The Cheyenne Social Club*, about a bordello, deplores the smutty pictures now coming out of Hollywood. He says his films are in good taste.

OCTOBER 24 Richard Burton buys a $1.1 million, 69.42-carat diamond for Elizabeth Taylor.

NOVEMBER 12 Saying that everyone should be willing to give up something to stop the Vietnam War, Paul Newman, Dennis Hopper, Jon Voight, and Alan Arkin ask fans to boycott their films on the 14th as a protest against business as usual. Theater owners are not happy with this. **14** Francis Ford Coppola incorporates his American Zoetrope Studio, named for the early nineteenth-century toy that created the illusion of a moving picture.

Movies

Dennis Hopper, and Jack Nicholson (in his breakthrough role) star in *Easy Rider*, a road film that becomes a metaphor for the Sixties, premiering in the U.S. at the Beekman. Nicholson is in the film only because Rip Torn, originally slated for the part of the lawyer, could not agree with director Hopper on the script. Bruce Dern didn't want to do it, so Nicholson, who has been in several low-budget films by Roger Corman and others, got his chance.

AUGUST 27 Haskel Wexler's *Medium Cool*, filmed on Chicago streets during the 1968 Democratic Convention, and starring Robert Foster and Verna Bloom, premieres at Loew's Tower East.

SEPTEMBER 23 *Butch Cassidy and the Sundance Kid*, starring Robert Redford, Paul Newman, and Katherine Ross, with Burt Bacharach's "Raindrops Keep Falling on My Head," premieres at the Roger Sherman Theater near Yale University. The reception is at Morey's, the famed undergraduate pub, where women are admitted for the first time.

OCTOBER 8 *Bob & Carol & Ted & Alice*, starring Robert Culp and Natalie Wood and Elliott Gould and Dyan Cannon, opens at the

Bob & Carol & Ted & Alice (l. to r. Elliot Gould, Natalie Wood, Robert Culp, and Dyan Cannon)
MOMA/© COLUMBIA PICTURES

Business and Society

sification into other businesses, such as the MGM Grand Hotel in Las Vegas, will mark his reign. **29** Stanley R. Jaffe is named to replace Martin S. Davis as head of Paramount.

NOVEMBER 24 Hal Wallis, who has produced independently and released through Paramount since 1944, will be moving to Universal, it is announced.

Births, Deaths, Marriages, and Divorces

DECEMBER • Lana Turner divorces Ronald Dante. **22** Director Josef von Sternberg d.

Also this year: • Cher is said to have married Sonny Bono this year when she became pregnant, although they maintain that they had married on October 2, 1964. • Glenn Close m. rock musician Cabot Wade. • Christopher Walken m. Georgianne Thon. • Woody Allen and Louise Lasser, Claire Bloom and Rod Steiger, Arlene Dahl and Alexis Lichine, and Victor Mature and Joy Urwick divorce.

DECEMBER 1 Barbra Streisand says that her application to buy a Park Avenue cooperative apartment was turned down because the residents feared the hullabaloo that a celebrity might bring. That's "ironic," she says, because in Hollywood she's criticized for not giving parties or even going to premieres. **16** Barbra Streisand, described by the *New York Times* as dressed like "an elegant Nefertiti," has to be extricated from her limousine by the police when she arrives at the Rivoli for the premiere of *Hello Dolly*, in which she stars. She has been besieged and imprisoned in the car by overzealous fans.

Paul Newman and Robert Redford star in *Butch Cassidy and the Sundance Kid*, the quintessential buddy film, directed by George Roy Hill, from a screenplay by William Goldman. It premieres September 23, 1969, at the Roger Sherman Theater near Yale University. *LC/© 20TH CENTURY FOX*

Cinema 1. "Consider the possibilities," say the ads. **22** Liza Minnelli stars in director Alan Pakula's first film, *The Sterile Cuckoo*, premiering at the Forum and Loew's Tower East.

DECEMBER 10 Jane Fonda, Michael Sarrazin, and Gig Young star in Sidney Pollack's *They Shoot Horses, Don't They?*, premiering at the Fine Arts. **15** *Cactus Flower*, Goldie Hawn's first major film, for which she will win an Oscar, premieres at the Paris and Astor Theaters. Walter Matthau and Ingrid Bergman are also in it. **18** *Anne of the Thousand Days*, starring Richard Burton and Genevieve Bujold, premieres at the Beverly Theater in Beverly Hills.

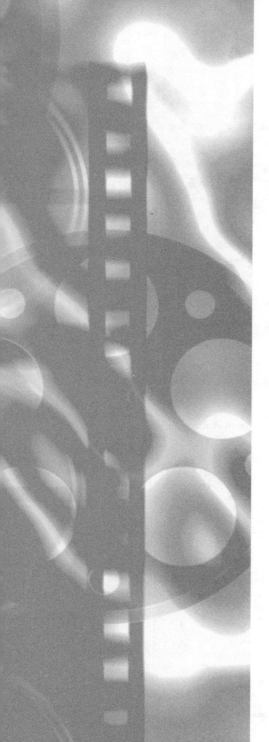

*T*he movie rating system is modified. Unemployment in Hollywood is averaging about fifty percent and in some IATSE locals is as high as seventy percent. Nevertheless, the industry begins to focus on improving minority employment, where it has been remiss. MGM auctions its props and costumes, sells part of its Culver City lot, and moves its executive offices from New York to Hollywood. Arnold Schwarzenegger makes his feature film debut, as "Arnold Strong," in *Hercules Goes Bananas*. Julie Andrews flops in *Darling Lili* and sees the bottom almost drop out of her flourishing career.

- Number of releases: 367
- TV owners with color sets: 39%
- Number of theaters: 13,750, of which 3,750 are drive-ins
- Average weekly attendance: 17,700,000
- Average ticket price: $1.55
- Box office receipts: $1,162,000,000

Top billing in Hollywood films by gender, according to *The Guinness Book of Movie Facts and Feats*:
men: 79%
women: 25%

Top stars at the box office, based on a Quigley Publications poll of exhibitors:

1. Paul Newman
2. Clint Eastwood
3. Steve McQueen
4. John Wayne
5. Elliot Gould
6. Dustin Hoffman
7. Lee Marvin
8. Jack Lemmon
9. Barbra Streisand
10. Walter Matthau

Top rental earnings, based on figures reported by *Variety*:

1.	*Airport*	$37,650,000
2.	*M*A*S*H*	22,000,000
3.	*Patton*	21,000,000
4.	*Bob & Carol & Ted & Alice*	13,900,000
5.	*Woodstock*	13,500,000

The New York Film Critics Circle Awards
Best Picture: *Five Easy Pieces*

The Golden Globe Awards
Best Picture (Drama): *Love Story*
Best Picture (Musical/Comedy): *M*A*S*H*

The Cannes Film Festival
Palme d'Or: *M*A*S*H*

The Academy Awards (presented April 15, 1971)
Best Picture: *Patton*
Actor: George C. Scott (*Patton*)
Actress: Glenda Jackson (*Women in Love*)
Supporting Actor: John Mills (*Ryan's Daughter*)
Supporting Actress: Helen Hayes (*Airport*)
Director: Franklin J. Schaffner (*Patton*)

January	February	March	April	May	June	
		26 Woodstock documentary		**3–20** MGM auctions props and costumes		
29 Barbra Streisand dating Prime Minister Trudeau	**4** *Patton*		**5** Warren Beatty fund-raising for George McGovern		**14** Sir Laurence Olivier made Lord Olivier	

July	August	September	October	November	December	
			23 Walt Disney World opens in Orlando		**16** *Love Story*	
1 Jean Seberg and Romain Gary divorce	**1** Frances Farmer d.	**11** Mia Farrow m. André Prévin		**5** Writers Guild drops 1954 non-communist requirement		

Personalities

JANUARY • Peter Bogdanovich, in a Van Nuys supermarket, spots Cybill Shepherd on the cover of *Glamour,* and now has his female lead for *The Last Picture Show.* • Bette Midler is performing on weekends, for $50 a night, at New York City's Continental Baths—a gay bath house—where Barry Manilow is the house pianist. **12** Sylvester Stallone signs to appear in a soft-core porno movie, tentatively called *The Party,* to be filmed in the next few days. **29** Barbra Streisand, who is dating Canadian Prime Minister Trudeau, watches him from the gallery of Parliament. An opposition member says he would like to ask Trudeau a question "if he can take his eyes and mind off the visitors gallery long enough to answer."

FEBRUARY 9 *Time* quotes MGM head James Aubrey on last year's *The Gypsy Moths*: "We can't make a picture with Burt Lancaster and Deborah Kerr groping with each other anymore. That's obscene. It's like watching a couple of grandparents pawing with each other."

MARCH 6 The explosion of a radical bomb factory in Greenwich Village severely damages the home of Dustin Hoffman next door. **15** Liza Minnelli is quoted in a New York *Daily News* interview: "If I read one more article where I'm described as being perky, I'll puke!" **20** Steve McQueen, his foot in a cast from a motorcycle mishap, is part of a team that takes first place in its class at the auto-racing Grand Prix at Sebring, Florida. **30** Lauren Bacall opens on Broadway in *Applause,* a musical based on the film, *All About Eve.*

APRIL 7 On Oscar night, the audience at the Dorothy Chandler Pavilion finds very amusing the casting of Raquel Welch as presenter of the Academy Award for Special Visual Effects. **15** Warren Beatty, in the midst of a sabbatical from films to work for George McGovern, stages a fund-raising concert for him in Inglewood, California, at which Barbra Streisand sings and Gene Hackman, Sally Kellerman, Jack Nicholson, and Julie Christie work as ushers.

MAY • Jill St. John begins to date Henry Kissinger. **3-20** MGM auctions off its props and costumes. Judy Garland's magic red slippers from *The Wizard of Oz* will bring $15,000, as will the boat from the 1951 musical, *Show Boat,* bought by Texas oil man Lamar Hunt.

Movies

JANUARY 25 Robert Altman's *M*A*S*H,* starring Donald Sutherland, Elliott Gould, and Sally Kellerman premieres at the Baronet. On March 16, the U.S. Army and Air Force will ban its showing at base theaters because it "reflects unfavorably" on the military.

FEBRUARY 4 *Patton* premieres at the Criterion. Attending are George C. Scott, Karl Malden, and General Omar Bradley (a consultant on the production), who Malden plays in the film. President Nixon, it is reported, watches it twice before sending troops into Cambodia in April.

MARCH 5 *Airport,* with an all-star cast including Burt Lancaster, George Kennedy, Dean Martin, and Helen Hayes, premieres at the Radio City Music Hall. **25** Ken Russell's *Women in Love,* starring Alan Bates, Oliver Reed, and Glenda Jackson, opens at the Fine Arts. **26** *Woodstock,* the documentary about last year's rock festival, premieres at the Trans-Lux East.

JUNE 10 Godfrey Cambridge and Raymond St. Jacques star in *Cotton Comes to Harlem,* opening at the DeMille and 86th St. East.

23 Thousands crowd Times Square outside the Criterion Theater to see Mae West arrive for the premiere of *Myra Breckenridge.* Raquel Welch, feuding with West, is also there. One of the muscular young men in the film is twenty-five-year-old Tom Selleck. *Time* finds the movie "about as funny as a child molester."

JULY 15 Peter Boyle is *Joe,* a resentful, right-wing hard-hat, premiering at the New Embassy Theater. Susan Sarandon debuts in this film.

SEPTEMBER 11 Joan Crawford ends her career with a horror film, *Trog,* premiering at

Business and Society

JANUARY 27 The movie rating system is modified. M is replaced by PG, suggesting parental guidance although admitting all ages. R now limits admission to those at least seventeen, rather than sixteen years old, unless accompanied by a parent or guardian. And X-rated films will be limited to those at least seventeen or eighteen rather than sixteen, depending on local laws.

MARCH 25 The first Jerry Lewis Cinema opens in a New Jersey mall. **31** Hollywood studios work out an equal-employment agreement with the Justice Department banning discrimination, and agree to take steps to increase minority employment.

APRIL • MGM moves its executive offices from New York to Hollywood. **28** The movie and TV industry announce the forming of a job pool for minority applicants.

JUNE 25 Warners announces that it will move its executive offices to Burbank.

JULY 28 Stanley Jaffe becomes president of Paramount Pictures.

AUGUST 26 The Screen Actors Guild agrees to work with an industry group called Justice for Chicanos to improve the image of Mexican-Americans in films.

SEPTEMBER 30 MGM announces the sale

Births, Deaths, Marriages, and Divorces

FEBRUARY 14 Jason Robards Jr. m. Lois O'Connor. **17** Composer Alfred Newman d. **24** Conrad Nagel d.

APRIL 29 Uma Thurman, whose mother was previously married to Timothy Leary, b. **30** The body of Inger Stevens, a suicide from a drug overdose, is discovered.

MAY 11 Sammy Davis Jr. m. Altovise Gore.

JULY • Rory Calhoun and Lita Baron are divorced. **1** Jean Seberg and Romain Gary are divorced.

Woody Allen   *MSN*

JUNE 14   Sir Laurence Olivier becomes Lord Olivier, the first actor to enter the House of Lords.   **16**   Alfred E. Knopf, publisher, buys actor Tom Tyron's first novel, *The Other.*

JULY 22   *Variety* reports Dennis Hopper's anger at *Life* magazine's June 19 cover story depicting him as a drug user. Hopper says "the only thing I shoot up with is Vitamin B-12, and my only habit-forming vice is cigarets [sic]."   **30**   Paul Newman breaks his ankle in a motorcycle spill during a rehearsal for *Sometimes a Great Notion.*

AUGUST 19   *Daily Variety* reports that Frank Sinatra will star in *Dirty Harry.*

SEPTEMBER 6   In a confrontation with Frank Sinatra's entourage, the casino manager at Caesars Palace is arrested for pulling a gun to back up his order to cut off Sinatra's credit at the high-stakes baccarat table. But the sheriff who makes the arrest also says of Sinatra: "He's through picking on little people in this town."   **30**   Otto Preminger is found not guilty of desecrating a Massachusetts cemetery in filming a nude scene with Liza Minnelli for *Tell Me That You Love Me, Junie Moon.*

OCTOBER 14   Woody Allen makes his formal, professional debut as a jazz clarinet player at Barney Googles in New York. Next year he will settle in for a long run at Michael's Pub.

NOVEMBER 3   Jane Fonda is arrested at the Cleveland airport for smuggling drugs—a substance later found to be vitamins. She also kicks a customs agent and is jailed for ten hours.

the Oriental Theater in Chicago.   **12**   *Five Easy Pieces*, starring Jack Nicholson, Karen Black, Sally Struthers, and Susan Anspach, has its theatrical premiere at the Coronet after opening at the New York Film Festival yesterday. Nicholson's off-screen affair with Anspach produces a baby boy.   **23**   *Tora! Tora! Tora!*, showing Pearl Harbor from both Japanese and American points of view, premieres in New York, Los Angeles, Honolulu, and Tokyo. It stars Martin Balsam, Jason Robards, E.G. Marshall, and Toshio Masuda.

NOVEMBER 9   David Lean's *Ryan's Daughter*, starring Robert Mitchum, Trevor

of one-third of its Culver City lot to a company that will build housing.

NOVEMBER 5   The Writers Guild drops its 1954 requirement that members not be communists.

DECEMBER 9   Fifty women visit the American Film Institute to protest the small number of grants and fellowships awarded to women by AFI—only six out of 150 so far.   **29**   20th Century Fox president

AUGUST 7   Albert Finney m. actress Anouk Aimée.   **1**   Frances Farmer d.   **24**   Peter Sellers m. Miranda Quarry.

SEPTEMBER 11   Mia Farrow m. André Prévin.

Ryan O'Neal and Ali Mcgraw in *Love Story*   *LC/ © PARAMOUNT PICTURES*

Personalities

DECEMBER 21 Elvis Presley meets President Nixon, who will appoint him an honorary agent in the war against drugs.

Movies

Howard, and Sarah Miles, premieres at the Ziegfeld. **10** Carl Reiner's *Where's Poppa?*, starring George Segal and Ruth Gordon, premieres at the Coronet.

DECEMBER 5 Robert Altman's *Brewster McCloud* premieres in the Houston Astrodome, where much of it was filmed. The audience of 23,900 is probably the biggest ever for the showing of a film. Stars Bud Cort, Sally Kellerman, Margaret Hamilton, and Michael Murphy attend. **14** Arthur Penn's *Little Big Man*, starring Dustin Hoffman, Faye Dunaway, and Chief Dan George, premieres at the Sutton Theater. **16** *Love Story*—"Love means never having to say you're sorry"— starring Ali MacGraw and Ryan O'Neal, premieres at Loew's State I. MacGraw attends with her husband, Paramount executive Robert Evans. The film, for which McGraw made $22,000, will gross $114 million. Tommy Lee Jones, in his screen debut, plays O'Neal's Harvard roommate (in reality, Jones was Al Gore's Harvard roommate).

Business and Society

Richard D. Zanuck and executive David Brown are forced to resign.

Births, Deaths, Marriages, and Divorces

OCTOBER 19 Lee Marvin m. Pamela Feely. **31** Dennis Hopper m. Michelle Phillips. It lasts eight days.

DECEMBER 4 George Sanders m. Magda Gabor, sister of his second wife, Zsa Zsa Gabor. It lasts six weeks. **18** Lee Remick m. British director William Gowens.

19 Sally Kellerman m. Richard Edelstein.

Also this year: • Billy Crystal m. Janice Goldfinger. • Jessica Lange m. Paco Grande. • Tom Selleck m. Jacquelyn Ray. • Joan Collins and Anthony Newley divorce.

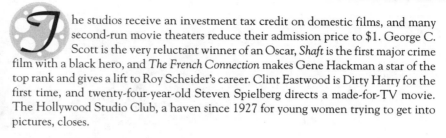

*T*he studios receive an investment tax credit on domestic films, and many second-run movie theaters reduce their admission price to $1. George C. Scott is the very reluctant winner of an Oscar, *Shaft* is the first major crime film with a black hero, and *The French Connection* makes Gene Hackman a star of the top rank and gives a lift to Roy Scheider's career. Clint Eastwood is Dirty Harry for the first time, and twenty-four-year-old Steven Spielberg directs a made-for-TV movie. The Hollywood Studio Club, a haven since 1927 for young women trying to get into pictures, closes.

- Number of releases: 432
- Total screens: 14,000, of which 3,720 are in drive-ins
- Average weekly attendance: 15,800,000
- Average ticket price: $1.65
- Box office receipts: $1,170,000,000
- Sean Connery's fee for *Diamonds Are Forever*: $1,200,000
- Number of films in which Clint Eastwood will play Harry Callahan, beginning this year with *Dirty Harry*: 5
- Age of Gene Hackman when he becomes a star in *The French Connection*: 40
- Production cost of *Deep Throat*: $25,000
- *Deep Throat* gross after two years: $4,600,000

Top stars at the box office, based on a Quigley publications poll of exhibitors:

1. John Wayne
2. Clint Eastwood
3. Paul Newman
4. Steve McQueen
5. George C. Scott
6. Dustin Hoffman
7. Walter Matthau
8. Ali McGraw
9. Sean Connery
10. Lee Marvin

Top rental earnings, based on figures reported by *Variety*:

1. *Love Story* $50,000,000
2. *Little Big Man*   15,000,000
3. *Summer of '42*   14,000,000
4. *Ryan's Daughter*   13,400,000
5. *The Owl and the Pussycat*   11,500,000

The New York Film Critics Circle Awards
Best Picture: *A Clockwork Orange*

The Golden Globe Awards
Best Picture (Drama): *The French Connection*
Best Picture (Musical/Comedy): *Fiddler on the Roof*

The Cannes Film Festival
Palme d'Or: *The Go-Between*

The Academy Awards (presented April 10, 1972)
Best Picture: *The French Connection*
Actor: Gene Hackman (*The French Connection*)
Actress: Jane Fonda (*Klute*)
Supporting Actor: Ben Johnson (*The Last Picture Show*)
Supporting Actress: Cloris Leachman (*The Last Picture Show*)
Director: William Friedkin (*The French Connection*)

January	February	March	April	May	June	
	20 Rex Harrison divorces Rachel Roberts			**31** Audie Murphy's body discovered in plane wreckage		
	27 Marlon Brando to star in *The Godfather*	**8** Harold Lloyd d.	**1** Paramount head Stanley R. Jaffe announces resignation		**18** Jean Peters divorced from Howard Hughes	

July	August	September	October	November	December	
2 *Shaft*			**3** *The Last Picture Show*		**22** *Dirty Harry*	
	23 River Phoenix b.	Nixon "Enemies List" includes Gregory Peck and Steve McQueen		**3** Warners to become major force in cable TV		

Personalities

JANUARY 11 Ali MacGraw, star of *Love Story*, is on the cover of *Time*, illustrating the article: "The Return to Romance." **21** Susan Hayward is rescued from a fire in her Ft. Lauderdale apartment, which started when she smoked and then passed out after drinking. **27** Paramount announces that Marlon Brando will play Don Vito Corleone in *The Godfather*. **29** "He has gorgeous blond hair that falls almost to his shoulders and I call him my hippie-dippie," says Brenda Vaccaro—quoted today in Earl Wilson's syndicated column—of her twenty-six-year-old live-in lover, Michael Douglas.

FEBRUARY • Steve McQueen joins Barbra Streisand, Paul Newman, and Sidney

Movies

MARCH 21 *The Andromeda Strain*, starring Arthur Hill and opening today at Cinema I, is the first film to feature computerized animation and is also the first filming of a Michael Crichton novel.

APRIL 18 *Summer of '42*, starring Jennifer O'Neill, premieres at the Fine Arts. **23** Melvin Van Peebles's *Sweet Sweetback's Baadasssss Song*, in which he stars, opens at three New York theaters, causing controversy for its tell-it-like-it-is black militancy.

Marlon Brando in *The Godfather*   *MSN/* © *PARAMOUNT PICTURES*

Business and Society

JANUARY 26 MGM president James T. Aubrey says that merger talks between his studio and 20th Century Fox (which Darryl Zanuck has denied ever took place) have been "discontinued." MGM also announces that Herbert Solow is out as its production head, to be replaced by a committee.

MARCH 1 Warners announces that Richard

D. Zanuck and David Brown are joining the company as executives. **19** The Italian-American Civil Rights League announces that the producers of *The Godfather* have agreed not to use the words "Mafia" or "Cosa Nostra" in the film.

APRIL 1 Stanley R. Jaffe announces that he will resign as head of Paramount, effective August 1, to return to independent producing. **5** President Nixon tells movie executives, who have described the industry

in California as "close to collapse," that they won't get the tax relief they have requested to boost U.S. production.

MAY 10 Frank Yablans becomes president of Paramount.

AUGUST 27 California Governor Ronald Reagan writes to President Nixon, urging him to grant tax relief to California's beleaguered film industry.

Births, Deaths, Marriages, and Divorces

JANUARY 20 Bronco Billy Anderson d.

FEBRUARY 20 Rex Harrison divorces Rachel Roberts.

MARCH 8 Harold Lloyd d. **16** Bebe Daniels d.

MAY 30 Jennifer Jones m. Norton Simon. **31** Audie Murphy's body is discovered in the wreckage of a plane crash.

JUNE 11 Hayley Mills m. director Roy Boulting. **18** Jean Peters is divorced from Howard Hughes.

JULY 6 Barbra Streisand and Elliott Gould divorce. **23** Van Heflin d.

AUGUST 13 James Mason m. Clarissa Kaye. **16** Paul Lukas d. **23** River

Poitier in First Artists. **23** The Hollywood YWCA announces the closing of the Hollywood Studio Club, built in 1927 to house young women trying to make it in the movies.

MARCH 1 At a Los Angeles auction of 20th Century Fox memorabilia, Debbie Reynolds bids unsuccessfully for Elizabeth Taylor's *Cleopatra* throne. **10** Otto Preminger adopts Erik Kirkland, his son by his 1944 affair with stripper Gypsy Rose Lee. Lee, who died last year, wanted Preminger's paternity kept secret. **16** Al Pacino, who on February 23 signed with MGM to appear in *The Gang That Couldn't Shoot Straight*, settles out of court Metro's suit against him for reneging on the deal so that he can play Michael Corleone in *The Godfather*. **24** Filming $ in Germany, Warren Beatty trips and falls onto a railroad track, manag-

ing to scramble away just before a train bears down on him. He suffers torn ligaments. **27** President Nixon visits the Beverly Hills home of the ailing Samuel Goldwyn to award him the Medal of Freedom. **29** Filming begins on Francis Ford Coppola's *The Godfather*.

APRIL 15 "Oh my God!" gasps Goldie Hawn on Oscar night as she opens the envelope containing the name of the winner for Best Actor. It *is* George C. Scott, for *Patton*, who in February said he wouldn't want it if he got it. The awards ceremony is at the Dorothy Chandler Pavillion.

JUNE 23 Debbie Reynolds's fourteen-year-old daughter, Carrie Fisher, makes her show business debut in her mother's act at the Nugget in Sparks, Nevada.

JULY 6 Barbra Streisand and Elliott Gould are the first celebrity couple to take advantage of the Dominican Republic's new quickie divorce law. Gould is in the Dominican Republic with Jennifer Bogart, who is pregnant with his child. **23** *Life* magazine's cover story says that "The world's favorite movie star is—no kidding—Clint Eastwood."

AUGUST 6 Burt Lancaster, arrested in Malibu on suspicion of drunken driving, refuses to take a sobriety test. **25** Elizabeth Taylor becomes a grandmother for the first time.

SEPTEMBER • Nixon aide Charles Colson sends to the president's lawyer, John Dean, a list of celebrities to be considered "enemies" of the administration. It includes: Jane Fonda, Steve McQueen,

JUNE 23 *Klute*, starring Jane Fonda and Donald Sutherland, premieres at the Cinerama and Murray Hill theaters. **24** Robert Altman's *McCabe and Mrs. Miller*, starring Warren Beatty and Julie Christie, premieres at the Criterion and Loew's Cine. **30** Mike Nichols's *Carnal Knowledge*, starring Jack Nicholson, Art Garfunkel, Ann-Margret, and Candice Bergen, premieres at the Cinema 1 and the National Theater in Westwood. In Georgia it will be declared obscene and banned.

JULY 2 Gordon Parks's *Shaft*, starring Richard Roundtree, a breakthrough commercial crime film with a black hero, opens at the

DeMille and the 72nd St. Playhouse. Isaac Hayes's recording of the title song is a hit. **13** Al Pacino and Kitty Winn star in *The Panic in Needle Park*, opening at Loew's Tower East. **28** *Billy Jack*, starring Tom Laughlin, a film he made in 1968, opens in New York at Loew's State I and Loew's Cine to tepid reviews. But the box-office strength it shows in the Midwest and West will lead to its re-release in 1973.

OCTOBER 3 Peter Bogdanovich's *The Last Picture Show*, starring Ben Johnson, Ellen Burstyn, Jeff Bridges, Cloris Leachman, Cybill Shepherd, and Timothy Bottoms, opens at the Cinema 1. On the set, Shep-

herd had a romance with Bridges and then with Bogdanovich, with whom she will stay for the next seven years. **7** Gene Hackman, Roy Scheider, and Fernando Rey star in, and William Friedkin directs, *The French Connection*, premiering at Loew's State II and Loew's Orpheum.

NOVEMBER 3 *Fiddler on the Roof*, starring Chaim Topol, premieres at the Rivoli. And Clint Eastwood debuts as a director and stars in *Play Misty for Me*, opening at Universal Showcase Theaters. **7** The first Los Angeles International Film exposition opens with the West Coast premiere of *The Last Picture Show* at Grauman's Chinese

SEPTEMBER 16 Gordon Stulberg is announced as the new president of 20th Century Fox.

OCTOBER 23 Walt Disney World opens in Orlando.

NOVEMBER 3 Steve Ross, president of Kinney Services, Warner's parent company, says that the company will become a major force in cable TV.

DECEMBER 10 President Nixon signs a tax bill granting Hollywood a seven-percent investment tax credit on domestic films, meant to encourage filming in the U.S. rather than abroad. **14** Los Angeles, facing competition from New York and other shooting locations, makes it easier for companies to get permits to film on the city's streets.

Phoenix b. **26** Rex Harrison m. Elizabeth Harris, ex-wife of Richard Harris. **27** Jean Peters m. producer Stanley Hough.

SEPTEMBER 10 The body of Pier Angeli, who died from an overdose of sleeping pills, is discovered. **17** The body of Bella

Darvi, a suicide, is discovered. **23** Yul Brynner m. Jacqueline De Croisset.

OCTOBER 29 Winona Ryder (Winona Horowitz) b.

NOVEMBER • Donald Sutherland and Shirley Douglas divorce.

Also this year: • Edward James Olmos m. Kaija Keel, daughter of Howard Keel. • Ellen and Neil Burstyn, Debra Paget and Ling Chieh Kung, and Natalie Wood and Richard Gregson divorce.

Personalities

Gregory Peck, Barbra Streisand, and Tony Randall. **14** Burt Reynolds begins to date Dinah Shore. **15** Angela Lansbury's arm is broken when she is hit by a truck in Cork, Ireland.

OCTOBER 3 "Nightclub Debut for Bette Midler" is the *New York Times* headlines over jazz columnist John Wilson's review of her act at Downstairs at the Upstairs (actually, she has already appeared at a few clubs). Wilson admires her talent but writes, "Does she know what to do with it or doesn't she?" The audience, which "had no doubts," loved her, as did Atlantic Records head Ahmet Ertegun, who hears her, signs her, and will release her first album next November: "The Divine Miss M."

NOVEMBER • A Los Angeles judge fines Hedy Lamarr $15,000 in damages for falsely accusing a man of raping her in 1967. • Donald Sutherland and Jane Fonda bring their FTA ("Free" The Army) antiwar show to areas near U.S. military bases in Southeast Asia. **13** The ABC Saturday night made-for-TV movie is *Duel*, starring Dennis Weaver. Its director is twenty-four-year-old Steven Spielberg, and this is his first feature-length movie.

DECEMBER • Robert Altman, Robert Mitchum, and Blake Edwards accuse MGM of mishandling their films.

Clint Eastwood in *Dirty Harry*   *LC*
© *WARNER BROTHERS*

Movies

Theater. Gregory Peck, Ryan O'Neal, Groucho Marx, and Andy Warhol are among those attending.

DECEMBER 14 George C. Scott stars in Paddy Chayefsky's dark comedy, *The Hospital*, premiering at the Sutton. **15** *$*, starring Warren Beatty and Goldie Hawn, opens at three New York theaters. **17** Sean Connery is James Bond again in *Diamonds Are Forever*, opening at showcase theaters. **19** Stanley Kubrick's X-rated *A Clockwork Orange*, starring Malcolm McDowell, premieres in New York, Toronto, San Francisco, and Hollywood. **22** Clint Eastwood is *Dirty Harry*, opening at Loew's State 2 and Loew's Orpheum.

Business and Society

Births, Deaths, Marriages, and Divorces

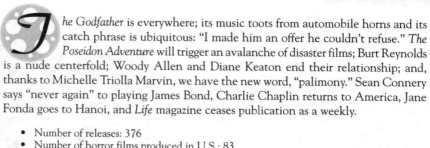

*T*he Godfather is everywhere; its music toots from automobile horns and its catch phrase is ubiquitous: "I made him an offer he couldn't refuse." *The Poseidon Adventure* will trigger an avalanche of disaster films; Burt Reynolds is a nude centerfold; Woody Allen and Diane Keaton end their relationship; and, thanks to Michelle Triolla Marvin, we have the new word, "palimony." Sean Connery says "never again" to playing James Bond, Charlie Chaplin returns to America, Jane Fonda goes to Hanoi, and *Life* magazine ceases publication as a weekly.

- Number of releases: 376
- Number of horror films produced in U.S.: 83
- TV owners with color sets: 53%
- Number of screens: 14,400, of which 3,700 are in drive-ins
- Average weekly attendance: 18,000,000
- Average ticket price: $1.70
- Box office receipts: $1,644,000,000
- Average production cost per film: 1,890,000
- Ship used to film *The Poseidon Adventure*: the *Queen Mary*
- U. S. popcorn crop this year: 519.7 million pounds

Top stars at the box office, based on a Quigley Publications poll of exhibitors:

1. Clint Eastwood
2. George C. Scott
3. Gene Hackman
4. John Wayne
5. Barbra Streisand
6. Marlon Brando
7. Paul Newman
8. Steve McQueen
9. Dustin Hoffman
10. Goldie Hawn

Top rental earnings, based on figures reported in *Variety*:

1. *The Godfather* — $81,500,000
2. *Fiddler on the Roof* — 25,100,000
3. *Diamonds Are Forever* — 21,000,000
4. *What's Up, Doc?* — 17,000,000
5. *Dirty Harry* — 16,000,000

The New York Film Critics Circle Awards
Best Picture: *Cries and Whispers*

The Golden Globe Awards
Best Picture (Drama): *The Godfather*
Best Picture (Musical/Comedy): *Cabaret*

The Cannes Film Festival
Palme d'Or: *The Mattei Affair* and *The Working Class Goes to Paradise*

The Academy Awards (presented March 27, 1973)
Best Picture: *The Godfather*
Actor: Marlon Brando (*The Godfather*)
Actress: Liza Minnelli (*Cabaret*)
Supporting Actor: Joel Grey (*Cabaret*)
Supporting Actress: Eileen Heckart (*Butterflies Are Free*)
Director: Bob Fosse (*Cabaret*)

January	February	March	April	May	June
1 Maurice Chevalier d.	**13** *Cabaret*	**15** *The Godfather*	• Burt Reynolds *Cosmopolitan*'s nude centerfold	• Desi Arnaz Jr. announces engagement to Liza Minnelli	**28** Judge orders Elliott Gould to pay medical expenses of photographer he hit

July	August	September	October	November	December
8 Jane Fonda arrives in Hanoi	• Shirley MacLaine is a delegate to the Democratic Convention	**10** Ann-Margret hurt in fall at Sahara Tahoe Hotel	**18** *Lady Sings the Blues*	**8** HBO's first movie is *Sometimes a Great Notion*	**29** *Life* ends publication as a weekly

Personalities

• A U.S. Department of Transportation TV ad features a man with white hair, saying: "I'm Dana Andrews, and I'm an alcoholic. I don't drink anymore, but I used to—all the time."

FEBRUARY 11 The Hollywood Chamber of Commerce votes to add a star for Charlie Chaplin to the Hollywood Walk of Fame. He has been kept out because of his radical politics. **14** Keefe Brasselle, 50s star most notable for *The Eddie Cantor Story*, is fined and given a three-year suspended sentence for shooting a man whom the actor thought was flirting with his wife in a bar last July 10. **14** Filming begins on *The Getaway*, during which one of Hollywood's hottest romances, between Steve McQueen

Movies

JANUARY 19 Sam Peckinpah's *Straw Dogs*, starring Dustin Hoffman and Susan George, opens at Loew's Tower East and Loew's State. Its violence causes considerable controversy.

FEBRUARY 13 Bob Fosse's *Cabaret*, starring Liza Minnelli, Michael York, and Joel Grey, premieres at the Ziegfeld.

MARCH 9 *What's Up, Doc?*, directed by Peter Bogdanovich and starring Barbra Streisand, Ryan O'Neal, and Madeline Kahn, premieres at the Radio City Music

Liza Minnelli in *Cabaret*   LC/© ALLIED ARTISTS

Business and Society

MARCH 22 Jay Silverheels ("Tonto" in *The Lone Ranger*) attacks the screen treatment of American Indians in a *Hollywood Reporter* interview.

JULY 20 Steven J. Ross becomes chairman of the board and CEO of Warner Communications.

AUGUST 8 Richard Zanuck and David Brown, who left Warners last month, begin producing films for Universal. **21** Columbia moves its executive offices from its Gower St. studio to the Burbank Studio it will share with Warner Bros. **24** In order to achieve an R rather than the X rating it has been given, director Stanley Kubrick withdraws *A Clockwork Orange* from release to make the necessary cuts. In many parts of the country, theaters will not show any film rated X and newspapers will not run ads for them.

Jay Silverheels as "Tonto"   LC

Births, Deaths, Marriages, and Divorces

JANUARY 1 Maurice Chevalier d.

FEBRUARY • George Peppard and Elizabeth Ashley divorce. **3** George C. Scott and Colleen Dewhurst divorce a second time.

16 Rhonda Fleming divorces Hall Bartlett.

MARCH 14 Steve McQueen and Neile Adams divorce. **19** Jean Seberg m. di-

and Ali MacGraw, is kindled. **16** Raquel Welch breaks her wrist while rehearsing for *Kansas City Bomber*, a picture about the roller derby, forcing a two-month delay in the start of filming. **22** Michelle Triola Marvin sues Lee Marvin for half the property they acquired while living together for six years. The lawsuit will introduce a new word into the language: "palimony." **27** On Elizabeth Taylor's fortieth birthday, celebrated in Budapest, Richard Burton gives her a yellow diamond once owned by the builder of the Taj Mahal. Ringo Starr and Princess Grace of Monaco attend her birthday dinner.

APRIL • Burt Reynolds is the nude centerfold in *Cosmopolitan*. **2** Charlie Chaplin is in the U.S. for the first time since the blacklist to be honored at Lincoln Center. **10** Charlie Chaplin's star in the Holly-

wood Walk of Fame is unveiled. In the week that it's been in place, it has already been defaced and someone tried to steal it. **10** The Academy Awards ceremonies are held at the Dorothy Chandler Pavilion, where George C. Scott, Oscar nominee for Best Actor for his role in *The Hospital*, does not get to turn down an award this year. **23** The *QE2* docks in Southampton, carrying the formerly married Natalie Wood and Robert Wagner, whose accidental meeting on board has relit the flame between them.

MAY • Desi Arnaz Jr. announces his engagement to Liza Minnelli. **8** Christian Brando, thirteen-year-old son of Anna Kashfi and Marlon Brando, returns to his father's custody following his mother's arrest for drunkenness and her alleged "kidnapping" of him to Mexico.

28 Nine-year-old Ally Sheedy, modeling children's clothing with her sister, appears on the cover of *Parade*, the Sunday supplement.

JUNE 23 Ed Begley Jr., standing outside a Los Angeles nightclub wearing a cop costume that is part of his club act, is arrested for "impersonating an officer." **28** A Los Angeles judge orders Elliott Gould to pay $6,000 in medical expenses to the photographer that the actor manhandled in 1968 when he tried to snap Gould and his then-wife Barbra Streisand leaving a theater.

JULY • Sean Connery is taking a "never again" position on playing James Bond. Candidates rumored for the next Bond film, tentatively called *Live and Let Live*, are Burt Reynolds, Paul Newman, and Roger Moore. **8** Jane Fonda arrives in Hanoi on a So-

Hall. **15** Francis Ford Coppola's *The Godfather*, starring Marlon Brando, Al Pacino, Diane Keaton, James Caan, and Robert Duvall, premieres at Loew's State I and four other theaters. The *New York Times* calls it "one of the most brutal and moving chronicles of American life ever designed within the limits of popular entertainment." It will gross a record $465,000 in the first week, with merchants near the theaters complaining that the long lines are blocking access to their stores.

APRIL 28 Ralph Bakshi's *Fritz the Cat*, advertised as "X-rated and animated,"—it's the first X-rated cartoon—opens at the Fine

Arts and United Artists East.

JUNE 21 Alfred Hitchcock's *Frenzy*, starring Jon Finch and Barry Foster, opens at New York area theaters. **29** Robert Redford stars in *The Candidate*, premiering at the Sutton.

JULY 26 John Huston's *Fat City*, starring Stacy Keach, Jeff Bridges, and Susan Tyrell, opens at the Columbia II. **30** Burt Reynolds, Jon Voight, and Ned Beatty (in his film debut) star in *Deliverance*, opening at Loew's Tower East. The "Dueling Banjos" theme becomes a hit.

Robert Redford stars in *The Candidate*, premiering June 21, 1972. *LC*

SEPTEMBER 7 Martin Ransohoff leaves Filmways to produce independently. **27** Rev. Jesse Jackson's Operation PUSH begins to pressure MGM, Columbia, and United Artists to start putting blacks in positions of power.

OCTOBER 2 Rod Steiger accuses producers of cheating many top-flight actors who agree to take a small amount up front and the rest as a percentage of profits.

NOVEMBER 8 HBO begins microwave broadcasts, but only 350 homes in Wilkes-Barre are equipped to receive its signals and its first movie, *Sometimes a Great Notion*

DECEMBER 29 *Life* magazine ends publication as a weekly, depriving the movies of a major source of publicity.

rector Dennis Berry. **29** Producer J. Arthur Rank d.

APRIL 5 Brian Donlevy d. **25** George Sanders, "bored," according to the note he leaves, commits suicide.

MAY • Dennis Hopper m. Daria Halprin.

JULY 6 Brandon De Wilde dies in an auto accident. **16** Natalie Wood and Robert Wagner remarry. **17** Ernest Borgnine and Donna Rancourt divorce.

SEPTEMBER 12 William Boyd d. **14** George C. Scott m. Trish Van de Vere.

OCTOBER 9 Miriam Hopkins d. **16** Leo G. Carroll d.

NOVEMBER 22 Yvette Mimieux m. producer-director Stanley Donen.

DECEMBER 9 Louella Parsons d.

Personalities

viet airliner. The North Vietnamese government has invited her to observe the results of U.S. bombing, and she will use the visit to attack the American war effort. The trip will turn many Americans against her, and it will be years before she emerges from the cloud of controversy it causes.

AUGUST • Shirley MacLaine is a delegate to the Democratic Convention. • Ann Rutherford is filming *They Only Kill Their Masters* on MGM's Lot No. 2, soon to be turned into a housing development. She's "living" in the same house that was hers in the Andy Hardy film series, on "Carvel St." **8** Sonny and Cher are named to the National Council on Drug Abuse. **14** Filming begins on *The Exorcist*. Linda Blair will spend two hours a day having her makeup applied. **17** Paramount launches its "Directors Co.," which will finance the work of Francis Ford Coppola, Peter Bogdanovich, and William Friedkin. **26** Actress Terry Moore, who serves on President Nixon's National Council on Drug Abuse, is arrested at the airport in New Orleans for possession of marijuana.

SEPTEMBER 10 Ann-Margret, appearing at the Sahara Tahoe Hotel, falls from scaffolding as she's about to go on, suffering a concussion, broken jaw, and broken arm. She will collect $1.5 million in an out-of-court settlement. **12** Dustin Hoffman joins Sidney Poitier, Paul Newman, Barbra Streisand, and Steve McQueen at First Artists.

DECEMBER 8 Running his Mercedes into a hillside near Malibu, Jason Robards Jr. arrives at the hospital with his heart stopped, his face smashed, and a finger partly severed. It will take three operations to put him back together again. **20** An unidentified woman pours red paint on Jane Fonda, who is in Stockholm, demonstrating against the Vietnam War.

Movies

AUGUST 1 *The New Centurions*, starring George C. Scott and Stacy Keach, premieres at the Cinema Hollywood Theater in Hollywood. **4** Ron O'Neal stars in Gordon Parks's *Superfly*, a popular film about drug dealers, opening at Loew's State 1 and Loew's Cine. Some black groups attack it for presenting a distorted picture of black America. **25** *Blacula*, starring William Marshall, the first major black horror film, opens at the Criterion and Juliet 2.

SEPTEMBER 24 Martin Ritt's *Sounder*, starring Cicely Tyson and Paul Winfield, premieres at the Plaza and New Embassy Theaters.

OCTOBER 18 Diana Ross makes her screen debut in *Lady Sings the Blues*, premiering at Loew's State 1 and Loew's Orpheum.

DECEMBER 10 *Sleuth*, starring Laurence Olivier and Michael Caine, premieres at the Ziegfeld. **12** *The Poseidon Adventure*, premiering at the National and Beekman Theaters, stars Gene Hackman, Shelly Winters, Ernest Borgnine, Jack Albertson, Stella Stevens, Red Buttons, Carol Lynley, Roddy McDowall, and Leslie Nielsen. The film kicks off a spate of 1970s disaster movies.

Business and Society

Births, Deaths, Marriages, and Divorces

Also this year: • William Hurt m. actress Mary Beth Supinger. • Divorces include Dean Martin and Jeanne Beigger, Liza Minnelli and Peter Allen, Terry Moore and Stuart Cramer III, and Raquel Welch and Patrick Curtis.

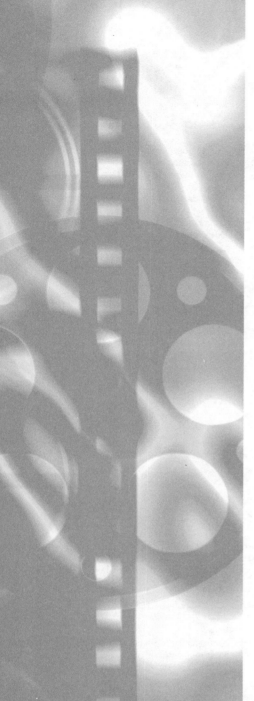

MGM is out of the distribution business, and the Supreme Court revises the rules on obscenity. Marlon Brando sends an Apache woman to reject his Oscar on Awards night. Roger Moore is the new James Bond; Linda Blair turns many heads (and certainly her own) in *The Exorcist*, a monster hit; and director Martin Scorsese leaps into the first rank of moviemakers with *Mean Streets*. The Jack Nicholson–Anjelica Huston and Barbra Streisand–Jon Peters relationships begin, and Jane Fonda marries Tom Hayden.

- Number of releases: 463
- Number of screens: 14,400, of which 3,650 are in drive-ins
- Average weekly attendance: 16,600,000
- Average ticket price: $1.77
- Box office receipts: $1,524,000,000
- TV program Linda Blair watches while having her makeup applied for *The Exorcist*: reruns of *The Flying Nun*

Top stars at the box office, based on a Quigley Publications poll of exhibitors:

1. Clint Eastwood
2. Ryan O'Neal
3. Steve McQueen
4. Burt Reynolds
5. Robert Redford
6. Barbra Streisand
7. Paul Newman
8. Charles Bronson
9. John Wayne
10. Marlon Brando

Top rental earnings, based on figures reported by *Variety*:

1. *The Poseidon Adventure*	$40,000,000
2. *Deliverance*	18,000,000
3. *The Getaway*	17,500,000
4. *Live and Let Die*	15,500,000
5. *Paper Moon*	13,000,000

The New York Film Critics Circle Awards
Best Picture: *Day for Night*

The Golden Globe Awards
Best Picture (Drama): *The Exorcist*
Best Picture (Musical/Comedy): *American Graffiti*

The Cannes Film Festival
Palme d'Or: *Scarecrow* and *The Hireling*

The Academy Awards (presented April 2, 1974)
Best Picture: *The Sting*
Actor: Jack Lemmon (*Save the Tiger*)
Actress: Glenda Jackson (*A Touch of Class*)
Supporting Actor: John Houseman (*The Paper Chase*)
Supporting Actress: Tatum O'Neal (*Paper Moon*)
Director: George Roy Hill (*The Sting*)

January	February	March	April	May	June	
		2 Women in Film founded		**22** Liza Minnelli has a one-month romance with Peter Sellers		
16 Jane Fonda divorces Roger Vadim	**11** Mysterious death on location of *The Man Who Loved Cat Dancing*				**7** Ali McGraw divorces Robert Evans	
	21 Jane Fonda m. Tom Hayden		**3** Edward G. Robinson art collection sold to Armand Hammer			

July	August	September	October	November	December	
	31 John Ford d.			**25** Laurence Harvey d.		
12 Steve McQueen m. Ali MacGraw		**17** MGM quits film distribution business			**26** *The Exorcist*	
			14 *Mean Streets*			

Personalities

• Jack Nicholson and Anjelica Huston meet and begin a long-term, non-exclusive relationship.

JANUARY 18 1940s movie tough guy Lawrence Tierney is hospitalized with stab wounds after being attacked outside a New York City bar.

FEBRUARY • Milton Caniff, who created the comic strip "Terry and the Pirates" in 1934, reveals that he modeled the appearance of the Dragon Lady after Joan Crawford. **11** On location in Arizona for *The Man Who Loved Cat Dancing*, David Whitny, Sarah Miles's business manager, is found dead in her bathroom of a drug overdose after roughing her up a few hours before. Burt

Reynolds, who had come to Miles's room last night when he heard a commotion, will be the subject of unfounded rumors of involvement with the actress and with Whitny's death. **16** Glenn Ford, in Sydney, Australia, at an awards dinner, speaks out against Australia's criticism of the U.S. in Vietnam.

MARCH 27 Oscar winner for Best Actor, Marlon Brando, who turned down a Golden Globe award in January for his role as Don Vito Corleone, stuns the Academy tonight at the Dorothy Chandler Pavilion by sending Apache Sacheen Littlefeather to say that he is turning down this Oscar, too, because of America's treatment of the Indians. **31** President Nixon presents John Ford with the Medal of freedom at an American Film Institute tribute to the director in Beverly Hills. Jane Fonda and Tom

Hayden are thwarted in their attempt to see Nixon to protest the Vietnam War.

APRIL • The South Carolina legislature calls upon theaters in the state to not show Jane Fonda's films because of her left-wing politics. **3** The Knoedler Art Gallery in New York buys the collection of the late Edward G. Robinson (on behalf of Armand Hammer), for $5.1 million. It includes works by Cezanne, Van Gogh, Gauguin, Renoir, and Toulouse-Lautrec. **17** Shirley MacLaine leads "a representative group of women," leaving for China to meet with Chinese women. Out of the trip will come MacLaine's documentary, *The Other Half of the Sky: A China Memoir*.

MAY 22 Liza Minnelli, in the midst of a one-month romance with Peter Sellers, confirms the end of her one-year engagement

Movies

FEBRUARY 1 Bernardo Bertolucci's sensational *Last Tango in Paris*, starring Marlon Brando and Maria Schneider, has its U.S. theatrical premiere at the Trans-Lux East. The $5 ticket price brings complaints from critics and the director. **23** *Walking Tall*, the violent story of Tennessee Sheriff Buford Pusser's war on corruption, starring Joe Don Baker, premieres at the Hollywood Pantages.

MAY 9 Warners re-releases *Billy Jack* after Tom Laughlin sued them (February 1,

1972) for mishandling the 1971 release. The film is now making big profits. **16** Peter Bogdanovich's *Paper Moon*, starring Ryan O'Neal and introducing O'Neal's nine-year-old daughter, Tatum, premieres at the Coronet. **17** *The Day of the Jackal*, starring Edward Fox, opens at three New York theaters.

JUNE 20 George Segal and Glenda Jackson are the stars of *A Touch of Class*, opening at the Baronet. **26** Roger Moore has taken over from Sean Connery as the new James Bond in *Live and Let Die*, premiering at the Chinese Theater in Hollywood. Paul McCartney sings the title song.

AUGUST 1 "Where were you in '62?" George Lucas's *American Graffiti*, starring Richard Dreyfuss and "Ronnie" Howard, premieres at the Avco Cinema Center in Los Angeles. **17** Martial arts artist Bruce Lee stars in the "chopsocky" classic, *Enter the Dragon*, opening at several New York theaters. **26** Robert DeNiro (in a role played by Paul Newman on TV) and Michael Moriarty star in *Bang the Drum Slowly*, premiering at the Cinema I. Danny Aiello is making his screen debut.

OCTOBER 13 Closing the New York Film Festival this year is Terence Malick's *Badlands*, starring Martin Sheen and Sissy

Business and Society

MARCH 2 Women in Film is founded in Hollywood to further opportunities for women filmmakers. **6** The Writer's Guild of America strikes the Association of Motion Picture and Television Producers in a jurisdictional dispute involving "hyphenates"—writer-producers.

APRIL 26 United Artists announces that it

will not advertise its X-rated *Last Tango in Paris* in the *Los Angeles Times*, which insists on grouping it with the porno movies.

MAY • 20th Century Fox begins the industry's shift of openings from Wednesdays to Fridays. The move is intended to cut down on expensive Sunday advertising and minimize the effect of bad reviews, which would appear on Saturdays.

JUNE 5 Lew Wasserman becomes chairman

of the board of MCA (Music Corproation of America), replacing Jules Stein. **5** Columbia announces that it will move its New York office to Los Angeles. **21** The Writers Guild of America strike is settled, with "writer" being more carefully defined. **21** The U.S. Supreme Court announces new guidelines under which states may censor movies, plays, books, and magazines. Material that appeals to "prurient interest" or is "patently offensive" may be banned if it appears that way

Births, Deaths, Marriages, and Divorces

JANUARY 8 Michael Caine m. Shakira Baksh. **16** Jane Fonda divorces Roger Vadim. **21** Jane Fonda m. Tom Hayden. **25** Edward G. Robinson d.

FEBRUARY 24 Ernest Borgnine m. Tove Traesnaes.

MARCH 23 Ken Maynard d.

APRIL 18 Karen Black m. Skip Burton. **21** Rod Steiger m. Sherry Nelson. **24** Dean Martin m. Catherine Hawn.

JUNE 7 Ali McGraw divorces Robert Evans.

JULY 2 Betty Grable d. **6** Joe E. Brown d. **7** Veronica Lake is dead. **11** Robert Ryan d. **12** Lon Chaney Jr. d. **12** Steve

to Desi Arnaz Jr. Liza is in Britain giving concerts to pay off her mother's debts.

JUNE • Second baseman Kurt Russell of the El Paso Sun Kings, a California Angels minor league club, sustains a career-ending shoulder injury while making a double play. He will now give up the Disney movies he's been appearing in during the off-season to try for a serious acting career. • John Wayne characterizes Watergate as "a damned panty raid." • Omar Sharif wins the Ladbroke World Master Bridge Championship. **12** Walking in New York's Chinatown with Dick Cavett, Marlon Brando, pursued by paparazzo Ron Galella, punches the photographer, breaking his jaw.

JULY 3 Elizabeth Taylor acknowledges that she and Richard Burton have separated.

AUGUST • Jon Peters, called to Barbra Streisand's home to do her hair, will end up as her live-in lover. **8** MGM, trying to boost the sagging box office of *The Man Who Loved Cat Dancing*, advertises the film as "Burt and Sarah in the torrid love story that shocked the country," with obvious echoes of events on location in February. Reynolds forces them to change it to "…that shocked the Old West." **30** Mark Frechette, twenty-five, star of Michelangelo Antonioni's only American film, *Zabriskie Point* (1970), is arrested in Boston after attempting to rob a bank. He will die in prison on September 27, 1975, allegedly from an accident while lifting weights.

SEPTEMBER 3 A Hong Kong coroner says that "cannabis poisoning" contributed to the death of Bruce Lee, a diagnosis about which American doctors are skeptical.

14 Gloria Swanson rededicates the HOLLYWOOD` sign on its fiftieth anniversary.

OCTOBER 1 Francis Ford Coppola's *The Godfather, Part II* goes into production. Filming of the Corleone family's Lake Tahoe home will be done at the former estate of auto magnate Henry J. Kaiser. "Hyman Roth," the Meyer Lansky–like character, is being played by Lee Strasberg, rather than Elia Kazan, Coppola's first choice, at the suggestion of Strasberg's Actors Studio pupil, Al Pacino.

NOVEMBER 7 Dennis Weaver becomes the first president of the Screen Actors Guild to be elected without being the candidate of the nominating committee. He defeated John Gavin.

DECEMBER 3 Bette Midler opens at the

Spacek in a movie about killer Charlie Starkweather and his girlfriend, Carol Fugate. **14** Martin Scorsese's breakthrough film about small-time hoods, *Mean Streets*, starring Robert DeNiro and Harvey Keitel, premieres theatrically at the Cinema I, after being a hit at the New York Film Festival. **16** *The Paper Chase*, starring Timothy Bottoms, Lindsay Wagner, and John Houseman, premieres at the Sack Cinema 57 Two in Boston. Harvard, where it was filmed, has declined to take part in the benefit premiere, and its faculty is said to dislike the picture. **17** Barbra Streisand and Robert Redford star in *The Way We Were*, premiering at Loew's State I.

Robert DeNiro and Harvey Keitel in *Mean Streets*   LC

to "average persons applying contemporary community standards." No longer will "redeeming social value" be a defense.

JULY 1 Ted Mann takes over the 267-house General Theater circuit, including its flagship, the former Grauman's Chinese Theater in Hollywood.

SEPTEMBER 4 David Begelman becomes president of Columbia's Motion Pictures Division. **17** MGM president James

McQueen and Ali McGraw marry. **20** Bruce Lee d.

AUGUST 9 Anthony Perkins m. Berinthia Berenson, sister of Marisa Berenson. **31** Director John Ford d.

OCTOBER • Sean Connery and Diane Cilento divorce. **9** Elvis Presley and

Priscilla Beaulieu divorce. **25** Marsha Mason m. playwright Neil Simon.

NOVEMBER 4 Sue Lyon m. Gary Adamson at the Colorado State Penitentiary, where he's serving time for murder and robbery. **14** Silent-screen star Lila Lee d. **23** Sessue Hayakawa and Constance

Talmadge die. **25** Laurence Harvey d.

DECEMBER 8 Elliott Gould m. Jennifer Bogart. **20** Bobby Darin d. **21** Marge and Gower Champion divorce.

Also this year: • Sally Field and Steve Craig divorce. • William Holden and Brenda Marshall divorce.

Personalities

Palace. **9** Elizabeth Taylor and Richard Burton reconcile. **31** Eighteen-year-old Debra Winger, almost killed in an amusement park truck accident, is left partially paralyzed and blind in one eye for several months.

Movies

DECEMBER 5 Al Pacino is an honest cop in Sidney Lumet's *Serpico*, premiering at the Forum and Baronet theaters. **12** Jack Nicholson, Otis Young, and Randy Quaid star in *The Last Detail*, premiering at the Bruin Theater in Westwood, Los Angeles. **16** *Papillon*, starring Dustin Hoffman and Steve McQueen, premieres at Loew's State I. **17** Woody Allen and Diane Keaton star in *Sleeper*, premiering at the Coronet and Little Carnegie. **18** James Caan and Marsha Mason star in *Cinderella Liberty*, premiering at the Columbia I.

25 *The Sting*, opening at many New York area theaters, promotes the revival of Scott Joplin's piano rags. The movie stars Paul Newman, Robert Redford, Robert Shaw, and Charles Durning. **26** *The Exorcist*, premiering in twenty-four theaters around the country, sets off a cycle of occult/horror films. It stars Linda Blair (with the voice of Mercedes McCambridge when Blair is feeling devilish), Ellen Burstyn, and Max von Sydow. The movie will spawn two sequels.

The Last Detail, premiering December 5, has a salty Robert Towne screenplay. Jack Nicholson, one of two sailors assigned to escort prisoner Randy Quaid to the brig, is sympathizing with him:

Nicholson: "They really stuck it to you, kid."

Quaid: "Yeah. Yes sir."

Nicholson: "Stick it in and break it off. Up your giggie with a wah wah brush. Stick it in and break it off."

Business and Society

Aubrey, saying that "the bottom has fallen out of the market," takes his studio out of the film-distribution business and announces that it will be making just a few "quality" pictures from now on.

OCTOBER 18 United Artists acquires releasing rights to MGM's films for the next ten years. **31** James Aubrey resigns as MGM's president, to be replaced by Frank E. Rosenfelt.

Births, Deaths, Marriages, and Divorces

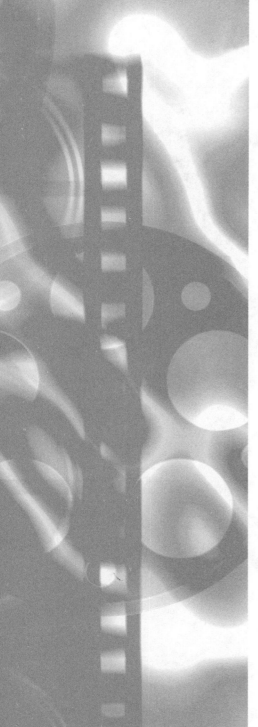

*T*he *Godfather Part II* is an extraordinarily successful sequel, MGM lives off its past in *That's Entertainment*, *Death Wish* makes Charles Bronson an American movie star, and Mel Brooks has two satirical hits in *Blazing Saddles* and *Young Frankenstein*. David Niven squelches a streaker at the Oscar ceremonies, Mia Farrow makes the cover of the first issue of *People*, Elizabeth Taylor and Richard Burton divorce for the first time, and Sam Goldwyn dies. TV executive Barry Diller is the new Paramount CEO.

- Number of releases: 550
- TV owners with color sets: 67%
- Number of screens: 14,400, of which 3,575 are in drive-ins
- Average weekly attendance: 19,400,000
- Average ticket price: $1.87
- Box office receipts: $1,909,000,000
- Average production cost per film: $2,500,000

Top stars at the box office, based on a Quigley Publications poll of exhibitors:

1. Robert Redford
2. Clint Eastwood
3. Paul Newman
4. Barbra Streisand
5. Steve McQueen
6. Burt Reynolds
7. Charles Bronson
8. Jack Nicholson
9. Al Pacino
10. John Wayne

Top rental earnings, based on figures reported by *Variety*:

1. *The Sting* — $68,450,000
2. *The Exorcist* — 66,300,000
3. *Papillon* — 19,750,000
4. *Magnum Force* — 18,300,000
5. *Herbie Rides Again* — 17,500,000

The New York Film Critics Circle Awards
Best Picture: *Amarcord*

The Golden Globe Awards
Best Picture (Drama): *Chinatown*
Best Picture (Musical/Comedy): *The Longest Yard*

The Cannes Film Festival
Palme d'Or: *The Conversation*

The Academy Awards (presented April 8, 1975)
Best Picture: *The Godfather Part II*
Actor: Art Carney (*Harry and Tonto*)
Actress: Ellen Burstyn (*Alice Doesn't Live Here Anymore*)
Supporting Actor: Robert Duvall (*The Godfather Part II*)
Supporting Actress: Ingrid Bergman (*Murder on the Orient Express*)
Director: Francis Ford Coppola (*The Godfather Part II*)

January	February	March	April	May	June
	7 *Blazing Saddles*	**4** Mia Farrow on cover of first issue of *People*		**2** Steven Spielberg's *Jaws* goes into production	
	27 Mercedes McCambridge wants credit for being the demon voice in *The Exorcist*		**24** Bud Abbott d.		**20** *Chinatown*

July	August	September	October	November	December
24 Mia Farrow wins libel suit against London tabloids		**15** Liza Minnelli m. Jack Haley Jr.		**14** Johnny Mack Brown d.	
	30 First Telluride Film Festival		• Karen Black and Skip Burton divorce	**11** *The Godfather Part II*	

Personalities

JANUARY • Thirty-four-year-old six-time world karate champion Chuck Norris, encouraged by Steve McQueen, retires from competition to try for an acting career • Peter O'Toole's cancer surgery and the breakup of his marriage to Sian Phillips sidetracks his career. • USC film student Robert Zemeckis wins awards at foreign film festivals for his *Field of Honor*.

JANUARY 15 John Wayne rides into Harvard Square aboard an armored personnel carrier to receive the *Harvard Crimson*'s "Brass Balls" award. **27** Harvey Keitel saves the life of Joan Alpert, wife of film critic Hollis Alpert, when she chokes on a piece of steak and loses consciousness at Sardi's in New York. Keitel holds her upside down until she coughs up the food.

Movies

FEBRUARY 7 Mel Brooks's *Blazing Saddles*, starring Cleavon Little and Gene Wilder, opens at the Sutton and in Los Angeles at the Avco Center Cinema in Westwood.

MARCH 27 *The Great Gatsby*, starring Robert Redford, Mia Farrow, Bruce Dern, and Sam Waterston, premieres at Loew's State I. Many reviewers find it a letdown after its big buildup. **31** Goldie Hawn and Ben Johnson star in Steven Spielberg's first theatrical feature film, *The Sugarland Express*, opening at the Cinema II and

Business and Society

MARCH 28 Richard F. Walsh, IATSE president for thirty-three years, resigns for reasons of health and is replaced by Walter Diehl. **29** Michael Medavoy is named production head at United Artists.

MAY 6 Fire destroys three sound stages at the Samuel Goldwyn Studios.

"I HAD TO THINK EVIL..."

Linda Blair   *LC*

Mercedes McCambridge   *LC*

JANUARY 27 Mercedes McCambridge, irked that Warner Bros. did not credit her with supplying the voice of the demon in *The Exorcist*, is now airing her grievance following reports in *Time* and *Variety* that she and not Linda Blair was speaking. "Does God want to punish me for playing the voice of the Devil?" she muses to a reporter. "I'm a product of 16 years of convent education and I am still a devout Catholic, so speaking those vile, blaspheming words was an *agony* for me.... I can't believe that Satan will sound like Mary Poppins, can I? So I had to *think* Evil. Every night when I came home I got down on my knees and gave thanks to God that I had been able to conjure up so much demonic personality.... Any child could have wiggled on the bed. *If there was any horror in the exorcism, it was me!*"

FEBRUARY 24 *Exorcist* director William Friedkin, replying to Mercedes McCambridge's claim of credit for bringing the Devil to life in the film with her voice, says that she did not ask for credit and none was specified in her contract. He claims that he was going to give her screen credit anyway but Warners overruled him, then changed its mind. The studio's ads in the trade press on January 22 thanked her for her work and recent prints of the movie give her credit. Friedkin also thinks that "Miss McCambridge's outrageous attempt to detract from Linda Blair's portrayal and push herself into the spotlight is the most unjustifiable and unprofessional action I have ever encountered as a filmmaker."

JUNE 24 The U.S. Supreme Court overturns a Georgia Supreme Court ruling that *Carnal Knowledge* is obscene. **30** Joseph Levine leaves Avco Embassy Pictures. He will be succeeded as president by William E. Chaikin.

JULY 1 Richard D. Heffner becomes head of the Code and Rating Administration of

the Motion Picture Association of America. **13** Chicago's Biograph theater, where John Dillinger was killed, closes. "The neighborhood theater is dead, just like Dillinger," the last owner quips.

AUGUST 19 The Screen Actors guild drops its noncommunist oath. **26** Warners

Births, Deaths, Marriages, and Divorces

JANUARY 2 Tex Ritter d. **24** Larry Fine of the Three Stooges d. **31** Jane Russell m. Calvin Peoples. **31** Samuel Goldwyn d.

APRIL 12 Sissy Spacek m. Jack Fisk. **15** Peter Fonda and Susan Brewer divorce. **18** Silent-film star Betty Compson d. **24** Bud Abbott d. **30** Agnes Moorehead d.

MAY 3 Gloria Grahame divorces Tony Ray. **25** Donald Crisp d.

JUNE 26 Elizabeth Taylor and Richard Burton divorce.

AUGUST 7 Faye Dunaway m. rock musician Peter Wolf of the J. Geils Band.

FEBRUARY • Betty Hutton, broke and emotionally frail, begins working as a cook at a Portsmouth, Rhode Island, church rectory. In December, she will have a nervous breakdown, eventually recover, and will begin a teaching career. **3** Interviewed about the plain and simple life she is now sharing with activist Tom Hayden, Jane Fonda says: "There's a contradiction between being involved in a movement for social change and also being a movie actress in Hollywood. I'm trying to reduce that contradiction as much as possible."

MARCH • Cuts sustained by Donald Sutherland when he falls through a glass door at home hold up shooting of *Day of the Locust* for a week. **4** Mia Farrow is on the cover of the first issue of *People* magazine, heralding "the year's next big movie," *The Great Gatsby*. **25** Henry Fonda

lends his support to daughter Jane's "Indo-China Peace Campaign" with a benefit performance of his Broadway play, *Clarence Darrow*.

APRIL • Senator Lowell Weicker reveals White House memos that show the IRS being used to give tax breaks to the Administration's friends, including John Wayne. (Wayne calls Weicker a "cheap politician.") **2** At the Academy Awards ceremony at the Dorothy Chandler Pavilion, David Niven is introducing Elizabeth Taylor when a naked man streaks across the stage. Without skipping a beat, Niven says that the man is "showing off his shortcomings." **3** William Peter Blatty, author and producer of *The Exorcist*, who won an Oscar last night for Best Screen Adaptation, says that the failure of the film to win for best picture and director is a "disgrace."

MAY 2 Steven Spielberg's *Jaws* goes into production. Charlton Heston, who wanted to do this film, has been passed over for lesser-knowns Roy Scheider and Richard Dreyfuss. Sterling Hayden, slated for the role of the shark hunter, has been sidelined by tax difficulties and replaced by Robert Shaw. The biggest star is Bruce, the largest of three mechanical sharks. The shark hunter's boat isn't supposed to sink when buffeted by Bruce, but when it does, the footage will stay in the movie. **8** *The Towering Inferno* goes into production. 20th Century Fox and Warner Bros., which found themselves developing similar films on the same subject, have joined forces—unprecedented for a feature film—to make it. Fire chief Steve McQueen was first offered the role of the architect, which went to Paul Newman after McQueen made his choice. Newman's son Scott will play one

National theaters.

APRIL 7 Gene Hackman stars in Frances Ford Coppola's *The Conversation*, which premieres theatrically at the Coronet. The film won the Grand Prize at Cannes.

MAY 1 *The Lords of Flatbush* premieres at the Baronet and the RKO Kenmore (on Flatbush Avenue in Brooklyn). "The real heart and guts of the movie is supplied by one Sylvester Stallone, a huge bull of an actor," the *Hollywood Reporter*'s review notes. Other unknowns in the film are Henry Winkler, Susan Blakely, and, in a minor part, Armand Assante. **17** MGM's

That's Entertainment premieres at the Beverly Theater in Beverly Hills. Stars attending the gala opening include Fred Astaire, Gene Kelly, Bing Crosby, Jimmy Durante, Ava Gardner, Groucho Marx, Liza and Vincente Minnelli, Margaret O'Brien, Elizabeth Taylor, and Johnny Weissmuller. Reminiscent of Hollywood's heyday, a four-thousand-foot-long, six-foot-wide red carpet runs from the theater across the street and down Wilshire Boulevard to the Beverly Wilshire Hotel. **22** *Benji*, starring Higgins the dog, Peter Breck, and Deborah Walley, premieres at the North Park Cinema in Dallas.

JUNE 19 Warren Beatty stars in Alan J. Pakula's story of a political assassination, *The Parallax View*, premiering at the Cinema I. **20** Roman Polanski's *Chinatown*, starring Jack Nicholson, Faye Dunaway, and John Huston, premieres at the Coronet and Loew's State I theaters. An evocation of film *noir*, in color, it has an acclaimed screenplay by Robert Towne, which will be the only part of the production that wins an Oscar, despite the film's 11 nominations.

JULY 14 Richard Dreyfuss stars in the Canadian film, *The Apprenticeship of Duddy Kravitz*, premiering in the U.S. at the Baronet and Forum theaters. **24** Charles

announces that, effective January 1, Frank Wells will become its chairman and CEO, and John Calley, its president. **30** The first Telluride Film Festival opens in Telluride, Colorado, and is immediately involved in controversy over its tribute to Hitler's filmmaker, Leni Riefenstahl. When Gloria Swanson arrives at the festival to accept an award, reporters ask her if she thinks that the honor being paid to Riefenstahl is inappropriate. "Why? Is Leni Riefenstahl waving a Nazi flag? I thought

Hitler was dead," says the former Mack Sennett bathing beauty. "Why don't you ask me about *me*? . . . There has been plenty of scandal and rumor about me. Why don't you ask me about that?"

SEPTEMBER • The American Film Institute chooses nineteen women for a workshop, financed by the Rockefeller Foundation, aimed at preparing them to direct feature films and TV shows. Participants include Lee Grant, Ellen Burstyn, Lily Tomlin, Julia

Phillips, and Margot Kidder. **21** Paramount announces that TV executive Barry Diller will become its chairman and CEO.

NOVEMBER 8 Paramount president Frank Yablans resigns.

DECEMBER 17 Former Johnson administration foreign policy advisor Walt Rostow fails to get an injunction to stop the opening of *Hearts and Minds*, a documentary about the Vietnam war that depicts Rostow

SEPTEMBER • Peter Sellers and Miranda Quarry divorce. **15** Liza Minnelli m. Jack Haley Jr. **21** Walter Brennan d.

OCTOBER • Karen Black and Skip Burton divorce.

NOVEMBER 14 Johnny Mack Brown d.

DECEMBER 28 Sylvester Stallone m. Sasha Czack.

Also this year: • Mickey Rooney and Carolyn Hockett divorce. • Omar Sharif and Faten Hamama divorce. • Gene Wilder and Mary Schutz divorce.

Personalities

of the firemen. It will be the second feature film for O.J. Simpson, former college and pro football star, who is parlaying his good looks and charm into a screen career.

JUNE–JULY Elliott Gould and Jennifer O'Neill get engaged, then disengaged.

JUNE • ** Richard Pryor serves a ten-day jail sentence for federal-income-tax evasion. **26 The Wall Street Journal reports that an oil-drilling scam has bilked Liza Minnelli, Walter Matthau, Barbara Streisand, and other celebrities.

JULY 23 Daily Variety reports that Larry Fishburne, age twelve, has signed to appear in Hit the Open Man [retitled Cornbread,

Earl and Me]. **24** Mia Farrow wins her London libel suit against The Sun, a scandal sheet, for its March article, "How Do You Kiss a Man You Can't Stand?" It claimed that she hated her Great Gatsby co-star, Robert Redford. **25** The Hollywood Reporter's gossip column notes Debbie Reynolds's "mixed feelings" about seventeen-year-old daughter Carrie Fisher "getting more space in the fan mags than Jackie O." Debbie is worried about kidnappers.

AUGUST 1 Twenty-two-year-old Christopher Reeve, just out of Cornell, joins the cast of the TV soap opera Love of Life. **21** Buford Pusser, the subject of Walking Tall, dies in an auto accident the day after it was announced that he would play himself in a sequel to the first film.

SEPTEMBER 15 Under the influence of something, David Carradine leaps naked from his car and assaults a woman on the street. He also breaks into a neighbor's home in Laurel Canyon and smashes windows and furniture. **18** Doris Day wins a $22.8 million suit against her former lawyer and manager, Jerome B. Rosenthal, for malpractice in handling her affairs. She eventually settles for $6 million. "My husband [Martin Melcher, who has died] trusted Rosenthal and I trusted my husband," she says.

OCTOBER 8 Yvette Mimieux stars in Hit Lady, a made-for-TV movie on ABC that she wrote herself.

**DECEMBER • ** The FBI, investigating film piracy, seizes the movie collection of Roddy McDowall on the grounds that he has

Movies

Bronson achieves U.S. stardom in Death Wish, premiering at Loew's Astor Plaza and Cine theaters. The film's violence and theme of vigilante action against crime stirs controversy.

AUGUST 12 Art Carney successfully bridges the gap between The Honeymooners and feature films with his role in Harry and Tonto, which was shown on August 9 at the Atlanta International Film Festival and today opens at the Plaza, where Carney is making a personal appearance. **21** Burt

Reynolds stars in The Longest Yard, premiering at three New York theaters.

OCTOBER 11 Tobe Hooper's The Texas Chain Saw Massacre, made for under $200,000, opens in 230 theaters across Texas. A sneak preview in San Francisco caused some revolted patrons to demand their money back. The movie will become a cult classic.

NOVEMBER 10 Dustin Hoffman and Valerie Perrine—repeating the role she played on the stage—star in Lenny, the story of Lenny Bruce, premiering at the Cinema I. **15** Earthquake, starring Charlton Heston,

Ava Gardner, and Genevieve Bujold, opens in theaters throughout the country in "Sensurround," with its low-frequency noises supposed to suggest a quake. **24** Albert Finney and Ingrid Bergman head the all-star cast in Murder on the Orient Express, premiering in the U.S. at the Coronet.

DECEMBER 9 Martin Scorsese's Alice Doesn't Live Here Anymore, starring Ellen Burstyn, Kris Kristofferson, Harvey Keitel, Diane Ladd, and Jodie Foster, premieres at the Avco Center Theater in Westwood. **11** Frances Ford Coppola's The Godfather, Part II premieres at five New York theaters. It stars Al Pacino, Robert DeNiro, Robert

Business and Society

unfavorably. The temporary restraining order he does get on December 31 will be vacated on January 22. **27** Gordon Stulberg resigns as president of 20th Century Fox.

Births, Deaths, Marriages, and Divorces

bought from Ray Atherton, who is known to have trafficked in unauthorized prints. McDowall will be cleared on June 2. **25** Esther Williams is arrested for speeding and drunk driving on the Ventura Freeway.

Duvall, Lee Strasberg, Diane Keaton, John Cazale, Abe Vigoda, Michael V. Gazzo, Harry Dean Stanton, Talia Shire, and Danny Aiello. **14** Mel Brooks's *Young Frankenstein*, starring Gene Wilder, Marty Feldman, Peter Boyle, and Madeline Kahn, opens at the Sutton at midnight tonight. **16** The Avco Theater in Westwood, Los Angeles, hosts the premiere of Irwin Allen's *The Towering Inferno*, with most of the cast attending. Stars in the film include Paul Newman, Steve McQueen, Faye Dunaway, William Holden, Fred Astaire, O.J. Simpson, Richard Chamberlain, and Jennifer Jones, in her last movie. Simpson plays a security guard.

PACINO AND DENIRO: FATHER AND SON IN *THE GODFATHER, PART II*

Robert DeNiro (above), plays the young Vito Corleone and Al Pacino (left), plays his son, Michael, in *The Godfather, Part II*, but they never appear in the same scene together. *LC/© PARAMOUNT PICTURES*

"P"roduct shortage" are the key buzz words, as production in Hollywood slows to a trickle. Sony demonstrates the Betamax, and Creative Artists Agency is formed. Sharks are in, as *Jaws* pioneers—and cleans up—in wide release. Olivia de Havilland and Joan Fontaine stop speaking to each other, Cher divorces Sonny Bono and marries Greg Allman (for a week), and Elizabeth Taylor and Richard Burton remarry. Ellen Burstyn is the first person to win an Oscar and a Tony in the same year (for her performances in the film *Alice Doesn't Live Here Anymore*, and the play *Same Time, Next Year*). And an FBI disinformation campaign against Jane Fonda is revealed.

- Number of releases: 604
- Number of screens: 15,000, of which 3,600 are in drive-ins
- Average weekly attendance: 19,900,000
- Average ticket price: $2.05
- Box office receipts: $2,115,000,000
- Size of "Bruce," the mechanical shark used in the filming of *Jaws*: 25 feet

Top stars at the box office, based on a Quigley Publications poll of exhibitors:

1.	Robert Redford	6.	Clint Eastwood
2.	Barbra Streisand	7.	Burt Reynolds
3.	Al Pacino	8.	Woody Allen
4.	Charles Bronson	9.	Steve McQueen
5.	Paul Newman	10.	Gene Hackman

Top rental earnings, based on figures reported by *Variety*:

1.	*Jaws*	$102,650,000
2.	*The Towering Inferno*	55,000,000
3.	*Benji*	30,800,000
4.	*Young Frankenstein*	30,000,000
5.	*The Godfather Part II*	28,900,000

The New York Film Critics Association Awards
Best Picture: *Nashville*

The Golden Globe Awards
Best Picture (Drama): *One Flew Over the Cuckoo's Nest*
Best Picture (Musical/Comedy): *The Sunshine Boys*

The Cannes Film Festival
Palme d'Or: *Chronicle of the Burning Years*

The Academy Awards (presented March 29, 1976)
Best Picture: *One Flew Over the Cuckoo's Nest*
Actor: Jack Nicholson (*One Flew Over the Cuckoo's Nest*)
Actress: Louise Fletcher (*One Flew Over the Cuckoo's Nest*)
Supporting Actor: George Burns (*The Sunshine Boys*)
Supporting Actress: Lee Grant (*Shampoo*)
Director: Milos Forman (*One Flew Over the Cuckoo's Nest*)

January	February	March	April	May	June	
20 Michael Ovitz and others leave William Morris to set up Creative Artists Agency	• Feuding sisters Olivia de Havilland and Joan Fontaine break off completely	**17** Barbra Streisand meets Queen Elizabeth	**14** Fredric March d.	**29** Sony demonstrates Betamax	**20** *Jaws*	

July	August	September	October	November	December	
29 Judge rules rights to images of Laurel and Hardy owned by their widows, not Hal Roach	**4** Dennis Hopper arrested in Taos for carrying a .357 Magnum	• Warren Beatty says press wants to push him into marriage with Michelle Phillips	**10** Elizabeth Taylor remarries Richard Burton **19** *One Flew Over the Cuckoo's Nest*	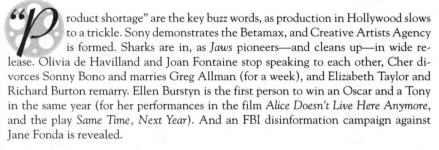	**9** Director William Wellman d.	

Personalities

JANUARY • In the ultimate revenge against its native son, who denigrated his birthplace, Philadelphia announces plans to use the image of W.C. Fields to promote the city. • The Hollywood Foreign Press Association names seventeen-year-old Melanie Griffith Miss Golden Globe for 1975.

FEBRUARY • Feuding sisters Olivia de Havilland and Joan Fontaine, each unhappy with the other's behavior as their mother is dying, break off relations completely. **18** The Justice Department acknowledges that the CIA monitored some of Jane Fonda's mail over several years.

MARCH 2 James Caan, who has worked the

W.C. Fields   LC

rodeo circuit since 1972 as a hobby, injures his hand while roping a steer at Los Alimitos. **17** A gloved Barbra Streisand, on meeting Queen Elizabeth, asks her: "Why do women have to wear gloves to meet you, but men don't?" The Queen says it's probably tradition. **24** Dan Dailey punches a San Francisco airport ground attendant who will not issue a boarding pass to the intoxicated actor. (Dailey's son recently committed suicide.)

APRIL 7 Richard Dreyfuss, Michael Moriarty, Peter Boyle, Jack Gilford, and other celebrities demonstrate in Washington for amnesty for war resistors. **8** Political controversy flares on Oscar night at the Dorothy Chandler Pavilion, with Bob Hope forcing the Academy to issue a disclaimer when Bert Scheider, producer of *Hearts and Minds*, winner for Best

Movies

FEBRUARY 11 *Shampoo*—"Your hairdresser does it better"—starring Warren Beatty, Julie Christie, Lee Grant, and Goldie Hawn, premieres at the Baronet.

MARCH 18 *Tommy*, the Who's rock opera, starring Ann-Margret, Oliver Reed, Elton John, and other rock stars, premieres at the Ziegfeld in "Quintaphonic [stereophonic] Sound." Present tonight are Ann-Margret, Elton John, Peter Townsend, and Tina Turner. The post-premiere party is being held in the 57th St. subway station.

MAY 18 *The French Connection II*, opening at three New York theaters, stars Gene Hackman and Fernando Rey.

JUNE 11 Robert Altman's *Nashville*, starring Ronee Blakely, Karen Black, Henry Gibson, Shelly Duvall, Keith Carradine, and Lily Tomlin, with Elliot Gould and Julie Christie playing themselves, premieres at the Cinema II and Baronet theaters. Heralded by many as a masterpiece, it has twenty-four main characters, improvising at times as they move through the worlds of country music and southern politics. It was filmed in less than two months for $2 million. Also premiering at many New York

theaters is Arthur Penn's *Night Moves*, starring Gene Hackman and Melanie Griffith. **20** Steven Spielberg's *Jaws*, which will gross $458 million, opens on 460 screens around the country. Heralded by a *Time* cover story last week and three days of heavy TV advertising, the film is a smashing success and helps to establish the pattern of opening major films in many theaters—even in smaller cities and towns—at once, known as "wide release." It stars Roy Scheider, Richard Dreyfuss, and Robert Shaw.

SEPTEMBER 21 Sidney Lumet's *Dog Day Afternoon*, starring Al Pacino and John

Business and Society

JANUARY 20 Five agents, including Michael Ovitz and Ron Meyer, leave the William Morris Agency to set up Creative Artists Agency (CAA) on $21,000 of borrowed money.

APRIL 11 Paramount production head Robert Evans resigns to produce independently.

MAY 29 Sony demonstrates for the press a new videotape machine called the Betamax. Capable of recording up to an hour and costing $2,295, it is characterized by the *New York Times* as for "the wealthy faddist market." It will be available in October. Over the next decade, videotape recorders will, in fact, spread to the masses, changing the way that many people see movies. **29** The Producers Guild votes to affiliate with IATSE.

JUNE 23 The Supreme Court strikes down a Jacksonville, Florida ordinance preventing drive-ins from showing films with nude scenes.

SEPTEMBER 3 Universal, dissatisfied with the handling of labor negotiations, leaves the Association of Motion Picture and Television Producers. United Artists (October 3) and Paramount (December 4) will follow its lead.

Births, Deaths, Marriages, and Divorces

JANUARY 30 George Peppard m. Sherry Boucher. **31** Merle Oberon m. Robert Wolders.

FEBRUARY 22 Drew Barrymore, granddaughter of John Barrymore, b.

MARCH 14 Susan Hayward d.

APRIL 14 Fredric March d. **15** Richard Conte d. **21** Malcolm McDowell m. Margot Dullea, ex-wife of Keir Dullea.

Documentary, reads a telegram from the Viet Cong.

MAY • Hollywood Ten blacklisted writer Dalton Trumbo is given the Oscar he won twenty years ago under the name "Robert Rich," for *The Brave One*.

JUNE 18 In a *Hollywood Reporter* interview, Brian Garfield, on whose novel *Death Wish* is based, decries the film's violence and says that director Michael Winner "made Charles Bronson, who was supposed to be evil, a knight on a white horse." **20** Director Sam Peckinpah, known for the violence in his films, is arrested at Los Angeles International Airport for punching a passenger agent in a dispute over his luggage. He will be fined and placed on probation.

JULY 29 A New York judge rules that the merchandising rights to the names and images of Laurel and Hardy are owned by their widows and not the Hal Roach Studios.

AUGUST • Karen Black is playing a male homosexual in a student film being made in Los Angeles. **4** Dennis Hopper is arrested in Taos for carrying a .357 Magnum. Last month he was fined for leaving the scene of an accident. **20** Richard Burton and Elizabeth Taylor, divorced last year, announce that they are back together again.

SEPTEMBER • Warren Beatty complains that the press is trying to push him into a marriage with Michelle Phillips. **9** With the premiere of TV's *Welcome Back, Kotter*, John Travolta, playing Vinnie Barbarino,

"I AIN'T GOT YOU, BABE": SONNY AND CHER DIVORCE THIS YEAR

LC

Cazale, premieres at the Cinema I. **24** *Three Days of the Condor* (working title: *Six Days of the Condor*) premieres at the Astor Plaza and Tower East theaters. It stars Robert Redford, Faye Dunaway, Max van Sydow, and Cliff Robertson.

OCTOBER 8 *Hearts of the West*, starring Jeff Bridges, Andy Griffith, Blythe Danner, and Alan Arkin, a quirky film about Hollywood B westerns, premieres at the Sutton.

NOVEMBER 6 George Burns and Walter Matthau are *The Sunshine Boys*, premiering at the Radio City Music Hall. Its Burns's first film in more than three decades.

OCTOBER • Columbia Pictures changes its logo from a woman holding a torch to a semi-abstract representation of only the rays from the torch. **28** Stanley Jaffe becomes production head at Columbia.

NOVEMBER 3 Kathleen Nolan becomes the first woman to win the presidency of the Screen Actors Guild.

Jack Nicholson plays McMurphy, a wisecracking mental asylum inmate, in *One Flew Over the Cuckoo's Nest*   MSN/© UNITED ARTISTS

MAY 4 Moe Howard, of the Three Stooges, d. **6** Sean Connery m. Micheline Rocquebrun.

JUNE 27 Cher divorces Sonny Bono. **30** Cher m. rock star Greg Allman, a

match that will not make it through the week.

JULY 4 Karen Black m. L. Minor (Kit) Carson. John Carradine m. Emily Cisneros.

OCTOBER 6 Jennifer Bogart divorces Elliott Gould. **10** Elizabeth Taylor and Richard Burton remarry.

DECEMBER 9 Director William Wellman d. **16** Rex Harrison and Elizabeth Harris

Personalities

is on his way to stardom. **12** Robert DeNiro leaves the cast of *Bogart Slept Here* over "artistic differences" with director Mike Nichols, shutting down production, which began last week.

OCTOBER 11 NBC's *Saturday Night Live*, from which Chevy Chase, Dan Aykroyd, John Belushi, Jane Curtin, Larraine Newman, Steve Martin, Bill Murray, Mike Myers, and Dana Carvey will launch film careers, premieres. Billy Crystal, whose seven-minute spot is cut to two minutes just before air time, walks out and goes home without appearing on the first show. **24** Clint Eastwood removes Phil Kaufman as director of *The Outlaw Josie Wales*, taking the reins himself.

NOVEMBER 20 Ronald Reagan announces his candidacy for the Republican nomination for president. FCC rules require equal time be given to his opponents if his old movies are shown on TV while he's running.

DECEMBER 15 Jane Fonda reveals that in 1970 the FBI tried to plant with *Daily Variety* columnist Army Archerd a fake document purporting to show that Fonda, at a Black Panther meeting, had called for President Nixon's assassination.

Movies

19 Jack Nicholson, Louise Fletcher, and Danny DeVito star in Milos Forman's *One Flew Over the Cuckoo's Nest*, premiering at the Sutton and Paramount Theaters and at the Regent in Westwood in Los Angeles. Adapted from Ken Kesey's dark satiric novel, the film was produced by Michael Douglas. It will sweep the 1975 Academy Awards (presented March 1976), taking best picture, actor, actress, director, and adapted screenplay awards.

DECEMBER 17 John Huston's *The Man Who*

Would Be King, opens at Loew's Astor Plaza and Coronet Theaters. It stars Sean Connery and Michael Caine. **18** Stanley Kubrick's *Barry Lyndon*, starring Ryan O'Neal and Marisa Berenson, premieres in the U.S. at the Ziegfeld and Baronet Theaters.

Business and Society

Births, Deaths, Marriages, and Divorces

divorce. **24** Composer Bernard Herrmann is dead the day after he finished recording the music for *Taxi Driver*.

Also this year: • Dudley Moore and Tuesday Weld marry. • Robert Duvall and Barbara Benjamin, Shirley Jones and Jack Cassidy, and Debbie Reynolds and Harry Karl divorce.

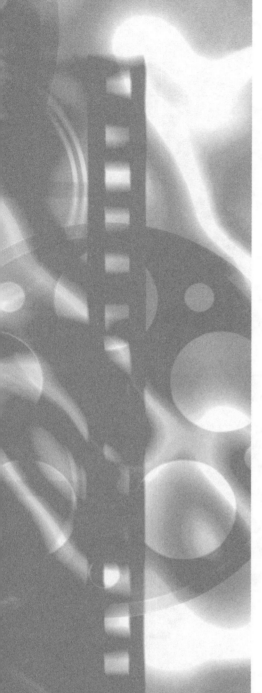

ylvester Stallone triumphs in *Rocky*; *The Rocky Horror Picture Show* is an entirely different kind of film; and *King Kong* is back, this time lusting after new star Jessica Lange, who offscreen begins an affair with the considerably more graceful Mikhail Baryshnikov. *Gone With the Wind* debuts on network TV. And Brooke Shields's photo is on the cover of a paperback novel advertised as "the story of a teenage nymph and the man who had to have her."

- Number of releases: 575
- TV owners with color sets: 74%
- Number of screens: 15,800, of which 3,635 are in drive-ins
- Average weekly attendance: 18,400,000
- Average ticket price: $2.13
- Box office receipts: $2,036,000,000
- Average production cost per film: $4,000,000
- Total number of films made by John Wayne: 153—142 in leading roles
- Number of words uttered in Mel Brooks's *Silent Movie*: one, "*non*," by pantomimist Marcel Marceau

Top stars at the box office, based on a Quigley Publications poll of exhibitors:
1. Robert Redford
2. Jack Nicholson
3. Dustin Hoffman
4. Clint Eastwood
5. Mel Brooks
6. Burt Reynolds
7. Al Pacino
8. Tatum O'Neal
9. Woody Allen
10. Charles Bronson

Top rental earnings, based on figures reported by *Variety*:
1. *One Flew over the Cuckoo's Nest* $56,500,000
2. *All the President's Men*   29,000,000
3. *The Omen*   27,850,000
4. *The Bad News Bears*   22,250,000
5. *Silent Movie*   20,300,000

The New York Film Critics Circle Awards
Best Picture: *All the President's Men*

The Golden Globes Awards
Best Picture (Drama): *Rocky*
Best Picture (Musical/Comedy): *A Star Is Born*

The Los Angeles Film Critics Association
Best Picture (tie): *Network* and *Rocky*

The Cannes Film Festival
Palme d'Or: *Taxi Driver*

The Academy Awards (presented March 29, 1977)
Best Picture: *Rocky*
Actor: Peter Finch (*Network*)
Actress: Faye Dunaway (*Network*)
Supporting Actor: Jason Robards Jr. (*All the President's Men*)
Supporting Actress: Beatrice Straight (*Network*)
Director: John Avildsen (*Rocky*)

January	February	March	April	May	June	
1 Marijuana fans change HOLLYWOOD sign to HOLLYWEED	**12** Sal Mineo stabbed to death **22** George Lucas begins filming *Star Wars*		**1** *Rocky Horror Picture Show* begins NYC midnight shows		**10** Shirley Temple Black becomes White House Chief of Protocol	

July	August	September	October	November	December	
30 Elizabeth Taylor and Richard Burton re-divorce	**30** Alan Ladd Jr. 20th Century Fox president	**10** David Begelman cashes check with forged signature of Cliff Robertson	**20** Former model Kim Basinger appears on TV's *Charlie's Angels*	**21** *Rocky*	**4** Elizabeth Taylor m. John Warner	

Personalities

JANUARY 1 Marijuana fans change the HOLYWOOD sign to HOLLYWEED. **7** Police, on a tip, raid the Los Angeles home of Ryan O'Neal and arrest him for possession of marijuana. Charges will be dropped after he completes a drug education program. **9** Filming begins on the first *Rocky* movie, in which the Steadicam, the trade name for a hand-held, body-braced camera that enables a photographer in motion to make fluid shots, is getting its initial use in a major feature film. Sylvester Stallone has spent five months sparring in the gym, preparing for the title role in the screenplay he wrote in four days. Butkus, Rocky's dog, is, in fact, Stallone's pet. **14** A day before production is to begin on his remake of *King Kong*, producer Dino De Laurentiis introduces the cast to the press on the jungle set at Paramount. One of the film's stars is an unknown model from New York with no movie experience: Jessica Lange.

FEBRUARY • Nick Nolte achieves stardom in his role as Tom Jordache in the TV mini-series, *Rich Man, Poor Man*. **7** Marlon Brando turns down an NAACP Humanitarian Award, saying that too many awards have been given to too many people who haven't done enough to achieve equality. **12** "Meryl Streep, a blonde beauty with a couple of college degrees, seems unaware that she's on the threshold of stardom," comments the New York *Daily News*. She graduated from Yale Drama School only last June and has already made her mark in several plays. **12** Sal Mineo is stabbed to death outside his West Holly-

Meryl Streep　　　　　LC

Movies

FEBRUARY 4 Paul Mazursky's *Next Stop, Greenwich Village*, starring Shelley Winters, Lenny Baker, Chistopher Walken, and Jeff Goldblum, opens at the Cinema I. **8** Robert DeNiro—"You talkin' to me?"— Cybill Shepherd, Harvey Keitel, and Jodie Foster star in Martin Scorsese's *Taxi Driver*, opening at the Coronet.

MARCH 11 Richard Lester's *Robin and Marian*, starring Sean Connery, Audrey Hepburn, Robert Shaw, and Richard Harris, opens at the Radio City Music Hall.

"LET'S DO THE TIME WARP AGAIN..."

The Rocky Horror Picture Show　　　　LC

APRIL 1 *The Rocky Horror Picture Show*, in which Susan Sarandon is seduced by a transvestite from outer space, begins a run of midnight showings at the Waverly Theater in New York's Greenwich Village. This satire featuring sex, transvestites, and rock music, will become a cult experience, in which audience members dress like the movie's characters and shout their lines before they are heard on the soundtrack.

Business and Society

JANUARY 29 A court in Rome rules that *Last Tango in Paris* is obscene and the producer, director, and actors, including Marlon Brando, are liable to arrest if they come to the city.

MARCH 9 Manhattan District Attorney Robert Morgenthau rules that the "snuff film," a pornographic movie in which the actual murder of a woman is said to be depicted, is a hoax. Prominent writers and feminists had called for an investigation into the film.

APRIL 1 The Boston Police Department says it will not ban *Snuff*, a film that purports to show the actual killing of several women, because "It is a film of violence with no flagellation or torture in sexual context..."

Births, Deaths, Marriages, and Divorces

JANUARY 13 James Caan m. Sheila Ryan. **23** Sidney Poitier m. Joanna Shimkus.

FEBRUARY • Melanie Griffith m. Don Johnson. **11** Lee J. Cobb d. **12** Sal Mineo d.

MARCH 14 Busby Berkeley d.

APRIL 5 Howard Hughes, reclusive producer, d. The 1980 film *Melvin and Howard* is a fantasy about someone who meets Hughes after he drops out of sight. **14** Doris Day m. Barry Comden. **25** Director Carol Reed d.

JUNE 11 Adolph Zukor is dead at age 103. **12** Cinematographer James Wong Howe d. **26** Raul Julia m. Merel Poloway in a Hindu ceremony.

wood apartment. On February 13, 1979, Lionel Williams will be convicted of killing him in the course of a robbery. **23** Elizabeth Taylor and Richard Burton announce another separation. **25** Tommy Rettig, 1950s child star who made seventeen films and was also featured on TV's *Lassie*, is sentenced to five-and-a-half years in prison for smuggling cocaine into the U.S.

MARCH 22 George Lucas begins filming the first of nine planned movies in the *Star Wars* epic. Mark Hamill's character, "Luke Skykiller," becomes "Luke Skywalker," as of today. Harrison Ford is a carpenter who has turned actor. **29** On Oscar night at the Dorothy Chandler Pavilion, Elizabeth Taylor is wearing, with her diamonds, a gown whose color Halston is calling "Elizabeth Taylor red."

APRIL 12 In a *Village Voice* interview, Robert Redford says that "Beverly Hills sucks." **16** Francis Ford Coppola fires Harvey Keitel from the lead role in *Apocalypse Now* in a contract dispute over when Marlon Brando will show up so that filming can proceed. Martin Sheen will get the part.

JUNE 1 *Apocalypse Now*, filming in the Philippines, is halted by the rainy season and Typhoon Olga, which has destroyed many of the sets. Production shuts down for several months.

JULY 1 Queen Elizabeth makes Bob Hope an honorary Commander of the British Empire. **1** Jack Lemmon, in his Rolls Royce, is arrested for drunken driving near Malibu.

AUGUST 7 Rod Steiger has heart-bypass surgery. **23** Sally Field and Burt Reynolds

have arrived in Atlanta to film *Smokey and the Bandit*. He asks her for a date that will begin a romance lasting into the early 1980s.

SEPTEMBER 21 TV star John Travolta signs with producer Robert Stigwood to make three films, the first of which is tentatively called *Tribal Rights of the New Saturday Night*.

OCTOBER • "Inside Woody Allen," a comic strip, debuts. • Unknown actor Joe Pesci stars in a low-budget film called *Death Collector*, showing in New York theaters, that will be seen by Martin Scorsese and Robert DeNiro, resulting in a part for Pesci in *Raging Bull*. **20** Former model Kim Basinger appears on TV's *Charlie's Angels* in an episode called "Angels in Chains."

NOVEMBER 16 Syndicated columnist Earl Wilson quotes bodybuilder Arnold

---

APRIL 6 *The Bad News Bears*, starring Walter Matthau, Tatum O'Neal, and Vic Morrow, premieres in New York and Los Angeles. **7** *All the President's Men*, starring Robert Redford, Dustin Hoffman, and Jason Robards Jr. has its theatrical premiere at five New York area theaters.

MAY 19 *The Missouri Breaks* opens at several New York theaters. Marlon Brando speaks with an Irish accent and wears a dress in this western directed by Arthur Penn. Jack Nicholson, Randy Quaid, and Harry Dean Stanton also star.

AUGUST 4 Clint Eastwood appears in his first

film with Sondra Locke, *The Outlaw Josie Wales*, opening at New York area theaters. **11** *The Shootist* opens at the Astor Plaza. John Wayne, actually dying of cancer, plays a gunfighter dying of cancer in this, his final film. The picture also stars Lauren Bacall, Ron Howard, James Stewart, and Richard Boone.

OCTOBER 3 *The Front*, starring Zero Mostel and Woody Allen, opens at the Coronet. The film is about the Hollywood blacklist, which kept many of the movie colony's creative people from working in the 1950s because of their previous political associations. Several people associated with this

film, including director Martin Ritt, were among those who were blacklisted. **6** *Marathon Man*, starring Dustin Hoffman and Laurence Olivier, premieres at Loew's State I and Tower East theaters.

NOVEMBER 14 Peter Finch, Fay Dunaway, William Holden, and Beatrice Straight star in Paddy Chayefsky's *Network*, a biting satire on the shallowness of TV, directed by Sidney Lumet and premiering at the Sutton. "I'm mad as hell, and I'm not going to take it anymore," is the film's catch phrase. **16** Brian DePalma's *Carrie*, starring Sissy Spacek, Piper Laurie, Amy Irving, Nancy Allen, and John Travolta,

---

MAY 1 Harry Reems (Herbert Striecher), the male star of the porno film *Deep Throat*, becomes the first actor ever convicted on federal obscenity charges.

JUNE 21 Andrew Heiskell, chairman of Time, Inc., announces that his company will be investing in films produced and distributed by Columbia Pictures.

AUGUST 3 Paramount and Sony announce that they will combine Sony's betamax

technology and the studio's film library to tap the home-entertainment market through the release of movies on tape. **21** In an article headlined "Hollywood Losing Glamour Image as Tawdriness Replaces the Tinsel," the *New York Times* describes the transformation of Hollywood Boulevard and its environs by the increasing number of adult bookstores and other sex-related businesses. **30** Alan Ladd Jr. becomes president of the feature film division of 20th Century Fox.

SEPTEMBER 10 David Begelman, president of Columbia Pictures, cashes a check on which he has forged the name of actor Cliff Robertson.

OCTOBER 25 Michael Eisner is named president and CEO of Paramount Pictures, effective November 15.

JULY 3 Goldie Hawn m. Bill Hudson. **11** Frank Sinatra m. Barbara Marx. **30** Elizabeth Taylor and Richard Burton divorce for a second time.

AUGUST 21 Richard Burton m. Susan Hunt.

NOVEMBER 28 Rosalind Russell d.

DECEMBER 4 Elizabeth Taylor m. John Warner. • Chevy Chase m. Jacquelin Carlin.

Also this year: • Robert DeNiro m. Diahnne Abbott. • Patrick Swayze m. Lisa Niemi. • Arlene Dahl and Rounsevelle Schaum, Goldie Hawn and Gus Trikonis,

and Haley Mills and Roy Boulting divorce.

Personalities

Schwarzenegger, about to be seen in the documentary *Pumping Iron*: "I find if you train the mind you can do anything. I can see myself going from top bodybuilder to top actor."

Movies

opens at "Red Carpet" theaters in New York. **21** Sylvester Stallone's *Rocky*, in which he stars with Burgess Meredith, Talia Shire, and Carl Weathers, premieres at Cinema II. There will be four sequels.

DECEMBER 5 David Carradine plays Woody Guthrie in *Bound for Glory*, premiering at the Coronet. **7** *Silver Streak*, premiering at Loew's Tower East, stars Gene Wilder, Jill Clayburgh, and Richard Pryor. **16** Dino De Laurentiis's *King Kong*, starring Jessica Lange, Jeff Bridges, and Charles Grodin, premieres at the Music Box Theater in Portland, Oregon, where the ushers dress as apes. **22** Clint Eastwood is Dirty Harry again in *The Enforcer*, also starring Tyne Daly and Harry Guardino, opening across the country.

Business and Society

> The Association of Asian-Pacific Artists, in a Hollywood trade paper ad, attacks typecasting: "Sinister Villains, China Dolls, Waiters, Laundrymen!"
>
> October 29, 1976

Births, Deaths, Marriages, and Divorces

"*A* long time ago, in a galaxy far, far away," begins the first of a scheduled nine films in the *Star Wars* epic; this one will garner ten Oscar nominations and get Harrison Ford's career underway. George Burns plays God, Diane Keaton is looking for Mr. Goodbar, John Travolta is dancing to disco, and Dolby stereo soundtracks are here to stay. Roman Polanski is arrested, and Martin Sheen has a heart attack, as the *Apocalypse Now* shoot in the Philippines runs into nothing but trouble. Charlie Chaplin, Joan Crawford, Bing Crosby, Elvis Presley, and Groucho Marx die. Columbia, discovering that film division head David Begelman is an embezzler, places him on leave.

- Number of releases: 560
- Number of screens: 16,050, of which 3,600 are in drive-ins
- Average weekly attendance: 20,400,000
- Average ticket price: $2.23
- Box office receipts: $2,372,000,000
- Total theater concession sales: over $400,000,000, of which popcorn accounts for 42%
- Approximate value of *Star Wars* merchandise sold: $2,500,000,000
- Number of copies the soundtrack album from *Star Wars* will sell: 3,000,000+

Top stars at the box office, based on a Quigley Publications poll of exhibitors:

1. Sylvester Stallone
2. Barbra Streisand
3. Clint Eastwood
4. Burt Reynolds
5. Robert Redford
6. Woody Allen
7. Mel Brooks
8. Al Pacino
9. Diane Keaton
10. Robert DeNiro

Top rental earnings, based on figures reported by *Variety*:

1. *Star Wars* — $127,000,000
2. *Rocky* — 54,000,000
3. *Smokey and the Bandit* — 39,750,000
4. *A Star Is Born* — 37,100,000
5. *King Kong* — 35,850,000

The New York Film Critics Association Awards
Best Picture: *Annie Hall*

The Los Angeles Film Critics Association
Best Picture: *Star Wars*

The Golden Globe Awards
Best Picture (Drama): *The Turning Point*
Best Picture (Musical/Comedy): *The Goodbye Girl*

Academy Awards (presented March 29, 1978)
Best Picture: *Annie Hall*
Actor: Richard Dreyfuss (*The Goodbye Girl*)
Actress: Diane Keaton (*Annie Hall*)
Supporting Actor: Jason Robards Jr. (*Julia*)
Supporting Actress: Vanessa Redgrave (*Julia*)
Director: Woody Allen (*Annie Hall*)

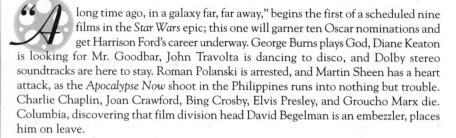

January	February	March	April	May	June
14 Peter Finch d.	• Bill Murray becomes a regular on NBC's *Saturday Night Live*	**1** Martin Sheen has a heart attack on location for *Apocalypse Now*	**11** *Newsweek's* cover story celebrates new star Sylvester Stallone	**25** *Star Wars*	**25–26** Mike Todd's body stolen from a Chicago cemetery

July	August	September	October	November	December
• Liza Minneli settles out-of-court with the *Harvard Lampoon*		**16** Elvis Presley d. **30** Columbia puts David Begelman on leave for nine weeks, for embezzlement	**14** Bing Crosby d. **16** *Close Encounters of the Third Kind*		**19** Roman Polanski under psychiatric observation for statutory rape conviction

Personalities

JANUARY • The publication of *The Films of Robert Redford* is being delayed by the star's desire to tone down the remarks he made to author James Spada about other actors.

FEBRUARY • Bill Murray becomes a regular on NBC's *Saturday Night Live*. **14** Sissy Spacek is on the cover of *Newsweek* as part of its story, "The New Actresses." Also profiled are Talia Shire, Shelley Duvall, Jenny Agutter, and Jill Clayburgh.

MARCH 1 Martin Sheen has a heart attack on location for *Apocalypse Now* in the Philippines. **11** Director Roman Polanski is arrested in Los Angeles and charged with raping a thirteen-year-old girl yesterday at the home of Jack Nicholson, who is away.

Anjelica Huston, who is breaking up with Nicholson, has come to collect her clothes and is arrested on an unrelated charge of cocaine possession. **23** "11-Year Old as a Child Harlot; Ivory Soap Alumnus," is *Variety*'s headline about the signing of Brooke Shields for Louis Malle's *Pretty Baby*. **27** The death from cancer of actress Diana Hyland leaves John Travolta, her fiancé, devastated. It is in this state of mind that he will finish filming *Saturday Night Fever*. **28** *Time*'s cover story is "New Queen of Comedy: Lily Tomlin." **29** Barbra Streisand escapes her fans with a James Bond caper when exiting the Oscar ceremonies tonight at the Dorothy Chandler Pavilion: she's hired a Barbra Streisand impersonator to draw them away.

APRIL 11 *Newsweek*'s cover story, "Rocky KO's Hollywood," is a six-page celebra-

tion of new star Sylvester Stallone. **19** Martin Sheen, recovered from his heart attack, is back filming *Apocalypse Now*.

MAY • Francis Ford Coppola puts up all his assets as collateral for a loan from United Artists so that he can finish *Apocalypse Now*. **1** The Los Angeles District Attorney announces that Anjelica Huston will testify for the state against Roman Polanski, and that the drug charges against her are being dropped. **10** The will of Joan Crawford, who dies today, concludes: "It is my intention to make no provision herein for my son Christopher or my daughter Christina for reasons which are well known to them." **17** Nick Nolte is the target of a palimony suit filed by Karen Eklund, whose five-year live-in relationship with the actor ended last year.

Movies

JANUARY 18 Carly Simon, James Taylor, Carroll Baker, and Tom Wolfe attend the premiere at the Plaza Theater of *Pumping Iron*, a documentary on bodybuilder Arnold Schwarzenegger.

FEBRUARY 6 *The Twilight's Last Gleaming*, starring Burt Lancaster, Paul Winfield, Richard Widmark, and Charles Durning, premieres at the Kennedy Center in Washington, D.C.

MARCH 31 *Black Sunday*, starring Bruce Dern, Robert Shaw, and Marthe Keller,

opens at Loew's State I.

APRIL 10 Premiering at the Coronet is Robert Altman's *Three Women*, starring Sissy Spacek, Shelley Duvall, and Janice Rule. **20** Woody Allen's *Annie Hall*, starring Allen, Diane Keaton, Tony Roberts, Carol Kane, Shelley Duvall, Paul Simon, Christopher Walken, and Colleen Dewhurst, as well as newcomer Sigourney Weaver in a brief role as Allen's date, premieres at seven United Artists Showcase theaters in New York.

MAY 19 The enormously successful *Smokey and the Bandit*, starring Burt Reynolds,

Jackie Gleason, and Sally Field, opens, followed by several sequels and imitations. **25** George Lucas's *Star Wars* opens in wide release. It stars Mark Hamill, Carrie Fisher, Harrison Ford, Alec Guinness, and the voice of James Earl Jones as Darth Vader; and opens to the strains of composer John Williams's music in Dolby stereo, and the words "A long time ago, in a galaxy far, far away…" Money pours into the box offices—more money, ultimately, than was made by *Jaws*.

OCTOBER 2 Jane Fonda and Vanessa Redgrave star in *Julia*, premiering at Cinema I. **7** *Oh, God*, opening in several New York

Business and Society

MARCH 9 Black Muslims take hostages at several Washington, D.C. theaters, demanding that *Mohammad, Messenger of God*, starring Anthony Quinn, be withdrawn. In New York and Los Angeles, where the film has opened today, theaters stop showing it at the request of the police. The Muslims will surrender tomorrow, and showing of the film will resume. **15** MGM announces

the promotion of Sherry Lansing to Vice President for Creative Affairs. **17** Dolby Labs announces that optical tracks in Dolby Stereo are now feasible without increasing the cost of prints. The process has been tested on a few prints of *Lisztomania* and *A Star Is Born* and will undergo its first major test in the upcoming *Star Wars*.

AUGUST 5 20th Century Fox announces that it has licensed its films for videotape. Fifty titles will go on sale in December,

including *M*A*S*H* and *The French Connection*. **15** *Daily Variety* quotes video cassette distributor John Ralston: "I don't think there ever will be a big market for major feature films."

SEPTEMBER 30 Columbia places film division head David Begelman on leave after discovering that he has embezzled over $60,000 from the company by cashing checks made out to others, including actor Cliff Robertson.

Births, Deaths, Marriages, and Divorces

JANUARY 7 Omar Sharif m. Sohair Ramzi, former wife of Prince Khaled of Saudi Arabia. **14** Peter Finch d.

FEBRUARY 8 Director William Friedkin m. French actress Jeanne Moreau. **18** Peter Sellers m. Lynne Frederick.

MARCH 20 Michael Douglas m. Diandra Lucker.

APRIL 14 Producer Robert Evans m. Phyllis George. **28** Ricardo Cortez d.

MAY • Peter Falk and Alice Mayo divorce. **10** Joan Crawford d.

JUNE 5 Jeff Bridges m. Susan Geston.

Joan Crawford dies in May, leaving her children nothing in her will. *LC*

JUNE • Asked by reporters about *A Party at Kitty and Stud's*, the porno film he made in 1970, now being rented for private parties at $10,000 per showing, Sylvester Stallone says: "Hell, for $10,000 forget the film. I'll be there myself." • Waitress Mary Steenburgen leaves her job at Manhattan's Magic Pan Creperie. Her boss, filling out her papers, notes: "termination—left to star in a movie with Jack Nicholson." (The movie is *Going South*.) **12** Paul Newman escapes injury when a sports car flips over and lands on the one he's driving in an Ohio Sports Car Club of America race. **25–26** Mike Todd's body is stolen over the weekend from a Chicago cemetery, a day after Elizabeth Taylor had visited the site with John Warner. It will be recovered on June 28. Police think that thieves assumed he had been buried with a diamond ring.

JULY • Liza Minnelli accepts an out-of-court settlement from the *Harvard Lampoon* for its publication of an especially tasteless illustration of her mother, Judy Garland.

AUGUST 8 Director Roman Polanski pleads guilty to "unlawful sexual intercourse" with a thirteen-year-old girl, for which he was arrested in March. **9** Roman Polanski breaks the camera of a photographer trying to get a picture of the director at the grave of his wife, Sharon Tate, on the eighth anniversary of her murder by the Manson "family."

SEPTEMBER 18 Richard Pryor confronts the audience at a gay-rights benefit at the Hollywood Bowl: "When the niggers was burning down Watts, you were doing what you wanted to do on Hollywood Boulevard—and didn't give a damn." Turn-

Star Wars   MSN/© 20TH CENTURY FOX

theaters, stars George Burns, John Denver, and Teri Garr. **19** Diane Keaton is the star of *Looking for Mr. Goodbar*, opening in New York, Los Angeles, and Toronto.

NOVEMBER 13 *The Turning Point* premieres at the Kennedy Center in Washington, D.C., where President Carter is introduced to Shirley MacLaine, Mikhail Baryshnikov, and Leslie Browne, who are in the film. Anne Bancroft also stars. **16** Steven Spielberg's *Close Encounters of the Third Kind*, starring Richard Dreyfuss, Teri Garr, Melinda Dillon, Francois Truffaut, and Bob Balaban, premieres at the Ziegfeld. **20** *The Goodbye Girl*, starring Marsha

DECEMBER 19 Columbia Pictures reinstates David Begelman as head of its movie and TV division. Columbia attributes his behavior to "emotional problems." The decision raises questions about how the studio has handled the affair and prompts allegations of widespread corruption in the industry.

AUGUST 16 Elvis Presley d. **19** Groucho Marx d.

SEPTEMBER 10 Glenn Ford m. Cynthia Hayward. **22** Richard Pryor m. Deboragh McGuire.

OCTOBER 14 Bing Crosby dies—on a golf course in Spain.

NOVEMBER • James Caan and Sheila Ryan divorce. **3** Florence Vidor d.

DECEMBER 2 Peter Falk m. Shera Danese. **25** Charlie Chaplin is dead. **26** Director Howard Hawks d.

Also this year: • Leslie Caron and Michael Laughlin, Melanie Griffith and

Don Johnson, Dean Martin and Catherine Hawn, and Jean Simmons and Richard Brooks divorce.

Personalities

ing his back, he invites them to "Kiss my happy, rich, black ass."

OCTOBER • Warren Beatty, his romance with Julie Christie already on shaky ground, now has to hold up filming of *Heaven Can Wait* because of the broken arm she sustained while roller skating. **8** The wire services carry a report that the Steve McQueen–Ali MacGraw marriage is headed for divorce. **11** John Wayne, who supports the treaty that would return the Panama Canal to Panama, writes to Ronald Reagan, who opposes it, accusing Reagan of "misinforming people."

DECEMBER • Aldo Ray, 1950s movie star, with no other job offers, stars in a hard-

core sex film, *Shy Dove*, although he is not in any of the explicit sex scenes. **19** Roman Polanski enters the California state prison at Chino for forty-two days of psychiatric observation. **20** Linda Blair is arrested in Connecticut on a Florida warrant charging her with conspiracy to buy cocaine on October 26 at the funeral of singer Ronnie Van Zant. When she's arrested, amphetamines are found in her handbag.

THE KING IS DEAD

Elvis Presley
January 8, 1935–August 16, 1977. *LC*

Movies

Mason and Richard Dreyfuss, premieres at Loew's Astor Plaza.

DECEMBER 15 *Saturday Night Fever*, opening in wide release, makes a movie star of John Travolta. The Bee Gees's music was used to pre-market the film: "How Deep Is Your Love?" is already at the top of the charts.

Business and Society

Births, Deaths, Marriages, and Divorces

Christina Crawford's *Mommie Dearest* portrays a Joan Crawford few knew. The first of four Superman films comes to the screen, and a Russian roulette scene in *The Deer Hunter* disturbs many. Roman Polanski flees the country; and Michelle Pfeiffer, nineteen, is chosen Miss Orange County (California). Richard Gere's visit to a refugee camp in Nepal leads to his interest in Tibetan Buddhism, his championing of Tibetan culture, and a friendship with the Dalai Lama. Electronics engineer Ralph Weingerr develops a colorization process for black-and-white films.

- Number of releases: 354
- Number of screens: 16,250, of which 3,600 are in drive-ins
- Average weekly attendance: 21,800,000
- Average ticket price: $2.34
- Box office receipts: $2,653,000,000
- Average production cost per film: $5,000,000
- Marlon Brando's fee for *Superman*: $2,225,000
- Number of letters received by John Wayne in the two months after he undergoes surgery: 150,000
- Title of Spanish-language version of *Grease*: *Vaselina*

Top stars at the box office, based on a Quigley Publications poll of exhibitors:
1. Burt Reynolds
2. John Travolta
3. Richard Dreyfuss
4. Warren Beatty
5. Clint Eastwood
6. Woody Allen
7. Diane Keaton
8. Jane Fonda
9. Peter Sellers
10. Barbra Streisand

Top rental earnings, based on figures reported by *Variety*:
1. *Grease* — $83,100,000
2. *Close Encounters of the Third Kind* — 54,000,000
3. *National Lampoon's Animal House* — 52,350,000
4. *Jaws 2* — 49,300,000
5. *Heaven Can Wait* — 42,500,000

The New York Film Critics Circle Awards
Best Picture: *The Deer Hunter*

The Golden Globe Awards
Best Picture (Drama): *Midnight Express*
Best Picture (Musical/Comedy): *Heaven Can Wait*

The Cannes Film Festival
Palme d'Or: *The Tree of Wooden Clogs*

The Academy Awards (presented April 9, 1979)
Best Picture: *The Deer Hunter*
Actor: Jon Voight (*Coming Home*)
Actress: Jane Fonda (*Coming Home*)
Supporting Actor: Christopher Walken (*The Deer Hunter*)
Supporting Actress: Maggie Smith (*California Suite*)
Director: Michael Cimino (*The Deer Hunter*)

January	February	March	April	May	June
1 New copyright act protects most films for seventy-five years	**5** *Coming Home*	**1-2** Charlie Chaplin's body stolen	**23** Paul Newman is part of U.S. delegation to United Nations Conference on Disarmament		**26** Jane Russell begins four-day jail sentence for drunk driving

July	August	September	October	November	December
• John Travolta on *McCall's* cover	**2** Hollywood Chamber of Commerce, under public pressure, announces star for Paul Robeson	**14** Premiere of *Mork and Mindy* TV show, starring Robin Williams	**19** Gig Young kills his wife and himself	**11** New HOLLYWOOD sign, costing $27,000 per letter, dedicated on network TV	**14** *Superman*

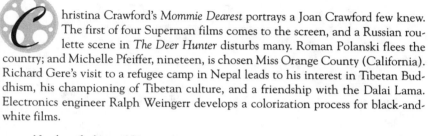

Personalities

JANUARY 1 Richard Pryor quarrels with his wife and her friends, chasing them out of the house, ramming their Buick with his Mercedes, and shooting up their car with at least ten shots. **9** *Time*'s cover story is "Hollywood's Honchos: Burt Reynolds and Clint Eastwood."

FEBRUARY • Dustin Hoffman sues First Artists for taking over *Agatha* and *Straight Time*, films Hoffman was making for a percentage instead of salary so that he could maintain artistic control. They say the films were over budget. **1** Roman Polanski flees the country just before he is to be sentenced for a sex offense. **13** "They're just rumors and it's just ridiculous," Sondra Locke says in *People*

about a possible romance between her and Clint Eastwood.

MARCH 1-2 During the night, Charlie Chaplin's body is stolen from a Swiss grave. It will be held for ransom, which the family refuses to pay, and will be recovered in two weeks. **14** According to *Daily Variety*, until recently, the only "bankable" female star in Hollywood was Barbra Streisand. But now Jane Fonda and Faye Dunaway have joined her, and not far behind are Jacqueline Bisset, Ali MacGraw, Diane Keaton, Jill Clayburgh, Genevieve Bujold, and Sally Field. **29** The Academy Awards ceremonies are held at the Dorothy Chandler Pavilion. Vanessa Redgrave, accepting the award for Best Supporting Actress in *Julia*, refers to demonstrators outside protesting her pro-Palestinian politics as "a small bunch of Zion-

ist hoodlums." Later in the evening she is denounced by Paddy Chayefsky.

MAY 23 Paul Newman is part of the U.S. delegation to the United Nations Conference on Disarmament, opening today.

JUNE • Sigourney Weaver, daughter of NBC president Sylvester "Pat" Weaver, and an off-Broadway actress who had a bit part in *Annie Hall*, leaves for London to make a film called *Alien*. **26** Jane Russell begins a four-day jail sentence in Santa Barbara for driving drunk while on probation for a similar offense. **28** Jim Brown is sentenced to a day in jail for beating and choking his golf partner last October.

JULY • John Travolta is the first man in *McCall*'s 102 years of publication to have the cover all to himself. And Mary

Movies

FEBRUARY 1 *Coma*, starring Genevieve Bujold, Michael Douglas, and Richard Widmark, with a bit part for Tom Selleck, premieres in several New York area theaters. **15** Hal Ashby's *Coming Home*, starring Jane Fonda, Jon Voight, and Bruce Dern, premieres at the Cinema I and in Los Angeles at the Avco.

MARCH 5 *An Unmarried Woman*, starring Jill Clayburgh and Alan Bates, premieres at five New York theaters. Louis Malle's *Pretty Baby*, which stars Susan Sarandon,

Keith Carradine, and twelve-year-old Brooke Shields, premieres at the Coronet.

APRIL 26 *The Last Waltz*, Martin Scorsese's documentary of The Band's last concert, premieres at the Ziegfeld.

JUNE 16 John Travolta and Olivia Newton-John are the stars of *Grease*, opening in wide release. **28** *Heaven Can Wait* starring Warren Beatty, Julie Christie, and James Mason, opens at thirty theaters around the country.

JULY 8 *Foul Play*, starring Goldie Hawn and Chevy Chase in his movie debut, gets a gala

premiere at the Palace of Fine Arts in San Francisco. **21** Gary Busey stars in *The Buddy Holly Story*, opening in New York at several theaters. **28** John Belushi stars in *National Lampoon's Animal House*, premiering in New York area theaters.

AUGUST 6 Woody Allen's *Interiors*, starring Diane Keaton, Geraldine Page, E.G. Marshall, and Maureen Stapleton, opens at the Baronet. **16** Claudia Weill's *Girlfriends*, starring Melanie Mayron and Eli Wallach, premieres at the Cinema I during a New York City newspaper strike. Weill, Mayron, and Wallach go out on the street to appeal to people to see the film.

Business and Society

JANUARY 1 A new copyright act takes effect, protecting most films for seventy-five years. **13** Arthur Krim, Robert Benjamin, and other executives at United Artists, unhappy with how parent company Transamerica is running UA, resign. Others, including Michael Medavoy, will leave tomorrow.

FEBRUARY • Five executives who recently resigned from United Artists form Orion Pictures. **5** David Begelman resigns from Columbia Pictures.

JUNE 1 Daniel Melnick becomes president of Columbia Pictures. **28** David Begelman, pleading guilty to grand theft, is fined and given probation.

JULY 20 Columbia Pictures Industries fires its president, Alan Hirschfield, in the wake

of the Begelman scandal. **31** *Star Wars* has surpassed *Jaws* in worldwide film rentals.

AUGUST 22 MGM announces that it is leaving the Association of Motion Picture and TV Producers.

OCTOBER • *Sneak Previews* debuts on PBS with Gene Siskel and Roger Ebert. **20** "Film Biz Wary of Home Video" says a *Daily Variety* headline. **24** Daniel Melnick steps down as president of Colum-

Births, Deaths, Marriages, and Divorces

FEBRUARY 14 Joan Bennett m. David Wilde.

MAY 10 Nick Nolte m. Sharon Haddad.

JULY 28 Mickey Rooney takes his eighth wife, Jan Chamberlain.

AUGUST 21 Robert Shaw d. **26** Charles Boyer commits suicide two days after his wife's death.

SEPTEMBER 9 Jack Warner d. **27** Gig Young m. Kim Schmidt. **30** Meryl Streep m. Donald Gummer.

OCTOBER 16 Dan Dailey is dead. **19** Gig Young shoots to death his wife of three weeks, Kim, and then kills himself.

Steenburgen and Malcolm McDowell meet on the set of *Time after Time* and fall in love. **10** The Hollywood Chamber of Commerce refuses a star for Paul Robeson on the Hollywood Walk of Fame because he's not a "household word," not, they insist, because of his leftist politics.

AUGUST 2 The Hollywood Chamber of Commerce, in the light of "additional information"—and a public outcry—announces that Paul Robeson will have a star on the Walk of Fame. **8** The old HOLLYWOOD sign is taken down, to be replaced by a new one.

SEPTEMBER 14 Robin Williams begins his rise to stardom with the premiere of the *Mork and Mindy* TV show.

OCTOBER 2 George Segal, who has the male

lead role in Blake Edwards's *10*, fails to show up for the first day of filming after a difference of opinion about the script. Edwards accuses Segal of lacking "character, courage, and morality." **10** A college student confesses an attempt to extort $150,000 from Walter Matthau by threatening to murder his son. **12** Joan Fontaine, in a *Hollywood Reporter* interview, says of her sister, Olivia de Havilland: "I married first, won the Oscar before Olivia did, and if I die first, she'll undoubtedly be livid because I beat her to it."

NOVEMBER • Armand Assante punches paparazzo Ron Galella, says the photographer, when Galella tries to snap the actor with girlfriend Dyan Cannon at JFK Airport in New York. **11** The new HOLLYWOOD sign, costing $27,000 per letter, is dedicated on network TV.

DECEMBER • Sid Luft, former husband of Judy Garland, auctions off her possessions, including a Mercedes that goes for $60,000, and loaded dice, a gift from Frank Sinatra, which brings $1,200. Liza Minnelli's suit to stop the sale was unsuccessful. **8** Neville Brand and John Carradine are each rescued from their homes in separate fires in the Los Angeles area. **11** "In her movie debut in something called *Halloween*," is how *People* begins an article titled "Another Hollywood Brat Breaks Through: It's Jamie Lee Curtis, Daughter of Janet Leigh and Tony Curtis."

---

25 *Who'll Stop the Rain*, starring Nick Nolte and Tuesday Weld, opens in New York.

SEPTEMBER 13 Terence Malick's *Days of Heaven*, starring Richard Gere and Brooke Adams, opens in New York.

OCTOBER 5 *The Boys from Brazil*, with Gregory Peck as the Nazi Dr. Mengele and Laurence Olivier as a Nazi hunter, and also starring James Mason, opens at the Ziegfeld. **6** *Midnight Express*, starring Brad Davis, with an Oscar-winning Oliver Stone screenplay, has its U.S. premiere in New York. **25** John Carpenter's *Halloween* opens in New York, Chicago, and Los An-

geles. Jamie Lee Curtis (paid only $8,000 for her movie debut role) and Donald Pleasance are the stars. Numerous sequels will follow.

DECEMBER 8 Michael Cimino's *The Deer Hunter*, starring Robert DeNiro, Christopher Walken, and John Cazale and Meryl Streep, who have been living together, premieres at Mann's National Theater in Westwood in Los Angeles. Cazale was dy-

ing of cancer during production. A number of deaths will be attributed to people trying to imitate the film's Russian roulette scene. **14** *Superman* premieres at Mann's Chinese Theater in Hollywood, with stars Christopher Reeve, Margot Kidder, Gene Hackman, and Ned Beatty present. Marlon Brando also stars as *Superman*'s father, and is reported to have received several million dollars for his twelve days of work and several minutes of screen time.

---

bia Pictures to return to producing.

DECEMBER 7 A fire at the National Archives destroys much of the newsreel collection donated by MCA–Universal. **15** The Philips–MCA video laser discs go on sale for the first time—in Atlanta. Available titles will include *Smokey and the Bandit* and *National Lampoon's Animal House*.

Robin Williams as "Mork"   *LC*

NOVEMBER 18 Cybill Shepherd m. David Ford. **23** Anouk Aimée divorces Albert Finney. **24** Dennis Quaid m. Pamela Soles.

DECEMBER 17 Rex Harrison m. Mercia Tinker.

Also this year: • Marriages include Kevin Costner and Cindy Silva, Rhonda Fleming and theater magnate Ted Mann, Tom Hanks and Samantha Lewes, and Jeremy Irons and actress Sinead Cusack (daughter of Cyril Cusack). • Elliott Gould and Jennifer Bogart remarry. • Robert DeNiro and Diahnne Abbott, Sidney Lumet and

Gail Jones, and Steve McQueen and Ali MacGraw divorce. • Clint Eastwood is divorced from Maggie Johnson, who receives a $25 million settlement.

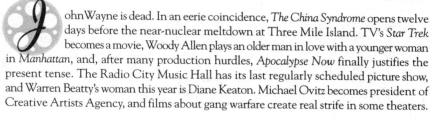

*J*ohn Wayne is dead. In an eerie coincidence, *The China Syndrome* opens twelve
days before the near-nuclear meltdown at Three Mile Island. TV's *Star Trek*
becomes a movie, Woody Allen plays an older man in love with a younger woman
in *Manhattan*, and, after many production hurdles, *Apocalypse Now* finally justifies the
present tense. The Radio City Music Hall has its last regularly scheduled picture show,
and Warren Beatty's woman this year is Diane Keaton. Michael Ovitz becomes president of
Creative Artists Agency, and films about gang warfare create real strife in some theaters.

- Number of releases: 214
- Number of screens: 16,900, of which 3,575 are in drive-ins
- Average weekly attendance: 21,600,000
- Average ticket price: $2.51
- Box office receipts: $2,806,000,000
- Substance used to simulate the monster's drool in *Alien*: K-Y Jelly
- Projected cost of *Apocalypse Now*: $12,000,000
- Actual cost of *Apocalypse Now*: $30,000,000
- U.S. gross of *Apocalypse Now*: $37,000,000

Top stars at the box office, based on a Quigley publications poll of exhibitors:

1. Burt Reynolds
2. Clint Eastwood
3. Jane Fonda
4. Woody Allen
5. Barbra Streisand
6. Sylvester Stallone
7. John Travolta
8. Jill Clayburgh
9. Roger Moore
10. Mel Brooks

Top rental earnings, based on figures reported by *Variety*:

1. *Superman*	$81,000,000
2. *Every Which Way but Loose*	48,000,000
3. *Rocky II*	43,050,000
4. *Alien*	40,100,000
5. *The Amityville Horror* and *Star Trek*	35,000,000

The New York Film Critics Circle Awards
Best Picture: *Kramer vs. Kramer*

The Lost Angeles Film Critics Association
Best Picture: *Kramer vs. Kramer*

The Golden Globe Awards
Best Picture (Drama): *Kramer vs. Kramer*
Best Picture (Musical/Comedy): *Breaking Away*

The Cannes Film Festival
Palme d'Or: *Apocalypse Now* and *The Tin Drum*

The Academy Awards (presented April 14, 1980)
Best Picture: *Kramer vs. Kramer*
Actor: Dustin Hoffman (*Kramer vs. Kramer*)
Actress: Sally Field (*Norma Rae*)
Supporting Actor: Melvyn Douglas (*Being There*)
Supporting Actress: Jane Alexander (*Kramer vs. Kramer*)
Director: Robert Benton (*Kramer vs. Kramer*)

January	February	March	April	May	June	
12 Director Brian DePalma m. Nancy Allen	**12** Two die in theaters playing *The Warriors*, teen gang film	**16** *The China Syndrome*	**25** *Manhattan* **29** Mary Pickford d.		**11** John Wayne d.	

July	August	September	October	November	December	
12 American International Pictures merges with Filmways **15** *Apocalypse Now*		**14** The FBI acknowledges a 1970 harassment campaign against Jean Seberg	• Religious groups protest Monty Python's *Life of Brian*	• More than 500,000 Bo Derek posters sold	**19** MGM names David Begelman to head film division	

Personalities

JANUARY • Paramount executive Barry Diller tells an interviewer about his studio's plans to re-edit *Saturday Night Fever* for a PG rating so that it might find a wider audience: "I don't think that people who go to see the PG version will feel cheated. They'll see the same story, hear the same music, see John Travolta—although he'll be more like the Travolta they've seen in *Grease*." • Gene Roddenberry, creator of TV's *Star Trek* is interviewed on the set of the first movie version of the program. He reflects that his budget was $186,000 an episode on television. "I always thought of what I could do if I had an extra five grand a week. This is everything I ever dreamed of." The budget for the film is $20 million. **15** Armand Assante is quoted

in *People* on his affair with Dyan Cannon: "She is the demonstration of my manhood, just as I am of her womanhood. It is va-ro-o-o-m."

MARCH 2 Anthony Franciosa pleads guilty in London to possession of cocaine and is fined $250.

APRIL 9 At the Dorothy Chandler Pavilion, John Wayne, with two months to live, hands out the Oscar for Best Picture to Michael Cimino for *The Deer Hunter*. **16** Michael Cimino, the Oscar-winning director of *The Deer Hunter*, begins to film an ambitious western: *Heaven's Gate*. **18** A Los Angeles judge rules in a celebrated "palimony" suit that Lee Marvin must pay Michelle Triola Marvin, his companion of six years, $104,000 to compensate her for time lost in her singing career. But she has no claims on Marvin's property.

22 A *New York Times* Sunday magazine article, "The Maturing of Woody Allen," states: "*Manhattan* testifies with eloquence and candor that Allen may . . . have a soft spot in his heart for young, young women. But there is little of Humbert (*Lolita*) Humbert here. Although sex is by no means devalued, the real attraction lies between kindred spirits. The older Allen grows, the more he seems to value innocence in women—not sexual innocence, but that shiningness of soul that age so often tarnishes." **26** The out-of-court settlement in Jane Fonda's privacy suit against the FBI provides that the agency will no longer try to disrupt her political or professional life.

MAY • Johnny Weissmuller, a patient at the Motion Picture Country Hospital, is disrupting other patients with his Tarzan calls

Movies

• With *Annie* and a remake of *The Champ* slated for production this year, the film industry is moving away from the 1970s theme of the child as demon, displayed in *The Exorcist*, *The Omen*, and *Rosemary's Baby*.

FEBRUARY 9 *Murder by Decree*, premiering in the U.S. at the Ziegfeld, stars Christopher Plummer, Genevieve Bujold, James Mason, Donald Sutherland, and John Gielgud.

MARCH 2 *Norma Rae*, starring Sally Field, Ron Leibman, and Beau Bridges, opens in New York at several theaters. **16** *The China Syndrome*, starring Jack Lemmon, Jane Fonda, and Michael Douglas, opens nationwide. In the film, there is a reference to a possible nuclear power plant accident that could "render an area the size of Pennsylvania uninhabitable." The near-meltdown at the Three Mile Island nuclear plant in Pennsylvania on March 28 will draw attention to the picture.

APRIL 25 Woody Allen's *Manhattan* opens at several New York theaters. Allen, Diane Keaton, Meryl Streep, Michael Murphy,

and Mariel Hemingway star in this movie in which Allen plays a forty-two-year-old man with a seventeen-year-old-girlfriend. **25** "Last Day" says Radio City Music Hall's newspaper ad for *The Promise*. But there is no "Next Attraction," because the world's most famous movie theater will now become a stage-show-only house, what it started out to be in the first place.

MAY 25 *Alien*, a science-fiction horror movie with vivid, stomach-turning special effects that will be imitated in other films, opens across the country in about ninety theaters. Sigourney Weaver has her first

Business and Society

FEBRUARY 12 A shooting and a stabbing leave two dead at theaters in Southern California playing *The Warriors*, a movie about New York teenage gangs. **22** The Soviet Bloc countries withdraw from the West Berlin Film festival over the showing of Michael Cimino's *The Deer Hunter*, which deals with the Vietnam War.

MARCH • Film critic Pauline Kael leaves *The New Yorker* for a position at Paramount, where she will stay for a year before returning to the magazine. • Columbia has begun what it calls "the first tease-by-television campaign in movie history." It is spending $3 million for five commercials which neither reveal the title of the film being advertised or say anything specific about its subject matter. The first shows a fireball with a voice-over: "*The China Syndrome*. It's not about China. It's about

choices. Between honesty and ambition, career and conscience, responsibility and profit. *The China Syndrome*. Today, only a handful of people know what it means. On March 16, so will you." **13** Creative Artists Agency announces that Michael Ovitz has been named president. **23** The opening of *Boulevard Nights*, a movie about Chicano gangs, brings stabbings and shootings at theaters in several Chicano neighborhoods in California, but no deaths.

Births, Deaths, Marriages, and Divorces

JANUARY • Olivia de Havilland and Pierre Galante divorce. **12** Director Brian De Palma m. Nancy Allen. **31** Mia Farrow divorces André Prévin.

MARCH 1 Dolores Costello d. **9** Jill Clayburgh m. playwright David Rabe. **11** The body of character actor Victor Killian, who was beaten to death, is discovered in Hollywood.

APRIL • Liza Minnelli and Jack Haley Jr. divorce.

MAY 26 George Brent d. **29** Mary Pickford is dead. **31** Jean Seberg m. Ahmed Hasni, although she never divorced her previous husband, Dennis Berry.

during the night. **20** Francis Ford Coppola, who yesterday showed his *Apocalypse Now* at Cannes as a "work in progress," denounces media coverage of the film's star-crossed production. "American journalism is the most decadent, most unethical, most lying profession you can encounter," he tells a press conference. **21** Maureen O'Hara tells a House subcommittee considering a gold medal to honor the dying John Wayne: "He is a hero, and there are so few left." The medal, later approved, will bear the inscription she suggests: "John Wayne, American." **24** Thirteen-year-old Brooke Shields "is in love with her horse," according to New York *Daily News* columnist "Suzy."

JUNE 11 Kenneth Tynan's *New Yorker* article on Louise Brooks, "The Girl in the Black Helmet," helps to spark a revival of

starring role, with Tom Skerritt, John Hurt, Yaphet Kotto, and Harry Dean Stanton also in the cast. Weaver, the only one left alive at the end of the film, will be back for two sequels.

JUNE 15 Sylvester Stallone's *Rocky II* is a very successful follow-up to Roman Numeral I. **22** Jim Henson's *The Muppet Movie* opens in forty-two theaters nationwide. **29** Roger Moore is James Bond in *Moonraker*, also starring Lois Chiles, Michael Londsdale, and Richard Kiel playing "Jaws." It opens in eight hundred theaters.

APRIL 12 Mann's Chinese Theaters II and III, built next to the original, and the first theaters constructed in Hollywood since the Cinerama Dome in 1963, open with the premiere of *Hurricane*. **18** The world's biggest movie theater complex, the 18-theater Cineplex in Toronto, opens.

JUNE • Fotomat begins to rent films on tape at its Southern California locations. **27** Warner Communications forms a videotape division to exploit its film library in

interest in the silent-screen star, whose silent films will begin to show up in the repertory theaters.

JULY 2 Sherry Steiger files a palimony suit against Rod Steiger to get part of the community property acquired when they lived together for three years before their 1973 wedding. She's hired Marvin Mitchelson, who represented Michelle Triola Marvin in her suit against Lee Marvin. The Steigers will settle it out of court. **20** The California State Senate rejects Governor Jerry

Brown's appointment of Jane Fonda to the State Arts Council.

AUGUST • Low-budget filmmaker Steve Lewicki receives Madonna Ciccone's application for a part in his *A Certain Sacrifice*. She writes that since the fifth grade, she "wanted to be a nun or a movie star." Ms. Ciccone, who will later drop her last name, gets the role. • Michael Cimino's *Heaven's Gate* is reported way over budget and behind schedule. **6** Warren Beatty begins to film *Reds*, during which, or shortly after,

APOCALYPSE NOW: THREE YEARS IN THE MAKING

"I love the smell of Napalm in the morning," says Lt. Col. Kilgore, played by Robert Duvall in Francis Ford Coppola's *Apocalypse Now*. Three disaster-strewn years in the making, plagued by horrendous conditions on location, and halted by the heart attack of Martin Sheen, here shown emerging from the water, this film both opened up the Vietnam War to cinematic depiction and connected it to what Coppola and many others saw as the dark underside of American culture.

Two years after completion of principle photography, *Apocalypse Now* premieres in New York, Los Angeles, and Toronto on August 15, 1979. It stars Martin Sheen, Marlon Brando, Robert Duvall, Frederic Forrest, Sam Bottoms, Dennis Hopper, and Larry Fishburne.

Photos LC/© UNITED ARTISTS

JUNE 11 John Wayne d.

JULY 13 Silent-screen star Corinne Griffith and "Our Gang" star Darla Hood die.

SEPTEMBER 8 The body of Jean Seberg, who took an overdose of pills, is discovered in the back of a car on a Paris street.

OCTOBER 1 Director Dorothy Arzner d.

NOVEMBER 11 Composer Dimitri Tiomkin d. **23** Merle Oberon d.

DECEMBER 4 Liza Minnelli m. Mark Gero. **11** Director William Friedkin and actress Jeanne Moreau divorce. **22** Darryl F.

Zanuck d. **25** Joan Blondell d.

Also this year: • Divorced are Morgan Freeman and Jeanette Bradshaw, Sian Phillips and Peter O'Toole, Susan and Chris Sarandon, and Rod Steiger and Sherry Nelson.

Personalities

his romance with costar Diane Keaton will come to an end. **24** Eleven-year-old Molly Ringwald, who has appeared on *The New Mickey Mouse Club*, is an original cast member of the TV sitcom *Facts of Life*, premiering tonight.

SEPTEMBER 5 Linda Blair is sentenced to do public service on her Florida conviction for cocaine possession. **10** Novelist Romain Gary, former husband of Jean Seberg, who committed suicide a few days ago, blames her death on the FBI. He contends the FBI undermined her mental health in 1970 by circulating to the media a false story that she had become pregnant by a member of the Black Panthers. (Depressed by her death, Gary will kill himself

Al Pacino in *Cruising*, being filmed in July in Greenwich Village.   LC
© UNITED ARTISTS

Movies

JULY 13 *Breaking Away*, starring Dennis Christopher, Dennis Quaid, and Daniel Stern, premieres at the Westwood Theater in Los Angeles.

AUGUST 3 Nick Nolte stars in *North Dallas Forty*, opening in wide release.

SEPTEMBER 14 Malcolm McDowell, David Warner, and Mary Steenburgen attend the U.S. premiere of *Time after Time* at the Regency I in San Francisco. **19** *The Onion Field*, starring James Woods, John

Savage, and Ted Danson, opens in New York. **29** John Huston's *Wise Blood*, starring Brad Dourif, Harry Dean Stanton, and Ned Beatty, premieres at the New York Film Festival.

OCTOBER 5 *10*, starring Dudley Moore, Julie Andrews, and "introducing" Bo Derek, opens in 650 theaters. **5** Burt Reynolds, Jill Clayburgh, and Candice Bergen star in *Starting Over*, premiering at several New York theaters.

NOVEMBER 7 Rose-colored searchlights herald the premiere of *The Rose*, Bette Midler's feature-film debut, at the Century

Plaza in Century City, Los Angeles. Co-starring Alan Bates and Frederic Forrest, the plot of the film was suggested by the life of rock star Janis Joplin.

DECEMBER 7 *Star Trek—The Motion Picture* opens throughout the country on its way to a $17 million domestic gross for the first week, a new record. This first of six films, derived from the TV show, stars William Shatner, Leonard Nimoy, and other familiar cast members. **14** Steve Martin gets his first starring role in *The Jerk*, opening in 503 theaters nationwide. He co-stars with Bernadette Peters, whom he is seeing offscreen as well. **19** Dustin Hoffman,

Business and Society

the new medium.

JULY 12 American International Pictures merges with Filmways. **25** Gays demonstrate in Greenwich Village against the filming in the neighborhood of *Cruising*, starring Al Pacino which, they say, gives a derogatory picture of their lives.

AUGUST 8 20th Century Fox announces that Sandy Lieberson will replace Alan Ladd Jr., who has announced that he will be leaving next year as head of its picture division. **17** HBO becomes available in the Los Angeles area.

OCTOBER • Monty Python's *Life of Brian*, a humorous parable about Jesus Christ, is met by religious protests at many theaters throughout the country. **16** IATSE head Walter F. Diehl calls a studio lawyer a

"kike" during labor negotiations. Diehl will apologize tomorrow only after the slur creates an uproar.

DECEMBER 5 Samuel Z. Arkoff resigns as head of American International Pictures. **19** MGM announces the appointment of David Begelman as president and CEO of its film division, effective January 15.

Births, Deaths, Marriages, and Divorces

on December 2, 1980.) **12** Jan-Michael Vincent surrenders to the Malibu police, who have a warrant for his arrest because of his greenhouse full of marijuana plants. **14** The FBI acknowledges a 1970 harassment campaign against Jean Seberg. **18** In response to gay protests over his filming of the crime novel *Cruising*, and his handling of its theme of sadomasochism, director William Friedkin says that his reaction to exploring the world in which the story takes place was largely positive. "What struck me was the level of energy, and the total dedication to this fantasy world. It seemed to me to be very exciting. . . . All the films I've made in one way or another deal with characters who are obsessed, driven, perhaps sexually confused, given over to a macho image, which is generally bluff, and living on the edge of danger."

Among his films are *The Night They Raided Minsky's*, *The Boys in the Band*, *The French Connection*, and *The Exorcist*. **23** Jane Fonda and Tom Hayden, at a huge antinuclear power demonstration in New York, begin a fifty-city tour to raise money for their Campaign for Economic Democracy.

OCTOBER 11 Christopher Walken is beaten near his New York City apartment when he asks two men to turn down their radio. His broken nose requires surgery, and he loses the use of a finger. **18** Blake Edwards, director of *10*, complains about how his film is being advertised. "Orion ran me over like a steamroller," he says of the studio releasing his comedy. "Whether you like the film or not, it is not a sexist movie. The visual advertising they chose is totally sexist. The ad shows Dudley Moore swing-

ing from a chain around the neck of a girl with a big pair of bosoms." **22** *Playgirl* names Woody Allen one of the ten sexiest men of the year.

NOVEMBER • More than 500,000 Bo Derek posters are sold in four weeks.

DECEMBER 3 The heirs of Bela Lugosi, contending that Universal is unfairly exploiting his image as Dracula by licensing it to appear on merchandise, lose their suit in California Supreme Court. **24** Former actor John Derek, whose photographs of wives Ursula Andress and Bo Derek have made him rich, is quoted in *People*: "I have an awkward image, peddling my wife for profit."

Bette Midler in *The Rose*

LC/© 20TH CENTURY FOX

Meryl Streep, Jane Alexander, and Justin Henry star in *Kramer vs. Kramer*, opening at Loew's State II and Tower East theaters. **20** Bob Fosse's *All That Jazz*, starring Roy Scheider, Jessica Lange, Ann Reinking, Ben Vereen, and Cliff Gorman, opens at Cinema I. *Being There*, starring Peter Sellers and Shirley MacLaine, premieres at the Coronet and in Los Angeles at the Regent in Westwood.

onald Reagan is the first movie star elected President of the U.S., and Sherry Lansing becomes the first woman to head a major studio when she becomes president of 20th Century Fox. The Writers Guild of America begins to supplement the pensions of members blacklisted in the fifties, to make up for their lost income. Woody Allen and Mia Farrow begin a romance. Alfred Hitchcock and Mae West die, and Macaulay Culkin is born.

- Number of releases: 245
- Percentage of TV households with VCRs: 2%
- Number of screens: 17,600, of which 3,550 are in drive-ins
- Total admissions: 1,021,500,000
- Average ticket price: $2.69
- Box office receipts: $2,748,500,000
- Average production cost per film: $9,400,000
- Amount of weight gained by Robert DeNiro for his role as Jake La Motta in *Raging Bull*: 50 pounds

Top stars at the box office, based on a Quigley Publications poll of exhibitors:
1. Burt Reynolds
2. Robert Redford
3. Clint Eastwood
4. Jane Fonda
5. Dustin Hoffman
6. John Travolta
7. Sally Field
8. Sissy Spacek
9. Barbra Streisand
10. Steve Martin

Top rental earnings, based on figures reported by *Variety*:
1. *The Empire Strikes Back* $120,000,000
2. *Kramer vs. Kramer*   60,500,000
3. *The Jerk*   43,000,000
4. *Airplane*   38,000,000
5. *Smokey and the Bandit II*   37,600,000

The New York Film Critics Circle Awards
Best Picture: *Ordinary People*

The Los Angeles Film Critics Association
Best Picture: *Raging Bull*

The Golden Globe Awards
Best Picture (Drama): *Ordinary People*
Best Picture (Musical/Comedy):
    Coal Miner's Daughter

The Cannes Film Festival
Palme d'Or: *Kagemusha*

The Academy Awards (presented March 31, 1981)
Best Picture: *Ordinary People*
Actor: Robert DeNiro (*Raging Bull*)
Actress: Sissy Spacek (*Coal Miner's Daughter*)
Supporting Actor: Timothy Hutton (*Ordinary People*)
Supporting Actress: Mary Steenburgen (*Melvin and Howard*)
Director: Robert Redford (*Ordinary People*)

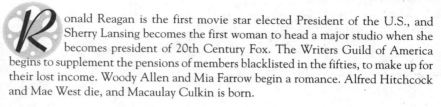

January	February	March	April	May	June
1 Sherry Lansing first woman to head major studio (20th Century Fox)		**15** Gays picket opening of *Cruising* in San Francisco **17** Polygram Pictures, with Peter Guber, chairman, formed	• Woody Allen and Mia Farrow begin courting		**9** Richard Pryor almost killed in explosion while free-basing cocaine **21** *The Empire Strikes Back*

July	August	September	October	November	December
24 Peter Sellers d.	**14** Dorothy Stratten's husband, enraged by her relationship with Peter Bogdanovich, kills her	**19** *Ordinary People*	**7** Producer Robert Evans gets year's probation on cocaine conviction	• Steve McQueen, Mae West, and George Raft d.	**31** Director Raoul Walsh d.

Personalities

JANUARY 14 James Garner, driving in Los Angeles's Coldwater Canyon, is forced to stop by the occupants of another car, who beat and rob him, sending him to the hospital. **29** The U.S. issues a stamp honoring W.C. Fields on the 100th anniversary of his birth.

FEBRUARY 11 Five-foot-two Dudley Moore meets almost-six-foot Susan Anton at an awards dinner, leading to a long-term relationship. **26** Dennis Hopper, high on drugs, slashes the finger of actress Sally Kirkland on the set of *Human Highway*.

MARCH • Bo Derek appears nude in *Playboy*.

APRIL 1 Robert Redford, on a skiing trip, lands by helicopter in the Mt. Timpanogos Scenic Area, and is cited by the U.S. Forest Service for operating a motorized vehicle where he shouldn't. **14** Competing for the Best Supporting Actor on Oscar night at the Dorothy Chandler Pavilion are Justin Henry, at nine, the youngest ever nominated, and a seventy-nine-year-old, who tonight will become the oldest person to win any Oscar—Melvyn Douglas. **17** Woody Allen and Mia Farrow begin courting with lunch at Lutèce, Manhattan's premier French restaurant. By next month the newspapers will be on to this new romance.

MAY • In his *Penthouse* magazine, publisher Bob Guccione, producer of the kinky film *Caligula*, says that during production Peter O'Toole "was strung out on something." • Robert Redford announces that he will set up a Sundance Film Institute in Utah to foster the making of independent films.

JUNE • Robert Young is hospitalized for "chemical depression." He's been doing TV commercials for Sanka decaffeinated coffee, in which he says: "I love coffee, but too much caffeine makes me nervous." **9** Richard Pryor almost kills himself in an explosion while free-basing cocaine.

JULY 17 Five minutes into his performance in *Camelot* at Lincoln Center, the curtain rings down on Richard Burton, who appears to be drunk. He says that medication caused his slurred speech and stumbling. **31** Steve McQueen enters a Mexican clinic to try an unconventional treatment for cancer.

Movies

FEBRUARY 1 *My Brilliant Career*, an Australian film directed by Gillian Armstrong and starring Judy Davis and Sam Neill, premieres in the U.S. at the Cinema I.

MARCH 7 *Coal Miner's Daughter* opens. Sissy Spacek (whose own voice is heard on the soundtrack) and Tommy Lee Jones star in this story of Loretta Lynn. **17** James Caan debuts as a director and stars in *Hide in Plain Sight*, premiering in Los Angeles at the Village Theater in Westwood.

Yoda and Luke Skywalker (Mark Hamill) in *The Empire Strikes Back*   MSN/© 20TH CENTURY FOX

Business and Society

JANUARY 1 Sherry Lansing becomes president of 20th Century Fox, the first woman to head a major studio.

FEBRUARY 6 Raphael Etkes replaces Samuel Z. Arkoff as president of American International Pictures, which will now be known as Filmways Pictures. **15** Gays picket the opening of *Cruising*, starring Al Pacino,

Births, Deaths, Marriages, and Divorces

JANUARY 16 Steve McQueen m. Barbara Minty.

APRIL 29 Alfred Hitchcock d.

MAY 11 Randy Quaid m. Ella Jolly.

JUNE 7 Mel Gibson m. Robyn Moore. **24** Fred Astaire m. jockey Robyn Smith.

JULY 5 Raquel Welch m. Andre Weinfeld. **7** Dore Schary d. **24** Peter Sellers d.

AUGUST 26 Macaulay Culkin, nephew of actress Bonnie Bedelia, b.

SEPTEMBER 27 Candice Bergen m. direc-

AUGUST 14 Playboy Playmate and actress Dorothy Stratten is murdered by Paul Snyder, her estranged husband, who is furious that she has taken up with director Peter Bogdanovich.

SEPTEMBER • Jodie Foster enters Yale. **5** Michelle Triola Marvin, who brought the "palimony" suit against Lee Marvin, is arrested for shoplifting at a Beverly Hills department store. **25** Chevy Chase, appearing on TV's *Tomorrow* show with Tom Snyder, jokingly refers to Cary Grant as a "homo." Grant will sue and collect about $100,000 from Chase.

OCTOBER 2 After persistently denying reports that he has cancer, Steve McQueen acknowledges that he does. **7** Producer Robert Evans, convicted of cocaine possession, is sentenced to a year's probation and

A STAR BECOMES PRESIDENT

Ronald Reagan becomes the President for a second time. First it was the Screen Actors Guild. Now it's the United States of America. Elected in 1980, he is shown here taking the oath of office as the 40th President in January 1981.

Photo courtesy LC

MAY 10 *Friday the 13th* opens. This horror film stars Betsy Palmer and introduces the character "Jason," who will be around for numerous sequels until finally, in 1993, *Jason Goes to Hell*. **21** *The Empire Strikes Back*, the second in a planned nine installments of the Star Wars saga, opens in wide release. It stars Mark Hamill, Harrison Ford, Carrie Fisher, Billy Dee Williams, Alec Guinness, and the voice of James Earl Jones. This installment introduces the Buddha-like Yoda. **23** Stanley Kubrick's *The Shining*, starring Jack Nicholson, Shelley Duvall, Danny Lloyd, and Scatman Crothers, opens at ten theaters in New York and Los Angeles.

JUNE 11 *Urban Cowboy*—"Hard hat days and honky-tonk nights"—starring John Travolta and Debra Winger, opens. It sparks a fad of mechanical bull riding in bars across America.

JULY 2 *Airplane!*, a spoof on *Airport*, starring Robert Hays, Julie Hagerty, Lloyd Bridges, and Leslie Nielsen, opens. **25** Brian DePalma's *Dressed to Kill*, starring Michael Caine (as a cross-dressing, deadly psychiatrist), Angie Dickinson, and Nancy Allen, opens.

SEPTEMBER 19 The opening of *Ordinary*

People, starring Mary Tyler Moore, Donald Sutherland, Judd Hirsch, and Timothy Hutton, marks Robert Redford's debut as a director.

OCTOBER 1 John Cassavetes's *Gloria*, co-winner of the Golden Lion Award at the Venice Film Festival and starring his wife, Gena Rowlands, premieres in the U.S. today at the Cinema I. **3** Anthony Hopkins, John Hurt, Anne Bancroft, John Gielgud, and Wendy Hiller star in *The Elephant Man*, opening in a limited engagement. **10** *Private Benjamin*, starring Goldie Hawn, opens. **17** *Melvin*

at the St. Francis Theater in San Francisco, charging that it depicts gay life as perverse.

MARCH 17 The Polygram Group announces its acquisition of Casablanca Record and Filmworks and the formation of Polygram Pictures, with Peter Guber, chairman. **20** Francis Ford Coppola announces the formation of Zoetrope Studios.

APRIL 8 Warner Bros. buys the Goldwyn Studios.

MAY 1 Paramount promotes Dawn Steel to Vice President for Production.

JULY • Martin Scorsese leads film professionals who urge Eastman Kodak to find a way to stop the fading of color negatives. **21** The Screen Actors Guild goes on strike over money issues, shutting down production.

AUGUST 1 Cinemax, HBO's all-movie cable TV channel, begins operations.

SEPTEMBER • The California Governor's Committee for the Employment of the Handicapped sets up a Hollywood office to help secure roles in films and on TV for people with disabilities. (In 1949 Jack Warner would not loan out Ronald Reagan to MGM for *The Stratton Story*, about a baseball player with one leg, because, he said, "There are two things movie audiences aren't interested in—baseball and cripples.")

tor Louis Malle. **29** A few days after his divorce from Margot Dullea, Malcolm McDowell m. Mary Steenburgen.

OCTOBER • Dudley Moore and Tuesday Weld divorce. **6** Dustin Hoffman and Anne Byrne divorce. **15** Dustin Hoffman m.

Lisa Gottsegen.

NOVEMBER • Chevy Chase and Jacqueline Carlin divorce. **7** Steve McQueen d. **22** Mae West d. **24** George Raft d.

DECEMBER 31 Director Raoul Walsh d.

Also this year: • Goldie Hawn and Bill Hudson divorce. • Tying the knot are Kim Basinger and Ron Britton, Jeff Goldblum and Patricia Gaul, and Sally Kellerman and Jonathan Krane.

Personalities

required to produce an antidrug film. **14** Jerry Lewis files for bankruptcy after his wife, Patti, sues for alimony.

NOVEMBER • Some TV stations ban ads in which Brooke Shields, modeling jeans, says "You know what comes between me and my Calvins? Nothing." **4** Former Warner Bros. contract player and SAG president Ronald Reagan is elected President of the United States. **15** June Lockhart, 1940s star, is hospitalized with a broken pelvis and broken ribs from a San Antonio auto accident.

DECEMBER • Philadelphia rejects a bronze statue of Sylvester Stallone, donated by him for placement on the steps of the city's art museum, à la *Rocky*. (But in 1982 it will stand there temporarily when *Rocky III* premieres.) • MGM's David Begelman fires Raquel Welch from *Cannery Row* for holding up production by taking three hours to put on her makeup. She says they just want to bring in Debra Winger, who won't cost as much. (Welch will win a $10.8 million judgment against MGM in 1986, only to have it thrown out by the California Supreme Court in 1989.) **2** In a TV interview with Barbara Walters, Burt Reynolds calls his early acting "a combination of Marlon Brando and Yvonne De Carlo." **15** Orion announces that Woody Allen is leaving United Artists to release through them.

Comedian Richard Pryor, known for his no-holes-barred comic routines, goes too far in his personal life, and nearly kills himself in June in an explosion while free-basing cocaine. He will later incorporate material from this experience into his comedy act and openly talk about it in interviews as well. *LC*

Movies

and Howard, starring Jason Robards Jr. and Paul LeMat in a story about Howard Hughes, which premiered at the New York Film Festival, has its theatrical debut at the Beekman Theater.

NOVEMBER 8 *Let There Be Light*, John Huston's 1945 documentary about mentally ill soldiers, suppressed by the military, is first publicly shown at the L.A. County Museum of Art. **14** Martin Scorsese's *Raging Bull*, the story of boxer Jake LaMotta, starring Robert DeNiro (who put on fifty pounds to play the role), Cathy Moriarity, and Joe Pesci, premieres in New York, Los Angeles, and Toronto. **19** Michael Cimino, director of the Academy Award-winning *The Deer Hunter*, brings a western, *Heaven's Gate*, to the screen, opening at the Cinema I. Almost as long as *Gone With the Wind*, it will play for a week, laying one of the biggest eggs in Hollywood history.

DECEMBER 19 Jane Fonda, Lily Tomlin, Dolly Parton, and Dabney Coleman star in *9 to 5*, opening today. **22** *Breaker Morant*, which has already won several Australian Academy Awards, opens at Cinema I. It stars Bruce Beresford and Edward Woodward.

Business and Society

OCTOBER 5 SAG members end the strike begun on July 21, having made economic gains.

Births, Deaths, Marriages, and Divorces

MGM buys United Artists. Films featuring violence and horror are popular, and for the first time more than half of films rated earn an "R." John Hinckley's attempted assassination of President Reagan drags Jodie Foster's name into the news. Mel Gibson, Jeremy Irons, Kathleen Turner, and William Hurt begin to leave their mark. William Holden, Natalie Wood, and director William Wyler die.

- Number of releases: 173 (major studios, only)
- Percentage of TV households with VCRs: 3%
- Number of screens: 18,050, of which 3,300 are in drive-ins
- Total admissions: 1,067,000,000
- Average ticket price: $2.78
- Box office receipts: $2,965,600,000
- Average production cost per film: $11,300,000
- Weight of the boulder in the opening sequence of *Raiders of the Lost Ark*: several hundred pounds; number of takes needed for the scene: 10
- Stuntman substituting for Harrison Ford in the scene: none, it's Ford
- Number of snakes used in filming *Raiders of the Lost Ark*: several thousand garden snakes and two cobras

Top stars at the box office, based on a Quigley Publications poll of exhibitors:

1. Burt Reynolds
2. Clint Eastwood
3. Dudley Moore
4. Dolly Parton
5. Jane Fonda
6. Harrison Ford
7. Alan Alda
8. Bo Derek
9. Goldie Hawn
10. Bill Murray

Top rental earnings, based on figures reported by *Variety*:

1. *Raiders of the Lost Ark* $90,450,000
2. *Superman II*   64,000,000
3. *Stir Crazy*   58,400,000
4. *9 to 5*   57,850,000
5. *Stripes*   39,500,000

The New York Film Critics Circle Awards
Best Picture: *Reds*

The Los Angeles Film Critics Association
Best Picture: *Atlantic City*

The Golden Globe Awards
Best Picture (Drama): *On Golden Pond*
Best Picture (Musical/Comedy): *Arthur*

The Cannes Film Festival
Palme d'Or: *Man of Iron*

The Academy Awards (presented March 29, 1982)
Best Picture: *Chariots of Fire*
Actor: Henry Fonda (*On Golden Pond*)
Actress: Katharine Hepburn (*On Golden Pond*)
Supporting Actor: John Gielgud (*Arthur*)
Supporting Actress: Maureen Stapleton (*Reds*)
Director: Warren Beatty (*Reds*)

January	February	March	April	May	June	
• Eddie Murphy becomes a regular on TV's *Saturday Night Live*	**30** John Hinckley, who shoots President Reagan, obsessed with Jodie Foster		**31** Stacy Keach m. Jill Donahue		
	• February Demi Guynes m. Freddie Moore, becoming Demi Moore		**3** President Reagan nominates John Gavin to be ambassador to Mexico		**12** *Raiders of the Lost Ark*	

July	August	September	October	November	December	
	28 *Body Heat*			**2** Ed Asner elected president of SAG	
28 MGM buys United Artists from Transamerica	**18** *The French Lietenant's Woman*		**15** MGM resurrects film division under Freddie Fields		• Demi Moore joins cast of TV soap opera *General Hospital*	

Personalities

JANUARY • Nineteen-year-old Eddie Murphy becomes a regular on TV's *Saturday Night Live*.

FEBRUARY 5 Told there is no money to pay them this week, five hundred cast and crew members working on Francis Ford Coppola's *One from the Heart* keep working anyway.

MARCH 26 Carol Burnett wins a $1.6 million libel suit (later reduced to $750,000) against the *National Enquirer*, which had portrayed her as a public drunk. **30** John Hinckley, who shoots President Reagan, is found to have an obsession with actress Jodie Foster, whom he has stalked. **31** The Oscar ceremonies at the Dorothy

Eddie Murphy   *LC*

Chandler Pavilion begin with filmed greetings from President Reagan, who would not have made it if his remarks were not pre-recorded since he was shot yesterday by John Hinckley.

APRIL • *Life*'s cover story is "Meryl Streep, America's Best Actress." On September 7 she will be on the cover of *Time*. **3** President Reagan nominates actor John Gavin to be ambassador to Mexico. **22** The House Committee on Narcotics Abuse and Control opens hearings on the use of drugs in the entertainment industry. But Hollywood celebrities, feeling they are being scapegoated and fearing that they will be asked to "name names" of those they know who use drugs, do not come forward to testify. **27** An Ontario court dismisses a charge of hashish possession against Sterling Hayden.

Movies

FEBRUARY 6 *Fort Apache, the Bronx*, starring Paul Newman, Ed Asner, Danny Aiello, and Pam Grier, opens. Latinos picket theaters in New York and other cities showing the film, charging it with "racism."

APRIL 3 Burt Lancaster and Susan Sarandon star in Louis Malle's *Atlantic City*, opening at Loew's Tower East. **10** John Boorman's *Excalibur*, a British film about King Arthur starring Nicole Williamson, Nigel Terry, Gabriel Byrne, and Liam Neeson, opens. **24** *Heavens Gate*, edited from

219 minutes down to 153, re-opens and flops again.

MAY 22 Alan Alda's *The Four Seasons*, starring Alda, Carol Burnett, Len Cariou, Sandy Dennis, and Rita Moreno, opens theatrically after an April 30 premiere at the Denver International Film Festival. **31** *Superman II*, starring Christopher Reeve, Margot Kidder, Gene Hackman, and Ned Beatty, premieres in the U.S. at the Uptown Theater in Washington, D.C. On Friday, June 19, it will begin playing at fourteen hundred theaters, where it will set a new opening-weekend record gross of $14,000,000.

JUNE 12 Steven Spielberg's *Raiders of the Lost Ark*, the first of three pictures featuring the exploits of Indiana Jones, opens. Paramount wanted Tom Selleck to star but couldn't get him released from his commitment to CBS for a new TV program called *Magnum P.I.* They settled for Harrison Ford, who is joined by Karen Allen and Denholm Elliott in a nonstop action epic evoking Saturday matinees of times past. The lively music accompanying it was written by John Williams. **26** *For Your Eyes Only*, starring Roger Moore as 007, James Bond, opens today. • Bill Murray and Sean Young star in *Stripes*, opening today.

Business and Society

APRIL 12 The Writers Guild of America goes on strike against the producers over money issues.

MAY 29 *Daily Variety* reports that Dolby "Surround-Sound" will soon be available on videotape and cable TV broadcasts.

JUNE 4 "Premiere" a distributing venture

through which Columbia, MCA/Universal, Paramount, and 20th Century Fox hoped to control distribution of films to cable TV, falls through because of Justice Department opposition on the grounds of monopoly. **8** Oil mogul Marvin Davis takes over 20th Century Fox.

JULY 11 The Writers Guild of America strike ends with economic gains for writers. **28** MGM buys United Artists from Transamerica Corp.

AUGUST 22 The national board of the Screen Actors Guild turns back an attempt to take away Ronald Reagan's membership because of his crushing of the air controller's strike.

SEPTEMBER • The Motion Picture Association reports that the 500 films that Jimmy Carter saw while he was President is more than twice the number any of his predecessors viewed. **14** *Entertainment Tonight* debuts, the first syndicated TV show to be beamed to stations by satellite.

Births, Deaths, Marriages, and Divorces

JANUARY 21 Bill Murray m. Mickey Kelly

FEBRUARY • Demi Guynes m. musician Freddie Moore, becoming Demi Moore

MAY 31 Stacy Keach m. Jill Donahue

JULY 27 Director William Wyler d.

AUGUST • Richard Pryor m. Jennifer Lee. **4** Melvyn Douglas d.

SEPTEMBER 27 Robert Montgomery d.

OCTOBER 5 Gloria Grahame d. **24** Costume designer Edith Head d.

JUNE 1 Richard Harris is knighted.

JULY 1 With the opening of *S.O.B.*, star Julie Andrews tries out a new screen persona. She curses and goes topless. **20** Eleven-year-old Christian Slater opens in the musical *Oliver!* at the Municipal Opera of St. Louis. **23** A Los Angeles judge places Rita Hayworth, who has Alzheimer's disease, in the care of her daughter, Princess Yasmin Khan. **24** Peter Fonda receives a summons at Denver's Stapleton Airport for

slashing a poster that says of his sister: "Feed Jane Fonda to the Whales."

AUGUST 11 The California State Court of Appeals reverses the 1979 award of $104,000 to Michelle Triola Marvin in her palimony suit against Lee Marvin. Triola was convicted of shoplifting last month. **28** Jim Bridges quits as director of *The Verdict*, in which Robert Redford is supposed to star, because Redford keeps fiddling with the script. Producers Richard

Zanuck and David Brown are talking about replacing Redford with either Jon Voight or Paul Newman.

SEPTEMBER 6 Today's Jerry Lewis Muscular Dystrophy telethon is protested by two groups of people with disabilities, who say that his shows depict people like themselves as "childlike and dependent."

OCTOBER • In a *Playboy* interview, Donald Sutherland reveals that he had a three-year affair with Jane Fonda. **27** Barbara Stanwyck is robbed and beaten in her Beverly Hills home.

NOVEMBER 2 Rock Hudson has quintuple heart bypass surgery. **7** Driving through upstate New York to meet with Paul Newman, Robert Redford receives his eighth speeding ticket in the last three years.

Harrison Ford in *Raiders of the Lost Ark*

JULY 17 *Arthur*, starring Dudley Moore, Liza Minnelli, and John Gielgud, opens.

AUGUST 19 Sidney Lumet's *Prince of the City* is a true story of police corruption in New York and what happened to the cop who blew the whistle on it. It stars Treat Williams and Jerry Orbach and premieres at Cinemas I, II, and III. **28** Peter Weir's *Gallipoli*, an Australian film starring Mark Lee and Mel Gibson, has its U.S. premiere at the Baronet and in Los Angeles at the Bruin in Westwood. **28** William Hurt and Kathleen Turner, in her screen debut, star in Lawrence Kasdan's *Body Heat*, which opens today.

OCTOBER 1 MGM president David Begelman shifts over to head the newly acquired United Artists. **15** MGM resurrects its film division under Freddie Fields.

NOVEMBER 2 Ed Asner is elected president of the Screen Actors Guild. **24** USC's new school of film and television is dedicated. George Lucas contributed $4.4 million of the $14 million needed to launch it. **30** Norman Lear and Jerry Parenchio buy

Avco Embassy Pictures and change its name to Embassy Communications.

NOVEMBER • Cicely Tyson m. jazz trumpeter Miles Davis. **15** Brenda Vaccaro m. Charles Cannizzaro. **16** William Holden's body is discovered in his Santa Monica apartment about a week after his death. **29** Natalie Wood falls from a boat and drowns.

Also this year: • Tommy Lee Jones m. Kim Cloughley. • Among those divorcing this year are Tony Curtis and Leslie Allen, Doris Day and Barry Comden, Angie Dickinson and Burt Bacharach, Piper Laurie and Joseph Morgenstern, and Cornel Wilde and Jean Wallace.

Personalities

23 James Caan will withdraw from making films for several years because of the death today of his sister Barbara, the strain of conquering a cocaine addiction, and stress from two recent divorces.

DECEMBER • Demi Moore joins the cast of the TV soap opera *General Hospital*. **7** *Newsweek*'s cover story, "A New Breed of Actor," featuring William Hurt, Elizabeth McGovern, and Treat Williams, finds them "less concerned with personality and more with honesty of craft...." **9** *Taps* was supposed to be a vehicle for Timothy Hutton, who currently has one of Hollywood's hot and bankable names. But the film and Hutton are incidental to the fact that it serves as a springboard to stardom for two members of the supporting cast, who steal the picture: Tom Cruise and Sean Penn.

Meryl Streep in *The French Lieutenant's Woman*
LC/© UNITED ARTISTS

Movies

SEPTEMBER 18 Meryl Streep and Jeremy Irons star in *The French Lieutenant's Woman*, premiering in New York, Los Angeles, and Toronto. Faye Dunaway plays Joan Crawford in *Mommie Dearest*, also opening. **25** The U.S. premiere of the British *Chariots of Fire*, directed by Hugh Hudson and starring Ben Cross and Ian Charleson, with music by Vangelis, opens the New York Film Festival. It opens at Cinema I tomorrow. Opening in New York, Los Angeles, and Toronto are Robert De Niro and Robert Duvall in *True Confessions*.

NOVEMBER 18 Katharine Hepburn, Henry Fonda, and Jane Fonda star in *On Golden Pond*, directed by Mark Rydell and premiering at the Motion Picture Academy of Arts and Sciences Goldwyn Theater in Beverly Hills. Henry Fonda was hospitalized yesterday for a heart condition. **19** Sydney Pollack's *Absence of Malice*, starring Paul Newman and Sally Field, opens at Loew's Tower East and in Los Angeles at the Regent.

DECEMBER 4 Warren Beatty's *Reds*, starring Beatty, Diane Keaton, (whose clashes with Beatty over her role hasten the end of their offscreen relationship), Maureen Stapleton, and Jack Nicholson, opens. This story of journalists John Reed and Louise Bryant also features present-day interviews with figures such as the writer Henry Miller, who actually knew Reed and Bryant.

Business and Society

Births, Deaths, Marriages, and Divorces

Coca-Cola buys Columbia Pictures. "E.T. phone home," is heard around the country, and the little alien's image is on merchandise everywhere. "Up Where We Belong," from *An Officer and a Gentleman*, is a hit; and *48 Hours* catapults Eddie Murphy to movie stardom in his first film. Jacqueline Bisset and ballet dancer–actor Alexander Godunov get together (in 1985, *People* will call them "the most torrid twosome in showbiz"). John Belushi overdoses; and Henry Fonda, Ingrid Bergman, and Grace Kelly die.

- Number of releases: 428
- Percentage of TV households with VCRs: 6%
- Number of screens: 18,000, of which 3,050 are in drive-ins
- Total admissions: 1,175,400,000
- Average ticket price: $2.94
- Box office receipts: $3,452,700,000
- Average production cost per film: $11,800,000
- Camera speed used for the explosion in *Star Trek: the Wrath of Khan*: 2,500 frames per second
- Number of extras in *Gandhi*: 250-300,000
- Amount Steven Spielberg is making from *E.T.* at the height of its popularity: $1,000,000 a day
- Cost of making the alien in *E.T.*: $1,500,000

Top rental earnings, based on figures reported by *Variety*:

1. *E.T., The Extra-Terrestrial* $187,000,000
2. *Rocky III*   63,450,000
3. *On Golden Pond*   63,000,000
4. *Porky's*   53,500,000
5. *An Officer and a Gentleman*   52,000,000

The New York Film Critics Circle Awards
Best Picture: *Gandhi*

The Los Angeles Film Critics Association
Best Picture: *E.T., The Extra-Terrestrial*

The Golden Globe Awards
Best Picture (Drama): *E.T., The Extra-Terrestrial*
Best Picture (Musical/Comedy): *Tootsie*

The Cannes Film Festival
Palme d'Or: *Missing*

The Academy Awards (presented April 11, 1983)
Best Picture: *Gandhi*
Actor: Ben Kingsley (*Gandhi*)
Actress: Meryl Streep (*Sophie's Choice*)
Supporting Actor: Louis Gossett Jr. (*An Officer and a Gentleman*)
Supporting Actress: Jessica Lange (*Tootsie*)
Director: Richard Attenborough (*Gandhi*)

January	February	March	April	May	June	
	8 Orion takes over Filmways		• "Jane Fonda's Workout" video released		**11** *E.T., The Extra-Terrestrial*	
		5 John Belushi found dead of drug overdose				
8 Danny DeVito m. Rhea Perlman					**14** *Conan the Barbarian*	

July	August	September	October	November	December	
	12 Henry Fonda d.		**10** Richard Dreyfuss crashes Mercedes into palm tree in Beverly Hills		**20** Sherry Lansing leaves 20th Century Fox to produce independently	
28 *An Oficer and a Gentleman*						
	28 Ellen Burstyn and Al Pacino co-artistic directors of the Actors Studio			**5** Elizabeth Taylor divorces John Warner		

Personalities

• Jacqueline Bisset and ballet dancer-actor Alexander Godunov get together (in 1985, *People* will call them "the most torrid twosome in show biz").

> *President Ronald Reagan says of today's films: "I liked it much better when the actors kept their clothes on."*
>
> January 27, 1982

FEBRUARY • Jessica Lange is ordered to pay alimony to her estranged husband, Pacho Grande, who has become blind.

MARCH 5 John Belushi is found dead at the Chateau Marmont of a drug overdose. Dan Aykroyd will lead the funeral procession on a motorcycle. **19** Louis Gossett Jr. is arrested at his Malibu home, on charges brought by his ex-wife, for possessing cocaine and giving it to his seven-year-old son and to his girlfriend's children. The charges involving the children will be dropped for lack of evidence and the possession charge dealt with by Gossett's enrollment in a rehabilitation program. **29** Warren Beatty escorts Diane Keaton to the Academy Awards ceremony tonight at the Dorothy Chandler Pavilion.

APRIL • "Jane Fonda's Workout" video is released. Brooke Shields fashion dolls go on sale. **1** The Boston Symphony Orchestra cancels Vanessa Redgrave's appearance to narrate Stravinsky's *Oedipus* because of negative reaction from the public and musicians in the orchestra toward her anti-Zionist statements. **21** Charlton Heston tells the Senate Judiciary Committee that videotape machines and blank videotape should carry a federal tax to provide payments to the creators of content of material taped off the air. **26** Burt Reynolds punches a photographer waiting outside the actor's house to photograph him with Loni Anderson.

MAY • Troy Donahue begins to pull himself out of an addiction to drugs and alcohol. **30** Ellen Burstyn is the first woman elected president of Actors Equity.

JUNE 5 Sophia Loren is released from jail in Italy after serving seventeen days for tax fraud. **9** Steven Spielberg pays $60,500 at auction for one of the several "Rosebud"

Movies

FEBRUARY 5 *Personal Best*, opening in Los Angeles, New York, and Toronto, stars Mariel Hemingway and Scott Glenn. **12** Costa-Gavras's *Missing*, starring Jack Lemmon and Sissy Spacek, opens.

MARCH 19 Blake Edwards's *Victor/Victoria*, starring Julie Andrews, Robert Preston, and James Garner, premiered three days ago at the Los Angeles International Film Exposition and today opens in theaters in New York, Los Angeles, and Toronto. *Porky's*, starring Bob Clark and Dan Monahan, opens in 1,148 theaters. It is a highly profitable exploitation of two popular subjects: high school and sex.

APRIL 2 Barry Levinson's *Diner*, which flopped at previews in Phoenix and St. Louis and was almost shelved by MGM-UA, premieres at the Festival Theater. A recent critic's screening and Pauline Kael's *New Yorker* review have now produced a favorable buzz. It stars Steve Guttenberg, Mickey Rourke, Daniel Stern, Kevin Bacon, and Ellen Barkin. **28** Mel Gibson stars in *Road Warrior*, opening today at the Festival Theater. He first played the role in *Mad Max* in 1979, which got buried in its original U.S. release but will now get a second life. **30** Rod Steiger, Maximilian Schell, and Robby Benson are the stars of *The Chosen*, opening at the Beekman and Cinema III.

MAY 14 Arnold Schwarzenegger stars in his first popular feature film, *Conan the Barbarian*, opening at 1,398 theaters nationwide.

JUNE 4 *Poltergeist*, starring Craig T. Nelson, JoBeth Williams, and Beatrice Straight, opens. *Star Trek II: The Wrath of Kahn*, with the cast of the TV show and Ricardo Montalban, opens in over one thousand theaters. **11** Steven Spielberg's *E.T.*,

Business and Society

• Video cassette reproduction of films begins to become an important factor in the financing of production. By the end of the year the average film is earning eight percent of its revenues from this source • The number of films made in New York City has tripled in the last five years. Illinois, Texas, Georgia, and Florida are also competing with Hollywood for the production dollar.

FEBRUARY 8 Orion takes over Filmways. **17** Screen Actors Guild president Ed Asner receives a phone call threatening his life because of his liberal politics. Asner is given police protection. **19** President Reagan says that he's "disturbed" by SAG president Ed Asner's support for Salvadoran rebels.

JUNE 8 Paramount announces that Jeffrey Katzenberg is its new production chief. **17** CBS and 20th Century Fox create a partnership to release videotapes. **22** Coca-Cola announces the completion of its purchase of Columbia Pictures.

JULY 12 On the publication date of David McClintick's *Indecent Exposure*, about the 1977 David Begelman scandal, MGM-UA announces that Begelman is no longer head of United Artists. **16** Cineplex opens its first U.S. house, a fourteen-screen Showcase cinema at the Beverly Center in Los Angeles.

Births, Deaths, Marriages, and Divorces

JANUARY 8 Danny DeVito m. Rhea Perlman.

FEBRUARY 12 Farrah Fawcett and Lee Majors divorce. **17** Lee Strasberg d.

MARCH 5 John Belushi is found dead.

MAY • Melanie Griffith m. Steven Bauer.

JUNE 19 Chevy Chase m. Jayni Luke. **29** Director Henry King d.

JULY 11 Robby Benson m. rock singer Karla de Vito. **23** Jessica Lange and Paco Grande divorce. **29** Director William Friedkin m. British actress Leslie-Anne Down.

AUGUST • Robert Duvall m. Gail Youngs. **1** John Malkovich m. Glenne Headly.

Arnold Schwarzenegger in *Conan the Barbarian* MSN

sleds used in *Citizen Kane*. **10** Under the headline "Fresh Face," the New York *Daily News* reports that "Holly Hunter, a newcomer to both New York and Broadway, has just replaced Mary Beth Hurt...in Beth Henley's "Crimes of the Heart....""

JULY 3 Eddie Murphy says in *TV Guide*: "I know I'm going to be a millionaire when I'm 22, maybe sooner." He is making $4,500 a show on *Saturday Night Live*. **23** Vic Morrow and two child actors are killed in a helicopter accident during the filming of *Twilight Zone—The Movie*. Director John Landis will be indicted for involuntary manslaughter for the incident.

AUGUST 20 The California Labor Commission orders Richard Pryor's ex-manager, David Franklin, to pay the star the

The Extra-Terrestrial opens in over one thousand theaters, grosses nearly $12,000,000 in its first three days, and will ultimately bring in $701.1 million. Universal licenses about fifty products to use the image of E.T., and "E.T., phone home" becomes a catch phrase. **25** Destined to become a cult classic, Ridley Scott's *Blade Runner*, a futuristic film *noir* set in Los Angeles, starring Harrison Ford, Rutger Hauer, Sean Young, Edward James Olmos, and Darryl Hannah, opens. Based on Phillip K. Dick's novel, *Do Android's Dream of Electric Sleep?*, it will be released in the director's cut in 1992.

SEPTEMBER • Neil Gabler and Jeffrey Lyons replace Siskel and Ebert on *Sneak Previews*.

OCTOBER 1 The Disney Company opens its Epcot Center in Florida.

NOVEMBER 26 The Disney Company signs an agreement with the NAACP to improve opportunities for blacks. MGM-UA will sign a similar agreement on December 23. **30** HBO and CBS, to insure a steady flow of movies for broadcast, join with Columbia Pictures to form Nova, a movie production company they will rename Tri-Star Pictures next year.

DECEMBER 20 Sherry Lansing resigns as president of 20th Century Fox to produce independently.

12 Henry Fonda d. **18** Silent-screen star Beverly Bayne d. **29** Ingrid Bergman d.

SEPTEMBER • Cybill Shepherd and David Ford divorce. **14** Grace Kelly—Princess Grace of Monaco—dies of injuries from yesterday's auto accident.

NOVEMBER 1 King Vidor d. **5** Elizabeth Taylor divorces John Warner.

DECEMBER 3 William Hurt and Mary Beth Supinger divorce.

Also this year: • Michael Keaton m. Caroline MacWilliams. • Michelle Pfeiffer m. Peter Horton. • Audrey Hepburn and Dr. Andrea Dotti and Tom Selleck and Jacquelyn Ray divorce.

Personalities

$3,000,000 he embezzled from him.

SEPTEMBER • Paul Newman enters the food business with "Newman's Own" salad dressing. He will donate some of the profits to progressive social causes. **5** A drunken driver in San Francisco smashes into the taxi carrying Janet Gaynor, her husband, Paul Gregory, Mary Martin, and her manager, Ben Washer. Washer is killed, and the others are seriously injured. **28** Ellen Burstyn and Al Pacino become co-artistic directors of the Actors Studio.

OCTOBER • Warren Beatty and nineteen-year-old Daryl Hannah are an item. • Robin Williams, his wife pregnant with their first child, gives up alcohol and co-caine—cold turkey. • Linda Blair appears nude in *Oui* magazine. **10** Richard Dreyfuss crashes his Mercedes into a palm tree in Beverly Hills. Police, extricating him, also find cocaine and Percodan in his possession.

DECEMBER • In a *Rolling Stone* interview, Bette Midler reveals that she once tried—unsuccessfully—to romance Bob Dylan. **7** Stella Stevens, skidding on an ice-slicked road in Washington state, collides with a logging truck. She's all right but her uncle, riding beside her, is killed. **8** At a postpremiere party for *That Championship Season*, Robert Mitchum, apparently irked at the demands of photographers, throws a basketball at *Time* photographer Yvonne Helmsley, breaking her glasses and camera and bruising her face. **19** Jodie Foster is fined $100 for possessing a small amount of cocaine at Boston's Logan Airport.

Movies

JULY 28 An *Officer and a Gentleman* opens. Directed by Taylor Hackford, it stars Richard Gere, Debra Winger, and Louis Gossett Jr., and features the song "Up Where We Belong." Onscreen lovers Winger and Gere did not get along on the set.

OCTOBER 1 Peter O'Toole stars in *My Favorite Year*, opening today.

DECEMBER 3 Jessica Lange stars in *Frances*, the story of screen actress Frances Farmer, premiering at the Cinema II. **8** Richard

Richard Gere stars in *An Officer and a Gentleman*, opening in July.　　　　LC

Attenborough's *Gandhi*, starring Ben Kingsley, Candice Bergen, Edward Fox, and John Gielgud, has its North American premiere in New York, Los Angeles, Toronto, and Washington. The enormously popular *48 HRS*, starring Eddie Murphy and Nick Nolte, opens across the country. And Sidney Lumet's *The Verdict*, starring Paul Newman, Charlotte Rampling, and James Mason, opens. **10** *Sophie's Choice*, starring Meryl Streep and Kevin Kline, opens. Streep, in an Oscar-winning performance, benefits from Nestor Alemendros's cinematography. **17** Sidney Pollack's *Tootsie*, starring Dustin Hoffman in drag, Jessica Lange, and Teri Garr, opens.

Business and Society

Births, Deaths, Marriages, and Divorces

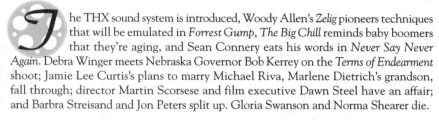

*T*he THX sound system is introduced, Woody Allen's *Zelig* pioneers techniques that will be emulated in *Forrest Gump*, *The Big Chill* reminds baby boomers that they're aging, and Sean Connery eats his words in *Never Say Never Again*. Debra Winger meets Nebraska Governor Bob Kerrey on the *Terms of Endearment* shoot; Jamie Lee Curtis's plans to marry Michael Riva, Marlene Dietrich's grandson, fall through; director Martin Scorsese and film executive Dawn Steel have an affair; and Barbra Streisand and Jon Peters split up. Gloria Swanson and Norma Shearer die.

- Number of releases: 495
- Percentage of TV households with VCRs: 10%
- Number of screens: 18,900, of which 2,850 are in drive-ins
- Total admissions: 1,196,900,000
- Average ticket price: $3.15
- Box office receipts: $3,766,000,000
- Average production cost per film: $11,900,000
- Number of times the word "shit" is used on the soundtrack of *Scarface*: 206

Top stars at the box office, based on a Quigley Publications poll of exhibitors:

1. Clint Eastwood
2. Eddie Murphy
3. Sylvester Stallone
4. Burt Reynolds
5. John Travolta
6. Dustin Hoffman
7. Harrison Ford
8. Richard Gere
9. Chevy Chase
10. Tom Cruise

Top rental earnings, based on figures reported by *Variety*:

1. *Return of the Jedi*	$165,500,000
2. *Tootsie*	94,500,000
3. *Trading Places*	40,600,000
4. *War Games*	36,600,000
5. *Superman III*	36,400,000

The New York Film Critics Circle Awards
Best Picture: *Terms of Endearment*

The Los Angeles Film Critics Association
Best Picture: *Terms of Endearment*

The Golden Globe Awards
Best Picture (Drama): *Terms of Endearment*
Best Picture (Musical/Comedy): *Yentl*

The Cannes Film Festival
Palme d'Or: *The Ballad of Narayama*

The Academy Awards (presented April 9, 1984)
Best Picture: *Terms of Endearment*
Actor: Robert Duvall (*Tender Mercies*)
Actress: Shirley MacLaine (*Terms of Endearment*)
Supporting Actor: Jack Nicholson (*Terms of Endearment*)
Supporting Actress: Linda Hunt (*The Year of Living Dangerously*)
Director: James Brooks (*Terms of Endearment*)

January	February	March	April	May	June	
24 Director George Cukor d.	• Kim Basinger on display in *Playboy*	**4** *Tender Mercies*	• Dennis Hopper paranoid and hallucinating from drugs in Cuernavaca, Mexico	• Richard Pryor signs a $40 million, 5-year deal with Columbia Pictures	**29** Sylvester Stallone leaves his prints outside Mann's Chinese Theater	

July	August	September	October	November	December	
29 Raymond Massey and David Niven d.	**16** Carrie Fisher m. singer Paul Simon	**30** *The Big Chill* / **15** Eddie Murphy on HBO draws criticism for gay-bashing and AIDS jokes	**23** *Terms of Endearment*		**9** *Scarface*	

Personalities

JANUARY 21 Dennis Morgan, 1940s star, and his wife are hospitalized when their car plunges down a fifty-foot ravine near Tracy, California. **26** An earthquake damages the Malibu homes of Rod Steiger, Bruce Dern, Dyan Cannon, and Burgess Meredith. **31** The *New York Post* reports that Clint Eastwood and William Shatner helped to finance a raid into Laos by retired Green Beret Col. James "Bo" Gritz, seeking to find and rescue American P.O.W.s. Shatner says he gave money to obtain movie rights to the story, but Eastwood won't comment.

FEBRUARY • Kim Basinger is on display in *Playboy*.

MARCH 14 Liza Minnelli, choking on food lodged in her throat, is rushed to a Dallas hospital. **17** Peter O'Toole becomes the father of a son, Lorcan, by girlfriend Karen Brown (who sometimes uses his last name but is not married to him). The child will become the subject of a bitter custody battle between the two in 1988. **31** With the Broadway opening of the play 'Night, Mother, Kathy Bates achieves stardom.

APRIL • Dennis Hopper, paranoid and hallucinating from drugs, runs naked in Cuernavaca, Mexico, after being fired from *Jungle Warriors*. **11** On Oscar night at the Dorothy Chandler Pavilion, Kristy McNichol is almost left speechless. Presenting the statuette for Best Animated Short Subject, she opens the envelope to discover that the winner is…Zbigniew Rybcyznski. The best she can manage with his last name is a feeble "Sky." **20** The *Terms of Endearment* company begins filming on location in Nebraska, where Debra Winger meets and begins a long-term romance with Governor Bob Kerrey. Her relationship with Shirley MacLaine, her mother in the film, is considerably less affectionate.

MAY • Richard Pryor signs a $40 million, five-year deal with Columbia Pictures. **8** Elizabeth Taylor and Richard Burton open on Broadway in *Private Lives*. He is visibly in decline, and the reviews are terrible. **28** Ryan O'Neal, trading punches with his son, Griffen, knocks out several of the teenager's teeth.

Movies

JANUARY 21 Mel Gibson, Sigourney Weaver, and Linda Hunt star in *The Year of Living Dangerously*, opening at Cinema I.

FEBRUARY 18 Martin Scorsese's *The King of Comedy*, starring Robert DeNiro and Jerry Lewis, opens at the Coronet.

MARCH 4 *Tender Mercies*, opening at Loew's Tower East, stars Robert Duvall, Tess Harper, Betty Buckley, Wilford Brimley, and Ellen Barkin. **25** Francis Ford Coppola's *The Outsiders*, a teenage drama

Business and Society

• Long-term contracts are making something of a comeback. Studios have granted them to Eddie Murphy, Richard Pryor, and Michael Keaton.

JANUARY 27 Paramount announces that Frank Mancuso is the new president of its picture division.

Robert Duvall in *Tender Mercies*   LC

Births, Deaths, Marriages, and Divorces

JANUARY • Meg Tilly m. producer Tim Zinnemann. **24** Director George Cukor d.

FEBRUARY 6 Keith Carradine m. Sandra Will. **13** Jerry Lewis m. Sandra Pitnick.

MARCH 14 Harrison Ford m. Melissa Mathison. **15** James Earl Jones m. Cecillia Hart. **20** Richard Dreyfuss m. Jeramie Rain.

APRIL • Yul Brynner, just divorced from Jacqueline De Croisset, m. Kathy Lee. **4** Gloria Swanson d. **11** Dolores Del Rio d. **29** Dan Aykroyd m. actress Donna Dixon.

JUNE 12 Norma Shearer d. **25** Denzel Washington m. Paulette Pearson.

JUNE 6 Dudley Moore plays the piano part in Beethoven's Triple Concerto with the St. Paul Chamber Orchestra at Carnegie Hall. **27** Paramount announces that Eddie Murphy has signed a five-year film contract—called "wildly lucrative" by *Variety*—that will bring him a total of $15,000,000 plus a percentage of the profits. **29** Sylvester Stallone leaves his hand and foot prints outside Mann's Chinese Theater.

JULY • Shirley MacLaine's New Age *Out on a Limb* becomes a bestseller. • Madonna's first album, "Madonna," is released. **15** Eddie Murphy signs a new contract with *Saturday Night Live*, giving him a reported $30,000 a show. **19** A car driven by a drunken driver hits Dudley Moore's Mercedes on the Santa Monica freeway, totaling it but leaving the actor unhurt. A passenger in the other car is killed.

AUGUST 7 Tom Selleck and his stepson survive with only cuts and bruises a three-story fall in a Jeep in a Honolulu parking garage. **13** Richard Gere receives a summons for urinating in the street on Broadway near his Greenwich Village apartment early this morning. According to the *New York Post*, the officer issuing the summons told the actor: "You ain't no officer and you ain't no gentleman." **15** *People*, in a profile of nineteen-year-old Rob Lowe, comments: "What Lowe hasn't yet figured out is how to combine an acting career with a love life."

SEPTEMBER 2 Charges of cocaine possession against Richard Dreyfuss stemming from last October's auto accident are dropped because he is doing well in a rehabilitation program. **5** Brooke Shields enters Princeton. **16** Wearing a red tie and blue-and-white striped suit, Austrian-born

Arnold Schwarzenegger becomes an American citizen.

Arnold Schwarzenegger becomes a U.S. citizen in September.   *LC*

showcasing several young actors, including Matt Dillon, Patrick Swayze, Rob Lowe, Emilio Estevez, and Tom Cruise, opens.

APRIL 15 "What a feeling!" Jennifer Beals stars in *Flashdance*, opening in one thousand theaters.

MAY 25 *Return of the Jedi*, the third Star Wars film, starring Mark Hamill, Harrison Ford, Carrie Fisher, Billy Dee Williams, Alec Guinness, and the voice of James Earl Jones, opens in one thousand theaters. Lucasfilms's THX sound system is first used with this movie in some theaters.

JUNE 8 Dan Aykroyd and Eddie Murphy are in *Trading Places*, starting today. **10** Roger Moore is back as James Bond in *Octopussy*, opening at thirteen hundred theaters. **26** *The Dresser*, starring Albert Finney, Tom Courtenay, Edward Fox, and Zena Walker, opens.

JULY 15 Woody Allen's *Zelig*, co-starring Mia Farrow, opens at the Beekman. **29** Chevy Chase stars in *National Lampoon's Vacation*, opening in wide release.

AUGUST 5 Tom Cruise and Rebecca De Mornay star in *Risky Business*, opening today. They are also playing featured roles

in each other's private life.

SEPTEMBER 21 *Educating Rita*, starring Michael Caine and Julie Walters, opens at Cinema II. **30** Lawrence Kasdan's *The Big Chill* opens. It stars Tom Berenger, Glenn Close, Jeff Goldblum, William Hurt, Kevin Kline, Mary Kay Place, Meg Tilly, and Jobeth Williams. The part of Alex, whose suicide is the reason for the gathering of former friends in the movie, was played by unknown Kevin Costner. He ended up on the cutting-room floor.

OCTOBER 7 Twelve years after turning in his license to kill, Sean Connery is back

APRIL 18 The Disney Channel begins broadcasting. **27** SAG and AFTRA refuse to support hiring quotas for minorities.

MAY 19 Nova becomes Tri-Star Pictures.

AUGUST 25 Paramount's New York City street set is destroyed by fire, which also damages sets for *Star Trek III*.

DECEMBER • Charlton Heston, who opposes a proposed merger of SAG and AFTRA,

attributes the death threats he's been getting to the effect of the inflammatory rhetoric of SAG president Ed Asner, who supports the merger.

> The dialogue in *The Big Chill* is full of before-and-after portraits of a generation:
>
> **Tom Berenger (to Kevin Kline):** "Who'd've thought we'd both make so much money? Two revolutionaries!"

JULY 3 Richard Burton m. Sally Hay. **5** Patricia Neal divorces Roald Dahl. **29** Raymond Massey and David Niven d.

AUGUST 3 Carolyn Jones d. **16** Carrie Fisher m. singer Paul Simon. **17** Lyricist Ira Gershwin d.

OCTOBER • Marsha Mason and Neil Simon divorce. **10** Ralph Richardson d. **15** Pat O'Brien d.

Also this year: • Divorcing are Richard Burton and Susan Hunt and Dennis Quaid and Pamela Soles. • Christine Lahti m. Thomas Schlamme.

Personalities

OCTOBER 3-4 Director Francis Ford Coppola shuts down production of *The Cotton Club* in a dispute with producer Robert Evans, with whom he does not have a written contract. **15** "Eddie Murphy Delirious" on HBO tonight draws criticism for his gay-bashing and jokes about AIDS. **24** The National Association of Theater Owners names Kim Basinger "Female Star of Tomorrow."

DECEMBER 5 Elizabeth Taylor enters the Betty Ford Clinic to deal with the effects of alcohol and overmedication. **22** A Christmas tree fire destroys the home (and Oscar) of Gene Kelly, burning him slightly. **29** Arnold Schwarzenegger and Maria Shriver escape with minor injuries when their Jeep, which he is driving, goes off a road and down an embankment. He's cited for driving without a license.

Movies

for one more time as 007, James Bond, in *Never Say Never Again*, opening today, with Kim Basinger, Max von Sydow, Barbara Carrera, and Klaus Maria Brandauer. **21** *The Right Stuff*, based on the Tom Wolfe bestseller about the U.S. space program and starring Sam Shepard, Scott Glenn, Ed Harris, and Dennis Quaid, opens.

NOVEMBER 18 Barbra Streisand produced, directed, and stars in *Yentl*, with Mandy Patinkin and Amy Irving, opening in New York, Los Angeles, and Toronto. **23** James Brooks, who directed TV's *The Mary Tyler Moore Show*, brings to the big screen *Terms of Endearment*, starring Debra Winger, Shirley MacLaine, Jack Nicholson, and Danny DeVito, opening today.

DECEMBER 9 Al Pacino, Michelle Pfeiffer, and Mary Elizabeth Mastrantonio star in Brian DePalma's *Scarface*, opening today. The "X" rating it earned on November 3 was changed to an "R" on November 8 on appeal. **14** *Silkwood*, starring Meryl Streep, Kurt Russell, and Cher, opens. This film about safety in a nuclear plant, based on a true story, is director Mike Nichols's first film in seven years.

Jack Nicholson stars opposite Shirley MacLaine in *Terms of Endearment.*   *LC*

Business and Society

Births, Deaths, Marriages, and Divorces

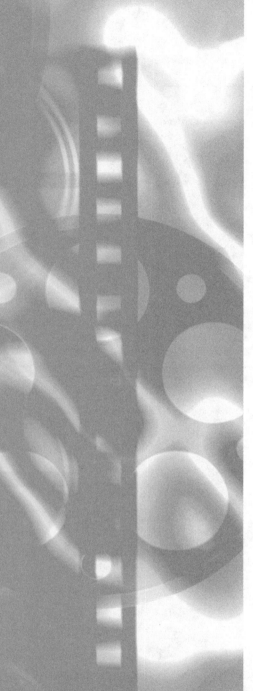

*G*hostbusters sets off a national craze for buttons that express negative views; they emulate the film's graphic of a ghost in a circle with a diagonal line through the ghost. IBM perpetuates the image of Charlie Chaplin's "Tramp" by using it in its advertisements. Dennis Hopper spends time in the psychiatric unit of Los Angeles's Cedars–Sinai Hospital, Tony Curtis and Liza Minnelli are at the Betty Ford Clinic dealing with substance-abuse problems, and Stacy Keach goes to prison on a cocaine charge.

- Number of releases: 536
- Percentage of TV households with VCRs: 18%
- Number of screens: 20,200, of which 2,850 are in drive-ins
- Total admissions: 1,199,100,000
- Average ticket price: $3.36
- Box office receipts: $4,030,600,000
- Average production cost per film: $14,400,000
- Length of this year's Academy Awards ceremony: 3 hours, 42 minutes
- Eddie Murphy's total compensation from *Beverly Hills Cop*: over $14,000,000

Top stars at the box office, based on a Quigley Publications poll of exhibitors:

1. Clint Eastwood
2. Bill Murray
3. Harrison Ford
4. Eddie Murphy
5. Sally Field
6. Burt Reynolds
7. Robert Redford
8. Prince
9. Dan Aykroyd
10. Meryl Streep

Top rental earnings, based on figures reported by *Variety*:

1.	*Ghostbusters*	$127,000,000
2.	*Indiana Jones and the Temple of Doom*	109,000,000
3.	*Gremlins*	78,500,000
4.	*Beverly Hills Cop*	58,000,000
5.	*Terms of Endearment*	50,250,000

The New York Film Critics Circle Awards
Best Picture: *Passage to India*

The Los Angeles Film Critics Association
Best Picture: *Amadeus*

The Golden Globe Awards
Best Picture (Drama): *Amadeus*
Best Picture (Musical/Comedy): *Romancing the Stone*

The Cannes Film Festival
Palme d'Or: *Paris, Texas*

The Academy Awards (presented March 25, 1985)
Best Picture: *Amadeus*
Actor: F. Murray Abraham (*Amadeus*)
Actress: Sally Field (*Places in the Heart*)
Supporting Actor: Haing Ngor (*The Killing Fields*)
Supporting Actress: Peggy Ashcroft (*A Passage to India*)
Director: Milos Forman (*Amadeus*)

January	February	March	April	May	June
	• Nick Nolte m. Becky Linger				**8** *Ghostbusters*
20 Johnny Weismuller d.		**5** William Powell d.	**9** Shirley MacLaine wins Oscar		**14** *Time* magazine's cover story is "Shirley MacLaine: Getting Her Kicks at 50"

July	August	September	October	November	December
16 Liza Minnelli checks into Betty Ford Clinic	**5** Richard Burton d.	**21** *Places in the Heart* and *Amadeus*	**12** *Blood Simple*		**7** Stacy Keach given nine months in jail for April 3 cocaine arrest in London
			9 *A Nightmare on Elm Street*		

Personalities

JANUARY 9 Glenn Close stars with Ted Danson in the ABC TV movie, *Something about Amelia*, about incest, watched by sixty million viewers. **13** France makes Jerry Lewis a commander in its Order of Arts and Literature. **27** Whoopi Goldberg's one-woman tour de force, *The Spook Show*, which gained her a following in the San Francisco area last year, opens at the Dance Theater Workshop in New York. It will lead to an HBO special and a role for her in *The Color Purple*. **29** Anthony Perkins is arrested at Heathrow Airport in London and will be fined for bringing marijuana and LSD into Britain.

FEBRUARY 24 Al Pacino resigns as co-artistic director of the Actors Studio.

Co-director Ellen Burstyn will remain in the position until 1988. **27** According to members of the production crew filming *Little Treasure* in Cuernavaca, Burt Lancaster and Margot Kidder get into a fist-fight, each drawing blood.

MARCH • Bill Murray is in an altercation with another patron at Piro's, a New York restaurant. **2** NBC announces that Eddie Murphy is leaving *Saturday Night Live* to concentrate on his movie career. **26** President Reagan awards James Cagney the Medal of Freedom. **29** Dustin Hoffman opens in an acclaimed Broadway production of the play, *Death of a Salesman*. John Malkovich, playing one of his sons, is called "spellbinding" by the *New York Times*. He is about to begin his film career with *Places in the Heart* and *The Killing Fields*.

APRIL • Susan Sarandon travels with a group of American women—MADRE—bringing baby food to mothers in war-torn Nicaragua. **3** Stacy Keach is arrested at Heathrow Airport in London, charged with smuggling a small quantity of cocaine. **9** The show must go on, and on, at the Oscar ceremonies tonight, which take almost four hours at the Dorothy Chandler Pavilion. Shirley MacLaine, taking the award for Best Actress in *Terms of Endearment*, hoists the Oscar and declares: "I deserve this." The audience loves it.

MAY 10 Jack Nicholson wins damages from *The Sun*, a supermarket tabloid, which had claimed that the actor had a "string of drug arrests." In fact, he's had none. **14** *Time* magazine's cover story is "Shirley MacLaine: Getting Her Kicks at 50." **21** The privately funded Hollywood Museum opens.

Movies

JANUARY 27 Woody Allen's *Broadway Danny Rose*, starring Allen, Mia Farrow, and Nick Apollo Forte, opens.

MARCH 2 Rob Reiner's rock group satire *This Is Spinal Tap* opens in a limited engagement. **9** *Splash*, starring Darryl Hannah, Tom Hanks, and John Candy, opens. **23** *Police Academy*, starring Steve Guttenberg, G.W. Bailey, and Bubba Smith, opens in 1,063 theaters. There will be five sequels. **30** Michael Douglas, Kathleen Turner, and Danny DeVito star in *Romancing the*

Stone, directed by Robert Zemeckis and opening today.

APRIL 6 *Moscow on the Hudson* opens. It stars Robin Williams. **13** *Swing Shift*, starring Goldie Hawn and Kurt Russell (who fell in love during filming and moved in together) and Christine Lahti, opens. Hawn clashed with director Jonathan Demme and supposedly changed part of the screenplay to aggrandize her character at the expense of Lahti's.

MAY 11 Barry Levinson's *The Natural*, starring Robert Redford, Robert Duvall, Glenn Close, and Kim Basinger, opens.

23 Harrison Ford and Kate Capshaw star in *Indiana Jones and the Temple of Doom* opening in 1,685 theaters. It will gross $45,709,328 in its first week, topping *Return of the Jedi*. *Indiana Jones and the Temple of Doom* has rapid-fire dialogue as well as nonstop action:

Kate Capshaw: "I thought archaeologists were funny little men searching for their mommies."
Harrison Ford: "Mummies."

Capshaw: "The entire place is crawling with living things."
Ford: "That's why they call it the jungle, sweetheart."

Business and Society

JANUARY 17 The Supreme Court rules that home video taping does not violate copyright laws.

FEBRUARY–MARCH • SAG president Ed Asner, who supports the merger of his union with AFTRA, feuds with Charlton Heston, who opposes it. Asner says that opponents promote a "master race" mentality among

actors. Heston attributes a recent threat against his life to this kind of rhetoric.

FEBRUARY 15 Walt Disney Productions announces the formation of Touchstone Productions.

APRIL 11 A conference on alcohol and drug abuse opens at the Burbank Studios, co-sponsored by Warner Bros. and Columbia.

MAY • Cineplex acquires the 297-theater

Odeon chain in Canada and becomes Cineplex Odeon.

JUNE 27 A PG-13 rating is instituted, requiring that children under thirteen admitted to films so classified be accompanied by an adult. The violence in *Indiana Jones and the Temple of Doom* had much to do with the creation of this category.

JULY 16 Jay Kanter is announced as the new head of production at MGM-UA.

Births, Deaths, Marriages, and Divorces

JANUARY • Director Brian DePalma and Nancy Allen divorce. **20** Johnny Weissmuller dies; a recording of his Tarzan ape call will be played at his burial on January 22.

FEBRUARY • Nick Nolte m. Becky Linger.

MARCH 1 Jackie Coogan d. **5** William Powell d.

APRIL • Tony Curtis m. Andria Savio. **26** Silent-screen star May McAvoy d.

MAY 25 Debbie Reynolds m. Richard Hamlett.

JUNE 16 Morgan Freeman m. Myrna Colley-Lee.

JUNE • Jane Fonda and Tom Hayden hold a meeting in their backyard of about fifty young Hollywood stars, including Eric Stoltz, Tom Cruise, and Rob Lowe, to mobilize them to work for liberal causes. **12** Los Angeles Lakers fan Jack Nicholson, watching a playoff game against the Boston Celtics in the Boston Garden from a sky box, "moons" nearby hostile fans, according to Celtics broadcaster Johnny Most. **13** Jan-Michael Vincent, in a bar fight in Malibu, knocks another customer unconscious.

JULY 14 Eddie Murphy is in a fight with another patron at a Sunset Strip club. Murphy's lip is cut, and the other man claims he was cut by a glass thrown by Murphy, who says the man made racial remarks to him. **16** Liza Minnelli checks into the Betty Ford Clinic in Rancho Mirage for seven weeks to deal with her drug and alcohol problem.

AUGUST • Edward James Olmos joins the cast of *Miami Vice*, which debuted on TV a few weeks ago. **31** Brenda Vaccaro is arrested at her West Los Angeles home for possession of cocaine, on a tip from her ex-boyfriend. The charges will be dropped when no proof is found that the drug belonged to her.

OCTOBER • Filming *Red Sonja*, Arnold Schwarzenegger has an affair with Brigitte Nielsen. **12** Charles Higham's *Audrey: The Life of Audrey Hepburn*, published today, reveals that at age thirteen she worked in the Dutch underground against the Nazi occupation of Holland. **31** Twenty-nine-year-old Robby Benson has open heart surgery to repair a valve.

DECEMBER 2 Barbara Goldsmith's interview with Robert DeNiro in *Parade* is the first he's given in ten years. He was suspicious and uneasy about being recognized or overheard at the Long Island restaurant where he insisted they meet, and reveals little. **7** Stacy Keach is sentenced to nine months in jail for his April 3 cocaine arrest in London. He will serve a total of six months, beginning immediately.

JUNE 1 Sergio Leone's *Once Upon a Time in America*, starring Robert DeNiro, James Woods, Elizabeth Mcgovern, Treat Williams, and Tuesday Weld, opens. Eighty-three minutes have been cut from the print shown at Cannes, and the confusing narrative has been rearranged in chronological order. The original 227-minute print is later released as well. **8** *Gremlins*, starring Zach Gilligan and Phoebe Cates, opens in 1,511 theaters. **8** Bill Murray, Dan Aykroyd, and Sigourney Weaver star in *Ghostbusters*, opening in 1,339 theaters. Before his untimely death, John Belushi had been set to team with Aykroyd in this film. **22** *The Karate Kid*, opening today, stars Ralph Macchio and Pat Morita.

AUGUST 15 *The Woman in Red*, opening today, stars Gene Wilder, Charles Grodin, Gilda Radner, and Kelly Le Brock, and features Stevie Wonder's "I Just Called to Say I Love You."

SEPTEMBER 14 *A Soldier's Story*, starring Howard E. Rollins Jr., Adolph Caesar, and Denzel Washington, opens in New York, Los Angeles, and Toronto. John Sayles's *The Brother from Another Planet* premieres at the Embassy 72nd St. **21** Opening in wide release today are Carl Reiner's *All of Me*, starring Steve Martin, Lily Tomlin, and Victoria Tennant; Robert Benton's *Places in the Heart*, starring Sally Field, Lindsay Crouse, Ed Harris, Amy Madigan, John Malkovich, and Danny Glover; and *Amadeus*, starring Tom Hulce, F. Murray Abraham, and Elizabeth Berridge. **28** The New York Film Festival opens with *Country*, starring Jessica Lange, Sam

SEPTEMBER 11 Barry Diller is named chairman of the board and CEO of 20th Century Fox, effective October 1. **12** Paramount names Frank Mancuso to replace the departing Barry Diller as studio head. Michael Eisner resigns when passed over for the spot. **22** Michael Eisner becomes chairman of Disney Productions, and on September 30 will name Jeffrey Katzenberg to head the Disney studio.

OCTOBER 1 The American Movie Classics

JULY 27 James Mason d.

AUGUST • Kathleen Turner m. Jay Weiss. **4** Silent-screen star Mary Miles Minter d. **5** Richard Burton dies; Elizabeth Taylor collapses when told the news.

Bill Murray (l.) and Dan Akroyd (c.) in *Ghostbusters*   LC/© COLUMBIA PICTURES

Personalities

A CLASSIC REVIVED: METROPOLIS

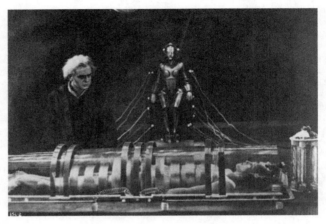

AUGUST 16 A reconstructed version of Fritz Lang's 1926 classic, *Metropolis*, with music by Giorgio Moroder, the first feature-length film presented in digital stereo, has its West Coast premiere at the Samuel Goldwyn Theater in Beverly Hills.   *MSN*

Movies

Shepard, and Wilford Brimley.

OCTOBER 12 Independents Ethan and Joel Coen's first feature film, *Blood Simple*, starring John Getz and Frances McDormand and brought in under $2 million, premieres at the New York Film Festival. **26** Arnold Schwarzenegger stars in *The Terminator*, opening in 1,005 theaters.

NOVEMBER 2 Sam Waterston, Haing Ngor, and John Malkovich star in *The Killing Fields*, directed by Roland Joffe, at the

Robert Englund stars as the horrific Freddie Krueger in *A Nightmare on Elm Street*, one of the most intelligent and terrifying horror films of the 1980s. *LC*
© *NEWS LINE*

Cinema I. **9** Robert Englund is Freddie Krueger in Wes Craven's *A Nightmare on Elm Street*, opening today and followed by numerous recurrent dreams in the form of sequels.

DECEMBER 5 Eddie Murphy is the star of *Beverly Hills Cop*, opening today. It will be the first movie to be shown on two thousand screens during its maximum saturation period. **14** David Lean's *A Passage to India*, starring Judy Davis, Victor Banerjee, Peggy Ashcroft, James Fox, and Alec Guinness, opens at the Ziegfeld.

Business and Society

(AMC) cable TV channel begins operations. **8** Ned Tanen is named head of Paramount's film division.

Births, Deaths, Marriages, and Divorces

SEPTEMBER 1 Glenn Close m. James Marlas. **14** Janet Gaynor d. **18** Gene Wilder m. Gilda Radner. **25** Walter Pidgeon d.

OCTOBER • Sigourney Weaver m. Jim Simpson.

DECEMBER • George Peppard, having been divorced from Sherry Boucher, M. Alexis Adams. **15** Sally Field m. Alan Greisman. Bette Midler and Martin von Haselberg are married in Las Vegas by an Elvis impersonator. **18** Jamie Lee Curtis m. Christopher Guest. **24** Peter Lawford d.

Also this year: • Arlene Dahl m. Marc Rosen, her sixth husband. • Carrie Fisher and Paul Simon, Glenn Ford and Cynthia Hayward, and Ida Lupino and Howard Duff divorce.

upert Murdoch takes over 20th Century Fox and film colorization begins on TV. Madonna steals *Desperately Seeking Susan* from Rosanna Arquette. Molly Ringwald is one of several young and promising stars becoming known as the "Brat Pack." Others in the group include Emilio Estevez and Ally Sheedy, who will appear with Ringwald in *The Breakfast Club*, and Tom Cruise, Matt Dillon, Patrick Swayze, Demi Moore, Kiefer Sutherland, Phoebe Cates, Lou Diamond Phillips, and Rob Lowe.

- Number of releases: 470
- Percentage of TV households with VCRs: 27%
- Number of screens: 21,150, of which 2,800 are in drive-ins
- Total admissions: 1,056,100,000
- Average ticket price: $3.55
- Box office receipts: $3,749,400,000
- Average production cost per film: $16,800,000
- Mayhem rate in *Rambo: First Blood Part II*: one killing every 2.1 minutes

Top stars at the box office, based on a Quigley Publications poll of exhibitors:

1. Sylvester Stallone
2. Eddie Murphy
3. Clint Eastwood
4. Michael J. Fox
5. Chevy Chase
6. Arnold Schwarzenegger
7. Chuck Norris
8. Harrison Ford
9. Michael Douglas
10. Meryl Streep

Top rental earnings, based on figures reported by *Variety*:

1.	*Back to the Future*	$94,000,000
2.	*Rambo: First Blood Part II*	80,000,000
3.	*Rocky IV*	65,000,000
4.	*Beverly Hills Cop*	50,000,000
5.	*Cocoon*	40,000,000

The New York Film Critics Circle Awards
Best Picture: *Prizzi's Honor*

The Los Angeles Film Critics Association
Best Picture: *Brazil*

The Golden Globe Awards
Best Picture (Drama): *Out of Africa*
Best Picture (Musical/Comedy): *Prizzi's Honor*

The Cannes Film Festival
Palme d'Or: *When Father Was Away on Business*

The Academy Awards (presented March 24, 1986)
Best Picture: *Out of Africa*
Actor: William Hurt (*Kiss of the Spider Woman*)
Actress: Geraldine Page (*The Trip to Bountiful*)
Supporting Actor: Don Ameche (*Cocoon*)
Supporting Actress: Anjelica Huston (*Prizzi's Honor*)
Director: Sydney Pollack (*Out of Africa*)

January	February	March	April	May	June	
	• Michael J. Fox replaces Eric Stolz in *Back to the Future*	**13** Alan Ladd Jr. becomes president and CEO of MGM-UA	**3** Last of original Brown Derby restaurants in Hollywood closes		**22** Fire damages Barbara Stanwyck's home	
		• Madonna meets Sean Penn on the set of her "Material Girl" video		**22** *Rambo: First Blood Part II*		

July	August	September	October	November	December	
25 Rock Hudson reveals he has AIDS	**16** Madonna m. Sean Penn		**2** Rock Hudson d. of AIDS	• *Miracle on 34th St.* is first colorized film widely shown on TV	**18** *The Color Purple*	
		23 Rupert Murdoch owns 20th Century Fox				

Personalities

• Carrie Fisher spends time in a drug rehabilitation clinic in southern California after an overdose of Percodan, which she says was accidental.

JANUARY • Halfway through filming *Back to the Future*, director Robert Zemeckis replaces Eric Stoltz with TV actor Michael J. Fox.

FEBRUARY • Madonna meets Sean Penn on the set of her "Material Girl" video. • Debra Winger, scheduled to star in *Peggy Sue Got Married*, is in traction with a back injury, and rumor has it that Kathleen Turner will be offered the role.

MARCH 3 Bruce Willis, off-Broadway actor and sometime waiter and bartender, co-stars

Movies

JANUARY 25 John Schlesinger's *The Falcon and the Snowman*, starring Timothy Hutton and Sean Penn, opens.

FEBRUARY 8 Harrison Ford, Kelly McGillis, Lukas Haas, and Alexander Godunov star in *Witness*, opening today. **15** Albert Brooks's *Lost in America*, starring Brooks and Julie Haggerty, opens in five cities.

MARCH 8 Peter Bogdanovich's *Mask*, starring Cher and Eric Stoltz, opens in New York, Toronto, and Los Angeles.

Rosanna Arquette and Madonna in *Desperately Seeking Susan*.　LC
© ORION

29 Orion opens *Desperately Seeking Susan*, starring Rosanna Arquette and Madonna, on 268 screens with a marketing campaign geared toward teenagers. But the film's producers were right: it's young adults who make it a hit. Madonna, on the heels of recordings "Like a Virgin" and "Material Girl," steals the film from Arquette.

Business and Society

JANUARY 21 MGM-UA names Alan Ladd Jr. to head United Artists.

MARCH 13 Alan Ladd Jr. becomes president and CEO of MGM-UA, replacing Frank Yablans. Jay Kanter will head MGM and Richard Berger, United Artists. **20** Rupert Murdoch buys fifty percent of 20th Century Fox.

APRIL 4 The Los Angeles Philharmonic Auditorium, once Clune's Auditorium, where D.W. Griffith's *Birth of a Nation* premiered in 1915, is reduced to rubble to make way for a hotel and office building. **15** Dawn Steel becomes Paramount's production chief. **15** ABC cancels the TV showing of Warren Beatty's *Reds* when Beatty wins an arbitration hearing on their plan to trim it by sixteen minutes to accommodate commercials. Beatty and Paramount lose $6.5 million on the cancellation.

MAY 6 20th Century Fox announces that its co-owners Marvin Davis and Rupert Murdoch will buy the Metromedia TV stations. Davis will later back out.

JULY 8 The Walt Disney company announces that it has secured from MGM-UA the right to use the MGM name, logo, and film clips for a Disney-MGM Theme Park at Walt Disney World.

AUGUST • Cineplex Odeon buys the Plitt

Births, Deaths, Marriages, and Divorces

MARCH 21 Michael Redgrave d.

APRIL • Dyan Cannon m. producer Stanley Fimberg.

MAY 9 Edmond O'Brien d. **13** Silent-screen star Leatrice Joy d. **16** Margaret Hamilton d.

JUNE 2 Hedy Lamarr divorces Lewis Boies Jr.

AUGUST 8 Louise Brooks d. **16** Madonna m. Sean Penn.

SEPTEMBER • Sylvester Stallone and Sasha Czack divorce. **27** Lloyd Nolan d.

OCTOBER 2 Rock Hudson dies of AIDS. **10** Orson Welles and Yul Brynner die.

with Cybill Shepherd in the pilot film for *Moonlighting* on the *ABC Sunday Night Movie.* **16** The widows of Carl Foreman and Michael Wilson are given the Oscars their blacklisted husbands should have received in 1957 for *The Bridge on the River Kwai* screenplay. **25** Amy Irving, single, clearly pregnant, and about to take part in the Oscar ceremony telecast from the Dorothy Chandler Pavilion, is almost scratched from the lineup when some Academy administrators worry about how it will look. But her partner, Steven Spielberg, scheduled to hand out an award, says that he will leave with her if it comes down to that, and so she goes on.

APRIL 1 *Playboy* publisher Hugh Hefner accuses director Peter Bogdanovich of seducing the seventeen-year-old sister of Dorothy Stratten, former Playmate and Bogdanovich girlfriend who was slain in 1980. Bogdanovich denies it. **3** The last of the original Brown Derby restaurants, in Hollywood on Vine St.—where Clark Gable romanced Carole Lombard in booth number five—closes.

JUNE 1 Brooke Shields celebrates her twentieth birthday in New York at Chippendales, the club where boys dance in g-strings. (Her contract with the publishers of *On Your Own*, her guide for young girls, stipulated that she remain a virgin until age twenty.) **15** The publication of Shaun Considine's *Barbra Streisand: The Woman, The Myth, The Music*, a critical portrait of an often difficult person, brings threats of a lawsuit from the star. **22** A fire does $1,800,000 worth of damage to Barbara Stanwyck's home, but she is unhurt.

JULY 11 *Playboy* goes on sale with nude photos of Madonna, beating *Penthouse* and its pictures to the stands by one day. **17** Madonna's application to buy a co-op apartment in the San Remo on New York City's Central Park West is rejected without explanation. Of the board members, only Diane Keaton votes "yes." **25** A spokesperson for Rock Hudson reveals that he has AIDS.

AUGUST 2 A judge dismisses Madonna's attempt to stop the release on video cassette of Steve Lewicki's 1979 *A Certain Sacrifice*, in which, she says, she was "second-rate." **12** Burt Reynolds denies persistent rumors that he has AIDS. He's in the midst of a three-year-screen hiatus—and has not been looking well—primarily because of a joint disorder brought on by a punch to the jaw he received while filming

MAY 22 In the biggest opening ever, *Rambo: First Blood Part II* appears on 2,074 screens. Sylvester Stallone's one-man army becomes the most controversial "hero" of the decade. **24** Roger Moore's latest James Bond film opens, *A View to a Kill*, with Christopher Walken and Tanya Roberts.

JUNE 14 Anjelica Huston achieves stardom in her father John Huston's *Prizzi's Honor*, also starring Jack Nicholson and Kathleen Turner, opening today. **21** *Cocoon*, opening on 1,140 screens, is directed by Ron Howard and stars Don Ameche, Wilford Brimley, Hume Cronyn, Jessica Tandy, Brian Dennehy, Gwen Verdon, and Jack Gilford.

JULY 3 Robert Zemeckis's *Back to the Future*, starring Michael J. Fox, Christopher Lloyd, and Crispin Glover, opens on 1,419 screens. It will be followed by two sequels. **10** *Silverado*, opening today, stars Kevin Kline, Scott Glenn, Rosanna Arquette, John Cleese, Kevin Costner, Danny Glover, Jeff Goldblum, and Brian Dennehy. **26** Hector Babenco's *Kiss of the Spider Woman*, starring William Hurt, Raul Julia, and Sonia Braga, premieres in the U.S. at Cinema I.

AUGUST 9 *Pee-Wee's Big Adventure*, starring Paul Reubens, opens.

SEPTEMBER 13 Jane Fonda, Anne Bancroft, and Meg Tilly star in *Agnes of God*, opening today in a limited engagement.

DECEMBER 6 Jon Voight, Eric Roberts, and Rebecca De Mornay star in *Runaway Train*, opening today. **18** Terry Gilliam's fantasy extravaganza, *Brazil*, opens, starring Jonathan Pryce, Kim Greist, and Robert De Niro. A faction at Universal felt it was not good enough to release, although four days ago the Los Angeles Film Critics voted it Best Picture. **18** Steven Spielberg's *The Color Purple* opens in a limited engagement and will go into wide release on December 20. Whoopi Goldberg, Oprah Winfrey,

Theaters, a six-hundred-house chain. • Michael Medved replaces Neil Gabler on *Sneak Previews.* **7** Ted Turner announces he has agreed to acquire MGM-UA. **16** Asian-Americans picket the New York opening of *Year of the Dragon*, claiming it perpetuates ethnic stereotypes.

SEPTEMBER 23 Rupert Murdoch buys out Marvin Davis to become sole owner of 20th Century Fox. **24** Dino De Laurentiis agrees to buy Embassy Pictures from Columbia.

NOVEMBER 19 Stepin Fetchit d. **27** Amy Irving m. director Steven Spielberg.

DECEMBER 12 Anne Baxter d. **15** Sylvester Stallone m. Brigitte Nielsen.

Also this year: • Divorced are Glenn Close and James Marlas, Melanie Griffith

and Steve Bauer, and Randy Quaid and Ella Jolly.

Orson Welles, the director who made film history in 1941 with *Citizen Kane*, dies on October 10, 1985. *LC*

Personalities

City Heat last year. He has also become addicted to Halcion. **16** The guests at Madonna's wedding to Sean Penn at a Malibu beach house include Cher, Andy Warhol, Tom Cruise, and David Letterman, who dine on pizza and curried oysters from Spago. When press helicopters hover, Penn carves a huge "FUCK OFF" in the sand and fires a warning shot.

OCTOBER • *Playgirl* publishes nude photos of Syvester Stallone—stills from his 1970 porno film. **17** Sean Penn pleads no contest in Nashville to charges that he assaulted two journalists in June, for which he draws a fine and suspended sentence.

Movies

Danny Glover, and Margaret Avery star. The film's negative treatment of black men stirs controversy. Also opening in the same release pattern is Sidney Pollack's *Out of Africa*, starring Robert Redford and Meryl Streep. **20** Geraldine Page, in an Oscar-winning performance, stars in *The Trip to Bountiful*, premiering at Cinema II. Peter Masterson directed this Horton Foote screenplay, which Foote based on his stage version.

NOVEMBER • Marlee Matlin moves in with William Hurt following completion of filming on *Children of a Lesser God*. **4** James Caan, attending a Mafia racketeering trial in New York to lend support to one of the defendants, Anthony Russo, an old friend of his, is subpoenaed himself to testify. **5** Patty Duke becomes the second woman elected president of SAG. **15** Peter

Bogdanovich declares bankruptcy.

DECEMBER 13 The barn that Cecil B. DeMille used to film *The Squaw Man* in 1914, which was moved from Paramount to a site opposite the Hollywood Bowl on February 15, 1983, is dedicated as the Hollywood Studio Museum.

ROCK HUDSON: "HOLLYWOOD'S MOST HANDSOME BACHELOR"

Throughout his film career, starting with Warners in 1948 through his time with Universal, Rock Hudson lived a lie that was carefully crafted for him by the studios. Linked in the gossip columns to starlets Vera Ellen and Piper Laurie; dubbed in a *Life* cover story "Hollywood's Most Handsome Bachelor"; and then part of a marriage that left Louella Parsons "shocked" when it broke up, the public Rock Hudson was never allowed to be himself. Thus the widespread shock when it is learned in July of this year that he is gay and has AIDS. The announcement convinces President Reagan of the seriousness of the AIDS epidemic. Hudson will die soon after.

Rock Hudson, early in his career.   LC

Business and Society

NOVEMBER–DECEMBER • *Miracle on 34th St.* is the first colorized (originally black-and-white) film widely shown on TV.

NOVEMBER 13 CBS announces that it will sell its share of Tri-Star.

Births, Deaths, Marriages, and Divorces

ed Turner, taking over MGM-UA, keeps its film library and sells the studio back to Kirk Kerkorian. MCA-Universal begins to buy into Cineplex Odeon and will eventually acquire forty-nine percent of it—part of a growing trend of producers and distributors becoming exhibitors as well, a small echo of Hollywood's Golden Age. Paul Hogan emerges from TV ads for Australian tourism into the surprise blockbuster hit, *Crocodile Dundee*. It grosses more than thirty times the $5.6 million it cost to make. And Cary Grant is dead.

- Number of releases: 451
- Percentage of TV households with VCRs: 37%
- Number of screens: 22,750, of which 2,800 are in drive-ins
- Total admissions: 1,017,200,000
- Average ticket price: $3.71
- Box office receipts: $3,778,000,000
- Average production cost per film: $17,500,000

Top stars at the box office, based on a Quigley Publications poll of exhibitors:

1. Tom Cruise
2. Eddie Murphy
3. Paul Hogan
4. Rodney Dangerfield
5. Bette Midler
6. Sylvester Stallone
7. Clint Eastwood
8. Whoopi Goldberg
9. Kathleen Turner
10. Paul Newman

Top rental earnings, based on figures reported by *Variety*:

1.	*Top Gun*	$82,000,000
2.	*The Karate Kid Part II*	56,950,000
3.	*Crocodile Dundee*	51,000,000
4.	*Star Trek IV: The Voyage Home*	45,000,000
5.	*Aliens*	42,500,000

The New York Film Critics Circle
Best Picture: *Hannah and Her Sisters*

The Los Angeles Film Critics Association
Best Picture: *Hannah and Her Sisters*

The Golden Globe Awards
Best Picture (Drama): *Platoon*
Best Picture (Musical/Comedy): *Hannah and Her Sisters*

The Cannes Film Festival
Palm d'Or: *The Mission*

The Academy Awards (presented March 30, 1987)
Best Picture: *Platoon*
Actor: Paul Newman (*The Color of Money*)
Actress: Marlee Matlin (*Children of a Lesser God*)
Supporting Actor: Michael Caine (*Hannah and Her Sisters*)
Supporting Actress: Dianne Wiest (*Hannah and Her Sisters*)
Director: Oliver Stone (*Platoon*)

January	February	March	April	May	June	
15 MCA-Universal begins to buy into Cineplex Odeon	**7** *Hannah and Her Sisters*	**25** Ted Turner takes over MGM-UA **8** Clint Eastwood elected mayor of Carmel			**6** Ted Turner announces sale of MGM, except for film library **18** Directors Guild of America award to Oscar Micheaux, pioneer black filmmaker	

July	August	September	October	November	December	
18 *Aliens*	**1** Tatum O'Neal m. tennis star John McEnroe	**6** Silent-screen star Blanche Sweet d.	• Chevy Chase at the Betty Ford Center	**13** John Huston denounces colorized version of *The Maltese Falcon*	**19** *Platoon*	

Personalities

JANUARY 30   Tom Laughlin is hospitalized with a severe concussion sustained in a fight scene in *The Return of Billy Jack*.

MARCH •   Sally Field, in a *Playboy* interview, says that in her relationship with Burt Reynolds she almost disappeared as an individual in trying to be whatever he wanted her to be. **8**   The Directors Guild of America, for the first time, gives its Outstanding Feature Film Achievement Award to a director not nominated for an Academy Award: Steven Spielberg, for *The Color Purple*. **24**   *The Color Purple* has been nominated for eleven Academy Awards. Its director, Steven Spielberg, although overlooked for a Best Director nomination, is at the Dorothy Chandler Pavilion tonight for the Oscar ceremonies.

Whoopi Goldberg in *The Color Purple*   LC
© *WARNER BROTHERS, photo by Gordon Parks*

APRIL 8   Clint Eastwood is elected mayor of Carmel-by-the-Sea, California.

MAY 18   The Directors Guild of America gives its first posthumous award—to Oscar Micheaux, pioneer black filmmaker, whose 1924 *Body and Soul* was Paul Robeson's first movie. **23**   Jan-Michael Vincent's drunken driving conviction gets him thirty days in jail for violating probation on a 1983 conviction for the same offense. **26**   "Meet Hollywood's new teen princess" says *Time*'s cover story on Molly Ringwald, Brat Pack veteran of *Sixteen Candles* (1984), *The Breakfast Club* (1985), and *Pretty in Pink* (1986)—the "Molly Trilogy."

SEPTEMBER 2   Cathy Smith, who injected John Belushi with cocaine and heroin just before his death, is sentenced to three years in prison. **6**   Barbra Streisand gives a

Movies

JANUARY 23   Bette Midler, Richard Dreyfuss, and Nick Nolte star in *Down and Out in Beverly Hills*, the remake of Jean Renoir's 1932 *Boudu Saved from Drowning*, opening today.

FEBRUARY 7   Woody Allen's *Hannah and Her Sisters*, starring Allen, Mia Farrow, Michael Caine, Carrie Fisher, and Barbara Hershey, opens.

MARCH 5   Oliver Stone's *Salvador*, starring James Woods and James Belushi, opens. **7**   Premiering at the Paris Theater is Mer-

chant–Ivory's *A Room with a View*, starring Maggie Smith, Helena Bonham-Carter, Daniel Day-Lewis, Denholm Elliott, Julian Sands, and Simon Callow. Daniel Day-Lewis also stars in Stephen Frear's *My Beautiful Laundrette*, opening at the Embassy.

MAY 16   Tom Cruise, Kelly McGillis, and Val Kilmer star in *Top Gun*, opening on 1,028 screens. It will gross $8,193,052 in its first three days. (Cruise, on actually flying in an F-14: "It's very sexual.")

JUNE 13   Rodney Dangerfield is most of the show in *Back to School*, opening in 1,605 theaters.

Kelly McGillis and Tom Cruise in *Top Gun*   LC
© *PARAMOUNT PICTURES*

Business and Society

MARCH 24   The Supreme Court rules that films with sex scenes may be banned from drive-ins if they can be seen from the outside. **25**   Ted Turner takes over MGM-UA, paying $1.5 billion for it, and makes Alan Ladd Jr. chairman of the board. Turner then sells United Artists back to Kirk Kerkorian.

APRIL 8   Jack Valenti, Motion Picture Association of America head, announces that profanity and drug use will automatically earn a movie at least a PG-13 rating.

MAY 20   *Daily Variety* reports that Ted Turner will colorize MGM's inventory of black and white films.

JUNE 6   Ted Turner announces the sale of MGM, except for its film library, back to Kirk Kerkorian for $490,000,000.

23   Columbia announces that David Puttnam will become its chairman and CEO, effective September 1.

SEPTEMBER 2   MGM Entertainment Co. becomes MGM-UA Communications.

Births, Deaths, Marriages, and Divorces

FEBRUARY 2   Brenda Vaccaro m. Guy Hector. **3**   Rod Steiger m. Paula Ellis. **10**   Brian Aherne d.

MARCH 10   Ray Milland d. **16**   Timothy Hutton m. Debra Winger. **30**   James Cagney d.

APRIL 23   Director Otto Preminger d. **26**   Arnold Schwarzenegger m. TV broadcaster Maria Shriver, President Kennedy's

niece. All the Kennedys attend the Hyannis wedding. • Broderick Crawford and silent-screen star Bessie Love d.

MAY 23   Sterling Hayden d. **24**   Stuntman Yakima Canutt d.

JUNE 3   Anna Neagle d. **22**   Stacy Keach m. Malgosia Tomassi.

1986 373

"Signs" of the Times

• Ali McGraw, at the Betty Ford Clinic to dry out, introduces herself to the other patients: "My name is Ali, and I am an alcoholic/male-dependent."

• Neither Judy Garland, Ann Rutherford, nor Lana Turner would have said anything like this in an Andy Hardy movie:

Molly Ringwald: "I can't believe I gave my panties to a geek." (*Sixteen Candles*)

• The Los Angeles Parks and Recreational Department fences off part of West Mullholland Drive to keep vandals away from the HOLLYWOOD sign.

JULY 18 Sigourney Weaver, playing a feminist science-fiction–horror heroine stars in James Cameron's *Aliens*, opening on 1,437 screens. Weaver calls her "Ripley" character "Rambolina."

AUGUST 8 Rob Reiner's *Stand by Me*, starring River Phoenix and Kiefer Sutherland, opens in a limited engagement before its wide release on August 22.

SEPTEMBER 19 David Lynch's celebration of strangeness, *Blue Velvet*, opens. It stars Kyle MacLachlan, Isabella Rossellini (Lynch's girlfriend), Dennis Hopper, Laura Dern, Hope Lange, and Dean Stockwell.

OCTOBER • Tri-Star Pictures agrees to buy the Loew's theater chain. **17** Ted Turner sells MGM's Culver City lot to Lorimar-Telepictures. Gulf and Western buys the Mann theater chain.

DECEMBER 7 The Screen Actors Guild votes to censure its former president, Charlton Heston, for supporting antilabor "right-to-work" laws. **14** Disney releases *Sleeping Beauty* on video cassette at $29.95 and sells over a million.

live concert for the first time in almost two decades when she sings at her Malibu home in a fund-raiser for progressive political causes. Listening are Bette Midler, Jack Nicholson, Anjelica Huston, and Robin Williams.

OCTOBER • Chevy Chase, who has kicked a cocaine habit, spends two weeks at the Betty Ford Center to get rid of an addiction to painkillers he has taken for back injuries caused by his TV pratfalls. • 1950s movie star Aldo Ray is suspended

by SAG for working in nonunion movies. **9** Richard Pryor, appearing on *The Tonight Show*, tells Johnny Carson that he's lost weight because of a sinus condition and not from AIDS, as rumors have it. (In fact, he has multiple sclerosis.)

NOVEMBER • The Hollywood Walk of Fame selection committee rejects the De Laurentiis Entertainment Group's request that a star be given to King Kong. **13** At a press conference, barely able to breathe because of emphysema, John

Sigourney Weaver and Carrie Henn in Aliens LC
© 20TH CENTURY FOX, *photo by Bob Penn*

JULY 25 Vincente Minnelli d.

AUGUST 1 Tatum O'Neal m. tennis star John McEnroe. • Jan-Michael Vincent m. Joanna Robinson.

SEPTEMBER 1 Whoopi Goldberg m. David Claessen. **6** Silent-screen star Blanche

Sweet d. **13** Rosanna Arquette m. James Howard.

OCTOBER • Richard Pryor m. Flynn Belaine. **5** Hal Wallis d. **14** Keenan Wynn d.

NOVEMBER 20 Steve Martin m. Victoria Tennant. **29** Cary Grant d.

DECEMBER 26 Elsa Lanchester d.

Also this year: • Jeff Goldblum and Patricia Gaul divorce, as do Gene Hackman and Fay Maltese, and director William Friedkin and Leslie-Anne Down.

Personalities

Huston denounces the colorized version of *The Maltese Falcon*, shown last night on the Turner Broadcasting System (TBS). **17** Martin Sheen is arrested as he leads protestors onto the government's nuclear weapons test site in Nevada.

DECEMBER • Debra Winger, in an *Esquire* interview, calls Taylor Hackford, her director in *An Officer and a Gentleman*, "an animal," and James Brooks, who directed *Terms of Endearment*, "crude." **6** Emilio Estevez and Demi Moore have put off the wedding they had set for today, ostensibly because of work-scheduling conflicts.

Dennis Hopper in *Blue Velvet*   *LC*

Movies

Dern and MacLachlan have developed a relationship offscreen. **26** Opening today is *Crocodile Dundee*. The surprise success of this film and its star, Paul Hogan, spokesperson for the Australian tourist industry, ushers in a season of Aussie chic in America. It will gross more than thirty times its $5.6 million cost. **30** Jazz great Dexter Gordon stars in *Round Midnight*, opening at the New York Film Festival. He and fellow musicians Herbie Hancock, Wayne Shorter, Ron Carter, and Tony Williams created the soundtrack on camera.

OCTOBER 3 *Children of a Lesser God* opens. In it, Marlee Matlin, a deaf woman playing a deaf woman (unlike *Johnny Belinda*, in which Jane Wyman acted deaf), becomes a star. William Hurt co-stars. **10** Francis Ford Coppola's *Peggy Sue Got Married*, starring Kathleen Turner and Nicolas Cage, opens. **17** *The Color of Money*, Martin Scorsese's sequel to *The Hustler*, opening today, stars Paul Newman, Tom Cruise, and Mary Eliza-beth Mastrantonio. **31** *The Mission*, starring Jeremy Irons and Robert DeNiro, opens at Cinema I.

DECEMBER 19 Oliver Stone's *Platoon*, which he shot in less than two months, for under $7 million, opens in about a dozen theaters prior to its January 2 wide release. Stars include Tom Berenger, Willem Dafoe, Charlie Sheen, and Forest Whitaker.

Business and Society

Births, Deaths, Marriages, and Divorces

*H*alf of American homes that have TVs have VCRs, and a similar percentage have cable. Hollywood's revenue from video cassettes will outpace box office profits for the first time. *Fatal Attraction* is discussed everywhere, from fan magazines to feminist journals; and *Wall Street*—"Greed is good"—also stirs widespread comment. Director John Landis is found innocent in the deaths of three actors during the production of *Twilight Zone: The Movie*. Demi Moore marries Bruce Willis; and Danny Kaye, Rita Hayworth, Fred Astaire, and John Huston die.

- Number of releases: 509
- Percentage of TV households with VCRs: 52%
- Number of screens: 23,550, of which 2,500 are in drive-ins
- Total admissions: 1,088,500,000
- Average ticket price: $3.91
- Box office receipts: $4,252,900,000
- Average production cost per film: $20,100,000
- Age of Lillian Gish, costarring with Bette Davis in *The Whales of August*: 93

Top box office stars, based on a Quigley Publications poll of exhibitors:
1. Eddie Murphy
2. Michael Douglas
3. Michael J. Fox
4. Arnold Schwarzenegger
5. Paul Hogan
6. Tom Cruise
7. Glenn Close
8. Sylvester Stallone
9. Cher
10. Mel Gibson

Top rental earnings, based on figures reported by *Variety*:
1. *Beverly Hills Cop II* $80,850,000
2. *Platoon*   66,700,000
3. *Fatal Attraction*   60,000,000
4. *Three Men and a Baby*   45,000,000
5. *The Untouchables*   36,850,000

The New York Film Critics Circle Awards
Best Picture: *Broadcast News*

The Los Angeles Film Critics Association
Best Picture: *Hope and Glory*

The Golden Globe Awards
Best Picture (Drama): *The Last Emperor*
Best Picture (Musical/Comedy): *Hope and Glory*

The Cannes Film Festival
Palme d'Or: *Under Satan's Sun*

The Academy Awards (presented April 11, 1988)
Best Picture: *The Last Emperor*
Actor: Michael Douglas (*Wall Street*)
Actress: Cher (*Moonstruck*)
Supporting Actor: Sean Connery (*The Untouchables*)
Supporting Actress: Olympia Dukakis (*Moonstruck*)
Director: Bernardo Bertolucci (*The Last Emperor*)

January	February	March	April	May	June
	20 Sean Penn is fined and placed on probation on battery charge	**3** Elizabeth Taylor becomes head of the American Federation for AIDS Research • *Vanity Fair* celebrates Dennis Hopper's return from alcoholism, drug addiction, and madness		**29** John Landis found innocent of involuntary manslaughter in filming *Twilight Zone: The Movie*	**22** Fred Astaire d.

July	August	September	October	November	December
24 Steve Martin on cover of *Time* • Cineplex Odeon's 18-screen cinema at Universal Studios draws 38,000 on opening weekend		 **18** *Fatal Attraction*	**1** A 6.1 earthquake hits Los Angeles	**21** Demi Moore m. Bruce Willis	**4** Director Rouben Mamoulian d.

Personalities

- Carrie Fisher's first novel, *Postcards from the Edge*, is published.

JANUARY 2   Jim Belushi, driving a friend's BMW, gets out, punches, and knocks down a Westwood, Los Angeles pedestrian who spat at the car in the belief that the actor had come too close to him. Assault charges against Belushi will be dropped in October when he settles out of court with the man.

FEBRUARY 20   Sean Penn pleads no contest to a battery charge for his April 12 attack on a man Penn accused of trying to kiss his wife, Madonna, in a Los Angeles night club. Penn is fined and placed on probation.

MARCH 3   Elizabeth Taylor becomes head of the American Federation for AIDS Research.   **6**   Audrey Hepburn and Sean Connery receive France's Commander of Arts and Letters award.   **26**   A back page ad in the *Hollywood Reporter* reads: "I'm an actor PLEASE…let me Act. *John Ireland*" It will bring the seventy-three-year-old a role in a TV movie.   **30**   On Oscar night at the Dorothy Chandler Pavilion, Marlee Matlin, who is deaf, presents the award for the Best Achievement in Sound and then sees her boyfriend, William Hurt, who is presenting the award for Best Actress, sign her name as the winner, for her role in *Children of a Lesser God*.

APRIL   • *Vanity Fair*'s cover story is "Dennis Hopper: How the Mad, Bad & Dangerous Movie Star Came Back from the Dead & Took the Town by Storm," celebrating his

Elizabeth Taylor becomes head of The American Federation for AIDS Research.   *LC*

Movies

MARCH 6   Barry Levinson's *Tin Men*, starring Richard Dreyfuss, Danny DeVito, and Barbara Hershey, opens in a limited engagement. *Lethal Weapon*, the first of three action films with Mel Gibson and Danny Glover, opens in 1,256 theaters.   **11**   Ethan and Joel Coen's *Raising Arizona*, starring Nicolas Cage and Holly Hunter, opens.

MAY 15   *Ishtar*, starring Dustin Hoffman and Warren Beatty, opens in 1,139 not-very-crowded theaters. This $51 million misfire will gross $4.3 million in its first week.

22   Eddie Murphy is at the peak of his popularity with *Beverly Hills Cop II*, released in 2,326 theaters. It will gross $33,014,153 in its first four days.

JUNE 3   Brian DePalma's *The Untouchables* (based on the TV program that debuted on October 15, 1959) opens. It stars Kevin Costner, Sean Connery, Andy Garcia, and Robert DeNiro.   **12**   Jack Nicholson, Cher, Susan Sarandon, and Michelle Pfeiffer star in *The Witches of Eastwick*, opening today.   **26**   *Full Metal Jacket*, opening today, starring Matthew Modine and Alec Baldwin, is director Stanley Kubrick's first film in seven years.

JULY 17   Peter Weller is *Robocop*, opening in 1,580 theaters, followed by several sequels.   **31**   Timothy Dalton, the new James Bond, stars in *The Living Daylights*, opening in 1,728 theaters.

AUGUST 17   *Dirty Dancing*, in which Jennifer Grey and Patrick Swayze star, opens.   **28**   John Sayles's $4-million *Matewan*, with only James Earl Jones's name easily recognizable in the credits, premieres at Cinema I to critical acclaim.

SEPTEMBER 18   *Fatal Attraction*, starring Michael Douglas, Glenn Close, and Anne Archer, opens today and adds a new ex-

Business and Society

APRIL 9   Columbia CEO Guy McElwaine resigns.

MAY 12   Woody Allen and Ginger Rogers appear before a Congressional panel to decry the colorizing of old films.

JULY   • Cineplex Odeon's eighteen-screen cinema at Universal Studios draws 38,000

to its opening on the July 4th weekend and will gross $369,254,000 in its first week.   **14**   *Daily Variety* and *Variety*, owned by the family of founder Sime Silverman since he founded *Variety* in 1905, will be sold to the Cahners Publishing Company, a British firm, it is announced today.   **20**   "Environmental sculptors" cover up the "H" in the HOLLYWOOD sign, making it OLLYWOOD to reflect the country's obsession with Oliver North.

SEPTEMBER   • The American edition of *Premiere*, the French movie magazine, begins regular publication.   **15**   Pope John Paul II, introduced by MCA's Lew Wasserman, tells an audience of entertainment industry executives at a hotel in Universal City that they have a special responsibility to help make this a better world. Someone has welcomed the Pope by converting the HOLLYWOOD sign to HOLYWOOD.   **16**   David Puttnam, who has made many enemies at Columbia, announces his resignation as

Births, Deaths, Marriages, and Divorces

JANUARY 15   Ray Bolger d.

MARCH   **2**   Randolph Scott d.   **3**   Danny Kaye d.   **22**   Robert Preston d.

APRIL   • Faye Dunaway and Terrence O'Neill divorce (they had married in secret).

MAY 9   Tom Cruise m. Mimi Rogers.   **14**   Rita Hayworth d.

JUNE 10   Elizabeth Hartman, who won an Oscar for her film debut in *Patch of Blue*, commits suicide.   **13**   Geraldine Page d.   **22**   Fred Astaire d.   **24**   Jackie Gleason d.

AUGUST 1   Silent-screen star Pola Negri d.   **7**   Tom Selleck m. Jillie Mack.   **17**   Director Clarence Brown d.

resurrected career in *Blue Velvet* and return from alcoholism, drug addiction, and madness. • Eddie Murphy settles out of court for reportedly $1.5 million a lawsuit for money owed to his former manager, who signed Murphy when he was sixteen.

MAY 25 Bruce Willis is arrested at his Hollywood Hills home when he attacks police responding to neighbor's complaints of a loud pool party. Carried struggling and shouting to a patrol car, Willis will have assault charges against him dropped for lack of sufficient evidence, but will be forced by a judge to apologize to his neighbors. **29** Director John Landis is found innocent of involuntary manslaughter in the helicopter death in 1982 of three people, including actor Vic Morrow, while shooting *Twilight Zone—The Movie*.

JUNE 9 Brooke Shields graduates from Princeton. **23** Sean Penn pleads no contest to reckless driving over Memorial Day and to assaulting an extra on the set of *Colors* on April 2. For violating his probation (imposed Feb. 20 for a battery charge), he draws two months in jail. He will serve thirty-three days, with a week's break to allow him to complete some film work. **29** Tom Cruise finishes fourteenth in his first professional auto race at the Atlanta Raceway. In another contest, Paul Newman finishes seventh.

JULY • James Caan, dining at La Dolce Vita in Beverly Hills with several local mobsters, brags that with the support of the Columbo crime family and of Meyer Lansky's widow, he will star in a film about Lansky.

AUGUST 5 Matthew Broderick, driving a

rented BMW in Northern Ireland with Jennifer Grey beside him, collides head-on with another car, killing the two women in it. Grey is slightly bruised, but Broderick is hospitalized with a leg fracture. **17** Jennifer Grey, injured two weeks ago in an auto accident, attends the premiere in New York of *Dirty Dancing* with her father, Joel. **24** *Time*'s cover story, "Steve Martin: He's Off the Wall," calls him "the '80s top comic actor." He starred in *Roxanne*, released two months ago. **25** Paramount signs a new five-picture deal with Eddie Murphy.

OCTOBER 12 Robert Redford announces that he will produce, and Cineplex Odeon will release, a series of independent, low-budget films, beginning with *A River Runs through It*.

Michael Douglas and Glenn Close in *Fatal Attraction*   MSN
© *PARAMOUNT PICTURES*

pression to the language—as in "Fatal Attraction Murder Case," in which a woman becomes obsessed with a man, driving her to kill. Paramount has added a slam-bang ending because preview audiences did not go for the suicide of Glenn Close's character.

OCTOBER 9 John Boorman's *Hope and Glory*, a British film starring Sebastian Rice-Edwards, opens at the New York Film Festival.

NOVEMBER 20 Bernardo Bertolucci's *The Last Emperor*, starring John Lone and Peter O'Toole, opens in six theaters. **25** Tom

head of the studio. Columbia says it has asked for his resignation.

OCTOBER The Cahner's Publishing Company buys *Variety* and *Daily Variety*. **1** A Los Angeles earthquake measuring 6.1 on the Richter Scale cause minor damage and delays at area studios. **8** SAG president Patty Duke says that ex-president Charlton Heston's support for a lawsuit to compel refunding of dues spent for political purposes constitutes "war" against the

28 Director John Huston d. **29** Lee Marvin d.

SEPTEMBER • Kiefer Sutherland m. Camilia Kath. **13** Producer-director Mervyn LeRoy d. **25** Mary Astor d. **27** Karen Black m. Steven Eckelbery.

OCTOBER 2 Madeleine Carroll d.

NOVEMBER 1 Geena Davis m. Jeff Goldblum. **21** Demi Moore weds Bruce Willis.

DECEMBER 4 Director Rouben Mamoulian d. **22** Silent-screen star Alice Terry d.

26 Louis Gossett Jr. m. Cyndi Reese.

Also this year: • James Spader m. Victoria Kheel. • Divorcing are Tom Hanks and Samantha Lewes and Sylvester Stallone and Brigitte Nielsen.

Personalities

NOVEMBER • Dennis Quaid, while filming *Everybody's All-American*, breaks his collar bone when tackled by former profootball star Tim Fox. **30** Christopher Reeve is in Chile to express solidarity with prominent people in the arts who are threatened with death by the extreme right.

DECEMBER • Columbia drops Burt Lancaster from *Old Gringo* and replaces him with Gregory Peck when the studio can't get cast insurance on Lancaster, who had heart surgery in 1983. **19** Mia Farrow and Woody Allen become the parents of a son, Satchel.

TAG LINES: UPSCALE AND BARGAIN BASEMENT

Advertising tag lines reflect the movies they are promoting, as these two 1987 examples show:

"Three beautiful women. One lucky devil." — *The Witches of Eastwick*

"Unwed! Untamed! Unleaded!" "Backseat Bimbos meet their Roadside Romeos" — *Hot Rod Harlots*

Movies

Selleck, Steve Guttenberg, and Ted Danson star in *Three Men and a Baby*, opening today.

DECEMBER 9 Steven Spielberg's *Empire of the Sun*, starring Christian Bale and John Malkovich, opens in a limited engagement and on December 11 will go into wide release. **11** Oliver Stone's *Wall Street*, starring Charlie and Martin Sheen and Michael Douglas as "Gordon Gekko" ("Greed is good"), opens. **16** *Moonstruck*, starring Cher, Nicolas Cage, Olympia Dukakis, Danny Aiello, and Vincent Gardenia, opens in seven theaters in New York, Los Angeles, and Toronto. It proves so popular that its wide release date will be moved up a week, to January 15. *Broadcast News* also opens in seven theaters (wide release on December 25). It stars William Hurt, Holly Hunter, and Albert Brooks. **17** John Huston's final film, *The Dead*, starring Anjelica Huston and Donal McCann, premieres in the U.S. at Cinema I. **23** Barry Levinson's *Good Morning Vietnam*, starring Robin Williams and Forest Tucker, opens for a limited engagement, with wide release on January 15.

Business and Society

union. **28** Dawn Steel is named president of Columbia Pictures.

NOVEMBER • New York's Mayor Ed Koch urges a boycott of Cineplex Odeon theaters, which have just raised admission from six to seven dollars. • TV signals are now delivered by cable in fifty percent of American homes that have TVs.

Births, Deaths, Marriages, and Divorces

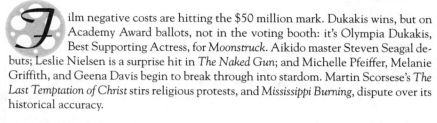

*F*ilm negative costs are hitting the $50 million mark. Dukakis wins, but on Academy Award ballots, not in the voting booth: it's Olympia Dukakis, Best Supporting Actress, for *Moonstruck*. Aikido master Steven Seagal debuts; Leslie Nielsen is a surprise hit in *The Naked Gun*; and Michelle Pfeiffer, Melanie Griffith, and Geena Davis begin to break through into stardom. Martin Scorsese's *The Last Temptation of Christ* stirs religious protests, and *Mississippi Burning*, dispute over its historical accuracy.

- Number of releases: 510
- Percentage of TV households with VCRs: 62%
- Number of screens: 23,250, of which 1,550 are in drive-ins
- Total admissions: 1,084,800,000
- Average ticket price: $4.11
- Box office receipts: $4,458,400,000
- Average production cost per film: $18,100,000
- Price paid at auction for one of four pairs of ruby-red slippers worn by Judy Garland in *The Wizard of Oz*: $165,000
- Number of names in the credits of *Who Framed Roger Rabbit*: 743

Top stars at the box office, based on a Quigley Publications poll of exhibitors:

1. Tom Cruise
2. Eddie Murphy
3. Tom Hanks
4. Arnold Schwarzenegger
5. Paul Hogan
6. Danny DeVito
7. Bette Midler
8. Robin Williams
9. Tom Selleck
10. Dustin Hoffman

Top rental earnings, based on figures reported by *Variety*:

1. *Who Framed Roger Rabbit* — $78,000,000
2. *Coming to America* — 65,000,000
3. *Good Morning, Vietnam* — 58,100,000
4. *Crocodile Dundee II* — 57,300,000
5. *Big* — 50,800,000

The New York Film Critics Circle Awards
Best Picture: *The Accidental Tourist*

The Golden Globe Awards
Best Picture (Drama): *Rain Man*
Best Picture (Musical/Comedy): *Working Girl*

The Cannes Film Festival
Palme d'Or: *Pelle the Conqueror*

The Academy Awards (presented March 29, 1989)
Best Picture: *Rain Man*
Actor: Dustin Hoffman (*Rain Man*)
Actress: Jodie Foster (*The Accused*)
Supporting Actor: Kevin Kline (*A Fish Called Wanda*)
Supporting Actress: Geena Davis (*The Accidental Tourist*)
Director: Barry Levinson (*Rain Man*)

January	February	March	April	May	June
• The *Hollywood Reporter* sold to Billboard Publications		• River Phoenix on cover of *Vegetarian Times*	**29** Burt Reynolds m. Loni Anderson		**17** Jane Fonda apologizes on TV for any hurt she caused with antiwar comments
15 Matthew Broderick fined for "careless" driving in last August's fatal accident			• Melanie Griffith at the Hazelden Foundation rehabilitation clinic		

July	August	September	October	November	December
16 Michael J. Fox m. Tracy Pollan		**27** President Reagan signs Film Preservation Act		**21** Art Buchwald sues Paramount over authorship of *Coming to America*	
11 Twenty-five thousand march on Universal Studios to protest *The Last Temptation of Christ*			**14** *The Accused*		**16** *Rain Man*

Personalities

JANUARY • The Directors Guild cites John Landis for unprofessional conduct in the accident that killed three people during the filming of *Twilight Zone: The Movie*. • Barbra Streisand, her romance with Baskin-Robbins ice cream heir Richard Baskin ended, is seen with Don Johnson. Arnold Schwarzenegger says of Sylvester Stallone in a *Playboy* interview: "He just hits me the wrong way…. There's nothing that anyone can do out there to save his ass and his image." When Stallone objects, Schwarzenegger will complain that he was misquoted.

FEBRUARY 4 Clint Eastwood announces that he will not seek another term as mayor of Carmel. **15** Matthew Broderick pleads guilty to "careless" driving in last August's fatal accident in Northern Ireland and is fined $175.

MARCH • River Phoenix is on the cover of *Vegetarian Times*.

APRIL 11 There will be no Dukakis in the White House this year, but one—Olympia Dukakis, presidential candidate Michael Dukakis's cousin—does win an Oscar at the Shrine Auditorium tonight for Best Supporting Actress.

MAY • Melanie Griffith dries out at the Hazelden Foundation rehabilitation clinic in Minnesota.

JUNE 17 Jane Fonda, interviewed by Barbara Walters on ABC's *20/20*, apologizes for any hurt she may have caused to

Jane Fonda apologizes to Vietnam veterans in June.   *LC*

Movies

MARCH 18 Edward James Olmos stars in *Stand and Deliver*, opening today. **30** Michael Keaton, Alec Baldwin, Geena Davis, and Winona Ryder are the stars of *Beetlejuice*, opening today.

APRIL 8 *Above the Law*, opens, introducing to the screen aikido master Steven Seagal. **15** The opening of Dennis Hopper's *Colors*, starring Robert Duvall and Sean Penn, is marred by the fear of gang violence. Fifteen theaters in California and New Jersey cancel its showing.

JUNE 3 Penny Marshall's *Big*, starring Tom Hanks and Elizabeth Perkins, opens. **15** Kevin Costner, Susan Sarandon, and Tim Robbins star in *Bull Durham*, opening today. Sarandon and Robbins, who almost wasn't hired because the studio thought moviegoers would find implausible a romance between him and Sarandon, began a romance during the film's production. **22** "Stay tooned," say ads heralding today's opening of *Who Framed Roger Rabbit*, starring Bob Hoskins, which combines live and animated action.

JULY 15 Bruce Willis (whose $5 million salary for the film disturbs some in Hollywood) and Bonnie Bedalia star in *Die Hard*, opening today in twenty-one theaters. Also debuting, in a limited engagement, is *A Fish Called Wanda*, starring John Cleese, Jamie Lee Curtis, and Kevin Kline.

AUGUST 12 Martin Scorsese's *The Last Temptation of Christ*, starring Willem Dafoe, Harvey Keitel, Barbara Hershey, and Harry Dean Stanton, opens in New York, Los Angeles, and Chicago. Also opening, in wide release, is *Young Guns*, starring Emilio Estevez, Kiefer Sutherland, Lou Diamond Phillips, and Charlie Sheen. **19** Jonathan Demme's *Married to the Mob* opens, starring Michelle Pfeiffer, Mercedes Ruehl, Dean Stockwell,

Business and Society

• Negative costs are beginning to hit $50 million with some regularity. This year *Rambo III*, *Coming to America*, *The Adventures of Baron Munchausen*, and *Who Framed Roger Rabbit* will run up that tab.

JANUARY • The *Hollywood Reporter* is sold to Billboard Publications. Last October, the Cahner's Publishing Company bought *Variety* and *Daily Variety*. All publications were bought from the families that started them.

MARCH 7 The Writers Guild of America strikes over money issues.

JUNE 8 *Daily Variety* reports that there has been a surge in Hollywood horror film production over the last three years. The industry shot 52 in 1985, 89 in 186, and 105 last year. Much of this is being driven by the demand for horror films at the video rental stores.

JULY • On TV's *Sneak Previews*, Michael Medved and Jeffrey Lyons begin to rate films for violence.

AUGUST 7 The twenty-two-week Writers Guild strike is settled. **11** According to police, about twenty-five thousand people, many fundamentalist Christians, march on Universal Studios to protest Martin Scorsese's *The Last Temptation of Christ*, which opens tomorrow. Many demonstrators use the parking lot for the Universal

Births, Deaths, Marriages, and Divorces

JANUARY 7 Trevor Howard d. **25** Silent-screen star Colleen Moore d.

FEBRUARY 21 Dudley Moore m. Brogan Lane.

APRIL 29 Burt Reynolds m. Loni Anderson. • Director Mike Nichols m. broadcaster Diane Sawyer. **30** Tom Hanks m. Rita Wilson.

JUNE 18 Ryan O'Neal, having divorced Leigh Taylor-Young, m. Farrah Fawcett.

JULY 16 Michael J. Fox m. Tracy Pollan.

AUGUST 9 Gossip columnist Jimmy Fidler d. **10** Adela Rogers St. John, Hearst

Vietnam veterans with her past antiwar comments.

JULY • Rosanna Arquette has left husband James Howard and begun a three-year affair with rock star Peter Gabriel. **27** Cher's live-in-lover, Robert Camilletti, is arrested at their Benedict Canyon home for allegedly attempting to use his Ferarri to try to run over a photographer taking pictures of the house. At a news conference tomorrow, Camilletti and Cher will say that the photographer has been harassing them. (Camilletti will be allowed to plead no contest to destroying the man's camera equipment.)

SEPTEMBER • Martin Sheen and Edward James Olmos each fast three days to support the United Farm Workers protest against dangerous conditions for farm workers.

OCTOBER • Kelly McGillis is interviewed on the occasion of the opening of *The Accused*, in which she stars with Jodie Foster. McGillis tells reporters that she was raped in 1982 and would not take the role of the victim, played by Foster, because it would have been too painful. • Elizabeth Taylor is back at the Betty Ford Clinic, where she meets Larry Fortensky. And Tuesday Weld, in *Interview* magazine, refers to her ex-husband, Dudley Moore, as "a major asshole." **4** According to the *New York Post*, Shirley MacLaine, taping the David Letterman show, responds to his kidding about her "channeling" with: "Maybe Cher was right. You are an asshole."

DECEMBER 4 Gary Busey is thrown from his motorcycle in Culver City and hits a curb head-first, requiring two hours of surgery to save his life. The actor, who actively opposes mandatory helmets for bikers, was not wearing one. **22** Thirteen-year-old

Willem DaFoe in *The Last Temptation of Christ*   LC

and Matthew Modine. **24** Amy Irving stars in *Crossing Delancy*, opening today at the Plaza.

SEPTEMBER 2 John Sayles's *Eight Men Out*, a film about the attempt to throw the 1919 World Series, starring Sayles, John Cusack, Charlie Sheen, and Studs Terkel, opens. **9** Sidney Lumet's *Running on Empty*, opening today in twenty-two theaters, stars Judd Hirsch, Christine Lahti, and River Phoenix. **23** Sigourney Weaver stars in *Gorillas in the Mist*, opening at the Beekman in 70mm.

OCTOBER 14 *The Accused*, starring Jodie Foster and Kelly McGillis, opens.

Studio Tour, pouring several thousand dollars into the company's coffers for the privilege of doing so. **26** Protestors in Utah steal and destroy a print of *The Last Temptation of Christ* and slash the screen of the theater showing it.

SEPTEMBER 27 President Reagan signs the Film Preservation Act, under which the government may designate twenty-five films as national treasures, requiring disclaimers, should they be colorized, that

reporter, known as "Mother Confessor of Hollywood," d.

OCTOBER 31 John Houseman d.

NOVEMBER 17 Hollywood gossip columnist Sheila Graham d. **27** John Carradine d.

DECEMBER 30 Peter Bogdanovich m. Louise Hoogstratton, sister of his murdered fiancée, Dorothy Stratten.

Also this year: • Ellen Barkin m. Gabriel Byrne. • Joe Pesci m. Martha Haro. • Michelle Pfeiffer divorces Peter Horton.

Personalities

Drew Barrymore's spokesperson announces that the actress has been released from an alcoholic rehabilitation center. **28** Madonna complains to the police that her husband, Sean Penn, beat her and tied her to a chair.

Jodie Foster wins the 1988 Best Actress Academy Award for her role in *The Accused*, based upon a real gang-rape incident. 　*LC/© PARAMOUNT PICTURES*

Movies

DECEMBER 2 Leslie Nielsen is the stumbling, stupid detective in *The Naked Gun*, a film based on an unsuccessful TV show, opening today at 1,576 theaters. **9** Alan Parker's *Mississippi Burning*, starring Gene Hackman and Willem Dafoe, opens in a limited engagement. There is controversy over its emphasis on the role of the FBI in this story of the investigation of the murder of civil rights workers. The only theater in Philadelphia, Mississippi, near where the murders occurred, will not show the film. Also opening today, in wide release, is *Twins*, starring Arnold Schwarzenegger and Danny DeVito. **16** Dustin Hoffman and Tom Cruise star in Barry Levinson's *Rain Man*, opening on 1,248 screens. It will take the Oscars for Best Picture, Best Actor, and Best Director. **21** *Working Girl*, starring Melanie Griffith, Harrison Ford, and Sigourney Weaver, opens. Opening in a limited engagement is *Dangerous Liaisons*, starring Glenn Close, John Malkovich, and Michelle Pfeiffer. (Pfeiffer and Malkovich are reported to have had an affair.) **23** William Hurt, Kathleen Turner, and Geena Davis, star in *The Accidental Tourist*, opening in several theaters.

Business and Society

they were originally in black and white and their creators have not consented to the change.

NOVEMBER 21 Humorist Art Buchwald and producer Alain Bernheim sue Paramount for $5 million, claiming that *Coming to America*, starring Eddie Murphy and Arsenio Hall, is based on an idea Buchwald submitted to the studio in 1983.

Births, Deaths, Marriages, and Divorces

*B*ette Davis and Laurence Olivier die. Time and Warner merge; and Sony buys Columbia, which has merged with Tri-Star. *Batman* is BIG—on licensed merchandise and at the box office. Idealism is central in *Field of Dreams*, *Dead Poets Society*, and *Parenthood*, but "stupid humor" also comes to the screen. *Sex, lies, and videotape*, *Drugstore Cowboy*, and *Roger & Me* go far on low budgets. Kim Basinger buys a town, Rob Lowe is in the wrong kind of film, Zsa Zsa Gabor slaps a Beverly Hills cop, Christian Slater does worse, and writer Joe Eszterhas says that superagent Michael Ovitz has been threatening him.

- Number of releases: 501
- Percentage of TV households with VCRs: 68%
- Number of screens: 23,150, of which 1,100 are in drive-ins
- Total admissions: 1,262,800,000
- Average ticket price: $3.97
- Box office receipts: $5,033,400,000
- Average production cost per film: $23,500,000
- Jack Nicholson's fee for playing The Joker in Batman: $11,000,000 plus a percentage
- First three days' gross for *Batman*: $40,489,746
- First ten days' gross for *Batman*: $100,000,000
- Value of merchandise with licensed Batman insignia sold this year: $375,000,000

Top stars at the box office, based on a Quigley Publications poll of exhibitors:

1. Jack Nicholson
2. Tom Cruise
3. Robin Williams
4. Michael Douglas
5. Tom Hanks
6. Michael J. Fox
7. Eddie Murphy
8. Mel Gibson
9. Sean Connery
10. Kathleen Turner

Top rental earnings, based on figures reported by *Variety*:

1.	*Batman*	$150,500,000
2.	*Indiana Jones and the Last Crusade*	115,000,000
3.	*Lethal Weapon 2*	79,500,000
4.	*Honey, I Shrunk the Kids*	71,100,000
5.	*Rain Man*	65,000,000

The New York Film Critics Circle Awards
Best Picture: *My Left Foot*

The Los Angeles Film Critics Association
Best Picture: *Do the Right Thing*

The Golden Globe Awards
Best Picture (Drama): *Born on the Fourth of July*
Best Picture (Musical/Comedy): *Driving Miss Daisy*

The Academy Awards (presented March 26, 1990)
Best Picture: *Driving Miss Daisy*
Actor: Daniel Day-Lewis (*My Left Foot*)
Actress: Jessica Tandy (*Driving Miss Daisy*)
Supporting Actor: Denzel Washington (*Glory*)
Supporting Actress: Brenda Fricker (*My Left Foot*)
Director: Oliver Stone, (*Born on the Fourth of July*)

January	February	March	April	May	June	
• Madonna withdraws her December 28 police complaint that Sean Penn beat her	**3** John Cassavetes d. **6** Columbia and Tri-Star merge		**26** Lucille Ball d.	**19** The mother of an underage girl accuses Rob Lowe of having sex with her daughter	**23** *Batman*	

July	August	September	October	November	December	
11 Laurence Olivier d.	**18** L.A. police acknowledge going easy on enforcing drug laws at location shooting sites	**27** Coca-Cola sells Columbia to Sony	**24** Zsa Zsa Gabor is sentenced to three days in jail for slapping a Beverly Hills cop	**11** Court rules that "Oscar," although copyrighted, has entered the public domain **13** *Driving Miss Daisy*		

Personalities

• In several appearances, including one on the *David Letterman Show*, Madonna and comedian Sandra Bernhard teasingly refer to what sounds like a sexual relationship between them. By next year, Madonna will refer to it as a joke and her friendship with Bernhard will be over.

JANUARY • Madonna withdraws her December 28 complaint to the police that estranged husband Sean Penn beat her.

FEBRUARY 9 Los Angeles police arrest an obsessive fan of Michael J. Fox, who has sent him more than a thousand letters "ordering" the star to divorce Tracy Pollan and go back to his old flame, Nancy McKeon. **12** James Caan is hospitalized with cracked ribs from a Santa Monica motorcycle accident. **15** Marc Christian, Rock Hudson's lover, wins a $14.5 million suit against the actor's estate—later reduced to $5.5 million—because Hudson never told Christian that he had AIDS. **15** Jane Fonda and Tom Hayden announce their separation. **22** The publication party for *King Kong* (1933) star Fay Wray's autobiography, *On the Other Hand*, is held on the eighty-sixth-floor observatory of the Empire State Building. **24** Timothy Hutton wins a $10 million suit against MGM for lying to him in 1983 when they cancelled *Roadshow*, in which he was to star, supposedly because of director Richard Brook's heart attack. The studio has already settled with Jack Nicholson and Mary Steenburgen out of court.

MARCH • Kim Basinger, with an investment of $900,000, heads a group that pays $20 million for the five-hundred-inhabitant town of Braselton, Georgia, near where Basinger was raised, with the aim of turning it into a tourist attraction and movie production center. **19** The *Los Angeles Times* reports that James Caan's intention of making a movie about Meyer Lansky with the support of the Columbo family has been blocked by the Gambino family (in the person of John Gotti, the FBI will later reveal). **29** On Oscar night at the Shrine Auditorium, a tradition is broken. Four previous times an actor or actress has been nominated in both the Best and Supporting Actor or Actress categories. Each time, the nominee won in the supporting category. But this year, Sigourney Weaver, nominated for Best Actress in *Gorillas in the Mist* and Best Supporting Actress for *Working Girl*, draws a blank. Geena Davis

Movies

FEBRUARY 17 *Bill & Ted's Excellent Adventure*, opening today, starring Keanu Reeves and Alex Winter, sets off a round of "stupid humor" films, including *Wayne's World* (1992).

MARCH 31 *Heathers*, starring Christian Slater, Winona Ryder, and Shannon Doherty, opens.

APRIL 21 Kevin Costner, Amy Madigan, Ray Liotta, and James Earl Jones star in *Field of Dreams*, opening today.

MAY 24 Sean Connery joins Harrison Ford in Steven Spielberg's *Indiana Jones and the Last Crusade*, opening at 2,327 theaters. It grosses $5,617,049 today, the third biggest opening day ever. Over the Memorial Day weekend it will take in more than half of all money spent on movies in the U.S. and Canada. But in this blockbuster summer, *Ghostbusters II* and *Batman* will match or break its box office records.

JUNE 2 Robin Williams stars in *Dead Poets Society*, which opens today. **23** Tim Burton's *Batman*, starring Michael Keaton, Jack Nicholson (stealing the film as "The Joker"), Kim Basinger, Billy Dee Williams, and Jack Palance, opens in 2,194 theaters. It will gross $40,489,746 in its first three days, which *Daily Variety* says "most likely has defined the outer limits of the b.o. for some time." Licensed merchandise adds to the kitty. Also opening today is *Honey, I Shrunk the Kids*, starring Rick Moranis. **30** Spike Lee's controversial look at race relations, *Do the Right Thing*, starring Lee, Danny Aiello, Ossie Davis, and Ruby Dee, opens.

JULY 12 Billy Crystal, Meg Ryan, and Carrie Fisher star in *When Harry Met Sally*, opening in a limited engagement. Soon after today's opening, President Bush, his wife away, will ask Jack Valenti of the Mo-

Business and Society

JANUARY 30 Alan Ladd Jr. announces that he will head the new Pathé Entertainment Company, controlled by Italian financier Giancarlo Paretti.

FEBRUARY 14 Turner Entertainment cancels the colorization of *Citizen Kane* when it discovers that Orson Welles's contract with RKO had given him total control over the film. **15** MGM-UA is forced to apologize to the Motion Picture Academy when the studio's ad celebrating the nomination of *Rain Man* for best picture runs in New York and Los Angeles papers as the nominations are announced. The studio says the ads were prepared in the hope of a nomination and were mistakenly run a day early.

MARCH 4 Warner Communications and Time, Inc., announce their merger to form

Spike Lee, Director of *Do the Right Thing*.

MSN

Births, Deaths, Marriages, and Divorces

FEBRUARY 3 John Cassavetes d. **19** Kate Nelligan m. Robert Reale.

MARCH 4 William Hurt m. Heidi Henderson, daughter of musician Skitch Henderson, whom he met at the Hazelden Center in Minnesota. **5** Kevin Kline m. Phoebe Cates.

APRIL 26 Lucille Ball d.

is Best Supporting Actress for *The Accidental Tourist*.

APRIL 3 Clint Eastwood informs Sondra Locke, who's directing *Impulse*, that he wants out of their thirteen-year relationship and also wants her out of the house the two have occupied since 1980. On April 10 he will have her locked out, and on April 26 she will file a palimony suit against him.

Michael Keaton in *Batman*

LC/© WARNER BROS.

tion Picture Association to screen it for him, and will find Meg Ryan's simulated orgasm hysterically funny.

MAY • Martin Sheen, named honorary mayor of Malibu, disturbs many of his constituents by declaring Malibu "a nuclear-free zone, a sanctuary for aliens and the homeless, and a protected environment for all life, wild and tame." **15** Producer Robert Evans is allowed to plead the Fifth Amendment in a hearing into the 1983 murder of Roy Radin, involved in production of Evans's *The Cotton Club*. Evans's

AUGUST 2 *Parenthood*, opening today, stars Steve Martin, Mary Steenburgen, Dianne Wiest, Tom Hulce, Rick Moranis, Jason

name was brought up by his ex-girlfriend, and newspapers refer to him as a "suspect," but he is never charged. **19** The mother of an underage girl accuses Rob Lowe of having sex with her daughter and videotaping it during the 1988 Democratic Convention in Atlanta. The tape, censored and uncensored, will be widely shown on TV in the next month, and Lowe will be sentenced to community service in lieu of jail time for the incident.

JUNE 26 *Time*'s cover story is "Kevin Costner: The new American hero—smart, sexy and on a roll."

JULY • Responding to criticism of his appearance in Colt 45 malt liquor ads aimed at the black community, Billy Dee Williams replies: "You can't legislate morality." **10** Mel Blanc, the voice of Bugs Bunny

Robards Jr., Martha Plimpton, and Keanu Reeves. **4** Steven Soderburgh's *sex, lies, and videotape*, starring James Spader, winner of the Golden Palm at Cannes, opens. **9** *The Abyss*, opening today, starring Ed Harris, Mary Elizabeth Mastrantonio, and Michael Biehn, an otherwise ordinary film, has extraordinary computerized special effects, which pave the way for *Terminator 2*.

OCTOBER 6 Matt Dillon stars in Gus Van Sant's *Drugstore Cowboy*, premiering at the Carnegie Hall Cinema. **13** Woody Allen's *Crimes and Misdemeanors*, starring Allen, Mia Farrow, Anjelica Huston, Martin Landau, Claire Bloom, Alan Alda,

Time Warner. **6** Columbia and Tri-Star merge. **30** The Disney Company sues the Academy of Motion Picture Arts and Sciences for copyright infringement because it used the character of Snow White during the Academy Award ceremonies without permission. The Academy's apology will end the suit.

APRIL 9 Gulf & Western announces the changing of its name to Paramount Communications.

MAY 1 The Disney–MGM Theme Park opens at Walt Disney World.

JUNE 16 Cineplex Odeon raises its weekend admission price in Manhattan theaters to $7.50.

AUGUST 1 Joe Roth becomes chairman of 20th Century Fox Films, replacing Leonard Goldberg, who resigned. **18** Some Los Angeles area police acknowledge they have stopped enforcing drug laws at location

shooting sites because of the state's desire to keep filming in California. **28** The Walt Disney Company announces the acquisition of Henson Associates (Jim Henson's Muppets).

SEPTEMBER 7 Barris Industries, Inc., which produced *Rain Man* and *Batman*, becomes Guber–Peters Entertainment Co., after its principles, Jon Peters and Peter Guber. **27** Coca-Cola's sale of Columbia to Sony for $3.4 billion is announced.

JUNE • Dennis Hopper m. Katherine La Nasa. **26** Melanie Griffith m. Don Johnson.

JULY 2 James Woods m. Sarah Owen. **11** Laurence Olivier d.

AUGUST • Kenneth Branagh m. Emma Thompson.

SEPTEMBER 22 Irving Berlin dies at age 101.

OCTOBER 5 Randy Quaid m. Evi Motolanez. **6** Bette Davis d. **15** Cornel Wilde d.

DECEMBER • Debra Winger and Timothy Hutton divorce. **6** John Payne d. **16** Lee Van Cleef dies. **31** Annabella

Sciorra m. Joe Petruzzi.

Also this year: • Rebecca De Mornay m. Bruce Wagner. • Kim Basinger will pay $9,000 a month alimony to Ron Britton following their divorce. • Amy Irving and Steven Spielberg divorce, with Irving receiving what is said to be the biggest

Personalities

and other Warners cartoon characters, dies. His tombstone will read: "That's All, Folks."

AUGUST • James Woods and Sean Young settle out of court his 1988 suit alleging that after working together on *The Boost*, Young sent him a voodoo doll and photos of dismembered animals to harass him. • Marlon Brando, who has just finished filming *The Freshman* and has his neck in a brace from a fall while ice skating for a scene in the film, pans the picture and says that he's retiring. **19** Elizabeth Taylor hosts a birthday party in Tangiers for wealthy publisher Malcolm Forbes, to which he has flown six hundred guests. Rumors have linked Taylor to Forbes.

OCTOBER 15 Preacher Billy Graham gets a star on Hollywood's Walk of Fame, based on his documentary films. **18** The Los Angeles *Herald-Examiner* breaks the story of screenwriter Joe Eszterhas's letter to Michael Ovitz, accusing the head of Creative Artists Agency of trying to ruin Eszterhas because he has switched to International Creative Management, a rival agency. **24** Zsa Zsa Gabor is sentenced to three days in jail for a June traffic incident in which she slapped a Beverly Hills cop when he stopped her Rolls Royce. During the trial, she said of a possible jail term: "I'm afraid of lesbians."

NOVEMBER 7 Ronald Reagan, at a Hollywood luncheon, apologizes for remarks he made on his recent trip to Japan in which he said that he hoped the Japanese might clean up the American film industry.

11 Eighty-five pieces from Billy Wilder's art collection bring $32.6 million at a Christie's auction in New York.

DECEMBER • Madonna's spokespeople deny reports that she and Warren Beatty, with whom she has worked on *Dick Tracy*, will wed or that she is pregnant by him. **20** Elvis Presley's daughter, Lisa Marie, after a decade of legal entanglement, inherits his $100 million estate, which will be managed by a trust until 1998. **29** Christian Slater, stopped the second time for drunken driving in Los Angeles, crashes his car while attempting to flee, runs from the police, and, when caught, kicks an officer. In July he will spend ten days in jail.

Movies

Joanna Gleason, and Jerry Orbach, opens on a limited basis. Also opening today is *Look Who's Talking*, starring John Travolta and Kirstie Alley.

NOVEMBER 8 Critics compare favorably Kenneth Branagh's *Henry V*, a British import opening today, to that of Laurence Olivier's 1945 version. **10** Daniel Day-Lewis and Brenda Fricker star in *My Left Foot*, an Irish production, opening in a few theaters after a September 23 showing at the New York Film Festival. **15** Opening

today are *Steel Magnolias*, starring Sally Field, Dolly Parton, Shirley MacLaine, Darryl Hannah, Julia Roberts, and Olympia Dukakis, and, in a limited engagement, the Disney Company's animated feature, *The Little Mermaid*.

DECEMBER 8 *The War of the Roses* opens. Directed by Danny DeVito, it stars DeVito, Michael Douglas, and Kathleen Turner. **13** *Driving Miss Daisy*, starring Morgan Freeman, Jessica Tandy, and Dan Aykroyd, opens, as does *Enemies, A Love Story*, starring Ron Silver and Anjelica Huston. **14** Matthew Broderick, Denzel Washington, and Morgan Freeman star in *Glory*, the

story of a white-led black unit of soldiers in the Civil War, opening today. **19** Michael Moore's *Roger & Me*, a documentary about General Motors, premieres in Flint, Michigan. It will gross $8 million, the most ever for any nonmusic documentary. **20** Oliver Stone's *Born on the Fourth of July*, starring Tom Cruise and Willem Dafoe, opens at the Ziegfeld.

Jessica Tandy and Morgan Freeman in *Driving Miss Daisy*   LC/© WARNER BROS.

Business and Society

OCTOBER 10 The sale of MGM-UA to the Australian company, Qintex, a deal first announced in March and seemingly completed on September 15, falls through.

NOVEMBER 9 Sony acquires the creative talents of Jon Peters and Peter Gruber for Columbia by merging with their company after settling with Warners, which had the

option on their services. **11** A U.S. District Court judge rules that Oscar, although copyrighted by the Motion Picture Academy, has entered the public domain because of the way the Academy has promoted and commercialized it.

DECEMBER 1 Following today's departure of its president, Garth Drabinsky, Cineplex Odeon will end its five-year period of constant expansion.

Births, Deaths, Marriages, and Divorces

settlement ever between Hollywood personalities. • Robert Duvall and Gail Young divorce, as do Madonna and Sean Penn, Chuck Norris and Diane Holecheck, Cliff Robertson and Dina Merrill, and Cicely Tyson and Miles Davis.

Matsushita buys MCA–Universal, Giancarlo Parretti takes control of MGM–UA, and "NC-17" replaces the "X" rating. Hollywood is turning some films into virtual series, as producers seek safety in sequels. This year's include *Back to the Future, Part III* (May 25), *Another 48 Hours* (June 8), *Gremlins 2: The New Batch* (June 15), *Robocop 2* (June 22), *Young Guns II* (August 1), *The Two Jakes* (August 10—the sequel to the 1974 *Chinatown*), *Texasville* (September 28—sequel to the 1971 *The Last Picture Show*), *Child's Play 2* (November 9), *Rocky V* (November 6), *Predator 2* (November 21), and *Look Who's Talking Too* (December 14). Greta Garbo dies.

- Number of releases: 410
- Number of screens: 23,700, of which 900 are in drive-ins
- Total admissions: 1,188,600,000
- Average ticket price: $4.23
- Box office receipts: $5,021,800,000
- Average production cost per film: $26,800,000
- Bruce Willis's fee as the voice of a baby in *Look Who's Talking Too*: a reported $10,000,000

Top stars at the box office, based on a Quigley Publications poll of exhibitors:

1. Arnold Schwarzenegger
2. Julia Roberts
3. Bruce Willis
4. Tom Cruise
5. Mel Gibson
6. Kevin Costner
7. Patrick Swayze
8. Sean Connery
9. Harrison Ford
10. Richard Gere

Top rental earnings, based on figures reported by *Variety*:

1. *Ghost* — $94,000,000
2. *Pretty Woman* — 81,900,000
3. *Home Alone* — 80,000,000
4. *Die Hard 2* — 66,500,000
5. *Total Recall* — 65,000,000

The New York Film Critics Circle Awards
Best Picture: *Goodfellas*

The Los Angeles Film Critics Association
Best Picture: *Goodfellas*

The Golden Globe Awards
Best Picture (Drama): *Dances with Wolves*
Best Picture (Musical/Comedy): *Green Card*

The Cannes Film Festival
Palme d'Or: *Wild at Heart*

The Academy Awards (presented March 25)
Best Picture: *Dances with Wolves*
Actor: Jeremy Irons (*Reversal of Fortune*)
Actress: Kathy Bates (*Misery*)
Supporting Actress: Whoopi Goldberg (*Ghost*)
Supporting Actor: Joe Pesci (*Goodfellas*)
Director: Kevin Costner (*Dances with Wolves*)

January	February	March	April	May	June	
20 Barbara Stanwyck d.	**19** Director Michael Powell d.	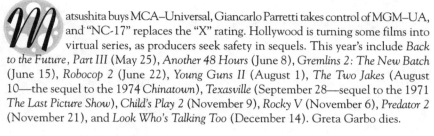 **23** *Pretty Woman*	**22** Elizabeth Taylor almost dies of pneumonia	**1** Film Foundation formed, dedicated to film preservation • Jane Fonda and Tom Hayden divorced		

July	August	September	October	November	December	
2 MCA–Universal buys the 18-screen Cineplex Odeon Universal City Cinemas	• Charlie Sheen enters a drug and alcohol rehabilitation program	**26** "NC-17—No Children Under 17 Admitted," replaces the "X" rating	**27** Director Peter Bogdanovich removed from *Another You*	**9** *Dances with Wolves*	**24** Tom Cruise m. Nicole Kidman	

Personalities

JANUARY • Charlie Sheen's live-in-girl-friend, Kelly Preston, is slightly wounded when a pistol accidentally discharges in their apartment. • Press agents for Arnold Schwarzenegger and Sylvester Stallone deny reports of a feud between the two stars. **22** President Bush appoints Arnold Schwarzenegger chairman of the President's Council on Physical Fitness and Sport. **25** Director Francis Ford Coppola and his Zoetrope Studio file for bankruptcy, the result of problems dating back to the 1982 film *One From the Heart*.

FEBRUARY • Forty-five filmmakers protest the lack of an Academy Award nomination to Michael Moore for his documentary, *Roger and Me*.

"I NEVER SAID 'I WANT TO BE ALONE'"

MSN

APRIL 15 Greta Garbo dies at age 84. "I never said 'I want to be alone,'" she had insisted. "I only said 'I want to be *let* alone.' There is all the difference."

Movies

MARCH 2 *The Hunt for Red October*, starring Sean Connery, Alec Baldwin, Scott Glenn, and James Earl Jones, opens. **23** Opening today is *Pretty Woman*, starring Richard Gere and Julia Roberts. By August 25 it will become the Disney Studio's highest grossing release ever. **30** *Teenage Mutant Ninja Turtles* opens today on 2,006 screens and appears on licensed products in toy stores everywhere.

APRIL 27 Sidney Lumet's *Q & A*, opening today, stars Nick Nolte, Armand Assante, and Timothy Hutton.

JUNE 1 *Total Recall* opens. *Daily Variety* says that "troubling questions about the film's ultraviolence recede in the harsh light of the unmistakable saleability of the product—Arnold Schwarzenegger on Mars!" Sharon Stone is on Mars, too. **15** Warren Beatty's *Dick Tracy*, opening in 2,332 theaters, is based on the comic strip that began in the *Detroit Mirror* on October 5, 1931. The film, which stars Beatty, Madonna, Al Pacino, Dustin Hoffman, James Caan, and other heavily made-up stars, cost $101 million and will generate ticket sales of $104 million, only about half that of the similarly expensive *Batman*.

JULY 3 Bruce Willis and Bonnie Bedalia are back for *Die Hard 2*, debuting on 2,507 screens. **13** Patrick Swayze, Demi Moore, and Whoopi Goldberg star in *Ghost*, opening today. **18** *Arachnophobia*, opening today, starring Jeff Daniels and John Goodman, was at one time called "Along Came a Spider." **20** Andrew Bergman's *The Freshman*, opening today, stars Matthew Broderick, Bruno Kirby, and Marlon Brando in a thinly veiled reprise of Don Vito Corleone. **27** *Presumed Innocent*, based on the Scott Turow bestseller, stars Harrison Ford, Raul Julia, Bonnie Bedalia, and Brian Dennehy.

Business and Society

JANUARY 8 A Los Angeles Superior Court judge rules that Art Buchwald and Alain Bernheim are entitled to nineteen percent of the net profits from *Coming to America*, the film starring Eddie Murphy and based on an idea submitted by Buchwald. • Dawn Steel resigns as Columbia Pictures president.

FEBRUARY 20 Mike Medavoy resigns as production head at Orion Pictures to head Tri-Star Pictures.

MARCH 6 Giancarlo Paretti, who controls Pathé Communications, negotiates an agreement to buy MGM–UA Communications. **30** Giancarlo Paretti is convicted in Rome of bankruptcy fraud and sentenced to prison.

APRIL 4 Dawn Steel signs a three-year agree-

ment to produce independently for Disney and Touchstone.

MAY 1 The creation of the Film Foundation, dedicated to film preservation, is announced by Martin Scorsese, Sydney Pollack, Steven Spielberg, George Lucas, Francis Ford Coppola, Woody Allen, Stanley Kubrick, and Robert Redford.

JUNE 7 MCA opens its Universal Studios Park in Florida.

Births, Deaths, Marriages, and Divorces

JANUARY 5 Arthur Kennedy d. **20** Barbara Stanwyck d. **25** Ava Gardner d.

FEBRUARY 19 Director Michael Powell d.

MARCH 17 Capucine commits suicide.

APRIL 15 Greta Garbo d. **23** Paulette Goddard d. **24** Character actor Albert Salmi murders his wife and commits suicide.

MAY • Glenn Ford m. Karem Johnson. **2** Claire Bloom m. novelist Philip Roth. **6** Charles Farrell d. **16** Sammy Davis Jr. d. **16** Jim Henson d. **18** Jill Ireland d. **26** Jill St. John m. Robert Wagner.

JUNE • Jane Fonda and Tom Hayden

MARCH 26 Billy Crystal takes over as host of the Academy Awards ceremonies. Kim Basinger, introducing film clips of the nominees for Best Picture at the Dorothy Chandler Pavilion, adds that Spike Lee's *Do the Right Thing* should have been one of them. According to *Women's Wear Daily*, this year's ceremonies are really the "Armani Awards." Nominees Jessica Tandy, Julia Roberts, and Michelle Pfeiffer appear Armani-clad for their possible moment in the spotlight, and Billy Crystal, Tom Hanks, Denzel Washington, Dennis Hopper, Steve Martin, and Jeff Goldblum are sporting Armani tuxedos. **27** Kathleen Turner, who has just opened to critical acclaim in a Broadway revival of *Cat on a Hot Tin Roof*, is besieged by reporters asking about her husband, Manhattan real estate developer Jay Weiss. He holds the lease on the Happy Land Social Club in the Bronx, which burned down two days ago, killing 87 people. (In 1992 he will plead guilty to a violation—insufficient sprinklers—and pay a fine.)

APRIL • Charlie Sheen's engagement to Kelly Preston is off, but she's not returning his $200,000 ring. **16** The Jack Nicholson–Anjelica Huston long-term but non-exclusive romance collapses for good when his current flame, Rebecca Broussard, has a baby and he sticks by her. **22** Fifty-eight-year-old Elizabeth Taylor almost dies of pneumonia. During her recovery, she will acknowledge her romance with twenty-three-year-old Julian Hobbs so that he can be at her side without causing a commotion.

MAY • Julia Roberts, filming *Sleeping with the Enemy*, refuses to strip to panties and a T-shirt for a scene unless the crew disrobes as well, which many of them do. **25** Nagoya, Japan, Los Angeles' sister city, dedicates a replica of Hollywood's Walk of Fame.

JUNE • Emilio Estevez, in Bolivia to scout sites for a movie he's considering, is temporarily detained for questioning by police investigating drug trafficking. **•** Gene Wilder begins to do TV commercials urging women to get tested for ovarian cancer, of which his wife, Gilda Radner, died on May 20 of last year. **8** John Cusack is fined $876 and has his license suspended for ninety days on a drunk driving conviction involving an accident on Santa Monica Blvd. on February 23. **18** *The Star*, a supermarket tabloid, prints nude photos of Arnold Schwarzenegger. **22** Carolco's record bid of $3 million at auction wins Joe Eszterhas's screenplay, called "Basic Instinct." **23** Gary Busey pays $242,000 at auction for one of Buddy Holly's guitars.

AUGUST 24 Nicolas Roeg's *The Witches*, starring Anjelica Huston and Mai Zetterling, opens.

SEPTEMBER 12 Mike Nichols's *Postcards from the Edge*, opening today, stars Shirley MacLaine, Meryl Streep, and Dennis Quaid. **19** Martin Scorsese's *Goodfellas*, starring Robert DeNiro, Ray Liotta, and Joe Pesci, opens today. **28** John Schlesinger's *Pacific Heights*, opening today, starring Melanie Griffith, Matthew Modine, and Michael Keaton, concerns an individual who insinuates himself into a couple's life and then turns demonic, a theme that will be repeated in next year's *Consenting Adults* and *Unlawful Entry*.

JULY 2 MCA–Universal buys the eighteen-screen Cineplex Odeon Universal City Cinemas.

SEPTEMBER 26 The Motion Picture Association announces that "NC-17—No Children Under 17 Admitted," will immediately replace the "X" rating. The first film rated NC-17 is *Henry and June*, opening October 5.

OCTOBER 23 Time Warner secures worldwide home video rights to United Artists's

Julia Roberts stars in *Pretty Woman*, opening in March.   *LC*

films for $125 million as part of the Pathé deal for MGM–UA, now being completed.

OCTOBER 5 Barry Levinson's *Avalon*, starring Armin Mueller-Stahl, Aidan Quinn, Elizabeth Perkins, and Joan Plowright, and the NC-17-rated *Henry and June*, starring Fred Ward and Uma Thurman, open in limited engagements. **17** *Reversal of Fortune* opens today in New York, Los Angeles, and Chicago. According to attorney Alan Dershowitz, Claus von Bulow's lawyer, Jeremy Irons makes a better von Bulow than his client.

NOVEMBER 9 Kevin Costner's *Dances with Wolves*, starring Costner and Mary McDonnell, with some of the dialogue subtitled in Sioux, opens. Financed abroad

NOVEMBER • Hollywood production companies begin a seven-month boycott of location shooting in New York City until the film craft union there makes concessions to cut costs. **1** Giancarlo Parretti completes his purchase of MGM–UA from majority stockholder Kirk Kerkorian for $1.3 billion, creating MGM–Pathé Communications. Almost immediately, the new company will start bouncing checks. **6** An arson fire at Universal causes millions in damages, including to a set for

divorce. **2** Rex Harrison d.

JULY 8 Howard Duff d. **15** Margaret Lockwood d. **24** Gene Kelly m. Patricia Ward. **26** Dudley Moore and Brogan Lane divorce.

SEPTEMBER • Raquel Welch and Andre

Weinfeld divorce. **4** Irene Dunne d. **9** James Caan m. Ingrid Hajek. **10** Burt Lancaster m. Susie Scherer. **22** Jim Belushi m. Marjorie Bransfield.

OCTOBER 20 Joel McCrea d.

NOVEMBER 12 Eve Arden d **23** Sean

Young m. Robert Lujan.

DECEMBER 7 Joan Bennett d. **24** Tom Cruise m. Nicole Kidman.

Also this year: **•** Divorces include Tom Cruise and Mimi Rogers, Geena Davis and Jeff Goldblum, Rebecca De Mornay and

Personalities

JULY • Screenwriter, director, and actor John Sayles is also a novelist. He has just sold *Los Gusanos* (*The Worms*), about Cuban exiles, to HarperCollins with the stipulation that it not be edited.

AUGUST • Charlie Sheen enters a thirty-day drug and alcohol rehabilitation program. **22** "I Am Not an Anti-Semite" is the headline over Spike Lee's *New York Times* rebuttal to those who see such bigotry in his recent *Mo' Better Blues*.

SEPTEMBER 24 *Forbes*'s cover story is on Madonna, "America's Smartest Businesswoman." **24** "Stars' Rocketing Salaries Keep Pushing the Envelope," headlines *Variety*. Arnold Schwarzenegger is reported

Kevin Costner in *Dances with Wolves*   LC

to have earned as much as $13 million for *Total Recall*.

OCTOBER 15 Margot Kidder, who played Lois Lane in the Superman films, sustains disabling nerve damage in an accident while filming a TV show. **27** Tri-Star removes director Peter Bogdanovich, who has been filming since September 17, from *Another You*, supposedly because of schedule delays. Rumor has it that star Gene Wilder won't work with him.

NOVEMBER 30 Burt Lancaster is hospitalized with a stroke he suffers while visiting Dana Andrews, an Alzheimer's patient, in a nursing home.

Movies

when no U.S. studio would open its coffers, it will become the first western since the 1931 *Cimarron* to win the Oscar for Best Picture. Costner, in addition to an Oscar for Best Director, is also awarded membership in the Sioux tribe. **16** Macauley Culkin catapults to stardom in *Home Alone*, opening today and costarring Joe Pesci and Daniel Stern. The film grosses almost $50 million in its first ten days and will become the third biggest moneymaker after *E.T.* and *Star Wars*. **23** Paul Newman and Joanne Woodward star in the

Merchant–Ivory production, *Mr. and Mrs. Bridge*, opening in a limited engagement. **30** *Misery* is what James Caan finds at the hands of Kathy Bates, opening today.

DECEMBER 5 Martin Scorsese's *The Grifters*, starring Anjelica Huston, John Cusack, and Annette Bening, opens. **7** Tim Burton's *Edward Scissorhands*, debuting today, stars Johnny Depp, Winona Ryder, and Dianne Wiest. Ryder and Depp are lovers off screen as well as onscreen. **14** Richard Benjamin directs Cher, Winona Ryder, and Bob Hoskins in *Mermaids*, opening today. **21** Penny Marshall's *Awakenings*, based on the work of psychologist Oliver Sacks

and starring Robin Williams and Robert DeNiro, opens. **22** Brian DePalma's *The Bonfire of the Vanities*, based on the Tom Wolfe novel, opens. This commercial and artistic disaster features Tom Hanks, Bruce Willis, and Melanie Griffith. **25** Al Pacino, Diane Keaton, and Andy Garcia star in Francis Ford Coppola's *Godfather, Part III*, opening at 1,820 theaters. The production of the film marked the end of the Pacino–Keaton offscreen romance.

> From *The Godfather III*, some wisdom you cannot refuse:
>
> **Al Pacino:** "Never hate your enemy. It affects your judgment."

Business and Society

Oscar, now filming with Sylvester Stallone, and to sets used on *The Sting, Airport, Back to the Future, Dirty Harry*, and *To Kill a Mockingbird*. The Universal Studio Tours will have to be temporarily shortened. **26** Matsushita buys MCA and, with it, Universal, for $6.13 billion. The deal was partly brokered by Michael Ovitz.

DECEMBER 1 The American Movie Classics cable TV channel goes to a twenty-four hours a day programming schedule, beginning with a Marilyn Monroe marathon. **13** The deal in which Disney was going to purchase Jim Henson's company breaks down over money.

Births, Deaths, Marriages, and Divorces

Bruce Wagner, Malcolm McDowell and Mary Steenburgen, John Malkovich and Glenne Headly, and Kiefer Sutherland and Camelia Kath.

Johnny Depp in *Edward Scissorhands*   LC
© 20TH CENTURY FOX

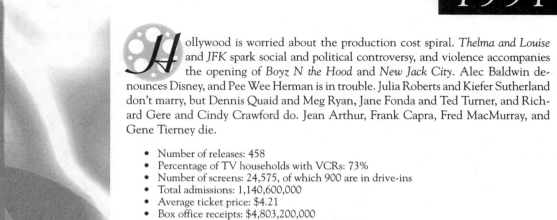

*H*ollywood is worried about the production cost spiral. *Thelma and Louise* and *JFK* spark social and political controversy, and violence accompanies the opening of *Boyz N the Hood* and *New Jack City*. Alec Baldwin denounces Disney, and Pee Wee Herman is in trouble. Julia Roberts and Kiefer Sutherland don't marry, but Dennis Quaid and Meg Ryan, Jane Fonda and Ted Turner, and Richard Gere and Cindy Crawford do. Jean Arthur, Frank Capra, Fred MacMurray, and Gene Tierney die.

- Number of releases: 458
- Percentage of TV households with VCRs: 73%
- Number of screens: 24,575, of which 900 are in drive-ins
- Total admissions: 1,140,600,000
- Average ticket price: $4.21
- Box office receipts: $4,803,200,000
- Average production cost per film: $26,100,000
- Amount spent on premiere party for *Terminator 2*: $450,000
- Arnold Schwarzenegger's fee for *Terminator 2*: a reported $15,000,000

Top stars at the box office, based on a Quigley Publications poll of exhibitors:

1. Kevin Costner
2. Arnold Schwarzenegger
3. Robin Williams
4. Julia Roberts
5. Macaulay Culkin
6. Jodie Foster
7. Billy Crystal
8. Dustin Hoffman
9. Robert DeNiro
10. Mel Gibson

Top rental earnings, based on figures reported by *Variety*:

1.	*Terminator 2*	$112,000,000
2.	*Robin Hood: Prince of Thieves*	86,000,000
3.	*City Slickers*	60,750,000
4.	*Home Alone*	60,000,000
5.	*The Silence of the Lambs*	59,900,000

The New York Film Critics Circle Awards
Best Picture: *The Silence of the Lambs*

The Los Angeles Film Critics Association
Best picture: *Bugsy*

The Golden Globe Awards:
Best Picture (Drama): *Bugsy*
Best Picture (Musical or Comedy): *Beauty and the Beast*

The Cannes Film Festival
Palme d'Or: *Barton Fink*

The Academy Awards (presented March 30, 1992)
Best Film: *The Silence of the Lambs*
Actor: Anthony Hopkins (*The Silence of the Lambs*)
Actress: Jodie Foster (*The Silence of the Lambs*)
Supporting Actor: Jack Palance (*City Slickers*)
Supporting Actress: Mercedes Ruehl (*The Fisher King*)
Director: Jonathan Demme (*The Silence of the Lambs*)

January	February	March	April	May	June	
13 Jeffrey Katzenberg memo on Hollywood's production cost spiral	**14** *The Silence of the Lambs*	**16** Giancarlo Parretti forced to hand over reins of MGM–Pathé to Alan Ladd Jr. **8** Opening of *New Jack City* brings violence at theaters	**17** Alec Baldwin accusations of bad treatment by Disney Studio		**11** Julia Roberts cancels wedding to Kiefer Sutherland	

July	August	September	October	November	December	
3 *Terminator 2*	• Demi Moore is pregnant and nude on the cover of *Vanity Fair*	**3** Director Frank Capra d.	**22** Planet Hollywood opens in New York	**5** Fred MacMurray d.	**25** *Prince of Tides*	

Personalities

JANUARY 13 Vanessa Redgrave's call for U.S. forces to stay out of the Persian Gulf is interpreted as pro-Iraq, causing her to take out an ad in today's *New York Times* explaining that she simply wants to see war avoided. **14** The New York Court of Appeals turns down Sandra Jennings' claim to have been the common-law-wife of William Hurt, with whom she lived from 1981 to 1984 and had a child. **19** Robert Young, after drinking all night, unsuccessfully attempts suicide.

FEBRUARY 13 Kirk Douglas is hospitalized when the helicopter in which he is flying collides with a plane and crashes. **28** "Perhaps I failed as a father," Marlon Brando tells a judge, asking leniency for his son Christian, who is about to receive ten years in prison for killing his half-sister Cheyenne's boyfriend.

MARCH 11 Jamie Lee Curtis acknowledges in *People* that when she was twenty, she did coke with her father, Tony Curtis. **18** *People* magazine reveals that in the years since she has been out of the public eye, Sandra Dee has fought alcohol and drug addiction and anorexia. **25** The approximately one thousand stretch limos bringing celebrities to tonight's Academy Awards ceremonies at the Shrine Auditorium are said to be a record. Security is unusually tight following the recently concluded Persian Gulf War. Everyone except Bob Hope is asked to pass through metal detectors.

APRIL • Tom Hanks, his career in the doldrums after duds such as *Bonfire of the Vanities* and *Joe Versus the Volcano*, presses the William Morris Agency to get him something good for a change.

MAY • The British press plays up stories about a romance between Keifer Sutherland, who has just announced his engagement to Julia Roberts, and go-go dancer Amanda Rice. **17** Alec Baldwin, in an *Entertainment Weekly* interview, says that Walt Disney tried to coerce him into not complaining about the poor way he contends he was treated on *The Marrying Man*. He calls Disney Studio head Jeffrey Katzenberg "the eighth dwarf—Greedy." Baldwin and Kim Basinger became an item during the movie's production. **23** Mickey Rourke, age thirty-four, debuts as a professional fighter, earning a unanimous decision over Steve Powell in Ft. Lauderdale. **29** Richard Pryor has heart bypass surgery.

Movies

FEBRUARY 14 Hannibal Lecter, psychiatrist and cannibal, played by Anthony Hopkins, makes his second screen appearance, in Jonathan Demme's *The Silence of the Lambs*, also starring Jodie Foster and opening today. The Lecter character was also in *Manhunter*, a 1986 film, where he was played by Brian Cox. In that movie a male police officer—the role parallel to Foster's in *Silence*—enlists Lecter's aid in probing the psyche of a serial killer, similar to what happens in the current film. Both movies are based on the fiction of Thomas Harris.

Anthony Hopkins and Jody Foster in *The Silence of the Lambs*   *LC/© ORION PICTURES*

Business and Society

• Hollywood is showing a new responsiveness to black filmmakers. Nineteen pictures by figures such as Spike Lee, John Singleton, Mario Van Peebles and others are scheduled for release this year.

JANUARY 13 The Disney Company's Jeffrey Katzenberg sends to his executives a memo on holding down costs. Leaked to the press, it will spark widespread discussion of the need to halt Hollywood's production cost spiral.

MARCH 8 The opening of *New Jack City*, about inner city drug violence, stirs youth to real life violence at theaters in Los Angeles, Las Vegas, New Jersey, and New York, where one person is killed. **20** Frank Mancuso leaves Paramount Pictures. **29** MGM–Pathé's creditors file an invol-

Births, Deaths, Marriages, and Divorces

JANUARY 12 Keye Luke, Charlie Chan's "Number One" son, d.

FEBRUARY 14 Dennis Quaid m. Meg Ryan

MARCH 18 Silent screen star Vilma Banky d. **27** Aldo Ray d.

APRIL • Kathy Bates m. Tony Campisi. **16** Director David Lean d. **20** Director Don Siegel d.

MAY 1 Robert Duvall m. Sharon Brophy. **4** Bing Crosby's son Dennis commits suicide. Another son, Lindsay, killed himself in 1989. **30** Douglas Fairbanks Jr. m. Vera Shelton.

JUNE 19 Jean Arthur d.

QUOTABLE CITY SLICKERS

Billy Crystal (to Bruno Kirby): "Ed, have you noticed the older you get, the younger your girlfriends get? Soon you'll be dating sperm."

Bruno Kirby: "A spaceship lands and the most beautiful woman you ever saw gets out. And all she wants to do is have the greatest sex in the universe with you."
Billy Crystal: "Could happen."
Kirby: "And the second it is over, she flies away for eternity. No one will ever know. You're telling me you wouldn't do it?"
Crystal: "No. Because what you're describing actually happened to my cousin Ronald, and his wife did find out about it at the beauty parlor. They know everything there."

Billy Crystal and Jack Palance, *City Slickers*
LC/© CASTLE ROCK

Billy Crystal: "Hi Curley! Kill anyone today?"
Jack Palance: "Day ain't over yet."

JUNE 11 Julia Roberts cancels her much-publicized wedding to Kiefer Sutherland, three days before it is to take place on the back lot at Fox. She then flies to Dublin with Jason Patric, Sutherland's friend and grandson of Jackie Gleason. **13** In *Rolling Stone*, Carrie Fisher interviews Madonna, who reveals that Sean Penn has his nickname for her, "Daisy," tattooed on his toe.

JULY • Sylvester Stallone wins damages and an apology from the London *Spectator*, which claimed he dodged the draft during the Vietnam War and did not go to Cannes in 1987 because he feared a terrorist attack. **16** Annette Bening, who won the role of Catwoman in *Batman Returns* over Cher, told Warner Bros. a few days ago that she can't do it because she's pregnant with Warren Beatty's baby. Sean Young, attempting to win the role, today comes to the

APRIL 22 A 70mm version of the 1960 *Spartacus* premieres at the Ziegfeld. A five-minute scene with homoerotic overtones between Laurence Olivier and Tony Curtis, cut from the original release and lacking Olivier's voice on the soundtrack, is dubbed by Anthony Hopkins. Tony Curtis, Jean Simmons, and Martin Scorsese attend.

MAY 9 Madonna documents her Blonde Ambition tour in *Madonna, Truth or Dare*, premiering at the San Francisco Film Festival.

JUNE 7 Billy Crystal, Jack Palance, Daniel Stern, and Bruno Kirby star in *City Slick-*

ers; and Wesley Snipes and Annabella Sciorra star in Spike Lee's *Jungle Fever*, opening today. **14** Kevin Costner and Morgan Freeman are the stars of *Robin Hood: Prince of Thieves*, opening today on 2,369 screens.

JULY 3 Arnold Schwarzenegger is back in *Terminator 2*, opening in 2,274 theaters. The film is notable for its spectacular stunts and use of computer "morphing" to physically transform its characters. **12** John Singleton's movie about Los Angeles street

City Slickers
LC/© CASTLE ROCK

untary bankruptcy petition against it.

APRIL 16 Giancarlo Parretti is forced by Crédit Lyonnais, his studio's biggest creditor, to hand over the reins of MGM–Pathé to Alan Ladd Jr. **17** The authorities in Dallas grant Oliver Stone's request to film in the Texas School Book Depository, from which Lee Harvey Oswald allegedly fired the shots that killed President Kennedy.

MAY 1 Paramount announces the appointment

JULY 2 Lee Remick d. **6** Director William Friedkin m. producer Sherry Lansing. **8** James Franciscus d. **22** Rob Lowe m. Cheryl Berkoff.

AUGUST • Martha Haro files for a divorce from Joe Pesci, but they continue to live together.

SEPTEMBER 3 Director Frank Capra d. **4** Tom Tryon d. **5** John Travolta m. Kelly Preston in a Scientology ceremony. **8** Gene Wilder m. Karen Webb.

OCTOBER 6 Elizabeth Taylor m. Larry Fortensky. **12** Steven Spielberg m. Kate Capshaw.

NOVEMBER 5 Fred MacMurray d. **6** Gene Tierney d. **9** Yves Montand d. **29** Ralph Bellamy d.

DECEMBER 12 Richard Gere m. model Cindy Crawford. **21** Jane Fonda m. Ted Turner.

Personalities

studio uninvited and dressed for the part. Director Tim Burton is unimpressed and annoyed, and she is escorted off the lot. **23** James Farentino is arrested in Vancouver for possession of cocaine. **26** Pee Wee Herman is arrested outside a Sarasota porno theater and charged with indecent exposure and masturbation while watching *Catalina Tiger Shark*.

AUGUST • Bruce Willis changes the name of his Hudson Hawk Films to Flying Heart Films following the large egg laid by his movie, *Hudson Hawk*. • Demi Moore, pregnant and nude, appears on the cover of *Vanity Fair*. • A group of black artists and intellectuals question Spike Lee's fitness to make a movie about Malcolm X.

ON THE ROAD WITH THELMA AND LOUISE

Brad Pitt   LC

MAY 24 *Thelma and Louise*, starring Susan Sarandon, Geena Davis, Harvey Keitel, and Brad Pitt in his first important role, opens. This feminist buddy–road film sets off another ripple in the ongoing debate about the relationship between men and women.

Brad Pitt: "Tell me something, Miss Thelma. How's it you ain't got any kids? I mean God give you something special. I think you ought to pass it on."

Geena Davis: Well, Daryl—that's my husband . . . he says he ain't ready yet. Say's he's still too much of a kid himself. Kind of prides himself on being infantile."

Susan Sarandon: "Got a lot to be proud of."

Movies

gangs, *Boyz N the Hood*, starring Larry Fishburne, Ice Cube, and Cuba Gooding, opens, and its merits are immediately overshadowed by violence related to its showing in twelve states, which leaves three dead. Nineteen theaters will pull the film.

AUGUST 21 Ethan and Joel Coen's *Barton Fink* opens. It stars John Turturro, John Goodman, and Judy Davis, and won the Golden Palm at Cannes.

SEPTEMBER 20 *Rambling Rose*, starring Laura

Dern, Robert Duvall, Diane Ladd, and Lukas Haas, opens, as does *The Fisher King*, in a limited engagement, starring Robin Williams, Jeff Bridges, Amanda Plummer, and Mercedes Ruehl. **29** River Phoenix and Keanu Reeves star in Gus Van Sant's story of male hustlers, *My Own Private Idaho*, opening today at the Waverly and Plaza Theaters after a September 27 debut at the New York Film Festival.

OCTOBER 9 *Little Man Tate*, opening today, is Jodie Foster's directorial debut. It stars Foster, Dianne Wiest, and Adam Hann-

Byrd. **11** Michelle Pfeiffer and Al Pacino are *Frankie and Johnny*, debuting today. Also opening is John Sayles's *City of Hope*, which stars Sayles, Vincent Spano, and Tony LoBianco.

NOVEMBER • Disney releases *Fantasia* on videocassette for fifty days only, promising to withdraw it forever afterward. It will sell over fourteen million copies. **13** In Martin Scorsese's *Cape Fear*, opening today, Robert DeNiro and Nick Nolte play roles originated in the 1962 version by Robert Mitchum and Gregory Peck. Jessica

Business and Society

of Brandon Tartikoff as its new chairman. **8** Jon Peters leaves Columbia to produce independently. **10** SoftVideo, software that will permit CD-Rom-based films to be shown on personal computers, is introduced.

JULY • The Arts and Entertainment cable TV network broadcasts "Naked Hollywood," a British documentary on the U.S.

film business. The film industry attacks it as unduly harsh criticism.

SEPTEMBER 4 Coca-Cola announces that it has hired Michael Ovitz's Creative Artists Agency as a marketing consultant because "We are in a global village and CAA represents the single greatest source in understanding that culture." **23** An NAACP report says that "white males" still call the shots in Hollywood, preventing minorities from gaining ground.

OCTOBER • Congressman Leon Panetta introduces legislation to limit foreign ownership of U.S. "cultural business enterprise" to fifty percent. **3** Mark Canton replaces Frank Price as Columbia Pictures chairman.

NOVEMBER • The Attorney General of California sues the Hollywood Chamber of Commerce for misusing money earmarked for trust funds to keep up the HOLLYWOOD sign and the Hollywood Walk of Fame. In

Births, Deaths, Marriages, and Divorces

Also this year: • Dyan Cannon and Stanley Fimberg and Edward James Olmos and Kaija Keel divorce.

1 Hedy Lamarr is arrested in Florida for shoplifting, but charges will be dropped when she signs a promise not to do it again. **8** Gary Oldman is arrested for drunken driving, with Kiefer Sutherland along for the ride.

SEPTEMBER • Barbra Streisand, promoting her *Prince of Tides*, gives her first magazine interview in eight years. It appears in *Vanity Fair*: "Streisand Now." • Actress and model Carré Otis is accidentally wounded in the shoulder by a .357 Magnum while visiting Mickey Rourke on the set of *White Sands* in Santa Fe. The gun was in a bag that she picked up.

OCTOBER • Mickey Rourke is quoted in the French edition of *Premiere*, now on sale: "When I look at a film of Kevin Costner's, I fall asleep out of boredom." **4** Jodie

Lange, and Juliette Lewis also star in this picture. And Walt Disney's popular animated feature *Beauty and the Beast* opens in a limited engagement. **22** *The Addams Family*, starring Anjelica Huston, Raul Julia, and Christopher Lloyd, opens. It will be followed by 1993's *Addams Family Values*.

DECEMBER 10 In spite of the participation of Dustin Hoffman, Robin Williams, and Julia Roberts, Steven Speilberg's *Hook*, a retelling of Peter Pan that debuts today in 2,197 theaters, is one of the year's disappointments. **13** Warren Beatty's *Bugsy*, with Beatty as Bugsy Siegel, co-starring

March the Chamber will agree to pay the disputed sum and relinquish some control over the trusts, without admitting guilt.

DECEMBER 11 Orion Pictures files for bankruptcy. **30** A judge in Delaware rules that control of MGM–Pathé rests with its main creditor, the Crédit Lyonnais Bank, and not with financier Giancarlo Parretti, now in an Italian prison on a tax evasion charge.

Foster cancels a *Today* show appearance when she's told that her introduction will include a mention of John Hinckley, who stalked Foster when she was at Yale and tried to kill President Reagan—a subject she refuses to discuss. **6** A one-hundred-person security force patrols the estate of Michael Jackson during the wedding of Elizabeth Taylor to Larry Fortensky—her seventh husband (and eighth marriage) but the first who is not a celebrity—where Roddy McDowall, who was also at Taylor's first wedding, provides continuity. **20** Tom Laughlin (*Billy Jack*), declares himself a candidate for President. **22** Planet Hollywood, the New York restaurant-as-Hollywood-theme-park, has a celebrity opening. Principal investors Arnold Schwarzenegger, Sylvester Stallone, and Bruce Willis, and six hundred other luminaries attend.

Annette Bening, Harvey Keitel, and Joe Mantegna, opens in New York, Los Angeles, and Chicago. **20** The opening of Oliver Stone's *JFK*, starring Kevin Costner, Sissy Spacek, Joe Pesci, Tommy Lee Jones, and Gary Oldman, provokes demands that all records related to the assassination of President Kennedy be opened to the public. Stone defends on the Op-Ed pages his film's view that the killing involved a conspiracy and a cover-up. **25** Barbra Streisand directs and stars in *Prince of Tides*, opening today. Nick Nolte co-stars. **27** Kathy Bates and Jessica Tandy star in the surprise hit film, *Fried Green Tomatoes*, opening today.

DECEMBER • Bette Midler, in a *Vanity Fair* interview, replies to Geraldo Rivera's recent claim in his book, *Exposing Myself*, that his "affair" with her revealed her to be insatiable. Calling him a "toad," she says that he and his producers came to her home, shoved her in the bathroom, "broke poppers under my nose and started to grope me." **9** In a *People* interview, Sarah Owen, James Wood's estranged wife, accuses him of verbal, physical, and sexual abuse, including some at gunpoint. He denies it.

americans will spend $4.9 billion to go to the movies this year, but $12 billion to buy or rent tapes. In the past five years, tape rentals have increased by thirteen percent, but sales are up thirty-one percent. Crédit Lyonnais takes full control of MGM-UA. Barbra Streisand leads Hollywood fund-raising for women senatorial candidates and for presidential candidate Bill Clinton. Woody Allen and Mia Farrow also hold the spotlight, but would rather not. Elizabeth Taylor (on February 27) and Debbie Reynolds (on April 1) turn sixty.

- Number of releases: 481
- Number of screens: 25,100, of which 875 are in drive-ins
- Percentage of TV households with VCRs: 76%
- Total admissions: 1,173,200,000
- Average ticket price: $4.15
- Box office receipts: $4,871,000,000
- Average production cost per film: $28,900,000

Top stars at the box office, based on a Quigley Publications poll of exhibitors, published in the *Motion Picture Almanac*:

1. Tom Cruise
2. Mel Gibson
3. Kevin Costner
4. Jack Nicholson
5. Macaulay Culkin
6. Whoopi Goldberg
7. Michael Douglas
8. Clint Eastwood
9. Steven Seagal
10. Robin Williams

Top rental earnings, based on figures reported by *Variety*:

1. *Home Alone 2: Lost in New York* $102,000,000
2. *Batman Returns* 100,100,000
3. *Lethal Weapon 3* 80,000,000
4. *Sister Act* 62,400,000
5. *Aladdin* 60,000,000

The New York Film Critics Circle Awards
Best Picture: *The Player*

The Los Angeles Film Critics Association
Best Picture: *Unforgiven*

The Golden Globe Awards
Best Picture (Drama): *Scent of a Woman*
Best Picture (Musical or Comedy): *The Player*

The Cannes Film Festival
Palme d'Or: *The Best Intentions*

The Academy Awards (presented March 29, 1993)
Best Picture: *Unforgiven*
Actor: Al Pacino (*Scent of a Woman*)
Actress: Emma Thompson (*Howard's End*)
Supporting Actor: Gene Hackman (*Unforgiven*)
Supporting Actress: Marisa Tomei (*My Cousin Vinnie*)
Director: Clint Eastwood (*Unforgiven*)

January	February	March	April	May	June	
	19 2,398-theater United Artists chain, nation's biggest, sold		**10** *The Player*		• FBI guarding Meg Ryan and Dennis Quaid against threats	
		20 *Basic Instinct*				
	22 Freddie Bartholomew d.		**6** Marlene Dietrich d.			

July	August	September	October	November	December	
1 MCA–Universal first studio to offer same-sex partners health insurance benefits		**16** Barbra Streisand hosts star-studded fund-raiser for candidate Bill Clinton			**31** Anthony Hopkins knighted	
	17 Woody Allen says he's in love with twenty-one-year-old, adopted daughter of Mia Farrow		**21** Madonna's *Sex* goes on sale		**25** *The Crying Game*	

Personalities

JANUARY 8 Warren Beatty becomes a father when Annette Bening—they're not married—gives birth to a girl. **13** Mia Farrow discovers nude photos of her adopted daughter, Soon-Yi, in Woody Allen's apartment.

MARCH 29 The Golden Raspberry Foundation awards Sean Young, who played twins in *A Kiss Before Dying*, "worst actress" for the twin who lives and "worst supporting actress" for the one who doesn't. **30** Seventy-two-year-old Jack Palance turns the Academy Awards ceremony at the Dorothy Chandler Pavilion into a workout, doing one-handed pushups. Several actresses allude to the fact that Barbra Streisand, whose *Prince of Tides* was nomi-

nated for Oscars in seven categories, was not nominated for Best Director. Many celebrities are wearing red lapel ribbons to support those who have AIDS.

Kim Basinger withdraws in June from *Boxing Helena* and is sued.   LC

APRIL • A brief fling between Sharon Stone and singer Dwight Yoakam leaves no afterglow for Stone, who says: "A dirt sandwich is better than Dwight Yoakam." • Whoopi Goldberg falls in love with Ted Danson on the set of *Made in America* • Marlon Brando, disturbed by "historical inaccuracies" in *Christopher Columbus: The Discovery* and by what he sees as financial irregularities connected to the film, demands that his name be removed from the credits. **5** Participants in today's Washington, D.C. Abortion Rights rally include Jane Fonda, Mary Steenburgen, Christine Lahti, and Joanne Woodward. **20** Time Warner announces a seven-year production deal with Madonna that could be worth as much as $60 million to her. **21** 20th Century Fox announces a twelve-film, $500 million deal with producer/director James Cameron, who directed the "Terminator"

Movies

MARCH 13 Merchant–Ivory's *Howard's End*, starring Anthony Hopkins, Emma Thompson, Helena Bonham-Carter, and Vanessa Redgrave, opens. **13** *My Cousin Vinny*, starring Joe Pesci and Marisa Tomei, opens. **20** *Basic Instinct*, opening today, stars Michael Douglas and Sharon Stone, in a part turned down by Kim Basinger, Michelle Pfeiffer, Ellen Barkin, Geena Davis, and Mariel Hemingway because it was too steamy. The film is a box-office success. Next year, Stone will call the film's sex scenes "ridiculous."

APRIL 10 Following its April 3 debut at the Cleveland Film Festival, Robert Altman's *The Player* has its theatrical opening. This satire on Hollywood stars Tim Robbins, with cameos for celebrities such as Whoopi Goldberg.

MAY 29 Whoopi Goldberg is a big hit in *Sister Act*, opening today.

JUNE 5 *Patriot Games*, based on the Tom Clancy bestseller and opening today at 2,365 theaters, stars Harrison Ford, Ann Archer, Richard Harris, and James Earl Jones. **16** Michael Keaton is the 180th star to leave his prints outside Mann's Chinese Theater in Hollywood as *Batman Returns* premieres. The film's other stars, Danny DeVito, Michelle Pfeiffer, and Christopher Walken are also there, as are Arnold Schwarzenegger, James Caan, Christian Slater, and Mickey Rooney. The post-premiere party is on the Warners soundstage that still sports sets of Gotham City and the Bat Cave. When the film opens across the country on June 19, it will

Business and Society

JANUARY 17 The opening of *Juice*, the first feature by black director Ernest Dickerson—Spike Lee's cinematographer—brings more violence at inner city theaters, including several shootings and a death.

FEBRUARY 19 Tele-Communications, Inc., agrees to sell the 2,398-theater United Artists chain, the nation's biggest, to a subsid-

iary of Merrill Lynch Capital Partners, Inc. **24** Barry Diller resigns as chairman of 20th Century Fox.

MARCH 16 Art Buchwald and producer Alain Bernheim are awarded $150,000 and $750,000, respectively, as final settlement of their 1988 suit against Paramount for *Coming to America*.

APRIL 1 Jack Valenti, an aide to President Kennedy and head of the Motion Picture

Association of America, calls Oliver Stone's *JFK* a "smear" and a "hoax."

MAY 7 Crédit Lyonnais formally takes control of MGM–Pathé Communications, renaming it Metro-Goldwyn-Mayer.

OCTOBER 29 Brandon Tartikoff resigns as chairman of Paramount Pictures. • Supporters of presidential candidate H. Ross Perot change the HOLLYWOOD sign in the Hollywood Hills to PEROTWOOD.

Births, Deaths, Marriages, and Divorces

JANUARY 3 Judith Anderson d. **22** Freddie Bartholomew d. **26** Jose Ferrer d. **27** Liza Minnelli and Mark Gero divorce.

MARCH 2 Sandy Dennis d. **12** Warren Beatty and Annette Bening announce that

they have married, but won't say when. **21** John Ireland d. **29** Paul Henried d.

APRIL 29 Emilio Estevez m. singer Paula Abdul.

MAY 3 George Murphy d. **6** Marlene Dietrich dies in Paris, the day before the opening of the Cannes Film Festival. **10** John Lund d. **23** Anjelica Huston m. Robert Graham.

JUNE • Mickey Rourke m. Carré Otis. **3** Robert Morley d.

movies. **25** Guests at Barbra Streisand's fiftieth birthday party include ex-husband Elliott Gould, ex-live-in-lover Jon Peters, and Frank Sinatra, Warren Beatty, Meryl Streep, and Goldie Hawn. **30** Hollywood studios close early out of fear of more violence after last night's outbreak following the verdict in the Rodney King beating trial, in which many people feel that the LAPD officers who beat him got off too easily. The Hollywood Women's Political Committee will send food to South-Central Los Angeles, hard hit by rioting. Barbra Streisand will send $100,000; and Edward James Olmos is in the streets, helping with the clean-up.

MAY 19 Spike Lee receives the money he needs to complete *Malcolm X* from prominent African-American entertainers and sports figures, including Oprah Winfrey, Bill Cosby, and Michael Jordan. **29** Alec Baldwin, seeking to prevent cruelty to horses, testifies at a New York City hearing on keeping hansom cabs off the streets. When the drivers boo him with obscenities, according to the *New York Post*, the actor, who is to participate in an AIDS walk tomorrow, invites one to step outside with "C'mon out here, you faggot."

JUNE • The FBI is guarding Meg Ryan, Dennis Quaid, and their infant son after their lives were threatened in anonymous letters. **10** Kim Basinger, who took over the lead role in *Boxing Helena* when Madonna passed it up, withdraws, for which she will be sued. The director, Jennifer Chambers Lynch, is the daughter of director David Lynch. **20** Waiters and bartenders (several of whom are actors) on strike against the Rainbow Room at New York's Rockefeller Center, tell the *New York Post* that Robert Duvall crossed their picket line this evening. When challenged, they say, he gave them "the finger" and called them "faggots." When they yelled that Marlon Brando wouldn't do this, Duvall called Brando an "asshole." **30** Francis Ford Coppola files for bankruptcy again.

JULY 1 Hollywood actresses, led by Lily Tomlin and Barbra Streisand, raise funds at a Beverly Hills luncheon for women Senate candidates. And MCA–Universal becomes the first movie studio to offer same-sex partners health insurance benefits. **8** Annette Funicello announces that she has had multiple sclerosis since 1987.

AUGUST • Demi Moore is again on the cover of *Vanity Fair*, this time wearing a "suit" painted on her skin. **4** Charlie Sheen

gross $42.7 million from 2,644 theaters on its first weekend. **25** The premiere of *A League of Their Own* at the Ziegfeld is attended by Madonna, director Penny Marshall, and Tom Hanks. Geena Davis also stars in this film about the women's baseball league begun during World War II. An all-woman jazz band entertains at the post-film party at Tavern on the Green.

AUGUST 7 Clint Eastwood's Oscar-winning western without heroes, *Unforgiven*, opens on 2,071 screens. It stars Eastwood, Gene Hackman, Morgan Freeman, and Richard Harris. **14** Bridget Fonda and Jennifer Jason-Leigh star in the psychological thriller *Single White Female*, opening today.

SEPTEMBER 4 Tim Robbins directs and stars in a political satire, *Bob Roberts*, opening today at eight theaters. **18** Tri-Star Pictures has moved up the opening of Woody Allen's *Husbands and Wives* from September 23 to today and enlarged the engagement from eight cities to nationwide booking on 865 screens, taking advantage of publicity surrounding Allen's romance with Mia Farrow's daughter. TV ads feature an excerpt from the film in which Farrow asks Allen: "Do you think we'd ever break up?" The movie stars Mia Farrow, Judy Davis, Sidney Pollack, Liam Neeson, and Juliette Lewis. **30** James Foley's *Glengarry Glen Ross*, based on the David Mamet play and starring Al Pacino, Jack Lemmon, Alec Baldwin, Ed Harris, and Alan Arkin, opens.

OCTOBER 23 In this "unusually good year for the discovery of first-rate American directors...add to the list the name of Quentin Tarantino," says the *New York Times* review of *Reservoir Dogs*, opening today. A former video store clerk and self-styled "film-geek," Tarantino, whose first name comes from the character Quint

NOVEMBER 2 Joe Roth, 20th Century Fox chairman, announces his resignation to produce independently at Walt Disney Studios. Peter Chernin replaces him at Fox. **4** Sherry Lansing is named to head Paramount Pictures. **5** Orion emerges from bankruptcy. **14** The "MGM" sign is removed from that studio's Culver City headquarters, which will be occupied by Sony Pictures Entertainment. MGM is moving to Santa Monica. **17** The Motion Picture Academy decides to stop awarding an

AUGUST 8 Barbara Hershey m. Stephen Douglas.

SEPTEMBER 10 George Peppard m. Laura Taylor. **12** Anthony Perkins dies of AIDS.

OCTOBER 6 Denholm Elliott d. of AIDS. **10** Ally Sheedy m. David Lansbury,

Tim Roth and Harvey Keitel in *Reservoir Dogs*

Personalities

pays $93,500 for the baseball that the New York Mets's Mookie Wilson hit to win the sixth game of the 1986 World Series. **6** Harold Russell sells at auction an Oscar he was awarded for playing the disabled veteran in *The Best Years of Our Lives* (1946). The statuette brings $60,500. **17** Fifty-seven-year-old Woody Allen announces that he is in love with the twenty-one-year-old, adopted daughter of Mia Farrow, Allen's former lover. He has sued Farrow (August 13) for custody of their biological child and the two children they adopted together; she has charged him with child abuse.

SEPTEMBER 12 Anthony Perkins dies of AIDS. In his last days he dictated a state-ment: "I choose not to go public about this, because to misquote *Casablanca*, I'm not much at being noble, but it doesn't take too much to see that the problems of an old actor don't amount to a hill of beans in this crazy old world." **16** Barbra Streisand serenades candidate Bill Clinton at a Beverly Hills fund-raiser. Also present are Jack Nicholson, Whoopi Goldberg, Dustin Hoffman, Danny DeVito, Michelle Pfeiffer, Chevy Chase, Warren Beatty, and David Geffen. Clinton says he wants them to be "part of the Administration, not just part of the winning campaign." **23** Their ten-year romance ended, Darryl Hannah and Jackson Browne have a violent (she says) confrontation in their Santa Monica home. She has taken up with John F. Kennedy Jr.

OCTOBER • Production begins on *Sliver*. Star Sharon Stone falls in love with Bill Macdonald, the film's co-producer, who leaves his wife Naomi, whom he only recently married. Naomi seeks consolation from *Sliver*'s screenwriter, Joe Eszterhas and his wife, Naomi's best friend. In April 1993, Eszterhas will leave his wife and take up with Naomi Macdonald. **21** Madonna's $49.95, shrink-wrapped book *Sex* goes on sale. **27** The *Los Angeles Times* turns down Spike Lee's request that only black reporters interview him on his upcoming *Malcolm X*.

NOVEMBER • Kit Culkin, Macauley's father, pressures 20th Century Fox to remove producer Laurence Mark from *The Good Son*. **18** Barbra Streisand asks the movie industry to boycott Colorado's vacation areas because of that state's voter-approved antigay-rights stance. Celebrities owning homes in progressive Aspen will pressure

Movies

Asper, played on TV's *Gunsmoke* by Burt Reynolds, was only last year playing an Elvis impersonator on *The Golden Girls*. *Reservoir Dogs*, which Tarantino wrote as well as directed, features in its cast Tim Roth, Harvey Keitel, and 1940s B-movie bad guy Lawrence Tierney. The film is marked by extreme violence.

NOVEMBER 11 *Aladdin*, an animated feature with Robin Williams doing the genie's voice, opens. The soundtrack, including the song "A Whole New World," is popular.

13 Francis Ford Coppola's *Bram Stoker's Dracula* opens on 2,491 screens. It stars Gary Oldman, Winona Ryder, Anthony Hopkins, and Keanu Reeves. **18** Spike Lee's *Malcolm X*, starring Denzel Washington, debuts. **25** Forest Whitaker, Miranda Richardson, Jaye Davidson, and Stephen Rea star in Neil Jordan's *The Crying Game*—he wrote and directed it—an "astonishingly good and daring" film, according to *Daily Variety*, opening at six theaters. Equally astonishing is the $62 million it will earn.

Business and Society

Oscar for nonfiction short subjects, which, once movie staples, are no longer a factor in the industry.

DECEMBER 24 Carolco Pictures announces that MGM has agreed to participate in a plan to finance the faltering studio in return for the right to distribute its films.

Stephen Rea and Jaye Davidson in *The Crying Game*   LC/© MIRAMAX

Births, Deaths, Marriages, and Divorces

nephew of Angela Lansbury. **22** Cleavon Little d.

NOVEMBER 2 Hal Roach dies at age 100. **19** Diane Varsi d. **22** Sterling Holloway d.

DECEMBER • Tatum O'Neal and John McEnroe separate. **17** Dana Andrews d.

Also this year: • Richard Dreyfuss and Jeramie Rains and Dennis Hopper and Katherine La Nasa divorce.

her to back off. **22** Appearing on TV's *60 Minutes*, Woody Allen says that Mia Farrow, "obsessed with Greek tragedy," has threatened to kill him and pluck out his eyes. **25** John Travolta's "Mayday" briefly clears the air space over all three Washington, D. C. airports as he pilots his malfunctioning private jet to an emergency landing at Dulles.

DECEMBER 31 Anthony Hopkins is knighted.

Madonna publishes her book, *Sex*, in October.   *LC*

DECEMBER 11 Opening simultaneously in over fifty countries and in 1,925 theaters in the U.S. is *A Few Good Men*, starring Tom Cruise, Jack Nicholson, and Demi Moore. **23** Martin Brest's *Scent of a Woman*, a remake of a 1974 Italian film, stars Al Pacino and opens today. **30** George Miller's *Lorenzo's Oil*, opening today, stars Susan Sarandon and Nick Nolte in a true story about parents of a desperately ill child who take it upon themselves to cure him.

SOME OF THE BEST MOVIE AD TAG LINES OF 1992

"No sex. No booze. No Men. No way." — *Sister Act*

"A family is like peanut brittle. It takes a lot of sweetness to hold all the nuts together." — *Used People*

"Allie's roommate is about to borrow a few things without asking. Her clothes. Her boyfriend. Her life." — *Single White Female*

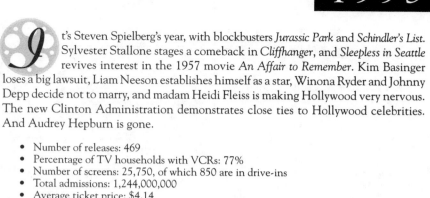

*J*t's Steven Spielberg's year, with blockbusters *Jurassic Park* and *Schindler's List*. Sylvester Stallone stages a comeback in *Cliffhanger*, and *Sleepless in Seattle* revives interest in the 1957 movie *An Affair to Remember*. Kim Basinger loses a big lawsuit, Liam Neeson establishes himself as a star, Winona Ryder and Johnny Depp decide not to marry, and madam Heidi Fleiss is making Hollywood very nervous. The new Clinton Administration demonstrates close ties to Hollywood celebrities. And Audrey Hepburn is gone.

- Number of releases: 469
- Percentage of TV households with VCRs: 77%
- Number of screens: 25,750, of which 850 are in drive-ins
- Total admissions: 1,244,000,000
- Average ticket price: $4.14
- Box office receipts: $5,154,200,000
- Average production cost per film: $29,900,000
- Price range of Forest Lawn Memorial Park plots, final resting place of many stars: $395 to $7,500

Top stars at the box office, based on a Quigley Publications poll of exhibitors:

1. Clint Eastwood
2. Tom Cruise
3. Robin Williams
4. Kevin Costner
5. Harrison Ford
6. Julia Roberts
7. Tom Hanks
8. Mel Gibson
9. Whoopi Goldberg
10. Sylvester Stallone

Top rental earnings (as of February, 1994), based on figures reported by *Variety*:

1.	*Jurassic Park*	$205,000,000
2.	*Mrs. Doubtfire*	98,350,000
3.	*The Fugitive*	92,600,000
4.	*The Firm*	77,050,000
5.	*Sleepless in Seattle*	64,950,000

The New York Film Critics Circle Awards
Best Picture: *Schindler's List*

The Los Angeles Film Critics Association
Best Picture: *Schindler's List*

The Golden Globe Awards
Best Picture (Drama): *Schindler's List*
Best Picture (Musical or Comedy): *Mrs. Doubtfire*

The Cannes Film Festival
Palme d'Or: *The Piano* and *Farewell to My Concubine*

The Academy Awards (presented March 21, 1994)
Best Picture: *Schindler's List*
Actor: Tom Hanks (*Philadelphia*)
Actress: Holly Hunter (*The Piano*)
Supporting Actor: Tommy Lee Jones (*The Fugitive*)
Supporting Actress: Anna Paquin (*The Piano*)
Director: Steven Spielberg (*Schindler's List*)

January	February	March	April	May	June	
	• L.A. takes over Egyptian Theater to preserve it		**30** Disney Studios announce purchase of Miramax			
		24 Producer of *Boxing Helena* wins $8.92 million suit against Kim Basinger	**24** Kim Basinger, with $5 million in assets, files for bankruptcy		**27** Julia Roberts m. Lyle Lovett	
20 Audrey Hepburn d.						

July	August	September	October	November	December	
		24 Child molestation charges against Woody Allen dropped		**5** Whoopi Goldberg and Ted Danson announce end of romance		
25 Alan Ladd Jr. fired at MGM; Frank G. Mancuso hired	**6** *The Fugitive*	**17** *The Piano*			**15** *Schindler's List*	

Personalities

JANUARY • Madonna buys the Castillo del Largo estate in the Hollywood Hills, once owned by Bugsy Siegel. **8** The U.S. Post Office issues an Elvis Presley commemorative stamp. Presley fans have opted for the young, slim Elvis in a Post Office poll in which the alternative image was the older, Las Vegas Elvis. **19** Barbra Streisand heads President-elect Bill Clinton's inaugural gala star list. Others at inaugural events are Warren Beatty, Jack Nicholson, Alec Baldwin, Kim Basinger, Chevy Chase, Whoopi Goldberg, Don Johnson, Melanie Griffith, Richard Dreyfuss, Sally Field, and Jack Lemmon.

FEBRUARY • Karina Lombard, filming *The Firm* with Tom Cruise in the Cayman Is-

Liam Neeson, responding to what people seem to want to know about him since he's become more well known, says in a *New York Times* interview: "Is this what's going to be on my tombstone? 'He dated Julia Roberts and Barbra Streisand.'" He also dated Brooke Shields, Jennifer Grey, and Natasha Richardson.

January 10, 1993

lands, complains that Cruise's wife, Nicole Kidman, appears to be hovering, to make sure that her mate is not tempted into an on-the-set romance.

MARCH 2 A seventy-five-foot Arnold Schwarzenegger balloon, inflated in Times Square yesterday, depicts him with a gun in one hand, two sticks of dynamite in the other. Today, in response to criticism that the image is inappropriate in the light of the February 26 bombing of the World Trade Center, this prop for the filming of *The Last Action Hero* is deflated and then reinflated with a badge replacing the dynamite. **18** Woody Allen announces that a team of child abuse specialists have cleared him of Mia Farrow's charges that he molested their seven-year-old daughter. **24** The U.S. Post Office issues a stamp honoring Grace Kelly. **24** In Los Angeles Superior Court, producer Carl Mazzocone wins an $8.92 million judgment against Kim Basinger, who has broken her verbal agreement to appear in his film, *Boxing Helena*. **29** The Academy Award ceremonies at the Dorothy Chandler Pavilion are dedicated to women in the in-

Movies

MAY 7 *Dave*, a political satire about a man who resembles the President, starring Kevin Kline and Sigourney Weaver, opens, as does Kenneth Branagh's *Much Ado about Nothing*, starring Branagh, Denzel Washington, Emma Thompson, Michael Keaton, and Keanu Reeves. **28** Sylvester Stallone stars in *Cliffhanger*, a comeback film for him after several consecutive flops.

JUNE 10 *Orlando*, based on the Virginia Woolf novel, directed by Sally Potter and starring Tilda Swinton, opens. **11** Steven

Spielberg's special-effects extravaganza about cloned dinosaurs, *Jurassic Park*, opens in 2,404 theaters, where it will take in $50.1 million on its first weekend. It stars Sam Neill, Laura Dern, Jeff Goldblum, and Richard Attenborough. Yesterday, coincidentally, the British journal *Nature* published an account of the extraction from amber of the oldest DNA yet recovered. **25** The opening today of *Sleepless in Seattle*, starring Tom Hanks and Meg Ryan, leads to an increase in sales and rentals of the 1957 *An Affair to Remember*, which the characters in the movie watch and talk about. **30** Tom Cruise in *The Firm*, directed by Syndey Pollack, opens on 2,393

screens across the country. It's based on the John Grisham best-seller.

JULY 9 *In the Line of Fire*, opening today, stars Clint Eastwood as a secret service agent and John Malkovich as an assassin. **16** *Free Willy*, starring Jason James Richter in a movie about a boy and a killer whale, opens and becomes a surprise hit. **30** Philip Kaufman's *Rising Sun*, starring Sean Connery and Wesley Snipes in a film adapted from a Michael Crichton novel, opens. As was the novel, it is criticized for Japan-bashing.

AUGUST 6 Harrison Ford and Tommy Lee

Business and Society

JANUARY • Major studios begin to release feature film videos on Wednesdays, just as they have been releasing many movies on Fridays.

FEBRUARY • The city of Los Angeles takes possession of the Egyptian Theater on Hollywood Boulevard, which opened on October 18, 1922 with the premiere of

Douglas Fairbanks's *Robin Hood*. The city wants to preserve the now-empty house.

MARCH 8 The Blockbuster chain of video stores announces that it is buying just under fifty percent of Spelling Entertainment Group, a film and TV production company. **25** Crédit Lyonnais hires Michael Ovitz's Creative Artists Agency for strategic advice on its more than $3 billion in entertainment industry investments, including MGM. Other agencies charge that

this creates a conflict of interest for CAA, which at the same time could be negotiating for its clients with MGM.

APRIL 20 A disgruntled former Universal employee opens fire at the MCA building, wounding several people. **30** Hollywood unions declare themselves satisfied that Creative Artists Agency will steer clear of conflicts of interest when consulting with Crédit Lyonnais. But Jeff Berg of International Creative Management is pursuing

Births, Deaths, Marriages, and Divorces

JANUARY 1 Halle Berry m. baseball player David Justice. **20** Audrey Hepburn d.

FEBRUARY 5 Joseph Mankiewicz d. **27** Lillian Gish d. **28** Ruby Keeler d. **28** Tony Curtis m. Lisa Deutsch.

MARCH 5 Glenn Ford, 76, m. 30-something Jeanne Baus. It will last a few weeks. **17** Helen Hayes d. **18** Eddie Murphy m. Nicole Mitchell. **31** Brandon Lee d.

JUNE 27 Julia Roberts m. musician Lyle Lovett.

30 George "Spanky" McFarland d.

JULY 20 Joe Petruzzi files for divorce from Annabella Sciorra.

AUGUST 16 Stewart Granger d. **19** Alec Baldwin and Kim Basinger get married. **29** Marlee Matlin m. Kevin Grandalski.

dustry, but the music welcoming celebrities as they arrive is "Thank Heaven for Little Girls." Presenters Susan Sarandon and Tim Robbins ask that Haitians with AIDS be admitted into the U.S., and Richard Gere attacks the Chinese violation of human rights in Tibet. **31** Brandon Lee, son of Bruce Lee, dies of gunshot wounds from a pistol intended to fire blanks, on the set of *The Crow*. (On October 26, 1984, *Daily Variety* ran a story: "Filming Injuries Caused by Blank-Loaded Weapons an 'Overlooked' Safety Area.")

APRIL • After meeting Boris Yeltsin in Vancouver, President Clinton socializes with Richard Dreyfuss, Sharon Stone, and Richard Gere, who urges Clinton to meet with the Dalai Lama. Clinton aide George Stephanopoulos has been dating Jennifer Grey. • Cher travels to Armenia, bring-

ing medical and other supplies on behalf of the United Armenian fund.

MAY • Geena Davis is dating director Renny Harlin, whose ex-girlfriend, Laura Dern, has been seeing Davis's former husband, Jeff Goldblum. **24** Kim Basinger, with $5 million in assets, files for bankruptcy to hold off paying the settlement ordered in March in the *Boxing Helena* suit.

JUNE • Winona Ryder's engagement to Johnny Depp is off. **7** A New York State Supreme Court judge settles the Mia Farrow–Woody Allen child custody battle in Farrow's favor, calling Allen a "self-absorbed, untrustworthy and insensitive" father. **11** Burt Reynolds announces that his marriage to Loni Anderson is "irretrievably broken." **11** Merchandising spinoffs from *Jurassic Park*, opening today,

include a toy resembling actor Sam Neill. Describing a situation more suggestive of Oedipus than Tyrannosaurus Rex, he says: "My kids will be able to rip the head off their father." **14** Warner Bros. pays Michael Crichton, author of the novel *Jurassic Park*, what is said to be $3.5 million for screen rights to his next, unpublished novel, about sexual harassment. **30** Barbra Streisand, at Wimbledon, sees Andrei Agassi eliminated from the tennis tournament. Their "friendship" has filled the British sports pages all week.

JULY 30 James Farentino is arrested for threatening and harassing, via fax, ex-girlfriend Tina Sinatra.

AUGUST 3 Hollywood police arrest Wesley Snipes when they come to his aid after he has a minor motorcycle accident and dis-

Jones star in *The Fugitive*, based on the TV program, opening today. Directed by Andrew Davis, the film is marked by vivid stunt work, notably in a train wreck, and by special effects, such as a plunge from a dam.

SEPTEMBER 8 *The Joy Luck Club*, based on the bestselling novel by Amy Tan, directed by Wayne Wang, and starring Kieu Chinh, Tsai Chin, and France Nuyen, opens at the Cinema I. **13** Martin Scorsese's *The Age*

Michelle Pfeiffer and Daniel Day-Lewis star in *The Age of Innocence*, opening in September. *LC/© COLUMBIA PICTURES*

Tommy Lee Jones in *The Fugitive*   *LC/© WARNER BROTHERS*

the issue with the Justice Department. **30** The Walt Disney Studios announce that they will buy the Miramax Film Corporation.

MAY 23 The 1992 cult movie *Wax: Or the*

SEPTEMBER Steve Martin and Victoria Tennant separate. **10** Loretta Young m. Jean Louis. **12** Raymond Burr d. **25** Geena Davis m. director Renny Harlin.

OCTOBER 22 James Coburn m. Paula Murad. **25** Vincent Price d. **31** River Phoenix d.

NOVEMBER • Barbara Hershey and Stephen Douglas separate, as do Ellen Barkin and Gabriel Byrne. **13** Michelle Pfeiffer m. producer David Kelley. **27** Teri Garr m. John O'Neil.

DECEMBER 6 Don Ameche d. **14** Myrna Loy d.

Personalities

cover that he's carrying a concealed gun. He will pay a fine and receive probation. **9** The arraignment of Heidi Fleiss, Beverly Hills madam, for narcotics possession and pandering, and the revelation that police have her address book and traveler's checks from a famous actor, has much of Hollywood nervous. **24** A slightly ill-looking Burt Reynolds goes on ABC's *Good Morning America: Evening Edition* to say that he did cheat on his wife, Loni Anderson, but that she cheated first.

SEPTEMBER 24 A Connecticut state's attorney, although claiming he has "probable cause" to prosecute Woody Allen for child molestation—and had made out an arrest warrant—decides, in consultation with Mia

Movies

of Innocence, starring Daniel Day-Lewis, Michelle Pfeiffer, and Winona Ryder and narrated by Joanne Woodward, opens. **29** Robert DeNiro debuts as a director and stars in *A Bronx Tale*. Chazz Palmenteri, who plays a gangster, also wrote the screenplay.

OCTOBER 1 Robert Altman's *Short Cuts*, based on Raymond Carver short stories, with an all-star cast featuring Tim Robbins, Andie MacDowell, Madeleine Stowe, Jack Lemmon, Matthew Modine, Lily Tomlin,

Farrow, to drop the charges in the child's interests. Allen denounces the entire investigation.

OCTOBER • Kit Culkin, unhappy with the addition of Kevin Kline's narrative to *The Nutcracker Suite*, which opens November 19, stops the film's star, his son, Macauley, from promoting it. **8** At a Friars Club

Holly Hunter and Anna Paquin in *The Piano*   LC/© MIRAMAX

and Tom Waits, premieres at the New York Film Festival. **17** Jane Campion's *The Piano*, starring Holly Hunter, Harvey Keitel,

roast of Whoopi Goldberg in New York, her boyfriend, Ted Danson, in blackface, offends many by trying to make racial slurs humorous. **31** River Phoenix collapses outside the Viper Room, a West Hollywood nightclub. He dies from a cocaine and morphine overdose.

NOVEMBER 2 Wildfires sweep Malibu, de-

Anna Paquin, and Sam Neill, is shown at the New York Film Festival. It has already shared the Golden Palm award at Cannes

Business and Society

Discovery of Television Among the Bees is the first film to be transmitted—at two frames per second—over the Internet, the global computer network.

JUNE • A Library of Congress report warns that acetate-based safety film, in use since the early 1950s, can deteriorate, and that Eastman color film will fade.

JULY 9 Responding to the complaints of Arab-Americans, The Walt Disney Co. agrees to change song lyrics in *Aladdin* that are said to disparage Arabs. **25** Crédit Lyonnais announces that it has fired Alan Ladd Jr. as head of MGM, replacing him with Frank G. Mancuso, and will restore operations at United Artists—all in consultation with Michael Ovitz.

AUGUST 17 Turner Broadcasting buys New Line Cinema and Castle Rock Entertain-

ment. **24** MGM names John Calley to head its United Artists division with the aim of increasing its output of films.

SEPTEMBER 20 Cable TV companies Viacom and QVC begin a bidding war for Paramount.

OCTOBER 19 The Disney Company says that it will remove from *The Program*, a film about college football, a scene involving teenagers lying in the road to show their

Births, Deaths, Marriages, and Divorces

stroying the homes of Sean Penn and Ali MacGraw. **5** Whoopi Goldberg and Ted Danson announce that their romance is over. **9** Elizabeth Taylor flies to Mexico to lend support to friend Michael Jackson, who may be charged with child molesting. On November 12 she will accompany him to London. **17** The Santa Monica Mountain Conservancy announces that Barbra Streisand has donated to it her twenty-four-acre, $15 million Malibu Estate.

DECEMBER 4 President Clinton attends a Democratic fund-raiser in Beverly Hills with a guest list controlled by the host, Michael Ovitz's Creative Artists Agency, upsetting those represented by other agents. **31** Barbra Streisand begins two nights of performances at the MGM Grand in Las Vegas. In her first commercial concerts in two decades, she plays to 26,210 people.

1993 IS SPIELBERG'S YEAR

Schindler's List receives numerous awards and Spielberg will take home the Academy Award for best director for 1993 at the Academy Awards Ceremony next year.

Photo Courtesy LC.

and will open next month in New York and Los Angeles theaters.

NOVEMBER 5 Merchant–Ivory's *The Remains of the Day* starring Anthony Hopkins, Emma Thompson, Christopher Reeve, and James Fox opens. **10** Brian DePalma's *Carlito's Way*, starring Al Pacino and Sean Penn, opens. **24** Clint Eastwood and Kevin Costner star in, and Eastwood directs, *A Perfect World*, opening today. Also opening is *Mrs. Doubtfire*, in which Robin Williams's performance in drag draws raves. Sally Field co-stars in this very popular film.

DECEMBER 15 Steven Spielberg's film about the Holocaust, *Schindler's List*, starring Liam Neeson, Ben Kingsley, and Ralph Fiennes, opens on twenty-five screens in eighteen cities. The *New York Times*'s review says that Spielberg "has this year delivered the most astounding one-two punch in the history of American cinema. *Jurassic Park*, now closing in on billion-dollar grosses, is the biggest moneymaker of all time. *Schindler's List*, destined to have a permanent place in memory, will earn something better." **17** Julia Roberts and Denzel Washington star in Alan J. Pakula's *The Pelican Brief*, the second John Grisham bestseller to make it to the screen this year, open-

ing today. **22** *Philadelphia*, Jonathan Demme's AIDS drama, opens. It stars Tom Hanks in an Oscar-winning performance as the lawyer with AIDS and Denzel Washington as the homophobic lawyer who defends him in a discrimination case. **29** Anthony Hopkins and Debra Winger star in Richard Attenborough's *Shadowlands*, about the writer C.S. Lewis in love; and Daniel Day-Lewis and Emma Thompson star in Jim Sheridan's *In the Name of the Father*, a drama set against the backdrop of the strife in Northern Ireland. Both films open in limited engagements.

courage, after at least one death is attributed to adolescents imitating it.

NOVEMBER 9 Sony Pictures Entertainment (Columbia) shows freshman members of Congress a restored copy of *Mr. Smith Goes to Washington*.

DECEMBER 15 The U.S. concludes talks with members of the General Agreement on Tariffs and Trade without reducing the French tax on American films.

Tom Hanks (l) and Denzel Washington (r) in *Philadelphia*   *LC/© TriStar*

*V*iacom buys Paramount. The Disney Company loses its president, Frank Wells, in a helicopter crash; its chairman, Michael Eisner, has heart surgery; and Disney Studio head Jeffrey Katzenberg quits to join Steven Spielberg and David Geffen in a new venture. Burt Lancaster, Jessica Tandy, and Raul Julia die. Paul Newman is still nobody's fool, but Jim Carrey is dumber than thou in several films, and Tonya Harding (*Breakaway*) and Joey Buttafuoco (*Cul-de-Sac*) make movies. John Waters satirizes suburbia and society's fascination with murderers in *Serial Mom*. Kevin Costner flops as Wyatt Earp. But for Robert Zemeckis, director of *Forrest Gump*, the year is as sweet as, well, as a box of chocolates.

Top grossing films:

1.	*The Lion King*	$306,000,000
2.	*Forrest Gump*	301,000,000
3.	*True Lies*	146,000,000
4.	*The Santa Clause*	142,000,000
5.	*The Flintstones*	131,000,000

The Golden Raspberry Awards
Worst Picture: *Color of Night*
Actor: Kevin Costner (*Wyatt Earp*)
Actress: Sharon Stone (*Intersection* and *The Specialist*)
Supporting Actor: O. J. Simpson (*Naked Gun 33* $^{1}/_{3}$)
Supporting Actress: Rosie O'Donnell (*Exit to Eden*, *The Flintstones*, and *Car 54 Where Are You?*)

The New York Film Critics Circle Awards
Best Picture: *Quiz Show*

The Golden Globe Awards
Best Picture (Drama): *Forrest Gump*

The Cannes Film Festival
Palme d'Or: *Pulp Fiction*

The Academy Awards (presented March 27, 1995)
Best Picture: *Forrest Gump*
Actor: Tom Hanks (*Forrest Gump*)
Actress: Jessica Lange (*Blue Sky*)
Supporting Actor: Martin Landau (*Ed Wood*)
Supporting Actress: Dianne Wiest (*Bullets Over Broadway*)
Director: Robert Zemeckis (*Forrest Gump*)

January	February	March	April	May	June
17 The L.A. earthquake destroys Barbra Streisand's antiques		**9** *Four Weddings and a Funeral*		**21** Cineplex-Odeon and Sony Theaters-Loews raise New York City ticket prices to $8.00	
	15 Viacom wins Paramount	**13** *Serial Mom*			**15** *The Lion King*

July	August	September	October	November	December
24 Jeffrey Katzenberg leaves Disney			**12** Steven Spielberg, David Geffen, and Jeffrey Katzenberg announce new studio		**16** Sony and Philips introduce new video compact disc format
6 *Forrest Gump*	**22** $8 million+ judgment against Kim Basinger overturned			**17** Sony to take $3.2 billion loss on Columbia and TriStar	

Kathleen Turner (above left) in John Waters's *Serial Mom* takes out her frustrations in an unusual way in this dark satire of suburbia, finding unique ways to kill those who offend her. Meanwhile, Jody Foster (above right) plays a scheming con artist in the comic western *Maverick*, based on the popular 1950s TV series.

*Photos courtesy LC/*Serial Mom © *SAVOY PICTURES;* Maverick © *WARNER BROTHERS*

Director Robert Redford revisits the 1950s TV scandal that rocked the nation in *Quiz Show*. Ralph Fiennes, fresh from his success in last year's *Schindler's List*, plays the quiz show contestant Charles Van Doren, who was the focus of the investigation in the 50s.

Photo courtesy LC/© HOLLYWOOD PICTURES

PULP FICTION: ROYALE WITH CHEESE

John Travolta and Samuel Jackson as two hit men exchange some of their most memorable dialogue early in the film (screenplay by Quentin Tarantino):

John Travolta: You know what they call a Quarter Pounder with Cheese in Paris?

Samuel Jackson: They don't call it a Quarter Pounder with Cheese?

JT: No man, they got the metric system. They wouldn't know what the fuck a Quarter Pounder is.

SJ: Well, what do they call it?

JT: They call it a *Royale* with Cheese.

SJ: *Royale* with Cheese.

JT: That's right.

SJ: What do they call a Big Mac?

JT: A Big Mac's a Big Mac, but they call it *le* Big Mac.

SJ: *Le* Big Mac. What do they call a Whopper?

JT: I don't know. I didn't go into Burger King.

Director Quentin Tarantino took home the Oscar for the Best Original Screenplay for *Pulp Fiction*, his flamboyant, innovative homage to film noir. John Travolta plays heroin-addicted hit man Vincent Vega, in a performance that established Travolta as a dramatic actor worthy of notice and revived his career.

Photo courtesy LC/© MIRAMAX

HOOP DREAMS: BOXED OUT OF THE OSCARS

Directed by Steve James, *Hoop Dreams* follows the careers of two hopeful, hardworking student athletes, William Gates (above left) and Arthur Agee (above right). Highly praised by the public and critics alike, the film was not nominated for an Academy Award. As a result of the outcry and controversy over its Academy exclusion, the Academy is changing its rules for nominating documentaries.

Photos courtesy LC/© FINE LINE FEATURES

BURT LANCASTER: 1913–1994

Burt Lancaster's multifaceted screen career included everything from swashbuckling adventure films to comedies to serious dramas. Lancaster actually began as a circus actor, but went on to not only act in films but to also produce them. In his later years he appeared in a number of lighter roles with his buddy Kirk Douglas, but some of his finest work was also done in the 1980s, in films such as Louis Malle's *Atlantic City*. His powerful screen presence will long be remembered. Shown here: Burt Lancaster in *The Crimson Pirate* (1952), and late in his career (above).

Photos courtesy LC

Bibliography

Annuals, Newspapers, and Periodicals:

American Film
Cineaste
Daily Variety
Entertainment Weekly
Film Daily Almanac
Film History
The Hollywood Reporter
International Motion
Picture Almanac
Life
Look
The Los Angeles Times
The New York Herald-Tribune

The New York Times
Newsweek
People
Premiere
Time
Variety
Vanity Fair
The Velvet Light Trap

Also: *The American Film Institute Catalog of Motion Pictures Produced in the United States* now includes volumes covering the years 1911–1920, 1921–1930, 1931–1940, and 1961–1970.

Books:

Adams, Leith, and Keith Burns, eds. *James Dean: Behind the Scene.* New York: Citadel Press, 1992 (orig. pub., 1990).

Adams, Les, and Buck Rainey. *Shoot-Em-Up: The Complete Reference Guide to Westerns of the Sound Era.* New Rochelle, NY: Arlington House, 1978.

Altman, Diana. *Hollywood East: Louis B. Mayer and the Origins of the Studio System.* New York: Carol Publishing Group, 1992.

Andersen, Christopher. *Citizen Jane: The Turbulent Life of Jane Fonda.* New York: Henry Holt and Company, 1990.

———. *Madonna Unauthorized.* New York: Simon & Schuster, 1991.

Arce, Hector. *Groucho.* New York: G.P. Putnam's Sons, 1979.

Arnold, William. *Shadowland.* New York: McGraw-Hill, 1978.

Bach, Steven. *Marlene Dietrich: Life and Legend.* New York: William Morrow and Company, 1992.

Balio, Tino. *United Artists: The Company Built by the Stars.* Madison, WI: University of Wisconsin Press, 1976.

———. *United Artists: The Company That Changed the Film Industry.* Madison, WI: University of Wisconsin Press, 1987.

———, ed. *The American Film Industry*, rev. ed. Madison, WI: University of Wisconsin Press, 1985.

Basten, Fred E. *Glorious Technicolor: The Movies' Magic Rainbow.* South Brunswick, NJ: A.S. Barnes and Company, 1980.

Baudy, Mary L., ed. *The Dawn of Sound.* New York: Museum of Modern Art, 1989.

Beauchamp, Cari, and Henri Béhar. *Hollywood on the Riviera: The Inside Story of the Cannes Film Festival.* New York: William Morrow and Company, 1992.

Bego, Mark, ed. *The Best of Modern Screen.* New York: St. Martin's Press, 1986.

Behlmer, Rudy, ed. *Inside Warner Bros.* New York: Fireside, 1987 (first published by Viking, 1985).

———, ed. *Memo from David O. Selznick.* New York: Viking, 1972.

Berg, A. Scott. *Goldwyn: A Biography.* New York: Alfred A. Knopf, 1989.

Bergreen, Laurence. *As Thousands Cheer: The Life of Irving Berlin.* New York: Viking, 1990.

Black, Shirley Temple. *Child Star: An Autobiography.* New York: McGraw-Hill, 1988.

Bodeen, DeWitt. *From Hollywood: The Careers of 15 Great American Stars.* South Brunswick, NJ: A.S. Barnes and Company, 1976.

Bowers, Q. David. *Nickelodeon Theaters and Their Music.* Vestal, NY: The Vestal Press, 1986.

Bowers, Ronald. *The Selznick Players.* Cranbury, NJ: A.S. Barnes and Company, 1976.

Bowser, Eileen. *The Transformation of Cinema: 1907–1915.* History of the American Cinema, vol. 2, ed. Charles Harpole. New York: Charles Scribner's Sons, 1990.

———, ed. *Biograph Bulletins, 1908–1912.* New York: Octagon Books, 1973.

———, ed. *Film Notes.* New York: The Museum of Modern Art, 1969.

Bradford, Sarah. *Princess Grace.* New York: Stein and Day, 1984.

Brady, Frank. *Citizen Welles.* New York: Charles Scribner's Sons, 1984.

Brown, Gene, ed. *The New York Times Encyclopedia of Film.* 14 vols. New York: Times Books, 1984.

Brownlow, Kevin. *Behind the Mask of Innocence.* London: Jonathan Cape, Ltd., 1990.

Brownstein, Ronald. *The Power and the Glitter: The Hollywood-Washington Connection.* New York: Pantheon Books, 1990.

Cabarga, Leslie. *The Fleischer Story*, rev. ed. New York: DaCapo Press, 1988.

Carey, Gary. *All the Stars in Heaven: Louis B. Mayer's M-G-M.* New York: E.P. Dutton, 1981.

Carr, Robert E., and R.M. Hayes. *Wide Screen Movies: A History and Filmography of Wide Gauge Filmmaking.* Jefferson, NC: McFarland & Co., 1988.

Cawley, John, and Jim Korkis. *The Encyclopedia of Cartoon Superstars.* Las Vegas: Pioneer Books, 1990.

Ceplair, Larry, and Steven Englund. *The Inquisition in Hollywood: Politics in the Film Industry, 1930–1960.* New York: Doubleday, 1980.

Cline, William C. *In the Nick of Time: Motion Picture Sound Serials.* Jefferson, NC: McFarland & Co., 1984.

Considine, Shaun. *Bette & Joan: The Divine Feud.* New York: E.P. Dutton, 1989.

Corey, Melinda, and George Ochoa, comps. *A Cast of Thousands: A Compendium of Who Played What in Film.* 3 vols. New York: Facts on File, 1992.

Corman, Roger (with Jim Jerome). *How I Made a Hundred Movies in Hollywood and Never Lost a Dime.* New York: Random House, 1990.

Cox, Stephen. *The Munchkins Remember: The Wizard of Oz and Beyond.* New York: Dutton, 1989.

Crowther, Bosley. *Hollywood Rajah: The Life and Times of Louis B. Mayer.* New York: Henry Holt and Co., 1960.

————. *The Lion's Share.* New York: Dutton, 1957.

Culbert, David, ed. *Film and Propaganda in America: A Documentary History.* World War II, vol. 3, part 2. New York: Greenwood Press, 1990.

Culhane, John. *Walt Disney's Fantasia.* New York: Abradale Press, 1987.

Curcio, Vincent, *Suicide Blonde: The Life of Gloria Grahame.* New York: William Morrow, 1989.

Curtiss, Thomas Q. *Von Stroheim.* New York: Farrar, Straus and Giroux, 1971.

Dalton, David. *James Dean: The Mutant King.* San Francisco: Straight Arrow Books, 1974.

Dalton, David, and Ron Cayen. *James Dean: American Icon.* New York: St. Martin's Press, 1984.

Dardis, Tom. *Harold Lloyd: The Man on the Clock.* New York: Viking Press, 1983.

————. *Keaton: The Man Who Wouldn't Lie Down.* New York: Scribner's Sons, 1979.

Davidson, Bill. *Spencer Tracy: Tragic Idol.* London: Sidgwick & Jackson, 1987.

de Cordova, Richard. *Picture Personalities: The Emergence of the Star System in America.* Urbana, IL: The University of Illinois Press, 1990.

Denisoff, R. Serge, and William D. Romanowski. *Risky Business: Rock on Film.* New Brunswick, NJ: Transaction Publishers, 1991.

DiOrio, Al. *Barbara Stanwyck.* New York: Coward-McCann, 1983.

Dixon, Wheeler, ed. *Producers Releasing Corporation: A Comprehensive Filmography and History.* Jefferson, NC: McFarland & Co., 1986.

Downing, David. *Robert Mitchum.* London: W.H. Allen, 1985.

Eastman, John. *Retakes: Behind the Scenes of 500 Classic Movies.* New York: Ballantine Books, 1989.

Edmonds, I.G. *Big U: Universal in the Silent Days.* South Brunswick, NJ: A.S. Barnes and Company, 1977.

Edwards, Anne. *Early Reagan: The Rise to Power.* New York: William Morrow & Co., 1987.

————. *A Remarkable Woman: A Biography of Katharine Hepburn.* New York: Pocket Books, 1985.

Eells, George. *Final Gig: The Man Behind the Murder.* San Diego: Harcourt Brace Jovanovich, 1991.

————. *Hedda and Louella.* New York: G.P. Putnam's Sons, 1972.

————. *Robert Mitchum: A Biography.* New York: Franklin Watts, 1984.

Everson, William K. *American Silent Film.* New York: Oxford University Press, 1978.

Eyman, Scott. *Mary Pickford: America's Sweetheart.* New York: Donald I. Fine, Inc., 1990.

Faith, William Robert. *Bob Hope: A Life in Comedy.* New York: G.P. Putnam's Sons, 1982.

Fernett, Gene. *Poverty Row.* Satellite Beach, FL: Coral Reef Publications, 1973.

Fielding, Raymond. *The March of Time, 1935–1951.* New York: Oxford University Press, 1978.

Finch, Christopher, and Linda Rosenkrantz. *Gone Hollywood.* Garden City, NY: Doubleday & Company, 1979.

Finler, Joel W. *The Hollywood Story.* New York: Crown, 1988.

Flamini, Roland. *Ava: A Biography.* New York: Coward, McCann & Geoghegan, 1983.

Ford, Dan. *Pappy: The Life of John Ford.* Englewood Cliffs, NJ: Prentice-Hall, 1979.

Fordin, Hugh. *The Movies' Greatest Musicals: Produced in Hollywood USA by the Freed Unit.* New York: Frederick Ungar Publishing Company, 1984.

Fountain, Leatrice Gilbert, with John R. Maxim. *Dark Star.* New York: St. Martin's Press, 1985.

Francisco, Charles. *You Must Remember This: The Filming of Casablanca.* Englewood Cliffs, NJ: Prentice-Hall, 1980.

Frank, Gerold. *Judy.* New York: Harper & Row, 1975.

Fricke, John, Jay Scarfone, and William Stillman. *The Wizard of Oz: The Official 50th Anniversary Pictorial History.* New York: Warner Books, 1989.

Friedrich, Otto. *City of Nets: A Portrait of Hollywood in the 1940's.* New York: Harper & Row, 1986.

Furmanek, Bob, and Ron Palumbo. *Abbott and Costello in Hollywood.* New York: Perigee Books, 1991.

Fussell, Betty. *Mabel.* New York: Limelight Editions, 1992.

Gardner, Gerald. *The Censorship Papers: Movie Censorship Letters from the Hays Office, 1934 to 1968.* New York: Dodd, Mead & Co., 1987.

Gelman, Barbara, ed. *Photoplay Treasury.* New York: Crown, 1972.

Golden, Eve. *Platinum Girl: The Life and Legends of Jean Harlow.* New York: Abbeville Press, 1991.

Gomery, Douglas. *The Hollywood Studio System.* New York: St. Martin's Press, 1986.

————. *Shared Pleasures: A History of Movie Presentation in the United States.* Madison, WI: The University of Wisconsin Press, 1992.

Goodman, Ezra. *The Fifty-Year Decline and Fall of Hollywood.* New York: Simon and Schuster, 1961.

Grobel, Lawrence. *The Hustons.* New York: Charles Scribner's Sons, 1989.

Grover, Ron. *The Disney Touch: How a Daring Management Team Revived an Entertainment Empire.* Homewood, IL: Richard D. Irwin, 1991.

Gussow, Mel. *Darryl F. Zanuck: Don't Say Yes Until I Finish Talking.* New York: Da Capo Press, 1971.

Hall, Benjamin. *The Golden Age of the Movie Palace: The Best Remaining Seats.* New York: Clarkson N. Potter, 1961.

Halliwell, Leslie. *Halliwell's Film Guide.* Seventh edition. New York: Harper & Row, 1989.

Harmetz, Aljean. *The Making of the Wizard of Oz.* New York: Alfred A. Knopf, 1981.

Harvey, Stephen. *Directed By Vincente Minnelli.* New York: The Museum of Modern Art and Harper & Row, 1989.

Haver, Ronald. *David O. Selznick's Hollywood.* New York, Bonanza Books, 1985 (first pub., 1980).

Heimann, Jim. *Out With The Stars: Hollywood Nightlife in the Golden Era.* New York: Abbeville Press, 1985.

Heston, Charlton. *The Actor's Life: Journals, 1956–1976,* ed. Hollis Alpert. New York: E.P. Dutton, 1978.

Higham, Charles. *Audrey: The Life of Audrey Hepburn.* New York: Macmillan, 1984.

————. *Brando: The Unauthorized Biography.* New York: New American Library, 1987.

————. *Cecil B. DeMille.* New York: Da Capo Press, 1980 (originally published, 1973).

————. *Howard Hughes: The Secret Life.* New York: G.P. Putnam's Sons, 1993.

————. *Kate: The Life of Katharine Hepburn.* New York: W.W. Norton & Co., 1975.

————. *Lucy: The Life of Lucille Ball.* New York: St. Martin's Press, 1986.

————. *Merchant of Dreams: Louis B. Mayer and the Secret Hollywood.* New York: Donald I. Fine, Inc., 1993.

————. *Orson Welles: The Rise and Fall of an American Genius.* New York: St. Martin's Press, 1985.

————. *Sisters: The Story of Olivia de Havilland and Joan Fontaine.* New York: Coward-McCann, 1984.

————. *Warner Brothers.* New York: Charles Scribner's Sons, 1975.

Holden, Anthony. *Olivier.* London: Weidenfeld & Nicolson, 1988.

Houseman, Victoria. *Made in Heaven: The Marriages and Children of Hollywood Stars.* Chicago: Bonus Books, Inc., 1991.

Howlett, John. *Frank Sinatra*. New York: Wallaby Books, 1979.

Jensen, Paul M. *Boris Karloff and His Films*. South Brunswick, NJ: A.S. Barnes and Company, 1974.

Jones, G. William. *Black Cinema Treasures: Lost and Found*. Denton, TX: University of North Texas Press, 1991.

Jowett, Garth. *Film: The Democratic Art*. Boston: Little, Brown and Company, 1976.

Karney, Robyn, ed. *Who's Who in Hollywood*. London: Bloomsbury Publishing Company, 1993.

Katz, Ephraim. *The Film Encyclopedia*. New York: Perigee Books, 1982.

Kobel, John. *Rita Hayworth: The Time, the Place and the Woman*. London: W.H. Allen, 1977.

Kindem, Gorham, ed. *The American Movie Industry: The Business of Motion Pictures*. Carbondale, IL: Southern Illinois University Press, 1982.

Koppes, Clayton R., and Gregory D. Black. *Hollywood Goes to War: How Politics, Profits, and Propaganda Shaped World War II Movies*. New York: The Free Press, 1987.

Koszarski, Richard. *An Evening's Entertainment: The Age of the Silent Picture, 1915–1928*. History of the American Cinema, vol. 3, ed. Charles Harpole, New York: Charles Scribner's Sons, 1990.

———. *The Man You Love to Hate: Erich von Stroheim and Hollywood*. New York: Oxford University Press, 1983.

LaGuardia, Robert, and Gene Arceri. *Red: The Tempestuous Life of Susan Hayward*. New York: Macmillan, 1985.

Lahue, Kalton C. *Continued Next Week: A History of the Moving Picture Serial*. Norman, OK: University of Oklahoma Press, 1964.

———. *Dreams for Sale: The Rise and Fall of the Triangle Film Corporation*. Cranbury, NJ: A.S. Barnes and Company, 1971.

———. *Kops and Custards: The Legend of Keystone Films*. Norman, OK: University of Oklahoma Press, 1968.

Lambert, Gavin. *Norma Shearer: A Life*. New York: Alfred A. Knopf, 1990.

Lasky, Betty. *RKO: The Biggest Little Major of Them All*. 2nd. ed. Santa Monica, CA: Roundtable Publishing, Inc., 1989.

Lasky, Jesse with Don Weldon. *I Blow My Own Horn*. Darden City, New York: Doubleday & Co., 1957.

Lax, Eric. *Woody Allen: A Biography*. New York: Alfred A. Knopf, 1991.

Leamer, Laurence. *As Time Goes By: The Life of Ingrid Bergman*. New York: Harper & Row, 1986.

Leaming, Barbara. *Bette Davis: A Biography*. New York: Simon & Schuster, 1992.

——— *If This Was Happiness: A Biography of Rita Hayworth*. London: Sphere Books, 1990.

——— *Orson Welles: A Biography*. New York: Viking, 1985.

Leff, Leonard J. *Hitchcock And Selznick: The Rich and Strange Collaboration of Alfred Hitchcock and David O. Selznick in Hollywood*. New York: Widenfeld & Nicolson, 1987.

Leigh, Wendy. *Arnold: An Unauthorized Biography*. Chicago: Congdon & Weed, 1990.

Lenburg, Jeff. *Peekaboo: The Story of Veronica Lake*. New York: St. Martin's Press, 1983.

Lenning, Arthur. *The Count: The Life and Films of Bela "Dracula" Lugosi*. New York: G.P. Putnam's Sons, 1974.

Leonard, Maurice. *Mae West: Empress of Sex*. New York: Birch Lane Press, 1992.

Life Goes To The Movies. New York: Wallaby Books, 1981 (orig. pub., 1975).

Linet, Beverly. *Ladd: The Life, The Legend, The Legacy of Alan Ladd*. New York: Arbor House, 1979.

Lloyd, Ann, ed. *Movies of the Silent Years*. London: Orbis, 1984.

McBride, Joseph. *Frank Capra: The Catastrophe of Success*. New York, Simon & Schuster, 1992.

MacCann, Richard Dyer. *The People's Films: A Political History of U.S. Government Motion Pictures*. New York: Hastings House, 1973.

McGee, Mark T. *Fast and Furious: The Story of American International Pictures*. Jefferson, NC: McFarland & Co., 1984.

McGilligan, Patrick. *George Cukor: A Double Life*. New York: St. Martin's Press, 1991.

Macgowan, Kenneth. *Behind The Screen: The History and Techniques of the Motion Picture*. New York: Dell, 1965.

MacGraw, Ali. *Moving Pictures*. New York: Bantam, 1991.

Madsen, Axel. *Gloria and Joe*. New York: Arbor House, 1988.

Maltin, Leonard. *The Great Movie Shorts*. New York: Crown, 1972.

———. *Of Mice And Magic: A History of American Animated Cartoons*, rev. & updated. New York: New American Library, 1987.

———, ed. *Leonard Maltin's Movie and Video Guide 1994*. New York: Signet, 1993.

Maltin, Leonard and Richard W. Bann. *Our Gang: The Life and Times of the Little Rascals*. New York: Crown, 1977.

Mank, Gregory W. *The Hollywood Hissables*. Metuchen, NJ: The Scarecrow Press, 1989.

———, *Karloff and Lugosi: The Story of a Haunting Collaboration*. Jefferson, NC: McFarland and Company, 1990.

Margolies, John and Emily Gwathmey. *Ticket to Paradise: American Movie Theaters and How We Had Fun*. Boston: Little, Brown and Company, 1991.

Marx, Arthur. *The Nine Lives of Mickey Rooney*. New York: Stein and Day, 1986.

Marx, Groucho and Richard J. Anobile. *The Marx Bros. Scrapbook*. New York: Harper Perennial Library, 1989 (first published, 1973).

Marx, Kenneth. *Star Stats: Who's Who in Hollywood*. Los Angeles: Price/Stern/Sloan, 1979.

Mast, Gerald, ed. *The Movies in Our Midst: Documents in the Cultural History of Film in America*. Chicago: University of Chicago Press, 1982.

Matzen, Robert D. *Carole Lombard: A Bio-Bibliography*. New York: Greenwood Press, 1988.

Mix, Paul E. *The Life and Legend of Tom Mix*. South Brunswick, NJ: A.S. Barnes and Company, 1972.

Moldea, Dan E. *Dark Victory: Ronald Reagan, MCA, and the Mob*. New York: Viking, 1986.

Monaco, James, and the editors of BASELINE, eds. *The Encyclopedia of Film*. New York: Perigee Books, 1991.

Monaco, James and the editors of BASELINE. *The Movie Guide*. New York: Perigee Books, 1992.

Mordden, Ethan. *Movie Star: A Look at the Women Who Made Hollywood*. New York: St. Martin's Press, 1983.

Murray, Ken. *The Golden Days of San Simeon*. Garden City, NY: Doubleday & Co., 1971.

Musser, Charles. *The Emergence of Cinema: The American Screen to 1907*. History of the American Cinema, vol. 1, ed. Charles Harpole, New York: Charles Scribner's Sons, 1990.

Nelson, Nancy. *Evenings with Cary Grant: Recollections in His Own Words and by Those Who Knew Him Best*. New York: William Morrow and Company, 1991.

Okuda, Ted. *The Monogram Checklist: The Films of Monogram Pictures Corporation, 1931–1952*. Jefferson, NC: McFarland and Company, 1987.

Parish, James Robert. *The Swashbucklers*. New Rochelle, NY: Arlington House, 1976.

Parish, James Robert, and William T. Leonard. *The Funsters*. New Rochelle, NY: Arlington House, 1979.

Parish, James Robert, and Gregory W. Mank. *The Best of MGM: The Golden Years (1928–59)*. Westport, CT: Arlington House, 1981.

Parish, James Robert, and Don E. Stanke. *The All-Americans*. New Rochelle, New York: Arlington House, 1977.

———. *The Forties Gals*. Westport, CT: Arlington House, 1980.

———. *Hollywood Baby Boomers*. New York: Garland Publishing Company, 1992.

Parish, James Robert, with Steven Whitney, *The George Raft File: The Unauthorized Biography*. New York: Drake Publishers, 1973.

Pastos, Spero. *Pin-Up: The Tragedy of Betty Grable*. New York: G.P. Putnam's Sons, 1986.

Peters, Neal, and David Smith. *Ann-Margret: A Photo Extravaganza and Memoir*. New York: Delilah Books, 1981.

Pickard, Roy. *The Hollywood Studios*. London: Frederick Muller Ltd., 1978.

Pratt, George C. *Spellbound in Darkness: A History of the Silent Film*, rev. ed. Greenwich, CT: New York Graphic Society Ltd., 1973.

Pratt, William. *Scarlett Fever: The Ultimate Pictorial Treasury of* Gone with the Wind. New York: Macmillan, 1977.

Resnick, Sylvia Safran. *Burt Reynolds: An Unauthorized Biography*. New York: St. Martin's Press, 1983.

Robertson, Patrick. *The Guinness Book of Movie Facts and Feats*. New York: Abbeville Press, 1991.

———. *Movie Clips*. 2nd ed. London: Guinness Books, 1989.

Robinson, David. *Chaplin*. New York: McGraw-Hill, 1985.

Rodriguez, Elena. *Dennis Hopper: A Madness to His Method*. New York: St. Martin's Press, 1988.

Saleh, Dennis. *Science Fiction Gold: Film Classics of the 50s*. New York: McGraw Hill, 1979.

Sands, Pierre Norman. "A Historical Study of the Academy of Motion Picture Arts and Sciences (1927–1942)," Ph.D. dissertation, University of Southern California, 1967. Reprint. New York: Arno Press, 1973.

Satchell, Tim. *Astaire: The Biography*. London: Hutchinson, 1987.

Schickel, Richard. *D.W. Griffith: An American Life*. New York: Touchstone, 1985 (orig. pub., 1984).

Schumach, Murray. *The Face on the Cutting Room Floor*. New York: William Morrow, 1964.

Shaler, Tom, et al. *The American Film Heritage: Impressions from the American Film Institute Archives*. Washington, D.C.: Acropolis Books, 1972.

Shepherd, Donald and Robert Slatzer with Dave Grayson. *Duke: The Life and Times of John Wayne*. Garden City, NY: Doubleday, 1985.

Shipman, David. *The Story of Cinema: A Complete Narrative History From the Beginnings to the Present*. New York: St. Martin's Press, 1982.

Skal, David J. *Hollywood Gothic: The Tangled Web of Dracula from Novel to Stage to Screen*. New York: W.W. Norton & Co., 1991.

Sklar, Robert. *Movie-Made America: A Cultural History of American Movies*. New York: Random House, 1975.

Skretvedt, Randy. *Laurel and Hardy: The Magic Behind the Movies*. Beverly Hills, CA: Moonstone Pr., 1987.

Slide, Anthony. *The American Film Industry: A Historical Dictionary*. New York: Limelight Editions, 1990 (orig. pub., 1986).

———. *Aspects of American Film History Prior to 1920*. Metuchen, NJ: The Scarecrow Press, 1978.

———. *The Idols of Silence*. South Brunswick, NJ: A.S. Barnes Company, 1976.

Slide, Anthony with Alan Gevinson. *The Big V: A History of the Vitagraph Company*, new, rev. ed. Metuchen, NJ: The Scarecrow Press, 1987.

Spada, James. *Peter Lawford: The Man Who Kept the Secrets*. New York: Bantam, 1991.

———. *Shirley & Warren*. New York: Collier Books, 1985.

Spoto, Donald. *The Dark Side of Genius: The Life of Alfred Hitchcock*. New York: Ballantine Books, 1984 (orig. pub., 1983).

———. *Laurence Olivier: A Biography*. New York: Harper Collins, 1992.

———. *Marilyn Monroe: The Biography*. New York: Harper Collins, 1993.

Stanley, Robert H. *The Celluloid Empire: A History of the American Movie Industry*. New York: Communication Arts Books, 1978.

Steinberg, Cobbett. *Film Facts*. New York: Facts On File, 1980.

Stenn, David. *Clara Bow: Runnin' Wild*. New York: Penguin Books, 1990 (orig. pub., 1988).

Sterling, Bryan B., and Frances N. Sterling. *Will Rogers in Hollywood*. New York: Crown, 1984.

Swanson, Gloria. *Swanson on Swanson*. New York: Random House, 1980.

Swindell, Larry. *Screwball: The Life of Carole Lombard*. New York: William Morrow & Co., 1975.

Taraborrelli, J. Randy. *Cher: A Biography*. New York: St. Martin's Press, 1986.

Terenzio, Maurice, with Scott MacGillvray and Ted Okuda. *The Soundies Distributing Corporation of America: A History and Filmography of Their "Jukebox" Musical Films of the 1940s*. Jefferson, NC: McFarland & Company, 1991.

Thomas, Bob. *King Cohn: The Life and Times of Harry Cohn*. New York: McGraw-Hill, 1990 (orig. pub., 1967).

Thomas, Nicolas. *International Dictionary of Films and Filmmakers*. 5 vols. Detroit: St. James Press, 1972.

Thomas, Tony. *Howard Hughes in Hollywood*. Seacaucus, NJ: Citadel Press, 1985.

Tornabene, Lyn. *Long Live The King: A Biography of Clark Gable*. New York: G.P. Putnam's Sons, 1976.

Tosches, Nick. *Dino*. New York: Doubleday, 1992.

Truitt, Evelyn. *Who Was Who on Screen*. New York: R.R. Bowker, 1984.

Tusca, Jon. *The Vanishing Legion: A History of Mascot Pictures, 1927–1935*. Jefferson, NC: McFarland & Co., 1989.

———, ed. *Close-Up: The Contract Director*. Metuchen, NJ: The Scarecrow Press, 1976.

Van Hise, James. *Serial Adventures*. Las Vegas: Pioneer Books, 1990.

Vaughn, Robert. *Only Victims: A Study of Show Business Blacklisting*. New York: G.P. Putnam's Sons, 1972

Walker, Alexander. *Elizabeth: The Life of Elizabeth Taylor*. New York: Grove Weidenfeld, 1990.

———. *Fatal Charm: The Life of Rex Harrison*. London: Weidenfeld and Nicolson, 1992.

———. *Joan Crawford: The Ultimate Star*. (Authorized by Metro-Goldwyn-Mayer) New York: Harper & Row, 1983.

———. *The Shattered Silents: How the Talkies Came to Stay*. London: Harrap, 1986 (orig. pub., 1978).

Warren, Doug. *Betty Grable: The Reluctant Movie Queen*. New York: St. Martin's Press, 1974.

Wayne, Jane Ellen. *Clark Gable: Portrait of a Misfit*. New York: St. Martin's Press, 1993.

Wiley, Mason, and Damien Bona. *Inside Oscar: The Unofficial History of the Academy Awards*. New York: Ballantine Books, 1988.

Wilkerson, Tichi, and Marcia Borie. *The Hollywood Reporter: The Golden Years*. New York: Coward-McCann, 1984.

Windeler, Robert. *Sweetheart: The Story of Mary Pickford*. New York: Praeger, 1974.

Woodward, Ian. *Audrey Hepburn*. New York: St. Martin's Press, 1984.

Zierold, Norman. *Garbo*. New York: Stein and Day, 1969.

Index

PAGE NUMBERS IN *ITALICS* REFER TO ILLUSTRATIONS AND PHOTOGRAPHS.